Lecture Notes in Computer Science 3331

Commenced Publication in 1973
Founding and Former Series Editors:
Gerhard Goos, Juris Hartmanis, and Jan van Leeuwen

T0180701

Kiyoharu Aizawa   Yuichi Nakamura
Shin'ichi Satoh (Eds.)

Advances in Multimedia Information Processing – PCM 2004

5th Pacific Rim Conference on Multimedia
Tokyo, Japan, November 30 – December 3, 2004
Proceedings, Part I

 Springer

Volume Editors

Kiyoharu Aizawa
Department of Frontier Informatics, The University of Tokyo
5-1-5 Kashiwanoha, Kashiwa, Chiba 277-8561, Japan
E-mail: aizawa@hal.t.u-tokyo.ac.jp

Yuichi Nakamura
Academic Center for Computation and Media Studies, Kyoto University
Yoshida-Honmachi, Sakyo-ku, Kyoto 606-8501, Japan
E-mail: yuichi@media.kyoto-u.ac.jp

Shin'ichi Satoh
National Institute of Informatics
2-1-2 Hitotsubashi, Chiyoda-ku, Tokyo 101-8430, Japan
E-mail: satoh@nii.ac.jp

Library of Congress Control Number: 2004115461

CR Subject Classification (1998): H.5.1, H.3, H.5, C.2, H.4, I.3, K.6, I.7, I.4

ISSN 0302-9743
ISBN 3-540-23974-X Springer Berlin Heidelberg New York

Springer is a part of Springer Science+Business Media

springeronline.com

© Springer-Verlag Berlin Heidelberg 2004
Printed in Germany

Typesetting: Camera-ready by author, data conversion by PTP-Berlin, Protago-TeX-Production GmbH
Printed on acid-free paper   SPIN: 11363200   06/3142   5 4 3 2 1 0

Preface

Welcome to the proceedings of the 5th Pacific Rim Conference on Multimedia (PCM 2004) held in Tokyo Waterfront City, Japan, November 30–December 3, 2004. Following the success of the preceding conferences, PCM 2000 in Sydney, PCM 2001 in Beijing, PCM 2002 in Hsinchu, and PCM 2003 in Singapore, the fifth PCM brought together the researchers, developers, practitioners, and educators in the field of multimedia. Theoretical breakthroughs and practical systems were presented at this conference, thanks to the support of the IEEE Circuits and Systems Society, IEEE Region 10 and IEEE Japan Council, ACM SIGMM, IEICE and ITE.

PCM 2004 featured a comprehensive program including keynote talks, regular paper presentations, posters, demos, and special sessions. We received 385 papers and the number of submissions was the largest among recent PCMs. Among such a large number of submissions, we accepted only 94 oral presentations and 176 poster presentations. Seven special sessions were also organized by world-leading researchers. We kindly acknowledge the great support provided in the reviewing of submissions by the program committee members, as well as the additional reviewers who generously gave their time. The many useful comments provided by the reviewing process must have been very valuable for the authors' work.

This conference would never have happened without the help of many people. We greatly appreciate the support of our strong organizing committee chairs and advisory chairs. Among the chairs, special thanks go to Dr. Ichiro Ide and Dr. Takeshi Naemura who smoothly handled publication of the proceedings with Springer. Dr. Kazuya Kodama did a fabulous job as our Web master.

September 2004

Kiyoharu Aizawa
Yuichi Nakamura
Shin'ichi Satoh
Masao Sakauchi

PCM 2004 Organization

Organizing Committee

Conference Chair   **Masao Sakauchi**
N II/The Univ. of Tokyo

Program Co-chairs   **Kiyoharu Aizawa**
The Univ. of Tokyo
Yuichi Nakamura
Kyoto Univ.
Shin'ichi Satoh
N II

Poster/Demo Co-chairs   **Yoshinari Kameda**
Univ. of Tsukuba
Takayuki Hamamoto
Tokyo Univ. of Science

Financial Co-chairs   **Nobuji Tetsutani**
Tokyo Denki Univ.
Hirohisa Jozawa
NTT Resonant

Publicity Co-chairs   **Noboru Babaguchi**
Osaka Univ.
Yoshiaki Shishikui
NHK

Publication Co-chairs   **Takeshi Naemura**
The Univ. of Tokyo
Ichiro Ide
Nagoya Univ.

Registration Chair   **Ryoichi Kawada**
KDDI

Web Chair   **Kazuya Kodama**
N II

USA Liaison   **Tsuhan Chen**
CMU

Korea Liaison   **Yo-Sung Ho**
K-JIST

Advisory Committee   **Sun-Yuan Kung**
Princeton Univ.
Hong-Jiang Zhang
Microsoft Research Asia
Masayuki Tanimoto
Nagoya Univ.

Mark Liao
Academia Sinica
Hiroshi Harashima
The Univ. of Tokyo

Program Committee

Masao Aizu
Canon
Laurent Amsaleg
IRISA-CNRS
Yasuo Ariki
Kobe Univ.
Alberto Del Bimbo
Univ. of Florence
Nozha Boujemaa
INRIA Rocquencourt
Jihad F. Boulos
American Univ. of Beirut
Tat-Seng Chua
National Univ. of Singapore
Chabane Djeraba
LIFL
Toshiaki Fujii
Nagoya Univ.
Yihong Gong
NEC Laboratories America
Patrick Gros
IRISA-CNRS
William Grosky
Univ. of Michigan, Dearborn
Alexander G. Hauptmann
CMU
Yun He
Tsinghua Univ.
Xian-Sheng Hua
Microsoft Research Asia
Takashi Ida
Toshiba
Hiroyuki Imaizumi
NHK-ES
Takashi Itoh
Fujitsu
Alejandro Jaimes
FX PalJapan, Fuji Xerox

Mohan S. Kankanhalli
National Univ. of Singapore
Norio Katayama
NII
Jiro Katto
Waseda Univ.
Asanobu Kitamoto
NII
Hitoshi Kiya
Tokyo Metropolitan Univ.
Byung-Uk Lee
Ewha Univ.
Sang-Wook Lee
Seoul National Univ.
Michael Lew
Univ. of Leiden
Mingjing Li
Microsoft Research Asia
Rainer Lienhart
Univ. Augsburg
Wei-Ying Ma
Microsoft Research Asia
Michihiko Minoh
Kyoto Univ.
Hiroshi Murase
Nagoya Univ.
Chong-Wah Ngo
City Univ. of Hong Kong
Satoshi Nogaki
NEC
Vincent Oria
New Jersey Institute of Technology
Rae-Hong Park
Sogang Univ.
Helmut Prendinger
NII
Jong-Beom Ra
KAIST

Takahiro Saito
Kanagawa Univ.
Philippe Salembier
Univ. Politecnica de Catalunya
Nicu Sebe
Univ. of Amsterdam
Timothy K. Shih
Tamkang Univ.
John Smith
IBM T.J. Watson Research Center
Kenji Sugiyama
Victor
Ming Ting Sun
Univ. of Washington

Seishi Takamura
NTT
Qi Tian
Institute for Infocomm Research
Luis Torres
Univ. Politecnica de Catalunya
Marcel Worring
Univ. of Amsterdam
Yoshihisa Yamada
Mitsubishi Electric
Naokazu Yokoya
Nara Institute of Science
    and Technology

Additional Reviewers

Frank Aldershoff
Hirofumi Aoki
Yukihiro Bandoh
Istvan Barakonyi
Stefano Berretti
Marco Bertini
Lei Chen
Keiichi Chono
He Dajun
Manolis Delakis
Takuya Funatomi
Guillaume Gravier
Keiji Gyohten
Reiko Hamada
Mei Han
Atsushi Hatabu
Ngoh Lek Heng
Xian-Sheng Hua
Lim Joo Hwee
Masaaki Iiyama
Mitsuo Ikeda
Kiyohiko Ishikawa
Hironori Ito

Yoshimichi Ito
Junko Itou
Wei Jiang
Wanjun Jin
Koh Kakusho
Masayuki Kanbara
Yutaka Kaneko
Ewa Kijak
Jonghwa Kim
Hideaki Kimata
Takahiro Kimoto
Koichi Kise
Masaki Kitahara
Takayuki Kitasaka
Zhiwei Li
Lie Lu
Yufei Ma
Keigo Majima
Takafumi Marutani
Yutaka Matsuo
Toshihiro Minami
Yoshihiro Miyamoto
Seiya Miyazaki

Kensaku Mori
Takeshi Mori
Satoshi Nishiguchi
Takayuki Onishi
Wei-Tsang Ooi
Jia-wei Rong
Tomasz M. Rutkowski
Shinichi Sakaida
Tomokazu Sato
Susumu Seki
Yuzo Senda
Fumihisa Shibata
Tomokazu Takahashi
Hung-Chuan Teh
Qiang Wang
Kaoru Watanabe
Joost van de Weijer
Jun Wu
Huaxin Xu
Keisuke Yagi
Itheri Yahiaoui
Kazumasa Yamazawa

Table of Contents, Part I

Volume I

Art

Network (I)

Sports (I)

Immersive Conferencing: Novel Interfaces and Paradigms for Remote Collaboration

Network (II)

Image Retrieval

Image Analysis (I)

Face, Gesture, and Behavior (I)

Virtual Reality and Computer Graphics

Content Production (I)

Intelligent Media Integration for Social Information Infrastructure

Approaches or Methods of Security Engineering

Multimedia Servers

Video Retrieval

Table of Contents, Part II

Volume II

Application of Video Browsing to Consumer Video Browsing Products

Watermarking (I)

User Interface (I)

Content-Based Image Retrieval

Sports (II)

Network (III)

Streaming (I)

Visual Content Mining in Multimedia Documents

Compression (I)

Face, Gesture, and Behavior (II)

Applications (I)

User Interface (II)

Image Analysis (II)

Face, Gesture, and Behavior (III)

Table of Contents, Part III

Human-Scale Virtual Reality and Interaction

Surveillance and Tracking

Image Analysis (III)

Compression (II)

Streaming (II)

Watermarking (II)

Content Production (II)

Applications (II)

Multimedia Analysis

Compression (III)

Watermarking (III)

Author Index

Categorizing Traditional Chinese Painting Images

Shuqiang Jiang[1,2] and Tiejun Huang[2]

[1] Digital Media Lab, Institute of Computing Technology, Chinese Academy
of Sciences, Beijing 100080, China
[2] Research Center of Digital Media, Graduate School of of Sciences,
Beijing 100039, China
{sqjiang, tjhuang}@jdl.ac.cn

Abstract. Traditional Chinese painting ("Guohua") is the gem of Chinese traditional arts. More and more Guohua images are digitized and exhibited on the Internet. Effectively browsing and retrieving them is an important problem need to be addressed. This paper proposes a method to categorize them into Gongbi and Xieyi schools, which are two basic types of traditional Chinese paintings. A new low-level feature called edge-size histogram is proposed and used to achieve such a high level classification. Autocorrelation texture feature is also used. Our method based on SVM classifier achieves a classification accuracy of over 94% on a 3688 traditional Chinese painting database.

1 Introduction

With the advances of network and computing technology, many organizations have a large digital images content available for online access. Various museums are constructing digital archives of art paintings and preserve the original artifacts. More and more artists attempt to exhibit and sell their productions on the Internet. Thus it is possible to access and appreciate art pieces in digitized format. Effective indexing, browsing and retrieving art images are important problems need to be addressed not only for computer scientists and art communities but also for common art fanners. Guohua dates back to the Neolithic Age, some 6,000 years ago. As an important part of the East Asian cultural heritage, it is highly regarded for its theory, expression, and techniques throughout the world. Guohua is generally classified into two styles: Xieyi (freehand strokes) and Gongbi ("skilled brush"). The Xieyi School is marked by exaggerated forms and freehand brush work. The essence of landscapes, figures and other subjects are rendered with a minimum of expressive ink (Fig.1 (a)(b)). In contrast, the brushwork in Gongbi paintings is fine and visually complex, it is characterized by close attention to detail and fine brushwork (Fig.1 (c)(d)).

In the literature, automatically image understanding and retrieval use content-based method. A variety of techniques and systems have been developed such as QBIC, Photobook, VisualSEEK, and WebSEEK [1]. The drawback of

K. Aizawa, Y. Nakamura, and S. Satoh (Eds.): PCM 2004, LNCS 3331, pp. 1–8, 2004.

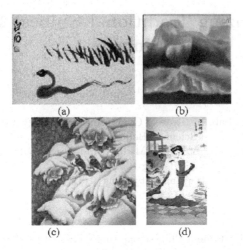

Fig. 1. Examples of Gongbi and Xieyi

this method is that low-level features used by them always could not be interpreted to high-level concepts that are commonly used by human. To overcome the drawback, semantic-sensitive image retrieval techniques have been introduced. Image semantic classification is a form of semantic image understanding. Its goal is to assign the image to semantic class, thus assisting image retrieval and related processing. Authors in [2][3] investigated on classifying indoor and outdoor scenes. Vailaya el al. [4] addressed the problem of classifying city versus landscape and further group landscape images into sunset, mountain and forest. The authors in [5][6] gave approaches to identify natural photographs versus artificial graphs generated by computer tools. Other examples of image semantic classification include face detection and objectionable image identification [7].

Processing on digitized art images is becoming an important research topic. The DELOS-NSF [8] working group discusses problems of retrieving art images and bridging the semantic gap, it points out that this area is still in the early stages of research. Li and Wang [9] use multi-resolution HMM method to characterize different drawing styles of artists. References [10] and [11] give techniques to identify Canvas painting and Traditional Chinese painting images respectively. A.D. Bimbo et al. [12] investigate on the problem of retrieving painting images using color semantics derived from the Itten color sphere.

As described in [8], constructing computer algorithms to learn to classify paintings of different styles is a promising step to bridging the semantic gap. Some works have been done in this domain [9,10,11]. Gongbi and Xieyi are two basic schools of traditional Chinese paintings. To characterize these two types of paintings may be of much help in analyzing traditional Chinese paintings and in retrieving them. In this paper, we propose a method to achieve this goal based on the investigations of visual differences of these two types of Guohua. This has not been explored before. Edge and texture features accompanied with SVM classifiers are used to achieve this high-level classification.

The rest of the paper is as follows. Image features are introduced in section 2 and implementation issues in section 3.Experimental results are given in section 4. And section 5 concludes the paper.

2   Image Features

Two distinguishable low-level texture and color features are employed. Edge-size histogram is first introduced in this paper. It measures the sparseness and granularity of edges of an image. An autocorrelation feature is a traditional texture feature that reflects coarseness of an image.

2.1   Edge-Size Histogram

Edge is regarded as an important feature to represent the content of the image. It conveys a large amount of visual information and human eyes are known to be sensitive to edge features for image perception. Edge histogram descriptor for MPEG-7 is well used in image matching [13]. Shim et al. [14] integrate color histogram and edge histogram for image retrieval. Edge-size histogram introduced in this paper is different from the above two method. It measures consistency and granularity of image edges. We give the formal description below.

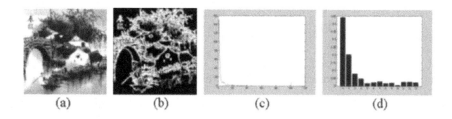

(a)   (b)   (c)   (d)

Fig. 2. Edge size histogram of an example image

Let I be a gray level image, $p(x,y)$ be pixels in I Edge detection is first performed using Sobel detector and generating k number of edges:$\{e_1, e_2, \ldots, e_k\}$. Let n_i be the size of the edge e_i: $n_i = |\{p|p \in e_i\}|$, where $|\bullet|$ denote the number of elements.The edge-size histogram is defined to have 13 dimensions. From 1 to 13, each dimension accumulates the number of edges that have the size of:$\{1, 2, \ldots, 10, [11,20], [21,100], [101,\infty]\}$,thus generating the vector$[EH_j]_{13}$. Edge-size histogram is computed by quantization of the above vector:$ESH_j = EH_j/k, j \in [0, 13]$.. To compute this kind of feature, image should first be resized to have same number of pixels. Figure 2 gives an example to compute this feature. Figure 2 (a) is the original gray-level image. 2(b) is the result of edge detection; there are totally 342 edges. Figure 2(c) is the edge size numbers from 1 to 101, the 101st dimension is the numbers that edges have the size larger than 100. Figure 2(d) is the final edge-size histogram.

As we know, color, saturation and luminance are three factors that artists used to create their productions. Thus we use HSL color space to represent images in the implementation. Edge-size histogram is computed on each of the 3 channels and a 39-bin feature is obtained.

It could be observed that Gongbi images generally have more detailed edges than Xieyi images, this is because the former is characterized by simple and bold strokes intended to represent the exaggerated likenesses of the objects, while the latter by fine brushwork and close attention to detail. The following figure shows this difference demonstrated by edge-size images. Figure 3 (a) (b) is the edge-size histogram of Xieyi paintings in figure 1 (a)(b). On the hue channel, small edges is less than that of figure 3(c)(d), which are edge-size histogram of two Gongbi images in Figure 1(c)(d). From data analysis, the other two channels may also be of some help to differentiate these two schools of traditional Chinese paintings.

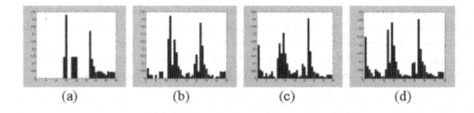

(a)   (b)   (c)   (d)

Fig. 3. Structure of the System in Fig.1

2.2   Autocorrelation Texture Features

Autocorrelation [15] measures the coarseness of an image by evaluating the linear spatial relationships between texture primitives. Large primitives give rise to coarse texture and small primitives give rise to fine texture. If the primitives are large, the autocorrelation function decreases slowly with increasing distance whereas it decreases rapidly if texture consists of small primitives. Autocorrelation function of an image is described as:

$$C_{ff}(p,q) = \frac{mn}{(m-p)(n-q)} \frac{\sum_{i=1}^{} \sum_{j=1}^{} f(i,j)f(i+p,j+q)}{\sum_{i=1}^{} \sum_{j=1}^{} f^2(i,j)}$$

(p,q) varied from (2,2) to (10,10) in a step of two, totally giving of 25 features.

It is conceivable that Gongbi images generally have finer textures than that of Xieyi. While in some cases, the margin part of Gongbi images is rather large, so the center part of the image is segmented to compute autocorrelation features

Fig. 4. Center part of an image

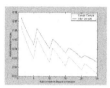

Fig. 5. Average autocorrelation feature values of typical Gongbi and Xieyi images

as illustrated in Figure 4. Xieyi images have larger feature values compared to Gongbi images. Figure 5 shows average result on 30 Gongbi and 30 Xieyi images selected from training set.

3 Implementation Issues

3.1 Classifier

Support vector machine is a two-class classification approach to learn linear or non-linear decision boundaries [16]. Given a set of points, which belong to either of two classes, SVM finds the hyper-plane leaving the largest possible fraction of points of the same class on the same side, while maximizing the distance of either class from the hyper-plane. This is equivalent to performing structural risk minimization to achieve good generalization. Assuming l examples from two classes,

$$(x_1, C_1)(x_2, C_2) \ldots (x_l, C_l), \ x_i \in R^N, \ C_i \in \{-1, +1\}$$

finding the optimal hyper-plane implies solving a constrained optimization problem using quadratic programming. The optimization criterion is the width of the margin between the classes. The discriminate hyper-plane is defined as:

$$g(x) = \sum_{i=1}^{d} a_i C_i k(x, x_i) + a_0$$

where $k(x, x_i)$ is a kernel function, x_i are so-called support vectors determined from the training data, C_i is the class indicator associated with each x_i, and a_i are constants which are also determined by training. Constructing the optimal hyper-plane is equivalent to finding all the nonzero a_i. The sign of $g(x)$ indicates the membership of x.

3.2 Dataset

The image database used in this experiment consists of 3688 traditional Chinese painting images collected from various sources and different artists in different periods. 1799 are Gongbi paintings and 1889 are Xieyi paintings. All these images are used as the test set. The training set includes 117 Gongbi images and 118 Xieyi images.

4 Experimental Results

We conducted a variety of experiments to measure classification performance. Overall classification accuracy criterion is used to evaluate the performance. Let K_g and K_x denote total number of Gongbi and Xieyi images respectively; C_g and C_x denote the number of correctly identified Gongbi and Xieyi images respectively. Thus detection precisions are described as follows:

P (G)= Precision (Gongbi) = C_g / K_g
P (X)= Precision (Xieyi) = C_x / K_x
P (O)= Precision (Overall) = (P (G)+ P (X))/2

Table 1. Result of classification method

	ESH	AC	ESH+AC
P(G)	85.2854%	77.2686%	95.5553%
P(A)	79.2523%	78.9172%	93.6644%
P(O)	82.2689%	78.0929%	94.6098%

Table 2. Comparison of different classifiers

	SVM	C4.5 Decision Tree	Naive Bayesian
P(G)	95.5553%	88.1601%	92.1623%
P(A)	93.6644%	83.748%	90.0476%
P(O)	94.6098%	85.9541%	91.105%

Table 1 shows the classification results of our method. The combined features of edge-size histogram (ESH) and autocorrelation (AC) give us better performance than one feature alone. The final overall classification accuracy of 94.6098% is achieved. The authors also compare SVM classifier with decision tree and Bayesian method, the features used here are combined edge-size histogram and autocorrelation. Results showed in table 2 validate that SVM has comparable or better performance among classification methods. Figure 6 shows some correctly classified image, and Figure 7 are some misclassified paintings.

(a) Correctly classified Gongbi paintings

(b) Correctly classified Xieyi paintings

Fig. 6. Correctly classified traditional Chinese paintings

(a) False classified Gongbi paintings

(b) False classified Xieyi paintings

Fig. 7. False classified traditional Chinese paintings

5   Conclusion

Although the two schools of Guohua try to achieve the same end: the creation of beauty, Gongbi and Xieyi images employ different drawing techniques. This paper gives a method to differentiate these two important categories of Chinese paintings using low-level image features. Encouraging results was obtained on a medium-sized dataset. Future works include establishing algorithms to identify other important semantic information for digitized Guohua images and other types of art images.

Acknowledgments. This work was partly supported by China-American Digital Academic Library (CADAL) project, and partly sup-ported by NEC-JDL video analysis and retrieval project.

References

1. Smeulders A.W.M., Worring M., Gupta A., Jain R.,: Content-Based Image Retrieval at the End of the Early Years. IEEE Trans. on Pattern Analysis and Machine Intelligence, vol. 22, no. 12, 2000
2. Szummer M., Picard R.: Indoor-Outdoor Image Classification. IEEE International Workshop on Content-based Access of Image and Video Databases, in conjunction with ICCV'98. Bombay, India, 1998
3. Serrano N., Savakis A., Luo J.: A Computationally Efficient Approach to Indoor/Outdoor Scene Classification. IEEE ICPR'02, Québec City, Canada, Aug. 2002
4. Vailaya A., Jain A., Zhang H.J.: On Image Classification:City vs. Landscape. IEEE Workshop on Content-Based Access of Image and Video Libraries, Santa Barbara, California, June21, 1998
5. Prabhakar S., Cheng H., Handley John C., Fan Z.G., Lin Y.W.: Picture-Graphics Color Image Classification. IEEE ICIP 2002
6. Wang J.Z., Li J., Wiederhold G., Firschein O.: Systems for Screening Objectionable Images. Computer Comm., vol.21, no.15, 1998
7. Fleck M., Forsyth D.A., Bregler C.: Finding Naked People. Proc. European Conf. Computer Vision, vol.2, 1996
8. Chen C.C., Bimbo A., Amato G., Boujemaa N.: Report of the DELOS-NSF Working Group on Digital Imagery for Significant Cultural and Historical Materials. DELOS-NSF Reports, December, 2002
9. Li J., Wang J.Z,: Studying Digital Imagery of Ancient Paintings by Mixtures of Stochastic Models. IEEE Transactions on Image Processing, vol. 12, no. 2, 15 pp., 2004
10. Leykin A., Cutzu F., Hammoud H.: Visual Properties Differentiating Art from Real Scenes. Technical Report No. 565, Computer Science Department, Indiana University
11. Jiang Shuqiang, Gao Wen, Wang Weiqiang: Classifying Traditional Chinese Painting Images. The 4th International Conference on Information, Communications and Signal Proc-essing - 4th IEEE Pacific-Rim Conference On Multimedia (ICICS-PCM2003)
12. Colombo C., Bimbo A.D., Pala P.: Semantics in Visual Information Retrieval. IEEE Multimedia, July-September 1999
13. International Organization for Standardization Organization International De Normalization ISO/IEC JTC1/SC29/WG11 Coding of Moving Pictures and Audio, ISO/IEC JTC1/SC29/WG11 N4031, Singapore, March 2001
14. Shim Seong-O, Choi Tae-Sun: Edge Color Histogram for Image Retrieval. IEEE ICIP 2002
15. Tuceryan M., Jain A.K.: Texture Analysis. In The Handbook of Pattern Recognition and Computer Vision (2nd Edition), by C. H. Chen, L. F. Pau, P. S. P. Wang (eds.), pp. 207-248, World Scientific Publishing Co., 1998. (Book Chapter)
16. Burges B.: Tutorial on Support Vector Machine for Pattern Recognition. Data Mining and Knowledge Discovery, vol.2, no.2, 1998

A Knowledge-Driven Approach for Korean Traditional Costume (Hanbok) Modeling*

Yang-Hee Nam, Bo-Ran Lee, and Crystal S. Oh

Div. of Digital Media, Ewha Womans University,
11-1 Daehyun-dong, Sodaemun-gu, Seoul, Korea
yanghee@ewha.ac.kr, vinery@hanmail.net, osjung8@hotmail.com
http://home.ewha.ac.kr/~yanghee/index.html

Abstract. Though garment simulation is now one of the important elements in broad range of digital contents, general users do not know well enough how to design a virtual costume that meets some requirements of its specific clothing pattern. In particular, hanbok-the Korean traditional costume- has many different characteristics against western ones in the aspect of its pattern design and of draping. This paper presents a knowledge-driven approach for supporting hanbok draping simulation without knowing how to design hanbok. Based on the analysis of designer's knowledge, we defined multi-level method of measurement construction according to the body shape features of different virtual actors. An experimental system is developed in the form of a Maya plug-in so that we can assure that time and effort for hanbok modeling is reduced and made easy.

1 Introduction

Garment simulation for virtual characters is now demanding in movies, animation, game and others. There have been several CAD systems developed for fashion industry, but they require fashion designer's expertise to complete the detail patterns of a given garment type. In particular, Korean traditional costume reveals great organizational difference against western clothing as describe in Table 1.

This paper proposes a knowledge driven approach for modelling 3D hanbok. We focused on the easy-to-use support for general users for creating hanbok draping simulation. Our approach can be summarized as three phases: First, based on the traditional hanbok design method, we provide *standard database of hanbok patterns*. By using this pattern database, general users without the knowledge of hanbok's design pattern can easily create virtual hanbok. Secondly, we constructed a knowledge-base on how to determine *major garment gauges* from a few body measurements. By this knowledge base, hanbok in several levels of sizes can be created from the same silhouette pattern. We also suggest the third step of *adjusting local measurements of hanbok* so that they

---

* This research was initially supported by Ewha Womans University in 2002.

K. Aizawa, Y. Nakamura, and S. Satoh (Eds.): PCM 2004, LNCS 3331, pp. 9–16, 2004.
© Springer-Verlag Berlin Heidelberg 2004

Table 1. Comparison of modelling process between hanbok and western clothes

Comparable factors	Hanbok	Western clothes
Garment cutting	2-D plane cutting	Curved cutting in 3-D
Fitting level of garment gauge	Flexible size with enough margin (refer to Fig. 1)	Well-fitting (showing body silhouette)
Garment fixation method & shape	Fixation by tying up with strings (flexible shape)	Fixation by button, hook, or zippers (intended shape)
Wearing method	Putting rich-size clothes around the body	Put body into the constrained volume of clothes

Fig. 1. Example wearing of hanbok

reflect various characteristics of individual body shapes that is far from standard body proportions. This detail adjustment level is required because someone can have a body shape that does not fit well with any of the standard levels of body proportion. This is important when we consider that some exaggerated or abnormal body features are often generated on purpose for synthetic characters. For example, hanbok resized by one of standard levels in the previous steps will be still awkward for a thin man with a big belly. The hanbok might be tight or torn around the belly and very loose for all other body parts. Supported by knowledge-base reflecting expert designer's experience, this third step enables individual body-shape dependent hanbok resizing without complex process of measurement re-evaluation.

All these modelling process can be carried out promptly and users can observe simulation results at the time of designing the clothing pattern. Thus, it reduces the mistakes that can be caused by non design experts.

The next chapter describes whole process of general garment design and reviews existing research on virtual garment modelling. The 3rd chapter introduces our proposed knowledge-driven method for hanbok modelling and describes in detail the multi-level adjustment of hanbok depending on character's body shape. Chapter 4 presents the implementation architecture of hanbok modelling system and the resulting hanbok modelling and simulation examples. Our conclusion and discussion on further research will be given in chapter 5.

2 Related Works

Generally, garment design process can be decomposed into several steps as in Fig. 2 Among these, our major concern is given to the steps of *pattern design, grading and draping*. *Pattern design* step is to design the garment cutting pattern. The next step is *grading* step where several standard levels of gauges are generated from a given pattern. The final *draping* step provides the correction of the design or the measurements by putting the garments on a human or mannequin body [1].

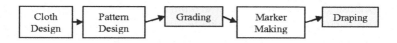

Fig. 2. Garment design steps [1]

Hanbok modelling also follows these steps where each of them involves various parameters and their application rules. However, expert's help is required for designing the cutting pattern and also for adjusting sizes according to the grading and draping rules[2][3][4].

Amongst the computer animation research of western clothes modelling, on-line clothing store done in Miralab is one of the recent remarkable works[5]. Though this work covered most of the process of garment modelling, it does not provide the draping step where the fine adjustment are carried out on the garment measurements according to the local body characteristics such as big belly, short neck, etc. Also, the reference gauges and method of measuring are different from those for hanbok. Therefore, it is not appropriate for applying their method to virtual hanbok modelling.

On the other hand, we appreciate the existing studies on real hanbok creation done by traditional costume designers. Some of these work give us applicable hints on hanbok grading rules[6][7][8][9]. To use them for digital hanbok creation, however, the rules should be analyzed in terms of body measurements and reconstructed as a retrievable knowledge-base. Also, the wearing simulation is better be provided so that it can show the resizing results right away. Since this resizing results only provide the adjustment of measurements for a few gauge levels of standard sizes, those grading rules should be combined with draping rules so that the measurements are adjusted by considering characters' local body shape features.

3 Knowledge-Bases for Hanbok Grading and Draping

This chapter introduces the proposed knowledge-driven modelling scheme that finally creates hanbok measurements according to body shape characteristics. As introduced in chapter 1, the knowledge base consists of two steps: the first one is calculating the standard levels of gauges for a given garment type (*grading*) and the second one is adjusting measurements according to the local characteristics of specific body shape (*draping*).

3.1 *Grading* Knowledge-Base: Resizing Rules for Standard Gauge Levels

Real hanbok pattern can be constructed from just two or three body measurements as its input parameters. Table 2 lists up those body sizes that their measuring is required for each of hanbok *Jogori* that corresponds to western shirt or jacket, and hanbok trousers, and skirt. However, specifying hanbok shape is related to more gauges than just a few input measurements. Meaning of terms representing each part of Jogori is indicated in Fig. 3. For helping non-designer's creation of hanbok pattern, we constructed a knowledge-base that provides how to produce garment gauges from a few body measurements.

Table 2. Kinds of body measurements required for Hanbok

Jogori(Shirt or Jacket)	Trousers	Skirt
Chest (male) or Upper-chest size (female), Back length, Hwa-jang (i.e., arm-length)	Hip size, Trousers length	Upper chest size, Skirt length

Table 3. The relationship between body measurements and gauges for *Jogori*

Body measurements for Jogori (ref. Chest size(**A**), Back length(**B**), Hwa-jang(**C**))			
Group	Gauges	Male	Female
1	Width of Jogori	A/4 +3	A/4 +1.5∼2
	Jindong (Width of a shoulder)	A/4 +2	A/4
	Godae (Width between the right and left sides of the neck)	A/10	A/10–0.5
	Width of a sleeve	A/4 +2	Jindong +3∼4
	Buri (Width of a cuff)	Jindong× 3 / 4	Jindong× 3 / 5
2	Jogori back length	B +10∼15	B
	Jogori front length	(Jogori back length) +1∼2	(Jogori back length) +3∼4
3	Length of a sleeve	C - (Jogori width)	C - (Jogori width)

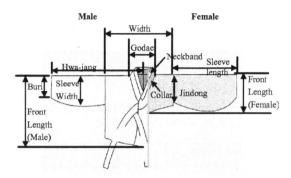

Fig. 3. Standard gauges of hanbok Jogori for both male and female

Table 3 is a summary of fuzzy mapping rules between a few body measurements and the evaluation method for resulting garment gauges. Group 1,2,3 are classified according to which body measurements are used for calculating the gauge values. Given this evaluation rules, the hanbok grading can be automatically established from a few body measurement inputs while keeping custom hanbok style.

3.2 *Draping* Knowledge-Base: Resizing Rules with Individual Body Characteristics

Even though the standard garment gauges are created in several levels, many of actual people do not have body shapes well matched to any of standard levels of global body size. Thus, though the grading rules given in the previous section enables gauge value construction for generally big or normal or small sizes, they do not work well with, for instance, short but fat body style or, in opposition, tall but thin body shape. In particular, Jogori style, for instance, is traditionally depending much on the shapes of face, neck and the line from chest to shoulder. Therefore, we need a second step resizing for such various characteristics of body shapes.

To provide this draping rules, we studied designer's guides where their empirical knowledge is expressed quite vaguely as : "for the fat body shape while short in height, the length of Jogori shouldn't be too long or short". Since such expert's knowledge is not computationally applicable, we classified the rules according to body characteristics: (1) global body shape (2) local body characteristics (3) face shape. In each category, we constructed a fuzzy knowledge base on how to adjust detail measurements of hanbok accordingly. To do this, we first classify the given character shape into one of the fuzzy descriptions in that category. This is accomplished by comparison of the standard and the given body shapes and clustering into fuzzy descriptions based on the difference scale. Once we find the given character's fuzzy description category, we apply the adjustment rules presented in Table 4. It shows the summary of final draping rules regarding various characteristic body shapes. In these rules, descriptive expressions such as 'reduce the length', 'reduce it a little', 'make it wider a bit' are transformed into the rules with fuzzy scale factor labeled as '*a, b, c, d*' respectively. These fuzzy-scale factors are applied for adjusting the garment measurements evaluated in the previous section in multiplicative manner.

Table 4. Local adjustment according to the individual body shape (Note: 'F.L.', 'B.L.'- front/back length, 'F.W.' ,'B.W.'- front/back width)

1. Categories of whole body shape						
(a=Narrowing, b=Narrowing a little,c=Widening a little, d=Widening)						

Measurements → Whole Body Shape ↓	Length of Jogori	Width of Jogori	Jindong (armhole)	Width of sleeves	Godae	Collar	Skirt
Short and fat	1	× b	× b	× b	× a	× c	Length× d Width× a
Short and thin	1	1	1	1	1	Width× c	Length× c
Tall and fat	1	1	1	1	× a	× c	1
Tall and thin	× c	× c	× c	× c	1	× b	× d
Body shape with its chest pushed out	F.L.× d B.L.× a	F.W.× d	1	1	1	1	1
Body shape with its chest bent in	F.L.× a B.L.× d	F.W.× d	1	1	1	1	1

2. Categories of local body shape							

Measurements → Local Body Shape ↓	Shoulder	Collar	Width	Skirt	Front Hanging	Godae	Dongjong
High shoulders	× c	Width× d Length× d	1	1	1	1	1
Drooping shoulders	× b	× d	1	1	1	1	1
Big chest	1	1	F.W.× d	Waist× c	× d	1	1
Big chest & belly	1	1	F.W.× d	1	× d	1	1
Big belly	1	1	Lower width× d	Waist× c Length× d	× d	1	1
Long neck	1	Width× a Length× d	1	1	1	1	× d
Short neck	1	Width× d Length× a	1	1	1	× d	× a

3. Categories of 'face' shape						

Face Shape ↓ Measurements→	Collar	Neckband	Skirt	Jogori	Width	Godae
Round shape	Width× a , Length× d	× a	1	1	1	1
Long face	Width× d , Length× a	× d	× d	× a	1	1
Square shape	Width× d	1	1	1	1	1
Inverse triangle shape	Width× d	× d	1	1	1	× a
With high cheekbones	Width× a , Length× d	× a	1	1	× d	1

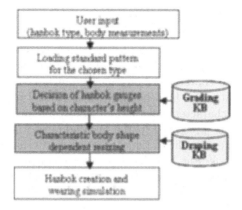

Fig. 4. Implementation architecture of knowledge-driven hanbok modeling

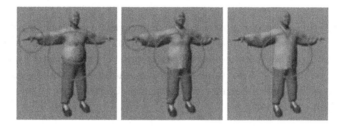

Fig. 5. Wearing simulation by sequentially applying 2-phase knowledge-bases

Fig. 6. Some results for different characteristic body shapes

4   Hanbok Modelling and Simulation: Some Results

Proposed hanbok animation system is implemented using MAYA API and MEL. The overall architecture is shown in Fig. 4. By selecting a character, initial body measurements are determined from the character. Since user also specifies hanbok type (*Jogori*, trousers, etc), the corresponding cloth pattern is loaded from pattern database. After this, the 1st step knowledge is applied to evaluate garment parameters from basic body measurements. Next step is adjusting the detail scale of local garment parameters according to characteristic body shapes and finally the created hanbok is shown as wearing simulation in MAYA.

Fig. 5 and Fig. 6 shows some of the experimental results for hanbok simulation based on our knowledge-driven approach. In the first picture of Fig. 5, we observe the character's belly area protruded outside his *Jogori*. Though this problem is somewhat corrected in the second picture by evaluating standard gauges from the given character's body measurements, the belly and the bust area is still tight. After the final adjustment is carried out based on draping knowledge-base, the character looks more comfortable and the hanbok silhouette is more natural as presented in the last figure of Fig. 5. In this manner, we can simulate clothes that fit to the character's body shape while keeping the inherent style of hanbok. Fig. 6 shows the wearing simulation results, where our approach is applied to several characters with different body shape characteristics.

5   Conclusions and Further Remarks

In summary, this paper proposed a knowledge-driven hanbok draping method that enables animators can create correct costume without hanbok design knowledge. Based on our knowledge based framework, learning based knowledge enhancing will be possible. Also, inherent wearing method of hanbok such as 'wearing by overlapping' and 'wearing by folding' will be studied to generate realistic digital hanbok animation.

References

1. Kim, S.J., Oh, S. W., Wohn, K.: Digital Fashion, Vol. 21. No. 2. J. of Korean Info. Sci. Soc. (2003) 35–42
2. Digital Fashion Ltd.: DressingSim (Software). http://www.dressingsim.com/
3. Syflex LLC.: Syflex-The Cloth Simulator (Software). http://www.syflex.biz/
4. Pad System Technologies Inc.: Pad System. http://www.padsystem.com/
5. Cordier, F., Seo, H., Magnenat-Thalmann, N.: Made-to-Measure Technologies for Online Clothing Store. IEEE CG&A., Vol. 23 (2003)38–48
6. Han, M.J., Song, M.K.: A Studies on the Automatic Drawing and Grading of Korean Man's Hanbok *Durumagi* using apparel CAD system. Journal of Korean Soc. of Clothing and Textiles, Vol. 24. No. 6. (2000) 799–809
7. Lee, J.W.: Revision: Making Hanbok (Korean). Kyungchoon Publishing Co. (1999)
8. Kang, S.J., Nam, Y.J., Cho, H.S., Hong, N.Y., Hwang, E.S.: Research on Measurement Standard for Ready-Made Hanbok Intended for Women in Their Twenties. Journal of Korean Society of Costume, Vol. 43. (1999)
9. Kang, S.J., Hong, N.Y., Nam, Y.J., Cho, H.S., Hwang, E.S.: Development of Men's Hanbok Jacket(jogori) and Trousers Patterns for Ready-Made Hanbok. Journal of Korean Society of Costume, Vol. 47. (1999)

Retrieval of Chinese Calligraphic Character Image

Yueting Zhuang, Xiafen Zhang, Jiangqin Wu, and Xiqun Lu

The Institute of Artificial Intelligence, Zhejiang University,
Hangzhou, 310027, P.R.China
{yzhuang,cadal,wujq,xqlu}@cs.zju.edu.cn

Abstract. Numerous collection of Chinese calligraphy is a valuable civilization legacy. However, it is very difficult to employ any existing techniques to retrieve them, because similarity measure is not a trivial problem for Chinese calligraphic characters. In this paper, a novel method is presented to retrieve Chinese calligraphic character images using approximate correspondence point algorithm. In this method, shapes of calligraphic characters are represented by their contour points. We first compute point contexts and find approximate point correspondence in the other character, and then retrieve calligraphic characters according to their accumulated matching cost. Finally, the efficiency of our algorithm is demonstrated by a preliminary experiment.

1 Introduction

Numerous collections of historical Chinese calligraphy are valuable resources serve to historians and calligraphy lovers who wish to learn from. For example, the collected works of the famous calligraphist Wang Xizhi were written about 1,650 years ago. These collections, although may be available through public libraries or Internet, cannot be retrieved by optical character recognition (OCR) which performs well on machine printed characters against clean backgrounds. The reason why no effective technique supports to retrieve Chinese calligraphic characters written in different styles lies in:

1) *Deformation*: The same writer under different moods can generate different styles of the same character. Sometimes a character is deformed consciously for a better artistic effect, such as the dry stroke.

2) *Complexity*: It has been estimated that an average character is composed of about 12.71 strokes (see [1]). The size of a stroke varies according to the total numbers of strokes composing the character, and the size of a stroke segment depends on the total number of segments composing the stroke. Also, strokes are written connectively in some calligraphic styles, making it even difficult to identify.

3) *Degradation*: Many ancient calligraphy works have been degraded by nature changes.

K. Aizawa, Y. Nakamura, and S. Satoh (Eds.): PCM 2004, LNCS 3331, pp. 17–24, 2004.

Conventional Chinese character recognition techniques (see [2]) share many same problems and solutions with calligraphic character retrieval. However, most of character recognition techniques are too rigid to be applied to calligraphic character retrieval.The primary contribution of this paper is to propose a novel calligraphic character retrieval approach using Approximate Point Correspondence, which we denoted by APC. The key issue is to find characters of similar shape based on user's query sample. In this paper, we assumed that it is not necessary to recognize a calligraphic character in order to retrieve it, since the purpose is to render the art beauty of different styles of the same character rather than the meaning of that character.

The remainder of this paper is organized as follows: Related work is surveyed in Section 2. In Section 3, our proposed approach for calligraphic character retrieval is described in detail. In Section 4, we present the experiment and evaluation. Conclusions and future works are given in the final Section.

2   Related Work

Numerous promising research works have been done on handwriting recognition, such as [3], uses word-matching technology to recognize George Washington's manuscripts, and [4] identifies ancient Hebrew manuscripts. However, no published research has done successfully on Chinese calligraphic character retrieval because it differs from other languages by its enormous numbers and complex structure of ideographs. A recent survey paper [5] gives good scientific background about handwriting recognition. In [6] Shi Baile et al. show a content retrieval method for one antique book. However, it is unknown how well this rigid visual similarity based method works on calligraphic characters in different styles written by many different people in many different dynasties.

Medial axis transformation (MAT) is often employed in off-line handwriting recognition. However, it will introduce noise to calligraphy because of its degraded image or dry brushes. Some important information will be lost and many critical structural features (for example, in [7], end points, hooks, T-shape, cross, and corner) cannot be detected. Our earlier work includes applying Projecting method and EMD method to Chinese calligraphic character retrieval.

- **Projecting Method**: Firstly, *2 dimensional data* of calligraphic character image is projected into *1 dimensional data* in several directions. Then pixel histograms are counted and compared using χ^2 test statistic. This is because most of Chinese characters are composed by five primitive strokes (see [1]): dot, dash, perpendicular down stroke, left falling stroke and right falling stroke, except dot the others have directions. If the projecting direction coincides with the stroke direction, then the position information of the stroke is remained after projecting. Also, we incorporate silhouette information of the character by projecting the margin from the border to the strokes.
- **EMD Method**: Earth Movers'Distance (EMD) is a partial distance measure between discrete and finite distributions [8]. One way to visualize this method is to imagine piles of dirt and holes in the ground, and the Earth Mover try

to fill all the holes with dirt. In case of the calligraphic character retrieval, imagine the sampled points from one character as piles of dirt and the points from the other character as holes in the ground. Then the less work the Earth Mover has to do to fill holes with dirt, the more similar these two characters are.

3 Matching Similar Chinese Calligraphic Characters

The key problem in calligraphic character retrieval is the matching of similar isolated characters, which we will describe begin with the preprocessing.

3.1 Preprocessing

The source data for similarity matching is obtained by the preprocessing, which includes the following steps.

1. **Binarization**: The image was smoothed and converted to binary image. This is because the colorful background of the image, which may interests readers, is not useful in the similarity matching process.
2. **Segmentation**: The segmentation of calligraphic characters is relative simple, because they were written by brush and the space between them are always exist. We use the minimum bounding rectangles to segment the original page into isolated characters as introduced in [9].
3. **Character scaling**: After isolated characters of different size are obtained, all the characters are normalized in order to keep scale invariant.In our work, the normalized scale size is 32×32 in pixels.
4. **Sampling**: We employ edge detector to get contour of the character. Then, store these contour points information in an array instead of store them in a 32×32 matrix.

3.2 Approximate Point Context

In terms of image comparisons, there are two categories of methods: intensity-based (color and texture) and geometry-based (shape). For calligraphic character retrieval, shape is far more interested than color or texture, though retrieve by shape is still a difficult aspect of content-base research (see [10] and [11]). Here, we use approximate points context to describe shape feature, since we're trying to find all the similar shapes not the exactly same shape.

As described earlier, Chinese characters are composed by five primitive strokes. Except the stroke of dot, the other strokes have directions. (Stroke of dash is horizontal, perpendicular down stroke is vertical, left falling stroke is slant approximately by $45°$ and right falling down stroke is slant approximately by $135°$). In terms of image, they are represented by pixels (or points). Therefore, the polar coordinates is more suitable to describe directional relationship of points than the Cartesian coordinates. Fig. 1 shows the coordinates we use.

For direction, we use 8 bins in equal degree size to divide the whole space into 8 directions. And for radius, we use 4 bins for $\log_2 r$(in our case the isolated character images are scaled to 32×32, so the chord is divided when r=2, r=4, r=8, r=16 and r=32). As you see not all the bins are in the same size, this is because the relationships with the nearby points are more important than with faraway points, and should be described in detail. Belongie et al. proposed an inspirational and similar approach to us in [12], yet it is much more complex at least for calligraphic character retrieval.

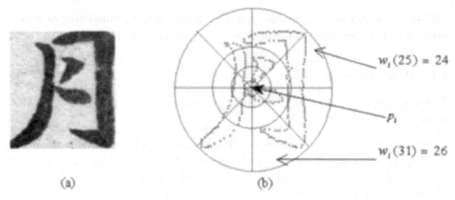

(a)   (b)

Fig. 1. Point context. (a) an original isolated calligraphic character example (b) the correspondence log-polar bins for point context computing when the point is p_i

For each point p_i of a given point set composed of n sampled points, we describe its approximate point context by it's relationship with the remainder $n - 1$ points using coarse k bins:

$$w_i(k) = \#\{q_j \neq p_i : q_j \in bin(k)\} \qquad (1)$$

Where p_i means the ith point which we are computing for the point context, k means the kth bin of point p_i. Fig.1(b). shows an example of how these bins are built and computed for a calligraphic character. The information of contour points which represent a character is kept in an array in advance. So, the point contexts of a character composed by n sampled points can be obtained in $O(n)$ time before shape matching process.

3.3   Finding Approximate Point Correspondence

For each given point p_i on the query example, if a point q_j is its corresponding point, then it subject to the following constrain:

$$dist = |p_i - q_j| = \sqrt{(x_i - x_j)^2 + (y_i - y_j)^2} \leq \frac{1}{3}length \qquad (2)$$

Where (x_i, y_i) and (x_j, y_j) denote the position of the point p_i and q_j, and $length$ is the scale size. This is because according to the calligraphy writing experience, very few stroke composer of a character will translate more than $\frac{1}{3}$ of the whole scale space, since an average character is composed by 12.71 strokes as mentioned above, and the size of a stroke depends on the number of strokes composing the character. Take advantage of this feature will greatly reduce the searching scope and also avoids finding some false corresponding point.

We still use the χ^2 test statistic to measure the matching cost. Let $C_{ij} = C(p_i, q_j)$ denote the matching cost of two points p_i and q_j (p_i is a point on the query example, and q_j is a point on a candidate calligraphic character), then the matching value of two points is defined as:

$$C_{ij} = C(p_i, q_j) = \frac{1}{2} \sum_{k=1}^{k=32} \frac{[w_i(k) - w_j(k)]^2}{w_i(k) + w_j(k)} \tag{3}$$

Where $w_i(k)$, $w_j(k)$ are the value of bin histograms at point p_i and point q_j, respectively. For each given point p_i in the query point set, if the point q_k has the minimum matching cost with point p_i, then it is regarded as the inexact (approximate) correspondence point for p_i, as in reality there's no exact corresponding point, except in the case that the candidate image is the same as the query. Therefore, the minimum point matching cost for p_i is:

$$PMC_i = min\{C(p_i, q_j) : j = 0, 1, 2...m\} \tag{4}$$

As the number of sampled points on each character is not in the same size, the mapping can't be one-to-one. One point in one set may have many counterpoints in the other set, or have no corresponding point (This will not happen since we can always find the point which has the minimum matching cost as the corresponding point. We don't need to reject those special points as [13] dose or add *dummy* nodes to the smaller point set as [12] does). The total matching cost of the two character images is defined as:

$$TMC = \sum_{i=1}^{i=n} (PMC_i + \alpha \|p_i - corresp(p_i)\|^2) \tag{5}$$

Where $\|p_i - corresp(p_i)\|^2$ is the Euclidean distance between point p_i and the approximate corresponding point $corresp(p_i)$ in a candidate calligraphic character. $\alpha = 0.1$. Thus the total matching cost of two characters can be obtained in $O(n^2)$ time compared with $O(n^3)$ time proposed by Belongie et al. This is because all the point contexts were computed in advance. They were computed only once and reused in the late matching process.

When all of the total matching cost of each candidate calligraphic character in the database with the query character were obtained, the retrieval can be done according to the matching cost. The less the matching cost is, the more similar the two calligraphic characters are.

3.4 Indexing Calligraphy Image

Another key problem in retrieval is how all the original data are indexed. In our work, we store large amount of raw data of original scanned paper image

Fig. 2. Two different retrieval examples by APC approach

in disk array according to its metadata such as the name of the author, the written time etc. The character's original position, which indicates where the isolated character located in original paper and where this original paper located in, also the associated contour information are stored in database on which the matching process performs. The disk cache is used to store regular used calligraphic character's raw data and features to speed up retrieval.

For the query sample, it can be an existing calligraphic character image imported from the disk. Or, if the user has no query sample initially, it can be scratched, or even typed in using keyboard. The shape feature of this query image is computed for the later matching process. Certain calligraphic character may have more deformation than others. We use feedbacks from user to navigator the user to change query step by step to get the calligraphic character that the user really want.

4   Experiments and Evaluation

4.1   Retrieval Result

In the experiment, approaches described above are tested with the same database and the same query examples. Different styles of the same character are considered relevant and should be retrieved. In this primitive experiment, we focus on 336 isolated characters in different styles, which belong to 150 character categories. They are chose from historical works randomly (the written time varies form 1650 years ago to 80 years ago). Fig.2 shows two retrieval examples by our APC approach. Similar retrieved characters are shown according to their matching cost. For the query example on the left part, there are 10 different instances of this character in the database, and some strokes were written in connected way as you can see. But all of them are retrieved. For the query on the right part, there are 20 different instances and all of them are retrieved.

Similar results obtained when we change to different query, even to the character scratched by user. Compared with Projecting approach and EMD approach, the performance of our proposed APC approach is the best, and that the relevance retrieve rate is higher compared with regular content-based image retrieval.

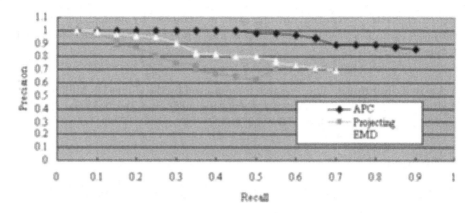

Fig. 3. Comparisons of average retrieval result of 20 randomly chose query samples

4.2   Measuring Retrieval Effectiveness

In order to quantitatively speculate on how well our approach does, we use recall and precision metrics for measuring retrieval effectiveness. They are defined as:

$$recall = \frac{|relevant \; \Box \; retrieved|}{|relevant|} \tag{6}$$

$$precision = \frac{|relevant \; \Box \; retrieved|}{|retrieved|} \tag{7}$$

It is easy to see that the point *(1,1)* on Recall-Precision coordinates is the ultimate goal for all researchers trying to reach, yet too difficult to touch in current time. Fig.3 is a Recall-Precision curve for the performance comparisons of APC approach, Projecting approach and EMD approach. It compares the average retrieval result (the average precision rate under the average recall rate) of 20 character queries randomly chose from the database. Each of them has more than 4 different calligraphic styles in the database. It shows that the performance of APC approach is better than EMD or Projecting approach. Especially, the recall rate is much higher. And the performance of EMD approach is a little better or similar to projecting approach.

5   Conclusions and Future Work

We propose an original and efficient approach to retrieve Chinese calligraphic characters by matching character images based on approximate point correspondence algorithm. While the experiment is somewhat preliminary, it works well and clearly demonstrates the applicability of our new approach to Chinese calligraphic character retrieval.

Our further development will include using adaptive histogram bins in order to make use of the context information of neighbor bins, and obtaining user desired character styles that do not exist in database by analogizing existing character examples based on their approximate point correspondence described in this paper.

Acknowledgements. This research is supported by the China-US Million Book Digital Library Project (see http://www.cadal.net), and the National Natural Science Foundation of China (No. 60272031).

References

1. Zhang Xi-Zhong, Chinese Character Recognition Techniques. Beijing: Tsinghua Uni-versity Press, 1992.
2. Wu You-Shou and Ding Xiao-Qing, Chinese character recognition: the principles and the implementations. Beijing: Advanced Education Press, 1992.
3. T.M. Rath, S. Kane, A. Lehman, E. Partridge and R. Manmatha, Indexing for a Digital Library of George Washington's Manuscripts: A Study of Word Matching Techniques, CIIR Technical Report, 2002.
4. Itay Bar Yosef, Klara Kedem, Its'hak Dinstein, Malachi Beit-Arie, Edna Engel: Classifi-cation of Hebrew Calligraphic Handwriting Styles: Preliminary Results. *In Proceedings of the First International Workshop on Document Image Analysis for Libraries (DIAL' 04)*, 2004, pp. 299-305.
5. R. Palmondon and S. N. Srihari, On-Line and Off-Line Handwriting Recognition: A Comprehensive Survey, *IEEE Transactions on Pattern Analysis and Machine Intelli-gence*, Vol. 22, No. 1, January 2000, pp. 63-84.
6. Shi Baile, Zhang Liang, Wang Yong, Chen Zhifeng, Content Based Chinese Script Re-trieval Through Visual Similarity Criteria, *Journal of Software in china* vol. 12 (9), 2001, pp. 1336-1342.
7. S. L. Xie and M. Suk, On machine recognition of hand-printed Chinese characters by feature relaxation, *Pattern Recognition*, vol. 21, no. 1, 1998, pp.1-7.
8. S. Cohen and L. Guibas. The Earth Mover's Distance under Transformation Sets. *In Proceedings of the 7th IEEE International Conference on Computer Vision*, Corfu, Greece, September 1999, pp. 173-187.
9. R. Manmatha and N. Srimal. Scale space technique for character segmentation in hand-written manuscripts. *In Pro. 2nd Int'l Conf. On Scale-Space Theories in Computer Vision*, 1999, pp. 22-33.
10. R.C. Veltkamp and M. Hagedoorn, State of the Art in Shape Matching, Technical Report UU-SC-1999-27, Utrecht, 1999.
11. Sven Loncaric. A Survey of Shape Analysis Techniques. *Pattern Recognition*, 31(8),1998, pp.983-1001.
12. S. Belongie , J. Malik , J. Puzicha, Shape Matching and Object Recognition Using Shape Contexts, *IEEE Transactions on Pattern Analysis and Machine Intelligence*, vol.24, No. 4, April 2002, pp.509-522.
13. Haili Chui, Anand, Rangarajan, A new point matching algorithm for non-rigid registra-tion, *Computer Vision and Image Understanding archive*, Volume 89, February 2003, pp. 114 - 141.

Random Channel Allocation Scheme in HIPERLAN/2

Eui-Seok Hwang[1], Jeong-Jae Won[2], You-Chang Ko[3], Hyong-Woo Lee[4], and
Choong-Ho Cho[1]

[1] Korea Univ. Dept. of Computer & Information Science
{ushwang,chcho}@korea.ac.kr
[2] Univ. of British Columbia Dept. of Electrical and Computers Engineering
wonjj@ece.ubc.ca
[3] LG Electronics Inc. UMTS Handset Lab.
ycko@lge.com
[4] Korea Univ. Dept. of Electronics & Information Engineering
hwlee@korea.ac.kr

Abstract. HIPERLAN/2 is one of the standards for high-speed wireless
LANs developed by ETSI BRAN. A mobile terminal(MT), when it has
messages to send in the uplink channel, may use contention slots, called
random access channels (RCHs), to send the resource request messages.
Based on successful resource request messages from the MTs, the access
point(AP) allocates uplink channel resources dynamically. The number
of RCHs in one MAC frame should be adjusted in such way that the
access delay for request messages is kept small without underutilizing
the RCHs. In this paper, we propose a new RCH allocation scheme using
the splitting algorithm, which dynamically adjusts the number of RCHs
according to the current traffic situation. The simulation results show
that our scheme performs well in terms of channel throughput, access
delay and delay jitter compared with previously proposed RCH allocation
schemes.

1 Introduction

As wireless LAN standards, ETSI BRAN's HIPERLAN/2 and IEEE's 802.11a
are currently suggested for providing raw data rates of up to 54 Mbps in the
5GHz band. The main differences between them occur at the MAC layer[2,4-
8]. While IEEE 802.11a uses a distributed MAC protocol that is based on a
CSMA/CA, HIPERLAN/2 is based on a TDMA/TDD approach using a MAC
frame with a period of 2ms[1].

In HIPERLAN/2, the MT, when it has messages to send in the uplink channel, may use contention slots, which are called RCHs, to send the resource request
message using the slotted ALOHA scheme. Based on successful resource request
messages from the MTs, the AP allocates uplink channel resources dynamically
considering message types. The number of RCHs in one MAC frame should be
adjusted in such way that the access delay for request messages is kept small

K. Aizawa, Y. Nakamura, and S. Satoh (Eds.): PCM 2004, LNCS 3331, pp. 25–32, 2004.
© Springer-Verlag Berlin Heidelberg 2004

without underutilizing the RCHs. It is desirable that the number of RCHs is dynamically adapted by the AP depending on the current traffic state. For example, the allocation of excessive RCHs may waste radio resources, and on the other hand, the allocation of insufficient RCHs may result in many collisions in access attempts.

In this paper, we propose a new adaptive random channel allocation scheme based on the splitting algorithm. The simulation results show that the proposed scheme achieves higher throughput, and incurs lower access delay and delay jitter than the previously proposed RCH allocation schemes.

This paper is organized as follows. In section 2, we describe HIPERLAN/2's MAC protocol and related research. A new random channel allocation scheme is proposed in section 3. Using the simulation, we show the performance of the proposed scheme in section 4. We conclude this paper in section 5.

2   Related Research

2.1   Basic MAC Frame Structure for HIPERLAN/2

One MAC frame of HIPERLAN/2 has fixed duration of 2ms and organized as shown in Fig.1[1].

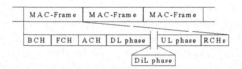

Fig. 1. Basic MAC frame structure for HIPERLAN/2

- BCH(Broadband CHannel : downlink) : conveys broadcast control information concerning the whole radio cell.
- FCH(Frame CHannel : downlink) : contains the information defining how the resources are allocated in the current MAC frame.
- ACH(Access feedback CHannel : downlink) : informs the MTs that have used the RCH in the previous MAC frame about the result of their access attempts.
- RCH(Random access CHannel) : is defined for the purpose of giving an MT the opportunity to request transmission resources in the uplink MAC frames. The number of RCHs of one MAC frame is in [1,31] [1].
- DL(DownLink), UL(UpLink), DiL(Direct Link)

2.2   The Previous Schemes for the RCH Allocation

The access to RCHs will be controlled by a contention window CW_a maintained by each MT. Each MT decides CW_a by the number a, where a is the number of retransmission attempts made by the MT. The CW_a is defined as follows, where n is the number of RCHs in the current MAC frame [1].

$$\diamond \text{ Initial attempt} : a = 0, \ CW_0 = n \tag{1}$$

$$\diamond \text{ Retransmission} : a \geq 1, \ CW_a = \begin{cases} 256 & 2^a \geq 256, \\ 2^a & n < 2^a \leq 256, \\ n & n \geq 2^a \end{cases}$$

The RCH used for the ath retransmission attempt including an initial transmission ($a = 0$) will be chosen by a uniformly distributed random integer value r within the interval $[1, CW_a]$. The MT shall start counting r from the first RCH in the MAC frame, in which the ACH indicates the failure of the previous access attempt. For initial transmission, the MT starts counting with the first RCH in the current frame. The MT shall not access the RCH before its counter has reached the RCH with the number equal to r. After receiving the ACH with a positive feedback, a will be reset to 0.

In [3], the number of RCHs is adaptively changed by the result of access attempts within the previous MAC frame. That is, the AP increases RCHs of next MAC frame as many as collided RCHs and decreases them by successful access attempts with weighting factor α. When there is no access attempt in the previous MAC frame, the AP reduces RCHs of the upcoming frame by one. The throughput of [3] can be increased to 37% when compared with fixed RCHs allocation schemes that perform at maximum 35% of channel throughput. This algorithm updating the number of RCHs is given by

$$r(t + 1) = r(t) + \alpha(N_f(t) - N_s(t))(1 - I_{idle}(t)) - I_{idle}(t) \tag{3}$$

where meanings of variables are as follows :

- $r(t)$: the number of allocated RCHs at MAC frame t
- α : weighting factor
- $N_f(t)$: the number of collided RCHs at MAC frame t
- $N_s(t)$: the number of successful RCHs at MAC frame t
- $I_{idle}(t)$: indication function of which value is 1 if there is no access attempt RCHs at MAC frame t ; otherwise its value is 0

Constrain the scope of allowable number of RCHs per MAC frame from minimum one to maximum R_{MAX} as Eq.4

$$r(t + 1) = \min\{\max\{r(t + 1), 1\}, R_{\text{MAX}}\} \tag{4}$$

3   New Random Channel Allocation Scheme

The AP controls the number of RCHs based on the splitting algorithm [9], by which the set of user involved in a collision is split into smaller subsets until individual users are singled out, and then can transmit without the risk of a collision. The number of RCHs of $(t + 1)^{th}$ MAC frame is given by

$$r(t + 1) = min\{N_a + 2 \times N_f(t), R_{\text{MAX}}\} \qquad (5)$$

where

- $r(t)$: the number of allocated RCHs at MAC frame t
- $N_f(t)$: the number of collided RCHs at MAC frame t
- N_a : the fixed number of RCHs allocated for newly arriving packets

As shown in Fig. 2, there are N_a RCHs for newly arriving request packets in each frame. For each collided RCH in the previous frame, additional two RCHs are allocated for collision resolution. For initial attempt, an MT randomly accesses one RCH within the interval $[1, N_a]$ as Eq. 6. The collided MTs in the previous MAC frame choose the RCH to access based on the location information of contention slots where collisions occur. That is, the MTs in the ith RCH among the collided RCHs in the previous MAC frame randomly access either $(2 \times i - 1 + N_a)^{th}$ or $(2 \times i + N_a)^{th}$ RCH as Eq. 7. In addition, if there are not enough RCHs in the current MAC frame, the retransmission occurs within the interval $[1, N_a]$ after a random delay[1] by frame unit as Eq. 8.

$\diamond$ Initial attempt: Random access within $[1, N_a]$ (6)
$\diamond$ Retransmission:

     Random access either $2i - 1 + N_a$ or $2i + N_a$ if $2i + N_a \leq R_{\text{MAX}}$ (7)
     Random access within $[1, N_a]$ after a random delay   if $2i + N_a > R_{\text{MAX}}$ (8)
         where i is the location of collided RCH in the previous MAC frame.

Fig. 2 shows an example of how the number of RCHs would be decided by the splitting algorithm, in which the number of RCHs for new requests is two and R_{MAX} is eight. If four RCHs are collided in the previous MAC frame, the number of RCHs will be 10 in the current MAC frame (two RCHs for new requests and eight RCHs that are splitted by four collided RCHs). However, the number of RCHs in the current MAC frame should be eight because R_{MAX} value is eight.

In the current MAC frame, new MTs can access the first or second RCH. The MTs collided on C_1 of the previous MAC frame randomly access either C_{11} or C_{12}. Similarly, the MTs involved in C_2 in the previous MAC frame can randomly access either in the fifth or in the sixth RCH in the current MAC frame. However, the MTs involved in C_4 in the previous MAC frame cannot access the RCH in the current MAC frame because the maximum number of RCHs is eight. Therefore, these MTs should access RCHs for new MTs after a random delay.

---

[1] When collided requests cannot be transmitted in the next frame, due to lack of RCHs, the requests are shceduled after a random delay uniformly distributed in $[RT_{\text{min}}, RT_{\text{max}}]$ in frames. These request are treated as if they are newly arriving requests.

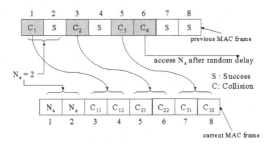

Fig. 2. An example of the splitting algorithm($N_a = 2$ $R_{\mathrm{MAX}} = 8$)

4   Simulation Results

This section presents some simulation results on the throughput, average delay and delay variance. In order to observe the presented performance issues, we examine the effects of the fixed number of RCHs allocated for new requests, N_a, and random delay experienced by MTs that should choose the RCHs out of the current MAC frame because there are not enough RCHs. The throughput(ρ) is defined as [3]

$$\rho = \frac{\text{total number of successful requests}}{\text{total number of RCHs allocated}} \tag{9}$$

For simulation, we assume that there is no transmission error due to radio channel environment, there are 50 MTs as a whole, and each MT's resource request message is generated according to Poisson process with rate λ per MAC frame. We also assume an MT cannot generate a new request message until the access attempt succeeds. We have simulated during 1000 seconds which contains 5×10^5 MAC frames.

In Fig. 3, we observe that the maximum throughput of the proposed scheme is 44%, while that of [3] is 37% when the weighting factor (α) in Eq. 3 is one. In general, when the packet arrival rate is low, the higher throughput can be achieved when N_a is low. That is, allocating many RCHs for new requests is a waste of resources when packet arrival rate is low. When the packet arrival rate is high, throughput can be improved when N_a is high. It is demonstrated that the system throughput can be reduced by increasing the number of collided requests in the case of allocating a few RCHs for new requests when the packet arrival rate is high.

Fig. 3 also shows the effects of random delay experienced by MTs that should choose the RCH out of the current MAC frame when R_{MAX} is 31. There is little difference in random delay (between 17 and 24 frames; between 25 and 32 frames) for the same value of N_a. The reason is that there are few occasions that the number of requested RCHs exceeds R_{MAX} in the system in the case when R_{MAX} is 31.

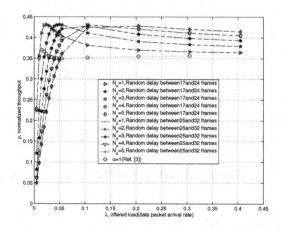

Fig. 3. Offered load versus throughput($R_{\mathrm{MAX}} = 31$)

Fig. 4 shows the throughput-delay characteristics of the proposed scheme. For example, the proposed scheme shows the delay within one frame when throughput is 3.5, however, the previous scheme [3] shows the delay beyond three frames. Concerning real-time traffic, the delay variance is also an important performance issue. Table 1 shows the delay variances of the previous work [3] and the proposed scheme. The proposed scheme performs well when compared with previously proposed schemes in terms of the mean delay and the dealy variance. The future wireless LAN should guarantee QoS of not only non-real-time traffic but also real-time traffic, that is, QoS of multi-media traffic. Therefore, we can expect that the proposed scheme can be useful in guaranteeing QoS of multi-media traffic in wireless LAN.

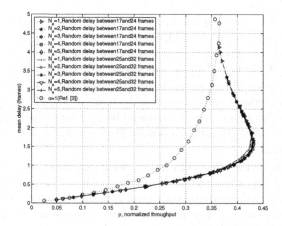

Fig. 4. Throughput versus Mean delay($R_{\mathrm{MAX}} = 31$)

Table 1. Comparison of delay variances of [3] and the proposed scheme

Arrival rate	[3] when $\alpha = 1$	Proposed scheme when $N_a = 2, R_{MAX} = 31,$ Random delay=[17,24]
0.02	1969.09	1.95896
0.03	1871.38	2.46129
0.04	1506.57	2.76634
0.05	1203.47	2.96508
0.105	484.129	3.38835
0.205	223.639	3.47065
0.305	150.943	3.5624

We have observed that the various random delay of MTs that exceeds R_{MAX} has little effect on the system performance when R_{MAX} is 31. However, when R_{MAX} is relatively small, random delay becomes a critical variable on the system performance. In Fig. 5, we see the effects of small R_{MAX}, that is, when N_a is 2 and R_{MAX} is 8. Even if the maximum throughputs associated with the various random delay approaches 44%, the system falls into an unstable state when random delay takes values from the range of 1 to 10 or 1 to 16. Therefore, we can expect that the system performance may be improved by increasing random delay rather than by increasing the range of random delay.

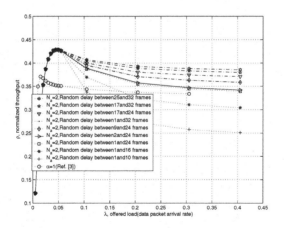

Fig. 5. Offered load versus Throughput ($R_{MAX} = 8$)

5   Conclusion

In this paper, we proposed a new random channel allocation scheme of HIPER-LAN/2 using the splitting algorithm. This scheme can reduce the complexity of MT because each MT does not need to maintain the retransmission attempts time and contention windows, and in addition, performs well in terms of throughput, mean delay and delay variance compared with the previously proposed RCH allocations schemes. From simulation results, we see that the throughput of our scheme is improved about 10% when compared with the fixed RCHs allocation scheme and the previous scheme[3]. In addition, we observed the effects of various random delay of MTs that exceeds the maximum number of RCHs and the number of reserved RCHs for new requests in a frame. For improving the throughput, the number of RCHs for new requests should be increased according to the traffic load. We also observed that the bigger random delay the better throughput.

The future wireless LAN should guarantee QoS of multi-media traffic. That is, in order to guarantee QoS for both non-real-time and real-time traffic, lowering delay and delay variance are needed for real-time traffic. Therefore, the proposed scheme can be applied for guaranteeing QoS of multi-media traffic in wireless LAN.

References

1. HIPERLAN/2 ; Data Link Control (DLC) Layer: Part 1, Basic Data Transport Functions, Broadband Radio Access Networks(BRAN), ETSI Standard TS 101 761-1 V1.3.1, Nov. 2001.
2. Jamshid khuun,et al., "HIPERLAN2: Broadband Wireless Communications at 5GHz", IEEE Communications Magazine, June 2002, pp.130-136.
3. Gyung-Ho Hwang, Dong-Ho Cho, "Adaptive Random Channel Allocation Scheme in HIPERLAN/2 ", IEEE Communications Letters, VOL. 6, NO. 1, JAN. 2002, pp. 40-42
4. Angela Doufexi, et al., "A Comparison of the HIPERLAN/2 and IEEE 802.11a Wireless LAN Standards", IEEE Communications Magazine, May 2002, pp. 172-180
5. R. Van Nee et al., "New High-Rate Wireless LAN Standards", IEEE Communications Magazine, Vol. 37, No. 12, Dec. 1999, pp. 82-88
6. A. Doufexi et al., "Throughput Performance of WLANs Operating at 5GHz Based on Link Simulations with Real and Statistical Channels", IEEE VTC '01 Spring
7. G. Anastasi, L. Lenzini, and E. Mingozzi, "MAC Protocols for Wideband Wireless Local Access: Evolution Toward Wireless ATM", IEEE Pers. Commun., Oct. 1999, pp. 169-74
8. A. Hettich and M. Schrother, "IEEE 802.11a or ETSI BRAN HIPERLAN/2: Who Will Win the Race for a High-Speed Wireless LAN Standard", Euro. WL Conf., Germany, Oct. 1999, pp 169-74
9. Bertsekas D, Gallager R. Data Networks. New Jersey: Prentice Hall, 2nd edition, 1992

A Two-Stage Queuing Approach to Support Real-Time QoS Guarantee for Multimedia Services in TDMA Wireless Networks

Ren-Hao Cheng[1], Po-Cheng Huang[3], Mong-Fong Horng[2], Jiang-Shiung Ker[1], and Yau-Hwang Kuo[3]

[1] Advanced Multimedia Internet Technology Inc., Yong Kang, Tainan, Taiwan
[2] CSIE, Shu-Te University, Kaohsiung, Taiwan
[3] CSIE, National Cheng Kung University, Tainan, Taiwan

Abstract. This paper presents a two-stage queuing approach (TSQA) to improve the quality of service when real-time service in wireless channels [1]. In the first stage, the required delay, bandwidth, lose and input rate of different traffic classes are considered to allocate resource. In the second stage, the channel condition of each host is involved to achieve the optimal bandwidth utilization and fairness between hosts. Finally, from the mathematical analysis and simulation results, we confirm that the TSQA really support QoS requirements of real-time multimedia services in the TDAM wireless networks

1 Introduction

As multimedia services become popular, the demand on real-time and reliable delivery is increasing. Multimedia services require certain quality of service (QoS) such as low packet delay, low packet loss and low delay jitter, etc [2]. With the evolution of wireless communication from GSM [3], GPRS [4] to 3G networks [5], the available bandwidth and capacity is continuously improved. Despite of that, how to utilize the network resource including bandwidth and capacity in an effective and efficient way is the focus of this paper.

In this work, we propose a two-stage queuing scheme operated in a TDMA base stations to support host stations with various service classes. The first stage queues are organized to meet the various services requirements. All incoming packets are classified into one of the first stage queue according to their service level agree (SLA). After the first stage, the packets are routed to the target host queue in the second stage. In such a scheme, there are two mechanisms to adapt the resource allocation; one is the stage-1 service allocator and the other is the slot scheduler. These two mechanisms implement a two-degree-of-freedom system to control the packet delivery according to the service class and the target host of the packets. The simulation results depict that the proposed approach has the ability to differentiate the delay and loss performances of various service traffics and demonstrate the superior efficiency as well as the feasibility.

K. Aizawa, Y. Nakamura, and S. Satoh (Eds.): PCM 2004, LNCS 3331, pp. 33–40, 2004.
© Springer-Verlag Berlin Heidelberg 2004

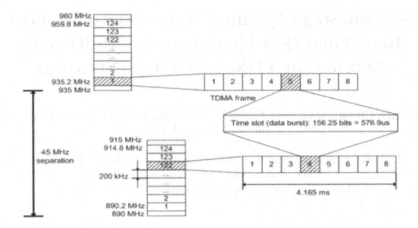

Fig. 1. Frequency division of GSM carrier and TDMA frames

This paper is organized as follows. The modeling of TDMA wireless system is presented in Section 2. In Section 3, a Two-Stage Queuing Approach (TSQA) is presented to detail the algorithm and operation. Then, four service classes including VoIP, VoD, Web browsing and File transfer, are used simultaneously to evaluate the performance of TSQA in Section 4. Finally we conclude this work in Section 5.

2   Modeling of TDMA Wireless Network

TDMA is one of the popular multiplexing technologies used in modern communication system. General Packet Radio Service (GPRS) is a typical and popular wireless data service. GPRS uses the same TDMA/FDMA method as GSM to form the physical channels [6]. Frequency channels are defined for the uplink and downlink direction, as shown in Fig. 1.Then, each frequency channel is divided into TDMA frames with a length of 4.165 ms. Moreover, each TDMA frame is split up into eight identical time slots. Each time slot is assigned to either GPRS for transmitting packet-switch data, or GSM for handling circuit-switch calls. The time slots used by GPRS are called as the packet data channel (PDCH). Radio block is denoted as a basic transmission unit of a PDCH. To transmit a radio block, four time slots in four consecutive TDMA frames are utilized and one radio block contains 456 bits. Due to forward error correction, there are fewer payload bits could be transmitted. The structure and the number of payload bits of a radio block depend on message type and coding scheme. There are four different coding schemes named as CS-1 to CS-4, with the data rate of 9kb/s, 13kb/s, 15kb/s and 21kb/s defined for the radio blocks carrying RLC data blocks [7]. The choice of one of four coding schemes depends on the quality of dynamic channel. Since the link quality is usually changing as the MS moving, the channel capacity certainly is time-varying. To model this time-varying channel, we use a Markov chain as shown in Fig. 2. In a Markov chain, state transition only depends on current state. The Memoryless property conforms to the channel dynamics caused by a mobile user. For GPRS, the Markov chain has four states denoting as CS-1 to CS-4 to represent the possible channel state. The transition probabilities between the states are discussed in [8].

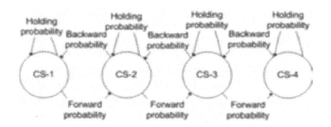

Fig. 2. Model for GPRS wireless channel.

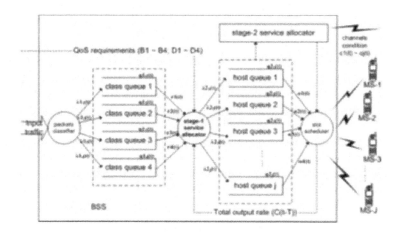

Fig. 3. The architecture of two-stage queuing approach

3   Two-Stage Queuing Approach (TSQA)

The proposed queuing architecture is shown in Fig 3 to support each mobile host (i.e., MS) with four traffic classes in the base station (i.e., BSS). Additionally, in the front of TSQA, the classifier routes the incoming packets to certain class queue according to service class definition. There are two stage managers to determine the resource allocation and indicate the rear slot scheduler to allocate the time slots for hosts. When a packet arrives at packet classifier, it is put into the corresponding class queue according to packet type. The stage-1 service allocation decides how much resource available for each class in this round, fetches packets from class queue and put them into host queue according to packet destination field. The slot scheduler then decides how many slots each host use in this round, encapsulates packet data into time slots and dispatches them to the air. In the followings, the operations of this architecture are illustrated in details.

3.1 Operation of Service Allocator in the First Stage

The objective of the first stage is to offer the specific quality levels for the various service classes. For example, VoIP needs the delivery of real-time and low packet loss and file transfer does not tolerate any packet loss. Because each service classes requires different delay bounds, the delay bound of each service class i denoted as Di is used as one of the parameters in bandwidth allocation. Additionally, in TDMA system, a host with a poor channel condition causes a demand of large slot number to likely degrade the packet delivery of the other hosts with better channel condition. Therefore, the real channel condition $C(t)$ is another important factor in slot scheduling to prevent inefficient slot allocation at the first stage. After determining the QoS requirements and obtaining the available channel capacity, the bandwidth allocated for each service class is given as

$$r_i(t) = C(t - T) * w_{1i}(t) \qquad (1)$$

where r_i, C_i and w_{ij} are the bandwidth allocated for host i, the channel capacity and the weight of class j used in the first stage, respectively. In Eq. 1, the allocate bandwidth not only depends on the available channel capacity but also the weight for each class. Since the available channel capacity of host i should serve all possible service classes, the weight w_{1i} is the significant operational parameter to determine the bandwidth allocation of service classes for one host.

The value of the class weight, w_{1i} , is determined by the Basically, the class with higher input rate require more resource to transmit their data and the weight should be larger than other classes. Then we get the weight of each class by

$$w'_{1i}(t) = \lambda_{1i}(t) / \sum_{i=1}^{4} \lambda_{1i}(t) \qquad (2)$$

But this is not a suitable value for QoS requirements because it does not take queuing delay into account. It goes without saying, while available channel capacity is scarce, the queuing delay will increase. At this moment, if we want to guarantee the QoS of real-time services, we have to sacrifice other service classes. The queuing delay is estimated by

$$d_i(t) = \frac{q_i(t - T) + [C(t - T) * w'_{1i}(t) - \lambda_i(t)] * T}{C(t - T) * w'_{1i}(t)} \qquad (3)$$

And the weights are obtained by

$$w_{1i}(t) = w_{1i}(t)' * \left\{ \exp\left[\frac{d_i(t)}{D_i}\right] - \alpha \right\} \text{ for i=1,2,3} \qquad (4)$$

$$w_{14}(t) = 1 - \sum_{i=1}^{3} w_{1i}(t) \tag{5}$$

In this way, if the queuing delay exceeds the class's delay bound, its weight will exponentially increase. If the available channel capacity is too scarce for all service classes to work well, the 4th class (i.e., background traffic) will be sacrificed.

3.2 Operation of Service Allocator in the Second Stage

Differing from the first stage objective of guaranteeing the QoS requirements of each class, the goals of the second stage are to improve the resource utilization, adapt radio resource allocation to link variation and achieve the link sharing of hosts as fair as possible. To achieve these goals, we need to know the current channel condition of each host. And we assume that, by control messages, BSS is aware of the channel condition $c_j(t)$ of active host j at time t. After determining the bandwidth of each class at first stage, packets will come with their associated bandwidth and then be put into the corresponding host queues by a rate of $\lambda_{2j}(t)$, where the j is host number and t is the current time. Since the output rate of each class is controlled according to their required QoS, even in the poor state of scarce resource, the real-time services is always guaranteed This also results in the increasing ratio of the allocated bandwidth of real-time service to total channel capacity. In second stage, at first, we need to know how many slots each hosts requires. This is obtained by

$$s_j(t) = \frac{q_{2j}(t-T) + \lambda_{2j}(t) * T}{c_j(t) * slot\_time} \tag{6}$$

where $q_{2j}(t-T)$ is the length of host queue j at last service round and $slot\_time$ is duration of one time slot. In viewpoint of channel utilization, we want to allocate the host with good channel condition more services. But on the other hand, we need to allocate more services for the host with a longer queue length in order to achieve fairness between hosts. However, according to Eq. 6, we find that the host with longer queue length and poor channel condition require more time slots to send its data. Since we want to keep the queue length effect but reduce the effect of channel condition in Eq. 5, we do a power computation on it and take the outcome for weight adjustment. Then the weight of each host queue will be

$$w_{2j}(t) = s_j(t)^{\beta} / \sum_{k=1}^{J} s_k(t)^{\beta} \tag{7}$$

where J is the total numbers of current hosts and β is a constant. Then the slots requested for host i is denoted as n_i and derived by

$$n_j(t) = N * w_{2j}(t) \tag{8}$$

where N is the total slot number in a service round. Finally, we have the output rate $o_j(t)$ of each host queue as

$$o_j(t) = n_j(t) * c_j(t) * slot\_time/T \qquad (9)$$

Equation 8 dervies the available channel capacity at first stage.

4 Simulation and Performance Evaluation

In simulation, each host connects the base station through its dedicated channel. We assume that each base station has 32 channels and the channel capacity varies with time. The input traffic used in simulation includes four classes of services conversational, streaming, interactive and background traffic classes. They are defined by ETSI for UMTS to distinguish the QoS specifications acquired by a wide variety of traffics [9]. The characteristics of each traffic class are shown in Table 1.

Table 1. Simulation Parameters

Service type	Traffic class	Gen. prob.	Data rate	Holding time
Voice over IP	Conversational	60%	11Kbps	60 ~ 180 sec
Video conference	Conversational	5%	40Kbps	60 ~ 180 sec
Video on demand	Streaming	5%	52Kbps	60 ~ 300 sec
Web browsing	Interactive	15%	10Kbps	0.5 ~ 6.5 sec
File transferring	Background	15%	10Kbps	10 ~ 60 sec

The generation probability is referred to the simulation environment in [10]. New call and hand-off call arrival rate are set to $0.1 \sim 0.5$ calls per second. The total call arrival rate is $0.2 \sim 1$ calls per second. The delay bound D_i of each class is 180, 500 and 2000 ms respectively and that of background traffic class is unspecified. The simulation results show that TSQA has great improvements on packet delay and,delay jitter. Generally speaking, the packet delay boundary is 180ms for voice service and 500ms for video service. Figure 4.(a-c) are packet delay of each traffic class under different link variation by using traditional scheduling method , and Fig. 4.(d-f) are resulted from TSQA. Obviously, TSQA presents a better packet delay control under 'bad' channel condition (channel model 3). And packet delay of traditional method increases rapidly while channel condition becomes worse.

Delay jitter is known as the variation of packet delay among packets. Delay jitter effects directly on the quality of streaming service. When delay jitter is large, discontinuity of video replaying appears. The limit of delay jitter is often less than twice of sample rate, which is usually 20ms to 40ms. Figure 5.(a) shows delay jitter of streaming service by using traditional method, and Figure. 5.(b) depicts the result of TSQA. Although both the two methods satisfy the

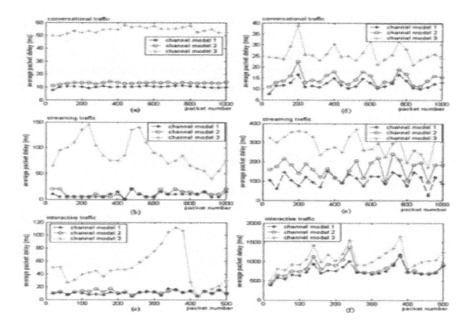

Fig. 4. Packet delay of each traffic class under different channel condition.

requirement, but TSQA demonstrates a better control while in a 'bad' channel condition (channel model 3). The reason is that the service allocation of traditional method more depends on the channel capacity than TSQA does.

5 Conclusion

So far, we have presented a two-stage queuing approach to support real-time QoS guarantee for multimedia services in TDMA wireless networks. There are several benefits of using TSQA. First, on the aspect of channel condition and service performance, the real-time service QoS is guaranteed.Second, slots utilization is highly improved. Thirdly, although background traffic is sacrificed in

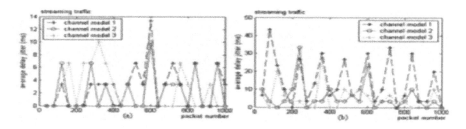

Fig. 5. Delay jitter of streaming traffic class resulted from traditional method and TSQA

a bad channel condition, once the channel condition recovers, the background traffic also will be repaid with higher throughput. Additionally, packet delay and throughput are not closely coupled. In most packet scheduling algorithms, the packet delay and throughput are taken into consideration simultaneously, but for real-time services, the throughput guarantee is not urgent as delay guarantee. In summary, TSQA demonstrates a new approach to the QoS design of future multimedia communication.

References

1. Clarke, F., Ekeland, I.: Nonlinear oscillations and boundary-value problems for Hamiltonian systems. Arch. Rat. Mech. Anal. **78** (1982) 315–333
2. Nomura N., Fujii T., and Ohta, N.: Basic Characteristics of Variable rate Video Coding in ATM Environment, *IEEE J. Select. Area Communication*, vol. 7 no. 5 pp.752-760, Jun. 1989.
3. M. Mouly and M. B. Pautet, "Current Evolution of the GSM Systems," *IEEE Personal Communications*, vol. 2, no. 5, pp. 9-19, Oct. 1995
4. J. Cai and D. J. Goodman, "General Packet Radio Service in GSM," *IEEE Communication Magazine*, vol. 35, pp. 122-131, Oct. 1997.
5. J. Gu and D. Yang, "Variability Study for 3G and Beyond Mobile Communications," *Wireless Communications, IEEE*, vol. 9, pp. 66-71, Apr. 2002.
6. ETSI, "Digital Cellular Telecommunication System (Phase 2+), General Packet Radio Service, Multiplexing and Multiple Access on the Radio Path," GSM 05.02 v6.60, Mar. 1999.
7. J. Cai and D. J. Goodman, "General Packet Radio Service in GSM," *IEEE Communication Magazine*, vol. 35, pp. 122-131, Oct. 1997.
8. J. S. Swarts and H. C. Ferreira, "On the Evaluation and Application of Markov Channel Models in Wireless Communications," *Proceeding of Vehicular Technology Conference*, vol.1, pp.117-121, Fall, 1999.
9. ESTI, "3rd Generation Partnership Project; Technical Specification Group Services and System Aspects; QoS Concept and Architecture (Release 1999)," 3GPP, 1999.
10. T. W. Yu and C. M. Leung, "Adaptive Resource Allocation for Prioritized Call Admission over an ATM-based wireless PCN," *IEEE J. Select. Areas Common.*, vol. 15, no. 7, pp. 1208-1225, Jul. 1997.
11. P. Mehta, and S. Udani, "Voice over IP," *Potentials, IEEE*, vol. 20, pp. 36-40, Oct. 2001.

Performance Evaluation of Adaptive Rate Control (ARC) for Multimedia Traffic

Surasee Prahmkaew and Chanintorn Jittawiriyanukoon

Department of Telecommunications Scince
Faculty of Science and Technology
Assumption University, Huamark, Bangkok, 10240, Thailand
{see, nin}@s-t.au.ac.th

Abstract. The paper presents an Adaptive Rate Control (ARC) mechanism to improve the performance of high-speed network to handle multimedia traffic by guaranteeing the cell loss ratio (CLR) for all cell streams. First, the cases in which a Tahoe, Reno, New Reno, SACK and Plain schemes are applicable in peak-cell-rate (PCR) are discussed. The ARC improves the performance by regulating the increment (up) and the decrement (down) of window size (flow control). Incoming traffic rate, number of cell drop, preset size of the window and estimated delay time are taken into account for this regulation. Simulations are used to investigate how Tahoe, Reno, New Reno, SACK and "Plain" can conduct, as congestion existed. Then we compare these results from four schemes to the "Plain" scheme (no flow control applicable) and to the proposed ARC. By altering windows size for the mentioned six schemes, we can obtain the supportive results.

Keywords: ATM, Tahoe, Reno, New Reno, SACK, Flow control, Sliding windows.

1 Introduction

Only a high-speed network can service multimedia traffic. The interface to Asynchronous Transfer Mode (ATM) or the architecture of ATM network would provide a multilevel of services. In networks as such, the multimedia information will be segmented into cells and the tremendous number of cells is traversed from sender to the destination via multiple hops transmission in the network. Not all traffic control methods are applicable to the high-speed networks such as ATM [1][12].

There are many previous studies involving flow control algorithms [3] and a source descriptor [2], however the behavior of each flow control scheme [12] with regulating window sizes is not found. In this paper, we proposed an ARC flow control that improves the performance of high-speed network such as ATM network by altering an appropriate size of the flow control window. Our proposed ARC against four existing flow control schemes that are Tahoe, Reno, New

K. Aizawa, Y. Nakamura, and S. Satoh (Eds.): PCM 2004, LNCS 3331, pp. 41–48, 2004.
© Springer-Verlag Berlin Heidelberg 2004

Reno, and SACK [4],[15] plus one "Plain" scheme are discussed. Finally the performance evaluation, especially in term of throughput, number of cells loss, mean time in queue, mean queue length and utilization of ATM link, between these six schemes will be compared.

2   The Model of Four Schemes

The existing congestion avoidance algorithms are discussed. Tahoe algorithm includes Slow Start, Congestion Avoidance, and Fast Retransmit. The Reno is the enhancement to Tahoe by softening the Fast Retransmit process with inclusive Fast Recovery. Selective Acknowledgments (SACK) has been presented to recover multiple segment losses by transmitting a duplicate acknowledgement. The information contains the out-of-sequence bytes SACK, RFC 2018, [5] has received. SACK also allows the transmitter to reconstruct the information about the non-received bytes at the destination. Farther detail can be found in [6][7]. Partial ACK takes Reno out of frame, deflates window size. Sender may have to wait for timeout before proceeding. In New Reno, partial ACK indicates lost packets and retransmits immediately. Retransmits 1 lost packet per round trip time until all lost packets from that window are retransmitted. New Reno also eliminates timeout (RFC 2583) [6].

Tahoe, Reno and New Reno, and SACK started window with an advertised size ranging from 1 to maximum size. It is increased by 1 (slow-start technique) for every successful transmission. When the window is topped up to the maximum size, most of input traffic would be discarded or tagged with the reason of capacity exceeding.

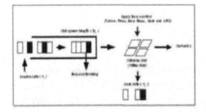
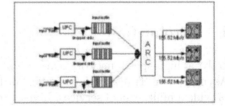

Fig. 1. ARC Flow control model.   **Fig. 2.** Simulation model.

3   Adaptive Rate Control Scheme

In the proposed ARC, we alleviate the number of cells by shrinking or expanding the window size automatically based upon source rate, cells drop, and cells delay. With ARC algorithm [16], it works like a control gate for all arriving cells. When cells arrive at gate and if no cell drop presents, the cell will be transmitted immediately (at no delay). If cell drop is present, the dropped cell will be firstly blocked in a cell queue (Qc) and waiting for a chance of retransmission as ARC finishes regulating the new windows size in order to conquer the cells drop. At the same time to maintain quality of service (QoS), the maximum cell delay time has been defined as CDVT. It means the cells have been waiting in the cell queue longer than CDVT will be discarded finally. Figure 1 illustrates the ARC flow control model for our analysis regarding the cell arriving process, conforming and non-conforming cells, window size adjustment and two states of problem for ARC.

In case that the arrival traffic (average arrival cell rate or traffic (λ_a) is less than the cell drop rate (λ_p) and cell drop is not yet present. ARC will initially set window size to be one (the minimum size).

On the other hand, if (λ_a) is larger than (λ_p) , ARC will regulate the window size with reference to cell drop rate (λ_p) and arrival traffic rate (λ_a). ARC will regulate the window size between one and three (three is the maximum size based on analytical model shown in figure 2). ARC algorithm is shown below.

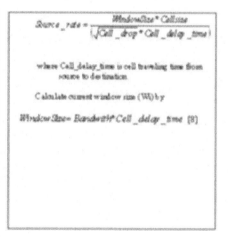

ARC algorithm

4   The Model of Plain Scheme

Unlike the proposed ARC, we are neither alleviating the number of cells by shrinking or expanding the window size automatically based upon source rate, cells drop, and cells delay nor applying any four schemes (Tahoe, Reno, New Reno and SACK) in the "Plain" scheme. We want to use this scheme for comparing the performance as well as to study what if all four (control) schemes and

ARC are transparent to the system. This will give the idea how much these flow control schemes will help ease the congestion

5 Simulation

Figure 2 demonstrates a simulation model utilized in the paper.

5.1 Input Traffic

The multimedia traffic can be basically classified into five categories: data, voice, video, image and graphics [14]. This research confines the discussion to mainly data, voice and video. Data sources are generally bursty in nature whereas voice and video sources can be continuous or bursty, depending on the compression and coding techniques used. Continuous sources are said to generate constant bit rate (CBR) traffic and bursty sources are said to generate variable bit rate (VBR)[9] traffic. Hence, only VBR traffic will be considered as an input for the study.

5.2 Characteristics of a Queuing Network Model

There are three components with certain characteristics that must be examined before the simulation models are developed.

5.2.1 Arrival Characteristics

The pattern of arrivals input traffic mostly is characterized to be *Poisson arrival processes*[11]. Like many random events, Poisson arrivals occur such that for each increment of time (T), no matter how large or small, the probability of arrival is independent of any previous history. These events may be individual cells, a burst of cells, cell or packet service completions, or other arbitrary events.

The probability of the inter-arrival time between event t, is defined by the *inter-arrival time probability density function (pdf)*. The following formula gives the resulting probability density function (*pdf*), which the inter-arrival time t is larger than some value x when the average arrival rate is λ events per second:

$$fx(t) = \begin{cases} e^{-\lambda t}, for\ t \geq 0 \\ 0, for\ t < 0 \end{cases} \tag{1}$$

$$p(t \leq x) = Fx(x) = \int_0^x e^{-\lambda x} dx = 1 - \lambda e^{-\lambda x} \tag{2}$$

$$p(t > x) = 1 - Fx(x) = \lambda e^{-\lambda x} \tag{3}$$

Queuing theorists call Poisson arrivals a *memoryless process*, because the probability that the inter-arrival time will be X seconds is independent of the memory of how much time has already expired. The formula of memoryless process is shown accordingly:

$$P(x > s + t | X > t) = P(X > s) = e^{-\lambda s}, \quad for \ s, \ t \ > 0 \tag{4}$$

This fact greatly simplifies the analysis of random processes since no past history, or memory, affects the processes commonly known as *Markov processes*. The probability that n independent arrivals occurs in T seconds is given by the formula Poisson distribution:

$$P(n, T) = (\lambda T)^n e^{-\lambda T} / n! \tag{5}$$

where:
$P(X)$ = probability of X arrivals,
n = number of arrival per unit of time,
λ = average arrival rate,
$E(n|T) = \lambda T$ = expected value of n for a given interval T, and e = 2.7183.

The combination of these two thoughts in a commonly used model is called the Markov modulated Poisson process (MMPP) or ON/OFF bursty model. In this paper, the burstiness is varied by altering the T_{ON} and T_{OFF}.

5.2.2 Service Facility Characteristics

In this paper, service times are randomly allocated by the *exponential probability distribution*. This is a mathematically convenient assumption if arrival rates are Poisson distributed. In order to examine the traffic congestion at output of ATM link (155.52 Mbps), the service time in the simulation model is specified by the speed of output link, given that a service time is 2.726 μs per cell.

5.2.3 Source Traffic Descriptor

The source traffic descriptor is similar to other previously published papers [10],[13],[16], that is $T = 1.0\mu s(1/999, 739s)$, $T = 2.0\mu s(1/499, 933s)$, $T = 3.0\mu s(1/333, 288s)$ and $T = 4.0\mu s(1/249, 966s)$.

6   Results

The comparison between four schemes namely Tahoe, Reno, New Reno, SACK, the proposed ARC and the "Plain" scheme is illustrated in graphs. The experiment has been set with the maximum window size of 3 for total six schemes.

With the burst/silence ratio 100:0, the average inter-arrival cell rate defines as 1, 2, 3, and 4 μs. Figure 3 illustrates the throughput against inter-arrival cell rate. Figure 4 illustrates mean time in queue against inter-arrival cell rate. Figure 5 illustrates mean queue length against inter-arrival cell rate. Figure 6 illustrates utilization of link against inter-arrival cell rate and Figure 7 illustrates cells drop against inter-arrival cell rate.

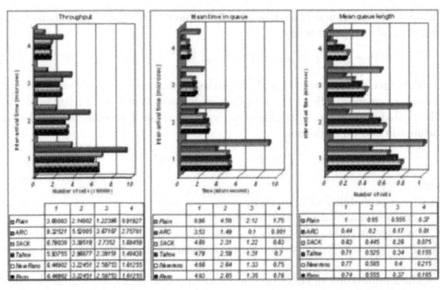

Fig. 3. Throughput.　　**Fig. 4.** Mean time in queue.　　**Fig. 5.** Mean queue length (cells).

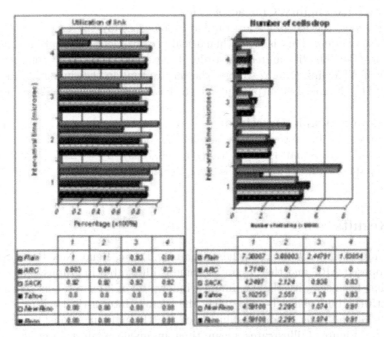

Fig. 6. Utilization of link.　　**Fig. 7.** Number of cells drop.

From figure 3, ARC offers the best performance, followed by SACK at any input data rates. Figure 4 describes mean time cells have to reside in the waiting room. Plain scheme gives the longest delay time in queue while ARC contributes the shortest time, followed by four schemes equally. ARC is a disarmingly short network residual time with a higher number of throughputs compared to other four schemes and the Plain scheme. From figure 5, Plain scheme is the poorest as there are huge number of cells waiting in the queue. This could possibly lead to bottlenecks in future. One of the most successful schemes is ARC by which most of the queue length is trivial, followed by SACK. As a result, the ARC provides a faster traverse time for variation of data rates over the high-speed network. To some extent, the performance ARC provides may be redundant, but from perspective of multimedia traffics it is clear that many users actually prefer working at a faster speed in transmission. Figure 6 illustrates how all schemes keep the high-speed link (155.52 Mbps) busy most of the simulation time duration, especially when the congestion ($inter-arrival time = 1\mu s$) nearly approaches. However, as the input rate drops the ARC seems to perform more efficiently than other five schemes. In figure 7, ARC will not have any problems with the dropped cells (cell loss). Plain scheme will and that could be a potential annoyance out of the way. With ARC, there might be an alternative solution to the multimedia traffics although it may raise some cell loss (but fewer) at the point of congestion.

7 Summary and Future Works

ARC will offer the highest performance in case of congestion (as the input arrival rate of multimedia traffic is higher than the ATM link capacity). Simulations demonstrate ARC outperforms compared to "Plain" and other four schemes. It does not have to be either costly or complicated but simply allows dropped cells to retransmit by regulating the window size directed to the arrival rate (λ_a) and number of dropped cells. On the other hand, ARC also gives remarkably better performance compared to five schemes (Tahoe, Reno, New Reno, SACK and Plain) in the case of non-congestion. There are many variations and the number of features available casts doubts on our future works. Predictably we have argued against this, so we would conduct some experiments on the extension of maximum window size. Different link capacities of high-speed networks and ARC extra-ordinary processing time will be further investigated. Also we plan to apply ARC scheme to the extent of low-speed wireless communication [17]. To conduct experiment with wider size of the windows we need a lot more modifications than the current simulation. In fact we are on that boundary then our experiences tell it will be hard pressed to provide a decent running platform for our future works.

References

[1] M. Allman, V. Paxson, and W. Stevens. "TCP Congestion Control", RFC 2581, 1999.

[2] Shigo Shioda and Hiroshi Satio, "Connection Admission Control Guaranteeing Negotiated Cell-Loss Ratio of cell Streams Passing through Usage Parameter Control," IEICE Trans. Commu, vol E80-B, no. 3, page 399-411,1997.

[3] Pitiporn P. et. al, "Performance Comparison of ATM Policy Mechanisms with Telecommunications Traffic", Proceeding of The 6th World Multiconference on Systematics, Cybernetics and Informatics, pp. 373-378, 2002.

[4] Ghanthiya L. et. al, "Performance Evaluation for TCP/IP over Satellite Communication with Sliding Window Algorithms, "Proceedings of the 4th International Conference on Intelligent Technologies (InTech'03),pp.17-24, 2003.

[5] M. Mathis, J. Mahdavi, S. Floyd and A. Romanow, "TCP Selective Acknowledgement Options", Internetdraft, RFC 2018, 1996.

[6] K. Fall and S. Floyd, "Simulation-based comparisons of Tahoe, Reno and SACK TCP", Computer Communication Review, vol 26, pp. 5-21, RFC 2583, 1996.

[7] Dannis Yang, "TCP performance and flow control", Candle computer report, vol 22. no. 2, 2000.

[8] Steven Low , "Equilibrium and Dynamic of TCP/AQM", Sigcomm, 2001, http://www.cds.caltech.edu/ doyle/Networks/TCPaqm.ppt

[9] D.D., Kouvatsos, "Performance Modelling and Evaluation of ATM Networks," Vol. 1. Chapman and Hall,1995.

[10] ATM Forum, "User-network interface (UNI) Specification version 3.1," The ATM Forum Technical Committee, Prentice Hall, 1995.

[11] B. Khoshnevis, "Discrete Systems Simulations," McGraw-Hill, 1994.

[12] E.P. Rathgeb, "Modelling and performance comparison of policing mechanisms for ATM networks," IEEE Journal on selected areas in communications, Vol. 9, No. 3, pp.325 - 334, 1991.

[13] M. Aida and H. Saito, "Traffic contract parameters and CAC guaranteeing cell-loss ratio in ATM networks," IEICE Trans. Commu., vol.E78-B,no.1, 1995.

[14] S.S. Al-Wakeel; N.-E. Rikli; and A.A. Al-Wehaibi, "Evaluation of Fairness Strategies for ATM Congestion Control Policing Mechanisms," IASTED Proceeding of International Conference on Applied Modeling and Simulation (AMP'99), 1999.

[15] Ghanthiya L. et. al, "Evaluation of TCP over Satellite Network with the Proposed Sliding Window Algorithms," Proceedings of the 6th IEEE International Conference on Advanced Communication Technology (ICACT'04),pp.917-922, 2004.

[16] S. Prahmkaew et. al, "A Study of Adaptive Rate Algorithm in ATM Network Flow Control," Proceedings of the International Conference on Parallel and Distributed Processing Techniques and Applications (PDPTA'04),pp.668-673, 2004.

[17] S. Prahmkaew et. al, "BTSnet: Model and Usage of Regular Traffic Patterns in Bangkok for Mobile Ad Hoc Networks and Inter-Vehicular Communications," Proceedings of the International Mobility Conference (MobiCon '04),S1-4, pp.1-9, 2004.

A Tennis Video Indexing Approach Through Pattern Discovery in Interactive Process

Peng Wang[1]*, Rui Cai[1], and Shi-Qiang Yang[2]

[1] Department of Computer Science and Technology
Tsinghua University, Beijing, 100084, China
{wangp01, cairui01}@mails.tsinghua.edu.cn
[2] Department of Computer Science and Technology
Tsinghua University, Beijing, 100084, China
yangshq@tsinghua.edu.cn

Abstract. Tennis game is a mutual and interactive process between the two opponents, and audiences are usually interested in how the players oppose and compete with each other. However, previous works on tennis video indexing are mainly based on analyses of player's behavior, such as movement and gesture, and seldom provide information of the match process. In this paper, a novel approach is proposed for tennis video indexing by mining the salient patterns in the match process. The match is first characterized by a time sequence of players' joint movements, based on which an unsupervised way is performed to extract the sub-sequences with high occurrence frequencies. These sub-sequences, called patterns, reflect the technical styles and tactics of the players, and offer an effective manner to organize the video. Evaluations on four hour broadcasting tennis videos show very promising results.

1 Introduction

Tennis game has been widely studied due to its numerous audiences and tremendous commercial potentials. Previous researches on tennis video analysis focus on parsing structural units[1]. To extract more elaborate information, current researches attempt to track motion of player and ball[2], and recognize human actions[3]. Based on these works, only the player's information is reserved for indexing. However, audiences still like to know more details about the match process, which consists of attack and defense between two players, called *Interactive Process* in this paper. With the interactive process, people can summarize the players' technical styles, their persistence capabilities, and the tactics to score a point. These information are useful for tennis players and coaches in training. Up to our knowledge, few works are reported in the literature on indexing the tennis video based on the characteristics of the interactive match process.

---

* This work was supported by the *National High Technology Development 863 Program* of China and the *National Grand Fundamental Research 973 Program* of China

K. Aizawa, Y. Nakamura, and S. Satoh (Eds.): PCM 2004, LNCS 3331, pp. 49–56, 2004.
© Springer-Verlag Berlin Heidelberg 2004

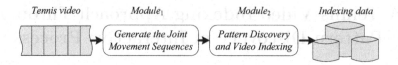

Fig. 1. The flowchart of the proposed indexing approach

In this paper, a novel approach is proposed to index tennis video by discovering repeated segments in the interactive process. These repeated segments are usually determined by the two players' technical styles. For instance, a player good at net game is used to take the net after each successful serve in match with a rival specialized in baseline game. However, there are two difficulties in detecting the repeated segments: 1) how to effectively characterize the interactive match process; and 2) little priori is known about the recurrent segments existing in the match. In a tennis match, since the players' positions and moving manners are important clues reflecting their technical styles, in this paper, we represent the interactive process with the two players' *Joint Movement Sequence*. The second problem is very like that faced in pattern discovery on DNA sequences, which has been well studied. Thus, similar techniques can be adapted to mine salient repetitive sub-sequences, also called *patterns*, in the joint movement sequence.

The system flowchart of the proposed indexing approach is shown in Fig. 1, which mainly consists of: generating joint movement sequences and pattern discovery. All the segments containing tennis court are first selected using a color-based algorithm[1], based on which the in-game shots are further identified with a court line detection algorithm [4]. For each in-game shot, we recognize the player's moving manners, which are then combined and sampled to generate the joint movement sequence. Based on all the joint movement sequences, pattern discovery algorithms are carried out to reveal the potential repeated patterns. Finally, video shots containing the same pattern are organized and re-grouped for browsing and retrieval.

The rest of this paper is organized as follows. Section 2 introduces the details of defining and generating the joint movement sequence. In Section 3, the pattern discovery algorithm and the indexing approach are described. Experiments and discussion are presented in Section 4. Finally, Section 5 gives the conclusion and our future works.

2   Generation of the Joint Movement Sequence

Players' position and moving manners directly represent their technical styles and tactics adopted in the match. By watching his rival's position and moving, the player decides how to return the ball, as well as the running direction in the next time slot. Thus the two players' movements depend on each other, and characterize the interactive match process together. In this section, we first introduce the recognition of single player's movement, and then describe how to combine the results to generate the joint movement sequence.

2.1   Recognition of Single Player's Moving Manners

Generally, there are two main moving styles in tennis match: running along the baseline (baseline game) and taking the net (net game). Considering the direction and magnitude of the speed, baseline game could be further divided into three manners, i.e., move left (L), move right (R) and hold still (S). Although net game also could be divided in similar way, the recognition may become difficult for that the speed is mainly toward the net (N) and relatively weak in horizontal. Thus, four moving manners are defined in this paper. The definition is coarse, but still reflect the main movement of the player. More importantly, the detection results are comparatively feasible, accurate and robust in practice.

A problem here is that the movements in tennis video are deformed due to the diagonally located camera, resulting in an inaccurate recognition. This is especially serious to the player in top half court. To solve this problem, a pinhole camera modelling has been proposed in our previous work [4]. First, motion vectors extracted from bit-stream are revised with the camera model. Then two temporal responses curves on horizontal and vertical motions [5] are generated based on the transformed motion vectors. These two response curves are then used as features to model and detect the moving manners with hidden Markov models (HMMs). More details could refer to [4].

With the recognition results, the single player's moving manner in a *Game Shot* is represented by the sequence:

$$G = \{(M_i, T_i)\}, i \in [1, D] \tag{1}$$

where $M_i \in \{S, L, R, N\}$ denotes the ith identified moving manner, T_i denotes the duration of M_i, and D is the total number of identified manner segments.

2.2   Joint Movement Analysis

For a *Game Shot*, the two players' moving sequences are obtained through the above procedure, as G_A and G_B illustrated in Fig. 2 (a). For each time slot within the shot, it is labeled by a pair of two players' moving manners. The moving manner pair, denoted as $M^2 = (M, M)$, where $M \in \{S, L, R, N\}$, provides a description to the players' joint movement. Different manner pairs can be considered as different joint movement types in the match. There is a 90-second period when players change sides, and the game statistics are simultaneously shown on screen. Therefore, the temporal and visual information is employed to identify players' changeover and generate manner pairs. Here, the the joint movement evolution is denoted as $\widetilde{G}$, as illustrated in Fig. 2 (b).

$$\widetilde{G} = \{(M_i^2, \widetilde{T}_i)\}, i \in [1, \widetilde{D}] \tag{2}$$

where M_i^2 is the ith segment with duration $\widetilde{T}_i$, $\widetilde{D}$ is the total segment number.

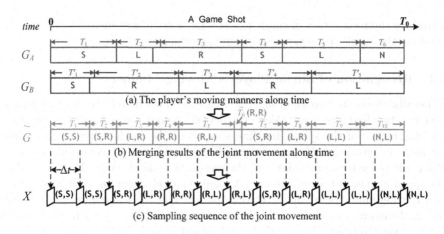

Fig. 2. Generation of the joint movement sequence

To facilitate the further works on pattern discovery, $\widetilde{G}$ should be converted to a symbol sequence, as the implementations of pattern discovery on discrete symbol list are more robust in practice than that on continuous stream. A simple way to generate such a symbol sequence is just keeping the M_i^2 in $\widetilde{G}$. However, the duration of each segment is also meaningful in describing the interactive match process. Same moving manner pairs with different persistence time would possibly present two different match processes. Thus in this paper, we adopt a periodic sampling to extract the symbol sequence. As shown in Fig. 2 (c), with a pre-defined time interval Δt, we record the manner pair every Δt to build the **Joint Movement Sequence** X:

$$X = \{M_j^2\}, j \in [1, \lceil T_0/\Delta t \rceil] \tag{3}$$

where T_0 is the *Game Shot* length, and Δt is set as 0.5 second in our current work. By using the sampling method, long segments in $\widetilde{G}$ will bring multiple symbols to X, and short segments are prone to be skipped, such as the $((R,R), \widetilde{T_6})$ in Fig. 2 (b). Discarding short segments will not affect the later pattern mining, as these segments give little contribution to the whole match process.

3   Pattern Discovery and Video Indexing

By extracting the joint movement sequence for each *Game Shot*, we obtain a set of symbol sequences for a given tennis video. In this Section, we introduce the indexing approach based on pattern discovery on the sequences in detail.

Fig. 3 gives an illustration of the repeated joint movement sequences, marked by rectangles. However, detecting these patterns automatically is a hard problem since their forms, as well as the number of potential pattern types, are both unknown in prior. Fortunately, similar problems have been studied in the domain of data mining, with the successful applications on computational biology and commercial data analysis. Most existing algorithms for pattern discovery are pattern driven approaches, which are based on enumerating candidate patterns and picking out the ones with high fitness. These approaches guarantee to find those best patterns with high efficiency. Among them, we employ the Teiresias algorithm proposed in [7] in this paper to solve our problem.

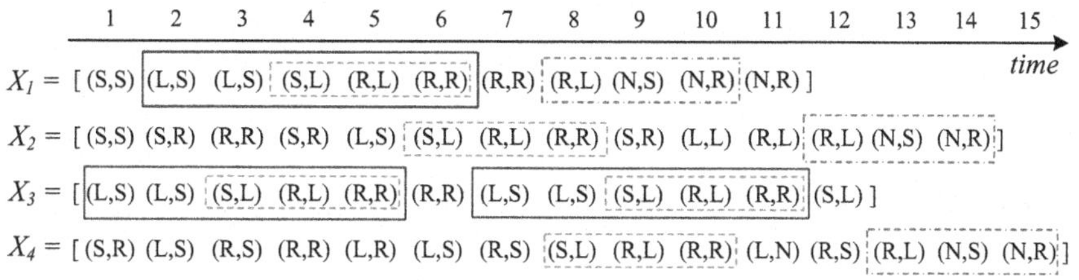

Fig. 3. An illustration of repeated patterns in joint movement sequences

Through pattern discovery in the joint movement sequences $\{X_1, X_2, \cdots\}$, we could obtain a group of repeated patterns and their occurrence frequencies. The frequency is especially important in our indexing work, because patterns with higher frequencies would reflect more typical playing styles and tactics of the players. Here a notation (p, f) is defined to express a pattern p and its frequency f together. For instance, there are three patterns in Fig. 3: $(p_1 = [(L, S)(L, S)(S, L)(R, L)(R, R)], f_1 = 3)$, $(p_2 = [(S, L)(R, L)(R, R)], f_2 = 5)$, and $(p_3 = [(R, L)(N, S)(N, R)], f_3 = 3)$. Note f_2 comprises two parts: 2 times from isolated p_2, and 3 times from p_2 embedded in p_1. In our works, p_1 and p_2 are considered representing different interactive processes, thus the frequency value should be recalculated to eliminate the count introduced by pattern nesting, as:

$$f_i = f_i - \sum_{j \in \Omega, j \neq i} f_j, \quad \Omega = \{k | p_i = sub(p_k)\} \tag{4}$$

where $sub(p_k)$ depicts a sub-sequence of p_k. In experiments, f_i is further normalized by the sequence number.

In the mining process, all video segments containing a certain pattern are located simultaneously. According to our assumption in this paper, these segments should describe similar interactive match process, and may be caused by the same tactic. Thus we could group all video segments containing the same pattern for further browsing and retrieval. Fig. 4 gives such an example. The indexing structure in Fig. 4 is tree-based, in which segments within the same group are first concatenated along time, and then tied to the node representing the related pattern. In order to make users' browsing more convenient, all these pattern nodes could be further sorted by their frequencies. That is, there are always $f_i \geq f_{i+1}$ in Fig. 4. Moreover, for two patterns with the same frequency, the one having longer duration would be placed in front, as longer patterns should include more information of the match process than short ones.

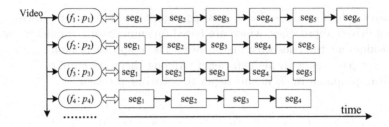

Fig. 4. An example of tennis video indexing based on detected patterns

4   Experiments

Four hour recorded live tennis videos are used in our experiments, which are collected from the games of A. Agassi and P. Sampras at US Open 2002 ($video_1$), and M. Safin and P. Sampras at Australian Open 2002 ($video_2$). The numbers of detected *Game Shots* in $video_1$ and $video_2$ are 316 and 329 respectively. For each *Game Shot*, we manually labelled the ground truth of moving segments for each player. Half of them are randomly selected as training data, and the remainders are used as testing.

First, we evaluate the performance of recognizing single player's moving manners. The precisions are calculated for each player with different manners respectively, as shown in Table 1. From Table 1, around 85% precision are obtained averagely in experiments. Comparatively, the performance of detecting "approaching to net"(N) is not as good as that of the other three. It is because the identification of vertical motion in tennis video is much harder than that of the horizontal. In our previous work [4], the performance for the player in top half court is generally lower than that in bottom half, nevertheless all players have similar performance in current experiments. The reason is that the precisions here are tied to certain player, and in the whole match the two players change their positions in turn. Although there are still about 15 % misclassification in system, these errors can be taken as random noise in following pattern mining, as they are not sufficient to construct any potential patterns.

Table 1. Identification results of player's moving manner

Movements	$video_1$		$video_2$	
	A. Agassi	P. Sampras	M. Safin	P. Sampras
S	92.54	88.73	90.36	93.04
L	87.50	83.33	87.10	90.22
R	87.10	86.36	86.67	85.11
N	73.91	84.62	80.43	76.47

Table 2. Comparison of discovered patterns for two videos

	$video_1$ (Agassi, Sampras)	$video_2$ (Safin, Sampras)
1	$([(S,S)(S,N)(R,N)], 0.23)$	$([(R,S)(S,L)(R,S)(S,L)(L,L)], 0.19)$
2	$([(N,S)(S,N)*(S,S)], 0.21)$	$([(L,L)*(R,R)(R,R)(S,L)(L,S)], 0.15)$
3	$([(L,S)(S,N)(R,N)(S,N)], 0.16)$	$([(S,S)(S,R)(L,S)(L,N)(R,S)(S,N)], 0.12)$
4	$([(S,L)(S,R)(R,S)(L,L)(R,L)], 0.09)$	$([(L,R)*(L,L)(R,L)], 0.11)$
5	$([(S,N)*(R,N)(L,N)], 0.07)$	$([(L,L)(L,R)(R,L)], 0.08)$

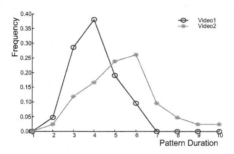

Fig. 5. Comparison of duration distributions for patterns in $video_1$ and $video_2$

Then, the pattern discovery is implemented on the joint movement sequences generated with the procedures in Section 3. We illustrate the obtained patterns with top five frequencies in Table 2. The most frequent pattern in $video_1$ is $[(S,S)(S,N)(R,N)]$, which means after the serve (S,S), Sampras rush to the net (S,N) and hit the ball towards the right side of Agassi, resulting in Agassi moves right long the baseline (R,N). Comparatively, the pattern at the first rank in $video_2$ is $[(R,S)(S,L)(R,S)(S,L)(L,L)]$, suggesting a persistent competition between the two opponents along the baseline. Other patterns can be explained in a similar way. The symbol $*$ here denotes an arbitrary joint movement symbol.

Moreover, we investigate the relations between pattern duration (the symbol number included) and occurrence frequencies in the two videos, and the results are shown in Fig. 5. The x-axis denotes the length varies from 1 to 10 symbols, and the y-axis denotes the sum of the frequencies for all the patterns in a given length. The curve of $video_1$ is more concentrated and patterns consisting of 4 symbols are with the highest frequency around 38%; and in $video_2$, pattern durations vary in a wide range and the peak locates at six. In $video_2$ there even exist patterns larger than 9, while no patterns in $video_1$ exceeds 7 symbols.

By combining the analyses of both the top five patterns and the duration distribution curves for $video_1$ and $video_2$, we could drive following useful inferences: (1) Sampras is in dominance in the match with Agassi. There are many $(-, N)$ in patterns from $video_1$, which suggests Sampras has many chances to take the net. And the pattern durations of $video_1$ are relatively shorter, which implies there are fewer strokes in a rally. (2) Sampras has little chance on net game in competition with Safin, as there is even no $(-, N)$ in the top two patterns in

$video_2$. Each serve in $video_2$ will persist a long time and it's hard for both sides to score a point. These conclusions are well consistent with the fact that Safin is younger than Agassi, and his hard and deep returns bring much troubles to Sampras in the match.

Above experiments have indicated that the playing styles can be effectively described by the discovered patterns. It also shows that the misclassification in single player's moving recognition brings little influence to the resulting patterns. Generally speaking, the results are very promising and encouraging.

5   Conclusion

This paper proposed a novel tennis video indexing approach by mining the salient patterns in the interactive match process. These patterns reflect players' technical styles and tactics in the game, and offer an effective way to organize the tennis video. Evaluations on four hours data indicate the method can achieve encouraging results in practice. In future work, we may focus on: (1) discovering more fine-grained patterns in tennis; (2) learning the mapping between high-level events and the patterns; and (3) extending the method to other sports videos.

References

1. G. Sudhir, John C.M. Lee, and Anil K. Jain, "Automatic Classification of Tennis Video for High-Level Content-Based Retrieval", *Proc. of 1998 International Workshop on Content-Based Access of Image and Video Databases*, pp. 81–90, 1998.
2. G.S. Pingali, Y. Jean, and I. Carlbom, "Real Time Tracking for Enhanced Tennis Broadcasts", *Proc. of 1998 IEEE Computer Society Conference on Computer Vision and Pattern Recognition*, pp. 260–265, Santa Barbara, CA, USA, Jun. 23–25, 1998.
3. H. Miyamori, "Improving Accuracy in Behaviour Identification for Content-based Retrieval by Using Audio and Video Information", *Proc. of the 16th International Conference on Pattern Recognition*, Vol. 2, pp. 826–830, Canada, Aug. 11–15, 2002.
4. P. Wang, R. Cai, B. Li, and S.-Q. Yang, "A Pinhole Camera Modeling of Motion Vector Field for Tennis Video Analysis", *to appear in Proc. of 2004 IEEE International Conference on Image Processing*, Singapore, Oct. 24–27, 2004.
5. G. Xu, Y.-F. Ma, H.-J. Zhang, and S.-Q. Yang, "Motion based Event Recognition Using HMM", *Proc. of the 16th International Conference on Pattern Recognition*, Quebec, Canada, Vol. 2, pp. 831–834, Aug. 11–15, 2002.
6. J.P. Caraca-Valente, Ignacio Lopez-Chavarrias, "Discovering Similar Patterns in Time Series", *Proc. of the 6th ACM SIGKDD International Conference on Knowledge Discovery and Data Mining*, pp. 497–505, Boston, USA, Aug. 2000.
7. I. Rigoutsos, A. Floratos, L. Parida, Y. Gao and D. Platt, "The Emergence of Pattern Discovery Techniques in Computational Biology", *Metabolic Engineering*, 2(3):159-177, July 2000. (http://cbcsrv.watson.ibm.com/Tspd.html)

Online Play Segmentation for Broadcasted American Football TV Programs[*]

Liexian Gu[1], Xiaoqing Ding[1], and Xian-Sheng Hua[2]

[1] Department of Electronic Engineering, Tsinghua University, Beijing, China
{lxgu, dxq}@ocrserv.ee.tsinghua.edu.cn
[2] Microsoft Research Asia, Beijing, China
xshua@microsoft.com

Abstract. This paper proposes an online segmentation scheme for broadcasted American football TV programs. The TV video streams are online partitioned into a series of play-break patterns with a relatively short delay. All the detected plays form an event-based summarization which contains complete information about the original match. The main contributions of the proposed scheme are twofold. First, an online adaptive field-color model is employed to deal with feature variations which may caused by court configurations and time-varying lighting conditions. Second, a temporal pattern based model is constructed to capture intrinsic features of football plays, which considerably increased the performance of the proposed scheme. Effectiveness of our approach is demonstrated by experiments on real recorded TV programs.

1 Introduction

Due to large potential applicable demands, sports video analysis has been an active research topic in recent years. Key techniques include highlights detection, automatic summarization, program structure parsing, etc. A typical application scenario can be described as follows: A busy-working football fan who will miss a live-broadcasted NFL game can get it recorded using personal video recorder (PVR) or other set-top devices. However when he has time to watch the recorded match, he may only want to enjoy the highlights or a shorter but complete summary, skipping those less interesting portions such as game pause, foul and various breaks. The so-called "smart playback" function has been approved appealing to end users with benefits of not only saving time but also bringing the feeling of being in control of what they watched[1].

In this paper we focus on broadcasted American football programs. According to the rules of football matches[2], a broadcasted game is generally composed of a series of attacking attempts with time-consuming breaks between them. Broadcasters often fill these breaking slots with close-ups, full-field views or audience scenes. Typically a complete NFL game will cost three hours but only about one hour is covered by real actions (which means that teams are truly

---

[*] This work was performed at Microsoft Research Asia.

K. Aizawa, Y. Nakamura, and S. Satoh (Eds.): PCM 2004, LNCS 3331, pp. 57–64, 2004.
© Springer-Verlag Berlin Heidelberg 2004

playing in the field). Those active segments, called plays, convey all contents for a football game in a considerable compressed manner. Hence we work on algorithms to automatically segment plays from broadcasted football video and concatenate them to form a compact summary of the whole game.

There have been a number of previous works for various types of sports videos based on different models. In [1], TV baseball game highlights were extracted on set-top devices using audio track features and probabilistic fusion. Xu et al.[3] employed HMMs to characterize motion pattern features, classifying basketball video into 16 basic events. Several probabilistic algorithms based on generic cinematic features to detect soccer goal events and basketball play-breaks were presented in [4][5]. However, little efforts have been made in football domain. Babaguchi[6] proposed an inter-modal collaboration scheme to detect football highlights through analyzing closed caption stream and a personalized retrieval and summarization system for sports video based on semantic metadata was presented in [7]. The most relevant research was reported by Li et al. in [8][9], where the start points of plays were determined by the scenes that players lined up; however, this model cannot cover a variety of plays which may started without such distinct pictures (some detailed analyses on this algorithm will be given in Sect. 2). Furthermore, none of the aforementioned approaches have the capability of online (means in real time or real time with a short period of delay) segmentation, which is important for many applications such as online skipping, namely, skipping forward or backward directly to previous or next interesting segment when watching buffered live TV programs.

The rest of this paper is organized as follows. Based on observed characteristics of various broadcasted football games and analyses on difficulties of existed algorithms, we propose a temporal pattern based online play detection scheme with adaptive field color models in Sect. 2. Performance evaluations are presented in Sect. 3, followed by conclusions in Sect. 4.

2   Our Approach

It is observed that in football games all plays are played in the field, which is green or near green and marked off by latitudinal stripes. Those field lines must be clearly discernable to the players and audiences since they measure the distance of ball advancing in each bout. Generally there are global views of the stadium, audience and other non-field frames in breaking intervals. Hence field scene is a strong indication of "play" events in football video. Nevertheless the dominant color of the field, green, is heavily depends on different courts. Moreover, it may vary significantly due to lighting conditions even in the same field since a football game often lasts three or more hours (for example, may from the afternoon to the evening). In [8][9], the green color of a specific game was calibrated using all potential field frames before the detection process. Such method lacks online detection capability and cannot adapt itself to the color drift along the game. To overcome this problem, in our system, the definition of green color is online dynamically updated. Furthermore, we model plays with their intrinsic temporal variations to make the detection scheme robustly applicable to various broadcasting patterns.

Diagram of our play segmentation system is shown in Fig. 1. Football video frames are fed into the adaptive color adjustment module and the play detection module simultaneously. As aforementioned, though the dominant color of the field is green, but the hue, saturation and brightness (in HSV color space) of this green color are not the same for different courts and even continue changing in the same court. Accordingly, the green color here is defined as a relatively wider (looser) interval in the color space in the initial stage and we will keep it updating dynamically to a relatively narrow interval when time is proceeding. Details of the adaptive field model and the play detection scheme are discussed in Sect. 2.1 and 2.2 respectively.

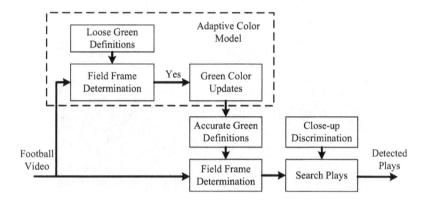

Fig. 1. Block diagram of our play-segmentation system for American football video

2.1   Adaptive Field Color Model

An authentic field frame is determined if it contains dominant green pixels and sufficient field lines. Field lines can be declared if there are more than two lines in a green background area, which should be sufficiently long and nearly parallel with each other. Although some field scenes cannot satisfy such strong constraints and are abandoned, those selected frames are sufficient to dynamically learn the accurate definition of the dominant color of the current game field in a sensitive and stable manner.

Our online adaptive green color adjustment procedure is described as follows:

1. For every incoming frame, count green pixels by the loose definition of "green". If green is not the dominant color of this frame, skip it, and then process the next one. Otherwise mark those green pixels with 1 and others are set to 0, and thus a green masked image is created.
2. Detect edges using Canny detector within the dilated green mask.

3. Find straight lines using Hough transform in the edge image.
4. If detected lines satisfy the aforementioned conditions, current frame is declared to contain fields. The color histogram of the green mask is cumulated into a buffer.
5. Seek those maximum dominant bins in accumulated histogram. The corresponding color range is the updated definition of field color.

Figure 2 shows an example where a frame is determined as field frame.

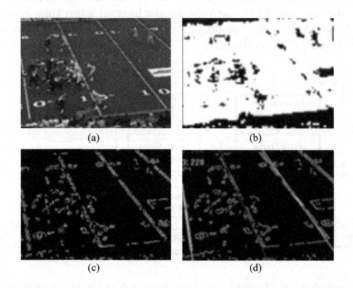

(a)   (b)

(c)   (d)

Fig. 2. An example of field frame selection by online green color learning procedure. (a) A sample frame image. (b) Dilated green mask image. (c) Masked edge image. (d) Detected field lines

2.2   Temporal Pattern Based Play Segmentation

In [8][9], the detection scheme for the start-of-play frames depends on the observation that all players line up to prepare the play while a side camera is capturing the scene, producing a picture similar to Fig. 3(a). Then combinational rules of dominant field color, field lines, clothes color, player lines and camera motion are employed to determine it. However, this is not the only pattern in broadcasted TV games. A play can be started with a medium close-up view of players captured by an end camera, as shown in Fig. 3(b), especially in replaying events and field goals. And place kicks are always started from end-zones in a global view, as shown in Fig. 3(c). In these situations, green color is not dominant and lines are often too weak to be correctly detected. Therefore the rule-based approach in a single frame would fail to recognize such plays.

(a)   (b)   (c)

Fig. 3. Various types of start-of-plays. (a) exhibits distinct visual pattern of a dominant green region with field lines. (b) is a typical replay. (c) is the first frame of a place kick

Though the start frame often does not contain sufficient field regions, a football play always contains typical field frames or segments in the middle. For instance, a place kick play begins with a frame image at low green ratio; however, after the ball is kicked out, the scene is usually switched to a view taken by a side camera to show events in the field, which can be detected as field frame rather easily. Such a typical temporal pattern depicted by the green-ratio curve and the number-of-lines curve is shown in Fig. 4. Then plays can be detected heuristically by searching these distinct patterns. Employing intrinsic correlations in temporal domain, it will be capable of detecting various types of football plays, as presented below.

1. Search segments including sufficient consecutive field frames.
2. From each segment, find the frame backwards where the green-ratio value has fallen beneath a predefined threshold. It is regarded as the start frame of this candidate play.
3. Take the following camera break as the end of current play because after a play the camera usually switches to capture non-action scenes.

Additional steps should be performed on those candidate plays to filter out false alarms. Close-up frames of certain players in the field also produce high green ratio values. From characterization of longest black runs in both horizontal and vertical directions, a frame containing heavy black blobs is recognized to be a close-up and should be removed from candidate plays. Sample images are shown in Fig. 5.

An event-based summary of a football game is then obtained through concatenating all detected plays. We have implemented a prototype system with which users can browse plays and randomly navigate among them efficiently for recorded TV football games.

3   Performance Evaluation

We have tested our play segmentation algorithms on three football video segments recorded from TV programs. The total length is about three hours. Videos are all encoded by MPEG-1 with 320×240 frame resolution. There are complex

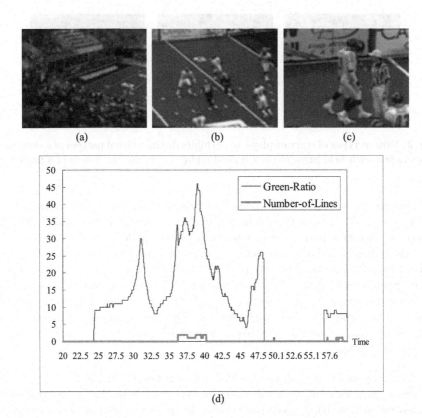

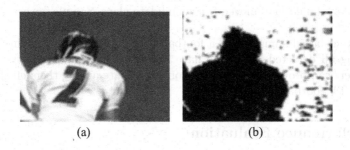

Fig. 4. The temporal pattern of a place kick play from 24s to 48s in a test video. (a) is the start frame of the play at 24s where green pixels are not dominant because it is captured from a global view camera. (b) is a middle frame at 37s where green pixels are dominant and field lines are distinct. (c) is the end frame at 48s. (d) depicts the temporal pattern of the whole play, where the segment from 36s to 40s can be firstly determined as field segment and then triggers the play detection module

Fig. 5. Samples of close-up detection. (a) A close-up frame. (b) Masked image to detect whether there are heavy black blobs

plays due to various broadcasting styles in our test videos, such as replays from different views and reviewing plays excerpted from historical games, which pose great challenges to detect it correctly and precisely. Detected plays are compared with manually labeled ground truth. To measure detection performance, two commonly used metrics, *recall* and *precision*, are defined as follows:

$$Recall = \frac{N_c}{N_c + N_m}, \qquad Precision = \frac{N_c}{N_c + N_f},$$

where N_c represents the number of correctly detected plays, N_m is the number of missed plays and N_f denotes the number of false detections.

Our experimental results are listed in Table 1. Compared with the system developed in [8][9], it achieved 0.68 recall, 0.87 precision in this test video set. It failed to detect those plays which started without distinct pictures of players lining up, for instance, it missed starts of all kickoff events. However, they could be detected successfully by our algorithms because the temporal pattern based play model handled these situations effectively. Therefore considerable improvements in recall rates were obtained.

Table 1. Test results of play segmentation

Video	Ground Truth	Detected Plays	Recall R	Precision P
03-16-I.mpg	70	89	0.857	0.700
03-23-I.mpg	88	106	0.750	0.708
03-23-II.mpg	88	112	0.796	0.661
Average	–	–	0.801	0.690

Most missed plays were those replaying shots captured from a different angle with low green-ratio and weak lines all the while so that no field scene segments could be determined. The precision was a bit lower because some non-action behaviors in the field are misclassified into plays.

4   Conclusions

We have presented an automatic online play segmentation and summarization system for broadcasted American football videos. Two major innovative contributions over previous approaches are the online field color learning scheme and the temporal pattern based modeling of football plays. Experiments on real-recorded programs have given promising results. We are investigating situations where the play model breaks down to further improve the detection performance. Moreover, it is more challenging to classify football plays into semantic classes such as Touch Down, Field Goal, Pass, Fumble, etc, which will be our future work.

References

1. Rui, Y., Gupta, A., Acero, A.: Automatically Extracting Highlights for TV Baseball Programs. Proc. ACM Multimedia. (2000) 105–115
2. American Football: Rules, http://www.allfootballs.com/afrules.html
3. Xu, G., Ma, Y.-F., Zhang, H.-J., Yang, S.: Motion Based Event Recognition Using HMM. International Conference on Pattern Recognition. (2002)
4. Ekin, A., Tekalp, A. M.: Generic Play-Break Event Detection for Summarization and Hierarchical Sports Video Analysis. IEEE International Conference on Multimedia and Expo. (2003)
5. Ekin, A., Tekalp, A.M., Mehrotra, R.: Automatic Soccer Video Analysis and Summarization. IEEE Transactions on Image Processing. 12(7) (2003) 796–807
6. Babaguchi, N.: Towards Abstracting Sports Video by Highlights. IEEE International Conference on Multimedia and Expo. (2000)
7. Babaguchi, N., Ohara, K., Ogura, T.: Effect of Personalization on Retrieval and Summarization of Sports Video. Proc. Fourth IEEE Pacific-Rim Conference on Multimedia. (2003)
8. Li, B., Sezan, M.I.: Event Detection and Summarization in Sports Video. IEEE Workshop on Content-Based Access of Image and Video Libraries (Joint with CVPR2001)
9. Li, B., Sezan, M.I.: Event Detection and Summarization in American Football Broadcast Video. Proc. SPIE Storage and Retrieval for Media Databases. vol. 4676 (2002) 202–213

Semantic Analysis of Basketball Video Using Motion Information

Song Liu, Haoran Yi, Liang-Tien Chia, Deepu Rajan, and Syin Chan

Center for Multimedia and Network Technology
School of Computer Engineering
Nanyang Technological University, Singapore 639798
{pg03988006, pg03763623, asltchia, asdrajan, asschan}@ntu.edu.sg

Abstract. This paper presents a new method for extracting semantic information from basketball video. Our approach consists of three stages: shot and scene boundary detection, scene classification and semantic video analysis for event detection. The scene boundary detection algorithm is based on both visual and motion prediction information. After the shot and scene boundary detection, a set of visual and motion features are extracted from scene or shot. The motion features, describing the total motion, camera motion and object motion within the scene respectively, are computed from the motion vector of the compressed video using an iterative algorithm with robust outlier rejection. Finally, the extracted features are used to differentiate offensive/defensive activities in the scenes. By analyzing the offensive/defensive activities, the positions of potential semantic events, such as foul and goal, are located. Experimental results demonstrate the effectiveness of the proposed method.

Keywords: Motion descriptors, scene detection and classification, video analysis.

1 Introduction

Content-based sports video analysis is becoming increasingly important due to the large amount of videos generated and distributed through networks. Generally, processing of sports video includes the following areas: analysis of the structure of a video, detection of important events or activities, following a specific player's actions and generating the summary. Video analysis aims to extract such semantic information within a video automatically. With such semantics, represented in terms of high level descriptors, indexing, searching and retrieving the video content can be improved.

Several sports video analysis and modelling methods have been investigated. In the literature, low-level soccer video processing algorithms and high-level event and object detection algorithms are utilized for automatic, real-time soccer video analysis and summarization [1]. In [2], color and motion features are used for dominant scene clustering and event detection. However, the above methods do not take the motion information which is an important cue for sports video

K. Aizawa, Y. Nakamura, and S. Satoh (Eds.): PCM 2004, LNCS 3331, pp. 65–72, 2004.

analysis into full consideration. In paper [3], the authors utilize the motion information for describing individual video object, but object segmentation for complex scenes like sports video is still a challenging problem. Thus, we propose an approach to differentiate camera motion and object motion from total motion without object segmentation.

This paper addresses the problem of content-based basketball video analysis for MPEG compressed videos. The problem has two related aspects: 1) analyze the structure of the basketball video and 2) locate the potential positions where an interesting event occurs. Since the semantic understanding of video content is highly dependent on the utilization of contextual information and domain rules, a basketball video analysis method is proposed based on both low-level features (color, texture and motion features) and domain specific knowledge. In the proposed method, a modified scene detection algorithm based on both visual and motion prediction information is introduced. New motion features are proposed to capture the total motion, camera motion and object motion respectively. The camera motion is estimated from the motion vectors in the compressed video using an iterative algorithm with robust outlier rejection. The reasons for using motion features are two folds: 1) motion information has strong relationship with semantic event, i.e. different events exhibit different motion patterns. 2) different events can be identified by motion features within a game and the video model generated by analyzing motion features is flexible enough to be applied in other classes of sports videos. However, to achieve detailed video analysis, we have combined the motion features with other low-level features: color and texture features.

The paper is organized as follows. Section 2 describes the three steps for the proposed basketball video analysis method - shot and scene boundary detection, scene classification and semantic video analysis for event detection. Section 3 presents the experimental results that quantify the performance of the proposed approach. Finally, conclusions are drawn in Section 4.

2   Basketball Video Analysis and Event Detection

The proposed video analysis algorithm consists of three stages: 2.1) shot and scene boundary detection, 2.2) scene classification and 2.3) video structure analysis for event detection. we will introduce the above stages in the following subsections.

2.1   Shot and Scene Boundary Detections

The shot and scene boundary detection is the initial step in our video analysis algorithm. Shot is the physical boundary of video, while scene is the semantic boundary of it [4,5]. Although there is a rich literature of algorithms for detecting video shot and scene boundaries, it is still a challenging problem for basketball video. As mentioned above, scene can be viewed as a semantic unit. Unlike other types of videos, e.g. movie, in which a scene is a group of shots which constitute the semantic unit, the scene in basketball video might be a segment of a shot. In basketball video, a single video shot could be a court-view camera that tracks the players or basketball for a significant amount of time without cuts or transitions but plenty of panning and some zooming. Generally, one or many meaningful semantics, like actions or events, e.g. *shot*, *goal* or *foul*, are contained in such kinds of shots. Since it is hard to extract the detail information for these actions or events from a single long camera shot, it is necessary to partition the shot into scenes further. After analyzing the structure of the long camera shot, we found the semantics in the shot have strong relationship with the global motion associated with the movement of the camera. For example, actions such as *shot* and *goal* will occur most likely when the camera motion is slow, while the fast camera motion often indicates offensive and defensive exchanging interval. Thus, we propose a video temporal segmentation algorithm based on color and motion prediction information to detect shot and scene boundaries simultaneously.

Utilizing the motion prediction information in MPEG video to detect the shot boundary has been proposed by [6]. Motion vectors are divided into four types and the number of each type of macroblocks (MBs) in a frame is used to indicate the similarity/dissimilarity of that frame with its neighboring frames. In our current algorithm, we extend the method in [6] to combine a color-based shot boundary detection method to detect the shot/scene boundaries in basketball videos simultaneously.

In the first step, we use the difference between the color histograms of the neighboring frames, D_h, as the feature, which is defined as

$$D_h = \frac{\sum_{i=0}^{N} |H_n(i) - H_{n-1}(i)|}{width \cdot height} > T_g \qquad (1)$$

where N is the number of bins in the color histogram, H_n and H_{n-1} are the color histogram of frame n and $n-1$ respectively, $width \cdot height$ denotes the pixel numbers in each frame, T_g is the threshold for detecting an isolated sharp peak in a series of discontinuity values of D_h.

To detect the scene boundary accurately and to address our purpose, we modified the original algorithm defined in [6]. Firstly, we modified the definition of Frame Dissimilarity Ratio (FDR) to provide a precise scene boundary detection when the boundary is located at P-frame and to eliminate some false detections. Secondly, we added one more restriction for I-frame into the original equation of dominant MB change (DMBC) to further filter out some false detections.

2.2   Scene Classification

Currently, to capture the structure of the video, we classify basketball scenes into six classes: 1) fast-motion court-view scenes, 2) slow-motion court-view scenes, 3) penalty scenes, 4) in-court medium scenes 5) out of court or close-up scenes, 6) bird-view scenes. The definitions and characteristics of each class are given below:

- *fast-motion court-view scene*: This scene displays a global view of the courts and has obvious global motion; hence, this type of scene can serve to differentiate the offensive and defensive exchange between the teams.

- *slow-motion court-view scene*: A scene that displays the global view of the court and has insignificant global motion; hence, this type of scene can be used to locate the interesting events.
- *penalty scene*: A scene that shows the taking of a penalty under the rim.
- *in-court medium scene*: A scene that focus on a whole player or players in a cluster. Generally, it is a zoomed-in court-view scene. In most cases, a replay is shown as in-court medium scene.
- *out of court or close-up scene*: Such scenes display the audience, coach and close-ups. This type of scenes usually indicate a break in the match or highlight the player who has just performed an exciting event.
- *bird-view scene*: A scene that shows a global view of the whole gymnasium and is usually taken from a stationary camera.

A series of texture and motion features are extracted for classifying a scene into one of the above six classes. In our initial experiment, the texture features were extracted from the key frame of a scene, which is an I-frame located at the central of the scene. Two texture features, *run length feature* [7] and *co-occurrence feature* [8] are generated from the key frame. The run length feature vector has four dimensions that are long run emphasis, shot run emphasis, run length entropy and run length energy. The co-occurrence feature vector has three dimensions that are contrast, energy and entropy respectively.

The second kind of features we use are motion features. We extracted three types of motion features: the amount of total motion (TM), the amount of camera motion (CM) and the amount of object motion (OM). First, we construct the frame by frame Motion Vector Field (MVF) using motion vectors[9]. Then we extract the frame by frame camera motion from the MVF. The camera motion is assumed to follow the classical 6 parameter affine model. We have developed an iterative algorithm with robust outlier rejection to estimate the affine parameters from compressed motion vectors directly (Please see [6] for the details).

Having determined the frame by frame global motion, we now elaborate our motion features for shot classification. The first type of motion features is *global camera motion description* including *camera horizontal motion* (CHD), *camera vertical motion* (CVD) and *camera zoom* (CZD). The definition of the above features are given below

$$CHD = \frac{\sum_{i=0}^{N} p_{3i}}{N} , CVD = \frac{\sum_{i=0}^{N} p_{6i}}{N} , CZD = \sum_{i=0}^{N}(p_{1i} + p_{5i})/2 \qquad (2)$$

where N is the number of frames included in a scene.

The second type of motion features are *total motion matrix, object motion matrix* and *camera motion matrix*, which describe the amount of total motion, object motion and camera motion for each macroblock. We first calculate total motion, object motion and camera motion matrixes for each frame and then accumulate their values across a shot. Finally, the projection values of these matrixes on the horizontal and vertical directions are used as feature vectors in our experiment.

A hierarchical SVM classifier is built for basketball scene classification. The structure of the classifier can be represented as: the basketball video scenes were classified into three classes, *court-view, bird-view* and *others* utilizing the texture-based features at the first run of the SVM classifier. The class *courts-view* was further divided into three classes, *fast-motion court-view scene, slow-motion court-view scene* and *Penalty scene,* based on the global camera motion information and TM, CM, OM matrixes. Lastly, the class *others* was divided into two classes, *in-court medium scene* and *out of court or close-up scene* based on the texture information and TM, CM, OM matrixes.

2.3 Basketball Video Structure Analysis

A high-level basketball video analysis algorithm has been designed to extract the semantic information based on the scene classification information. Therefore, a good approximation of the types of scene and structure of the basketball game has been achieved. The next step is to look at the type and order of scene change to infer another level of semantic information.

Based on the types and orders of changes in the scenes plus 1) a good understanding of the structure of a basketball video, 2) an understanding of the typical camera movement and position for a sport video, we can detect for events like which team is on the offensive and which team is on the defensive in a video segment. The global camera motion is a good feature for extracting this semantic, because the camera will keep on tracking the players or basketball in the game. Since the camera may sway when tracking the basketball, the camera motion does vary continually and may be hard to analyze, detecting the segment of offensive and defensive exchanging interval (ODI) become the main criteria for extracting this semantic. Two types of ODI can be detected from the video. One type is left to right change and the other is right to left change. After detecting the ODI scene, we can further infer the offensive and defensive activities (ODA) for each court-view scene. Our shot/scene boundary detection and scene classification program can provide an overview for a segment of video, and tell us in which part of video the ODI may occur. However these are not enough for accurately extracting ODA since the program can only tell the differences in the amount of motion between the scenes. So, an additional ODI information, modified accumulated camera motion in time (MACM), was calculated to improve the accuracy of ODA extraction, which is defined as the product of accumulated camera motion in time (ACM) and dominant camera motion filter (DCMF) as follows

$$MACM = ACM \times DCMF > T_\alpha \qquad (3)$$

where T_α is a threshold, i.e. if MACM is above the T_α, an ODI is detected.

$$ACM = \begin{cases} (CHD - CVD) \cdot e^{-CZD} \cdot D_s, \text{ If } CHD \cdot CVD > 0 \\ (CHD + CVD) \cdot e^{-CZD} \cdot D_s, \text{ If } CHD \cdot CVD < 0 \end{cases} \qquad (4)$$

where the D_s is the time duration for a single scene.

$$DCMF = \begin{cases} 1 \text{ The first ODI scene in the long court-view shot} \\ 1 \text{ } if \text{ } (ACM_{perviousODE})(ACM_{currentODE}) < 0 \\ 0 \text{ All out of court view scenes \& others} \end{cases} \qquad (5)$$

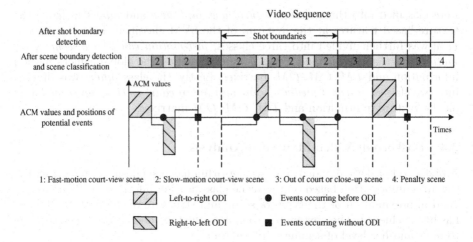

Fig. 1. Example for ODI detection and event detection.

From domain knowledge of basketball game, DCMF is utilized to filter out the conflicting ODI scenes since no two neighboring ODI scenes will have the same camera motion direction within a single shot.

The camera might focus on a player when the ODI occurred, some ODIs may not be captured by the camera in the video. To detect these non-captured ODIs, the detected ODI sequence is refined further. The refinement is based on the observation that left to right change and right to left change should alternate in the video. We will add a scene to ODI scenes if there is a court-view scene between two conflict scenes, otherwise we will delete the second scene of the two conflict scenes. Two scenes are deemed as conflict scenes if they have the same direction of camera motion. After that, an algorithm is applied to generate ODA for each court-view scene. From ODA, we can further infer the positions for the potential event or activities by combining the scene classification and ODA information. Currently, two classes of events are defined and can be detected from basketball video, which are *events before the ODI* and *events without ODI*. The first class of events includes *shot, goal, steal ball* and *offensive foul*, which will lead to a ODI. The second class of events include *defensive foul*. To detect the potential positions that these two kinds of events will occur, an algorithm is designed to look through the basketball video and locate the position based on some rules that are generated from domain knowledge of basketball game, i.e. a penalty sequence will follow from a foul committed by the opposing player. Figure 1 shows an example of ODA generation and event detection.

3   Experimental Result

In this section, we present the results of our algorithm for shot/scene detection, scene classification and video analysis. The test videos are two basketball videos

Table 1. Classification rates for level 1 and level 2 classes

Classes	Correct classification rate (%)	Classes	Correct classification rate (%)
Court-view	95.2	Bird-view	99.8
Others	95.0	Penalty scene	83.4
Slow-motion court-view scene	87.0	Fast-motion court-view scene	91.3
In-court medium view scene	88.0	Out of court or close-up scene	88.2

Table 2. The statistics about the appearance of ODI detection

Performance	Ground-truth	Correct	False	Miss	Recall (%)	Precision (%)
Before refining	93	85	6	8	91.4	93.4
After refining	93	91	8	2	97.8	92.0

and total length of the videos is about fifty minutes. The frame structure of the MPEG compressed test videos follows the standard GOP.

The performance of the algorithm for hard-cut boundaries and gradual transitions is tabulated together. In the test videos, wipes and dissolves were utilized in the replay and close-up shot. Overall, the algorithm achieves 84.3% recall and 97.5% precision rates over 286 shot boundaries. We got a low recall rate since our color-based shot detection algorithm could not detect the gradual transitions accurately. However, the scene detection algorithm do help to reduce the none-detection of gradual transitions. Since the scene detection is a very important stage for generating the data which are utilized in the scene classification and semantic video analysis algorithms, the results of these subsequent algorithms can be used to measure the performance of scene boundary detection indirectly.

Currently, a two-classes SVM classifier was implemented to handle the scene classification. For the case of multiple-classes classification, the classification rate of target class vs. others is used as the experimental results. Table 1 shows the results of scene classifications for the level 1 and level 2 scenes over a total of 1053 scenes. In the experiments, half of data set were used as training set and the remainder were used as test set.

Table 2 shows the results of ODI detection. The first row of the table shows the results of ODI detection using $MACM$ and the second row of the table shows the results after applying the refining algorithm. The ground-truth, in Table 2, was defined as the actual number which ODI occurred including the captured and non-captured one. The results of potential event detection is shown

Table 3. The statistics about the appearance of potential event detection

Events	Ground-truth	Correct	False	Miss	Recall (%)	Precision (%)
Events before the ODI	85	74	6	11	87.0	92.5
Events without the ODI	29	23	7	6	76.6	76.7

in Table 3. From the table, we can see the arbitrary number of events have been detected and classified to correct classes.

4   Conclusion

We have presented a new approach for basketball video analysis and event detection. The motion prediction and global motion information were utilized first to handle shot and scene boundary detection, second, for scene classification and last, to generate the features for semantic video analysis and event detection. Experimental results have demonstrated the effectiveness of the propose method. The method can generate a detailed description for video structure and detect an arbitrary number of events in a basketball game. Moreover, the motion related part of the method is applied directly on the MPEG compressed video without complete decoding of each frame. The information generated by the proposed method can be further combined for high-level video-content description and that information can subsequently be utilized to index, search and retrieval video-contents.

References

1. Ekin, A., Tekalp, A.M., Mehrotra, R.: Automatic soccer video analysis and summarization. IEEE Trans. on Image Processing 12 (2003) 796–807
2. Lu, H., Tan, Y.P.: Content-based sports video analysis and modeling. In: Proceedings of Seventh International Conference on Control, Automation, Robotics And Vision. (2002) 1198–1203
3. Fu, Y., Ekin, A., Tekalp, A., Mehrotra, R.: Temporal segmentation of video objects for hierarchical objectbased motion description. IEEE Trans. on Image Processing 11 (2002) 135–145
4. Nam, J., Tewfik, A.H.: Combined audio and visual streams analysis for video sequence segmentation. In: Proceedings of IEEE International Conference on Acoustics, Speech, and Signal Processing. Volume 4. (1997) 2665–2668
5. Saraceno, C., Leonardi, R.: Identification of story units in audio-visual sequences by joint audio and video processing. In: Proceedings of IEEE International Conference on Image Processing. (1998) 358–362
6. Yi, H., Rajan, D., Chia, L.T.: A unified approach to detection of shot boundaries and subshots in compressed video. In: Proceedings of IEEE International Conference on Image Processing. (2003)
7. Siew, L., Hodgson, R., Wood, E.: Texture measures for carpet wear assessment. IEEE Trans. Pattern Analysis and Machine Intelligence 10 (1988) 92–105
8. Haralick, R., Shanmugam, K., Dinstein, I.: Textural features for image classification. IEEE Trans. Systems, Man and Cybernetics 3 (1973) 610–612
9. Milanese, R., Deguillaume, F., Jacot-Descombes, A.: Video segmentation and camera motion characterization using compressed data. Multimedia Storage and Archiving Systems II(SPIE Proceedings) 3229 (1997)

Reach-Through-the-Screen: A New Metaphor for Remote Collaboration

Jonathan Foote, Qiong Liu, Don Kimber, Patrick Chiu, and Frank Zhao

FX Palo Alto Laboratory Inc., 3400 Hillview Ave., Palo Alto, CA 94304 USA

Abstract. For some years, our group at FX Palo Alto Laboratory has been developing technologies to support meeting recording, collaboration, and videoconferencing. This paper presents several systems that use video as an active interface, allowing remote devices and information to be accessed "through the screen." For example, SPEC enables collaborative and automatic camera control through an active video window. The NoteLook system allows a user to grab an image from a computer display, annotate it with digital ink, then drag it to that or a different display. The ePIC system facilitates natural control of multi-display and multi-device presentation spaces, while the iLight system allows remote users to "draw" with light on a local object. All our systems serve as platforms for researching more sophisticated algorithms to support additional functionality and ease of use.

1 Introduction

The Immersive Conferencing group at FX Palo Alto Laboratory investigates novel technologies for communication and collaboration. At FXPAL, our approach is to extend commodity hardware and software with novel approaches and interfaces that add functionality and simplify ease of use. Our work depends on a long tradition of research in this area by workers at Xerox PARC, MIT, Sony, UNC, Stanford, and elsewhere, and we apologize that space does not permit more than a cursory review of related work.

1.1 "Reach-Through-the-Screen" Interaction

Many of our systems are unified by a common interaction metaphor we call "RTS," for "reach-through-the-screen." In RTS, a video image of a particular location becomes an active user interface. We use the intuition that "things on the network are closer than they appear:" that is, devices visible in the video are available for control over the network, even if they are in a remote location. Devices and functions visible in the video image become available for the user to control via the video. For example, the video image of a display device becomes an active interface to that device: via RTS, a user may drag and drop a presentation file onto the video image, where it is then displayed. Similarly, dragging a file onto a printer image will case the printer to print that file. By

K. Aizawa, Y. Nakamura, and S. Satoh (Eds.): PCM 2004, LNCS 3331, pp. 73–80, 2004.

interacting with an image, users are not encumbered with headgear or special eyeglasses. This is a non-immersive "window-on-the-world" (WoW) style of augmented reality [1]. Figure 1 shows some of the interaction possibilities available with RTS (though we have not fully implemented all of them). For example, right-clicking on an audio device could call up the control panel for that device. A hallmark of RTS interaction that in many cases it gives remote participants richer control than local users. In this paper, we review four related systems that use the RTS metaphor. The FlySPEC system allows a camera to be controlled by pointing or circling regions of interest in the video. The NoteLook system allows presentation graphics to be "dragged" from a video image, annotated, and then "dropped" onto a display device to display the annotations. The ePIC system allows simple control of multi-screen presentation displays and devices using the RTS metaphor, while the iLight camera-projector system allows real-world objects to be annotated from a video image. Drawing on the video image causes the drawn annotations to be projected onto the scene. With all these systems, we have implemented a basic robust version as a platform for both use and research. In many cases, we plan to augment the systems with automatic functionality from computer vision, sensors, and/or machine learning techniques.

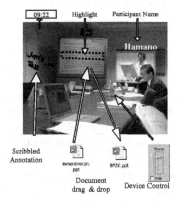

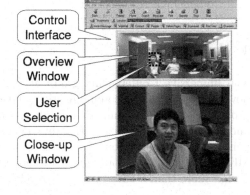

Fig. 1. "Reach through the screen" interface allows device access through an active video window.

Fig. 2. FlySPEC user interface. Circling a region in the panoramic video points the PTZ camera for a close-up view

2   The FlySPEC Camera System

A traditional pan/tilt/zoom (PTZ) camera system cannot allow multiple remote users to point the camera to different positions at the same time. To serve different viewing requests, a straightforward approach is to capture the event with a panoramic camera that covers every possible view and serve different viewing requests through electronic pan/tilt/zoom. However, a panoramic camera generally lacks the required resolution. FlySPEC is the name of our SPot Enhanced Camera system constructed by combining motorized PTZ cameras with a panoramic camera [3]. Using this combined system, users view a low-resolution panoramic view of a scene simultaneously with a customized close-up video. The panoramic video is the same for all users. The close-up video for a user is selected by marking a region in panoramic video with a gesture. Thus the panoramic video serves as an interface: clicking or circling objects in the panorama yields a zoomed-in video close-up.

Fig. 3. Multiple user requests for SPEC camera zoom

2.1   Camera Management and Automatic Control

A FlySPEC system has a limited number of physical PTZ cameras. A basic function of the FlySPEC system is to minimize conflicting PTZ requests and maximize the view quality for all remote users. This is done by serving view requests with a combination of cropped and zoomed images from both cameras. Each user therefore controls a "virtual camera" that behaves like a personal PTZ camera, (but may have reduced resolution). This is a problem for remote applications like classes, seminars, or sports games. To tackle the problem caused by multiple users, we optimize the view returned to each user by maximizing a cost function. Our FlySPEC system currently uses the overall electronic zoom factor as the cost function. Specifically, our management software tries to move PTZ cameras to positions that minimize the average electronic zoom for all users, thus resulting in the best images for all [2]. For example, Figure 2 shows multiple human zoom requests as rectangles; this is satisfied by zooming the camera to the bounding box of all requests. Our current research is to use machine learning to associate sensor data with human control actions to automatically develop good camera control strategies. For example, given motion and audio sensors, we could learn that motion near the podium results in camera movement from human controllers, while motion near the door does not.

Fig. 4. NoteLook pen annotation client

Fig. 5. NoteLook pen annotation interface showing active panoramic image with hotspots

2.2   Camera Registration and Calibration

Panoramic video is supplied by the FlyCam system developed at our lab, which employs multiple cameras and stitches the video images together [4]. A two-camera system provides a panoramic video with a horizontal field of view of approximately 110 degrees. (Recently, we have been constructing cheaper but low-resolution panoramic cameras by equipping inexpensive webcams with wide-angle lenses.) A chief asset of the panoramic camera is that it is fixed with respect to the scene. This allows sophisticated functions without having to compensate for camera motion. For example, registering devices with the areas they appear in the panoramic image allows them to be manipulated through that area without having to locate them with expensive and fragile computer vision techniques.

2.3   Devices and Hotspots

Availability and accessibility of devices are graphically depicted by the hotspots overlaid on the active video window. In practice, we used the fixed panoramic video image, and define hotspots to be particular regions of this image. The possible device operations are indicated by colors and styles of the highlight borders. We are currently working on automatically registering the PTZ camera image with the panoramic image, so that hotspots become active in the zoomed-in video as well.

3   The NoteLook Collaboration System

The NoteLook annotation system is designed to be run on a wireless pen tablet [5]. NoteLook allows collaboration and annotation around digital presentation

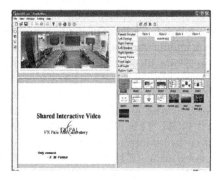

Fig. 6. ePIC presentation authoring and control system

graphics, using digital ink. In operation, the NoteLook system displays a thumbnail view of the conference room in the top left corner. Panoramic video shows a view of the environment with hotspots overlaid on the displays appearing in the video image. "Hotspots" that correspond to active devices are outlined with colored rectangle overlays on the live video image. Besides the two video channels from the front and back meeting room cameras, additional channels may be hooked up during a teleconference to interact with displays at a remote location. A user can grab an image of a slide showing on one of the wall displays by dragging from that display's hotspot into the note page area. The image appears in full resolution, and can be drawn upon with digital ink. After annotating the slide, the user can send the annotated image up to a selected wall display with a drag-and-drop operation. Users may also scribble notes on blank note pages with the pen. The image of any note page, whether it contains an annotated slide or only ink strokes, can be "beamed up" to any wall display. At the end of a session, the user can save the note pages for publishing on the Web. Note pages are time-stamped and automatically associated with any recorded meeting video in a Web interface, such that clicking on a particular annotation starts video playback at the time the annotation was made. More details and features of NoteLook are described in [6].

4 The ePIC Presentation Control System

Today, more and more meeting environments are equipped with a richer variety of displays, often including secondary or multiple projectors or large-screen displays. This gives a presenter richer options for conveying information to others. For example, a presenter can use the primary display for a text presentation, while using another display to show a supporting figure or video. Existing authoring tools, such as PowerPoint, are excellent for creating presentations for a single display, but provide no support for multiple devices, or remote presentations. To enable better use of media-rich environments, we designed ePIC, a tool for authoring and replaying presentations on arbitrary device configurations, that also supports real-time control [7] (as in FlySPEC and Notelook).

EPIC complements, but does not replace tools used to author specific media. It can organize media prepared for simple devices and synchronously present them in one or more multimedia venues. For example, the EPIC system can import a conventional PowerPoint file and re-author it for effective presentation on multiple displays. Our prototype supports arbitrary configurations of displays, printers, speakers and room lights. EPIC, which stands for Environment Picking Image Canvas, uses live or static images of the presentation environment as a graphical user interface (GUI). This allows users to visually select and control presentation devices, even in remote locations. Users may drag slides or media files onto a visual representation of the intended device. For example, a user can drag a slide thumbnail on top of any of the displays visible in Figure 8 to show a slide on that display. The live panoramic video is especially useful for remote presentations, as it allows the presenter to see exactly what the audience is seeing at any time. Figure 8 shows the ePIC user interface. At top left is the active video canvas, showing room control hotspots (besides displays, ePIC can control other room features such as loudspeakers, printers, cameras, and even room lighting.) At top right is the slide timeline. Users can arrange slides and room control actions by time in the presentation and device. The bottom left panel shows a detailed slide view, or zoomed video image from the PTZ camera. At bottom right the slides in a PowerPoint presentation are available either for immediate drag-and-drop operations or for arranging into a multiscreen presentation. EPIC provides both a preview mode and a playback mode. In the preview mode, the actual room devices are not controlled. Rather, a preview of the presentation is rendered in the video image canvas. By displaying slide thumbnails in the hotspot bounding boxes (see Figure 4), the user can navigate the presentation using the usual controls, and see a visual indication of what slides are rendered on each display device. The image canvas can contain a rendering of a VRML model of the venue, if available. In this case, slide thumbnails are rendered in 3-D on the display surfaces. Because the rendering viewpoint can be selected, the user can preview the presentation from any point in the venue. Figure 9 shows an example of a VRML output, including a pop-up menu for selecting the viewpoint. Users may also zoom in and out of the rendering to see details or overviews of the presentation. Currently, we are investigating ways to incorporate machine learning to assist multi-screen presentations and optimal slide placement [9].

5   The iLight Projection Drawing System

The iLight system allows remote users to draw using light projected on a real-life object or scene [8]. Using an aligned camera/projector system, live video from the scene is presented as a drawable video image to one or more remote users. Graphics drawn on the video canvas are projected onto the scene visible in the video. Thus remote users may annotate particular scene objects or features for local viewers, and can also display text and project arbitrary digital images. Unlike related systems, there are no video feedback problems, nor

Fig. 7. Previewing ePIC presentations on video (left) and VRML (right) representations

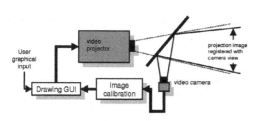

Fig. 8. iLight camera/projector system

Fig. 9. iLight user interface. User drawings on the video window are projected onto the actual scene.

are computer vision techniques required to detect objects or actions. Imagine a shared whiteboard as an example scenario. The iLight system's video projector "draws" remote images on a local whiteboard, while sending live whiteboard video to the remote drawer. In operation, remote users draw on the camera image with familiar graphical tools such as rectangles and (digital) pens, while local users draw directly on the whiteboard using (physical) dry-erase markers. The local projector, fixed with respect to the video camera, projects the remotely drawn images onto the whiteboard. Because the iLight camera and projector are exactly aligned, the projected image is drawn exactly where the remote user intends. Local users see the ink and projected light intermixed on the whiteboard, while remote users see a camera image of the same. Thus local and remote users can freely draw and annotate each other's work as if they shared a local whiteboard. Though neither can erase the other's marks, the remote user has functionality not available with physical ink. For example, the remote user may project any arbitrary image, as well as copy-and-paste regions of the camera image. We are currently investigating using camera feedback to enhance the projection onto surfaces with nonuniform reflectivity. By monitoring the reflection visible in the camera image, it is possible to modify the projected image to compensate for color and brightness variations in the scene. For example, when projecting on a checkerboard surface, the projection can be brightened in the dark squares and dimmed in the light squares to result in a more uniform perceived illumination.

6   Conclusion

We have presented four systems that support remote communication and collaboration, using a powerful and intuitive "reach-through-the-screen" interface. Perhaps most importantly, these systems serve as platforms for investigating algorithms, such as computer vision and machine learning, that will hopefully support additional advanced functions and ease of use.

References

1. M. Tani, K. Yamaashi, K. Tanikoshi, M. Futakawa, and S. Tanifuji, "Object-oriented video: Interaction with real-world objects through live video." In *Proc of CHI '92*, ACM Press, pp. 593–598
2. Q. Liu and D. Kimber, "Learning Automatic Video Capture from Human Camera Operations." In *Proc. IEEE Intl. Conf. on Image Processing*
3. Q. Liu, D. Kimber, J. Foote, L. Wilcox, and J. Boreczky. "FLYSPEC: A Multi-User Video Camera System with Hybrid Human and Automatic Control." In *Proc. ACM Multimedia 2002*, pp. 484–492, Juan-les-Pins, France, December 1-6, 2002.
4. J. Foote and D. Kimber, "FlyCam: Practical Panoramic Video." In *Proc. IEEE Intl. Conf. on Multimedia and Expo*, vol. III, pp. 1419–1422, 2000.
5. P. Chiu, Q. Liu, J. Boreczky, J. Foote, T. Fuse, D. Kimber, S. Lertsithichai, and C. Liao, "Manipulating and Annotating Slides in a Multi-Display Environment." In *Proc. of INTERACT '03*, pp. 583–590
6. P. Chiu, A. Kapuskar, S. Reitmeier, and L. Wilcox. "NoteLook: Taking Notes in Meetings with Digital Video and Ink." In *Proc. ACM Multimedia '99*, Orlando, Florida, November 1999.
7. C. Liao, Q. Liu, D. Kimber, P. Chiu, J. Foote, and L. Wilcox, "Shared Interactive Video for Teleconferencing. In *Proc. ACM Multimedia 2003*, pp. 546–554
8. J. Foote and D. Kimber, "Annotating Remote Reality with iLight," in preparation.
9. Q. Liu, F. Zhao, and D. Kimber, "Computer Assisted Presentation Authoring for Enhanced Multimedia Venues," in preparation.

Working Documents

Paul Luff[1], Hideaki Kuzuoka[2], Christian Heath[1],
Jun Yamashita[3], and Keiichi Yamazaki[4]

[1] Work Interaction and Technology, The Management Centre, King's College, London
150 Stamford Street, London, UK
{Paul.Luff, Christian.Heath}@kcl.ac.uk
[2] Graduate School of Systems and Information Engineering, University of Tsukuba
1-1-1 Tennoudai, Tsukuba, Ibaraki 305-8573, Japan
kuzuoka@esys.tsukuba.ac.jp
[3] Research Center for Advanced Science and Technology, The University of Tokyo
4-6-1 Komaba, Meguro-ku, Tokyo 153-8904 Japan
jun@cyber.rcast.u-tokyo.ac.jp
[4] Faculty of Liberal Arts, Saitama University
255 Simo-ohkubo, Sakura-ku, Saitama, Japan
yamakei@post.saitama-u.ac.jp

Abstract. Enhancing video-mediated communication has been a continual concern for developers of collaborative technologies ever since the emergence of CSCW. However, despite numerous attempts with a great variety of related technologies it is hard to find sustained examples of video-based technologies providing synchronous and symmetrical resources to support collaborative work. We consider enhancements to such systems focused around supporting work with material documents. By drawing on explorations with the use of this technology we consider the resources participants use and require undertaking detailed distributed collaborative activities in media space.

1 Introduction

There has been a long-standing interest in CSCW (Computer Supported Cooperative Work) in developing systems to support real time, synchronous collaboration amongst individuals based in different locations. In this paper we wish to introduce two prototype systems designed to support interaction and collaboration with and around document and other material resources. In particular we discuss the design and development of two solutions to enable individuals based in different physical locations to undertake various activities in collaboration with each other which rely upon accessing, examining, referencing, annotating and creating material documents including plans, pictures, papers and the like.

2 Background

One of the important developments within research on media space and video connectivity was the realisation that the conventional 'face to face' view found in

K. Aizawa, Y. Nakamura, and S. Satoh (Eds.): PCM 2004, LNCS 3331, pp. 81–88, 2004.
© Springer-Verlag Berlin Heidelberg 2004

most commercial systems does not provide support for many forms of collaboration. A range of workplace studies (e.g. [1]) demonstrated that almost all forms of synchronous collaboration in the workplace relied upon the participant's access to and use of various resources within the immediate environment. Perhaps the most important of these resources, is the material document, an object or artefact, whether plan, image or text, which pervades interaction and collaboration in many organisational activities. In consequence, it is increasingly recognised that media spaces have to provide systematic support for document-focused collaboration and furthermore evidence suggests that tangible material paper documents have qualities that support collaboration that may not necessarily be found in digital documents, at least as they currently configured and displayed [2,3]. Video conductivity therefore becomes critical in creating environments for cooperation and collaboration since we can begin to provide participants with access to each others material documents and provide opportunities to enable those documents to be referred to and transformed using conventional materials and bodily actions.

3   Requirements for Supporting Paperwork on a Desk

In earlier research, we identified a number of demanding, yet key, requirements that a coherent environment designed to support distributed, synchronous collaborative work needs to address. These requirements were drawn from a series of workplace studies undertaken over a number of years in a diverse range of settings including control centres, doctors surgeries, news rooms, architectural practices and trading rooms [4]. These include:

- providing resources through which participants can discriminate the actions of others. Actions involve shifts in orientation, and reference to the space and a range of objects, artefacts and features;
- considering ways in which participants can refer to, invoke, grasp, manipulate, address, and in various ways animate properties of the space, and coordinate such actions with the real-time conduct of others.

Refining these requirements with respect to configurability and assemblies of documents we could focus on a simple motivating example, say the kinds of support required by a pair of individuals collaboratively working, writing on and reading a set of documents. In order to support this remotely the system should provide:

- the ability to view a number of paper documents and types of documents in the remote domain;
- multiple forms of access to another's documents, including focused collaborative activities such as shared writing, private work with documents and 'semi-shared' activities where items may be referred to, but their details are not necessarily made public to the other;
- easy ways of moving between different forms of access.

In order to support these requirements, we developed from the existing Agora system built at the University of Tsukuba [5] a system that has developed upon a number of related initiatives that augment media space, such as VideoDraw [6], TeamWorkstation [7] and DigitalDesk [8]. These refinements on Agora discussed here are called AgoraPro and AgoraG and aim to support two participants interacting with a range of paper documents. Since we have already introduced the AgoraG in [9], the aim of this paper is to introduce the AgoraPro and to briefly describe the comparison of two systems.

Fig. 1. Agora System

4   The Agora System

Figure 1 and 2 shows the basic configuration of the Agora system. The most noticeable feature of the Agora system is the 60-inch screen that is situated along one side of the desk. Life-size image of the remote participant as they sit (or stand) at the desk is projected on the screen. This provides a view of the other as well as some a small portion of the desk in front of them. The camera associated with this view is attached to the screen; it is small enough for it not to be obtrusive. As well as this view, Agora also has three other areas:

– a private space where documents are only available to the local participant.
– a semi-shared document area (66cm x 49cm) where documents and hand gestures on and over the desktop are captured by a video camera above the desk, transmitted to a remote site, and projected onto the remote desktop from beneath. In order to eliminate infinite video feedback, polarised films are placed both on the desk surface and in front of the camera lens. The resolution in this area is relatively low and with the polarised films rather dark. Also, since the image is projected from beneath, documents on the local desktop cover the image of documents on the remote one.
– a shared document area provides an area where both participants can collaborate over details of documents. Images are captured from Digital Video cameras positioned above an area the same size as an A3 piece of paper (42x30cm) on each desk. These are mixed together and displayed on the shared document monitor in front of the participants.

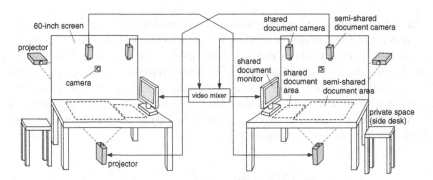

Fig. 2. Outline diagram of the Agora system.

The two sites connected through the system are 200m apart and they are connected via a high band width network (155Mbps ATM). Although not shown in the figure, each site is equipped with a microphone and a speaker to allow the participants to talk to and hear one other.

Since the document camera also captures participants' hand gestures over the shared document, images of the hands can also be seen in the shared document monitor. However, one of the problems of the original Agora system was that participants occasionally pointed to the shared document monitor when the object was actually on their own desk. Since such pointing actions cannot be captured by the document camera, images of the hands are not seen in the shared document monitor.

Supporting this kind of activity is critical for 'reaching into' the remote domain. This is why we investigated two different ways of displaying 'gestures' in the remote space. These variations are called AgoraPro and AgoraG.

4.1   AgoraPro

In AgoraPro we add a camera and projector to Agora which captures and shows hand gestures (Fig 3). A camera captures the local participant's gestures and the image is projected down to a shared document area at the remote site (see Fig. 4). In order to eliminate infinite video feedback a polarised film is placed in front of this camera so that the camera captures only a hand image. Since the remote document camera captures projected hand gestures and shows them on the shared document screen, a local participant can see that his or her own hands are projected at the remote site. For the remote participant, he/she can see the other participant's hand gestures projected both over the real document and on the shared document monitor. The projected image of the hand, although still in colour, appears lighter and whiter than the images of other hands captured through the camera.

In this way, a participant can point both at the real document (in their own space) and at the document displayed in the shared document monitor.

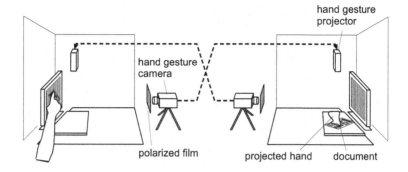

Fig. 3. Additional cameras and projectors for AgoraPro.

Fig. 4. The remote participant's hand is projected on a local document and the screen (AgoraPro).

Fig. 5. The laser spot pointing to a photograph on the shared screen (AgoraG).

4.2 AgoraG

In the AgoraG variation we use a more visually simple device – a remote control laser pointer. We also use a LCD with a touch panel as the shared document monitor. The laser pointer is controlled so that it enables a remote participant to point at 'real' documents when he or she touches the appropriate locations on the shared document monitor.

As the video image of the projected laser pointer is captured by the document camera it can be seen on the shared document monitors at both sites (Fig. 5). Thus the local participant can see that the laser pointer is actually pointing at the appropriate location, whilst the remote participant can see the laser spot both on the actual document on the desk and in the shared monitor.

5   Preliminary Observation of the System Usage

To examine how participants accomplished a range of tasks we developed a number of tasks that involved the use of a wide variety of documents – maps, photographs and textual documents. We chose tasks that involve different kinds

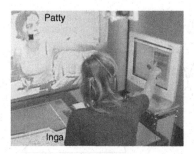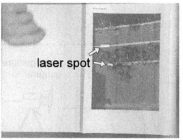

Fig. 6. Patty and Inga are orienting toward their shared screens and pointing together (left). Right photo shows the image on the shared document monitor.

of writing and reading activities – note-taking, drawing, annotating, writing lists and brief reports. In this paper, due to the space limitation, we do not describe the detail of the experiment. Rather, we only introduce two example scenes to help readers understand how the system support communication.

One of the interesting features of Agora are the ways in which the participants are able to interweave a range of resources and spaces within the developing course of a particular activity. For example relatively subtle shifts in orientation, the delicate onset of particular actions, and shifting glances between particular objects and domains, are not only available to the co-participant, but are oriented to in sequentially relevant ways. In other words, participants are able to retrieve the sense and significance of particular actions from the standpoint of the co-participants and thereby produce a sequentially appropriate action. This sense and sensibility is achieved through the ways in which co-participants interweaved the visibility of co-participants' actions on different displays and in different locales, so that for example, a shift in orientation on the large projected display and the beginnings of an arm movement towards the co-participant's screen, can be seen to prefigure some activity on a document - either on one's own shared screen or on a document on the desk. In Fig. 6, Inga first looks up towards Patty and then, finding Patty is pointing to her own 'shared' screen, Inga turns to her 'shared' screen where (as it is in the AgoraG configuration) the laser dot appears.

Interestingly, AgoraG and AgoraPro have very different implications for the range of actions in which the participants are able to engage. With AgoraG, we have noticed that participants are often able to make unproblematic and simple references to objects within the remote environment, in particular when they are attempting to differentiate one item from another. For certain tasks this may be a critical facility. Indeed, some recent experiments suggest that it is easier to use this to point to and recognise pointings to small objects. On the other hand, AgoraPro enables participants to overlay remote objects with a complex array of gestures and accomplish actions which involve much more than simple reference. For example, gestures can be used to demarcate different elements of an object, to exaggerate features and characteristics, and to animate and embed action in materials, so that they gain a significance, then and there,

Fig. 7. Using the projected gesture, the participant is indicating the width of the road on the photo. Right photo shows the image on the shared document monitor.

that they might not otherwise have (Fig. 7). Indeed, as in more conventional environments, AgoraPro provides participants with the resources to animate and annotate material objects through bodily action and thereby accomplish a range of actions which are ordinarily precluded when the participant's body is either unavailable or disassociated from the material objects with which it is 'engaged'.

The significance of visible gestures to the organisation of collaboration however goes far beyond the ability to animate material objects. It has some bearing on the ways participants coordinate their actions with each other. The single dot or cursor simply appears in the relevant location on the document, whereas the hands emerge progressively, within the developing course of the activity. So for example, we find that participants are able to form and reform the shape and movement of the hands with regard to emerging demands of the activity and in particular the co-participation of the other. The hands are sensitive to the shifting character of the activity, and their sensitivity is visible and oriented to by the co-participant. More fundamentally, rather than simply appearing in a location, the hands prospectively inform the co-participant; they provide sense of where they are going, what they are doing, and what it will take for their action to be complete. The prospective orientation of the hands' work enables the co-participant to envisage and anticipate the actions of the other, and to align towards those actions within the developing course of their articulation. The single dot or cursor is denuded of its temporal and spatial development, whereas the hands enable the co-participant to envisage their character and completion and thereby produce sequentially appropriate conduct right at the point and moment at which it becomes relevant. The hands therefore do not simply provide resources for the elaboration of material objects, but, through their prospective orientation, enrich the ways in which participants are able to produce, recognise and coordinate their actions with one another.

6 Summary

AgorPro and AgoraG proved surprisingly successful, at least within the framework of the small scale experiments we have undertaken so far. However the system and its arrangement has certain drawbacks. The media spaces consist of a complex configuration of cameras, projectors, filters, monitors and screens and although the system is only intended as experimental it is indeed somewhat cumbersome. More importantly perhaps, at least in the present context, the system appears particularly suitable for relatively intense forms of document focused collaboration, where it is critical that participants require subtle and fine-grained access to each others' actions. In this respect AgoraG and AgoraPro are configured to support a different order of activity than addressed in earlier work on media spaces and CVEs. In this case, we find a system which, as a consequence of its design and the quality of equipment, is able to support highly intensive forms of materially mediated collaboration but not focused on broader access to the participants' immediate environments. Thus our next challenge is to develop a simpler system that can be used for more general tasks.

Acknowledgements. This research was supported by Oki Electric Industry Co. Ltd., the Venture Business Laboratory (VBL) of the Ministry of Education, Culture, Sports, Science and Technology, and International Communications Foundation, Grant-in-Aid for Scientific Research (B), 2004, 16300261. The Anglo-Japanese collaboration was supported by the Daiwa Anglo-Japanese Foundation. The research at King's College was supported in collaboration with the Palcom project funded by the European Community Sixth Framework Programme (FP6-002057-PALCOM).

References

1. Nardi, B., Schwarz, H., Kuchinsky, A., Leichner, R., Whittaker, S., Sclabassi, R.: "Turning Away from Talking Heads: The Use of Video-as-Data in Neurosurgery". In: Proc. of INTERCHI'93. (1993) 327–334
2. Luff, P., Heath, C., Greatbatch, D.: Tasks-in-interaction: Paper and screen based documentation in collaborative activity. In: Proc. of CSCW '92, ACM Press (1992) 163–170
3. Sellen, A.: The Myth of the Paperless Office. MIT Press (2002)
4. Heath, C., Luff, P.: Technology in Action. Cambridge University Press (2000)
5. Kuzuoka, H., Yamashita, J., Yamazaki, K., Yamazaki, A.: Agora: A remote collaboration system that enables mutual monitoring. In: Extended Abstracts of CHI'99. (1999) 190–191
6. Tang, J., Minneman, S.: Videodraw: A video interface for collaborative drawing. ACM Transactions on Information Systems **9** (1991) 170–84
7. Ishii, H.: "TeamWorkStation: Towards a Seamless Shared Workspace". Technical report, NTT (1990)
8. Wellner, P.: "The DigitalDesk: Supporting Computer-based Interaction with Paper Documents". In: Proc. of Imagina. (1993) 110–119
9. Yamashita, J., Kuzuoka, H., Inoue, N., Yamazaki, K.: Development of a remote collaboration system that support communicational feedbacks (in japanese). Information Processing Society of Japan Transactions **45** (2004) 300–310

Immersive Meeting Point

An Approach Towards Immersive Media Portals

Ralf Tanger, Peter Kauff, and Oliver Schreer

Fraunhofer Institute for Telecommunications, Heinrich-Hertz-Institut,
Einsteinufer 37, 10587 Berlin, Germany
{Ralf.Tanger,Peter.Kauff,Oliver.Schreer}@hhi.fraunhofer.de

Abstract. Natural and realistic video communication and collaboration across long distances is an essential requirement in the context of
globalization. Against this background this paper presents a next generation system - the immersive meeting point- which bridges the gap between cutting-edge technology available from research laboratories and
advanced prototype systems beeing close to the market. The aim is to
provide immersive tele-presence and natural representation of all participants in a shared virtual meeting space to enhance quality of human-
centred communication. This system is based on the principle of a shared
virtual table environment, which guarantees correct eye contact and gesture reproduction. The current system design and details of the algorithms as well as the software concept are presented.

1 Introduction

The migration of immersive media to telecommunication continues to advance
and to become cheaper through digital representation. It is widely accepted that
this trend is going to have a strong impact on the appearance of daily life and
that it has much to contribute to the definition of new communication styles.
The ability to evoke a state of "being there" and/or of "being immersed" will
no longer remain the domain of flight simulators, CAVE systems, cyberspace
applications, theme park rides or IMAX theatres. It will arise in offices, venues
and homes and it has the potential to enhance quality of life in general.

The recent developments in the area of videoconferencing are the best proof
for this evolution. State-of-the-art videoconferencing systems already offer dedicated tele-presence capabilities to achieve most natural communication conditions. They use large plasma displays or large screen projections to present
people in life-size. Especially equipped conference rooms are going to reproduce
large table meetings by integrating projections walls seamlessly into real meeting
room environments. However, this evolution from first videoconference devices to
today's telepresence systems is only the beginning of a new era in telecommunication. Presence research and in particular presence engineering have developed
a lot of concepts to exceed the limitations of traditional communication and various international research efforts have investigated how to utilise these concepts

K. Aizawa, Y. Nakamura, and S. Satoh (Eds.): PCM 2004, LNCS 3331, pp. 89–96, 2004.
© Springer-Verlag Berlin Heidelberg 2004

for an improvement of physical presence (spatial closeness despite of distance) in video conferencing.

In this context our paper briefly points out the state of the art and explains the particular focus of the immersive meeting point (im.point) in this business segment. The im.point architecture is then described in detail and we conclude with an outlook on its significance for future work towards immersive media portals.

2   State of the Art

The spadework of immersive videoconferencing has definitively been done by the development of the experimental tele-cubicle platform within the US National Tele-Immersion Initiative (NTII) [1]. In this system single remote participants appear in life-size on separated stereo displays arranged symmetrically around a table. The current head position of the local user is tracked through sensory devices, and the stereo rendering of the remote partners is carried out in dependence of the tracked head position. As a consequence, the local user watches all remote partners under a correct perspective view - an outstanding feature that ensures an optimal reproduction of eye contact, body postures and gestures. A further interesting experimental system for immersive videoconferencing is the blue-C development of the Technical University of Zurich (ETH) in Switzerland [2]. It has a strong focus on 3-dimensional video analysis and rendering in a CAVE-like mounting. Its scientific objectives are close to the original NTII work, but blue-c uses latest technology and, with it, a system architecture that is even more complex than the one of NTII. It enables a number of participants to perceive the photo realistic three-dimensional image of their collaboration partners in real-time, while interacting and collaborating inside an immersive, virtual world. The key technology is a special screen, which can be switched from opaque state for display to transparent state for acquisition. Hence a complex synchronisation between screen, projectors, active illumination, stereo glasses and acquisition hardware has been developed.

Although both, NTII and blue-C still hold their particular merits, they are of experimental use only. In both systems 3D video acquisition and rendering are based on voxel representation formats, which are computationally expensive and require a cluster of high-end processor systems therefore. Moreover, both systems use complex display mountings. Special tracking devices are needed to adapt 3D rendering to the user's head position and the users have to wear special glasses to perceive the stereo cue. Obviously, that is not suitable for a marketable prototype system. Therefore the European IST project VIRTUE has proposed a semi-immersive and transportable desktop solution for immersive video conferencing [3]. It uses a 61-inch plasma system to be able to present a virtual conference scene in life-size at one common screen (see Fig. 1). The remote partners appear as natural video objects in the virtual scene. Thus, the local user gets the impression of a seamless transition between real work-spaces and shared virtual environment. Although the internal scene representation is based on an

Fig. 1. im.point conferencing terminal

entire 3D date structure, the display is restricted to 2D images to avoid the bearing of stereo glasses. Nevertheless, the 3D-to-2D rendering is adapted to the tracked head position of the local user. The intention of this processing was to support depth perception by head-motion parallax-viewing instead of stereo.

Another convincing approach to eliminate the notion of distances is the Telepresence Wall by France Telecom R&D [4]. This system is under test between two sites of France Telecom. 2D video images of the remote site are projected in real-time on the wall in long corridors and local people are captured by a reflecting-mirror based video module. Real-size display, echo cancellation and rendering of spatial audio provides important features to support natural communication.

3 Focus of im.point Development

Research systems such as the ones mentioned in section 2 usually need expensive hardware and are dedicated to a particular research topic. As a consequence, they are not really suitable to develop prototypes that are close to the market.Furthermore it is often not clear what features and components are a must for human-centered communication, what features are a "nice to have" and what features only make systems expensive without additional benefits for the user.

The ambition of the im.point development was therefore to bridge this gap between a system with already stable algorithms which can suit as basis for a marketable product on one hand and an experimental setup which provides researchers with a challenging platform to develop solutions in particular in the field of 3D video analysis and -synthesis on other hand. Along this bridge several components can be evaluated towards their necessity for future video-conferencing systems. All configurations of the im.point system provide at least a correct line of sight and a natural reproduction of gestures. The solutions are completely implemented in software and run on standard PCs in real time.

As shown in Fig. 1, the im.point is based on the concept of a shared virtual table environment (SVTE) that has originally been proposed by the European research project VIRTUE. The local user of the im.point system gets the impression that the real table in front of the terminals seamlessly extends into the virtual scene. The video objects of the remote partners appear in a natural manner behind the shared virtual table. However, taking into account the experience from VIRTUE, the system architecture has been considerably reduced and completely re-designed to achieve an optimal trade-off between performance, flexibility and complexity. All components proving a failure have been removed. That especially applies to the usage of head tracking and adapted 3D-to-2D rendering. The effect of depth perception by head-motion parallax viewing was quite limited in the VIRTUE set-up and changing the viewing perspective was sometimes more annoying than gainful. Similar holds for 3D video processing, which allows a perfect reproduction of eye contact on one hand but may also introduce new and annoying artefacts on the other hand. Reflecting these experiences, the im.point design has been built on a scalable and flexible system architecture using the MPEG-4 standard for video coding, scene description and multimedia integration framework. The system is entirely implemented in software on standard PC technology. Due to its flexibility the im.point system can be scaled from simple 2D video to full 3 D video processing, depending on the application and he performance requirements.

4   The im.point System Architecture

4.1   The Shared Virtual Table Environment (SVTE)

Basically, the im.point follows the SVTE concept. The idea is to place suitable video reproductions of all participants at predefined positions in a shared virtual environment. For a typical three-party conference these positions are located at the corners of an equilateral triangle enclosing the round table. The right illustration in Fig. 2 shows such a SVTE arrangement with three participants. The lines indicate the placement of the displays corresponding to the user with the same number. In addition, the mounting of cameras is shown as an example for user 1. Note that bottom camera captures the view for user 2 and, respectively, the top camera the view for user 3. Following this illustration, it can be understood that the distance between the head of a remote participant and the corresponding camera can be kept quite small. Thus, the lack of eye contact (difference between viewing direction and camera axis) is less than 10 degrees. Furthermore, the passive eye contact is supported as well, meaning that, when the two remote participants are looking at each other, the local user perceives it as he would do in a real conference situation. Due to these viewing conditions, a simple 2D video capturing is sufficient to achieve natural communication to the greatest possible extent. Therefore im.point scalability offers a commercial low-complexity version where the video representation of the conferees is limited to 2D video streams. However, for more experimental reasons and the purpose of long-term studies it also offers a 3D option where conferees are captured by

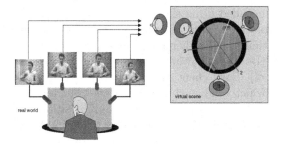

Fig. 2. Multi-view capturing for a 3 party conference

a multiple camera set-up, typically consisting of four cameras (see Fig. 2). In this case, disparities can be estimated from each camera pair, representing the dynamic 3D surface of the captured person. This 3D information can be used to reconstruct an intermediate view of a virtual camera that is located at the direct viewing line between two partners . This 3D video processing can be considered as an add-on feature allowing perfect eye contact between the partners.

4.2   System Components

Figure 3 outlines the current version of a fully featured im.point system. Each terminal consists of a server and a client. On the server the multi-view captured video frames are first segmented to separate the person's silhouette from the background. The separation is necessary for the seamless integration of the person into the virtual scene. For extraction of the depth information the video streams are pairwisely rectified to speed up the following disparity analysis. The disparities and the shaped video objects are then combined to one compact representation using joint texture and disparity maps. Texture and disparities

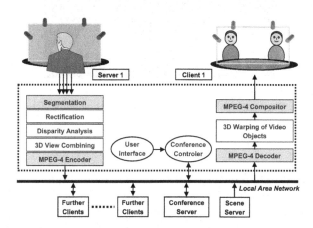

Fig. 3. Outline of im.point system

can be efficiently encoded using the MPEG-4 multimedia standard with binary shape encoding for the texture objects and gray-scale auxiliary planes for the disparity information. Data is then transmitted to the clients of the other terminals using DMIF (Delivery Multimedia Integration Framework) and UDP (User Datagram Protocol). Each client provides a BIFS (Binary Format for Scenes) compliant player which renders the virtual scene. The incoming MPEG-4 video streams are decoded. Depending on the default position of the user's head a final 3D warp is calculated using image-based-rendering techniques and the resulting individual view of each participant is integrated behind the virtual table. The BIFS scene itself is loaded during an initialization phase. Down-scaling for commercial low-complexity applications is achieved through by-passing the 3D processing modules (see shaded boxes in Fig. 3). In this case two cameras are used instead of four.

Segmentation. For a seamless integration into the virtual scene, the person must first be separated from the background. The segmentation algorithm basically follows a change detection approach, comparing the current image of a conferee with the corresponding background which was captured during an initialization phase [5]. To cope with slight changes of illumination the reference image with the background is permanently updated. Figure 4, left shows a segmentation result for a typical video conferencing scenario. A particular problem of this setup are heavy shadows on the table which lead to a significant amount of faulty segmentation. Therefore, a dedicated module has been developed to detect such shadows. The right hand side of Fig. 4 shows the final result including shadow detection [6]. For CCIR601 resolution, the whole segmentation runs with 70 fps on a single logical CPU of a Xeon 3GHz.

Fig. 4. Segmented object without and width shadow detection

Rectification and Disparity Estimation. On each terminal two camera pairs independently capture left and right stereo views of the local participant (see Fig. 2). Due to the small viewing distance, the camera mounting is highly convergent. To ease the subsequent disparity analysis under the given time constraints, the images are first rectified [7]. In rectified stereo images, the corresponding pixels

Fig. 5. Segmented original images (left two) and rectified images (right two)

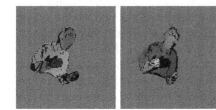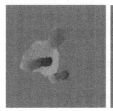

Fig. 6. Result of consistency check with unreliable disparities marked as black (left two) and final result after post processing (right two)

are to be found on the same scan line. The result of rectification is depicted in Fig. 5. To extract the required 3D representation, the depth of the captured video object is analysed on the basis of the rectified images. This is done by so-called disparity matching between multi-view images - a process searching for pixel correspondences referring to projections of the same 3D point onto different position in the image planes. For im.point a real-time stereo matching algorithm was developed, which provides spatially and temporally consistent disparities for full CCIR 601 resolution. It is based on a hybrid recursive matching (HRM) algorithm which has additionally been applied successfully to fast motion estimation in formats conversion and MPEG coding [8].

A crucial point is to provide accurate disparities for the complete image, including occluded as well as homogeneous or less structured regions. The disparities are first estimated on a 4x4 grid. Then mismatches are detected using a special consistency check (see left two images in Fig. 6). The arisen holes are then filled by a segmentation driven interpolation and extrapolation scheme. Homogeneous regions are interpolated. Around a detected depth discontinuity missing disparities are extrapolated towards the boundaries of segmentation masks determined in parallel. The right two images in fig. 6 show the final result after post-processing. More details about the disparity estimation approach can be found in [9].

System Integration. The system was entirely written in C++ using strictly a modular approach. In total 70 libraries were developed with about 500k lines of code. The server has to deal with the highest computational load, therefore all server modules were integrated using a data flow driven architecture to allow easy use of multi threading to distribute the components on all four logical CPUs of a current double processor Pentium Xeon system with 3 GHz. To provide an intuitive basis for future algorithmic developments all significant parameters of the used algorithms can be tuned without stopping the system allowing an online evaluation of new results.

5   Outlook

A new PC based immersive media portal has been presented, whose components are implemented purely in software. The modularity of the architecture design allows an easy integration of future tele-collaboration services beside the classical video conferencing. Due to the full compliance to the MPEG-4 standard, the system is open to other applications and easy to extend. The im.point provides the technology to evaluate and test effectively future real-time communication and tele-colaboration applications. Hence, human factors and presence research topics can be investigated.

References

1. Chen, W.C. et al.: Toward a Compelling Sensation of Telepresence: Demonstrating a portal to a distant (static) office. Proc. of IEEE Visualization, Salt Lake City, UT, USA, Oct. 2000, pp.327-333.
2. Gross M., Würmlin S., Naef M., Lamboray E., Spagno C., Kunz A., Koller-Meier E., Svoboda T., Van Gool L., Lang S., Strehlke K., Vande Moere A., Staadt O.: blue-c: A Spatially Immersive Display and 3D Video Portal for Telepresence. Proceedings of ACM SIGGRAPH, 2003, pp.819-827.
3. Schreer, O., Hendriks, E., Schraagen, J., Stone, J., Trucco, E., Jewell, M.: Virtual Team User Environments - A Key Application in Telecommunication. Proc. of eBusiness and eWork, Prague, Cech Republic, October, 2002.
4. www.rd.francetelecom.com/en/galerie/mur_telepresence/index.php
5. Feldmann, I., Askar, S., Brandenburg, N., Kauff, P., Schreer, O.: Real-Time Segmentation for Advanced Disparity Estimation in Immersive Video conference Applications. Proc. of 9th Int. Conf. on Computer Graphics, Visualization and Computer Vision (WSCG), Plzen, Czech Republic, Feb. 2002.
6. Schreer, O., Feldmann, I., Goelz, U., Kauff, P.: Fast and Robust Shadow Detection in Video conference Applications. Proc. of 4th EURASIP IEEE Int. Symposium on Video Processing and Multimedia Communications, Zadar, Croatia, June 2002.
7. Fusiello, E., Trucco, E., Verri, A.: Rectification with Unconstrained Stereo Geometry. British Machine Vision Conference, Essex, 1997, pp.400-409.
8. Kauff, P., Schreer, O., Ohm, J.R.: An universal algorithm for real-time estimation of dense displacement vector fields. Proc. of Int. Conf. on Media Futures, Florence, Italy, May 2001.
9. Atzpadin, N., Kauff, P., Schreer, O.: Stereo Analysis by Hybrid Recursive Matching for Real-Time Immersive Video Conferencing. Trans. on Circuits and Systems for Video Technology, Special Issue on Immersive Telecommunications, Vol.14, No.3, 2004, pp.321-334.

EnhancedTable: Supporting a Small Meeting in Ubiquitous and Augmented Environment

Hideki Koike[1], Shin'ichiro Nagashima[1], Yasuto Nakanishi[2], and Yoichi Sato[3]

[1] Graduate School of Information Systems, University of Electro-Communications,
1-5-1, Chofugaoka, Chofu, Tokyo 182-8585, Japan
koike@acm.org, naga@vogue.is.uec.ac.jp
[2] Faculty of Technology, Tokyo University of Agriculture and Technology,
2-24-16, Nakamachi, Koganei, Tokyo 184-8588
yasuto@cc.tuat.ac.jp
[3] Institute of Industrial Science, The Universitiy of Tokyo,
4-6-1 Komaba,Meguro-ku, Tokyo 153-8505, Japan
ysato@iis.u-tokyo.ac.jp

Abstract. This paper describes our design and implementation of an augmented table interface for small group meetings. The system was designed to be used by multiple users in the ubiquitous environment, where people do not need to bring their laptop PCs. With effective use of the advantage of computer vision, we implemented the concept of *ubiquitous desktop* as personal workspace and *virtual Chinese table* as shared workspace. User can share/personalize files by drag-and-dropping icons to/from the shared workspace. The system also provides capabilities for interactive image capturing and finger position sharing, both of which would be useful for the group meetings.

1 Introduction

As personal computers become more and more and popular, changes have occurred in the style of small group meetings. Traditionally, paper documents and white boards have been the main elements in such small meetings. On the other hand, people often bring their laptop PCs to the meeting in order to take notes and to show presentation slides to other participants. In addition, people also download electronic files, such as PDF documents, from the Internet during the meeting. Other participants may copy these files from his/her PC by using file transfer tools such as FTP.

Although such digitally enhanced meetings have succeeded in introducing efficiency, we often feel a little inconvenienced. For example, laptop PCs brought by the participants require a relatively large area of the space assigned to each participant on the meeting table. Little space remains in which to place other objects such as paper documents, and it is sometimes hard for participants to write memos in their notebooks.

When exchanging electronic files, people need to know the IP address of the computer from which the files are downloaded They have to make a connection to the computer, and copy the files onto their own PCs.

K. Aizawa, Y. Nakamura, and S. Satoh (Eds.): PCM 2004, LNCS 3331, pp. 97–104, 2004.
© Springer-Verlag Berlin Heidelberg 2004

Fig. 1. Typical meeting scene.   **Fig. 2.** EnhancedTable in use.

On the other hand, much research is being conducted to realize the ubiquitous computing environment proposed by Mark Weiser[11]. In the ubiquitous environment, a large number of computers are embedded in the environment and will support users' activity implicitly and/or explicitly by enabling communication with each other. If such environments were to be established, users would not need to carry their laptop PCs, which are heavy but contain important data. The users' data would be stored in network file servers which are in a safe place, and would be retrieved when necessary. It is, moreover, expected that the environment would recognize the user's position and show appropriate information at the appropriate position. However, the traditional interaction framework such as GUI, which uses a keyboard and mouse as standard input devices will not be appropriate in such a ubiquitous environment. Then the Perceptual User Interface (PUI) which utilizes several recognition technologies such as image recognition and speech recognition are focused on as the next generation interaction framework.

This paper describes our design for an augmented table system in a ubiquitous and augmented environment and its implementation. The system aims to support effective face-to-face meeting by allowing users natural and intuitive operation of digital files.

2   Meeting in Ubiquitous and Augmented Environment

To date, many augmented systems have been developed [3,4,12]. Most of them were designed for being used by a single user or for sharing one screen by multiple users. On the other hand, our interest is in integrating each user's personal workspace and a shared workspace on one screen. The key features of our system are as follows.

Integrating ubiquitous personal workspaces and shared workspace:
In the ubiquitous environment that we imagine, the user do not need to carry heavy laptop PCs which contain important files. When a user puts an object (e.g., a mobile phone) which identifies him/her on the table, the system identifies the user and displays his/her desktop with his/her personal files, which are stored

in a networked file server, at that user's position. The user directly manipulates the displayed objects by using his/her own hand and fingers instead of using a mouse or trackpad.

At the center of the table, a special shared workspace is projected. When a user drags his/her personal file from his/her workspace to the shared workspace, the file becomes a shared file. Other users can copy this shared file just by drag-and-dropping the file from the shared workspace onto their own personal workspaces. Moreover, this shared workspace serves as a presentation screen when the user previews particular file as we describe later.

Enhancing paper documents using vision-based augmented reality:
As we described in [3], paper documents and digital documents will co-exist for the time being. The paper documents are easier to carry, easier to read, easier to add notes to, and so on. However, it is much more difficult to make copies and send them to other people quickly. By effective use of the advantages of vision-based augmented reality, we implemented the following features which enhance the paper documents. One is interactive image capturing. The user can make a digitized image of a part of or all of a paper document just by showing a rectangle gesture. Another is finger position sharing. When the users enable the finger position sharing mode, each user's finger position is projected on the document.

3   EnhancedTable

In order to explore the interaction framework described above, we developed an augmented table system, named EnhancedTable, which allows parallel interactions by multiple users (Fig.2). The system uses a normal white table as a screen and interaction space. One of the important features of our system (and this feature is essential to support meeting) is the ability to allow parallel interaction by multiple users. Traditional touch panel systems do not allow such multiple interaction. Although some recent touch panel systems can detect multiple pointing, they still do not allow users to put some objects such as mug cups on the panel. It is also difficult or expensive to make a much larger table. On the contrary, our system naturally allows multiple interaction and could be extended to accommodate larger displays.

3.1   Personal Workspace: Ubiquitous Desktop

When the user sits at the table and put his/her mobile phone on the table, the system recognizes the mobile phone and identifies the user. Then it automatically projects the user's personal workspace such that the mobile phone is on the top-left (or top-right) corner of the workspace. Unlike other meeting systems which have embedded displays, the users can sit anywhere they want to because the projection coordinate is decided based on the position of the mobile phone.

There are data icons and operational icons in the personal workspace (Fig. 3). The data icons represent text files, image files, or audio files owned by the

Fig. 3. Private workspace and shared workspace.

Fig. 4. Users can preview files on the shared workspace.

Fig. 5. Interactive image capturing.

Fig. 6. Finger position sharing.

user. Users can drag these icons by using their fingers. The operational icons include trash icon, preview icon, etc. The users can perform a certain operation by drag-and-dropping the data icon on the operational icon.

3.2 Shared Workspace: Virtual Chinese Table

On the center of the table, a circular shared workspace is always displayed (Fig. 3). When a user drags his/her personal file from his/her workspace and drops onto the shared workspace, the file becomes a shared file. Other users can copy this shared file just by drag-and-dropping the file from the shared workspace to their own personal workspace. The user can rotate the circular shared workspace by hand as with a Chinese dining table in a Chinese restaurant (or with a lazy susan in a regular restaurant). The user in any position can reach every file in the shared workspace by rotating that space.

The shared workspace also plays a role as a presentation screen. When a user drags-and-drops any image file on the preview icon, that file is magnified at the shared workspace and all users can see and rotate the image (Fig. 4). When we use the traditional presentation screen, if one user wants to point to the presentation slide, he/she needs to stand up and go to the presentation screen. On the other hand, the users of our system can point to the slide without leaving their seats. However, all users cannot see the slide from the right angle simultaneously.

3.3   Interactive Image Capturing

In the current meetings, we sometimes want to digitize a part of or all of the paper document and send it to all participants during the meeting. In order to do this in the current meetings, we need to go to a PC connected to an image scanner, scan the file, and send it as an attachment file. It is a time-consuming task. On the other hand, our system provides interactive image capturing. When the user makes a rectangle with the thumb and pointing (index) finger of both hands and waits for three seconds, the CCD camera on the ceiling zooms into the rectangle area, and saves its image in JPEG format (Fig. 5). The reason why we used the third CCD camera is to obtain high resolution images when capturing the image.

3.4   Finger Position Sharing

When a user enables the finger position sharing mode, a grid is shown in the personal workspace. If the user aligns a paper document on the grid, other users' finger positions are projected on the document (Fig. 6). Different colors are assigned to each user to identify whose finger position they belong to.

4   Implementation Detail

4.1   Overview

On top of the table, there are two LCD projectors (PLUS V-1080) for displaying images, two CCD cameras (SONY EVI-D100) for finger/hand tracking, and one CCD camera (SONY EVI-D30) for image capturing. A LCD projector, a CCD camera (EVI-D100), and a PC (Pentium 4 2.80MHz: 512Mb memory: Linux) with an image processing board (HITACHI IP5005) make a unit. Currently we have installed two units. Each unit covers a half of the table. The reason why we use two units is to get enough resolution for displaying and capturing image.

4.2   User Identification

To recognize a mobile phone, we used a method for object registration and recognition using an RGB color histogram[5]. We first capture the image of an object by 60x60 pixels. The registration system scans each pixel and calculates RGB values of the pixel in 256 colors. If the value of the pixel is (r, g, b), where $0 \leq r, g, b \leq 8$, the system increments the value $H(r, g, b)$ by one. After scanning all the pixels in the image, this three dimensional matrix H is registered as a model of the object (Fig. 8). In the recognition process, the system looks for an object which has the size of usual mobile phones. When the system find

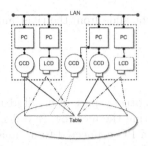

Fig. 7. System architecture.

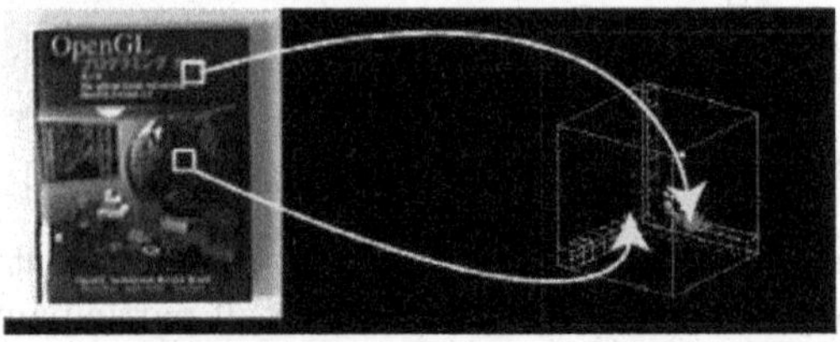

Fig. 8. RGB histogram.

the object, it calculates the RGB histogram of the object by using the same algorithm described above, and compares this histogram to those registered in the system. If the system finds a model whose histogram is close enough to the object's histogram, the object is regarded as matched to the model.

4.3   Finger Recognition

To detect hand regions, the system calculates the difference between the initial image and the current image of the tabletop. After the binarization operation, objects which are larger than a threshold are recognized as hand regions. Since the hand regions must cross the edge of the image, the system investigates every pixel of the four edges and determines the direction of finger tips. After the hand regions are detected, a certain area from the fingertips is recognized as the palm. By repeating the shrink operation to the palm region, the final pixel is determined to be the center of the palm. Then, using template matching with a circle template, the system finds the fingertips [7]. Currently the system can detect and track eight hands in 20 frame/sec. If the CPU becomes much faster, the system can track more hands faster.

After detecting the hands on the table, it is necessary to decide to whom each hand belongs. To do this, the system currently uses the distance between the identified object and the center of gravity of the hand region and the center of the palm.

1. If the center of gravity of hand region is in the personal workspace, the hand is recognized as the owner of the personal workspace.
2. If the center of palm is in the personal workspace, the hand is recognized as the owner of the personal workspace.

The reason why we need the first rule is that the center of the palm goes outside of the personal workspace when the user moves his/her hand to the shared workspace.

5   Discussion

Through the experimental use in our laboratory and the demonstrations to the visitors, we found that most of the people want to use the system in the real meetings. The first reason is its natural and intuitive interface for exchanging digital files. In particular, our users preferred to use the virtual Chinese table. However, some people claimed that it is unnatural to use fingers during the meeting because they usually hold a pen. So it might be better to use pen instead of finger to manipulate digital objects, such as seen with tablet PCs. The second reason is that people felt much closer to each other during the meeting because there is no physical fence or barrier (i.e., LCD displays of the laptop PCs) between users. In the current meetings, we do not know what other users are doing because of these barriers. Although this is nice to keep our privacy, it sometimes interferes with our mutual understanding.

We used color information of the mobile phones to identify users. This object recognition system gave 92 % correct answers for a hundred different images in our experiment. If the number of users is small and they use phones with different appearances, this identification works. However, if the number of users is larger and they use phones with similar appearance, this identification system would fail. For the better identification, there are some alternative methods, such RFID tag. This method is accurate for detecting who is in the environment. However, it is not appropriate for detecting where the user sits. One solution would be to use an object sensor behind the table to detect the precise position of the user.

6   Related Work

"Office of the future"[8] proposed an augmented office with some projectors. The users can see information on the desk or on the wall of the office. However, the developers did not mention how to interact in such a ubiquitous environment. "EasyLiving"[1] proposed an intelligent living room in the future. The environment always tracks users in the room and displays the users' desktop at appropriate screens. The interaction, however, is done using the traditional mouse and keyboard.

Our work is mostly inspired by Rekimoto's Augmented Surface[6], which smoothly integrates the desktop of laptop PCs and augmented table surface and wall. Augmented Surface is, however, a design prototype based on the current framework. It assumes an environment where people carry their own PCs. On the other hand, our system is a design prototype based on the ubiquitous environment of the near future. In particular, the ubiquitous desktop is a unique concept. Augmented Surface's vision system, called DeskSat, takes 30 seconds to scan the table surface. On the other hand, our vision system processes eight hands and other object in 20 frame/sec (i.e. 0.05 sec).

Another related work which should be mentioned is the "I/O bulb" concept in [9]. Unlike the normal bulb which has just the ON/OFF state, the "I/O bulb" has the ability of data projection and image capturing. As we described previously, EnhancedTable consists of two unit which includes a LCD, a CCD camera, and two PCs. This unit is a concrete implementation of the I/O bulb concept. We carefully designed our hardware and software so that each unit works by itself and is extensible. As a result, it is easy to add other units to the system in order to make a larger table (or room).

7 Conclusions

This paper described our design and implementation of an augmented table system, called EnhancedTable. The system was designed to be used in the ubiquitous environment in the near future, where people do not need to carry laptop PCs. We proposed and implemented the ubiquitous desktop as personal workspace and the virtual Chinese table as shared workspace. Users can easily exchange their files via the shared workspace in a natural and intuitive manner. We also implemented interactive image capturing and finger point sharing capabilities.

References

1. B. Brumitt, S. Shafer. Better Living Through Geometry. Personal and Ubiquitous Computing, Vol.5, Issue 1, 2001.
2. P.H. Dietz, D.L. Leigh. DiamondTouch: A Multi-User Touch Technology, ACM Symp. on User Interface Software and Technology (UIST), pp. 219-226, November 2001.
3. H. Koike, Y. Sato, Y. Kobayashi. Interactive Textbook and Interactive Venn Diagram: Natural and Intuitive Interfaces on Augmented Desk System. *ACM Conf. on Human Factors in Computing System (CHI2000)*, pp. 121-128, 2000.
4. M. Kruger. *Artificial Reality.* Addison-Wesley, 2nd edition, 1991.
5. T. Nishi, Y. Sato, H. Koike. SnapLink:Interactive Object Registration and Recognition for Augmented Desk Interface. *IFIP INTERACT'01*, pp. 240-246, 2001.
6. J. Rekimoto, M. Saitoh. Augmented Surfaces:A Spatially Continuous Work Space for Hybrid Computing Environments. *ACM Conf. on Human Factors in Computing System (CHI'99)*, pp. 378-385, 1999.
7. Y. Sato, Y. Kobayashi, H. Koike. Fast Tracking of Hands and Fingertips in Infrared Images for Augmented Desk Interface. *IEEE Int. Conf. Automatic Face and Gesture Recognition (FGR2000)*, pp. 462-467, 2000.
8. R. Raskar, G. Welch, M. Cutts, A. Lake, L.Stesin, H.Fuchs. The office of the future: a unified approach to image-based modeling and spatially immersive displays, Proc. of the 25th Annual Conf. on Computer Graphics and Interactive Techniques, ACM, 1998.
9. J. Underkoffler, H. Ishii. Illuminating light: An optical design tool with a luminous-tangible interface. In *ACM Conf. on Human Factors in Computing System (CHI'98)*, pp. 542–549, 1998.
10. F. Vernier, N. Lesh, C. Shen. Visualization techniques for circular tabletop interfaces. *(AVI'2002)*, pp. 257-265, 2002.
11. M. Weiser. The Computer for the 21st Century. Scientific American, Sep. 1991.
12. P. Wellner. Interacting with Paper on the DigitalDesk. *(Comm. of the ACM)*, pp. 86-96, 1993.

Remote Collaboration on Physical Whiteboards

Zhengyou Zhang and Li-wei He

Microsoft Research, One Microsoft Way, Redmond, WA 98052, USA

Abstract. A whiteboard provides a large shared space for the participants to focus their attention and express their ideas, and is therefore a
great collaboration tool for information workers. However, it has several
limitations; notably, the contents on the whiteboard are hard to archive
or share with people who are not present in the discussions. This paper
presents our work in developing tools to facilitate collaboration on physical whiteboards by using a camera and a microphone. In particular, our
system allows a user to take notes of a whiteboard meeting when he/she
wants or in an automatic way, to transmit the whiteboard content to
remote participants in real time and in an efficient way, and to archive
the whole whiteboard session for efficient post-viewing. Our system can
be retrofit to any existing whiteboard. With the help of a camera and a
microphone, we are effectively bridging the physical and digital worlds.

1 Introduction

The work presented in this paper focuses on the particular meeting scenarios
that use whiteboard heavily such as brainstorming sessions, lectures, project
planning meetings, and patent disclosures. In those sessions, a whiteboard is
indispensable. It provides a large shared space for the participants to focus their
attention and express their ideas spontaneously. It is not only effective but also
economical and easy to use – all you need is a flat board and several dry-ink
pens.

While whiteboard sessions are frequent for knowledge workers, they are not
perfect. The content on the board is hard to archive or share with others who
are not present in the session. People are often busy copying the whiteboard
content to their notepads when they should spend time sharing and absorbing
ideas. Sometimes they put "Do Not Erase" sign on the whiteboard and hope
to come back and deal with it later. In many cases, they forget or the content
is accidentally erased by other people. Furthermore, meeting participants who
are on conference call from remote locations are not able to see the whiteboard
content as the local participants do. In order to enable this, the meeting sites
often must be linked with expensive video conferencing equipments. Such equipment includes a pan-tilt-zoom camera which can be controlled by the remote
participants. It is still not always satisfactory because of viewing angle, lighting variation, and image resolution, without mentioning lack of functionality of
effective archiving and indexing of whiteboard contents.

K. Aizawa, Y. Nakamura, and S. Satoh (Eds.): PCM 2004, LNCS 3331, pp. 105–113, 2004.

Our system was designed with three purposes:

1. to alleviate meeting participants the mundane tasks of note taking by capturing whiteboard content automatically or when the user asks;
2. to communicate the whiteboard content to the remote meeting participants in real time using a fraction of the bandwidth required if video conferencing equipment is used;
3. to archive the whole meeting in a way that a user (participants or not) can find efficiently the desired information.

In the remainder of the paper, we describe the techniques used in each part. Because of space limitation, only a high-level description is provided.

To the best of our knowledge, all existing systems that capture whiteboard content in real time require instrumentation either in the pens or on the whiteboard. Our system allows the user to write freely on any existing whiteboard surface using any pen. To achieve this, our system uses an off-the-shelf high-resolution video camera which captures images of the whiteboard at 7.5Hz. From the input video sequence, our algorithm separates people in the foreground from the whiteboard background and extracts the pen strokes as they are deposited to the whiteboard. To save bandwidth, only newly written pen strokes are compressed and sent to the remote participants.

2   Whiteboard Scanning and Image Enhancement

Because digital cameras are becoming accessible to average users, more and more people use digital cameras to take images of whiteboards instead of copying manually, thus significantly increasing the productivity. The system we describe in this paper aims at reproducing the whiteboard content as a faithful, yet enhanced and easily manipulable, electronic document through the use of a digital (still or video) camera.

However, images are usually taken from an angle to avoid highlights created by flash, resulting in undesired perspective distortion. They also contain other distracting regions such as walls. The system we have developed uses a series of image processing algorithms. It automatically locates the boundary of a whiteboard as long as there is a reasonable contrast near the borders, crops out the whiteboard region, rectifies it to a rectangle with the estimated aspect ratio, and finally correct the colors to produce a crisp image.

Besides image enhancement, our system is also able to scan a large whiteboard by stitching multiple images automatically. Our system provides a simple interface to take multiple images of the whiteboard with overlap and stitches them automatically to produce a high-res image. The stitched image can then be processed and enhanced as mentioned earlier.

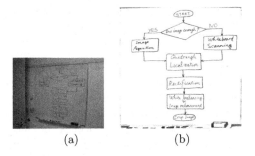

(a)   (b)

Fig. 1. Diagram of the system architecture drawn on a whiteboard. (a) Original image; (b) Processed one.

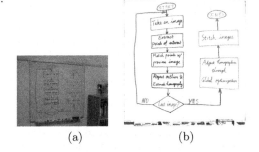

(a)   (b)

Fig. 2. Diagram of the scanning subsystem: (a) Original image; (b) Processed image.

2.1   Overview of the System

Let us take a look at Figure 1. On the top is an original image of a whiteboard taken by a digtal camera, and on the bottom is the final image produced automatically by our system. The content on the whiteboard gives a flow chart of our system.

As can be seen in Fig. 1b, the first thing we need to decide is whether it is enough to take a single image of the whiteboard. If the whiteboard is small (e.g., 40' by 40') and a high-resolution digital camera (e.g., 3 mega pixels) is used, then a single image is usually enough. Otherwise, we need to call the whiteboard scanning subsystem, to be described in Section 2.2, to produce a composite image that has enough resolution for comfortable reading of the whiteboard content. Below, we assume we have an image with enough resolution.

The first step is then to localize the borders of the whiteboard in the image. This is done by detecting four strong edges. The whiteboard in an image usually appears to be a general quadrangle, rather than a rectangle, because of camera's perspective projection. If a whiteboard does not have strong edges, an interface is provided for the user to specify the quadrangle manually.

The second step is image rectification. For that, we first estimate the actual aspect ratio of the whiteboard from the quadrangle in the image based on the fact that it is a projection of a rectangle in space. From the estimated aspect ratio, and by choosing the "largest" whiteboard pixel as the standard pixel in the final image, we can compute the desired resolution of the final image. A planar mapping (a 3× 3 homography matrix) is then computed from the original image quadrangle to the final image rectangle, and the whiteboard image is rectified accordingly.

The last step is white balancing of the background color. This involves two procedures. The first is the estimation of the background color (the whiteboard color under the same lighting without anything written on it). This is not a trivial task because of complex lighting environment, whiteboard reflection and strokes written on the board. The second concerns the actual white balancing. We make the background uniformly white and increase color saturation of the pen strokes. The output is a crisp image ready to be integrated with any office document or to be sent to the meeting participants.

Figures 1 and 2 each show the original image on the left and the processed image on the right.

2.2   Whiteboard Scanning Subsystem

The major steps of the Whiteboard Scanning system is illustrated in Figure 2. The mathematic foundation is that two images of a *planar* object, regardless the angle and position of the camera, are related by a plane perspectivity, represented by a 3×3 matrix called *homography* $\mathbf{H}$. The stitching process is to determine the homography matrix between successive images, and we have developed an automatic and robust technique based on points of interest. An example of whiteboard scanning is shown in Fig. 3.

Due to space limitation, the reader is referred to [3] for details.

3   Real-Time Whiteboard Processing and Collaboration

Sometimes, meeting participants who are on conference call from remote locations are not able to see the whiteboard content as the local participants do. In order to enable this, the meeting sites often must be linked with expensive video conferencing equipments. Such equipment includes a pan-tilt-zoom camera which can be controlled by the remote participants. It is still not always satisfactory because of viewing angle, lighting variation, and image resolution, without mentioning lack of functionality of effective archiving and indexing of whiteboard contents. Other equipment requires instrumentation either in the pens or on the whiteboard. Our system allows the user to write freely on any existing whiteboard surface using any pen. To achieve this, our system uses an off-the-shelf high-resolution video camera which captures images of the whiteboard at 7.5Hz. From the input video sequence, our algorithm separates people in the foreground from the whiteboard background and extracts the pen strokes as they are deposited to the whiteboard. To save bandwidth, only newly written pen strokes are compressed and sent to the remote participants.

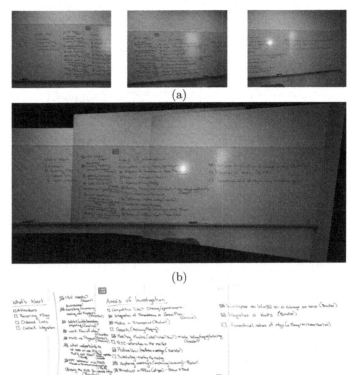

Fig. 3. A second example of whiteboard scanning. (a) Three original images; (b) Stitched image; (c) Final processed image.

3.1   Real-Time Processing

The input to our real-time whiteboard system is a sequence of video images, taken with a high-resolution video camera. There are a number of advantages in using a high-resolution video camera over the sensing mechanism of devices like Mimio or electronic whiteboard. They are: 1) Without requiring special pens and erasers makes the interaction much more natural. 2) Since it is taking images of the whiteboard directly, there is no mis-registration of the pen strokes. 3) As long as the users turn on the system before erasing, the content will be preserved. 4) Images captured with a camera provide much more contextual information such as who was writing and which topic was discussing (usually by hand pointing). However, our system has a set of unique technical challenges.

Since the person who is writing on the board is in the line of sight between the camera and the whiteboard, he/she often occludes some part of the whiteboard. We need to segment the images into foreground objects and whiteboard. For that, we rely on two primary heuristics: 1) Since the camera and the whiteboard are stationary, the whiteboard background cells are stationary throughout the sequence until the camera is moved; 2) Although sometimes foreground objects (e.g., a person standing in front of the whiteboard) occlude the whiteboard, the pixels that belong to the whiteboard background are typically the majority.

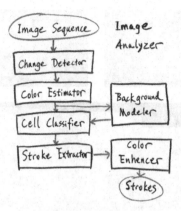

Fig. 4. The image sequence analysis process

We apply several strategies in our analysis to make the algorithm efficient enough to run in real time.

First, rather than analyzing the images at pixel level, we divide each video frame into rectangular cells to lower the computational cost. The cell size is roughly the same as what we expect the size of a single character on the board (16 by 16 pixels in our implementation). The cell grid divides each frame in the input sequence into individual cell images, which are the basic unit in our analysis.

Second, our analyzer is structured as a pipeline of six analysis procedures (see Figure 4). If a cell image does not meet the condition in a particular procedure, it will not be further processed by the subsequent procedures in the pipeline. Therefore, many cell images do not go through all six procedures. At the end, only a small number of cell images containing the newly appeared pen strokes come out of the analyzer.

The third strategy is specific to the video camera, Aplux MU2, that we use in our system. The Aplux MU2 allows the video frames to be directly accessed in Bayer format, which is the single channel raw image captured by the CMOS sensor. In general, a demosaicing algorithm is run on the raw image to produce an RGB color image. By processing the cell images in raw Bayer space instead of RGB space and delaying demosaicing until the final step and running it only on the cells containing new strokes, we save memory and processing by at least 66%. An additional benefit is that we can obtain a higher quality RGB image at the end by using a more sophisticated demosaicing algorithm than the one built into the camera driver.

3.2   Teleconferencing Experience

We have implemented our system as a plug-in to the Whiteboard applet of the Microsoft Windows Messenger (see Figure 5). The Whiteboard applet allows the users at two ends of a Windows Messenger session to share a digital whiteboard.

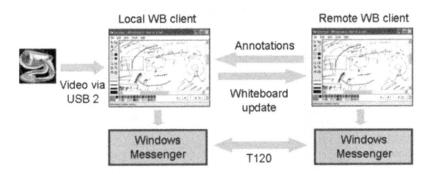

Fig. 5. Real-time whiteboard system inside the Windows Messenger

The user at one end can paste images or draw geometric shapes and the user at the other end can see the same change almost instantaneously. Usually, the user draws objects with his mouse, which is very cumbersome. With our system, the user can write on a real whiteboard instead.

The changes to the whiteboard content are automatically detected by our system and incrementally piped to the Whiteboard applet as small cell image blocks. The Whiteboard applet is responsible for compressing and synchronizing the digital whiteboard content shared with the remote meeting participant. The remote participant can add annotations on top of the whiteboard image using the mouse. When used with other Windows Messenger tools, such as voice conferencing and application sharing, whiteboard sharing becomes a very useful tool in communicating ideas.

A video capturing the working of our real-time whiteboard system will be shown during the conference. The reader is referred to [2] for details.

4   Whiteboard Archiving

As with the previous system, we point a high-resolution digital still camera to the whiteboard and continuously capture its images. Additionally, we also capture the audio discussions with a microphone. During the post-processing stage, our system distills a small set of key frame images from the captured image sequence. A key frame represents the maximum content on the whiteboard before each erasure. Time stamps of the pen strokes contained in the key frames are also computed. The users can view the key frame images, print them as notes, or cut and paste them into documents. If the users want to find more about the discussion on a particular topic, our browsing software allows them to click some pen stroke associated with that topic and bring up the audio at the moment when the stroke was written. Therefore the whiteboard content serves as a visual index to efficiently browse the audio meeting.

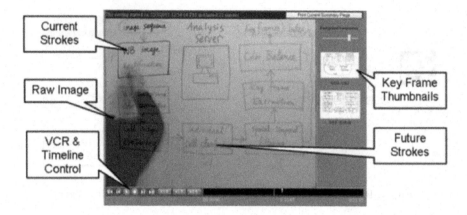

Fig. 6. Browsing interface. Each key frame represents the whiteboard content of a key moment in the recording. The main window shows a composition of the raw image from the camera and the current key frame. The pen-strokes that the participants are going to write in the future (Future Strokes) are shown in ghost-like style.

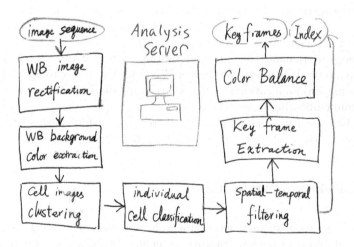

Fig. 7. The image sequence analysis process

4.1 Browsing Interface

Since most people probably do not want to listen to the recorded meeting from start to end, we provide two browsing features to make non-linear accessing of the recorded information very efficient (see Fig.6 and its caption). 1. Key Frames: Key frame images contain all the important content on the whiteboard and serve as a summary to the recording. They can be cut and pasted to other documents or printed as notes. 2. Visual Indexing: We provide two levels of non-linear access to the recorded audio. The first is to use the key frame thumbnails. The user can click a thumbnail to jump to the starting point of the corresponding key frame. The second is to use the pen strokes in each key frame. Together with the standard time line, these two levels of visual indexing allow the user to browse a meeting in a very efficient way.

4.2   Technical Challenges

The input to the Whiteboard Capture System is a set of still digital images (see Figure 2). We need to analyze the image sequence to find out when and where the users wrote on the board and distill a set of key frame images that summarize the whiteboard content throughout a session. Compared to other systems, our system has a set of unique technical challenges: 1) The whiteboard background color cannot be pre-calibrated (e.g. take a picture of a blank whiteboard) because each room has several light settings that may vary from session to session; 2) Frequently, people move between the digital camera and the whiteboard, and these foreground objects obscure some portion of the whiteboard and cast shadow on it. Within a sequence, there may be no frame that is totally unobscured. We need to deal with these problems in order to compute time stamps and extract key frames. Rather than analyzing images on per-pixel basis, we divide the whiteboard region into rectangular cells to lower computational cost. The cell size is roughly the same as what we expect the size of a single character on the board (about 1.5 by 1.5 inches). Since the cell grid divides each frame in the input sequence into cell images, we can think of input as a 3D matrix of cell images.

Figure 7 shows an outline of the algorithm. Due to space limitation, the reader is referred to [1] for details. A demo will be shown during the conference.

Acknowledgement. The authors are grateful to Zicheng Liu for his contribution and discussions in developing the whiteboard system.

References

1. L. He, Z. Liu, and Z. Zhang, "Why take notes? use the whiteboard system," in *Proc. International Conference on Acoustics, Speech, and Signal Processing (ICASSP'03)*, Hong Kong, Apr. 2003, vol. V, pp. 776–779.
2. L. He and Z. Zhang, "Real-Time Whiteboard Capture and Processing Using a Video Camera", Technical Report, Microsoft Research, 2004.
3. Z. Zhang and L. He, "Notetaking with a Camera: Whiteboard Scanning and Image Enhancement", in *Proc. International Conference on Acoustics, Speech, and Signal Processing (ICASSP 2004)*, May 17-21, 2004, Montreal, Quebec, Canada.

Aggressive Traffic Smoothing for Delivery of Online Multimedia*

Jeng-Wei Lin[1,3], Ray-I Chang[2], Jan-Ming Ho[1], and Feipei Lai[3,4]

[1] Institute of Information Science, Academia Sinica, Taipei, Taiwan
{jwlin, hoho}@iis.sinica.edu.tw
[2] Dept. of Engineering Science and Ocean Engineering,
[3] Dept. of Computer Science and Information Engineering, and
[4] Dept. of Electrical Engineering, National Taiwan University, Taipei, Taiwan
{rayichang, flai}@ntu.edu.tw

Abstract. Traffic smoothing is an efficient means to reduce the bandwidth requirement for transmitting a VBR video. For live video applications, Sen et al. present an online algorithm referred to as $SLWIN(k)$ to compute the transmission schedule on the fly. $SLWIN(k)$ looks ahead W frames to compute the transmission schedule for the next k frametimes, where $k \leq W$. Note that W is upper bounded by the initial delay of the playback. The time complexity of $SLWIN(k)$ is $O(W * N/k)$ for an N frame live video. In this paper, we present an $O(N)$ online traffic smoothing algorithm denoted as ATS (Aggressive Traffic Smoothing). ATS aggressively works ahead to transmit more data as early as possible for reducing the peak rate of the bandwidth requirement. We compare the performance of ATS with $SLWIN(k)$ based on several benchmark video clips. Experiment results show that ATS further reduces the bandwidth requirement, especially for interactive applications in which the initial delays are small.

1 Introduction

A growing number of applications such as digital libraries and newscasts require real-time multimedia to be accessed on networks. For continuous playback, the client player must render a new frame after one *frametime* has passed. To prevent the client from starvation, the video server has to transmit the video data into the client buffer before it is going to be rendered. However, video streams are compressed and often exhibit significant burstiness of *frame sizes* on many time scales due to the encoding frame structure and their natural variations within and between scenes [12][13]. This burstiness complicates the design of a multimedia system for high resource utilization, such as network bandwidth and the client buffer.

For a prerecorded video, the video server knows all the frame sizes. The server can use a traffic smoothing algorithm that takes advantage of the knowledge of upcoming large frames and starts more data transmission in advance of

---

* This paper was partially supported by NSC, Taiwan, under grants NSC91-2416-H-008-008-, NSC92-2416-H-002-051-, and NSC93-2213-E-002-086-.

K. Aizawa, Y. Nakamura, and S. Satoh (Eds.): PCM 2004, LNCS 3331, pp. 114–121, 2004.
© Springer-Verlag Berlin Heidelberg 2004

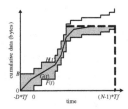
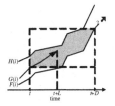

Fig. 1. A feasible transmission schedule.

Fig. 2. Looking ahead in a live video.

the burst. By working ahead, traffic smoothing is proved efficient at reducing the bandwidth requirement for VBR video transmission [1]-[9]. In live video applications, however, the server has limited knowledge of frame sizes at any one time. Sen et al. introduce a sliding-window traffic smoothing algorithm referred to as $SLWIN(k)$ that computes the transmission schedule on the fly [11]. Given an initial delay, $SLWIN(k)$ looks ahead a window of W frames and uses an offline traffic smoothing algorithm to compute the transmission schedule for the next k frametimes, where $k \leq W$. Note that W is upper bounded by the initial delay. For an N frame live video, the time complexity of $SLWIN(k)$ is $O(W * N/k)$. In this paper, we present an $O(N)$ traffic smoothing algorithm denoted as ATS (Aggressive Traffic Smoothing) that online computes the transmission schedule for live video applications. ATS generates the transmission schedule that works ahead as aggressively as possible without raising the peak rate of the transmission schedule. Experiment results show that ATS further reduces the bandwidth requirement and utilizes the client buffer more efficiently.

The remainder of this paper is organized as follows. A formal definition of the online traffic smoothing problem for live video is illustrated in Section 2. Section 3 presents our ATS algorithm and its time complexity proof. Section 4 shows the experiment results. Finally, in section 5, we give conclusions.

2   Online Traffic Smoothing for Live Video

For an N frame video $V=\{f_0, f_1, f_2, \ldots, f_{N-1}; T_f\}$, which uses f_i bits to encode the i-th frame and T_f is the frametime, a playback schedule can be represented as a cumulative playback function (CPF) $F(t) = F_i$ for $i * T_f \leq t < (i+1) * T_f$, where $F_i = 0$ for $i < 0$ and $F_i = F_{i-1} + f_i$ for $0 \leq i \leq N - 1$. At time $i * T_f$, the client player will have played F_{i-1} bits and will continue playing f_i bits in the next frametime. Given a D frametime playback delay, the video server can transmit media data at rate r_i from time $i * T_f$ to $(i+1) * T_f$ according to a transmission schedule $S=\{r_{-D}, r_{-D+1}, r_{-D+2}, \ldots, r_{N-2}\}$. The cumulative transmission function (CTF) is defined as $G(t) = 0$ for $t \leq -D * T_f$ and $G(t) = G(i * T_f) + r_i * (t - i * T_f)$ for $i * T_f < t \leq (i+1) * T_f$. To guarantee continuous playback at the client, S should satisfy $F(t) \leq G(t)$ for $t \leq (N - 1) * T_f$. We assume the client provides a B-bit buffer. The cumulative buffer function (CBF) is defined as $H(t) = F_{i-1} + B$ for $i * T_f < t \leq (i+1) * T_f$. To avoid

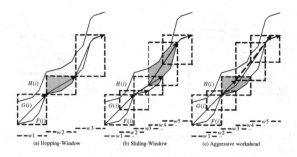

(a) Hopping-Window   (b) Sliding-Window   (c) Aggressive workahead

Fig. 3. Smoothing across window boundaries.

buffer overrun, S should also satisfy $G(t) \leq H(t)$ for $t \leq (N-1)*T_f$, as shown in Fig. 1. Without loss of generality, we consider a discrete time model at the granularity of a frametime. Assuming $T_f = 1$, we simplify the definition of $F(t)$, $G(t)$ and $H(t)$ as follows.

$$
\begin{aligned}
CPF: \quad & F(i) = 0, & & i < 0 \\
& F(i) = F(i-1) + f_i, & & 0 \leq i \leq N-1 \\
CBF: \quad & H(i) = F(i-1) + B, & & i \leq N-1 \\
CTF: \quad & G(i) = 0, & & i \leq -D \\
& G(i) = G(i-1) + r_{i-1}, & & -D < i \leq N-1
\end{aligned}
$$

For a prerecorded video stream, a traffic smoothing algorithm knows each frame size and can offline compute the transmission schedule such that $F(i) \leq G(i) \leq Min(H(i), F(N-1))$ for $-D \leq i \leq N-1$. For live video, however, a traffic smoothing algorithm has limited knowledge of frame sizes because future frames have not been generated. At any one time $t + D$, the algorithm knows f_{t+1}, $f_{t+2}, \ldots, f_{t+D}$ and has no idea about f_{t+D+1}, $f_{t+D+2}, \ldots, f_{N-1}$. Any L ($1 \leq L \leq D$) frametime transmission schedule $S^t = \{r_t, r_{t+1}, \ldots, r_{t+L-1}\}$ is feasible if S^t satisfies $F(i) \leq G(i) \leq Min(H(i), F(t+D))$ for $t < i \leq t + L$, as shown in Fig. 2. While the video server executes S^t, new frames are generated. After L frametimes have passed and S^t has therefore finished, L new frames have been generated. The traffic smoothing algorithm can incorporate new frame size information to compute the next transmission schedule S^{t+L}.

$SLWIN(k)$ fixes L to a pre-assigned constant k ($k \leq W$). In this paper, we assume $W = D$ so that $SLWIN(k)$ looks ahead as more frames as possible. When $k = W$, $SLWIN(W)$, also referred to as the hopping-window approach, is fast. However, it has drawbacks of smoothing traffic across window boundaries, as shown in Fig. 3(a). Intuitively, the bandwidth allocated for transmitting each frame should be decided with as much information as possible. As shown in Fig. 3(b), when using a smaller k, $SLWIN(k)$ computes the transmission schedule of a smaller bandwidth requirement. Sen et al. showed that $SLWIN(1)$ outperforms other $SLWIN(k)$ algorithms [11]. However, $SWLIN(1)$ computes the transmission schedule independently for each window. Therefore, the computing cost is large. In addition, $H(i)$ is suppressed by $F(t + D)$, as shown in Fig. 2. $SLWIN(k)$ may lower the transmission rate unnecessarily since it always selects the smallest bandwidth requirement for each window. As shown in Fig. 3(b), the transmission rate decreases in the third window and then increases in the fourth window. However, if the video server aggressively transmits more data in the third window, the bandwidth requirement for the fourth window can be reduced, as shown in Fig. 3(c). Since the server works ahead more aggressively, less data is buffered in the server. Therefore, the server can use a lower transmission rate to transmit the upcoming large frame.

3   Our Algorithm and Time Complexity Analysis

Like $MVBA$ [1] (the offline smoothing algorithm used by $SLWIN(k)$), ATS tries to find the shortest path between $F(i)$ and $MIN(H(i), F(i+D))$. To reduce the suppression effect, ATS heuristically generates the transmission schedules that work ahead as aggressively as possible without raising the peak rate. Since the suppression will be looser after a new frame is generated, aggressive workahead lasts for one frametime. To minimize the computing cost, ATS processes each frame once. It remembers useful computational results for the next window by the help of a funnel data structure.

As shown in Fig. 4(a), from the starting point $s=(t, G(t))$ of the window, ATS maintains the candidates for transmission schedules within a convex upper chain $U=\{u_0 = s, u_1, \ldots, u_m\}$ and a concave lower chain $V=\{v_0 = s, v_1, \ldots, v_n\}$. $u_1, \ldots, u_m$ are on H and $v_1, \ldots, v_n$ are on F. Note that U is convex if and only if $0 \leq m < 2$ or $Rate(u_j, u_{j+1}) < Rate(u_{j+1}, u_{j+2})$ for $0 \leq j < m - 2$, where $Rate(x, y)$ is the slope of the line from x to y. U and V form a funnel. For $t + 1 \leq a \leq t + D$, ATS iteratively considers unprocessed $F(a)$ and $H(a)$ once and modifies V and U, respectively, as shown in Fig. 4(b) and (c). By triangle inequality, we can prove that the shortest path is in the funnel.

ATS first considers to append the point $x=(a, F(a))$ onto V. ATS may remove some points from V so that the resultant chain V' is still concave. If V' will not cross U, as shown in Fig. 4(b), ATS continues processing $H(a)$. If V' will cross U, as shown in Fig. 5(a), ATS deterministically generates the transmission schedule according to the line segments on U that are under the dashed line (s, x) and then maintains the funnel, as shown in Fig. 5(b). It is easy to prove these line segments are parts of the shortest path. The detail procedure follows.

As shown in Fig. 6(a), along V, ATS tries to find a point v_i from v_n to v_1 so that $Rate(v_{i-1}, v_i) > Rate(v_i, x)$. If such a point is found, ATS removes $v_{i+1}, \ldots, v_n$ from V and adds x to the tail of V. As shown in Fig. 6(b), the resultant chain $V'=\{v_0, \ldots, v_i, x\}$ is concave. V' and U maintain the funnel. In this case, ATS does not generate the transmission schedule. If there is no such point, along U, ATS tries to find a point u_j from u_0 to u_m so that the edge $u_j x$ will not cross U, as shown in Fig. 6(c). ATS replaces V with $V'=\{u_j, x\}$. If $j \neq 0$, ATS generates the transmission schedule according to the chain $\{u_0, \ldots, u_j\}$ and then removes $u_0, \ldots, u_{j-1}$ from U. The resultant chain $U'=\{u_j, \ldots, u_m\}$ is convex. V' and U' maintain the funnel again, as shown in Fig. 6(d).   □

ATS then considers to append $x'=(a, H(a))$ onto U if $H(a) \leq F(t + D)$. Similarly, ATS may remove some points from U so that the resultant chain U' is convex. If U' will not cross V, as shown in Fig. 4(c), ATS continues processing

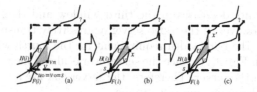

Fig. 4. ATS iteratively considers $F(i)$ and $H(i)$ to maintain the two chains.

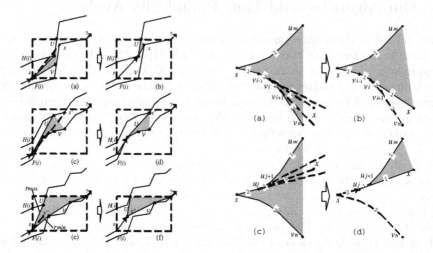

Fig. 5. Generating the schedule.   **Fig. 6.** Processing x.

the next frame. If U' will cross V, as shown in Fig. 5(c), ATS deterministically generates the transmission schedule according to the line segments on V that are above the dashed line (s, x') and then maintains the funnel, as shown in Fig. 5(d). Again, we can prove these line segments are parts of the shortest path. We omit the detail procedure since it is similar to the process of x.

Saturation may occur if ATS does not decide the transmission schedule after the $(t + D)$-th frame is considered, as shown in Fig. 5(e). Unlike $MVBA$, which always generates the transmission schedule according to V, ATS uses the aggressive workahead scheme to reduce the suppression effect. It generates the transmission schedule according to the dashed line (s, x''), where $x''=(t + 1, G(t) + MAX(MIN(r_{peak}, r_{max}), r_{min}))$, r_{min} and r_{max} are the minimal and maximal feasible transmission rates from the point s and r_{peak} is the current peak rate. Note that x'' is definitely in the funnel and the length of the transmission schedule is one frametime. ATS then reconstructs the funnel again by removing some points and adding x'' at the head of V and U, as shown in Fig. 5(f). We omit the detail procedure again.

The primary factor of the ATS time complexity is the funnel maintenance. We assume each edge on the funnel associates with a counter. The counter is initialized as zero and increases by one whenever the edge is scanned.

Lemma 1. *The counter of an edge that is added onto the funnel and removed later is read as two. The counter of an edge that remains on the funnel is read as one.*

Proof. We first consider the process of appending x onto V. ATS starts scanning the edges of V from the tail. If there is a point v_i $(1 \leq i \leq n)$ such that $Rate(v_{i-1}, v_i) > Rate(v_i, x)$, the scan stops. The edges of the chain $\{v_i, \ldots, v_n\}$ have been scanned and removed and their associated counters increased by one to two. The point x is then added to the tail of V. At this point, the readings of the two associated counters on the chain $\{v_{i-1}, v_i, x\}$ are two and zero. We can amortize the two counters so that each counter is reset to one, as shown in Fig. 6(a) and (b). If there is no such point, ATS starts scanning the edges of U from the head, as shown in Fig. 6(c) and (d). Again, we can apply similar amortized analyses. Therefore, we prove that lemma 1 holds after ATS completes the process of appending x onto V. It is easy to extend this proof and show that lemma 1 holds after ATS ends.   □

Lemma 2. ATS *adds a maximum of* $4 * N$ *edges onto the funnel.*

Proof. ATS iteratively considers $F(i)$ and $H(i)$ once for $0 \leq i \leq N - 1$. Each time, ATS adds one edge onto the funnel and may remove some edges. Since the number of transmission schedules generated will be N, at the most, ATS reconstructs the funnel at most N times. Each time, ATS may add two edges onto the funnel and remove some edges. In total, ATS adds a maximum of $4 * N$ edges onto the funnel.   □

Theorem 1. *The time complexity of* ATS *is* $O(N)$.

Proof. It can be derived from lemma 1 and 2.   □

4   Experiment Results

In this section, we examine the performance of ATS. The study focuses on network and client resources by measuring the peak rate and buffer occupancy. The peak rate of a transmission schedule determines its worst-case bandwidth requirement across the path from the video server to the client player. Practically, data packets may get lost in the network. If the client can detect the data lost early enough, it can request a retransmission. A transmission schedule that has a high occupancy of the client buffer usually implies that there is a high probability the client will detect the data lost early.

We simulated the transmission of several MPEG video clips [14] to compare the performance of ATS and $SLWIN(1)$. Fig. 7 and 8 show the peak rates and buffer occupancies of the schedules for transmitting Star Wars and News, respectively, with different initial delays and client buffer sizes. To demonstrate the lower bound of the peak rate, these figures also show the optimal offline schedules obtained by [1]. When the initial delay (D) is small, ATS is more likely to use the aggressive workahead scheme to generate the transmission schedule. As shown in Fig. 7 and 8, the peak rates of the ATS schedules are significantly smaller than $SLWIN(1)$ when D is smaller than 30 frametimes. The aggressive workahead scheme successfully reduces the suppression effect. Since there is not much data, the buffer occupancies are around 30% to 50%. As D increases, the

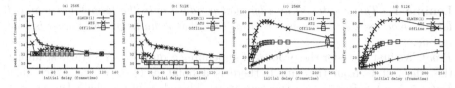

Fig. 7. Star Wars, B=256K and 512K.

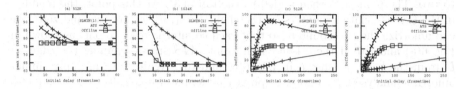

Fig. 8. News, B=512K and 1024K.

ATS schedules may have the same peak rates as *SLWIN*(1). The buffer occupancies of *ATS* schedules keep increasing to 80% or more and then slowly decrease back to the offline optimal. When *D* increases beyond a certain point, *ATS* always deterministically generates the transmission schedule in every window. In such situation, *ATS* generates the same transmission schedule as *SLWIN*(1). When *ATS* works on Star Wars, an interesting phenomenon occurs, as shown in Fig. 7(a) and (b). *ATS* dramatically reduces the peak rate to around 32 Kbytes per frametime when *D* is between 12 and 32 frametimes. Analyzing Star Wars, we find there are two bursts close to one another. The second is slightly burstier than the first. When *D* is smaller than 32 frametimes, *ATS* cannot smooth the first burst. *ATS* therefore raises the peak rate. Since *ATS* aggressively works ahead and keeps less data in the video server, it can smooth the second burst. When *D* is larger than 32 frametimes, *ATS* is able to smooth the first burst without raising the peak rate. However, *ATS* cannot smooth the second burst even by using the current peak rate. Therefore, the peak rate increases.

When the initial delay is small, enlarging the client buffer does not help *SLWIN*(1) reduce the peak rate. The suppression effect eliminates the benefits from a larger buffer. As shown in Fig. 7 and 8, when the client buffer size doubles, the peak rates of the *SLWIN*(1) schedules further decrease only when *D* is larger than 120 and 30 frametimes, respectively. On the other hand, the aggressive workahead scheme uses the buffer more efficiently. The peak rates of the *ATS* schedules are further reduced even *D* is small.

5 Conclusion

In this paper, we present an efficient traffic smoothing algorithm *ATS* for live video transmission. Unlike *SLWIN*(*k*), which computes the smallest bandwidth requirement for each window independently, after *ATS* generates the transmission schedule for the current window, it remembers useful computational results for the next window by the help of a funnel data structure. The total time complexity of ATS is $O(N)$. Note that $O(N)$ is a trivial lower bound to online smooth an N frame live video. To reduce the suppression effect caused by the lake of future frame sizes, ATS heuristically uses the aggressive workahead scheme to generate the transmission schedule. We have evaluated ATS by transmitting several benchmark video clips. Experiment results show that ATS further reduces the peak bandwidth requirement and better utilizes the client buffer, especially for interactive applications in which the initial delay is small.

References

1. James D. Salehi, Zhi-Li Zhang, Jim Kurose, Don Towsley, "Supporting Store Video: Reducing Rate Variability and End-to-End Resource Requirement Through Optimal Smoothing," *IEEE/ACM Trans. Networking*, Vol. 6, No.4, Aug. 1998.
2. W. Feng and S. Sechrest, "Critical Bandwidth Allocation for Delivery of Compressed Video," *Computer Communications*, pp. 709-717, Oct. 1995.
3. W. Feng, F. Jahaian and S. Sechrest, "Optimal Buffering for the Delivery of Compressed Video," *IS&T/SPIE MMCN*, pp. 234-242, 1995.
4. R. I. Chang, M. Chen, M. T. Ko and J. M. Ho, "Optimization of stored VBR video transmission on CBR channel," *SPIE, VVDC*, pp. 382-392, 1997.
5. R. I. Chang, M. Chen, M. T. Ko and J. M. Ho, "Designing the On-Off CBR Transmission Schedule For Jitter-Free VBR Media Playback in Real-Time Networks," *IEEE RTCSA*, pp. 1-9, 1997.
6. J. M. McManus and K. W. Ross, "Video On Demand over ATM: Constant-Rate Transmission and Transport," *IEEE INFOCOM*, March 1996.
7. J. M. McManus and K. W. Ross, "Dynamic Programming Methodology for Managing Prerecorded VBR Sources in Packet-Switched Networks," *SPIE VVDC*, 1997.
8. M. Grossglauser, S. Keshav and D. Tse, "RCBA: A Simple and Efficient Service for Multiple Time-Scale Traffic," in *Proc. ACM SIGCOMM*, pp 219-230, Aug. 1995.
9. Wuchi Feng, Jennifer Rexford, "A Comparison of Bandwidth Smoothing Techniques for the Transmission of Prerecorded Compressed Video," in *Proc. IEEE INFOCOM*, pp. 58-66, April 1999.
10. J. Rexford, S. Sen, J. Dey, W. Feng, J. Kurose, J. Stankovic, and D. Towsley, "Online Smoothing of Live, Variable-Bit-Rate Video," in *Proc. International Workshop on Network and Operating Systems Support for Digital Audio and Video*, pp. 249-257, May 1997.
11. Subhabrata Sen, Jennifer L. Rexford, Jayanta K. Dey, James F. Kurose, Donald F. Towsley, "Online Smoothing of Variable-Bit-Rate Streaming Video," *IEEE Trans. Multimedia*, Vol. 2, No.1, March 2000.
12. M. Garrett and W. Willinger, "Analysis, Modeling and Generation of Self-similar VBR Video Traffic," in *Proc, ACM SIGCOMM*, Sep. 1994.
13. M. Krunz and S. K. Tripathi, "On the Characteristics of VBR MPEG Streams," in *Proc. ACM SIGMETRICS*, pp. 192-202, June 1997.
14. http://www3.informatik.uni-wuerzburg.de/MPEG/traces/.

Distributed Video Streaming Using Multicast (DVSM)*

Ramesh Yerraballi and ByungHo Lee

Department of CSE, University of Texas at Arlington,
P.O. Box 19015, Arlington TX 76019, USA
{ramesh, blee}@cse.uta.edu

Abstract. The Internet is a packet switched best effort service, which does not provide guarantees of reliability and timely packet delivery. Video streaming, requiring high bandwidth and low delay is not naturally suited for such a network. Distributed Video Streaming (DVS) takes note of this fact and attempts to provide a more reliable (and timely) way of streaming using multiple senders to stream a video to a receiver simultaneously. The essence of this approach involves utilizing path diversity of multiple senders. If a path from a sender to a receiver is congested, alternate paths are exploited to maintain the required throughput of the video stream. In this paper we report, Distributed Video Streaming using Multicast (DVSM) a research extending the protocol suggested by DVS. Many current video streaming protocols use multicast to efficiently utilize the available bandwidth of the network. DVSM operates in this vein by applying multicast to DVS thus enhancing its functionality. We discuss and evaluate modifications to the protocols and algorithms required to transition from DVS to DVSM.

Keywords: Distributed Multimedia, Multicast, Path Diversity

1 Introduction

A logical extension to DVS, one that would better utilize the bandwidth of the Internet is to use Multicast to stream to multiple receivers. This logical extension, termed Distributed Video Streaming using Multicast (DVSM) is by no means trivial. Specifically, it involves revisiting the problems of rate-allocation, packet partitioning and buffering that are components of a DVS solution. Rate allocation decides which senders send at what rates, based on the feedback received from the multiple receivers. Packet- partitioning [2] finds a schedule for which segments of the video each server sends. Buffering facilitates smooth playback of video by buffering out-of-order segments and scheduling their playback appropriately.

---

* This work is sponsored by a grant from NSF for the MavHome Research Project(NSF-ITR 0121297)

K. Aizawa, Y. Nakamura, and S. Satoh (Eds.): PCM 2004, LNCS 3331, pp. 122–130, 2004.
© Springer-Verlag Berlin Heidelberg 2004

The rest of the paper is organized as follows; Section 2 discusses related work and the contributions of our work. Section 3 gives the specifics of various algorithms that make up the proposed DVSM solution. In Section 4 a simulation study performed to validate and evaluate our solution is presented, followed by conclusions in Section 5.

2   Related Work

Video Streaming over the Internet faces several challenges owing to the high data rate demands, delay sensitivity and loss tolerance characteristics of media. Research meeting these challenges falls into two categories: (i) Solutions that cope with the best-effort nature of the Internet. Solutions in this category include, Source Coding [3], Forward-Error Correction [4], TCP-friendly Streaming [5] and Multicasting [1], and (ii) Adapt the Internet to cope with Streaming Media. Solutions in this category include, Content Distribution Networks [6], End-to-end Routing [7] and Network QoS support [8]. Two of the research efforts that are specific to exploiting path diversity are [9] and [2]. In [9], specialized nodes determine which path packets should travel to reduce latency. In [2], multiple description coding and relay nodes transmit data using path diversity. While these two techniques call for changes, either in the infrastructure or in the video coding itself, DVS [1] exploits path diversity by suitably positioning multiple servers relative to a receiver.

DVS uses path diversity of multiple senders to achieve reliable delivery adjusting to congestion in the Internet. The DVS design constitutes three algorithms, bandwidth estimation, rate allocation and packet partitioning. A receiver periodically monitors delay and loss rate of the connection from each sender, using this to estimate the bandwidth from each sender. If the change in estimated bandwidth exceeds a predefined threshold, the rate-allocation algorithm is run to allocate new sending rates for each sender. This information is passed on to the senders from the receiver through control packets. On receiving control packets, senders run the packet partitioning algorithm, which divides the sequence of packets among multiple senders so there will be no missing or duplicate packets. The subject of this paper is a proposal to enhance DVS with Multicast capability. More specifically, DVSM extends DVS to have senders simultaneously stream video to multiple receivers. We note that this entails revisiting and adapting the algorithms for bandwidth estimation, rate allocation and packet partitioning.

3   DVSM Design

As in DVS, all senders have the complete Video, however their responsibility is to serve specific segments of the video. Each sender sets up a multicast group for its segments of the particular video, and invites all receivers interested in the video to join the group. A receiver subscribes to multiple groups that together provide the complete video. The problem of Multicast group formation and maintenance is a significant research issue in itself and beyond the scope of this paper, interested readers may find the following papers relevant:[10,11].

In DVS, the single recipient monitors delays and losses from each of the senders and makes rate re-allocations when significant changes occur. In DVSM, having multiple receivers, network status concerning a sender may differ among the receivers and therefore no single receiver has all the necessary information to make a globally consistent decision. We therefore transfer the responsibility for rate-allocation to the senders. Accordingly, a receiver periodically monitors the network condition and sends out control packets when there is significant change in the estimated available bandwidth. All senders run rate-allocation algorithms and decide on new sending rates. Packet partitioning is followed to split up the sending sequence of the requested video among the senders. As the control packets may arrive in different order among the senders, we need a process for guaranteeing that all the senders will compute consistent sending rates.

3.1   Bandwidth Estimation

Bandwidth estimation is done at a receiver to find out the available bandwidth that exists for a path from a sender to a receiver. The formula used to estimate the bandwidth (B) operates on the same lines as in DVS. Specifically we use the TCP friendly sending rate estimation formula proposed in [12]:

$$B = \frac{s}{R\sqrt{\frac{2p}{3}} + T_{rto}(3\sqrt{\frac{3p}{8}})p(1 + 32p^2)} \tag{1}$$

where, T_{rto} is the TCP timeout, R is the estimated round trip time in seconds, p is the estimated loss rate and s is the TCP segment size in bytes. A receiver estimates bandwidth B_j corresponding to each sender j, that it receives segments of the video from. These estimates are conveyed to the senders in control packets. A control packet contains several triples of Delay (D_j), loss rate (L_j) and estimated bandwidth (B_j) corresponding to each sender j that this receiver receives from. The last entry in the control packet is the Sync (Sy), which represents the synchronization sequence number used in packet partitioning. Note that, the control packets themselves are multicast and therefore are received by all senders.

The sender keeps a copy of a control packet for each receiver and the stored copy is the latest one that was received. When a control packet is received, the sender consolidates the bandwidth information received with current values (refer to Figure 1(a)). Information from each control packet received is put into the matrix S at the designated row based on the receiver it was sent from. Row i stores the control packet from Receiver i, which contains the Loss, Delay and Bandwidth triples (L_{ij}, D_{ij}, B_{ij}) for each sender j that the receiver is receiving from. When a new packet is received and the row is updated, we compute the minimum available bandwidth vector B by taking the minimum of a column representing available bandwidth (B_{ij}) for a sender j as reported by each receiver i. This vector is used in deriving the new sending-rates that the senders have

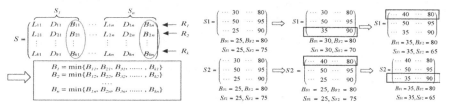

(a) Consolidating estimated bandwidths.

(b) Convergence of consolidation by minima at senders $S1$ and $S2$.

Fig. 1. Bandwidth Estimation

to use. As each receiver sends its control packet independently, they may arrive in different orders at the senders. By taking the minimum estimated available bandwidth, there may be short periods of discrepancies if control packets arrive in different order, however the senders will eventually come to the same conclusion. For example, let's assume that there are two senders ($S1$ and $S2$) and three receivers (Figure 1(b)). Only the estimated available bandwidth columns are shown. B_{S1} and B_{S2} are the computed minimum bandwidths (kbps) and S_{S1} and S_{S2} are the allocated sending rates (kbps) derived from B_{S1} and B_{S2} respectively. We assume in this case that the total sending rate (which in-practice depends on the actual video-rate) should add up to 100 kbps. At some point $t1$, $S1$ and $S2$ have consistent bandwidth computations of 25 and 80 respectively. Around time $t2$, say, $S1$ receives a control packet from the third receiver and $S2$ receives a control packet from the first receiver leading to inconsistent computed bandwidths and therefore sending rates. However, once the delayed packets arrive (at say $t3$) the minima will prevail and both senders will reach consistent values (35 and 80). The reader will note that, there is no claim of optimality in the consolidation mechanism. The overriding design criteria for the consolidation is consistency.

3.2 Rate Allocation

We stated in the previous section that the Sending rates are derived from the consolidated estimated bandwidth (available bandwidth). The idea is to compensate the sending rate of a congested sender by leveraging the rates of less congested sender(s). The compensation works by first choosing the server with the lowest loss rate and raising its sending rate to equal its available bandwidth. If this sender's available bandwidth isn't enough for meeting the loss, this process is continued with the next sender (with the lowest loss rate) until the reduced bandwidth is fully compensated. Figure 2 shows an example where the loss in bandwidth (x) of sender $S3$ is compensated by an increase at $S1$ (y) and $S2$ (z) in that order.

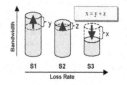

Fig. 2. Rate allocation example

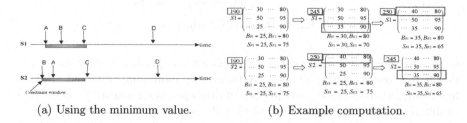

(a) Using the minimum value.   (b) Example computation.

Fig. 3. Synchronization Sequence Number

3.3   Packet Partitioning and Synchronization Sequence Number

The Synchronization Sequence Number (SSN) is a reference point for running the packet partitioning algorithm. The receivers convey their packet receipt status through a control packet containing the SSN. In DVS, this is an indicator to the sender as to where in the video stream this receiver has progressed. Senders use this number as the reference for packet partitioning. In DVSM we have to change the interpretation of this number to cope with having multiple receivers. Improper choice of the reference point for packet partitioning results in duplicate packets being transmitted. Figure 3(a) illustrates the problem, $S1$ and $S2$ represent two senders and the timelines for when control packets are received are marked A, B, C and D. A constraint window is used to group control packets instead of reacting to each packet independently. Control packets received within a window are considered in determining the effective SSN to use. In order to show how the effective SSN is determined we first show that a simple minima of all the SSNs within a window is not a good choice. Let's assume the SSN in control packets are ordered as follows: $B < C < A$. At $S1$, A is received first, followed by B and C. All three are within the constraint window so B is chosen as the SSN. However, at $S2$, C falls outside the window, and in a window of its own. This results in the effective SSN being that in B first, but immediately overwritten by that in C. Note that using a cumulative minima is not a valid solution either, as this will retain the oldest control packet's SSN across windows, making the use of the window concept useless. To solve this issue, a rather counter-intuitive solution is given. The semantic of the SSN sent in a control packet is changed (from that in DVS) to be an estimate of sequence number the receiver expects the sender to send. It is not for retransmission of missing packets (as in DVS) but used as a reference point for doing packet partitioning. Taking these two facts into consideration, we choose the maximum value of SSN as the reference in packet partitioning. Figure 3(b) shows the working of the effective SSN computation using the maximum, on the example presented in the previous section. At $S1$, when a control packet with SSN value of 245 is received it is found to be higher than the current one in use (195), it is therefore selected as a new synchronization sequence number for doing packet partitioning. The second control packet received by $S1$ has SSN value of 250. This is still greater than current value of 245, so a new value is chosen and packet partitioning is done based on 250. For $S2$, the reception of the SSNs is in reverse. It is important to note what happens when second control packet containing a lower SSN is received. Since it is of a lower value, 250 is retained as the effective SSN. However the sending rates among the senders has changed, so packet partitioning algorithm has to be run.A simulation study was performed using, NS2 [13], to test the viability of DVSM and compatibility with DVS. We consider two scenarios, the first to validate DVSM by showing that it reduces to DVS when a single receiver is used. The second scenario is used to demonstrate the effectiveness of DVSM. In each scenario, congestion is simulated by shared TCP traffic on intermediate links.

3.4   First Simulation Scenario

In the first simulation scenario, there are two senders streaming video packets to a single receiver (as in DVS) and 20 TCP connections share congested links with each sender. Congestion paths are represented with dotted lines. $B(i)$ is the estimated bandwidth for sender i computed using equation 1.. We use the concept of systolic window introduced in DVS [1] to minimize the number of control packets sent by a receiver. The estimated bandwidth is sampled periodically ($\phi = 100ms$) within a systolic window($w = 0.1 \times B_i$). Each time the estimate is above/below the previously computed bandwidth by a small tolerance value, we increment/decrement a count. When the count reaches a threshold ($\pm\gamma \ (= 30)$), a control packet is sent to indicate a significant change in the bandwidth.

In Figure 4(a), $TS1 \sim TS20$ and $TS21 \sim TS40$ represent the TCP servers and $TR1 \sim TR20$ and $TR21 \sim TR40$ represents the TCP clients (receivers). At time $t = 0.1s$ senders $S1$ and $S2$ start streaming their videos. At time $t = 10s$ twenty TCP connections sharing a link with $S1$ start to transmit data. Congestion occurs on link X and the loss rate for $S1$ at the receiver increases. Observing a significant change in B/W, the receiver sends out control packets to the senders. Upon receiving the control packets, the senders adjust their sending rates. At $t = 50s$, ten of these TCP connections stop transmission. At $t = 70s$ four more TCP connections stop transmission and again at $t = 90s$ four more TCP transmissions stop, leaving only two connections sharing a link with $S1$. At $t = 100s$ twenty TCP connections sharing a link with $S2$ start transmission. This causes congestion on link Y and the receiver sends out control packets. At $t = 150$ fifteen TCP connections sharing link Y stop transmission.

Figure 4(c) shows the loss rates of $S1$ and $S2$ measured at the receiver R. Higher loss rate for $S1$ is observed when there are TCP connections transmitting on a shared link X before $t = 100s$. Likewise, higher loss rate for $S2$ is observed when there are TCP connections transmitting on a shared link Y after

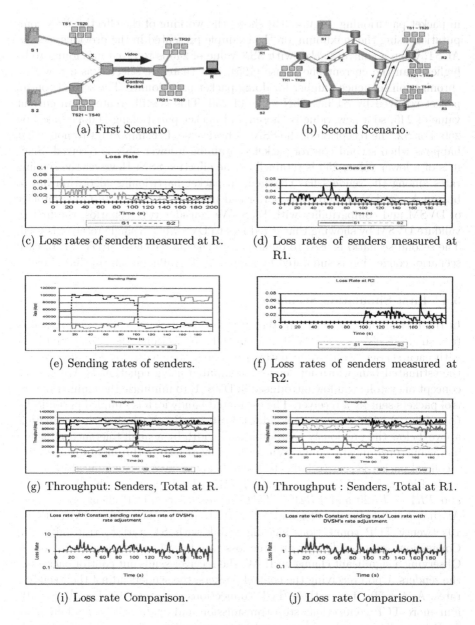

(a) First Scenario

(b) Second Scenario.

(c) Loss rates of senders measured at R.

(d) Loss rates of senders measured at R1.

(e) Sending rates of senders.

(f) Loss rates of senders measured at R2.

(g) Throughput: Senders, Total at R.

(h) Throughput : Senders, Total at R1.

(i) Loss rate Comparison.

(j) Loss rate Comparison.

Fig. 4. Simulation Scenarios

$t = 100s$. Figures 4(e) and 4(g) show the sending rates measured at each sender and, throughput measured at the receiver respectively. As number of TCP connections decrease at $t = 50s$, $t = 70s$ and $t = 90s$, available bandwidth of $S1$ continuously increases. Sending rate of $S1$ adjusts accordingly with the increase in available bandwidth. At $t = 100s$, congestion occurs for $S2$ and sending rate of $S2$ is lowered to adjust to the congestion. At $t = 150s$, 15 TCP connections stop transmission and sending rate of $S2$ rises slightly to reflect the change. Overall results show that sending rates adjust fairly well to network congestion. Throughput measured is consistent with the sending rate with slight oscillations caused by changing values in delay. These results are consistent with those reported in [1]. Figure 4(i) shows a comparison of the loss rate at the receiver using rate adjustment of DVSM against that without any rate adjustments (i.e., constant sending rate). It is observed that DVSM generally has lower loss rate indicating that congestion is controlled better using multiple senders.

3.5   Second Simulation Scenario

Figure 4(d) is a graph of loss rates of $S1$ and $S2$ measured at the receiver $R1$. High loss rate for $S1$ is observed when there are TCP connections transmitting on a shared link X before $t = 100s$. Figure 4(f) is a graph of loss rates of $S1$ and $S2$ measured at the receiver $R2$. High loss rate for $S2$ is observed when there are TCP connections transmitting on a shared link Y after $t = 100s$. Figure 4(h) shows the throughput measured at the senders and the receiver $R1$. As number of TCP connections decrease at $t = 50s, t = 70s$ and $t = 90s$, available bandwidth of $S1$ rises continuously. Sending rate of $S1$ adjusts accordingly with the increase in available bandwidth. At $t = 100s$, congestion causes $S2$'s sending rate to fall. At $t = 150s$, 15 TCP connections stop transmission and the sending rate of $S2$ is rises slightly to reflect the change. Overall result shows that sending rates adjust fairly well to network congestion. The throughput measured is consistent with the sending rate with slight oscillations caused by changing values in delay. Figure 4(j) compares the loss rate of a sender using rate adjustment of DVSM with that without any rate adjustments (constant sending rate). It is observed that DVSM generally has lower loss rate indicating that congestion is controlled better using multiple senders.

To summarize the results, the first scenario using a single receiver demonstrated that DVSM adjusts its sending rate to network congestion successfully mimicking the behavior of DVS [1]. The second scenario was used to show how DVSM performs with multiple receivers. Following the strategies described in Section 4, DVSM successfully adjusts its rate to congestions spread among multiple receivers. Also a comparison with and without rate adjustment demonstrated the effectiveness of DVSM. An important question that one can raise about the mechanism proposed in this paper, is with regards to its scalability. That is, will the mechanism scale well with increase in number of clients? We are currently working on building a prototype of the system that should help us answer this and other related questions.

References

1. Nguyen, T.P., Zakhor, A.: Distributed video streaming over the internet. In: Multimedia Computing and Networking. (2002)

2. Apostolopoulos, J.G., Tan, W., Wee, S.J.: Performance of a multiple description streaming media content delivery network. In: ICIP. (2002)
3. Lee, K., Puri, R., Kim, T., Ramchandran, K., Bharghava, V.: An integrated source coding and congestion control framework for video streaming in the internet. In: IEEE INFOCOM. (2000)
4. Nguyen, T., Zakhor, A.: Path diversity with forward error correction (pdf) system for packet switched networks. In: IEEE INFOCOM. (1999)
5. Tan, W., Zakhor, A.: Real-time internet video using error-resilient scalable compression and tcp-friendly transport protocol. In: IEEE Transactions on Multimedia. Volume 1. (1999) 172–186
6. Almeida, J.: Provisioning content distribution networks for streaming media. In: IEEE INFOCOM. (2002)
7. Paxson, V.: End-to-end routing behavior in the internet. Volume 5(5). (1997) 601–615
8. Shin, J., Kim, J., Kuo, C.J.: Qulaity of service mapping mechanism for packet video in differentiated services network. In: IEEE Trans. on Multimedia. Volume 3(2). (2001) 219–231
9. Steinbach, E.G., Liang, Y.J., Girod, B.: Packet path diversity for tcp file transfer and media transport on the internet. In: IEEE INFOCOM. (2002)
10. Levine, B.N., Garcia-Luna-Aceves, J.J.: A comparison of reliable multicast protocols. Multimedia Systems **6** (1998) 334–348
11. EL-Sayed, A., Roca, V., Mathy, L.: A survey of proposals for an alternative group communication service. IEEE Network Magazine special Issue on Multicasting: An Enabling Technology (2003)
12. Floyd, S., Handley, M., Padhye, J., Widmer, J.: Equation-based congestion control for unicast applications. In: Applications, Technologies, Architectures and Protocols for Computer Communication,. (2000) 43–56
13. ISI: (The network simulator 2 (ns2) - http://www.isi.edu/nsnam/ns/)

Centralized Peer-to-Peer Streaming with PFGS Video Codec

Ivan Lee[1] and Ling Guan[2]

[1] School of Electrical and Information Engineering, University of Sydney, NSW,
Australia
ivanlee@ieee.org
[2] Department of Electrical and Computer Engineering, Ryerson University, ON,
Canada
lguan@ee.ryerson.ca

Abstract. This paper addresses the bottleneck of the conventional video streaming using the client-server approach, and an innovative centralized peer-to-peer approach is proposed. In order to achieve the best perceived quality of service, combination of layered source coding and distributed network adaptation is proposed in this paper. The proposed technique features centralized management, guaranteed perceived quality of service, while offloading the bottleneck traffic loads among the peers. The performance of the centralized peer-to-peer streaming protocol is benchmarked against the differential service technique, by using the H.264 video codec with the progressive fine granular scalable extension.

1 Introduction

With the growing popularity of the personal computer industry, highly computerized world leads to the demand of computer interactions. Popular applications such as video conferencing and video on demand require effective video transmission over the internet. Video streaming, which requires higher network bandwidth and possesses tighter real-time constraints, is one of the enabler technologies for such applications.

Today, most of the video streaming techniques are based on the client/server architecture, where a centralized server is responsible for the entire transmission requests. Typically, this dedicated streaming server possesses longer uptime, higher bandwidth, and higher processing power. However, the client/server architecture does not scale to the growing audiences. In addition, the current internet is a heterogeneous collection of networks, and the QoS guarantee is missing by default. These characteristics present the bottleneck for video streaming using the client/server approach. To address these limitation, numerous techniques in transmission feedback control, adaptive source encoding algorithm, efficient packetization, resource allocation, and error control coding have been proposed to improve the quality of the video communication on today's Internet [1] [2]. Popular approaches such as traffic prioritization using DiffServ [3] and transmission bandwidth reservation using RSVP [4] are widely studied and realized in some commercial products.

K. Aizawa, Y. Nakamura, and S. Satoh (Eds.): PCM 2004, LNCS 3331, pp. 131–138, 2004.
© Springer-Verlag Berlin Heidelberg 2004

Distributed media streaming is another approach to address the limitations of client/server based streaming. A popular information exchange approach in the P2P framework is the simultaneous streaming from multiple senders. This approach yields higher throughput and increases the tolerance to loss and delay due to congestion [5]. The P2P multimedia streaming and caching service also reduces the initial delay for the playback, and minimizes the delay jitter during playback [6]. Deshpande et al. [7] proposed an application-layer multicast architecture called SpreadIt. The requesting nodes are formed peering layers on-demand, which builds up a multicast tree. Each node within the tree is responsible for forwarding the data to its descendants. Like typical multicast applications, SpreadIt does not restrict to video payload data, and it is designed for real-time delivery of any data type. SpreadIt aims to reduce the loss during the transmission, and there is no quality guarantee when video is transmitted using its framework. Tran et al. [8] also investigated application-layer multicast tree building, and proposed the ZIGZAG algorithm featuring short end-to-end delay, low control overhead, efficient join and failure recovery, and low maintenance overhand.

Centralized Peer-to-Peer Streaming Protocol (P2PSP) was first introduced to combine layered multimedia codec with distributed streaming infrastructure [9]. The performance of P2PSP compares to the client-server approach was evaluated using a 3D-DCT based video codec with vector quantization [10]. In this paper, we analyze the performance of centralized Peer-to-Peer Streaming Protocol (P2PSP), benchmarked against the DiffServ technique. H.264 FPGS is the video codec under our investigation.

2   Client/Server Versus Centralized Peer-to-Peer Streaming

The Client/Server network is the de-facto architecture for video streaming, because historically clients do not possess sufficient bandwidth or computational power to forward requests from neighbourhood peers. Client/Server streaming is illustrated in Fig. 1(a), and the protocol is summarized in Fig. 2(a). The Client/Server architecture consists of several limitations:

1. **Single point of failure** - the centralized streaming server is the only mean for data distribution, and it is therefore the target for the attack to deteriorate the service. While duplicating the servers and providing redundant network infrastructure could help to resist from the failures, however, it is not cost effective and is vulnerable to a large scale Denial of Service (DoS) or Distributed DoS (DDoS) attacks.
2. **Scalability problem** - despite the fact that techniques such as multicast was proposed to utilize the network resources, it is not designed for non-synchronized media streaming. This problem escalates when interactive media streaming applications are widely available to the audiences.
3. **Inefficient utilization of the network resources** - the Client/Server architecture was derived from historical computing infrastructure where huge

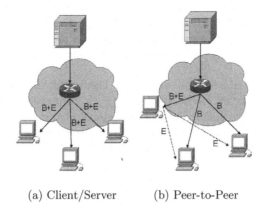

(a) Client/Server   (b) Peer-to-Peer

Fig. 1. The network topology for the simulation, where B denotes the base-layer stream and E denotes the enhancement layer streams

and expensive mainframe computers serves thin clients or dumb terminals. With the rapid growth of the computing and networking industries, the clients are capable of high computational task and the broadband access to the Internet has become affordable, and such trend will continue in the foreseeable future. Deploying these computational power and bandwidth within the Client/Server framework will underutilize the available resources.

The Peer-to-Peer (P2P) network empowers the peers to act the server's function to communicate between each other. In a fully decentralized P2P network, theneed of a central server is completely eliminated. Video streaming over the P2P network presents a feasible alternative to the Client/Server architecture, for offloading the traffic from the bottleneck link to the underutilized links. Although the P2P architecture has the potential to overcome some limitations raised by the Client/Server architecture, the P2P system possesses different constraints due to the following characteristics:

- **Heterogeneous**: Different peers have different bandwidth and processing capacity.
- **Unpredictable**: Each peer is free to join and leave the service at any time. There is no reinforcement to guarantee the service from the peers.

Both the heterogeneous and unpredictable behavior can severely impact the quality of the streaming video. Therefore, we propose a hybrid client/server and P2P streaming infrastructure, named centralized P2PSP. Centralized P2PSP uses the neighbourhood peers to offload the traffic load from the bottleneck link, while the server's roles in centralized management for authentication, authorization, and accounting are reserved. Centralized P2PSP is design for streaming any media type coded in base/enhancement layers, as illustrated in Fig. 1(b). The detailed protocol handshake for centralized P2PSP is shown in Fig. 2(b).

Step 1. The request peer P_{req} sends a setup message to the central server. The server firstly validates the AAA for P_{req}. Once the P_{req} is successfully validated, the server forwards the request to a nearby supplying peer P_{sup}. If no nearby peer has cached the video content, the server will also act as P_{sup}.

Step 2. P_{req} send the request signal for the video. The server commences streaming base-layer video, whereas P_{sup} is responsible for streaming the enhancement-layer video. The server updates P_{req} in the database.

Step 3. The server and P_{sup} continuously streams the video contents to P_{req}, until the media control signal (such as pause, play) or the session termination signal is received from the P_{req}.

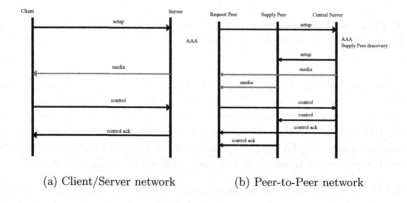

(a) Client/Server network   (b) Peer-to-Peer network

Fig. 2. Handshake of the video streaming for Client/Server and peer-to-peer network

3   P2PSP with PFGS

The H.264 PFGS coding consists of a base-layer and multiple enhancement layers. The enhancement layers are based on a low-complexity DCT-like bit-plane scheme. Different quality levels are achieved by decoding different levels of layers. In PFGS, each base-layer is always predicted by the base-layer from the previous frame, whereas an enhancement layer is predicted from the second or third enhancement layer of the previous frame. Details of the PFGS algorithm can be found in [11]. High coding efficiency and flexible scalability makes PFGS ideal evaluating centralized P2PSP.

As discussed previously, the client/server streaming model consists a network bottleneck. Let n_r denotes the number of receivers, r_{base} denotes the average transmission rate for the base layer video, and r_{enh} denotes the enhance layer video. The average bandwidth requirement of the bottleneck link b_{cs} is illustrated in Equation (1).

$$b_{cs} = n_r \left(r_{base} + \sum_{\forall EnhLayers} r_{enh} \right) \qquad (1)$$

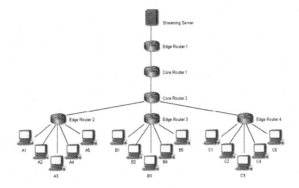

Fig. 3. Network topology for the simulation

For P2PSP, since the streamer server does not supply enhancement layers, the average bandwidth requirement at the bottleneck link, b_{p2psp}, is shown in Equation (2).

$$b_{p2psp} = n_r r_{base} + \sum_{\forall EnhLayers} r_{enh} \tag{2}$$

The traffic reduction on the bottleneck link is therefore:

$$b_{cs} - b_{p2psp} = (n_r - 1) \sum_{\forall EnhLayers} r_{enh} \tag{3}$$

Equation (3) indicates that the average bandwidth requirement for client/server and P2PSP approaches will only be equal (1) if there is only one receiving node (n_r equals 1), or (2) there is no enhancement layers ($\sum r_{enh}$ equals 0). For any other scenario, video transmission with the P2PSP approach will outperform the client/server approach.

A common technique for improving the streaming quality is to buffer the traffic. Let t denotes the time, t_0 denotes a reference starting time, and t_b is the buffering period. Let $r_{base,t}$ denotes the base-layer transmision rate at time t, and $r_{enh,t}$ denotes the enhancement-layer transmission rate at time t. The average bandwidth requirement $b_{cs,t}$ for client/server model is:

$$b_{cs,t} = \frac{n_r}{t_b} \sum_{t=t_0}^{t_0+t_b} (r_{base,t} + \sum_{\forall EnhLayers} r_{enh,t}) \tag{4}$$

Similarly, the average bandwidth requirement $b_{p2psp,t}$ for P2PSP model is:

$$b_{p2psp,t} = \frac{n_r}{t_b} \sum_{t=t_0}^{t_0+t_b} r_{base,t} + \frac{1}{t_b} \sum_{t=t_0}^{t_0+t_b} r_{base,t} \sum_{\forall EnhLayers} r_{enh,t} \tag{5}$$

The average bandwidth saving on the bottleneck link by using P2PSP with buffering is:

$$\frac{n_r - 1}{t_b} \sum_{t=t_0}^{t_0+t_b} \sum_{\forall EnhLayers} r_{enh,t} \tag{6}$$

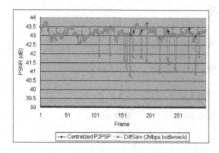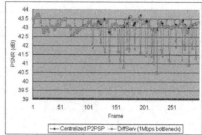

(a) Bottleneck bandwidth 2Mbps   (b) Bottleneck bandwidth 1Mbps

Fig. 4. Video quality with different bottleneck bandwidth

(a) DiffServ video output: frame   (b) Centralized P2PSP video out-
138 (PSNR=41.335dB)   put: frame 138 (PSNR=42.759dB)

Fig. 5. Output frame comparison for DiffServ and P2PSP

4   Simulation

The simulation is performed using NS-2, with the network topology shown in
Fig. 3. The bottleneck link is located between Core Router 1 and Core Router 2,
with the buffering period t_b in Equation. 4 and 5 equals 5ms. In the client/server
mode, the streaming server transmits the entire video traffic to each of the receiving nodes. DiffServ is experimented in the client/server mode. Each video frame
is packetized in a fixed size packet, to generate CBR traffic for the simulation.

Fig. 4 shows the comparison of the receiving video quality between P2PSP
and DiffServ, under different bottleneck bandwidth. Both Fig. 4(a) and Fig. 4(b)
indicate that the buffering technique at the bottleneck link reduces the packet
dropout rate, evidenced by no packet dropout initally before the buffer is fully
loaded. Once the buffer is over-loaded, DiffServ start to dropout packets and

therefore degrades the received video quality. Comparing Fig. 4(a) and Fig. 4(b), we observe that when the bottleneck bandwidth is reduced, DiffServ experiences more severe quality degrade. In comparison, P2PSP always result equal or better video quality. An example frame output is shown in Fig. 5.

5   Conclusions

In this paper, we proposed a distributed approach for video streaming. Centralized Peer-to-Peer Streaming Protocol addresses the bottleneck of the conventional Client and Server Streaming technique, to achieve higher perceived quality of service. Compares to competing technologies such as DiffServ, centralized P2PSP does not require software or hardware upgrade on the existing internet backbone. Centralized P2PSP offloads video traffic from the bottleneck link and decentralizes the processing power from the streaming server, while maintaining the high integrity in terms of authentication, authorization, and accounting. Simulations results show that centralized P2PSP can provide a consistent video quality at the receiver site, while DiffServ starts to dropout packets and degrades the video quality. We conclude that implementing centralized P2PSP video streaming is a cost-effective and highly scalable solution.

References

1. Dapeng Wu, Yiwei Thomas Hou, Wenwu Zhu, Hung-Ju Lee, Tihao Chiang, Ya-Qin Zhang, and H. Jonathan Chao, "On end-to-end architecture for transporting mpeg-4 video over the internet," *IEEE Trans. Circuits Syst. for Video Technology*, 2000.
2. Dapeng Wu, Yiwei Thomas Hou, Wenwu Zhu, Ya-Qin Zhang, and Jon M. Peha, "Streaming video over the internet: Approaches and directions," *IEEE Trans. on Circuits and Systems for Video Technology*, 2001.
3. S. Blake, D. Black, M. Carlson, E. Davies, Z.Wang, and W.Weiss, "An architecture for differentiated services," in *IETF RFC 2475*, December 1998.
4. Lixia Zhang, Steve Deering, Deborah Estrin, Scott Shenker, and Daniel Zappala, "Rsvp: A new resource reservation protocol," in *IEEE Network Magazine*, September 1993.
5. T. Nguyen and A. Zakhor, "Distributed video streaming over the internet," in *Proc. of SPIE Conference on Multimedia Computing and Networking*, Jan 2002.
6. Won J. Joen and Klara Nahrstedt, "Peer-to-peer multimedia streaming and caching service," in *Proc. of IEEE International Conference on Multimedia and Expo*, Aug 2002.
7. H. Deshpande, M. Bawa, and H. Garcia-Molina, "Streaming live media over a peer-to-peer network," Tech. Rep. 2002-21, Stanford University, March 2002.
8. Duc A. Tran, Kien A. Hua, and Tai T. Do, "Zigzag: An efficient peer-to-peer scheme for media streaming," Tech. Rep., University of Central Florida, 2002.
9. Ivan Lee and Ling Guan, "A scalable video codec design for streaming over distributed peer-to-peer network," in *Proc. of IEEE Global Telecommunications Conference (GLOBECOM)*, November 2002.

10. Ivan Lee and Ling Guan, "Centralized peer-to-peer streaming with layered video," in *Proc. of IEEE International Conference on Multimedia and Expo (ICME)*, July 2003.
11. Yuwen He, Feng Wu, Shipeng Li, Yuzhuo Zhong, and Shiqiang Yang, "H26l-based fine granularity scalable video coding," in *Proc. ISCAS*, May 2002.

Buffer Level Estimation for Seamless Media Streaming in Mobile IPv6 Networks

Dongwook Lee[1] and JongWon Kim[2]

Gwangju Institute of Science and Technology (GIST), Gwangju, 500-712, Korea
[1] UFON Research Center and [2] Networked Media Lab.
{dulee,jongwon}@gist.ac.kr

Abstract. In case of one-way streaming media applications over IP networks, it is well known that pre-buffering at the receiver side is very effective in overcoming network fluctuations. However, under the mobile IP situation that faces intermittent handoff of several seconds, it is not trivial to sustain seamless playback if latency requirement is stringent. Inaccurate and conservative choice on the required margin of buffering can waste limited latency budget, resulting in overall quality degradation. Thus, in this paper, we introduce a novel scheme that helps estimate the required pre-buffer size more accurately by considering both handoff duration and transient packet losses. Network simulation shows that the proposed scheme can provide an appropriate guideline on the buffer parameters and thus can facilitate the seamless streaming over the mobile IPv6 networks.

Keywords: Seamless media streaming, Mobile IP, Handoff transient time, and Pre-buffering.

1   Introduction

Mobile and wireless technologies have accelerated wide-spread adoption of multimedia services to mobile computers. In streaming applications, media streams have to be transmitted continuously, overcoming the fluctuation of network resources. The delay, jitter, and busty packet losses are usually addressed by adopting sufficient buffering at the clients prior to playout [1]. This buffering called "pre-buffering" smoothes network variations and gives a retransmission opportunity for lost packets. Under mobile networks, available bandwidth is scarce and even fluctuating severely. In addition, Transmission itself is paused when a handoff occurs. In fact, several mechanisms are proposed to reduce the blackout period due to handoff [2, 3]. However, these schemes are limited since they require special arrangements such as MAC bridge, additional resources, and corresponding signaling. Even with the fast handoff situations described in [7], packet losses are still present due to the weak signal strength around the handoff. Thus, we need to overcome possible shortage of buffer by adopting pre-buffering techniques. However, inaccurate and conservative choice on the required buffering margin can waste limited latency budget, resulting in overall quality degradation.

K. Aizawa, Y. Nakamura, and S. Satoh (Eds.): PCM 2004, LNCS 3331, pp. 139–146, 2004.

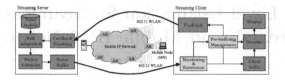

Fig. 1. Seamless media streaming framework in mobile IP networks.

In this paper, we introduce a seamless streaming framework by estimating the accurate prebuffer size to compensate the handoff latency and by adapting rate-shaping scheme to overcome the shortage of bandwidth around the handoff. We calculate the handoff latency by extending the previous work in [4] from the application point of view assuming the mobile IPv6 networks with fast handoff. Network simulation shows that the proposed scheme can provide appropriate guideline on the buffer parameters and thus can provide seamless streaming.

2   Seamless Media Streaming Framework

Fig. 1 shows the seamless media streaming framework under the mobile IPv6 networks [5], where IEEE 802.11 devices are configured as a wireless LAN infrastructure. A streaming application on a mobile node (MN) receives packets from a media server, while keeping an amount of packets in the client buffer to overcome resource fluctuations of network: available bandwidth, delay, and loss. The streaming server reacts to the feedback informed by the streaming client and performs quality adaptation, and packet schedule. The streaming client sends it's status information to the server, which includes current buffer occupancy, receiving rate, error rate, and etc. Many studies on the relationship between feedback and reaction have been reported in [8].

In this work, we are focusing on the movement of client, handoff, which interrupts media delivery and spoils client's streaming budget. Under the mobile IP networks, a MN that currently plays the streaming content can move beyond the reach of access router (AR) shown in Fig. 2(a). According to the received signal level, the MN initiates the handoff. At the beginning of the handoff, management frames are exchanged for a link-layer (L2) handoff between the MN and the wireless access point (AP) attached to the ARs. After the L2 handoff process, a network-layer (L3) handoff can be initiated. For the L3 handoff process, *'Binding Update'* (BU) message is used to inform both a corresponding node (CN) and a home agent (HA) about a new location information of the MN. After the CN receives the *BU* message, it changes the route path from the old route destined to the previous AR (PAR) (*old stream*) to the new one destined to the new AR (NAR) (*new stream*). The packets in the old route are forwarded to the NAR via the PAR according to the fast handoff procedure. Thus, to receive the packets from the old stream, the MN should wait for an additional time as well as the L2 handoff delay. Moreover, it is known that the change of route path causes the packet sequence disruption [4].

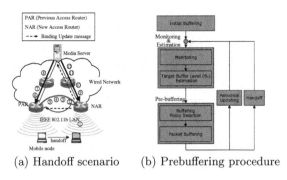

(a) Handoff scenario   (b) Prebuffering procedure

Fig. 2. Pre-buffering scenario.

In our framework, the handoff transient time is estimated before the hand-off occurs. To estimate the handoff transient time, the mobile client monitors network conditions such as link delay, flow rate, and queue status of the neighbor ARs. The handoff protocol and related signaling procedure are analyzed to get the handoff transient time. After estimating the handoff transient time, the streaming client tries to prepares enough data to compensate the estimated interruption time during the handoff. To acquire the estimated buffer level, target buffer level, which is estimated based on the given handoff transient time, the streaming client tries to collect packets, while keeping playback of the received media packets. There are two choices to boost required target level: increasing sending rate at the streaming server or decreasing the playback speed. It depends on the policy of pre-buffering management module.

The estimated buffer level can be varied along the time. Every ARs will have different required buffer level for handling handoff transient time. Even in the AR, network traffic condition can change the required buffer level. Thus, it is needed to keep the exact buffer level not to stop playback during the handoff. In Fig. 2(b), the estimation and buffer-level adjustment are performed periodically. To summarize, the pre-buffering scenario consists of buffer-level estimation procedure and buffer-level adjustment procedure as shown in Fig. 2(b). In the following section, we will analyze the handoff procedure to get handoff transient time which will be used to estimate target buffer level for pre-buffering.

3   Target Buffer Level Estimation for Pre-buffering

Handoff latency estimation: In this section, handoff latency and out-of-order packet period are estimated, which is based on the results of previous work [4]. Under the mobile IPv6 networks with fast handoff, a MN has a time period when it can not send and receive packets during handoff. We define this blackout period as the STP (silence time period). Also, we define the UTP (unstable time period) during when the packet sequence could be mis-ordered. Depending on the location of PAR and NAR, the timing between the old and new streams can be classified into three cases. As shown in Fig. 3, we can associate the transient

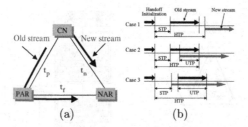

Fig. 3. Possible packet orderings observed at the MN during the handoff (for the traffic from the CN to the MN).

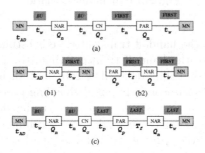

Fig. 4. Message flows and associated link delays for various packet streams (for the case when the MN moves from the PAR to the NAR): (a) the first packet of the new stream (for T_{f_new}), (b) the first packet of the old stream (for T_{f_old}); (b1) forwarded packet is already arrived at the NAR at the end of L2 handoff, and (b2) forwarded packet is not arrived at the NAR, and (c) the last packet of the old stream (for T_{l_old}).

time periods (i.e., STP, UDP, and HTP) according to link delays in NAR, PAR, and CN. For example, the 'Case 1' illustrates the situation where a MN moves to the far-away (in network routing sense) NAR from its CN. Thus, by setting the time when the MN leaves the PAR to zero, the STP, UTP, and HTP can be denoted by

$$STP = min(T_{f\_old}, \ T_{f\_new}), \tag{1}$$

$$UTP = max(0, T_{l\_old} - T_{f\_new}), \tag{2}$$

$$HTP = UTP + STP + |T_{f\_new} - T_{f\_old}|, \tag{3}$$

where T_{f_new} is the time when the first packet of new stream arrives to the MN and T_{f_old} and $T_{l\_old}$is the time when the first packet and the last packet of the old stream is delivered to the MN, respectively. The link delays between CN - PAR, CN - NAR, and PAR - NAR are denoted by t_p, t_n, and t_f, respectively. A handoff is started when a MN moves from the PAR. The bidirectional tunnel is already established between the NAR and the PAR. After the departure, there is a delay until the moved MN sends a RS message and the NAR responses it with a RA message. This delay consists of handoff latency in a link layer and a packet

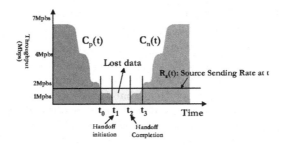

Fig. 5. Handoff scenario based on channel throughput.

transmission delay. We denote the L2 handoff delay as t_{L2}. The propagation delay of wireless link is denoted by t_w. Queueing delay of a packet in NAR, PAR, and CN is denoted by Q_n, Q_p, and Q_c respectively. The MN can receive a packet after L2-handoff completion and RS and RA packet exchange between MN and NAR. This attachment delay is set by $t_{AD} = t_{L2} + 2t_w$. According to the delay of each message flows shown in Fig. 4, the T_{f_new}, T_{f_old}, T_{l_old} can be described as follow.

$$T_{f\_new} = t_{L2} + 4t_w + 2Q_n + Q_c + 2t_n, \tag{4}$$
$$T_{f\_old} = max(t_{L2} + 3t_w, t_f + Q_p + Q_n + t_w), \tag{5}$$
$$T_{l\_old} = t_{L2} + 4t_w + 2Q_n + t_n + Q_c + t_p + Q_p + t_f. \tag{6}$$

Packet loss estimation: Handoff is performed based on the received signal strength of received data. Fig. 5 describes a throughput profile when a MN moves to a NAR from a PAR. When a MN is moving to a NAR from an PAR, the signal strength (and related transmission throughput) from the PAR decreases [6]. It is clear that the transmission throughput of IEEE 802.11b is smallest when the MN is around handoff. The streaming client should consider the throughput degradation around a handoff as wall as the handoff processing delay described in previous section. Streaming application may not guarantee required bandwidth (so called the source sending rate at time t, $R_s(t)$), around a handoff. Accordingly, when the throughput is less than $R_s(t)$, the packets sent by a streaming server will be lost. The throughput of the PAR channel is less than $R_s(t_0)$ at t_0 and the MN starts a handoff at t_1. While the handoff is finished at t_2, the channel throughput of the NAR is less than $R_s(t_2)$ until t_3. The total packet loss caused by handoff can be divided into three losses: pre-loss, post-loss, and handoff-loss. The pre-loss, L_{pre}, and the post-loss, L_{post}, are packet losses during periods before and after the handoff, respectively. The handoff-loss, $L_{handoff}$, is data losses during handoff duration. Then, the total loss, L_{total}, can be presented by $L_{total} = L_{pre} + L_{handoff} + L_{post}$, where $L_{pre} = \int_{t_0}^{t_1}(R_s(t) - C_p(t))dt$, $L_{post} = \int_{t_2}^{t_3}(R_s(t) - C_n(t))dt$, and $L_{handoff} = \int_{t \in STP} R_s(t)dt$, where $C_p(t)$ and $C_n(t)$ is the throughput function of channel in the PAR and in the NAR at time t, respectively.

Channel adaptation by feedback: The packet losses caused by decreased signal strength can be reduced by adopting a rate shaping method [8]. Using the feedback sent by the client, the streaming server can adjust $R_s(t)$ to the rate constrained by channel condition. For example, the streaming server reduces $R_s(t)$ to $C_p(t_0)$ at t_0 in Fig. 5. Generally, after a handoff, the received signal strength from the NAR is bigger than that from the PAR. Thus, $C_p(t_1) <= C_n(t_2)$. Then, there is no pre-loss and post-loss, since the $R_s(t_0) = C_p(t_0)$ and $C_p(t_0) = C_p(t_1) < C_n(t_2)$. Consequently, the total loss includes only the handoff-loss.

Fast handoff - no packet losses: In the fast handoff [7], during STP, the packets in the old stream are stored in the PAR and forwarded to a NAR. Hence, the handoff-loss does not exist in the fast handoff, if the ARs have enough buffer space to save the packets in the old stream during the STP.

Minimum buffer size to overcome handoff latency: We now describe the minimum buffer size that the client can tolerate the handoff latency. The video and audio data are first packetized at the server. For simplicity we assume that the media data is compressed such that one video frame and associated audio fit into one service frame. The service frame is segmented into n packets and the packets are transmitted at a constant rate. The packets are stored in the receiver buffer until the buffer reaches the target buffer size B_{Target}. When media playback is started, n packets are collected to reconstruct one service frame. Playback time of each service frame corresponds to inter-frame spacing, t_F, at the sender. The buffered packets can be played during T_p and it can be denoted by $T_p = \lfloor \frac{B_{Target}}{n} \rfloor \cdot t_F$, where $\lfloor x \rfloor$ represents the largest integer smaller or equal to x. Once the receiver faces buffer underflow, it stops playing media and stores incoming packet to the receiver buffer until the receiver buffer size reaches B_{Target}. The target buffer size is calculated according to the burst error length [1]. They figured out that the minimum buffer size, B_{loss}, to recover all lost packets can be written as

$$\lfloor \frac{B_{loss}}{n} \rfloor > T_{retx}(L_B) = \frac{\lfloor \frac{L_B}{t_{RTT}} \rfloor t_{RTT} + t_{RTT}}{t_F}. \tag{7}$$

where t_{RTT}, L_B, $T_{retx}(x)$ represent the round trip time, burst error length, and retransmission time of all x packets, respectively. The packet losses caused by decreased signal strength around handoff can be overcome by rate shaping controlled by client's feedback information. Also, the fast handoff of mobile IPv6 reduces the handoff loss. Then, the streaming application can only consider the STP to calculate prebuffer size. If we add the condition to Eq. (7), the target buffer level, $B_{Target} = B_H$, that can tolerate the handoff and provide seamless playback is

$$\lfloor \frac{B_H}{n} \rfloor = \begin{cases} T_{retx}(L_{total}), & \text{w/o rate shaping} \\ T_{retx}(L_{handoff}), & \text{with rate shaping} \\ \frac{STP}{t_F}, & \text{with rate shaping \& fast handoff.} \end{cases} \tag{8}$$

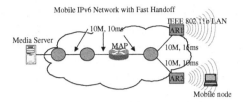

Fig. 6. Simulation scenario ($R(s)_t$ = 2.4Mbps, n = 10packets, packet size = 1Kbyte, and t_F = 0.03sec).

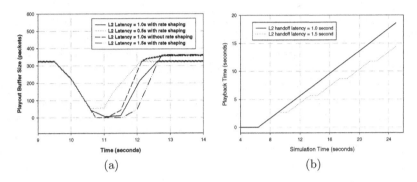

Fig. 7. (a) Buffer consumption rate and (b) Playback time with respect to the L2 handoff latency where the B_H is 330 packets (33 frames).

4   Simulation Results and Discussion

The simulation was based on the Network Simulator (NS-2). Fig. 6 shows the simulation scenario and parameters. Under the rate shaping option, the STP is main variable to calculate the B_{Target}. In Eq. (1), the T_{f_old} is selected as the STP in our simulation. Thus, L2 handoff latency (t_{L2}) is a main control variable to calculate the B_{Target}. The L2 handoff latencies of each ARs are configured variously between 0.5 and 1.5 seconds. The IEEE 802.11b PHY is operated with 11Mbps in normal condition. However, it changes the mode to 1Mbps in the PAR before 0.5 seconds of handoff initiation. After the end of handoff, it continues 1Mbps data rate and the mode is changed to 11Mbps after 0.5 seconds later. In our simulation, the 10% additional margin is added to the B_{Target}. The maximum buffer limit is 10% bigger than the B_{Target}. Only the streaming traffic is emitted to the link, and other traffic are not introduced in the simulation, which makes queueing delay at ARs ignorable.

Fig. 7(a) represents the buffer consumption ratio with respect to the L2 handoff latency variation under the B_{Target} is 330 packets(t_{L2}=1.0 seconds). The buffer drain rate is linearly increases according to the t_{L2}. When the t_{L2} is 1.5 seconds, 1.0 second, and 0.5 seconds, 330 packets, 326 packets, and 268 packets in the buffer are drained respectively. However, when the t_{L2} is 1.0s without the rate shaping, the whole packet, 330 packet, are consumed. The results are meet the result of the Eq. (8) well. The media playback time of a streaming client is shown in Fig. 7(b) where the target buffer level is 330 packets and maximum buffer limit is 363 packets that is estimation result for 1 second of L2 handoff latency. When the L2 handoff latency is 1 second, the playback is not interrupted but continuously served. However, we can observe that playback is interrupted whenever a handoff happens under it's L2 handoff latency is 1.5 seconds.

5   Conclusion

We introduced the seamless streaming framework by estimating the accurate buffer level for pre-buffering to compensate the handoff latency. We calculated the handoff latency in application point of view under the mobile IPv6 with fast handoff environment. The packet losses caused by decreased signal strength around handoff can be overcome by rate shaping controlled by client's feedback information. Also, the fast handoff of mobile IPv6 reduces the handoff loss. Thus, the streaming application can only consider the STP to calculate the target buffer level. The simulation result shows that the handoff aware streaming has no playback discontinuity while keeps a minimal pre-buffer size.

Acknowledgements. This work was supported by grant R05-2004-000-10987-0 from the Basic Research Program of the Korea Science & Engineering Foundation (KOSEF).

References

1. E. Steinbach, N. Farber, and B. Girod, "daptive playout for low latency video streaming," in *Proc. IEEE ICIP '01*, 2001.
2. H. Yokota, A. Idoue, T. Hasegawa, and T. Kato, "Link layer assisted mobile IP fast handoff method over wireless LAN networks," in *Proc. ACM MobiCom '02*, Atlanta, Georgia, Sep. 2002
3. T. Zhang, J. C. Chen, and P. Agrawal, "Distributed soft handoff in all-IP woreless networks," in *Proc. of 3GWireless '01*, San Francisco, May 2001.
4. D. W. Lee and J. Kim, "Out-of-sequence packet analysis in mobile IP handoff and its enhancement," in *Proc. 3G Wirelesss '02*, San Francisco, CA, May 2002.
5. D. Johnson and C. Perkins, "Mobility support in IPv6," Internet Engineering Task Force, RFC 3344, Aug. 2002.
6. J. D. Pavon and S. Choi, "Link adaptation strategy of IEEE 802.11 WLAN via received signal strength measurement ," in *Proc. IEEE ICC '03*, 2003.
7. R. Koodli, "Fast handovers for mobile IPv6," Internet Draft, Internet Engineering Task Force, March. 2003.
8. G. J. Conklin, et. al, "Video coding for streaming media delivery on the Internet," *IEEE Trans. on Circuits and Systems for Video Technology*, vol. 11, no. 3, pp. 269-281, 2001.

Dynamic Walks for Searching Streaming Media in Peer-to-Peer Networks

Zhou Su[1], Jiro Katto[1], and Yasuhiko Yasuda[1]

School of Science and Engineering, Waseda University, Ohkubo, 3-4-1, Shinjuku-ku,
169-0072, Tokyo, Japan
suzhou@waseda.jp

Abstract. With the advance of network technologies, availability and
popularity of streaming media contents over the P2P (Peer-to-Peer) Networks have grown rapidly in recent years. However, how to efficiently
search a requested steaming media among P2P peers is still a problem which causes a serious user delay and limited hit ratio. This paper presents an efficient search method for streaming media in P2P,
which reduces user response delays and exchange overhead simultaneously. Based on an analytical formulation of both streaming media and
P2P peers'characteristics, we derive a search algorithm which solves the
next two problems quantitatively. (1) How to decide the number of walkers (queries) at each step of search? (2) How to decide the length of walkers (queries) at each step of search? Simulation results verify that the
proposed algorithm efficiently resolves the above problems and provides
much better performance than conventional methods.

1 Introduction

Over the past several years, Peer-to-Peer computing has emerged as a popular
model aiming at further utilizing Internet information and resources. Unfortunately, the mechanism of how to search a requested object among P2P peers is
still a problem causing the serious user delay and limited hit ratio.

This so-called search algorithm has attracted many researches such as
Flooding, *Expanding Ring* and *Random Walks*. However, most of the current available algorithms were proposed regardless of the type of Web Contents.
These search methods designed for general Web objects are not appropriate for
streaming media. It is because streaming media has several inherent properties.
(1) The size of streaming media is usually larger than non-streaming files by
orders of magnitude [1][11][17][18]. (2) User access behavior shows quite different characteristics. For example, clients often stop watching a stream without
watching all of the parts [5][10][19][20]. (3) Different from conventional web objects, streaming media do not require to be delivered at once. Instead, streaming
servers continuously send data packets to clients in a (quasi) synchronized manner on the Internet[12][21].

For these reasons, the search mechanisms without the consideration for
streams' properties can't be efficiently applied to streaming media such as video

K. Aizawa, Y. Nakamura, and S. Satoh (Eds.): PCM 2004, LNCS 3331, pp. 147–156, 2004.
© Springer-Verlag Berlin Heidelberg 2004

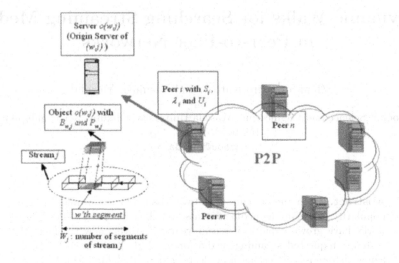

Fig. 1. Proposed P2P Architecture for Searching Streaming Media

and audio. Furthermore, it has also been showed that almost 80% of the network traffic in P2P network is caused by streaming data. Therefore, how to propose an algorithm to efficiently search streaming media in P2P networks becomes very important.

Here, we then propose a novel search algorithm for streaming media in P2P network based on the analysis of streaming media and P2P node'characteristics. The proposed algorithm is called Dynamic Streaming Walker (DSW), because both the number and the length of each walker in our proposal are varied according to the situation of the requested stream and neighbor peers. It is different from other conventional methods where each query is sent to a randomly chosen neighbor at each step. In this paper, our work focuses on how to decide both the number and the length of each walker at each step dynamically in order to reduce system overhead and improve user hit ratio simultaneously.

2   Previous Work

There are numerous works on how to search the requested objects in P2P networks.

The *Flooding* [6] is an algorithm where a node sends queries to all its connecting neighbors at each step. A *TTL* (Time To Live) is used to control the number of hops that a query can be propagated. However, the value of *TTL* is fixed and is hard to select properly. Furthermore, there are too many duplicate messages and network interrupts introduced by the *Flooding*.

In the *Expanding Ring* [4], a node starts a flood with a small *TTL*, and waits to see if the search is successful. If it is, then the node stops. Otherwise, the node increases the value of TTL and starts another flood. The process repeats until the object is found. Although this algorithm solves the TTL selection problem, it does not address the massage duplication issue inherent the *Flooding*.

Recently the *Random Walks* algorithm has been verified its better performance than others as it ingredients in protocols addressing searching and topology maintenance of unstructured P2P networks [7]. In the *Random Walks*, a requesting node sends k query messages (walkers), and each query message takes its own random walk. The expectation is that k walkers after T steps should reach roughly the same number of nodes as 1 walker after kT steps. However, the parameters of k and T are not automatically changed at different steps or for different objects during the searching process. Furthermore, its design has not take the property of streams into consideration.

We ourselves proposed an integrated pre-fetching and replacing algorithm to search the hierarchical (graceful) image in Content Delivery Networks for users [2]. We also presented a scheme for stream caching by using hierarchically distributed proxies with adaptive segments assignment, where the streaming data can be searched and provided quickly to the users [3]. However, the former did not deal with video streaming, and the latter was for the "global-scope" server cooperation for distributed streaming contents, instead of P2P Networks, as a future work.

3   Theoretical Analysis and Proposed Algorithm

In this section, firstly how to decide the number and length of each walker at each step for searching streams are introduced in Sect.3.1 and Sect.3.2 respectively. Then, the proposed search algorithm is presented in Sect.3.3. Finally, how to reduce the computational complexity is discussed in Sect.3.4.

3.1   How to Decide the Number of Each Walker at Each Step

We consider a P2P community with I peers (nodes). Each Peer i (i=1,..., I), which might be a powerful workstation, a personal computer, or a PDA an so on, has Si bytes of storage capacity and has clients that request objects at aggregate rate λi. A up ratio Ui is defined as the fraction of the time that Peer i is up (on line). We assume that there are J streams and each stream (stream$j, j = 1, ..., J$) is encoded into Wj segments. Bw, j denotes the data size of the w-th segment ($w = 1, ..., Wj$) of stream j. A parameter Pw, j is defined as the request probability for the w-th segment of stream j and Xi, w, j is denoted to be a parameter which takes a binary value of

$$X_{i,w,j} = \begin{cases} 1, (\text{if the } w\text{-th segment of stream } j \text{ is available at peer } i) \\ 0, (\text{otherwise}) \end{cases} \tag{1}$$

$$\sum_w \sum_j B_{w,j} \cdot X_{i,w,j} \leq S_i \tag{2}$$

As [1] showed that 80% of the requests to streaming media were served by only top 4% most popular servers. That is to say: popular servers store a quite large percentage of Web contents. Therefore, it is suggested that we should firstly send queries to these popular nodes at each search-step. In this paper we define these popular peers in P2P networks as *Active Peers*.

Let $\hat{} = \sum \lambda_i$, be the total request rate of all peers. Then, we can obtain the relative popularity of each peer as:

$$\lambda_i / \sum_i \lambda_i = \lambda_i / \wedge \tag{3}$$

Since a given peer may be up (online) or down (offline) at a given time, queries should be firstly sent to the peer with high online ratio Ui, because this peer should be likely to have connections with other peers and then stores more Web objects. We define the active degree of Peer i in P2P networks as Ai:

$$A_i = U_i \cdot \lambda_i / \sum_i \lambda_i = U_i \cdot \lambda_i / \wedge \tag{4}$$

On the other hand, except the peer active degree, the link condition should also be considered. To keep the load balance and reduce response time, firstly sending query to the neighbor peer with fast link should be advocated. Assume that Peer i has Li different links with its neighbor peers, each neighbor peer has a serial number l ($l=1,..., Li$), let's denote each link's RTT value as R_l. ($l=1,..., Li$).

Finally, we define a query number priority (QNP) for each neighbor peer i as follows:

$$QNP(l) = {}^{\beta}/R_l + (1 - \beta) \cdot A_l \tag{5}$$

In the above quation, β is a smoothing constant . After being given Ai in Eq.4, we can obtain:

$$QNP(l) = {}^{\beta}/R_l + (1 - \beta) \cdot U_l \cdot \lambda_l / \wedge \tag{6}$$

If a peer with high QNP, the query will first send this peer because it has both a high active ratio and fast link.

3.2   How to Decide the Length of Each Walker at Each Step

Performance evaluation of the search is given by the value of Search Hit-ratio. If a miss hit happens, new queries (walkers) need to be sent to other peers. It will incur network transmission cost, overhead and user delay. Therefore, for the walker-length, our goal is to selectively decide different walker-length for different streams so as to maximize the total Search Hit-ratio.

We assume that each streaming media is divided into segments based on the result of shot boundary detection. In our definition, the segment represents a sequence of frames that can be decoded by itself. For the MPEG compressed data, for example, it consists of a group-of-pictures (GOP) or multiple GOPs.

If a segment of one stream is requested from a peer and P2P networks also fetch this requested segment from other peers to it, we assume that this peer will keep this segment in itself. As sometimes not all the requested streams will be completely observed by clients, the peer only keeps the watched segments of the requested stream in. And the corresponding cache policy will also remove the unobserved segments from this peer quickly to save the storage resource for the future request.

In the case when a peer A keeps storing the first k segments of stream j, if a user requested this stream from peer B and stopped watching it after the playback of w segments, the probabilistic form of the Search Hit-ratio (Peer B gets w segments of stream j by sending a walker to Peer A) is given by:

$$p_{s\_hit} = \sum_{j,w,k} p(w \leq k \,|w,j)p(w,j) \tag{7}$$

Where $P(w \leq k \mid w,j)$ is the conditional probability distribution, or cpdf for short, that means the user is satisfied after watching the playback of total w segments already stored in the peer A. $P(w,j)$ is the pdf that a user requests the w segments of stream j. And $P(w,j)$ can be decomposed into $P(w \mid j)$ and $P(j)$. Then, Eq.(7) is rewritten as:

$$p_{s\_hit} = \sum_{j,w,k} p(w \leq k \,|w,j)p(w\,|j)p(j) \tag{8}$$

With an infinite amount of storage, $P(w \leq k \mid w,j) = 1$ when the first w segments of stream j with the pdf $P(w \mid j) = 1$ are stored in one peer.

In practice, however, peer capacity is finite and not all segments of all streams can be stored in one peer. Therefore, if the correct $P(w,j)$ of the top-ranked segments of the streams can be estimated and then stored in the cache, more clients' requests will be satisfied and then high $P(w \leq k \mid w,j)$ and a high Segment Hit-ratio can be obtained.

If a user's requested data is not stored in the cache of a peer and this cache is also full, replacement is required to make room for incoming data. Let the indices of the removed segments of the streams from the cache be $\wedge 3$. If the k-th segment of the stream f is removed, $\wedge 3 = \{(k,f)\}$. Besides, the new coming segments are $k+1$ to l segments of the stream m. We denote the set of indices $\{(k+1,m),(k+2,m),...,(l,m)\}$ as $\wedge 2$.

Then the Search Hit-ratio after the above replacement can be written as follows:

$$\begin{aligned} p_{s\_hit} = &\sum p(w \leq k/w,j)p(w,j) \\ &+ \sum p(r \leq k/l,m)p(r,m) \\ &- \sum p(s \leq k/r,n)p(s,n) \end{aligned} \tag{9}$$

Where (r,m) belongs to $\wedge 2$ and (s,n) belongs to $\wedge 3$. Since only the third term is controllable by the peer in the above equation, the maximization of P_{s_hit} is equivalent to the minimization of the third term. Therefore, $\wedge 3$ is the set of indices of the segments of the streams with the lowest pdf $P(s,n)$.

Therefore, the segment of one stream with the lowest $P(w \mid j)P(j)$ should be removed first. The above replacement rule also decides the available ratio of each segment of each stream. If a stream has high available ratio, we only need to send short-length walker to search it. Otherwise, for a stream with low available ratio, the walker' length should be long. This is a kind of dynamic walker, which the length is varied according to different streams.

How to efficiently calculate the available ratio of each segment of each stream $P(w \mid j)P(j)$ is also a problem considered by us. As there are numberless segments of different streams, keeping the request records for all segments of all streams is not realizable. Here, we introduce a method to obtain $P(w \mid j)$ by just keeping the stopping viewing point of stream j within several past requests.

Assume that stream j has been requested by Q times within a fixed period and each time the client stopped watching stream j after the playback of segment $S_{q,j}, (q = 1, ..., Wj), (j = 1, ..., J))$. $P(w \mid j)$ can be then computed as follows:

$$p(w, j) = |\{S_{q,j} \mid w \leq S_{q,j}\}| / Q \tag{10}$$

where $| \cdot |$ denotes the number of elements of a set.

On the other hand, $P(j)$ is the request frequency of stream j. It can be obtained by calculating the accumulative request times within one testing period. However, as the popularity may change over time, a stream with high access frequency in the last period may not be popular currently. Therefore, how to decide the testing period is very important.

We define TST as the number of total queries sent by users in a test period. Let v_j denote the request times of the request for stream j during the above period. Then, we can get:

$$p(j) = g(j)/(\sum_w g(w)) \tag{11}$$

$$g(j) = v_j/TST \tag{12}$$

Hence, the priority index of segment can be decided by

$$p(w \mid j)p(j) = (|\{S_{q,j} \mid w \leq S_{q,j}\}| / Q)g(j)/(\sum_w (g(w))) \tag{13}$$

As Q, TST and the summation of $g(w)$ over w are identical for all streams in the above Equation, for convenience, we define a query length priority (QLP) for the query of segment w of steam j as follows:

$$QLP(w, j) = |\{S_{q,j} \mid w \leq S_{q,j}\}| v_j/TST \tag{14}$$

3.3   Proposed Algorithm

The proposed search algorithm is to resolve the following two problems: (1) How shall we decide the number of walkers at each search-step? (2) How shall we decide the length of walkers at each search-step? To solve these problems, we give algorithm as follows:

When a peer i $(i=1, ..., I)$ sends queries (walkers) to its neighbor peer l $(l=1, ..., L_i)$ to request the w-th segment of stream j,

1) $QNP(l)$ in Eq.(6) is calculated. A threshold T_{QNP} is set up, if $QNP(l)$ $\geq T_{QNP}$, peer i will send query (walker) to peer l, otherwise, the query will not be sent. Then, the number of walkers can be controlled

2) A query to peer l ($l=1,..., L_i$) is decided to be sent, the total length of this query (walker) will be calculated by the $QLP(w, j)$ in Eq.(14). If we denote the total number of the search-step as ST, then the length at each step is $QLP(w, j)/ST$.

The above algorithm is different from the conventional method, *Random Walks* algorithm, which forwards a query message to a randomly chosen neighbor at each step. Since both the number and the length of each walker in our proposal are varied according to the situation of the requested stream and neighbor peer, we name the proposed algorithm *Dynamic Streaming Walker*.

3.4   Consideration on Computational Complexity

As there are numerous segments of streams in a peer, it is unrealistic to manage all segments of all streams' available ratios. Also, since the scale of P2P is being increased recently, to manage all peers' active ratios will cause a great amount of computational complexity in our algorithm.

Fortunately, previous researches showed that the distribution of web requests from a fixed group of users follows a Zipf-like distribution [9]. It has been proved that most web requests to a server are for a very small set of objects, for example top 10%. Because of this property, it is enough to only manage the aforesaid set of streams. Other recent studies also showed that client load is heavily skewed towards popular servers. In [1], it had been found that 80% of the requests to streaming media were served by only top 4% most popular servers. Therefore, to reduce computation complexity of our P2P, it is suggested that we only need to care about popular servers and popular streams.

Let F_i and F_j represent access frequency of peer i and stream j in last period, respectively. Then we apply

If F_i or F_j exceeds a pre-specified threshold, the system will execute the search algorithm for the coming period.

If not, the system just keeps access records and does not carry out any calculation.

The threshold is an access frequency of the stream (or the peer) of which ranking is Top 10, for example. Accordingly, the system only needs to manage a very small set of streams and peers, leading to reduction of computation complexity.

4   Evaluation of Policies

4.1   Simulation Conditions

In simulation experiments, we assume following conditions: There are 1000 nodes (peers) in our network simulator. As the recent study showed that most communication networks have Power-Law link distributions [8], network topology in

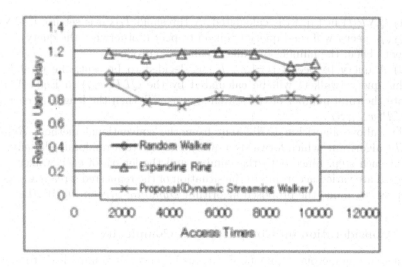

Fig. 2. Relative User Delay among Different Search Algorithms

our simulation is decided according to the Power-Law Random Graph: the i-th most connected node has Ω/r_i^β neighbors, and β is set to be 0.8 [4].

The distribution of web request is decided by Zipf distribution, which states that the relative probability of a request for the j-th most popular page is proportional to Ω/r_j^α. Besides, the parameter of Zipf distribution is 0.8 [9].

As for the streaming contents, there are 1000 different streams with the rate of 384kbps. The length of each stream is uniformly distributed from one minute to ten minutes and the size of one segment is 288kbyte [1]. In our simulation, clients often stop watching a streaming content after playback. The position where a client stops watching a stream is decided at random. Client requests arrive according to a Poisson process. The total request times in the simulations are 10000. Note that we set the number of total queries (walkers), which can be used in the following three algorithms, to be the same, if the available queries are used up, the simulation will also be ended. That is to say: we test the performance of each algorithm based on the same condition, where the available resource (query) is fixed.

There are three search algorithms we will study:
Expanding Ring
Random Walks
Proposal (Dynamic Streaming Walker)

4.2   Simulation Results

In Fig. 2, relative user delay is shown with respect to the *Random Walks* algorithm. From this figure, we can find that the *Expanding Ring* achieved the poorest relative performance. In *Expanding Ring*, the query is firstly sent with a small TTL value. If the requested stream can not be found within this small TTL period, then the TTL is increased and the query is continued to send to next peers. Although the TTL value is varied in *Expanding Ring*, its value only changes once after being set. Furthermore, its value is decided without analysis of network situation either. Therefore, its user delay is the worst among these three algorithms.

The *Random Walks* obtains a slight better performance than the *Expanding Ring*. The result can be explained as follows: In *Random Walks*, a requesting node sends k query messages (walkers), and each query message takes its own random walk. However, its own random walker doesn't make difference among different streams. As different streams have different available ratio, the needed queries of finding different streams are also different. Therefore, because of the poor efficiency of using the fixed number of queries, the user delay is lower than our proposal.

We can find that the proposed method substantially reduces user delay by almost 20% compared with *Random Walks* in Fig.2. The reason is because the proposal decides whether a query should be sent to its neighbor peers by considering many aspects such as peer activity, stream request frequency and peer status (link). This reason also results in an effective utilization of the fixed number of queries when the request times are increased. For our proposal, the relative user delay keeps being decreased with the request times increased.

5   Conclusions

This paper discussed how to optimally search streaming contents among P2P networks. Based on mathematical analysis, we proposed presented an efficient search scheme to reduces user response delays and exchange overhead simultaneously. Simulation results showed that the proposed method substantially reduced average user delay by 20% compared with the conventional ones.

There are a number of works to be done as further researches. Precise design of control packets exchanged among peers and its quantitative overhead evaluation should be carried out from the practical viewpoint. Furthermore, theoretical modeling and search algorithms should be expanded and sophisticated.

References

1. M. Chesire, A. Wolman, G.M. Voelker, and H.M. Levy: Measurement and Analysis of a Stream Media Workload, USITIS'01, San Francisco, CA, Mar. 2001.
2. Z. Su, T. Washizawa, J. Katto and Y. Yasuda, Integrated Pre-fetching and Caching Algorithm for Graceful Image Caching, IEICE Trans. on Commun, Vol.E86-B, No.9, Sep.2003.
3. Z. Su, J. Katto, T.Nishikawa, M.Murakami and Y. Yasuda: Stream Caching Using Hierarchically Distributed Proxies with Adaptive Segments Assignment, IEICE Trans. on Commun, Vol.E86-B, No.6, pp 1859-1869, Jun.2003.
4. Q. Lv, P. Cao, E. Cohen, K. Li and S. Shenker: Search and Replication in Unstructured Peer-to-Peer Networks. ISC2002

5. S. Acharya and B. Smith and P. Parnes: Characterizing User Access To Videos on the Videos On the World Wide Web, SPIE/ACM MMCN 2000, San Jose, CA, Jan 2000.
6. Gnutella, www. gnutella.co.uk
7. C. Jkantsidis, M. Mihail, A. Saberi, Random Walks in peer to Peer Networks, IEEE INFOCOM '04, HK, Mar.2004.
8. L. A. Adamic, B. Humberman, R. Lukose, and A. Puniyani, Search in Power Law Networks, Phys. Rev. E, Vol. 64, 2001.
9. L. Breslao, P. Cao, L. Fan, G. Phillips, and S. Shenker, Web Caching and Zip-like Distributions: Evidence and Implications, IEEE INFOCOM'99, New York, April, 1999.
10. V.N. Padmanabhan, H.J. Wang, P.A. Chou, Resilient Peer to Peer Streaming, IEEE ICNP Nov. 2003
11. S. Sen, J. Rexford and D. Towsley,Proxy Prefix Caching for Multimedia Streams, IEEE INFOCOM'99, New York, NY, Mar.1999.
12. I. Cidon, S. Kutten, and R. Soffer, Optimal Allocation of Electronic Content, IEEE INFOCOM 2001, Anchorage, AK, Apr.2001.
13. B. Li, M.J. Golin, G.F. Italiano, and X. Deng, On the Optimal Placement of Web Proxies in the Internet, IEEE INFOCOM'99, New York, NY, pp 21-25, Mar.1999.
14. L. Qiu, V.N. Padmanabhan, and G.M. Voelker, On the Placement of Web Server Replicas, IEEE INFOCOM 2001, Anchorage, AK, pp 22-26, Apr.2001.
15. J. Apostolopoulos, T. Wong, W. Tan, and S. Wee, On Multiple Description Streaming with Content Delivery Networks, IEEE INFOCOM, June 2002
16. M. Sasabe, N. Wakamiya, M. Murata and H. Miyahara, Proxy Caching Mechanisms with Video Quality Adjustment, SPIE ITCom, Feb.2001.
17. Z. Su, J. Katto and Y. Yasuda, Optimal Replication Algorithm for Scalable Streaming Media in Content Delivery Networks, IEICE Trans. on Information and Systems, Vol.E87-D, No.12, Dec.2004.
18. Z. Su, T. Washizawa, J. Katto and Y. Yasuda, Performance Improvement of Graceful Caching by Using Request Frequency Based Prefetching Algorithm, IEEE TENCON2001, Singapore, pp 370-376, Aug, 2001
19. Z. Su, T. Washizawa, J. Katto and Y. Yasuda, Hierarchical Image Caching in Content Distribution Networks, IEEE TENCON02, pp 786-790, Aug, 2001
20. Z. Su, J. Katto, T. Nishikawa, M. Murakami and Y. Yasuda, An integrated Scheme to Distribute Segmented Streaming Media over Hierarchical Caches, ICITA02, pp 240-14, Australia, Dec, 2002
21. Z. Su, J. Katto and Y. Yasuda, Replication Algorithms to Retrieve Scalable Streaming Media over Content Delivery Network, the 5th ACM SIGMM, Multimedia Information Retrieval (MIR2003), Berkeley, CA, USA, pp255-261, Nov, 2003

An Image Retrieval Scheme Using Multi-instance and Pseudo Image Concepts

Feng-Cheng Chang and Hsueh-Ming Hang*

Department of Electronics Engineering, National Chiao Tung University,
Hsinchu 300, Taiwan, R.O.C.,
fcchang.ee88g@nctu.edu.tw, hmhang@mail.nctu.edu.tw

Abstract. Content-based image search has long been considered a difficult task. Making correct conjectures on the user intention (perception)
based on the query images is a critical step in the content-based search.
One key concept in this paper is how we find the user preferred image
characteristics from the multiple samples provided by the user. The second key concept is that when the user does not provide a sufficient number of samples, how we generate a set of consistent "pseudo images". The
notion of image feature stability is thus introduced. In realizing the preceding concepts, an image search scheme is developed using the weighted
low-level image features. At the end, quantitative simulation results are
used to show the effectiveness of these concepts.

1   Introduction

The dramatically growing size of digital contents creates the demand for highly
efficient multimedia content management. Each content-based image retrieval
(CBIR) application requires a different set of configurations[1], including the
selected image features and the processing architecture, to achieve the desired
matching accuracy. There are no general guidelines in designing a good matching criterion; thus, many CBIR systems have been proposed to bridge the gap
between image feature space and human semantics.

In this paper, we will focus on the content-based image retrieval (CBIR)
methods. In sec. 2, we briefly discuss the concept of multiple instances and
common problems when using this technique. Based on a few assumptions, we
propose a straightforward yet effective method that incorporates multiple samples and image multi-scale property in estimating user intention in sec. 3. Then,
the subjective and objective performance of the proposed scheme is shown in
sec. 4. At the end, we conclude this presentation with sec. 5.

---

* This work is partially supported by the Lee & MTI Center for Networking Research
at National Chiao Tung University and by National Science Council (Taiwan, ROC)
under Grant NSC 91-2219-E-009-041

K. Aizawa, Y. Nakamura, and S. Satoh (Eds.): PCM 2004, LNCS 3331, pp. 157–164, 2004.

2   Motivations

In a typical Query-by-Example (QBE) CBIR system with relevance feedback function, it analyzes the user query images and/or relevant feedback images to derive the search parameters. The search parameters are often defined in terms of the image features pre-chosen in the system. Then the system searches the database and returns a list of the top-N similar images for further relevance feedback. This process can be repeated and hopefully it will eventually produce the satisfactory results to that particular user and query. In such a system, multiple samples (query and feedback) help the system to make a better "guess" on the user intention.

The problem is how one utilizes multiple image features and multiple query instances (images) to derive the proper search parameters. Multiple features and multiple instances represent two different aspects. The former is how we describe an image in an application; the latter is how we guess the user intention using the given instances. There exist many proposals on combining multiple features for image search such as [2]. Methods of combining multiple instances are usually considered as a part of a relevance feedback function. There are several existing CBIR proposals containing relevance feedback such as MARS[3,4] and iPURE[5].

In our previous project, we developed an MPEG-7 test bed [6] and thus have used it to examine several low-level MPEG-7 features. We observed that subjectively similar pictures tends to be close (near) in one or more feature spaces. Another observation is that a low-level feature often has (somewhat) different values when it is extracted from the same picture with different spatial resolutions and/or picture quality (SNR scalability). Our investigation finds that people often design a QBE system with feedback under the assumption that a sufficient number of query instances or feedback iterations can be provided by the user. However, this assumption is not always true in a real-world application[7]. Often, the sample size is very small (one to three) and the information contained in various samples may not be all consistent. Based on our observations, we are motivated to develop a distance-based user perception estimation algorithm, which tries to produce a correct conjecture on the user intention based on the small number of samples (instances) provided by the user.

3   Weighting on Low-Level Features

In the following discussions, we focus on a statistical approach that combines multiple low-level features together to form a "good" metric for retrieving "similar" images. We first describe the feature weights produced by multiple instances (query set) in sec. 3.1. Then, the approach of generating pseudo images using multiple (resolution or SNR) scales is described in sec. 3.2. In sec. 3.3, we present a CBIR architecture that uses the multi-instance and pseudo image concepts. It solves the feature space normalization problem, and reduces the impact of insufficient user feedback information.

3.1   User Perception Estimation

There are several ways to combine different low-level features. Here we use a straightforward one: weighted sum of feature distances. This method is simple because we use the ready-to-use distance functions, and the user perception is expressed by a weighting vector. Note that the weighting vector is derived from the multiple instances provided by the user.

Similar to many other image retrieval schemes, we assume the following conditions are satisfied:

- All the basic feature distance metrics are bounded.
- Two perceptually similar images have a small distance in at least one feature space.
- Low-level features are locally inferable[8]. That is, if the feature values of two images are fairly close, then the two images are perceptually similar.

In addition to the above assumptions, we add another conjecture: if two images have a large distance value in a specific feature space, we cannot determine the perceptual similarity of them based merely on this feature. Note that this feature space is simply irrelevant to our perception. It does not necessarily decide dissimilarity in perception.

Different from several well-known CBIR systems, our system does not rely on *a priori* feature distributions. These distributions may help to optimize inter-feature normalization, as in [3], to produce better performance in accuracy. However, they often introduce overheads and degrade system performance in speed. Even if feature distributions are available, they may not lead to appropriate normalization. Thus, we try to design our method to be independent of feature distributions as shown below. The need of normalization is eliminated because of the way we define distance function.

In summary, our feature weighting and combination principle is: *given two user-input query images, if they are farther apart in a certain feature space, this feature is less important in deciding the perceptual similarity for this particular query.* Suppose we have a query image set with n samples, $Q = \{q_i \mid i = 1..n\}$, and an available basic feature set $F = \{F_j \mid j = 1..m\}$. Let f_{ij} denotes the feature F_j value for image q_i. The normalized distance function for feature F_j is $d_j(f_{1j}, f_{2j}) = n_j * D_j(f_{1j}, f_{2j})$, where $D_j(f_{1j}, f_{2j})$ is the designated distance function for F_j, and n_j is the normalization factor for F_j, which sets the normalized value $d_j(f_{1j}, f_{2j})$ in the range of $[0, 1]$. Though n_j is an *a priori* information, we will see that it can be safely discarded at the end of this section.

We next define the feature difference between image i and all the other images in Q for feature F_j as follows:

$$diff_{ij} = \mu_{ij} + \sigma_{ij},$$

where

$$\mu_{ij} = \frac{1}{n-1} \sum_{k=1, k \neq i}^{n} d_j(f_{ij}, f_{kj})$$

$$\sigma_{ij}^2 = \frac{1}{n-1} \sum_{k=1, k \neq i}^{n} (d_j(f_{ij}, f_{kj}))^2 - \mu_{ij}^2.$$

The extra term (standard deviation) is added into the difference measure because experiments indicate that an "inconsistent" feature (large standard deviation) is less important. Then we express the scatter factor as the maximum difference in this feature space: $s_j = \max_{\forall i} \textit{diff}_{ij}$. The scatter factors can be considered as the importance indicator of that feature. Based on the previously mentioned rule, we give less perception weight to a more scattered feature (F_j):

$$w_j = (s_j * \sum_{k=1}^{m} \frac{1}{s_k})^{-1}.$$

The distance function combining m features is then defined as

$$D(q_1, q_2) = \sum_{j=1}^{m} w_j * d_j(f_{1j}, f_{2j}).$$

Finally, the distance function between image I and n query instances (Q) is defined by

$$D(I, Q) = \min_{i=1..n} D(I, q_i).$$

Note that the normalization factor n_j is canceled in every $w_j * d_j(f_{1j}, f_{2j})$ term. This implies that we can safely ignore the distance normalization problem as long as all the feature metrics are bounded.

3.2 Pseudo Query Images

In case that the number of query images is too small, we use the multi-scale technique to create pseudo query images. The term "scale" here refers to either the spatial resolution or the SNR quality. It is based on the conjecture that the down-sampled or noise-added images are subjectively similar to the original version. We also observe that a low-level feature may have different values at different scales (in spatial and in SNR).

An unstable (sensitive) feature tends to yield a large distance value when the distance is computed based on different scales of the same image. The quantitative difference in stability can be measured by the scatter factor s_j defined in sec. 3.1. Therefore, we adopt another principle: *we have a higher matching confidence (more weight) on the distance metric associated with a stable feature.* Now, we can include the stability estimation into the perception estimation by adding these pseudo images to the query set. The combined procedure thus puts less weight on more scattered features, which may be due to either perceptual irrelevance or feature instability.

3.3   Architecture

The proposed CBIR query system architecture is summarized in Fig. 1. The original query (input) images are processed to produce pseudo-images. Together they form the query set. The query set is fed into the user perception analysis process to estimate the weighting factors. Then, the query set and the weighting factors are sent to the image matching process to compute image similarity. At the end, the process generates the top-N list.

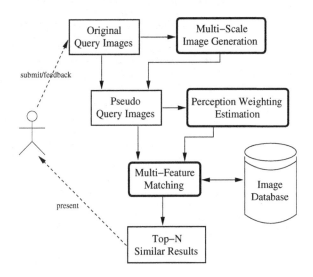

Fig. 1. Proposed perception estimation and query system

4   Experiments and Discussions

In this section, we examine our design using both subjective and objective measures. The screenshot shown on Fig. 2 is an application program running on our MPEG-7 test bed [6]. Three image global features defined by MPEG-7 are used. They are scalable color, color layout, and edge histogram. The query images are displayed on left panel. The right panel shows the top-25 query results.

4.1   ANMRR

We adopt the *Average Normalized Modified Retrieval Rank* (ANMRR)[9] metric in measuring the accuracy of our method. The ANMRR is used in the MPEG-7 standardization process to quantitatively compare the retrieval accuracy of different competing visual descriptors. For a query image, this measurement favors a matched ground-truth result and penalizes a missing ground-truth or

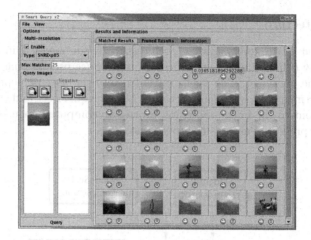

Fig. 2. Subjective results

a non-ground-truth result. We briefly describe the formula of ANMRR in the following paragraphs. Details can be found in [9][10, pp.183-184].

For a query q with a ground-truth size of $NG(q)$, we define $rank(k)$ as the rank of the kth ground-truth image on the top-N result list. Then,

$$Rank(k) = \begin{cases} rank(k) & \text{if } rank(k) \le K(q) \\ 1.25 \cdot K(q) & \text{if } rank(k) > K(q) \end{cases}$$

$$K(q) = \min\{4 \cdot NG(q), 2 \cdot \max[NG(q), \forall q]\}.$$

The average retrieval rank is then computed and normalized with respect to the ground-truth set to yield the *Normalized Modified Retrieval Rank* (NMRR):

$$NMRR(q) = \frac{\frac{1}{NG(q)} \sum_{k=1}^{NG(q)} Rank(k) - 0.5 \cdot [1 + NG(q)]}{1.25 \cdot K(q) - 0.5 \cdot [1 + NG(q)]}.$$

The range of $NMRR(q)$ is $[0, 1]$. The value 0 indicates a perfect match that all the ground-truth pictures are included in the top-rank list. On the other hand, the value 1 means no match. Finally, we have the *Average Normalized Modified Retrieval Rank* (ANMRR):

$$ANMRR = \frac{1}{NQ} \sum_{q=1}^{NQ} NMRR(q),$$

where NQ is the number of queries.

4.2   Experiments and Results

Our test images are pure scenic images. We collect 38 sets of scenic images as the ground truth. Each set of ground-truth images is taken on the same spot with slightly different camera pan and tilt angles. The size of a ground-truth set varies from 4 to 10. With additional randomly selected images, the database contains 1050 images in total.

Two multi-scale schemes are simulated: spatial and SNR. The spatial scaling factor (both width and height) for each down-sampled image is defined as follows: the n-th scale factor is $\alpha^n (\alpha = 0.7)$. In Fig. 3(a), we examine the effect of different pseudo/input image ratios. Under the same pseudo/input ratio, the more the input images (user provided), the better the query accuracy. For the same number of input images, pseudo images can improve the accuracy, especially when the input images is one or two. However, when input (query) images are higher in number, the addition of pseudo images may lower the matching accuracy. Fig. 3(b) shows the results of using SNR-scaled pseudo images. The noisy versions (pseudo images) are generated by applying JPEG compression with a quality factor of $\beta^n (\beta = 0.4)$ for the n-th scaled version. The SNR results are similar to those of spatial-scaled, with the exception that the average ANMRR is better in SNR multi-resolution approach.

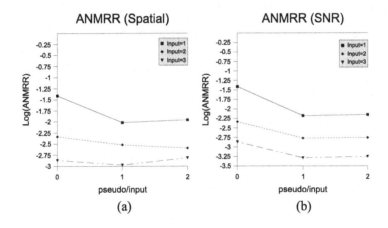

Fig. 3. Simulation results

5   Conclusion

In this paper, the problem associated with multi-instance image retrieval is investigated. The main contributions of this paper are (1) propose a distance-based method to estimate user perceptions based on the given multiple instances, and (2) generate consistent pseudo images when the query set is too small. The first concept is realized by analyzing the scattering of the query instances in feature space. Our conjecture is that a scattered feature implies less importance in deciding the perceptual similarity. The second concept is realized through the notion of feature stability. Our conjecture is that a stable image feature (for a particular image) has similar numerical values (small scatter factor) at different spatial or SNR scales of the same image. Therefore, pseudo images are created by scaling the original image at various spatial and SNR resolutions.

All the preceding concepts can be integrated into one algorithm using the same basic structure – adjusting the weights of features. We examined the performance of our scheme using MPEG ANMRR. Simulations show that multiple instances are helpful in achieving better query accuracy. In the case that the user input set is small, the synthesized pseudo images also improve the results in most cases. There are several parameters and/or distance measures can be further fine-tuned to produce better results.

References

1. Smeulders, A.W., Worring, M., Santini, S., Gupta, A., Jain, R.: Content-based image retrieval at the end of the early years. IEEE Trans. Pattern Analysis and Machine Intelligence **22** (2000) 1349–1380
2. Jeong, S., Kim, K., Chun, B., Lee, J., Bae, Y.J.: An effective method for combining multiple features of image retrieval. In: IEEE TENCON. Volume 2. (1999) 982–985
3. Rui, Y., Huang, T.S., Ortega, M., Mehrotra, S.: Relevance feedback: A power tool for interactive content-based image retrieval. IEEE Trans. Circuits Syst. Video Technol. **8** (1998) 644–655
4. Rui, Y., Huang, T.S., Mehrotra, S.: Content-based image retrieval with relevance feedback in MARS. In: Proc. IEEE Int. Conf. Image Processing. (1997) 815–818
5. Aggarwal, G., V., A.T., Ghosal, S.: An image retrieval system with automatic query modification. IEEE Trans. Multimedia **4** (2002) 201–214
6. Chang, F.C., Hang, H.M., Huang, H.C.: Research friendly MPEG-7 software testbed. In: Image and Video Communication and Processing Conf., Santa Clara, USA (2003) 890–901
7. T.V., A., Jain, N., Ghosal, S.: Improving image retrieval performance with negative relevance feedback. In: ICASSP. (2001) 1637–1640
8. Zhang, C., Chen, T.: An active learning framework for content-based information retrieval. IEEE Trans. Multimedia **4** (2002) 260–268
9. Committe, M., ed.: Subjective Evaluation of the MPEG-7 Retrieval Accuracy Measure (ANMRR). ISO/IEC JTC1/SC29/WG11, M6029, MPEG Committee (2000)
10. Manjunath, B.S., Salembier, P., Sikora, T., eds.: Introduction to MPEG-7. John Wiley & Sons Ltd., Baffins Lane, Chichester, West Sussex PO19 1UD, England (2002)

Representation of Clipart Image Using Shape and Color with Spatial Relationship

Jeong-Hyun Cho[1], Chang-Gyu Choi[2], Yongseok Chang[2], and Sung-Ho Kim[3]

[1] Division of Computer Technology, Yeungnam College of Science & Technology,
Daegu, Korea
petercho@ync.ac.kr
[2] Dept. of Computer Engineering Kyungpook National University, Daegu, Korea
{cgchoi, ysjang}@borami.knu.ac.kr
[3] Dept. of Computer Engineering Kyungpook National University, Daegu, Korea
shkim@knu.ac.kr

Abstract. This paper presents a method of extracting shape and color information from clipart images, then measuring the similarity between different clipart images using the extracted shape and color information. To represent the shape of clipart images, the proposed method expresses the convex and concave aspects of an outline using the ratio of a rectangle. The shape outline is then expressed using a rectangle representation and converted into a chain code. Meanwhile, the color is represented by color values quantized into HSV color coordinate, the location information between the color regions, and the size of the color regions. These color information can more appropriate for representing clipart images, which have a smaller number of colors than nature images. Experimental results showed that the proposed method is superior in expressing shape and color information than previous methods.

1 Introduction

With the increasing use of the internet and multimedia technologies, there is a need for technologies that can automatically extract, store, transmit, and search for multimedia data, as such, image content based retrieval systems have already been developed that can automatically extract, store, and search for images using color, texture, and shape.

The proposed system extracts shape and color feature vectors from the clipart image. The extraction methods that use shape features can basically be categorized as either outline-based methods or region-based methods [1~3]. Freeman and Davis were the first to represent the outline of an arbitrary shape using a Chain Code [4]. However, since a chain code will vary according to its rotation and size, several modified methods have also been introduced, including the Derivative Chain Code [5] and the Pace Code [6]. Persoon and Fu proposed a Fourier transform [7] and the EGFD was introduced in [8]. Finally, the UNL Fourier features [9] are invariant to size and translation, but variant to rotation. Thus, a 2-D Fourier transform is used to solve this problem. As a result, these

K. Aizawa, Y. Nakamura, and S. Satoh (Eds.): PCM 2004, LNCS 3331, pp. 165–173, 2004.
© Springer-Verlag Berlin Heidelberg 2004

methods are invariant to size, translation, and rotation, although the time cost remains the main shortcoming.

The contents-based retrieval systems that use color can be classified into histogram methods and color clustering methods [10~12]. However, these methods attempt to reduce the color information, resulting in a trade-off between the accuracy of the information and the amount of color information. Yet, a clipart image does not involve complicated color when compared with a nature image, thus a more appropriate format of color information is need.

The current paper proposes a new method that expresses the convex and concave aspects of an outline using the ratio of a rectangle, thereby expressing superior shape information than previous outline-based feature methods. And, to extract color features, the proposed system quantizes the HSV color coordinates, performs color labeling to create separate color regions, and calculates the spatial similarity between color regions. As such, the spatial similarity represents features that are invariant to translation, size, and rotation based on an angle of relative position.

The remainder of this paper is organized as follows. Section 2 outlines the proposed system and preprocessing methods. Section 3 describes the two feature vectors, shape rectangle representation, chain code and color, and estimation of similarity. Section 4 presents the experiment results, and section 5 gives some final conclusions and suggests areas for future work.

2   Outline of Proposed System and Preprocessing Steps

The proposed system extracts two feature vectors, shape and color, from a clipart images, saves them in a database, then measures the similarity between clipart images. Fig.1 shows the structure of the proposed system. The shape feature is extracted based on an outline of the clipart image and its conversion into a polygon. Next, the proposed rectangle representation uses the polygon information, which is changed into a chain code and saved as a feature vector in a DB. To extract the color features, the color coordinate is changed RGB into HSV, the HSV color quantized, and the quantized color labeled. The labeled color is then represented as relative color information and changed to a vector. Finally, the similarity between the features of a query clipart image, extracted in the same way as mentioned above, and the features stored in the DB is measured. To extract the outline of shape, a start point pixel is selected in the left-top part of the original image, then sampling pixels are extracted in proportion to the ratio of the image size to make a polygon. The sampling interval is determined by Eq. (1). Unlike human eyes, an image outline includes noise, which can be removed through the sampling interval. However, there is a trade-off, as if the sampling interval is too large, information will be lost, conversely, if the sampling interval is too small, the noise will be not be removed. Therefore, S is decided by τ and the image size. And, since S is decided according to the size of the image, the proposed method is invariant to size. Starting with the left-top pixel, the pixels located at the sampling interval represent the outline of the image following a

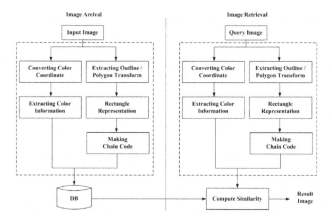

Fig. 1. Diagram of proposed system

clockwise direction.

$$S = \frac{2(W + H)}{\tau} \tag{1}$$

where, S is the sampling interval, W is the image width, H is the image height, and τ is the variable.

3   Extraction of Shape and Color Information

3.1   Shape Information

After extracting the outline and converting the original image into a polygon image, as mentioned in section 2, the proposed method uses a rectangle representation to express the convex or concave sections of the polygon image. Before proceeding to the rectangle representation, a step is included that decides whether a polygon's vertex is convex or concave in a clockwise direction [13]. The vertex is convex when the next vertex is located to the right in a clockwise direction, otherwise the vertex is concave, i.e. the next vertex is located to the left.

Before initiating the steps for creating rectangle representation, a determination is made whether the polygon's vertexes are convex or concave in a clockwise direction. If the first selected point, starting from the top-left point of the polygon image, is concave, the next search is for the first convex point in a counter clockwise direction. From this convex point to the next convex point, a point by element set is then included one by one in a clockwise direction. If the first selected point is convex, the width and height of the rectangle is calculated, where the width of the rectangle, W, is the length of the end-to-end convex points and the height, H, is the maximum length between the end-to-end convex points and other concave points. These steps are executed until all points are included in the rectangles.

To measure the similarity between the shapes of clipart images, a modified chain code is constructed from the rectangle representation using two symbols, one representing a convex rectangle and the other representing a concave rectangle, and a real value that represents the ratio of the width to the height of the rectangle. The real value is used to express the extent of the convexity or concavity. Symbol C is used to represent a concave rectangle, while V represents a convex rectangle. The real value is calculated based on the ratio of the height of the rectangle, H, to the width of the rectangle, W, i.e. H/W. Fig. 2 shows an example of a rectangle representation and the associated chain code. The chain code is constructed from the start rectangle following a clockwise direction and consists of the real value a_i, which is the ratio value, and the symbol C or V related to each rectangle. As such, the chain code is constructed based on an arrangement of real values and symbols. For example, the chain code '1V' in Fig. 2 (b) means that the ratio of the rectangle is 1 and that the rectangle is convex.

The use of a rectangle representation and chain code produces information that is invariant to size and translation. For example, when two shapes are the same, the same chain codes will be constructed even if their size or location is different. However, the information is not invariant to rotation, as the start point will differ for the outline extraction and translation into a polygon.

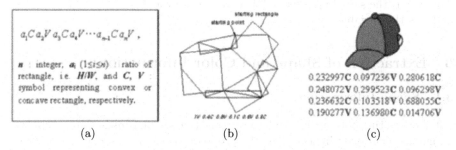

(a)   (b)   (c)

Fig. 2. Example of chain code: (a) form of chain code string, (b) example of converting rectangle representation into chain code and (c) example of chain code

3.2   Measurement of Shape Similarity

Using the vectors in the chain code, the similarity step is as follows. First, the same chain code length is created for comparative clipart images, since the length of two clipart images may be different or the same. Second, the similarity between a query clipart image and the database is measured. To make the same chain code length for two images, the length of the longer chain code between two clipart images is shortened, thereby modifying its shape. In this paper, to make the same length, concave regions are eliminated. However, when a concave region is removed, this results in a loss of shape information, therefore, a weight is needed when comparing with other clipart images. To obtain the minimum weight, d is determined as the minimum sum of the distance between d and each point, a_{k-1}, a_k, and a_{k+1}. The minimum weight is thus the minimum cost to modify a concave region, which is located in the center, and the convex regions, which are located at the end-to-end sides. And, a_{k-1}, a_k, and a_{k+1} are regarded as a positive value (a_{k-1}, a_{k+1}) in the case of a convex region, otherwise a negative value (a_k), and the chain code length can be shortened to calculate the minimum weight between d and the three values. Let A be the weight when removing the region and W_t be the similarity, while d, A, and W_t are defined as follows.

$$d = \begin{cases} \dfrac{a_{k-1} - a_k + a_{k+1}}{3}, & if \dfrac{a_{k-1} - a_k + a_{k+1}}{3} \geq 0 \\ 0 & , \quad otherwise \end{cases}$$

$$A = \sqrt{(d - a_{k-1})^2 + (d + a_k)^2 + (d - a_{k+1})^2} \tag{2}$$

$$W_t = \frac{1}{1 + A}, \qquad a_{k-1}, a_k, a_{k+1} \geq 0$$

This procedure is repeated until the two chain codes are the same length, where W_t is 0~1. As the next step, the similarity between the two chain codes with the same length is measured by rotating the two real values for each chain code, i.e. the ratio of the rectangle and calculating the distance between the two chain codes. Here, the real values of the chain code are considered as a vector, so the distance is calculated between two vectors [1]. As such, the rotation of the chain code is solved by the use of a chain code, and the use of two characters matches the same region, i.e. a convex region or concave region.

Let one chain code be S_1, the other chain code that is rotated to ith be S_2^i, and the length of the chain code be n. The similarity is then defined using Eq. (3), where W_s is a value between 0 and 1. The final similarity between a query clipart image and the database is the sum of W_s and W_t. For normalization, this sum is divided by 2, thus Eq. (4) is the similarity.

$$S_1 = a_1 C a_2 V \ldots a_{n-1} C a_n V,$$

$$S_2^i = b_{2i-1} C b_{2i} V \ldots b_{(2i+n-3) \bmod n} C b_{(2i+n-2) \bmod n} V$$

$$v_1 = (a_1, a_2, \ldots, a_n), \quad v_2^i = (b_{2i-1}, b_{2i}, \ldots, b_{(2i+n-2) \bmod n}) \tag{3}$$

$$d_i = \sqrt{(a_1 - b_{2i-1})^2 + (a_2 - b_{2i})^2 + \ldots + (a_n - b_{(2i+n-2) \bmod n})^2}$$
$$w_s^i = \frac{1}{1 + d_i}, \quad W_s = min\{w_s^i\}, i = 1, 2, \ldots, \frac{n}{2}$$

$$SIM_W = \frac{W_s + W_t}{2} \tag{4}$$

3.3   Extraction of Color Feature Vectors and Its Similarity

A clipart image is translated into HSV color coordinate, which is more precious than RGB. And, the HSV color coordinate system is used, as a clipart image has fewer colors than a nature image and hue is more important than the saturation value. To quantize the HSV components, the RGB colors are translated [13] into HSV quantized values, as in Eq. (5), where the function $int(r)$ converts a real value, r, into an integer value. Our color features are based on the HSV quantized values.

$$H = int(\frac{H}{11.25}) \times 11.25, S = \begin{cases} 0.5, & if S \geq 0.5 \\ 0, & otherwise \end{cases}, and V = \begin{cases} 0.2, & if V \geq 0.2 \\ 0, & otherwise \end{cases} \quad (5)$$

The first step in creating the color feature vector is calculating the center point of the clipart image, O, which is represented by $((\sum_{i=1}^{N} x_i)/N, (\sum_{i=1}^{N} y_i)/N$), where N is the number of pixels and (x_i, y_i) is each coordinate in the clipart image. After obtaining the center point, each pixel is labeled to extract representative colors. If the ratio of the color occupation calculated by the labeling process, is lower than 0.1 or 10 %, this representative color is removed, as it is not important. Next, the labeling process selects a pixel that does not currently have a label, then compares this pixel with the color regions established by the previous labeling process and includes it in a color region where the color values are the same. Otherwise, a new color region is made based on this pixel's color value. This process is ended when all pixels are included in the color regions.

The center point of the labeling color region, O_C, is $((\sum_{i=1}^{N_C} x_i^C)/N_C, (\sum_{i=1}^{N_C} y_i^C)/N_C)$, where N_C is the number of pixels in the labeling color region. The relative spatial feature is calculated based on the difference between the center points of the clipart image and the labeled color region, i.e. $vc = O_C - O$ (of course, an Euclidian distance). To extract an invariant feature, the proposed system then calculates the ratio of the clipart image to each labeled color region, i.e. $A_C = N_C/N$, finally producing the color feature vector $CF = \{f | f = (H_C, S_C, V_C, A_C, vc), c \text{ is integer}\}$. To measure the similarity between a query image and a DB image, the same number of elements CF elements needs to be established, as the CF will be different in each image. Thus, a smaller CF or equal CF set is selected. The color similarity of each element in the smaller CF is then calculated using a Euclidian distance and the subset with the highest similarity among the CF set is selected. As such, the CF is composed of the closest color elements and this procedure is repeated until all the elements in smaller CF are mapped to the elements in the larger CF set. Let the feature vector of the query image be CF_q and that of the DB image be CF_d, then the similarity SIM_C is Eq. (6). Since $1/(1 + CD_i)$ and AR_i are 0~1, the SIM_C is 0~1.

$$CF_d = \{f_i^d | f_i^d = (H_i^d, S_i^d, V_i^d, A_i^d, v_i^d), i = 1, 2, \ldots, n\}$$

$$CF_q = \{f_i^q | f_i^q = (H_i^q, S_i^q, V_i^q, A_i^q, v_i^q), i = 1, 2, \ldots, n\}$$

$$SIM_c = \frac{1}{n} \sum_{i=1}^{n} \frac{AR_i}{1 + CD_i} \quad where \ AR_i = \begin{cases} A_i^q/A_i^d, & if A_i^q < A_i^d \\ 1, & otherwise \end{cases} and \quad (6)$$

$$CD_i = \sqrt{(H_i^d - H_i^q)^2 + (S_i^d - S_i^q)^2 + (V_i^d - V_i^q)^2}$$

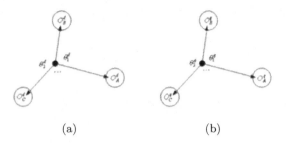

Fig. 3. Illustration of CF set: (a) is database and (b) is query image

This system has no spatial information, but rather uses the color between the labeled color regions. As such, the angle (θ, see Fig. 3) between the regions is calculated to obtain the spatial information, while the spatial similarity is obtained based on the angle between the query image and the DB image, θ is calculated based on the v in the CF, and the spatial similarity SIM_S is calculated using Eq. (7). Eq. (8) shows the final result of the color similarity.

$$SIM_S = \sum_{i=1}^{n} \frac{1 + cos(\theta_i^d - \theta_i^q)}{2} \tag{7}$$

$$SIM = \frac{SIM_C + SIM_S}{2} \tag{8}$$

4   Experimental Results

The experiment involved 880 clipart images, consisting of 172 original images, along with the same 172 images reduced 25% and 50%, and rotated 90° and 315°. To compare with other methods, a Chain Code, Fourier descriptor and UNL Fourier descriptor were selected and the performance results summarized in terms of the *Precision* and *Recall* [1]. The query image was selected from the 172 original images and the performance calculated based on the average *Precision* and *Recall* value.

Fig. 4 shows the system performance based on τ and α. The shape information was extracted by applying a rectangle representation and the similarity calculated by changing . The performance was superior when τ was 45, as seen in Fig. 4 (a), as too much shape information was lost when τ was too small, and no noise removed when τ was too large. The performance of the proposed system was also analyzed when adding a color feature vector. As mention in section 3, the shape similarity SIM_W and the color similarity SIM were both used to determine the final similarity, as illustrated in Eq. (9), where α is the weight and a larger α indicates more significant information for the retrieval system.

$$T = \alpha SIM_W + (1 - \alpha)SIM \tag{9}$$

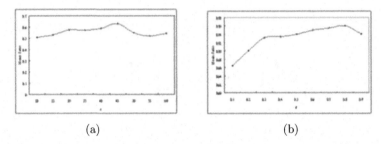

(a)   (b)

Fig. 4. System performance: (a) standard deviation of retrieval ratio vs. τ and (b) retrieval ratio vs. α (when $\tau=45$)

Table 1. Mean retrieval ratio for each method using shape and color information

Method	Mean retrieval ratio
Proposed method ($\tau= 45$)	0.632
Proposed method with color	0.761
Chain Code	0.473
Fourier descriptor	0.493
UNL Fourier feature	0.509

The performance was superior when α was 0.8, but this performance was limited to this test DB (see Fig. 4 (b)). Although the shape information performance was superior to the color information performance when using the same alpha, the former performance was lower. Table 1 showed the mean retrieval ratio when τ was 45 and α was 0.8, which revealed that the performance was superior when we added the color feature vectors.

5   Conclusion

This paper presented and implemented a system that can extract shape and color information, save the information in a database, and measure the similarity between clipart images. The proposed system consists of three steps for shape extracting; creating a polygon image from the original image, rectangle representation of the polygon image, and conversion into a chain code. The rectangle representation provides a more detailed representation of the shape than other outline-methods. And, the proposed method is invariant to rotation based on the use of a chain code. The color information is based on extracted color values and spatial features and is measured using the spatial similarity. As such, the proposed system can represent color, even when the size, location, or translation is variant. The experimental performance was 76.1% when using a combination of the rectangle representation and the color spatial similarity. However, the proposed system is presently limited to clipart images, as applying the proposed system to a natural image is difficult, due to problems extracting the outline.

Further studies will focus on indexing for effective searching and saving with a large DB.

References

1. B. Mehtre, M. Kankanhalli, and W. Lee, "Shape measures for content based image retrieval: A comparison," Information Processing & Management, vol.33, no.3, pp. 319-337, 1997.
2. A. Jain and A. Vailaya, "Shape-Based Retrieval: A case study with trademark image databases," Pattern Recognition, vol.31, no.9, pp. 1369-1390, 1998.
3. Z. Wang, Z.Chi and D. Feng, "Shape based leaf image retrieval," IEE Proc.-Vis. Image Signal Process, vol. 150, No. 1, pp. 34-43, 2003.
4. H. Freeman and L. Davis, "A corner finding algorithm for chain coded curves," IEEE Trans. on Computers, vol. 26, pp. 297-303, 1977.
5. E. Bribiesca and A. Guzman, "Shape description and shape similarity for two dimensional region," International conference on Pattern Recognition, 1978.
6. H. T. Wu, Y. Chang, and C. H. Hsieh, "Coding of arbitrarily shaped objects using pace code," International workshop on Image and Signal Processing and Analysis, pp. 119-124, 2000.
7. E. Persoon and K. Fu, "Shape discrimination using Fourier descriptors," IEEE Trans. On System, Man and Cybernetics, pp. 170-179, 1977.
8. D. Zhang and G. Lu, "Enhanced generic fourier descriptors for object-based image retrieval," Proceeding of ICASP 2002, vol. 4, pp. 3668-3671, 2002.
9. T. Rauber and S. Steiger-Garcao, "Shape description by UNL Fourier features an application to handwritten character recognition," International Conference on Pattern Recognition, 1992.
10. C. Djeraba, "Association and content-based retrieval," IEEE Trans. on Knowledge and Data Engineering, vol. 15, pp. 118-135, 2003.
11. L. Xiuqi, C. Shu-Ching, S, Mei-Ling, and B. Furht, "An effective content-base visual image retrieval system," Proceeding of COMPSAC 2002, pp. 914-919. 2002.
12. R. C. Gonzalez and R. E. Woods, Digital Image Processing 2nd, 2001.
13. F. Preparata and M. Shamos, Computational Geometry, Springer-Verlag New York Inc., 1985.

Automatic Categorization for WWW Images with Applications for Retrieval Navigation

Koji Nakahira, Satoshi Ueno, and Kiyoharu Aizawa

Department of Frontier Informatics
The University of Tokyo
{nakahira, ueno, aizawa}@hal.k.u-tokyo.ac.jp

Abstract. We propose a novel categorization for web images based on their image and text data, and propose new applications using this categorization. We have defined eight categories of images used in web pages, constructed a tree structure for the categorization, and applied Support Vector Machines (SVMs) to each stage of the categorization. We then conducted experiments to categorize a large number of web images, collected from the web sites of 130 listed Japanese companies, and found that they were well categorized with 90% precision. We discuss new applications using the image categories to help users navigate web pages. In addition to this, we examined a correlation with the image categories and the classification of web pages, and conducted an experiment to construct an object from web image.

1 Introduction

Web pages contain text and image information. Images provide important visual structure, however general WWW search engines such as Google do not use them to analyze web page information. As images are often large, they are always discarded before web pages are analyzed, and only their text information is used. So, to analyze web images deeply leads to a new approach to WWW. There are two kinds of information each web image has. One is the contents of them, and another is role which images play on web pages. In our research, the letter is main.

In this paper, we propose a novel categorization scheme for web images, and discuss new applications. Web images have a role and meaning, in contrast to natural images. For this research, we first categorized the roles of images into eight classes, and then applied Support Vector Machines (SVMs) in a tree-structured manner. We performed experiments using 20,000 images gathered from 130 web sites chosen from listed Japanese companies.

We then demonstrated two new applications using this image categorization: image-based navigation of web pages, and image-based summarization. We believe image categories can provide new features for web mining. In order to analyze web pages with abundant images, in all experiments, we targeted only company sites.

K. Aizawa, Y. Nakamura, and S. Satoh (Eds.): PCM 2004, LNCS 3331, pp. 174–181, 2004.

To date, images have been used in search engines such as Google's Image Search, which stores photos and figures from web pages. These images are collected using text analysis only, and retrieved by keyword [1]. We propose a different direction for applications using images, which requires a more thorough analysis of image information. There has been some research on web photo images, looking at improving the comprehension of natural images [2], and improving conventional image searches [3,4,5]. For example, in [5], content-based image retrieval was proposed for image searching, but this offered little improvement over a conventional image search. We believe our work is a first attempt to use various types of web images, including logos, banners, and photos, to enhance web navigation.

2   Categorization of Web Images

2.1   Tree Structured Categorization Using SVMs

Generally, images are classified according to their content, such as into "animal" or "flower" categories. However, in contrast to natural images, images in web pages have both a role and a meaning. For example, an image used as a link can indicate the content of the linked site. A figure that appears in a body of text indicates the content of the text. We believe that these image categories provide important information when analyzing web information. We have attempted to categorize web images automatically according to their roles, using SVMs [6]. SVMs are learning machines that can perform binary classification.

We defined some categories for the roles of images, and investigated images collected from 10 major company sites. From the use of each image, we defined eight categories: "photo figure", "non-photo figure", "main-title", "section-title", "icon for menu", "logo", "advertising image", and "segmented image". While finer classification is possible, we initially defined these eight broad categories, as we wished to perform a layered classification.

Figure 1 shows the tree structure that we used for the categorization. Images are categorized along this tree using SVMs with a Radial Basis Function (RBF) kernel. The use of SVMs results in a binary classification system, so this tree structure is necessary.

Example images corresponding to the categories are shown in Figure 2 and 3. We defined a 'main-title' image as one that indicates the theme of a page, and is often located at the top of the page. Many pages are organized by sections and subsections. A "section title" image is defined as the one that indicates the theme of these sections and subsections. "Photo figures" and "non-photo figures" are images in the body of text that show the content of the text. An "icon for menu" is an image that is arranged as a menu (consisting of a group of icons, with each linking to different content). A "segmented image" is an image that is divided into a number of pieces. At present, we do not use these images.

Global image features, tag features, and contextual features were used for the classification. We tried using only these rough features:

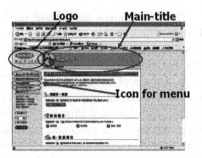

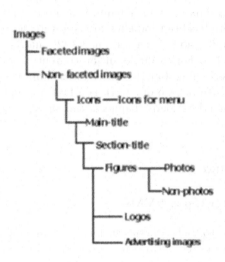

Fig. 1. Categorization Tree

Fig. 2. Example of "logo", "icon for menu", and "main-title" categories

Fig. 3. Example of "logo", "icon for menu", and "main-title" categories

- Size of the image
- Number of pixels in the image
- Aspect ratio
- Number of colors
- File type
- Existence of a link
- Location of the image in the page
- Length of comments added to the image
- Existence of the same image in the same page

"Size", "number of pixels", "aspect ratio", and "number of colors" were used as global image features, while "file type" and "existence of a link" were used as tag features, and "location in a page", "length of comments", and "existence of the same image in the same page" were used as contextual features. "Location of an image in the page" is a value between 0 and 1, with 0 indicating the image is located on the top of the page, and 1 indicating the image is located on the bottom of the page. Thinking intuitively about web images, if an image is an icon or part of a segmented image, for example, it is smaller, uses fewer colors, and the file is usually in GIF or PNG format. If it is a main-title, the aspect ratio

Table 1. Results of experiments using SVMs

Category	Number (%)	Precision	Recall
Figure (photos)	1521 (7.9%)	0.80	0.15
Figure (non-photos)	337 (1.8%)	0.87	0.10
Icons for menu	3345 (17.4%)	0.97	0.90
Section-title	1761 (9.2%)	0.90	0.87
Main-title	233 (1.2%)	0.92	0.25
Logos	306 (1.6%)	0.76	0.36
Segmented images	791 (3.7%)	0.93	0.77
Advertising images	709 (4.1%)	0.82	0.91
Classification failure	9933(51.8%)	—	—

is often large, and it is generally located at the top of a page. Similar patterns of menu-icon images often exist.

We calculated and compared more than 10 features that were thus used for classification. For example, the distribution of the value of "location of an image in the page" for the categories "figure", or "section-title", the distribution is uniform, compared with the category of "main-title" where the distribution inclines towards zero, and in the category of "advertising image", the distribution inclines towards zero and one. The nine features described above result from selecting the features where large deviations appear for some categories.

2.2 Categorization Experiments

We randomly selected 130 web sites from listed Japanese companies, and used images from these sites. The number of these images was 19,324. Among them, 1,500 images were used for training the SVMs with an RBF kernel. We categorized the images into the eight categories shown in Figure 1. Table 1 shows the number of pictures assigned to each category, the experimental precison results, and the experimental recall results. The average precision of the categorization is 0.90 and the average recall is 0.32. The average recall is but. However, precision and recall will be sufficient if the learning classification into the eight categories can be performed for the category "classification failure". Looking at the recall of each category, it can be seen that the images in category "classification failure" should belong to categories "figure (photos)", "figure (non-photos)", "main-title", or "logos". If analyzed using the content of the images (e.g., color histograms) they may be classified with higher accuracy, and the average recall may increase.

2.3 Evaluation Experiment

In order to confirm the worth of information of the classification of the web images based on their role, we experimented of classification of web pages. We used the CSJ index [7] as an index of the category of this web classification.

CSJ index is a service register web pages according to their own categories, manually. The category can be trusted enough for this experiment. We used the classification categories of the base, "News", "Life", "Information", "Search", "Hobby", "Computer", "Business", and "Learning". We randomly selected 15 web sites from listed Japanese companies, and used 560 pages from these sites. Among them, 150 pages were used for training the SVMs with an RBF kernel. First, as the features, we used only the word vector extracted using morphological analysis. The rate of a correct answer of this experiment was 74.9%. Next, we classified images in each page into eight categories described above, and used the classification ratio and the word vector as the features. The rate of a correct answer of this experiment was 82.3%. It was admitted that there was correlation with the image categories and the classification of web data, and this information serves many uses. The advantage of using images is that this classifying doesn't depend on language, and the fault is that web pages which have no images couldn't be classified.

2.4   Applications for the Use of Image Categories

Based on the image categorization above, we can propose new applications such as image-based navigation and image-based web summarization. We describe below three applications we have constructed.

– Menu navigation

A main-title image is a symbol image of a page, and shows the subject of the page. A section-title image is a symbol image of a section and shows the section content, while a group of menu icons shows the structure of a page with each icon having a link to a corresponding page. Many company sites use these images to effectively guide users. One of the applications we constructed navigates users using images only.

Figure 4 shows an example using the icon images for a menu. This navigation page is automatically generated. If one of the sites is clicked, the list of icons for the menu in the site is displayed. From this menu, one may quickly determine the structure of the site. When the user clicks one icon from the menu, they are taken immediately to the corresponding page.

– Page summarization

We can summarize web pages by using categorized images. Figure 5 shows an example using section-title images. A section-title image shows the content of the section. When a page has section-title images, showing them only will produce a summarization of the page. We rearranged the page so that the body text appears when the user clicks one of the section-title images. Thus, the user quickly gets an idea of the content of the page using this summarization, and can read the body text by clicking a section title of interest.

Fig. 4. Menu navigation

3 Constructing Object

There are two kinds of information each web image has. One is the contents of them, and another is role which images play on web pages. When we deal with the contents, it is a difficult problem to construct an object from a natural image. However, if this is possible, since the noise information of the background field can be omitted, the value as information on the images increases very much. Then, we assumed that if there are photo images which are in a near position in company sites, one of the background field or the object field of them is similar in a color or a pattern. It is because that in many case, such photo images are often photographed in same background, changed only the objects. If the objects are for example, heavy industrial machines, the background is changed, but in many case, the objects are similar in a color or a pattern. We conducted a experiment target to these 10 samples of a set of photo images. We compared the hue color histograms of them. If the histograms are overlapped in area beyond a value, the field corresponding to the color area is constructed from the photo image. If the field is located near the center of the photo image, it will be considered that it is an object, and if the field is located near the circumference of the photo image, it will be considered that it is a background. Figure 6 is one of the results of this experiment. The left are original photo images, the center are after above-mentioned processing , and the right are after noise removal. The rate of images was 30 percent the object can be extracted roughly, judged subjectively. The edge of the object was not able to be extracted finely, because only the color information was used. This will be enough if only the color information of an object is required. If the shape information of the object is required, we need

Fig. 5. Page summarization

Fig. 6. Constructing object

to consider a way using the pattern information or the edge information of the image to extract the outline of the object.

4   Conclusion

In this paper, we proposed automatic categorization of web images into various categories, based on text and image data, and proposed new applications for this categorization. The precision of categorization was high enough, and it was confirmed that these categories could be used effectively to realize new services, such as image-based navigation or summarization of web pages. And, we conducted an experiment to construct an object from photo image.

We are now attempting to categorize images more finely and account for more content-oriented information about images, and analyze web data by using the arrangement and layout of web images.

References

1. Sergey Brin and Lawrence Page, "The Anatomy of a Large-Scale Hypertextual Web Search Engine," in Computer Networks and ISDN Systems pp.107-117, vol. 30, 1998
2. Keiji Yanai, "An Experiment on Generic Image Classification Using Web Images," in IEEE Pacific Rim Conference on Multimedia, 2002
3. S. Sclaroff, M. LaCascia, S. Sethi, and L. Taycher, "Unifying textual and visual cues for content-based image retrieval on the World Wide Web," in Computer Vision and Image Understanding, 75(1/2):86-98, 1999
4. Keiji Yana, "Image collector II: A system gathering more than one thousand images about one keyword from the Web," in Proc. of IEEE International Conference on Multimedia and Expo, 2003
5. John R. Smith and Shin-Fu Chang, "Visually searching the Web for content," in IEEE Multimedia, 4(3):12-20, 1997
6. C. Cortes and V. Vapnik, "Support-Vector Networks, Machine Learning," in Vol. 20, pp. 273-297, 1995
7. CSJ index [http://www.csj.co.jp/csjindex/]

Region-Based Image Retrieval with Scale and Orientation Invariant Features

Surong Wang, Liang-Tien Chia, and Deepu Rajan

Center for Multimedia and Network Technology
School of Computer Engineering
Nanyang Technological University, Singapore 639798
{pg02759741, asltchia, asdrajan}@ntu.edu.sg

Abstract. In this paper, we address the problem of image retrieval when the query is in the form of scaled and rotated regions of images in the database. The solution lies in identifying points that are invariant to scaling and rotation and determining a robust distance measure that returns images that contain the query regions. We use the Harris-Laplacian detector to detect the interest points which are then matched with similar points in the image database using a novel fuzzy distance measure. Images with closely matching interest points are further refined using a cross-correlation measure that results in the final set of retrieval images. Experimental results show the effectiveness of the proposal image retrieval strategy.

Keywords: Scale-invariant, Region-based, Image retrieval, point matching.

1 Introduction

Since its advent, content-based image retrieval (CBIR) has become an important tool to automatically search and organize large number of images. In the last few years, scale and orientation invariant features for CBIR systems has been investigated [1][2]. The main idea in extracting scale and orientation features consists of two steps. First, some scale-invariant points, called interest points, are detected using point detectors. Next, some orientation-invariant features are calculated at these points. These scale and orientation invariant features represent the whole image and are used in image retrieval.

Recently region and object based image retrieval has attracted great research attention. Users usually focus on part of the image, which can be represented as the Region-Of-Interest (ROI). The difficulty in object-based image retrieval is the identification of an object under different viewing conditions. In this case, the query might contain objects at a different scale and orientation from those present in the database. Hence, for retrieval, this factor should also be considered in addition to the common visual features, such as color, texture and shape.

In this paper scale invariant features are used for region-based query and an efficient search algorithm based on interest point matching is discussed. Each

K. Aizawa, Y. Nakamura, and S. Satoh (Eds.): PCM 2004, LNCS 3331, pp. 182–189, 2004.
© Springer-Verlag Berlin Heidelberg 2004

region will represent an object at a different scale and orientation. In these regions the interest points and feature vectors are calculated based on [1]. We will use these features to query and improve the retrieval process. In [1] a voting algorithm is used to select the most similar images in the database. The distance between two matched points is evaluated to vote, with the image getting highest number of votes being the most similar result. Our proposed robust matching and retrieval procedure includes two steps. First, the vote algorithm is adapted to a fuzzy distance measure. The matching degree of each voted point is evaluated to measure the similarity. Second, the cross-correlation is calculated to reject some mismatched image and obtain the retrieval results.

The paper is organized as follows. In section 2 the details of the matching algorithm is described. Experiment results are presented in section 3. Finally conclusions are given in section 4.

2   Robust Matching and Retrieval with Scale and Orientation Invariant Features

The objective of this work is to apply scale and orientation invariant features to region-based image retrieval and to find the most similar images with a scaled and rotated region. The scale-invariant points are detected by the Harris-Laplacian detector in a multiple scale representation of image which is built by the convolution with a series Gaussian kernel. In the multi-scale space first the Harris detector is used to detect the robust points in a 2D plane. Then the scale-invariant points are selected from the robust points at which a local Laplacian measure is maximal over scales. The corresponding derivatives at the scale-invariant points are calculated as orientation-invariant feature vectors [1]. Up to 4th order Gaussian derivatives at the point are computed to form a 12-dimension feature vector. Rotation invariance is obtained by selecting the derivatives in the gradient direction.

These feature vectors are calculated for the images in database as well as for the query regions. Our work is mainly about how to compare and find the most similar images with a scalable and rotated region efficiently. The query regions are cropped from the images in database manually and each region represent one or more objects. Querying with regions that are cropped from an image makes it difficult to match its interest points with those in the database. This is due to the fact that cropped regions have fewer interest points, which could easily lead to mismatches. At the same time, we would like a point matching technique that is not computationally intensive so that the retrieval is fast as well as accurate.

The proposed region-based image retrieval algorithm consists of identifying the interest points in the query image and determining similar images from the database using a fuzzy distance measure. The results at this stage are further refined using a cross correlation method to obtain the final retrieval images.

2.1   Fuzzy Measure of Matching Degree

In [1] a voting algorithm is used to select the most similar images in the database. For each point of a query image, its descriptor is compared to the descriptors in the database. If the distance is less than a fixed threshold, the vote of that image in database is increased by one. This will be repeated for each scale-invariant point. The images with the highest number of votes are retrieved as the most similar results. Using this method, the results greatly depend on the selection of distance threshold. In fact it is very difficult to find a suitable fixed threshold for all images. If this method is applied to region-based retrieval, a new problem *occurs* because a simple region usually does not have enough scale-invariant points. It could be very easy to match the small number of scale-invariant points in the region. When there are several images all have the same high rank, it cannot distinguish the most similar one and get the correct results.

To resolve this problem, a matching degree is applied to measure the similarity of each voted point. It is based on the assumption that if the two images are correctly matched, the distance between the matched points of these two images will be very small. The matching degree reflects the real distance between the matched points of images. It is a fuzzy concept to measure the similarity and is of a value in the range $[0, 1] \subset \Re$, whereby 1 means these two points are equivalent and 0 means the distance is no less than the threshold. In the retrieval procedure, the matching degree of all matched points is accumulated and the average of accumulated matching degree is the final similarity distance between current image and the query region.

Currently a simple linear function is used to map the distance to a matching degree:

$$f(x_i) = 1 - \frac{x_i}{threshold} \tag{1}$$

where *threshold* is the fix threshold and x_i is the ith computed distance. In our approach, the common Euclidean distance is used as the distance measure between any two interest points.

With equation 1, the average matching degree *avgd* of current image in database will be:

$$avgd = \frac{1}{N}\sum_i f(x_i)$$

$$= 1 - \frac{1}{N}\sum_i \frac{x_i}{threshold} \tag{2}$$

where N is the number of matched points of current image. From our experiment, it can be seen that the results of using a matching degree are better than using vote number only.

2.2   Cross Correlation

As mentioned in previous section, there are large number of interest points in the whole image. So it is possible that the average matching degree is large enough but in fact the region is not similar to any part of the whole image. This is because the matched points may distributed in the whole image and not centralized on part of the image. These points are wrongly matched and there will be no similar region. While the correct selected image always has a similar region with the query region and the correct matched points will concentrate on that region. So the spatial location of matched points can be further detected to reject some mismatched images. To evaluate the spatial location of the matched interest points, cross correlations between the feature vectors of the query region and database images are calculated. Cross-correlation is a standard method to estimate the degree to which the query region and the region in database image being sought are correlated.

In our system the features are represented by a series of points sort according to the spatial location in the image or region. The cross-correlation between the two series of points of image and region separately is calculated with various delay. The peak value of cross-correlation series is determined as the cross-correlation between current image and the query region. If the cross-correlation is less than a threshold, the image cannot be similar with the query region and will be rejected. Instead of using a fixed threshold, the average of all the cross-correlation is used as the threshold. Cross-correlation measure is suitable for using a region to query a whole image. It can identify a subset from the whole image which is similar with the query region.

The rejection procedure is shown as follows:

1. Calculate cross-correlation series between the query region and the image in database with different delay.

2. Select the peak value of cross-correlation series as the cross-correlation value

3. Calculate the average cross-correlation $avgcorr$ for this query region as the threshold.

$$avgcorr = \frac{1}{M} \sum_i corr(i) \tag{3}$$

where M is the whole number of images in the database and $corr(i)$ is ith cross-correlation.

4. If $corr(i)$ is less than $avgcorr$, the image will be rejected.

3   Experimental Result

In this section some experimental results are presented to show the performance of the retrieval algorithm. The image database includes about 1500 images randomly selected from the standard Corel Photo Library and 300 regions. We manually crop these 300 regions from our database of 1500 images. Each image has about 800 feature vectors and each region has about 100 feature vectors corresponding to each interest point. Some small regions contain only 10-20 feature vectors.

At first a small region without scale change is used to find the original image. 300 regions are tested and more than 290 corresponding original images can be found at the top rank successfully. Others are all in the top 10 results. Figure 1 shows some retrieval examples. It can be seen that even when the region is very small and simple, or there are many additional points in target image, the original image also can be found successfully. The matched points and all detected points are also shown and most of them are matched properly. The calculation is very fast because of the small number of the interest points.

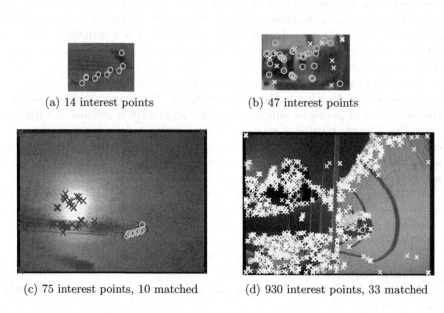

(a) 14 interest points   (b) 47 interest points

(c) 75 interest points, 10 matched   (d) 930 interest points, 33 matched

Fig. 1. Query with small regions. (a) and (b) are the query regions and (c) and (d) are the corresponding top rank results. The numbers shown are the whole number of interest points detected in the region or image. 'o' means matched points and 'x' means unmatched points.

In the second part of the experiment, new regions are formed from existing regions by different scale and rotation. Figure 2 is a example for query using rotated and scale-change region. The query region and top five results are shown here. The query region is rotated in 20 degree and changed with a 2.4 scale factor. It is a simple region and only has 39 interest points. The original image is correctly found and some regions in other scale are also found in high rank. Rank 3 and 4 are two very similar image and region regardless of the color information. Currently the feature vectors are not represent any color information. Another example is given in Figure 3.

Table 1 shows the summarized retrieval results under different scale factor, "1.4","1.8","2.4" and "2.8". A total of 100 regions are used for test and each region is changed with these four scale factors. Some regions also rotated up to ± 20 degree. The performance is evaluated as the average percentage when the original image is present as the first image or in the top five or in the top ten

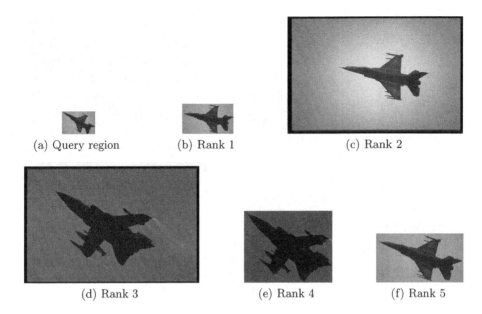

(a) Query region   (b) Rank 1   (c) Rank 2

(d) Rank 3   (e) Rank 4   (f) Rank 5

Fig. 2. Top 5 results of querying with scale and orientation changed region. (a) is the query region, scale=2.4, rotated $20°$, 39 interest points. (b) scale=1.8, 62 interest points, 17 matched. (c) is the original image , 126 interest points, 19 matched. (d) is a similar image, 209 interest points, 20 matched. (e) is a similar region, 181 interest points, 16 matched. (f) scale=1, rotated $15°$, 112 interest points, 21 matched

Table 1. Retrieval results based on region in different scale for all 100 regions. All regions are rotated with $10°$-$20°$ separately.

	Scale factor (rotation $10°$-$20°$)				
Retrieved rank	1	1.4	1.8	2.4	2.8
Top rank	97%	85%	76%	64%	52%
Top 5	100%	100%	90%	74%	66%
Top 10	100%	100%	94%	81%	70%

of the result set. It can be seen that even if the scale is changed up to 2.8, the results are good. We compare our results with the voting algorithm of [1] and the results of the voting algorithm are shown in Table 2. Table 2 shows the results presented in [1] which are querying with the whole images and Table 2 shows the query results of using the same regions and images of our image database. Here only the percentage of results in top 10 rank is evaluated. It can be seen that the results of region-based retrieval is not satisfied. Compared with the results of vote algorithm, it can be seen that the results of our method are better.

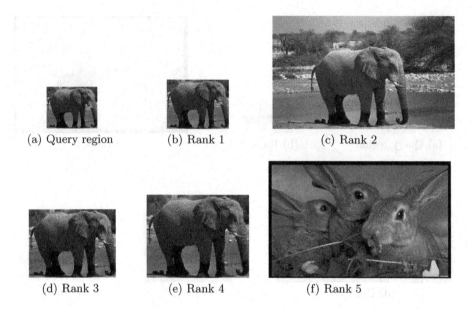

(a) Query region   (b) Rank 1   (c) Rank 2

(d) Rank 3   (e) Rank 4   (f) Rank 5

Fig. 3. Top 5 results of querying with scale and orientation changed region. (a) is the query region, scale=2.8, 213 interest points. (b) scale=2.4, 299 interest points, 167 matched. (c) is the original image, 1761 interest points, 149 matched. (d) scale=1.8, 484 interest points, 137 matched. (e) scale=1.4, 699 interest points, 148 matched. (f) is a wrong matched image, 1362 interest points, 152 matched.

Table 2. Retrieval results using vote algorithm [1]

(a) The results of using whole images presented in [1]

Retrieved rank	Scale factor (rotation 10°-20°)			
	1.4	1.8	2.4	2.8
Top rank	60%	60%	60%	50%
Top 5	100%	90%	60%	80%
Top 10	100%	100%	90%	90%

(b) The results of using the same Corel regions and images in our image database

Retrieved rank	Scale factor (rotation 10°-20°)				
	1	1.4	1.8	2.4	2.8
Top 10	50%	30%	20%	None	None

4   Conclusion

This paper has introduced an initial work for using scale-invariant information in region-based retrieval. From the experiment results, it can be seen that fuzzy matching degree measure can greatly improve the retrieval performance, especially for small set of interest points, because the matching degree is more important when there are not enough interest points to vote. Cross-correlation can further reject some mismatched images. How to obtain the matching points efficiently from very different numbers of points still need more investigation. In our future work, for some objects which has obvious edges, the edge information will be involved to improve retrieval efficiency and region or object will be determined automatically. Furthermore, some more efficient mapping functions for evaluating matching degree will be used.

References

1. Mikolajczyk, K., Schmid, C.: Indexing based on scale invariant interest points. In: Proceedings of the 8th International Conference on Computer Vision, Vancouver, Canada (2001) 525–531
2. D.G.Lowe: Object recognition from local scale-invariant features. In: Proceedings of the International Conference on Computer Vision, Corfu, Greece (1999) 1150–1157
3. Perwass, C., Sommer, G.: A fuzzy logic algorithm for dense image point matching. In: Proceedings of Vision Interface 2001. (2001) 39–47
4. Schmid, C., Mikolajczyk, K.: Image retrieval in the presence of important scale changes and with automatically constructed models. In: Multimedia Content-based Indexing and Retrieval Workshop. (2001)
5. Baumberg, A.: Reliable feature matching across widely separated views. In: Proceedings of the Conference on Computer Vision Pattern Recognition, South Carolina, USA (2000) 774–781

SOM-Based Sample Learning Algorithm for Relevance Feedback in CBIR

Tatsunori Nishikawa, Takahiko Horiuchi, and Hiroaki Kotera

Graduate School of Science and Technology, Chiba University
Chiba 263-8522, Japan,
mountposition@graduate.chiba-u.jp
{Horiuchi, Kotera}@faculty.chiba-u.jp

Abstract. Relevance feedback has been shown to be a very effective tool for enhancing retrieval results in text retrieval. In recent years, the relevance feedback scheme has been applied to Content-Based Image Retrieval (CBIR) and effective results have been obtained. However, most of the conventional feedback process has the problem that updating of metric space is hard to understand visually. In this paper, we propose a CBIR algorithm using Self-Organizing Map (SOM) with visual relevance feedback scheme. Then a pre-learning algorithm in the visual relevance feedback is proposed for constructing user-dependent metric space. We show the effectiveness of the proposed technique by subjective evaluation experiments.

1 Introduction

With the recent advance in the multimedia technology and growing amount of the multimedia data, content-based retrieval of multimedia data is becoming more and more important. Specifically, in Content-Based Image Retrieval (CBIR) system, visual contents of the image such as color, texture and shape as well as text annotation are used for searching the similar images [1]. However, there is much difficulty in mapping high-level concepts of similarity to such low-level image features in CBIR. Concept of "similarity" changes with users. Furthermore, concept of "similarity" changes with user's purposes even if it is the same user. Hence, it is difficult to search the optimal similar picture to a user's purpose by the fixed computer-centric CBIR.

To address those problems, interactive relevance feedback techniques have been proposed, which automatically update the metric space through the users' feedback. They broadly fall into one of two categories, namely weight update and query shifting [2]. Weight update techniques are based on a weighted similarity metric where relevance feedback information is used to update the weight associated with each feature in order to model user's need. Examples include decision tree learning [3], Bayesian learning [4], and kernel based learning [5]. Query shifting aims at moving the query towards the region of the feature space containing the set of "relevant" images and away from the region of the set of "non-relevant" images [6]. Some systems incorporated both techniques [7],[8].

K. Aizawa, Y. Nakamura, and S. Satoh (Eds.): PCM 2004, LNCS 3331, pp. 190–197, 2004.
© Springer-Verlag Berlin Heidelberg 2004

In those systems, image retrieval is considered as two class (positive and negative) problems. However, user's high level concepts are often hard to be expressed with only two classes of image examples. Besides, it is difficult to obtain an effective result from a small number of sample images. Therefore, a heavy iteration procedure in relevance feedback will be required.

This paper proposes a novel relevance feedback approach which can realize relevance feedback visually. At first, a CBIR system using Self-Organizing Map (SOM) [9] is proposed in the following section. Some SOM-based relevance feedback approaches have been proposed [10],[11]. However, those approaches still solved this problem as a two class problem and did not give us a visual solution. In our approach, multi-dimensional features extracted from an image is projected onto two-dimensional metric space by SOM. Then, the proposed relevance feedback scheme is built to the metric space. Since the SOM can express a user's similarity measure between images visually, the user can give evaluation and correction easily on the metric space. In this paper, we also develop a pre-learning algorithm.

2   CBIR Algorithm Using SOM

This section explains a proposed SOM-based CBIR algorithm. The SOM is an unsupervised learning method which can organize classification network based on sample data. In our system, two-dimensional layer of output units are used as metric space, which expresses the relation of n-dimensional reference features. By using the property, a relevance feedback which is easy to understand the metric space visually can be built. The degree of similarity is determined from the Manhattan distance on the metric space, and it uses for image retrieval. The construction of the SOM in our system is shown in Fig.1.

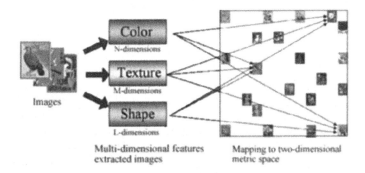

Fig. 1. The construction of the SOM in our CBIR.

2.1 Construction of 2D Metric Space

This subsection describes how to build two-dimensional metric space from the n-dimensional features extracted from images.

Let $\boldsymbol{x} = (x_1, x_2, x_3, \cdots, x_n)$ be an n-dimensional feature extracted from an input image. Two-dimensional metric space has $k \times k$ units arranged on the lattice point. Each of this unit (i, j) has an n-dimensional vector ($\boldsymbol{m}_{i,j} = (m_{i,j}^{(1)}, m_{i,j}^{(2)}, m_{i,j}^{(3)}, \cdots, m_{i,j}^{(n)})$ which is called *reference vector*. The metric space is constructed by the following steps.

(**STEP 1.**) A random vector is assigned to $\boldsymbol{m}_{i,j}(t = 0)$ which is the initial value of $\boldsymbol{m}_{i,j}$.

(**STEP 2.**) The Euclidean distances $\| \boldsymbol{x}(t) - \boldsymbol{m}_{i,j}(t) \|$ between an input data vector $\boldsymbol{x}(t)$ and all reference vectors $\boldsymbol{m}_{i,j}(t)$ are calculated, and a unit with the minimum distance becomes the winner unit (i^*, j^*).

(**STEP 3.**) The winner unit and the neighbouring units are updated by the following equation:

$$\boldsymbol{m}_{i,j}(t+1) = \begin{cases} \boldsymbol{m}_{i,j}(t) + \alpha_{i,j}(t)[\boldsymbol{x}_n - \boldsymbol{m}_{i,j}(t)] : (i,j) \in N_{i^*,j^*}(t) \\ \boldsymbol{m}_{i,j}(t) \qquad\qquad\qquad : (i,j) \notin N_{i^*,j^*}(t) \end{cases}, \quad (1)$$

where $N_{i^*,j^*}(t)$ means a region of the neighbouring units defined with the function. So, only the units within the region $N_{i^*,j^*}(t)$ are updated. The region is considered as a monotonically decreasing function for t, and converges on zero at $t \to \infty$. $\alpha_{i,j}(t)$ means a learning coefficient. $\alpha_{i,j}(t)$ considers as the monotonically decreasing function for t, and converges on zero at $t \to \infty$. In this paper, $\alpha_{i,j}(t)$ was set up with

$$\alpha_{i,j}(t) = \left(1 - \frac{t}{T}\right) \left(1 - \frac{\| (i,j) - (i^*,j^*) \|}{\| (I(t), J(t)) - (i^*,j^*) \|}\right), \quad (2)$$

where T means the number of iterations. $(I(t), J(t)$ expresses a boundary unit in $N_{i^*,j^*}(t)$, and it approaches toward the coordinates of the winner unit (i^*, j^*) with time progress. $\alpha_{i,j}(t)$ decreases in inverse proportion to distance with the winner unit. That is, vectors within a wide range are updated greatly when the iteration number is small. As the number of iteration becomes large, the range and the quantity of update become also small. From the above, similar vectors are arranged as the neighboring units. By setting each image on a unit with the nearest vectors, images with the similar feature become near and the images which are not similar keep away. This becomes an initial metric space.

(STEP 2) and (STEP 3) repeats T times. The reference vectors assigned at random become a systematic map which has continuity among adjacent units. The two-dimensional metric space construction is schematized in Fig.2.

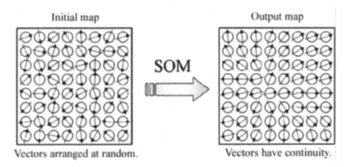

Fig. 2. Two-dimensional metric space construction.

2.2   Proposed CBIR Algorithm

The following is our CBIR algorithm.

(STEP 1) Construction of an Initial Metric Space
    Feature primitives such as color, texture and shape are extracted from a
    sample image chosen from the database images. The initial metric space is
    built by the SOM algorithm described in Sec.2.1.
(STEP 2) Pre-learning
    The sample images, which are arranged on the created metric space, are
    shown to a user. The user confirms the similarity visually, and corrects the
    image arrangement according to the user's similarity subjectivity. The sys-
    tem updates the metric space for adapting to the user's correction. The
    detailed algorithm for pre-learning will be pro posed in the next section.
(STEP 3) Image Retrieval
    The user inputs a new query image. The system projects the query image
    onto the metric space. Then the system selects near images from the database
    images by Manhattan distance on the metric space as shown in Fig.3.
(STEP 4) Post-learning
    If the output image is irrelevant to the user, he rearranges the query image
    on metric space, and the system reconstructs the metric space.

By iterating (STEP 3) and (STEP 4), the metric space iss adapted for the user.

3   Pre-learning Algorithm

In this section, we propose a pre-learning algorithm described in the previous
section.

    In (STEP 1), two-dimensional metric space was constructed as an initial
metric space. In order to adapt the metric space for a user, he corrects the
arrangement of the sample images on the initial space. This correction can be
realized by moving sample images on other units considered that the user is

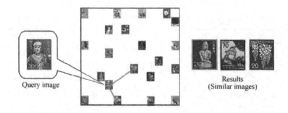

Fig. 3. Image retrieval process.

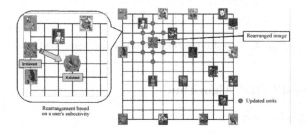

Fig. 4. Image retrieval process.

more suitable. The system updates unit vectors by Eq.(1) so that the unit with the moved sample image turns into a winner unit. Note that the update region $N_{i*,j*}(t)$ will be taken as the largest size which does not affect other units with sample images as shown in Fig.4. The number of iteration $T = 1$. From the above, the metric space is adapted by the supervised training.

4 Experiments

In order to verity the proposed technique, an evaluation experiment was performed. In order to investigate the fundamental characteristics of the technique, in this paper, color feature is used, which may be the most powerful feature of the image retrieval. A color clustering algorithm in Ref.[12], which is k-means-based algorithm in L*a*b* space, was used for extracting color features. In this paper, each average vector of three clusters was made into the representation color, and L*a*b* value of the representation color is made into an input vector of the SOM.

The following is the procedure of our experiment.

(1) We prepared 100 Japanese stamps as database images. The size of each image is 90 × 75. As a preliminary experiment, 100 images are mapped on two-dimensional metric space based on three clustered color values L*a*b*. Twenty images were chosen as sample images so that there might be no deviation (see Fig.5). Ten images were chosen as test images from the eighty remaining images at random. Test images are shown in Fig.6.

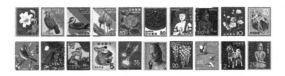

Fig. 5. Sample images.

Fig. 6. Test images.

(2) Three representation colors were extracted from each sample image by the method in Ref.[8], and three kinds of initial metric space were created. Those spaces are created by using only one representation color with the largest area in the image (three-dimensional vector), two colors (six-dimensional vectors), and three colors (nine-dimensional vectors), respectively. Why three spaces are created is to make correction easy by selecting one of spaces. The number of units was set to 12 × 12, and the number of iterations T was set to 1000. The initial range of the neighbouring units will be set to 12, and it will be made to converge on zero at $T = 1000$ linearly.

(3) A user may choose one metric space from three spaces subjectively based on the sense of relevant about color. Then, the user rearranges images on the selected space so that the arrangement meets suitable for user's similarity measure. The specific metric space for the user's retrieval can be built by this pre-learning.

(4) After the pre-learning to (3) was completed, the user was shown ten test images and arranged each test image to the most suitable unit on the metric space. The system also arranges the test images to each winner unit. An adaptation degree is evaluated for each test image by the following Manhattan distance between the unit (x_1, y_1) of user's decision and the winner unit (x_2, y_2) estimated by the system:

$$d = |x_1 - x_2| + |y_1 - y_2|. \tag{3}$$

That is, the degree d becomes small when the system is working effectively. Image retrieval results by the proposed algorithm and conventional algorithm without pre-learning in Ref.[12] were compared.

The evaluation experiment was conducted as mentioned above. Fourteen persons were selected as subjects. As the initial metric space, four subjects chose the two-color space and ten subjects chose the three-color space. No one chose the one-color space. Tables 1 and 2 show Manhattan distance for test images. The average of Manhattan distance for three-color space was 3.9 in 12 × 12 units and it was smaller than the distance for two-color space. In order to create effective metric space, some features may be needed. In the case of test image 8, the

Table 1. The Manhattan distance for 4 users who selected the initial space by two colors.

Subject Image No.	A	B	C	D	Max	Min	Average
1	7	5	3	4	7	3	4.75
2	2	7	4	2	7	2	3.75
3	6	5	4	7	6	4	5.50
4	4	2	2	1	4	2	2.25
5	8	5	6	11	8	5	7.50
6	3	4	3	3	4	3	3.25
7	9	11	13	9	13	9	10.50
8	12	9	10	10	12	9	10.25
9	3	3	6	6	6	3	4.50
10	9	8	10	4	10	8	7,75
Average	6.3	5.9	6.1	5.7	7.7	4.8	6.00

Table 2. The Manhattan distance for 10 users who selected the initial space by three colors.

Subject Image No.	E	F	G	H	I	J	K	L	M	N	Max	Min	Average
1	2	6	8	1	1	0	7	11	1	11	8	0	4.80
2	6	5	3	1	0	1	3	1	0	5	6	0	2.50
3	7	8	3	7	7	6	1	4	4	10	8	1	5.70
4	2	2	1	1	1	2	2	1	0	2	2	1	1.40
5	3	4	8	4	4	7	5	4	1	5	8	3	4.50
6	8	2	3	0	0	1	3	3	1	12	8	0	3.30
7	9	12	5	5	7	5	10	6	6	7	12	5	7.20
8	0	1	1	0	0	0	1	1	5	0	1	0	0.90
9	4	6	1	2	3	4	1	2	3	3	6	1	2.90
10	9	3	9	1	3	9	9	9	4	2	9	1	5.80
Average	5.0	4.9	4.2	2.2	2.6	3.5	4.2	4.2	2.5	5.7	6.8	1.2	3.90

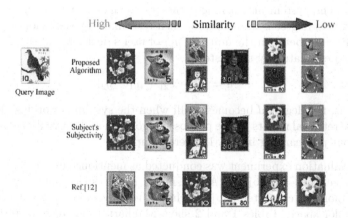

Fig. 7. Image retrieval results.

average distance for three-color space is 0.90. This means that suitable metric space was created by the pre-learning. Figure 7 shows an example of the image retrieval result for Subject H. The query test image is No.6. The top line shows the result by the proposed method. The middle line shows the result selected by the user subjectively. The bottom line shows the result by the conventional method without pre-learning in Ref.[12]. As shown in Fig.7, the similar ranking of the image based on the user's subjectivity and the result image of the system was in agreement by performing pre-learning. This shows that the similar image retrieval is realized by adopting user's subjectivity with pre-learning algorithm.

5   Conclusions

This paper proposed an SOM-based pre-learning algorithm for relevance feedback in CBIR. In our algorithm, users can create their similarity sense visually. The evaluation experiment was performed by color-based image retrieval, and the effectiveness of the proposed method was confirmed. In future works, we will apply the proposed system to other features, and develop a post-learning algorithm.

References

1. Feng, D., Siu, W.C., Zhang,H.J. (Eds.): Multimedia Information Retrieval and Management. Springer (2003)
2. Rocchio, Jr.,J.J.: Relevance feedback in information retrieval. SMART Retrieval System: Experiments in Automatic Document Processing (G. Salton eds.), Prentice-Hall (1971) 313–323
3. MacArthur, S.D., Brodley, C.E., Shyu, C.-R.: Relevance feedback decision trees in content-based image retrieval. Proc. IEEE Workshop on Content-based Access of Inage and Video Libraries (2000) 68–72
4. Vasconcelos, N., Lippman, A.: Learning from user feedback in image retrieval system. Proc. NIPS'99 (1999)
5. Tong, S., Chang, E.: Support vector machine active learning for image retrieval. Proc, 9th ACM conference on multimedia (2001)
6. Rui, Y., Huang, T.S., Mehrotra, S.: Content-based image retrieval with relevance feedback: in MARS. Proc. IEEE ICIP (1997) 815–818
7. Hesterkamp, D.R., Peng, J., Dai, H.K.: Feature relevance learning with query shifting for content-based image retrieval. Proc. ICPR2000 (2000) 250–253
8. Ishikawa, Y., Subramanya, R., Faloutsos, C.: Mindreader: Querying databases through multiple examples. Proc. 24th Int. Conf. Very Large Data Bases (1998)
9. Kohonen, T.: Self-organization and Associative Memory. 3rd ed. Springer (1989)
10. Laaksonen, J., Koskela, M., Laakso, S., Oja, E.: PicSOM – content-based image retrieval with self-organizing maps. Pattern Recognition Letters —bf 21, 13-14 (2000) 1199–1207
11. Koskela M., Laaksonen J., Oja E.: Implementing relevance feedback as convolutions of local neighborhoods on Self-Organizing Maps. Proc. ICANN 2002 (2002) 981–986
12. Asami, S., Kotera, H.: Content-Based Image Retrieval System By Multi-Dimensional Feature Vectors. Proc. IS&T's NIP19 (2003) 841–845

Classification of Digital Photos Taken by Photographers or Home Users[*]

Hanghang Tong[1], Mingjing Li[2], Hong-Jiang Zhang[2], Jingrui He[1], and Changshui Zhang[3]

[1] Automation Department, Tsinghua University, Beijing 100084, P.R.China
{walkstar98, hejingrui98}@mails.tsinghua.edu.cn
[2] Microsoft Research Asia, 49 Zhichun Road, Beijing 100080, P.R.China
{mjli, hjzhang}@microsoft.com
[3] Automation Department, Tsinghua University, Beijing 100084, P.R.China
zcs@tsinghua.edu.cn

Abstract. In this paper, we address a specific image classification task, i.e. to group images according to whether they were taken by photographers or home users. Firstly, a set of low-level features explicitly related to such high-level semantic concept are investigated together with a set of general-purpose low-level features. Next, two different schemes are proposed to find out those most discriminative features and feed them to suitable classifiers: one resorts to boosting to perform feature selection and classifier training simultaneously; the other makes use of the information of the label by Principle Component Analysis for feature re-extraction and feature de-correlation; followed by Maximum Marginal Diversity for feature selection and Bayesian classifier or Support Vector Machine for classification. In addition, we show an application in No-Reference holistic quality assessment as a natural extension of such image classification. Experimental results demonstrate the effectiveness of our methods.

1 Introduction

With the ever-growing advance of digital technology and the advent of Internet, many home users have collected more and more digital photos. However, due to the lack of expertise, the images taken by home users are generally of poor quality compared with those taken by photographers (an example in Fig.1). Automatically grouping images into these two semantically meaningful categories is highly desirable for [11][13][19]: 1) to efficiently store and retrieve digital content; 2) to help home users better manage digital photos or assess their expertise in photographing; 3) to evaluate and compare the qualities of different images with different content.

Finding discriminative enough features and training with a suitable classifier are always the key steps in image classification [11][13]. In the past several

---

[*] This work was performed at Microsoft Research Asia.

K. Aizawa, Y. Nakamura, and S. Satoh (Eds.): PCM 2004, LNCS 3331, pp. 198–205, 2004.
© Springer-Verlag Berlin Heidelberg 2004

years, there has been a lot of related work. For example, Serrano et al in [13] proposed using texture and color features and training with Support Vector Machine (SVM) for indoor/outdoor images. Oliveira et al in [11] proposed a set of features, including the prevalent color, the farthest neighbor and so on; and using Itemized Dichotomizer 3 (ID3) for photographs and graphics. Compared with these existing image classification problems, grouping images into 'by photographer' and 'by home user' is much more difficult for the following reasons: 1) it is not completely known what kinds of high level factors make the images 'by photographer' different from those 'by home-user' although it is easier for a subject to tell them apart; 2) how to express these factors (if we know them) as appropriate low-level features might be very difficult.

To address these issues, in this paper we solve our problem in a manner of 'black box' model. That is, we let the algorithm automatically find out those most discriminative features from some high-dimensional feature space in which the images belongs to these two classes might be separable; and feed them to a suitable classifier. To this end, firstly, we investigate a set of low-level features explicitly related to such high level semantic concept together with a set of general-purpose low-level features and the combination of them makes up the initial feature set. Next, to find out those most discriminative features and feed them to a suitable classifier, we propose two different schemes: one is boosting based in which situation the feature selection and classifier training are performed simultaneously, benefited from its powerful ability in combining weak learners; for the other method, we make use of the information of the label by Principle Component Analysis (PCA) [5] for feature re-extraction and de-correlation, followed by Maximum Marginal Diversity (MMD) [20] to select those most discriminative features which can be subsequently fed to Bayesian classifier or SVM [5]. While the former is very simple, the latter one is more sophisticated and leads to better performance for our problem. As a natural extension, we will show an application of such image classification in No-Reference holistic quality assessment. Experimental results on 29540 digital images and on a systematic subjective image quality assessment procedure demonstrate the effectiveness of our methods.

The rest of the paper is organized as follows: in Sect.2, we present our classification method in detail. Its application in No-Reference holistic quality assessment is shown in Sect.3. Section 4 gives the experimental results. Finally, we conclude the paper in Sect.5.

2   Grouping Image into 'by Photographer' and 'by Home User'

2.1   Initial Feature Extraction

Despite of the difficulties mentioned above, it is still possible to represent some high level concepts explicitly related with whether a given image is taken 'by photographer' or 'by home user' as suitable low-level features. We have performed extensive experiments and have come up with the following low-level features:

* **Blurness:** We use a two-dimensional feature $blur_i = [ib, be]^T$ proposed in our previous work [19] to indicate whether image i is blurred (ib) and to what extent it is blurred (be).
* **Contrast:** At current stage, we use a two-dimensional feature $contrast_i = [p_u, p_l]^T$ to indicate whether image i is over-bright (p_u) or over-dark (p_l).
* **Colorfulness:** The colorfulness of image i is measured by a one-dimensional feature $colorful_i$ [4].
* **Saliency:** We use a three-dimensional feature $saliency_i = [s_1, s_2, s_3]^T$ to indicate the saliency of image i, where s_1, s_2 and s_3 are the mean, variance and third-order moment of its saliency map (SM) [8].

To compensate for the limited understanding of the relationship between the high level concepts and its low-level features, a set of general-purpose low-level features are also used as Table 1:

Table 1. General-purpose low-level features

Category	Name	Dim.	Category	Name	Dim.
	Band Difference[1]	1		MRSAR[10]	15
	Color Moment [15]	9		Tamura[17]	18
	Color Histogram[16]	64	**Texture**	Wavelet[21]	18
Color	Lab Coherence[12]	128		WaveletPwt[9]	24
	Luv Coherence[12]	128		WaveletTwt[2]	104
	HSV Coherence[12]	128		Canny Histogram[6]	15
	Correlogram[7]	144	**Shape**	Sobel Histogram	15
Energy	DFT moment	6		Laplace Histogram	15
	DCT moment	6			

Note that 1) "Sobel Histogram" and "Laplace Histogram" are the modified versions of "Canny Histogram" which use Sobel and Laplace operators to detect edges instead of Canny operator, respectively; 2) "DFT moment" and "DCT moment" contains the mean and variance of the coefficients of Discrete Fourier Transformation and Discrete Cosine Transformation for red, green and blue channels, respectively.

The combination of all above features makes up the initial feature set for classification which contains 21 different kinds of low-level features and is 846-dimensional.

2.2 Finding Discriminative Features and Feeding to Classifier

It is always a challenge to select a good feature set for image classification [10][13]. We propose two different schemes for our task in this paper.

Boosting Based Scheme. Recent developments in machine learning field have demonstrated that boosting based methods may have a satisfactory combined performance by combing weak learners [3][5]. Furthermore, the boosting procedure can also be viewed as a feature selection process if the weak learner uses a single feature in each stage. Benefiting from such cherished properties, our first scheme is very simple. That is, we just use some boosting based method to train on the initial low-level feature set and in this context, boosting performs both feature selection and classifier training simultaneously. To be specific, we will examine both Ada-Boost and Real-AdaBoost for our classification task.

Feature Re-extraction Based Scheme. There are two other kinds of effective classifiers: one is Bayesian classifier which theoretically produces the minimum classification error; the other is SVM which has not only strong theoretical foundations but also excellent empirical successes. However, we can not directly apply these classifiers to our task since the dimensions of the initial feature set is very high. In such high-dimensional feature space, the following two issues become very difficult: 1) the high accuracy of probability estimation that is necessary for Bayesian classifier; and 2) the optimization of quadratic problem in SVM. To take the advantage of Bayesian classifier or SVM, we have to select a small subset from the initial feature set, whose elements are most discriminative.

On the other hand, we find out by experiments that the discriminative power for most features in the initial feature set is too weak, which means a small subset of it might not be adequate for a satisfactory classification performance.

Based on the above observations, we propose the following algorithm to re-extract some more discriminative features from the initial feature set, select those most discriminative ones by MMD and feed them to Bayesian classifier or SVM, hoping to further improve the classification performance compared with the first scheme. For denotation simplicity, we use S^+ and S^- denote the subset of images taken 'by photographer' and 'by home user'; N^+ and N^- denote the number of images in S^+ and S^-; and Σ^+ and Σ^- are the covariance matrices for S^+ and S^-, respectively.

Algorithm 1. Feature re-extraction based scheme

---

1. Normalize the feature $F(i)(i = 1, 2, \ldots, (N^+ + N^-))$ on each dimension to $[0, 1]$;
2. Calculate covariance matrix Σ [5]:

$$\Sigma = (N^- \cdot \Sigma^- + N^+ \cdot \Sigma^+)/(N^- + N^+) \qquad (1)$$

3. Perform PCA on Σ. Let $u_j(j = 1, 2, \ldots, 846)$ denote the jth principle axis;
4. The new feature set is denoted as $F'(i) = [x_1, x_2, \ldots, x_{846}]^T$, where $x_j(j = 1, 2, \ldots, 846)$ denote the projection of $F(i)$ on u_j;
5. Use MMD to select the most N discriminative feature $F'_s(i)$;
6. Feed $F'_s(i)$ to Bayesian classifier or SVM.

Note that by taking the covariance matrix as (1), we can make use of the information of the label in PCA to re-extract some more discriminative features from the initial feature set. Moreover, de-correlation on different dimensions by PCA also makes the subsequent feature selection step more reliable.

2.3 Application in No-Reference Holistic Quality Assessment

No-Reference (NR) quality assessment is a relatively new topic. Compared with the traditional assessment methods, it dose not require any kind of reference information and can be applied when the original un-distorted image might not exist or be very difficult to obtain. In recently years, it has been attracting more and more research attention.

However, due to the limited understanding of HVS (Human Vision System), most, if not all, of the existing NR assessment algorithms are based on the following philosophy [14][18]: "*all images are perfect, regardless of content, until distorted*". While this philosophy simplifies NR into measuring the introduced distortion, it can not evaluate the holistic quality for different images with different content since cognitive and aesthetic information within images is ignored in these methods and all undistorted images are treated as equally perfect.

As a natural extension of our image classification problem, we might solve NR holistic quality assessment from another point of view. Generally speaking, the images taken 'by photographer' are of relatively higher quality than those taken 'by home user'. Thus we have actually got a classifier which separates the images of 'high quality' and those of 'low quality' in Sect.2. By converting the output of the classifier to a continuous value, we get a confident coefficient indicating a given image i being of 'high quality' or being of 'low quality', which can be used as its holistic quality metric.

$$Qm(i) = \sum_{t=1}^{T} h_t(F(i)) \qquad (2)$$

where $h_t(t = 1, 2, \ldots, T)$ denote the tth weak learner of Real-AdaBoost; T is the total number of weak learners; and $F(i)$ is the initial feature vector for image i.

Finally, the quality score of the given image $Ps(i)$ can be predicted as (3) so that it will be consistent with the result given by human observers [18]:

$$Ps(i) = \alpha + \beta \cdot Qm(i)^{\gamma} \qquad (3)$$

where α, β and γ are unknown parameters and can be determined by minimizing the MSE (mean-square-error) between prediction scores and mean human scores.

3 Experimental Results

3.1 Image Classification

We examine our classification methods on a large image database: 16643 images from both COREL and Microsoft Office Online compose the subset of the images 'by photographer', and 12897 images taken by the staff in Microsoft Research Asia compose the subset of the images 'by home user'.

A set of parameters and operations need to be set:

- For both Ada-Boost and Real-AdaBoost, the bin number $bin = 20$; and the weak learner number $T = 100$;
- The number N of features selected in Algorithms 1 is determined by the elbow point on the plot of MMD of the feature $F'_s(i)$ in descending order;
- The adopted kernel function in SVM is the RBF kernel; the scale factor $\sigma = 0.05$ in the kernel and penalty factor $C = 10$;
- The probabilities for Bayesian classifier are obtained by Parzen Window Density Estimation [5]; and $P(S^+)/P(S^-) = N^+/N^-$.

We have performed 5-fold cross-validation on all 29540 images. The testing error is given in Table 2. It can be shown that 1) both schemes are effective; 2) SVM and Bayesian classifier produce better performance than Ada-Boost and Real-AdaBoost.

Table 2. The cross-validation results for image classification

	Ada-Boost	Real-AdaBoost	SVM	Bayesian
testing error	8.9%	6.6%	6.1%	4.9%

3.2 NR Holistic Quality Assessment

A systematic subjective experiment is performed on 379 images which possess different content. The subjective experiment is conducted in a similar way as [14] did: 16 human observers (8 men and 8 women) are asked to rate each image as 'Bad', 'Poor', 'Fair', 'Good' or 'Excellent' on the same computer. The images are displayed on the gray-level background one by one in a random order. Mean human scores are acquired after normalizing the original raw scores and removing outliers. All these 379 images are divided randomly into two sets: one as "training set" to determine the parameters in (3); and the other as "testing set" to examine the performance of our method for NR holistic quality assessment.

The result is encouraging: the linear correlation value between the prediction result and mean human score on "testing set" is 84.7%. The MSE between the prediction result and mean human score on "testing set" is 11.1. An example of applying our algorithm to evaluate holistic quality of different images is shown in Fig.1.

4 Conclusion

In this paper, we have dealt with a specific image classification problem: i.e. to group images according to the person who takes them: 'by photographer'

(a) $Ps = 9.5 \; Mhs = 11.7$ (b) $Ps = 28.6 \; Mhs = 36.7$

(c) $Ps = 65.3 \; Mhs = 70.0$ (d) $Ps = 82.6 \; Mhs = 78.3$

Fig. 1. An example of evaluating the holistic quality for different images. Ps: the prediction result; Mhs: the mean human score. Note that (a) and (b) are taken by 'home user'; while (c) and (d) are taken by 'photographer'.

or 'by home user'. A set of low-level features which are explicitly related to such specific high level semantic concept are investigated together with a set of general-purpose low-level features. To find out those most discriminative features and feed them to suitable classifiers, we propose two different schemes: one is boosting based, in which situation we make use of the cherished properties of boosting methods to perform feature selection and classifier training simultaneously; the other is feature re-extraction based, in which context we resort to PCA in a supervised manner to re-extract some more discriminative features from the initial weak features; then we use MMD to select those most discriminative ones and feed them to SVM or Bayesian classifier. Moreover, de-correlation on different dimensions of features by PCA also makes the subsequent feature selection step more reliable. While the first scheme is very simple, the latter one is more sophisticated and produces higher performance for our problem. As a natural extension, we show an application of such image classification in No-Reference holistic quality assessment. Experimental results on 29540 digital images and on a systematic subjective image quality assessment procedure demonstrate the effectiveness of our method.

Acknowledgements. This work was supported by National High Technology Research and Development Program of China (863 Program) under contract No.2001AA114190.

References

[1] Athitsos, V., et al: Distinguishing photographs and graphics on the World Wide Web. IEEE Workshop on CBAIVL (1997)

[2] Chang, T., et al: Texture analysis and classification with tree-structured wavelet transform. IEEE Trans. on Image Processing **2** (1993) 429-441

[3] Friedman, J., et al: Additive logistic regression: a statistical view of boosting. The Annual of Statistics **28(2)** (2000) 337-374

[4] Hasler, D., et al: Measuring colorfulness in real images. SPIE **5007** (2003) 87-95

[5] Hastie, T., et al: The Elements of Statistical Learning. Springer Verlag (2001)

[6] He, J.R., et al: W-Boost and its application to web image classification. Proc. ICPR (2004)

[7] Huang, J., et al: Image indexing using color correlogram. Proc. CVPR (1997) 762-768

[8] Ma, Y.F., et al: A user attention model for video summarization. ACM Multimedia (2002) 533-542

[9] Mallat, S.G.: A theory for multiresolution signal decomposition: the wavelet representation. IEEE Trans. on PAMI **11** (1989) 674-693

[10] Mao, J. et al: Textureclassification and segmentation using multiresolution simultaneous autoregressive models. Pattern Recognition **25** (1992) 173-188

[11] Oliveira, C.J.S., et al: Classifying images collected on the World Wide Web. SIGGRAPH (2002) 327-334

[12] Pass, G.: Comparing images using color coherence vectors. ACM Multimedia (1997) 65-73

[13] Serrano, N., et al: A computational efficient approach to indoor/outdoor scene classification. Proc. ICPR (2002) 146-149

[14] Sheikh, H.R., et al: Blind quality assessment for JPEG2000 compressed images. ICSSC (2002)

[15] Stricker, M., et al: Similarity of color images. SPIE **2420** (1995) 381-392

[16] Swain, M., et al: Color indexing. Int. Journal of Computer Vision **7(1)** (1991) 11-32

[17] Tamura, H., et al: Texture features corresponding to visual perception. IEEE Trans. on SMC **8** (1978) 460-473

[18] Tong, H.H., et al: No-reference quality assessment for JPEG2000 compressed images. Proc. ICIP (2004)

[19] Tong, H.H., et al: Blur detection for digital images using wavelet transform. Proc. ICME (2004)

[20] Vasconcelos, N., et al: Feature selection by maximum marginal diversity. Proc. CVPR (2003) 762-769

[21] Wang, J.Z., et al: Content-based image indexing and searching using Daubechies' wavelets. IJDL **1** (1998) 311-328

Background Modeling Using Phase Space for Day and Night Video Surveillance Systems

Yu-Ming Liang[1], Arthur Chun-Chieh Shih[2], Hsiao-Rong Tyan[3], and
Hong-Yuan Mark Liao[2]

[1] Department of Computer Sciene and Information Engineering,
National Chiao-Tung University, Taiwan
ulin@iis.sinica.edu.tw
[2] Institute of Information Science,
Academia Sinica,
Nankang, Taipei 115, Taiwan
{arthur, liao}@iis.sinica.edu.tw
[3] Department of Computer Engineering,
Chung-Yuan Christian University, Taiwan
tyan@ice.cycu.edu.tw

Abstract. This paper presents a novel background modeling approach
for day and night video surveillance. A great number of background
models have been proposed to represent the background scene for video
surveillance. In this paper, we propose a novel background modeling approach by using the phase space trajectory to represent the change of
intensity over time for each pixel. If the intensity of a pixel which originally belongs to the background deviates from the original trajectory
in phase space, then it is considered a foreground object pixel. In this
manner, we are able to separate the foreground object from the background scene easily. The experimental results show the feasibility of the
proposed background model.

1 Introduction

Visual surveillance has become an important research issue in recent years. Since
the price of video sensors keeps going down, a great number of researchers have
devoted themselves to the development of video surveillance systems [1,2]. A
good visual surveillance system should be able to function day and night. However, most of the existing visual surveillance systems cannot work twenty four
hours using only one sensor. In order to make a visual surveillance system function well during the night, a night vision sensor is indispensable [3]. In [3], Owens
and Matthies proposed to use a night vision sensor (which is actually an infrared
sensor) to perform monitoring during the night. However, a visual system that
is inexpensive and is able to operate either at the day time or at night is always
preferable. A star-light camera, under these circumstances, becomes a good candidate that best fits our requirements.

In the development of a conventional visual surveillance system, foreground
object detection is usually the first step that requires to be handled. A correct

K. Aizawa, Y. Nakamura, and S. Satoh (Eds.): PCM 2004, LNCS 3331, pp. 206–213, 2004.

foreground object extraction process is fairly important because a false detection will make the subsequent processes, such as tracking and recognition, become invalid. The background subtraction approach [1,2,4,5,6] is commonly adopted in most of the existing video surveillance systems [1,2]. This approach extracts the foreground components by comparing a new frame with the background model, which is represented by a pre-determined background scene. Under the circumstances, an efficient foreground object extraction process depends heavily on a successful background modeling.

In this paper, we propose a novel background modeling approach for day and night video surveillance by using a star-light camera. A star-light camera is able to acquire clear images even under very poor lighting conditions. A star-light camera uses Auto Gain Control (AGC) and Auto Electronic Shutter Control (AESC) to maintain the video level on a fixed IRE value, and therefore it can acquire images with similar brightness under various lighting conditions. Fig. 1 shows the acquired images taken by a conventional camera and a star-light camera, respectively, under three different lighting conditions. It is clear that the images taken by a star-light camera can maintain with a satisfactory brightness even under very poor lighting conditions. However, a star-light camera also has its drawback when encountering a light source which changes with respect to time. For example, if the light source is a fluorescent tube, then a star-light camera will activate AGC and AESC mechanism to compensate the changing lighting conditions all the time. As a consequence, the above mentioned compensation will cause the output video signal unstable. Fig. 2(a) illustrates the phenomenon that the intensity of a pixel over time forms a quasi-periodic signal, and Fig. 2(b) indicates that the intensity contributed by the foreground may replace the signal of the background. Having the above mentioned problem at hand, we are not able to use the existing background modeling methods [1,2,4, 5,6] to solve the problem. Since a star-light camera is inexpensive and has been widely used, we shall propose a new background modeling method to increase its accuracy. First, we shall transform the intensity signal from the time domain to the phase space. Then, a phase space trajectory is used to represent the intensity change over time for every pixel in the background scene. By observing the change of this trajectory, one is able to separate the foreground from the background easily.

2   Phase Space

In the nature, most dynamic systems are nonlinear, and they are usually difficult to be solved by analytical methods. Under the circumstances, the phase space approach [7] is one of the possible ways that can be applied to analyze the behavior of nonlinear dynamic systems. Fig. 2 shows that the intensity of a pixel over time is actually a nonlinear dynamic problem. Therefore, the phase space method can be applied to analyze the change of intensity over time for each pixel. Suppose the intensity value and the rate of change of intensity are represented by the X-axis and Y-axis, respectively, in the phase space. Fig. 2(c) shows the

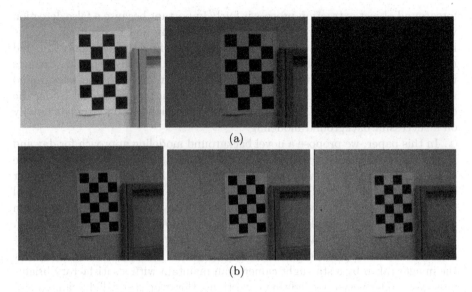

Fig. 1. Images taken by (a) a conventional camera, and (b) a star-light camera, respectively, under three different lighting conditions.

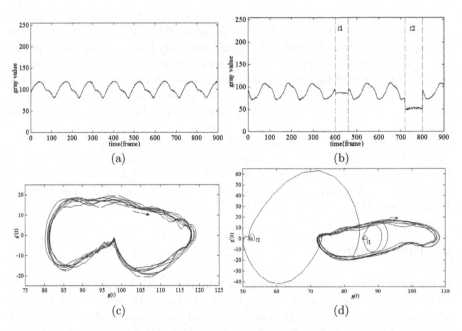

Fig. 2. The intensity of a pixel over time, (a) only background signal; (b) the composite signal that includes background and foreground signals; (c) the phase space diagram corresponding to the signal shown in (a); (d) the phase space diagram corresponding to the signal shown in (b).

phase space diagram that is corresponding to the signal shown in Fig. 2(a). It is clear that the phase space diagram has a particular appearance and trajectory.

It has been made clear that the goal of foreground detection is to separate the foreground from the background. In Fig. 2(b), it is obvious that the background and the foreground are represented by different signals (the durations of $t1$ and $t2$ are foreground and the rest are background). Fig. 2(d) shows the phase space of the signal shown in Fig. 2(b). When some foreground objects appear at the time intervals $t1$ and $t2$, the corresponding trajectories are significantly deviated from the original trajectory. From the above observed phenomenon, it is apparent that the phase space model is indeed a very good tool for modeling the background scene. From the trajectories shown in the phase space, it is very easy to separate a foreground object from the background scene.

3   The Proposed Method

In this paper, the phase space trajectory is applied to represent the change of intensity over time for each pixel in the background scene. Therefore, the task of background modeling is to model the phase space trajectory. For the purpose of efficiency, we apply the B-spline curve fitting approach to model the phase space trajectory.

3.1   Background Modeling

Suppose the change of intensity over time for each pixel is an intensity signal function of time, and the phase space is a two-dimensional space that consists of the intensity function (the X-axis) and its first order derivative (the Y-axis). Since a derivative is quite sensitive to noise, a smoothing process applying to the intensity signal function in advance is necessary. For each pixel x, we let the measured intensity signal function be $g_x(t)$ after executing a Gaussian smoothing process. The measured function $g_x(t), 1 \leq t \leq N$, can be used as a training signal to model the phase space trajectory.

Fig. 2(c) illustrates that a cycle of the phase space corresponds to one period in the intensity signal. Though the periodic durations of the same intensity signal are close to each other, they are not exactly the same. Therefore, a representative period which is the average period of all periods should be decided and then used to represent the period of the signal.

In order to derive the average period, we extract all peaks (or valleys) in a training signal $g_x(t)$, and then use all its constituent peaks to segment $g_x(t)$ into $k - 1$ periods:

$$P_i(t) = \begin{cases} g_x(t) & \text{if } t_i \leq t \leq t_{i+1} \\ 0 & \text{otherwise} \end{cases}, i = 1, ..., k - 1, \qquad (1)$$

where k is the number of extracted peaks and t_i represents the instant of the ith peak in $g_x(t)$. We use $T_i = t_{i+1} - t_i$ to represent the duration of the ith period, and then we calculate the average period from these k-1 periods:

$$T = \frac{1}{k-1}\sum_{i=1}^{k-1}T_i, \tag{2}$$

$$P(t) = \frac{1}{k-1}\sum_{i=1}^{k-1}P_i(\frac{t-t_k+T}{T}T_i+t_i), t_k - T \leq t \leq t_k, \tag{3}$$

where T is the duration of the average period. Fig. 3 illustrates an example showing how an average period looks like in two different diagrams.

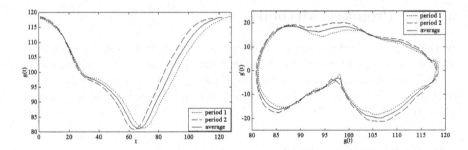

Fig. 3. An example showing how an average period looks like in two different diagrams.

After an average period is calculated, we apply uniform cubic B-spline curve fitting [8] to model it:

$$G_x(u) = \sum_{j=0}^{n+M-1} N_{j,M}(u)Q_{j\bmod(n+1)}, k_{M-1} \leq u \leq k_{n+M}, \tag{4}$$

where $N_{j,M}(u)$ are the jth B-spline function of order $M = 4$, Q_j is the jth control point, and the set of knots are as follows:

$$k_i = \frac{i-M-n}{n+1}T + t_k, i = 0,1,...,n+2M-1. \tag{5}$$

Finally, we use $B_x(u) = \left((G_x(u), G_x'(u)\right)$ to represent the phase space trajectory of any single pixel x.

In addition to background modeling, background updating is also an important task, because the background scene won't stay still forever. In this work, we update the phase space trajectory while a new period emerges. We use the previously derived average period to calculate the new average period and then use it as a new average period.

3.2 Foreground/Background Determination

After the training signal is modeled by a phase space trajectory, the trajectory model can be used in the foreground/background determination process for subsequent signals. Fig. 2(d) illustrates clearly that the trajectory deviates from its original (background) path when some foreground objects cover this pixel. In order to make a correct judgement on whether a pixel is occupied by a foreground object or by a background scene, we need to fully utilize the trajectories of the phase space. Suppose the phase space trajectory of the original intensity signal is $v_x(t) = \left(g_x(t), g_x'(t)\right)$, and the trajectory model is $B_x(u) = \left(G_x(u), G_x'(u)\right)$. In Fig. 4, it is clear that $v_x(t)$ cannot completely fit $B_x(u)$, but $v_x(t)$ will encircle along the surrounding of $B_x(u)$ following the time order. Thus we can calculate the shortest distance from $v_x(t)$ to $B_x(u)$ under the time order constraint. The distance can be taken as the criterion for determining foreground or background, and the trajectory point $B_x(u)$ with the shortest distance can be represented as the predicted point.

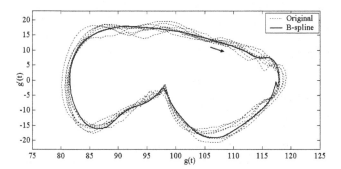

Fig. 4. The phase space trajectory of the original intensity signal and the established trajectory model using B-spline fitting.

Assume that the previously predicted point is $B_x(u')$, and then we calculate u to make the distance from $v_x(t)$ to $B_x(u)$ the shortest under the constraint $u' < u < u' + r$. r here is a given maximum possible change. Therefore, the distance can be calculated as follows:

$$d = \sqrt{(G_x(u) - g_x(t))^2 + (G_x'(u) - g_x'(t))^2}, \tag{6}$$

$$d^2 = (G_x(u) - g_x(t))^2 + (G_x'(u) - g_x'(t))^2. \tag{7}$$

When the distance is minimal, the first derivative of d is zero.

$$0 = (G_x(u) - g_x(t))\frac{G_x(u)}{du} + (G_x'(u) - g_x'(t))\frac{G_x'(u)}{du}. \tag{8}$$

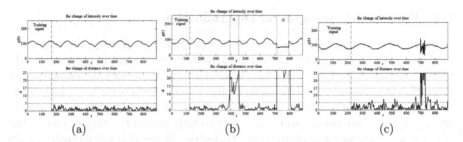

Fig. 5. The distance estimation for (a) a background signal; (b) a synthetic intensity signal, including background and foreground signals; (c) a real intensity signal, including background and foreground signals.

The order of this equation is five, and it is hard to compute. Thus, we use linear interpolation to estimate u. Finally, the pixel can be classified as foreground if $d > T$, where T is a given threshold. Otherwise, the pixel is a background pixel. The physical meaning of the above formulation is as follows. When a pixel is part of the background, its corresponding intensity won't deviate from the original trajectory too far. On the other hand, if there is a foreground object covering this pixel, its corresponding intensity will soon jump away from the original background trajectory.

4   Experimental Results

We have conducted a series of experiments to test the effectiveness of the proposed method. The upper half of Fig. 5(a) shows the intensity signal of a background pixel. The lower half of Fig. 5(a) shows the estimated distance to the background trajectory. We used the first period of the signal as the training signal to model the background trajectory. After the training process, it is clear that at each instant the estimated intensity distance to the background trajectory was non-zero, but very close to zero. In the second part of the experiment, we used a synthetic signal to conduct the experiment. The upper half of Fig. 5(b) shows a synthesized intensity signal with $t1$ and $t2$ durations replaced by other signals (this is equivalent to placing an object on the background). Again, we used the first period to train the system. From the estimated distances shown in the lower half of Fig. 5(b), it is apparent that the estimated distances located in $t1$ and $t2$ durations were much larger than those located in other durations. This means whenever there are any non-periodic signals occurred and some durations of the original periodic background signals were replaced, the corresponding estimated intensity distances of these replaced durations would jump to significantly high. Therefore, we are able to easily separate the foreground from the background by examining the estimated distance change. In the last part of the experiment, we used a real intensity signal to conduct the experiment. From $t = 220$ to $t = 690$, the real intensity signal corresponds to the background. At the duration from $t = 700$ to $t = 730$, a foreground object emerged and it covered the target pixel. It is clearly seen in the lower half of Fig. 5(c) that the estimated distances between $t = 700$ to $t = 730$ were significantly high in comparison with the estimated distances measured at other instants.

5 Conclusion

We have proposed a novel background model for day and night video surveillance. We use the phase space trajectory to represent the change of intensity over time for each pixel in the background scene. Furthermore, we detect the foreground by determining whether the current trajectory deviates from the background trajectory or not. The experimental results show the feasibility of the proposed background model. Since there are many issues in the background modeling, such as waving trees and shadows, our future work is to solve these issues based on the proposed background model.

Acknowledgments. The authors would like to thank the Department of Industrial Technology, Ministry of Economic Affairs, Taiwan for financially supporting this research under Contact no. 93-EC-17-A-02-S1-032.

References

1. W. E. L. Grimson, C. Stauffer, R. Romano, and L. Lee, "Using Adaptive Tracking to Classify and Monitor Activities in a Site," *Proceedings of IEEE Conference on Computer Vision and Pattern Recognition*, Santa Barbara, CA, pp. 22-29, 1998.
2. I. Haritaogul, D. Harwood, and L. S. Davis, "W^4: Real-Time Surveillance of People and Their Activities," *IEEE Transactions on Pattern Analysis and Machine Intelligence*, Vol. 22, No. 8, pp. 809-830, 2000.
3. K. Owens and L. Matthies, "Passive Night Vision Sensor Comparison for Unmanned Ground Vehicle Stereo Vision Navigation," *Proceedings of IEEE Conference on Robotics and Automation*, San Francisco, CA, 2000.
4. C. Wren, A. Azarbayejani, T. Darrell, and A. Pentland, "Pfinder: Real-Time Tracking of the Human Body," *IEEE Transactions on Pattern Analysis and Machine Intelligence*, Vol. 19, No. 7, pp. 780-785, 1997.
5. A. Elgammal, R. Duraiswami, D. Harwood, and L. S. Davis, "Background and Foreground Modeling Using Nonparametric Kernel Density Estimation for Visual Surveillance," *Proceedings of the IEEE*, Vol. 90, No. 7, July, 2002.
6. C. Ridder, O. Munkelt, and H. Kirchner, "Adaptive Background Estimation and Foreground Detection using Kalman-Filtering," *Proceedings of International Conference on Recent Advances in Mechatronics (ICRAM)*, pp. 193-199, 1995.
7. W. K. Tang, Y. K. Wong, and A. B. Rad, "Qualitative phase space modeling of nonlinear electrical dynamic systems," *Proceedings of IEEE Midnight-Sun Workshop on Soft Computing Methods in Industrial Applications*, Kuusamo, Finland, pp. 140-145, 1999.
8. F. Yamaguchi, "Curves and Surfaces in Computer Aided Geometric Design," Springer-Verlag, 1988.

Sequential Robust Direct Motion Estimation with Equal Projective Basis

Jong-Eun Ha[1], Dong-Joong Kang[1], and Muh-Ho Jeong[2]

[1] Tongmyong University of Information Technology
{jeha,djkang}@tit.ac.kr
[2] Korea Institute of Science and Technology
mhjeong@kist.re.kr

Abstract. This paper presents sequential robust direct motion estimation algorithm for the processing of uncalibrated dynamic image sequences. Through the propagation of the projective structures of the first two frames, we guarantee projective information under an equal basis. Since proposed algorithm yields projective information under equal basis, we could directly use these outputs for the metric recovery through self-calibration and motion segmentation using trifocal tenor.

Keywords: Uncalibrated, projective basis, sequential motion estimation

1 Introduction

Recent interesting applications such as virtual reality, augmented reality, and multimedia require the metric recovery and grouping into meaningful contents from the dynamic image sequences. Typically, those sequences are captured without knowing the parameters of cameras, and also there are both camera motion and independently moving objects. Some algorithms start from the computation of the dense optic flows, which requires various steps for the metric recovery. Since direct methods [1][2] explicitly impose motion model in the processing, in particular if we use uncalibrated 3D motion model, we could obtain the projective projection matrices and projective depths at each pixel. These quantities could be converted to the metric through the self-calibration [3]. But, these algorithms require large displacements between frames and more than three images according to the assumption. In this paper, we propose sequential robust direct motion estimation algorithm, which produces projective information under an equal basis. By this, we could directly apply self-calibration algorithm on the processing or could obtain more accurate motion segmentation using geometric constraints among three images - trifocal tensor.

2 Robust Direct Motion Estimation

In this section, we review the robust direct method [4] for the processing of two input images. Direct model-based motion estimation computes the motion field

K. Aizawa, Y. Nakamura, and S. Satoh (Eds.): PCM 2004, LNCS 3331, pp. 214–221, 2004.
© Springer-Verlag Berlin Heidelberg 2004

through the minimization of the registration error using the motion model explicitly. Robust estimation of motion field is obtained through the minimization of the following equation.

$$E = \sum_i \rho_D(I_2(x_i + u_i, y_i + v_i) - I_1(x_i, y_i), \sigma_D) + \sum_i \sum_{t \in N_i} \rho_S(\mathbf{u}_t - \mathbf{u}_i, \sigma_S) \; (1)$$

where the function ρ is the robust M-estimator, σ is the scale parameter of the robust function, and N_i represents the neighborhood of the current pixel and we consider four neighborhoods of east, west, south and north. For the discontinuities preserving optic flow, the last term of (1) is added. We can use various motion models according to a specific application. We use the uncalibrated 3D motion model that is proposed by [5] and [6] to cope with unknown parameters of cameras and to deal with the perspective effect.

$$u(x_1, y_1) = \frac{m_0 x_1 + m_1 y_1 + m_2 + z(x_1, y_1)m_8}{m_6 x_1 + m_7 y_1 + 1 + z(x_1, y_1)m_{10}} - x_1$$

$$v(x_1, y_1) = \frac{m_3 x_1 + m_4 y_1 + m_5 + z(x_1, y_1)m_9}{m_6 x_1 + m_7 y_1 + 1 + z(x_1, y_1)m_{10}} - y_1 \quad (2)$$

where $\mathbf{m} = \{m_1, ..., m_{10}\}$ are the motion parameters of an uncalibrated camera and is the projective depth. Motion model of (2) is valid for any pinhole camera model and even can cope with time varying internal camera parameters. Previous direct approaches [1], [2] using 3D motion model computes the depth through the local smoothing, which result in erroneous flows at the depth discontinuities. [7] shows that robust ρ-functions are closely related to the traditional line-process approaches for coping with discontinuities. For many ρ-functions it is possible to recover an equivalent formulation in terms of analog line processes. Based on this observation, through the second term in (1), we can take into account the discontinuity in the robust direct estimation with uncalibrated 3D motion model. Therefore, we can impose a global constraint for the image motion through the uncalibrated 3D motion model and at the same time can recover optic flow preserving discontinuities. The objective function of (1) has a non-convex form and it has many local minima. We use the Graduated Non-Convexity (GNC) algorithm by [8] to minimize this non-convex object function. GNC algorithm finds the solution by varying the functional form. In the robust estimation, this adjustment of the functional form is possible through the adjustment of the scale parameters. In each fixed scale, a gradient based method can find the local minimum. We use the Simultaneous Over Relaxation (SOR) as the local minimizer.

3   Sequential Robust Direct Motion Estimation Algorithm

Robust direct method in previous section deals with two frames as input. Simple extension to the sequence is to apply the same algorithm to the each set consisting of successive two images. In this case, the outputs of projective projection

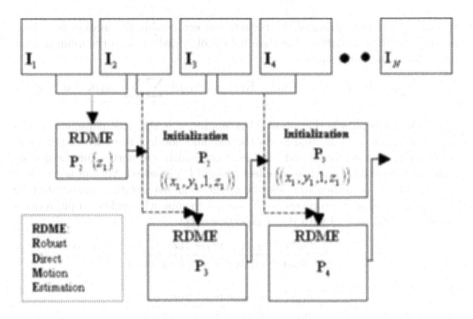

Fig. 1. Overall scheme of the proposed sequential robust direct motion estimation algorithm

matrices and projective structures of the corresponding points have different projective basis, which requires additional steps to have consistent projective information. In this section, we present sequential robust direct algorithm that yields projective information under an equal basis. This is done through the propagation of the projective structures computed from the first two images. For the next frame, we only update the motion parameters. This imposes the minimization process to find the motion parameters with projective structures computed from first two frames. By this, we could obtain projective projection matrices under equal basis in projective space. The overall scheme of the proposed algorithm is shown in Figure 1.

First we propagate the result of previous two frames $\{\mathbf{I}_{i-1}, \mathbf{I}_i\}$ to the next two frames $\{\mathbf{I}_i, \mathbf{I}_{i+1}\}$ for the initialization. Robust direct motion estimation gives projective depth of each pixel of the first camera and the projective projection matrix of the second camera. Also, algorithm compute solution scanning the pixel of the first image. For the initialization, we transform the result into the representation with respect to the each pixel of the second camera. And this is done using the forward mapping and interpolation. This process is shown in Figure 2. We compute the corresponding points of the first image, and then we accumulate this at the pixel of the second image using interpolation and averaging. Finally, through interpolation or triangulation using the computed projective projection matrix and correspondences from the forward mapping, we could obtain the projective structure of each pixel of the second image. Projective structures take the form of $(x_1, y_1, 1, z_1)^T$, which are consisted of the

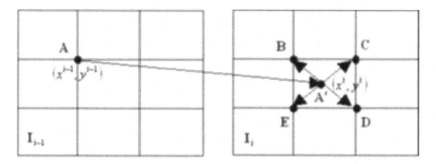

Fig. 2. Forward mapping of the displacement using the result of $\{\mathbf{I}_{i-1}, \mathbf{I}_i\}$.

Fig. 3. Input image sequence: image 1, 9, 13 from total 14 images.

corresponding points of the first image and the projective depth of that pixel. We initialize the projective projection matrix of the first image of the next two frames $\{\mathbf{I}_i, \mathbf{I}_{i+1}\}$ as the values computed using $\{\mathbf{I}_{i-1}, \mathbf{I}_i\}$. Projective depth of each pixel of is initialized as the projective structures computed using $\{\mathbf{I}_{i-1}, \mathbf{I}_i\}$. First two frames of image sequence are processed using the following motion model.

$$\begin{pmatrix} x_1 \\ y_1 \\ 1 \end{pmatrix} \cong \begin{pmatrix} 1 & 0 & 0 & 0 \\ 0 & 1 & 0 & 0 \\ 0 & 0 & 1 & 0 \end{pmatrix} \begin{pmatrix} x_1 \\ y_1 \\ 1 \\ z_1 \end{pmatrix}$$

$$\begin{pmatrix} x_2 \\ y_2 \\ 1 \end{pmatrix} \cong \begin{pmatrix} m_0^2 & m_1^2 & m_2^2 & m_8^2 \\ m_3^2 & m_4^2 & m_5^2 & m_9^2 \\ m_6^2 & m_7^2 & 1 & m_{10}^2 \end{pmatrix} \begin{pmatrix} x_1 \\ y_1 \\ 1 \\ z_1 \end{pmatrix} \tag{3}$$

$\{m_i^2\}$ are the motion parameters of the second camera. After computing using the motion model of (3), we obtain projective depth of each pixel of the first image and uncalibrated motion parameters. These results are used for the processing of next two frames. We could obtain the corresponding coordinates of the second image with respect to the each pixel of the first image. After using previous mentioned method, we initialize projective structures and projective projection matrix of the first image of the next two images. For the next two frames, the following motion model is used.

$$\begin{pmatrix} x_2 \\ y_2 \\ 1 \end{pmatrix} \cong \begin{pmatrix} m_0^2 & m_1^2 & m_2^2 & m_8^2 \\ m_3^2 & m_4^2 & m_5^2 & m_9^2 \\ m_6^2 & m_7^2 & 1 & m_{10}^2 \end{pmatrix} \begin{pmatrix} x_1 \\ y_1 \\ 1 \\ z_1 \end{pmatrix}$$

$$\begin{pmatrix} x_3 \\ y_3 \\ 1 \end{pmatrix} \cong \begin{pmatrix} m_0^3 & m_1^3 & m_2^3 & m_8^3 \\ m_3^3 & m_4^3 & m_5^3 & m_9^3 \\ m_6^3 & m_7^3 & 1 & m_{10}^3 \end{pmatrix} \begin{pmatrix} x_1 \\ y_1 \\ 1 \\ z_1 \end{pmatrix} \tag{4}$$

Projective structures of the second image at the highest pyramid level are sub-sampled from the original image level. Uncalibrated motion parameters of the highest pyramid level are set using the motion parameters propagation of [4] in reverse. But, this algorithm has the following shortcomings. We process all the sequence with respect to the first frame, and there are no mechanisms for the effective use of the redundant information in the sequence. Also, by experimental results we found that robust direct method with only update of motion parameters gives larger registration error than update both the motion parameters and the projective depth at each pixel. This is due to the fact that we start the minimization with the initialization of no motion between two images. Due to the initialization from the assumption of no motion between two images, though we know the projective structure of each pixel of the first image, the minimization starts at nearly equal distance from the ground truth as we process first two frames of the sequence where we do not know the projective depth of each pixel and motion parameters. One possible method is to use motion model in time domain such as the constant motion or linear motion, which might shift the starting position of the minimization more closely to the ground truth. Though proposed algorithm gives slightly large error, it could be effectively used in the processing of the sequence by applying this algorithm to the sub-group of the sequence.

4   Experimental Results

Figure 3 shows four images from original 14 images. They are acquired with hand-held camcorder where two objects move independently relative to the motion of the camera. Figure 4 shows the original difference image and the compensated difference image by proposed sequential algorithm. We used the same settings of the parameters in the sequence. Proposed method well compensates only the dominant motion of the camera. From these compensated difference images, we could start motion segmentation. Figure 5 shows the original sequence containing calibration box. Figure 6 represents the absolute mean difference per pixel of the original image, off-line, and on-line method. Off-line method applies robust direct method to the successive two images. Proposed sequential method gives slightly larger error than the off-line method. Transferred pixel errors by trifocal tensor are shown in Table 1. Trifocal tensor is computed using the projective projection matrices of first, i-th, and (i+1)-th camera. 48 points are selected

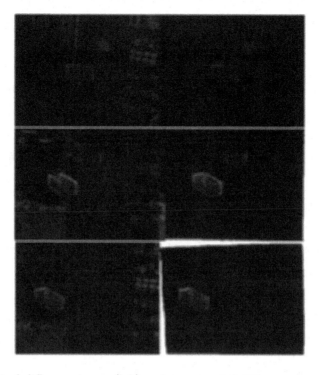

Fig. 4. Original difference image (left) and compensated difference image (right) by proposed sequential robust direct method.

Fig. 5. Input image sequence: image 1, 7, 10 from total 11 images

from the cross points of the calibration box for the computation of errors. As sequence goes on the registration errors accumulate, which results in the large transfer errors at the end of the sequence. These outputs could directly be used in the motion segmentation using trifocal tensor and metric recovery through self-calibration. For this goal, we must reduce the compensated residual error comparable to the off-line method. One possible method is to use the motion model in time do-main such as constant motion or linear motion.

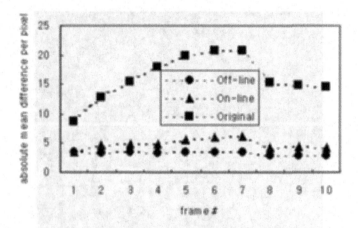

Fig. 6. Absolute mean difference per pixel by sequential robust direct method and off-line processing of the successive two images.

Table 1. Transfer pixel errors by trifocal tensor of images (1,i,i+1)

i	Transferred error (mean/std)		Original displacement (mean/std)		Relative Error(%)	
	x	y	x	y	x	y
2	0.202/0.166	0.205/0.127	1.487/0.448	0.391/0.302	13.6	52.5
3	0.542/0.189	0.207/0.161	2.796/0.874	0.855/0.682	19.4	24.2
4	0.839/0.264	0.713/0.302	4.72/1.345	1.498/1.121	17.7	47.6
5	1.263/0.373	1.426/1.08	7.388/2.115	2.410/1.802	17.1	59.1
6	1.224/0.289	2.799/2.00	10.52/2.989	3.127/2.415	11.6	89.5
7	2.02/0.487	3.92/2.97	14.21/3.839	3.621/2.623	14.2	108.2
8	5.33/1.31	3.87/2.84	16.04/4.298	3.925/2.709	33.2	98.6
9	9.56/2.30	4.12/2.62	17.69/4.723	4.331/2.967	54.6	95.1

5   Conclusion

We have presented sequential robust direct method for the processing of the general sequence containing independently moving objects under moving camera. For this, we used uncalibrated 3D motion model in robust direct method. Proposed algorithm pro-duces projective information under an equal basis, which provides many opportunities for the efficient processing of the sequence. Currently we are considering the use of motion model in time domain and the smart integration of the trifocal tensor in the processing for the improvement of the proposed algorithm.

References

1. Szeliski, R. & J. Coughlan: Spline-Based Image Registration, International Journal of Computer Vision, (1997) 199-218
2. Sawhney, H.S. & Ayer, S.: Compact representations of videos through dominant and multiple motion estimation, IEEE Transactions on Pattern Analysis and Machine Intelligence, (1996) 814-830
3. Pollefeys, M., Koch, R. & Van Gool, L.: Self-calibration and metric reconstruction in spite of varying and unknown camera paramters, Sixth International Conference on Computer Vision, (1998) 90-95
4. Ha, J.E. & Kweon, I.S.: Robust direct motion estimation considering discontinuity, Fourth Asian Conference on Computer Vision (2000)
5. Hartley, R., Gupta, R.& Chang, T.: Stereo from uncalibrated cameras, IEEE Conference on Computer Vison and Pattern Recognition, (1992) 761-764
6. Faugeras, O.D.: What can be seen in three dimensions with an uncalibrated stereo rig?, Second European Conference on Computer Vision, (1992) 563-578
7. Black, M.J. & Rangarajan, A.: On the unification of line processes, outlier rejection, and robust statistics with applications in early vision, International Journal of Computer Vision, (1996) 57-91
8. Blake, A. & Zisserman,A.: Visual Reconstruction, The MIT Press, (1987)

Generation of 3D Urban Model Using Cooperative Hybrid Stereo Matching

Dong-Min Woo[1], Howard Schultz[2], Young-Kee Jung[3], and Kyu-Won Lee[4]

[1] Myongji University, Yongin, 449-728, Korea
dmwoo@mju.ac.kr
[2] University of Massachusetts, Amherst, MA 01003, USA
hschultz@cs.umass.edu
[3] Honam University, Gwangju, 506-090, Korea
ykjung@honam.ac.kr
[4] Taejon University, Taejon, 300-716, Korea
kwlee@dju.ac.kr

Abstract. We present a new hybrid stereo matching technique in terms of the co-operation of area-based stereo and feature-based stereo to build 3D site model from urban images. The core of our technique is that feature matching is carried out by the reference of the disparity evaluated by area-based stereo. Since the reference of the disparity can significantly reduce the number of feature matching combinations, feature matching error can be drastically minimized. One requirement of the disparity to be referenced is that it should be reliable to be used in feature matching. To measure the reliability of the disparity, in this paper, we employ the self-consistency of the disparity. Our suggested technique is applied to the detection of 3D line segments by 2D line matching using our hybrid stereo matching, which can be efficiently utilized in the generation of the rooftop model from urban images. Since occlusions are occurred around the outlines of buildings, we use multi-image stereo scheme by fusing 3D line segments extracted from several pairs of stereo images. The suggested method is evaluated on Avenches data set of Ascona aerial images. Experimental results indicate that the extracted 3D line segments have an average error of 0.5m and can be efficiently used to the construction of 3D site models using a simple 3D line grouping.

Keywords: Stereo matching, 3D site model, urban images

1 Introduction

3D site model of urban environment is one of the most useful multimedia data. It has been traditionally utilized in urban change detection, environmental preservation. Recently, its usage is expanding to new applications, which include virtual city touring and simulation of urban development. An efficient technique to generate 3D site model of broad urban area is stereo processing of aerial or satellite images. There has been a significant body of research in stereo matching technique, which is broadly divided into area-based method [1,2] and feature-based method [3,4].

K. Aizawa, Y. Nakamura, and S. Satoh (Eds.): PCM 2004, LNCS 3331, pp. 222–229, 2004.

Area-based method is especially useful in the generation of 3D natural terrain model, since it can generate dense elevation map for each grid in the area. The current state of area-base method has been advanced to achieve a very precise terrain model. However, this method is not very successful in the site model generation, since it generates smoothed elevation around the boundaries or edges of buildings by the nature of correlation or SSD(Sum of Squared Difference) necessarily incorporated in the area-based stereo matching. Feature-based method might be basically effective in the site model generation, since the matching process is based on the features such as corner point, edge, line segment, zero-crossing, etc. Those features can be core elements constructing building rooftops. One of difficulties in the feature-based stereo matching of complex urban images is a increasing number of possible feature matching combination, which may lead to the high possibility of false feature matching, as well as significant computational cost.

In this context, there has been a necessity for a research on how to incorporate area-based method with feature-based method. This type of hybrid stereo matching method [5,6] has been studied mainly as the combination of area-based and feature-based methods. These combinational hybrid methods assume that features should be similarly extracted in both images, which can be hardly achieved in the real situation. Also, perspective distortion [2] cannot be avoided, since correlation window or SSD window needs to be used in the stereo matching process. As a result, an accurate disparity cannot be obtained in the boundaries of building with this approach. To resolve these problems, in this paper, we suggest a new hybrid stereo matching technique, which utilizes area-based method and feature-based method in a cooperative fashion. The core of this cooperation is that the feature matching is directed by the reliable disparity evaluated by area-based method. Since possible matched features are selected by the reference of the disparity of area-based method, the number of possible matched feature pairs can be drastically reduced, and the accurate feature matching can be achieved. In this paper, we use a line segment as the feature. Our hybrid stereo matching technique can process the accurate and rapid matching of 2D line segments. Matching result of 2D line segments constructs 3D line segments which can be key elements to build 3D model.

2   Cooperative Hybrid Stereo Matching

2.1   Disparity Reference

Our hybrid stereo matching scheme is based on the reference of disparity to the line matching. A line segment in the real world is appeared on the different position in both stereo images. If we use disparities on the line segment in one image, we can easily search the matched line segment in the other image. Fig. 1 shows the principle of disparity reference. If a line segment A of the reference image is translated by the disparities d_1 and d_2 along epipolar lines, it is approaching to a line segment B of target image. As the disparities d_1 and d_2 are close to the real values, the matching of line segments A and B are obviously carried out.

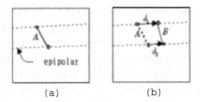

Fig. 1. Disparity reference in feature matching: (a) reference (b) target

2.2   Reliability Assessment of Disparity

The preliminary requirement for the disparity is its reliability sufficiently to be referenced. However the disparity evaluated by area-based stereo can be an outlier due to the matching error. In this context we evaluate the reliability of the disparity before it is used in feature matching.

To measure the reliability of the disparity, we employ the concept of self-consistency [7]. The original idea is based on the fact that two elevations evaluated by swapping the role of the reference and the target in the stereo matching process should be the same if the matches are correct. Therefore, the difference of the elevations provides a measure of consistency and reliability. In this paper, we extend this idea to the image space self-consistency [8] to determine the reliability of disparity.

3   3D Line Extraction

3.1   2D Line Detection

To detect 2D lines from epipolar image, edge detection is carried out first and then 2D lines are formed from edges. We employed Canny edge detector, since it is optimal according to the criteria where edge is defined and comes up with thin edges. To obtain 2D line segment, we use Boldt algorithm [9] based on token grouping. The method extracts an basic line element, token, in terms of the properties of line a and construct 2D line using grouping process. It is efficient in detecting 2D lines of large structure appeared in urban image.

3.2   2D Line Matching

2D lines detected in epipolar resampled images are matched by the disparity reference. Fig. 2 show how 2D line matching is carried out. If a line segment A in the reference image has n reliable disparities $d_1, d_2, \ldots, d_n$ at the points $a_1, a_2, \ldots, a_n$, these n points can be translated into the points in the target image by Eq. 1.

$$a_i^{'} = a_i + d_i \tag{1}$$

The line A' from a'_1 through $a'_2, \ldots$ to a'_n cannot be a straight line, since disparity has an error even though it is reliable. However, the points constructing the line A' are very adjacent to the line B in the target image frame. The errors between points in line A' and B are defined as Euclidean distance, as shown in Eq. 2.

$$e_i = |b_i - a'_i| \tag{2}$$

To define the criteria to match line A and line B, we calculate the average of the error shown in Eq. 2 and normalize it with regard to the length of the line, $|b|$. Thus, the matching criteria can be defined as Eq. 3.

$$J = \frac{1}{|b|n} \sum_{i=1}^{n} e_i \tag{3}$$

To match the lines in the reference and target images, we compare the calculated value of J with the threshold and determine the matching pair of lines. However, when we find the matched line we should not calculate J for all lines in the target image. Since the reliable disparity has a very small error, we can limit the possible matched lines in the target image by using only starting and ending points. With this scheme, 2D line matching can be promptly carried out.

3.3 Improvement of 2D Line Matching

One of difficulties in the feature-based stereo is that the same feature cannot be always similarly appeared in the reference and target image. As for the line feature matching, a line in the reference image can be appeared as disconnected or not existent in the target image. If a line is appeared in only one of images, our hybrid scheme does not generate false matched line and come up with no matched pair instead. If a line is appeared as disconnected and partially existent, we can improve the 2D matching result in terms of line extension and line linking. Line extension is for the partially appeared line in one image. As shown in Fig. 2, the part of line A is not detected. Line A from a_1 to a_n is matched to the part of line B from b_1 to b_n. The complete line B points from b_0 to b_n. This case we can extend line A to a_0, because the extended line segment from a_0 to a_1 can correspond to the part of line segment B from b_0 to b_1. The disconnected line is a frequently occurred case in the line. In this case, if two lines in one image

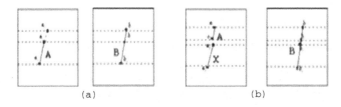

(a)   (b)

Fig. 2. Extension and linking of 2D line segment matching: (a) line extension (b) line linking

are matched to one line in the other image, we can connect two lines into one by line linking. Two lines A and X in the reference image are matched to the portions of one line B in the target image. Then lines A and X in the reference image are linked to form a new line pointing form a_1 to a_4, and this news line are matched to the whole line of B from b_1 to b_4.

3.4   3D Line Generation

After performing line extension and linking to the 2D line matching result, we obtain the improved 2D line matching result. The application of triangulation calculation to the starting points and the ending points of the matched lines come up with 3D line segment. In this paper, the generated 3D line segments can be also linked again using 3D perceptual grouping.

For 3D line linking, we represent 3D line segments in vector form. Then the direction of two vectors is calculated by inner product of two vectors over the product of the magnitudes of two vectors. If the direction of two vectors is similar and their points are adjacently aligned, we link two vectors into one vector, which is appeared as a linked 3D line segment.

4   Experimental Results

The experimental environment is set up, based on Ascona aerial images of Avenches area. Since Avenches data include 3D models of terrain and build-ings, these data can be efficiently utilized for the analysis and the accuracy assessment of the suggested hybrid scheme. In this experiment, four images are used, as shown in Fig. 3.

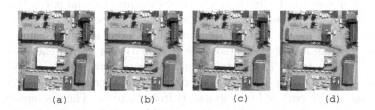

(a)   (b)   (c)   (d)

Fig. 3. Four Ascona aerial images used in the experiment: (a) image A (b)image B (c)image C (d)image D

Area-based stereo matching is performed on the epipolar resampled images. We obtain two disparity maps by exchanging the roles of reference and target images. Fig. 4 (a) shows the disparity map D_{AB} by applying area-based stereo to reference image A and target image B. Fig. 4 (b) is the result of the disparity map D_{BA} by exchanging the roles of reference and target images. [t] In the suggested hybrid stereo, only reliable disparities should be referenced to the feature matching. To measure the reliability, we calculate the difference of D_{AB}

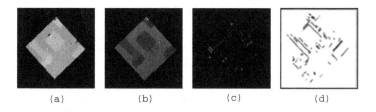

Fig. 4. Disparity maps and their reliability assessment: (a)D_{AB} (b)D_{BA} (c)self-consistency (d)reliable position

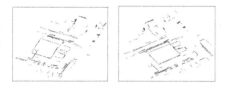

Fig. 5. Two views of fused 3D line segments

and D'_{AB}, the resampled D_{BA} into reference frame A. Fig. 4 (c) represents this difference in gray scale image, where the dark part shows a high consistency or reliability in disparity. In this experiment, we set the threshold to be 1, which means the disparity difference within 1 pixel can be determined as reliable. Fig. 4 (d) represents the position on the extracted line segment, where the disparity is determined as reliable by self-consistency. Dark lines show the position with high self-consistency.

By the nature of the binocular stereo processing, the occlusion should occur around the boundaries of building. To obtain all the 3D line segments in this experiment, in this paper, we use multi stereo processing by the fusion of 3D lines extracted from 4 images A, B, C and D, each of which is acquired 45 degrees apart each other. All 3D lines extracted from image pairs AB, BC, CD, DA are fused and in this process we perform a grouping of similar 3D line segments. Similarity of 3D line segments are calculated by the average distance. The grouped 3D lines are evaluated as a single 3D line in terms of least squared error. Fig. 5 represents the rendering of fused 3D line segments from 2 viewpoints. Table 1 shows the comparison between the extracted 3D line segments and the ground truth line segments. To represent the quantitative accuracy of 3D line segments extracted by our suggested scheme, we obtain the error by calculating the average distance between the extracted 3D line segments and the ground truth line segments as in Eq. 4.

$$E = \frac{\sum \frac{e_{1i}+e_{2i}}{2} \times d_i}{\sum b_i} \qquad (4)$$

In Eq. 4, e_{1i} is the distance from the starting point of line segment i to the ground truth 3D line, while e_{2i} is the distance from the end point of line segment i to the

Table 1. Average errors of detected 3D line segments (unit: meter)

image pair	suggested hybrid method	area-based method
AB	0.8827	2.1534
BC	0.4664	2.1679
CD	0.6138	2.1290
DA	0.4738	2.0904
Fusion result	0.5796	N / A

ground truth 3D line and d_i is the length of line segment i. Error analysis show that 3D lines from image pair BC are most accurate with the average error of 0.47m and that 3D lines from image pair AB have a little more errors relatively with the average error of 0.88m. The fused 3D lines from 4 pairs of images have the average error of 0.58m, which is similar to the average error of 3D lines from 4 pairs of images. To verify the effectiveness of the suggested hybrid stereo, we compare our result with elevation obtained by area-based stereo. On the boundaries of the buildings, i.e. lines of 3D model, elevations have average errors of 2.0m - 2.2m, which are 4 times more than our errors. Furthermore, area-based method has even more errors near the boundaries of the builds, because the nature of its matching by correlation or SSD.

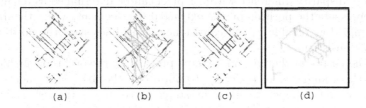

(a)   (b)   (c)   (d)

Fig. 6. 3D grouping to obtain the rooftop model: (a) corner points (b) hypothesis (c) rooftop (d) 3D view

To show the applicability of our suggested method to the site model, we try an experimental 3D model generation by using a fundamental 3D grouping scheme. The used 3D grouping scheme assumes that the rooftop consists of rectangular elements. Under this very limited assumption, we carry out 3D grouping by junction extraction and rooftop generation based on properties of building and hypothesis generation. Fig. 6 (a) and (b) show junctions detected from 3D lines and the hypothesis of the rooftop. Each hypothesis is verified by the properties of rooftop we define, and the building rooftop is generated as in Fig. 6 (c). From the 3D rendering of rooftop, shown in Fig. 6 (d), we find that the suggested hybrid stereo can be very effectively applied to the 3D modeling of urban area.

5 Conclusions

In this paper we suggest a new hybrid stereo matching technique. We utilize area-based stereo and feature-based stereo in a cooperative fashion, while other hybrid scheme is constructed in a combinational way. The core of our scheme is that the feature matching is referenced by the disparity in area-based stereo. With the scheme, we can extract 3D lines accurately and promptly. To show the applicability of our suggested method to the generation of 3D model of urban area, we perform the experiment on multi-image hybrid stereo system and build 3D rooftop model using a fundamental 3D grouping scheme. Since the generated 3D rooftop model reflects the shape of actual building, our suggested method can be very effectively utilized in the 3D site modeling from urban image. In this paper 3D grouping is carried out under the very limited assumption. We conclude that the future work should be focused on the extended research on more generalized 3D grouping.

Acknowledgement. This work was supported by grant No. R01-2002-000-00336-0 from the Basic Research Program of the Korea Science & Engineering Foundation.

References

1. Panton, D. J.: A Flexible Approach to Digital Stereo Mapping. Photogrammetric Engineering and Remote Sensing, Vol. 44 (1978) 1499-1512
2. Mostafavi, H.: Image Correlation with Geometric Distortion Part II: Effects on Local Accuracy. IEEE Trans. Aerospace and Electronic, Vol. 14 (1978) 494-500
3. Grimson, W.: Computational Experiments with Feature Based Stereo Algorithm. IEEE Trans. Pattern Analysis and Machine Intelligence, Vol. 7 (1985) 17-3
4. Marr, D., Poggio, T.: A Computational Theory of Human Stereo Vision. Proc. Royal Society of London Vol. 204 of B (1979) 301-328
5. Kanade, T., Okutomi, M.: A Stereo Matching Algorithm with an Adaptive Window: Theory and Experiment. IEEE Trans. Pattern Analysis and Machine Intelligence, Vol. 16 (1994) 920-932
6. Han, K., Bae, T., Ha, Y.: Hybrid Stereo Matching with a New Relaxation Scheme of Preserving Disparity Discontinuity. Pattern Recognition, Vol. 33 (2000) 767-785
7. Leclerc, Y., Luong, Q., Fua, P.: Self-consistency: A Novel Approach to Characterizing the Accuracy and Reliability of Point Correspondence Algorithms. DARPA Image Understanding Workshop (1998)
8. Schultz, H., Hanson, A., Riseman, E., Stolle, F., Zhu, Z., Woo, D.: A Self-consistency Technique for Fusing 3D Information. Proc. Information Fusion (2002) 1106-1112
9. Boldt, M., Weiss R., Riseman, E.: Token-based Extraction of Straight Lines. IEEE Trans. Systems Man Cybernetics, Vol. 19 (1989) 1581-1594

Segmentation of Interest Objects Using the Hierarchical Mesh Structure

Dong-Keun Lim[1] and Yo-Sung Ho[2]

[1] Digital Media R & D Center, Samsung Electronics
416 Maetan-3dong, Youngtong-gu, Suwon, Gyeonggi-do, 442-742, Korea
dk2003.lim@samsung.com
[2] Gwangju Institute of Science and Technology(GIST)
1 Oryong-dong, Buk-gu, Gwangju, 500-712, Korea
hoyo@gist.ac.kr

Abstract. The object boundary of an image plays an important role for image analysis and interpretation. The watershed algorithm and the region growing algorithm are popularly employed for image segmentation. These give reasonable performances, but require a large amount of computation time and sometimes fail to obtain continuous linkage of object boundary. In this paper, we introduce hierarchical mesh-based image segmentation. In each hierarchy, we employ neighborhood searching and boundary tracking methods to refine the initial boundary estimate. The proposed algorithm increases the robustness of linkage of object boundaries by overlooking and estimating connectivity and gives new modified chain coding. Reliable segmentation of objects can be accomplished by the proposed low complexity technique.

1 Introduction

The MPEG-4 international standards try to provide a solution to the challenging task in multimedia environment. It gives the broad range spectrum of requirements and applications through implementing content-based functionalities. One of the prerequisite condition is the ability to encode arbitrarily shaped VOs(Video Object). That skill is generally called image segmentation. In recent years, several algorithms for image segmentation have been proposed for certain applications, such as video conferences, where only one or two speakers exist in the static background [1][2].

Typical image segmentation algorithms include thresholding, region growing, split and merge, watersheds, or edge-based operations. Each operation has its own peculiar features and advantages. Initial segmentation is performed on the first frame of the video sequence by partitioning the frame into homogeneous regions based on image prosperities. The watershed algorithm [3][4] and the region growing algorithm [4-6] are popularly employed for initial segmentation; however, both of them require a large amount of computation time and they sometimes fail to obtain continuous linkage of object boundary. In order to overcome these problems, we propose a hierarchical approach for image segmentation using mesh

K. Aizawa, Y. Nakamura, and S. Satoh (Eds.): PCM 2004, LNCS 3331, pp. 230–238, 2004.

structures. The proposed algorithm also increases the robustness of linkage of object boundaries by overlooking and estimating connectivity at higher hierarchical levels and gives a new modified chain coding method which is applied to natural images, not limited to binary images.

2   New Segmentation Algorithm

2.1   Algorithm Overview

The proposed segmentation algorithm is based on hierarchical mesh classification with a pyramid data structure. The advantage of the hierarchical approach lies in the possibility of making a rough classification at a coarse level and then continuing into finer resolution to improve the segmentation accuracy. Our algorithm focus on interesting parts along object boundaries. The proposed algorithm is computationally efficient since only a fraction of all pyramid nodes is processed during the top-down classification [1][6].

Fig. 1 shows the flow diagram of the hierarchical image segmentation, which is similar to the divide-and-conquer algorithm for boundary detection.

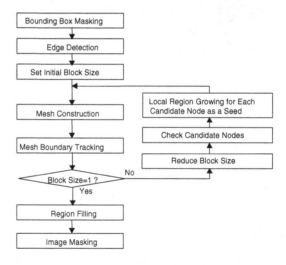

Fig. 1. The flow diagram of the proposed hierarchical mesh-based segmentation

We construct a hierarchical structure of meshes of different sizes using the edge information. Meshes are constructed by connecting the centroid of each candidate block. To follow the mesh boundary, we use a left-hand or a right-hand rule of a maze search based on the previous search direction. The algorithm works counterclockwise for the left-hand rule or clockwise for the right-hand rule along the meshes on the object boundary. The resulting boundary meshes are candidates of the next process in the mesh hierarchy. The candidate meshes are split into smaller meshes. We apply the mesh boundary tracking method and link the mesh boundary. This process continues iteratively until we reach one pixel resolution. In each level, local searches are carried out on the previous approximate boundaries. Since the resulting object boundary may not be accurate, we need to correct the boundary. We employ a local region growing algorithm to refine the boundary starting from the previous boundary as a seed. A segmentation mask is obtained by filling the refined object boundary.

2.2   Bounding Box Masking

Due to semantic ambiguity and content complexity, automatic segmentation algorithms are applied only on specific situation. For general applications, the user usually defines the object at the initial time. Semantic objects in the video frame can be identified.

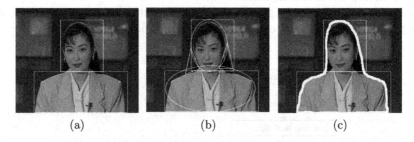

(a)   (b)   (c)

Fig. 2. Boundary of Region of Interest: (a) multiple bounding boxes, (b) boxes, circles and polygons, and (c) hand-drawn curve

As shown in Fig. 2, multiple rectangular boxes, circles and hand-drawn lines can be used to define the region of interest (ROI). We can also combine those bounding shapes with some choosing rule such as intersection, union, XOR, etc.

2.3   Boundary Tracking

An image can be represented by a mesh structure [2]. Meshes are generally located on long object boundaries, which are important in the hierarchical structure since they provide the meaning of the objects. After we find locations of candidate boundary points, we refine the object boundaries. Fig. 3 explains a mechanism of hierarchical mesh construction and boundary linking. At Level k, edges are located in three quadrants. Those regions are candidates for Level k+1. In the same way, at Level k+1, edges are located in seven regions, which are candidate locations for Level k+2.

A mesh structure can be generated by linking the centroid (center of mass) position of each block. Since edge information does not change according to the

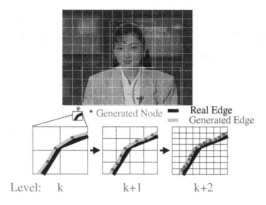

Fig. 3. Object locations at different levels or hierarchies: where k means the level

variation of luminance and has more object boundary information than luminance intensity one, we use edge information to obtain the centroid instead of luminance information.

As shown in Fig. 4, fragmentation problems in boundary tracking can arise when contours and boundaries are not smooth or have broken pieces.

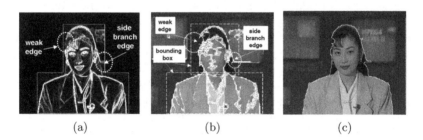

Fig. 4. Boundary Linkage Problem due to Fragmentation: (a) edge image, (b) mesh overlayed image of (a), and (c) segmented image with several problems that include fragmentation and meaningless side branch

One of the advantages using hierarchical mesh structures can be explained from Fig. 5. From link1 to link3 in level (k+1), we can not estimate the broken link directly without the related link information in level k. Since general edge link and follow algorithms cannot estimate the broken edge within very small region for estimation, they fail to find a continuous linkage. Although they increase the region for estimation to increase the robustness of a continuous linkage, the computational time and ambiguity of linkage may be increased.

In the proposed hierarchical approach, the linkage information in level k gives the estimated path of the broken links in level (k+1). From that information, we

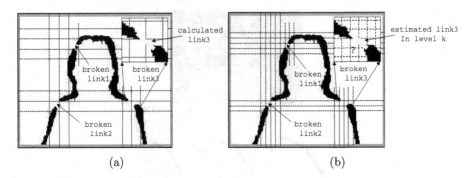

Fig. 5. Continuous Boundary Linkage in Hierarchical Level: (a) at level k, and (b) at level (k+1). The missing edge blocks at level (k+1) can be estimated using the calculated links in level k

reduce the estimation time of a continuous linkage and increase the robustness of the linkage. The following algorithm can effectively find the object boundary.

a) Starting from the upper left corner of the image, we perform raster scanning line by line until we reach the position of an edge block. This position is used as the starting point of boundary tracking. The left-hand rule is initially applied for searching.

b) Check the 3×3 neighborhood of the current position to find an edge block according to the priority of candidates. This procedure is explained in Fig. 6. If we miss a link before we have a complete closed loop, we return to the previous last starting position. We try another search with a different searching rule for the opposite direction of the object boundary.

c) At each edge block position, we define a value, DIR, which stores the direction of the motion for change to the current edge block position along the edge boundary. The next boundary position is searched among candidate edge blocks located in the priority tables, which are determined by DIR.

d) Reduce the edge block size and perform local region growing for the object boundaries. The range of region growing is limited to the previous block size.

e) The process from (b) to (d) is repeated until we obtain the object boundary at pixel accuracy. We can finish it when the result meets a certain condition.

Fig. 7 shows an example of boundary tracking, and summarizes edge positions and directions. We start with the left-hand scan. When we reach the image boundary at No. 18, we switch to the right-hand scan. The next position can be found among the candidates which are located as the priority in Fig. 6, determined by the previous direction(DIR) value. A side branch, which exists from No. 13 to No. 16, should be removed to generate a closed segmentation mask. It sometimes is not required to remove side branches such as antenna, tail, horn and thin-narrow objects.

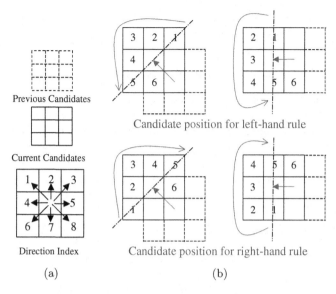

Fig. 6. The Rule of Boundary Tracking: (a) definition of DIR, and (b) two examples for left-hand and right-hand rule

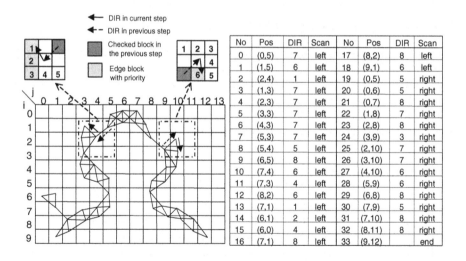

No	Pos	DIR	Scan	No	Pos	DIR	Scan
0	(0,5)	7	left	17	(8,2)	8	left
1	(1,5)	6	left	18	(9,1)	6	left
2	(2,4)	1	left	19	(0,5)	5	right
3	(1,3)	7	left	20	(0,6)	5	right
4	(2,3)	7	left	21	(0,7)	8	right
5	(3,3)	7	left	22	(1,8)	7	right
6	(4,3)	7	left	23	(2,8)	8	right
7	(5,3)	7	left	24	(3,9)	3	right
8	(5,4)	5	left	25	(2,10)	7	right
9	(6,5)	8	left	26	(3,10)	7	right
10	(7,4)	6	left	27	(4,10)	6	right
11	(7,3)	4	left	28	(5,9)	6	right
12	(8,2)	6	left	29	(6,8)	8	right
13	(7,1)	1	left	30	(7,9)	5	right
14	(6,1)	2	left	31	(7,10)	8	right
15	(6,0)	4	left	32	(8,11)	8	right
16	(7,1)	8	left	33	(9,12)		end

Fig. 7. An Example of Boundary Tracking: direction(DIR), position values(Pos), and scan methods(Scan)

2.4   Mesh Construction

It is desirable to have mesh boundaries aligned with object boundaries and edge information of the image to achieve better perceptual quality. There exist several algorithms for constructing mesh structures including uniform triangulation, Delaunay triangulation. In this paper, to construct the mesh structures, we connect two nearest vertices according to the 8-connectivity rule.

2.5   Edge Detection and Region Growing

A contour pixel is defined as a local maximum in the output of an edge detector or the first derivative operator. Since image edges characterize object boundaries, they are important for image segmentation. The goal of image segmentation is to find edge segments whose contours have significant contrast changes.

Region growing is a simple scheme for image segmentation. If the gray-level difference between two adjacent pixels is below a threshold value, those pixels are merged. We can use a statistic of object segments, instead of the pixel difference[4-6].

Both edge detection and region growing are two different aspects of the same process under the assumption of step edges and smooth brightness distribution within regions. Homogeneity for each region may be measured in terms of color, texture, motion, depth, etc. We examine gray-level changes. When we perform local region growing, we use the output of the Sobel edge detector as a seed. The output of the local region growing method is an initial candidate for the object boundary tracking in the next level.

2.6   Region Filling and Image Masking

In order to find the segmentation mask, we fill each region based on object boundary information. To fill a region with a certain gray value, we set each pixel lying on a scan line running from the left edge to the right edge to the same pixel value. The general polygon scan-conversion algorithm [7] handles both convex and concave polygon. In order to obtain image objects, we apply the AND operation with the original image and the segmentation mask.

3   Simulation Results

Computer simulation is performed on video conferencing images of the CIF(352 × 288) and QCIF(176 × 144) format. We use several kinds of head and shoulder images such as CLARE, AKIYO, Mother and Daughter.

Fig. 8 shows the hierarchical mesh generation and boundary tracking process for two-level. The object boundary and mesh are refined as proceeding to the next level. In the first hierarchical level, we partition the image into 16 × 16 blocks and generate meshes in the region of interest. Meshes are mainly distributed around edges. Using the boundary tracking process, we find object boundaries to generate closed contours at each hierarchical level. In the next level, we use 8 × 8 blocks and smaller meshes to refine the object boundaries. The local region growing method increases robustness of closed contour generation. Since meshes are only distributed around object boundaries, it reduces the computation time in the next level.

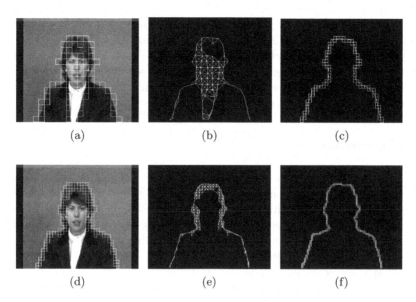

(a)   (b)   (c)

(d)   (e)   (f)

Fig. 8. Hierarchical Mesh Generation and Boundary Tracking for Two Level: (a) edge candidate blocks with 16×16 block size, (b) generated meshes with (a), (c) boundary meshes after boundary tracking with (b), (d) edge candidate blocks with 8×8 block size after local region growing with (c) as local seeds, (e) generated meshed with (d), and (f) boundary meshes after boundary tracking with (e)

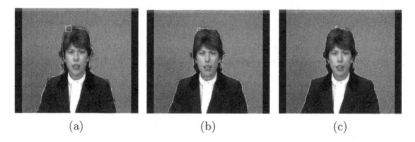

(a)   (b)   (c)

Fig. 9. Segmentation Results for CLAIRE: from 16×16 Block Size(a) to 4×4 block size(c), where they contain small rectangular block in the beginning of boundary tracking

(a)   (b)   (c)   (d)

Fig. 10. Segmentation Results for AKIYO and Mother and Daughter: (a) and (c) for 16×16 Block Size, (b) and (d) for 1×1 block size or one pixel resolution

From Fig. 9 and Fig. 10, we can see the results including two-level meshes of different block sizes for CLAIRE, AKIYO, and Mother and Daughter, respectively. These show the results at each level, where each frame uses a different block size. The square in the Fig. 9 indicates the block size at each level. As proceeding to the next level, we refine object boundaries. We obtain computational reduction by concentrating the meshes on the object boundary.

4   Conclusions

In this paper, we propose a new image segmentation algorithm using hierarchical meshes. Reliable segmentation of objects is obtained by the proposed low complexity method. The proposed algorithm increases the robustness of linkage of object boundaries by overlooking and estimating connectivity at higher hierarchical levels and gives a new modified chain coding method which is applied to natural images, not limited to binary images. Experimental results indicate that reliable segmentation of objects can be accomplished by the proposed low complexity technique, since it reduces the number of processing candidates as proceeding to the next level. We obtain the shape information of the image object from the intermediate results and data that can be used for constructing triangular mesh inside the object. Therefore, the proposed method can be used for continuous sequential processing based on mesh coding on MPEG-4 visual coding standard.

References

1. Westberg, L.: Hierarchical contour-based segmentation of dynamic scenes, IEEE Trans. Pattern Analysis and Machine Intelligence, vol. 14, no. 9 (September 1992) 946-952
2. Altunbasak, Y.: Object-scalable mesh-based coding of synthetic and natural image objects, ICIP'97 (October 1997) 94-97
3. Vincent, L., Soille, P.: Watersheds in digital spaces: An efficient algorithm based on immersion simulations, IEEE Trans. Pattern Analysis Machine Intelligence, vol. 13 (June 1991) 583-598
4. Hojjatoleslami, S.A., Kittler, J.: Region growing: a new approach, IEEE Trans. Im-age Processing, vol. 7, no. 7 (July 1998) 1079-1084
5. Pavlidis, T., Liow, Y.T.: Integrating region growing and edge detection, IEEE Trans. Pattern Analysis and Machine Intelligence, vol. 7, no.3 (September 1992) 225-233
6. Tabb, M., Ahuja, N.: Multiscale image segmentation by integrated edge and region detection, IEEE Trans. Image Processing, vol. 6 (May 1997) 642-655
7. Foley, J.D., (ed.): Introduction to computer graphics, Addison-Wesley (1994)

A Rapid Scheme for Slow-Motion Replay Segment Detection

Wei-Hong Chuang, Dun-Yu Hsiao, Soo-Chang Pei, and Homer Chen

Department of Electrical Engineering, National Taiwan University,
Taipei, Taiwan 10617, R.O.C.,
{r92942040, r92942028}@ntu.edu.tw,
{pei, homer}@cc.ee.ntu.edu.tw

Abstract. Efficient data mining for digital video has become increasingly important in recent years. In this paper, we present a new scheme for automatic detection of slow-motion replays in sports video. Several slow-motion features and some newly discovered characteristics of slow-motion segments are exploited to aid the detection. The first step of our method is based on the macroblock motion vector information, while the second step makes use of frame-to-frame difference under an MC-DCT structure to verify the output of the first step. The last step is applied to refine the segment boundaries. Unlike previous approaches, our method has great improvement in both speed and accuracy and a balance between efficiency and simplicity.

1 Introduction

As recent advances in digital video coding and transmission have made digital video very popular, It becomes more and more difficult for end users to go through all received video information. Sports video programs are a good example. Someone may be interested in many games played in a day but does not have the time to watch all of them or even one of them throughout. A tool for automatic detection of important events in sports video and for summary presentation will thus be very useful. Many approaches to event detection have been proposed [2], [6], [7], [10]. Besides these existing ideas, slow-motion replays usually represent the occurrence of important events, too. If these replay segments could be detected effectively, we can extract them from the original video and present them as a meaningful kind of highlights. In this paper, we propose a new scheme for slow-motion replay segments detection (SMRSD). First, we apply a novel procedure by scanning macroblock reference directions to find slow-motion replay segment candidates. Next, a DCT-domain procedure is used to refine the candidates and discard false ones. This method also checks frame differences but avoids inverse DCT operations. Lastly, the resulting replay segments are concatenated and presented to the viewer. This detection scheme performs completely in the compressed domain. With this scheme, the time cost will be low and results will be reliable.

K. Aizawa, Y. Nakamura, and S. Satoh (Eds.): PCM 2004, LNCS 3331, pp. 239–246, 2004.
© Springer-Verlag Berlin Heidelberg 2004

2   Previous Work

The SMRSD issue has been addressed in the literature by some researchers [1], [4], [10]. In general, there are two ways to generate slow-motion effects. For videos captured by a standard-speed camera, the slow-motion effect can be generated by frame repetition or frame interpolation [2]. (Note: The frame repetition method is more widely adopted because of its simplicity and maturity.) For videos recorded with a high-speed camera, the slow-motion effect can be generated by simply playing out the video at the normal speed.

Since standard-speed cameras are much more widely used (and cheaper) than high-speed cameras [1], in this paper, we concentrate on slow-motion videos "generated by frame repetition." Pan et.al [1] proposed an approach to detection of slow-motion segments. They defined the frame difference as

$$D(n) = \sum_{p=1}^{M} \sum_{q=1}^{N} (I_n(p,q) - I_{n-1}(p,q))^2,$$

where $I_n(p,q)$ denotes a macroblock in frame n. In a slow-motion region, because of the existence of repeated frames, $D(n)$ would have more abrupt changes than what it has in the normal play region. An example is shown in Fig.1, where it can be seen that $D(n)$ exhibits a clear pattern in which a large value is followed by several "near zero" values.

That is, $D(n)$ will cross its mean value in a slow-motion segment more often than in a standard-speed segment. In other words, $D(n)$ has a higher "zero-crossing rate" in slow-motion segments. Pan [1] defined the zero-crossing as

$$Z_c(n, \theta_k) = \sum_{i=1}^{L-1} trld(D(n-i) - \overline{D}(n), D(n-i-1) - \overline{D}(n), \theta_k)$$

where

$$trld(x, y, t) = \begin{cases} 1 \text{ if } x \geq t \text{ and } y \leq -t \\ 0 \text{ if } x \leq -t \text{ and } y \geq t \end{cases}.$$

Accordingly, $p_{zc}(n)$ is defined as a measure of the fluctuation of $D(n)$:

$$p_{zc}(n) = \arg \max_k Z_c(n, \theta_k) \geq \beta.$$

As suggested in [2], threshold values are set to:

$$L = 7, \theta_k = k, \beta = 1$$

The reader is referred to [1], [2],and [4] for more details.

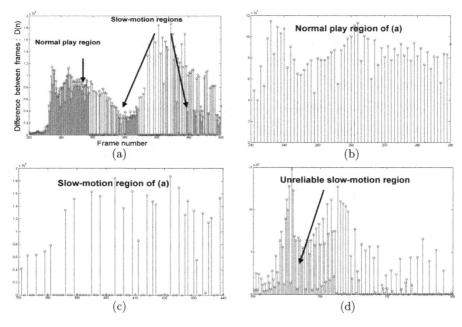

Fig. 1. (a) $D(n)$ of a video segment consisting of a normal play region and a slow-motion region, (b) the zoomed-in view of the normal play region, and (c) the zoomed-in view of the slow-motion region. (d) is a slow-motion segment which has a portion of weak zero-crossing pattern.

3   New Discovery and Compressed Domain SMRSD

Our tests told us that the zero crossing is a prevalent characteristic of slow-motion segments. But we have also noted that some slow-motion segments have weak zero-crossing patterns (as displayed in Fig. 1(d)). In such cases, purely rely on the zero-crossing may not give satisfactory results. Based on the observation of many sports videos, we have found that slow-motion segments would likely begin and end with a scene change such as logo flashing and scene wiping. These scene changes work as a clue of the appearance of slow-motion segments. If the segment boundaries are detected first, one may improve the computational efficiency by localizing the zero-crossing operations to only a few frames within each segment. Pan et al. [1] used an HMM model to detect the segment boundaries. This method requires training an HMM model. However, different kinds of video may have different characteristics. One HMM model is not general enough to work for all different kinds of videos.

The method developed by Pei and Chou in [5] detects the scene change based on the reference direction of each macroblock of bi-directional prediction (B) frames. The B frames before and after a scene change tend to have different reference directions, as shown in Fig. 2. This method performs consistently well for typical videos such as MTV, TV commercials, etc, but it generates incorrect

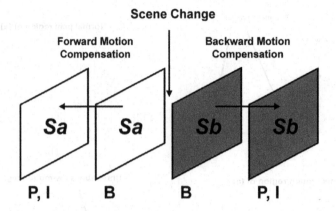

Fig. 2. Scene change detection based on the reference direction of bi-directional prediction (B) macroblocks. P stands for prediction macroblock, and I for intra macroblock.

results for sports video where there is a significant amount of motions due to camera panning or zooming.

While the detection method described in [5] fails for the specific application targeted in this paper, we found that it exhibits a distinctively different behavior for slow-motion segments: The number of scene changes it detects is far more than that for the normal play regions. This discovery inspires us to develop the new SMRSD scheme discussed here. The false alarms for scene changes generated by the detection method [5] signals the existence of slow-motion replay segments. That is, the more scene changes it detects, and the closer between scene changes, the more likely the segment is a slow-motion segment. This is illustrated in Fig. 3.

After further examining the phenomena described above, we found that slow-motion segments usually exhibit a particular pattern. The frame will remain still for some time then change to the next one. Freeze and play is ubiquitous in slow-motion plays, thus motion vectors of the macroblocks are likely to refer to different directions (most macroblocks of one frame refer forward, and most macroblocks of the adjacent frame refer backward) when abrupt shift between frames takes place. Hence it makes sense to detect slow-motion segments in a video by detecting the great change in reference direction of macroblocks.

3.1   Step I. Slow-Motion Segment Detection

The purpose of this step is to obtain an initial segmentation of the video sequence. High-density occurrence in Fig. 3 is an implication of the existence of a slow-motion region. Thus we extract those high density segments of the detection of large difference in reference direction change from the input video sequence. This includes an analysis of the spacing between occurrences generated by the detection method [5]. A threshold is applied to select slow-motion segments from all possible candidates. To obtain better detection results, we have many voting rules to account the amount of change in reference direction, then we discarded

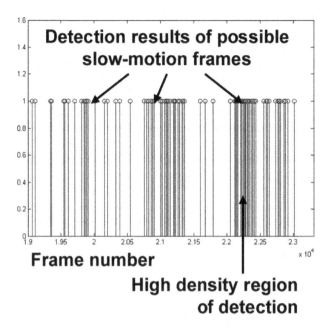

Fig. 3. The occurrence of scene changes detected by the method described in [5]. In those detection regions with high density, we found that there are great possibility that slow-motion segments reside.

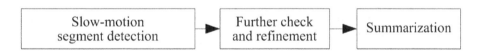

Fig. 4. A block diagram of the new SMRSD scheme. It consists of three steps as described in the following.

or added voting rules regarding to their contribution to detection results and emphasis on the most effective one, which is the reference pattern shown in Fig. 2. This greatly enhances the performance of the method and made much difference than any other kinds of slow-motion detection methods. After such a refinement, it is powerful in detecting jerky changes in video sequences, which is the phenomenon that exhibits in slow-motion segments. In this step, neighboring slow-motion segments are merged to account for the fact that, in practice, scene change can happen in a slow-motion replay. Slow-motion segments that are very short (for example, less than 1 second) are discarded. The candidates generated by this step usually have an accuracy of 70% in detection including miss and false alarm rate. To improve this result, we use the following step to reduce error rate and still preserve a high speed in detection.

3.2 Step II. Refinement

This refinement step, applied to those candidates found in Step I, is based on the zero-crossing measure [1]. There are two points to be noted. First, our goal is to develop a technique in the compressed domain; however, the zero-crossing method is applied to video frames in the spatial domain. We know that DCT is a unitary transform, and mathematically it makes no difference to calculate frame difference in either spatial domain or transform domain. The other point is that, in an MPEG stream, the DCT coefficients of predicted frames are the transform values of prediction error. Hence, we need to modify the calculation of $D(n)$ in Section 2. Chang et al. [8] suggest using a decoding structure as shown in Fig. 5.

This decoder structure is equivalent to the original decoder in that it generates the same decoding results. Under this decoding structure, the motion compensation is performed before the inverse DCT. This way, $D(n)$ and the zero-crossing method can be performed in the compressed domain. This step consists of the following operations that are applied to each candidate segment found in Step I to refine the segment boundary: Find all frames of the segment such that p_{zc} is greater than a preset threshold. For each frame near the segment boundary (both inside and outside the segment), make a merge or discard decision based on its p_{zc} value. Merge two segments if they are close (for example, within 30 frames) to each others.

3.3 Step III. Summarization

This step involves the following operations: 1) Choose a key frame from each slow-motion replay segment [7], [9] . 2) Include extra thirty seconds before and after each segment.

4   Experiment Results

Our scheme is fast because it uses only motion vector and coefficient information and does not need any decompression operation. This section presents the experimental results of our SMRSD scheme. To see the validity of this scheme, we use three different video clips generated by three different producers in two different countries, as shown in Table 1. The total duration is more than half an hour.

Table 1. SMRSD Test Data

Sequences	Length in min:sec	Length in frames
1016	13:14	23841
1106	11:08	20047
Final	08:09	14659

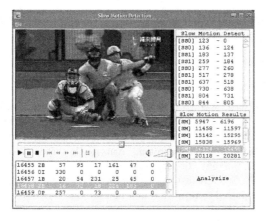

Fig. 5. SMRSD System Interface.

Table 2. SMRSD Results

Sequences	# of replay segments	Correct	False	Miss	Inaccuracy boundary	Time saved
1016	9	9	0	0	1	94.58%
1106	10	9	0	1	0	94.16%
Final	1	1	0	0	0	98.57%

We also developed a user interface which aids the user browsing the extraction SMRSD results, as follows:

The SMRSD results are shown in Table 2. Our results are and visually pleasant. Long segments can be represented effectively by very short ones. Particularly, because the operations are completely in the compressed domain and only use motion vectors most of time, the scheme is very suited for huge amount of data.

5 Conclusions

A new scheme for slow-motion replay segment detection has been described in this paper. We have tested this system in a computer environment that is similar to that in ordinary families, and the system (without optimization) runs far faster than real time. Experimental results show that this scheme is effective and superior to other schemes in that it allows a good balance between accuracy and efficiency. Users don't have to take a long time to watch the entire video of races or games, instead, they could watch the generated summaries to save their time.

Acknowledgement. We thank for those who gave us comments. These advices make this paper more complete and we are very grateful.

References

1. H. Pan, P. van Beek, and M. I. Sezan, "Detection of slow-motion replay segments in sports video for highlights generation," in *Proc. ICASSP'01*, pp. 1649–1652, 2001.
2. A. Ekin, M. Tekalp, and R. Mehrotra, "Automatic soccer video analysis and summarization," *IEEE Trans. Image Proc.*, Vol 12, No 7, pp.796–807, 2003.
3. J. Song and B.-L. Yeo, "A fast algorithm for DCT-domain inverse motion compensation based on shared information in a macroblock," *IEEE Trans. CSVT*, Vol 10, No 5, pp.767–775, 2000.
4. H. Pan, B. Li, and M. I. Sezan, "Automatic detection of replay segments in broadcast sports programs by detection of logos in scene transitions," in *Proc. ICASSP'02*, pp.3385–3388, 2002.
5. S.-C. Pei and Y.-Z.Chou, "Efficient MPEG compressed video analysis using macroblock type information," *IEEE Trans. Multimedia*, Vol 1, No 4, pp.321–333, 1999.
6. Y. Rui, A. Gupta, and A. Acero, "Automatically extracting highlights for TV baseball programs," in *Proc. of 8th ACM Inter. Conf. on Multimedia*, pp.105–115, 2000.
7. Y.-F. Ma, L. Lu, H.-J. Zhang, and M.J. Li, "A User Attention Model for Video Summarization," in *Proc. of 10th ACM Inter. Conf. on Multimedia*, pp.533–542, 2002.
8. S.-F. Chang, and D.G. Messerschmitt, "Manipulation and compositing of MC-DCT compressed video," *IEEE J. Select. Areas Commun.*, Vol 13, pp.1–11, Jan.1995.
9. T. Liu, H.-J Zhang, and F.Qi, "A novel video key-frame-extraction algorithm based on perceived motion energy model," *IEEE Trans. CSVT*, Vol 13, No 10, pp.1006–1013, 2003.
10. V. Kobla, D. DeMenthon, and D. Doermann, "Detection of slow-motion replay sequences for identifying sports videos," in *Proc. IEEE Third Workshop on Multimedia Signal Processing*, pp. 35–140, 1999.

Recognition of Very Low-Resolution Characters from Motion Images Captured by a Portable Digital Camera

Shinsuke Yanadume[1], Yoshito Mekada[2], Ichiro Ide[1], and Hiroshi Murase[1]

[1] Graduate School of Information Science, Nagoya University
Furo-cho, Chikusa-ku, Nagoya, Aichi, 464-8603 Japan
yanadume@murase.nuie.nagoya-u.ac.jp, {ide,murase}@is.nagoya-u.ac.jp
[2] Life System Science and Technology, Chukyo University
101 Tokodachi, Kaizu, Toyota, Aichi, 470-0393 Japan
y-mekada@life.chukyo-u.ac.jp

Abstract. Many kinds of digital devices can easily take motion images such as digital video cameras or camera-equipped cellular phones. If an image is taken with such devices under everyday situations, the resolution is not always high; moreover, hand vibration can cause blurring, making accurate recognition of characters from such poor images difficult. This paper presents a new character recognition algorithm for very low-resolution video data. The proposed method uses multi-frame images to integrate information from each image based on a subspace method. Experimental results using a DV camera and a phone camera show that our method improves recognition accuracy.

1 Introduction

Recently, opportunities for taking videos with such portable equipments as digital video cameras (DV camera) or camera-equipped cellular phones (phone camera) continue to increase. If a system could automatically recognize the characters from such video data, it could become a key piece of technology for the next generation of human-machine interfaces. For example, in the future, we will easily be able to scan and input URLs from magazines by phone cameras or send text by e-mail by recognizing characters from the images of captured notes. Many character recognition methods have already been proposed[1]. However, such methods generally assume that the image quality of characters is quite high. On the other hand, the quality of characters captured by portable digital cameras is often not sufficient to apply these methods; the image of the characters might be too small when a full document is captured in a single shot. Moreover, hand movement or poor lens quality might blur the image. It is difficult to recognize such low-quality characters from a single image. Eims et al.[9] proposed a method to recognize low-quality images from a image scanner, but this method is not sufficient in our case when the resolution of a single image is not enough. When we capture a character on video, we obtain a variety of character images

K. Aizawa, Y. Nakamura, and S. Satoh (Eds.): PCM 2004, LNCS 3331, pp. 247–254, 2004.
© Springer-Verlag Berlin Heidelberg 2004

as a sequence of motion images. If we properly use such information, recognition of very low-resolution characters may become possible, even if we cannot recognize them from a single image.

In this paper, we propose a method that recognizes characters from poor quality video images. Cheeseman et al.[2] generated an image with higher resolution from multi-frame low-resolution images. Thus restoration of low-resolution images is one solution[10]. On the other hand, we take information directly from multi-frame images at the recognition step and integrate that information with a subspace method[3,4,5,6,7]. We generate subspaces that approximate a set of a large number of training images and compute the degree of similarity of the subspace. Finally, we use the multi-frame images input for recognition.

The proposed method consists of the following three parts: gathering training data, constructing subspaces, and recognizing characters from input images. In the training step, our method uses many variations of characters that are segmented from sequences of videos at various resolutions. The recognition step does not need to estimate camera movements to recognize a character, unlike a previously proposed method by Sawaguchi et al.[8].

We describe the characteristics of the characters in the video data in section 2, propose the algorithm in section 3, and show the experimental results in section 4.

2   Characters in Video Data

2.1   Portable Digital Cameras

Figure 1(c) shows a typical example of a character captured by a portable digital camera that is obviously difficult to recognize from the single image shown. When we photograph a full document with a common portable camera, as shown in (Fig.1 (a)), each character is in low-resolution. Our aim is to recognize such poor quality characters as shown in Fig.1(c) by using the information from multi-frame images.

2.2   Characteristics of Videodata

When we take a video using a portable handy camera, hand movement slightly shifts and rotates the camera, making it difficult to fix the camera position difficult. Therefore, a large variation generally exists in a sequence of video images, even for the same character. If we can properly integrate the information from these images, recognition of a very low-resolution character may become possible, even if we cannot recognize it from a single image. Figure 2 shows character "A" obtained from two frames captured by a digital video camera. Typical character recognition algorithms might not be able to recognize these characters from a single image. However, the subtle difference between these two images provides a clue to improving the recognition accuracy.

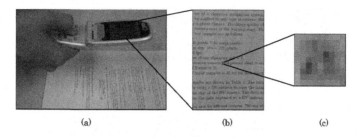

(a)   (b)   (c)

Fig. 1. Taking document image with a phone camera. (a): Taking an image with a phone camera. (b): Captured document image. (c): Segmented image of character "a".

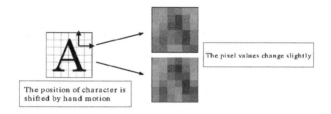

Fig. 2. Changes in pixel values due to hand motion.

3   Recognition of Characters from Motion Images

The proposed method consists of the following three parts: gathering training data, constructing subspaces, and recognizing characters from input images. We used character images captured by a portable camera as training data that helps achieve a high recognition rate and includes various cases of characters to be recognized. Eigenvectors were computed from the training data to be used to recognize input characters.

Training data and input data were generated from character images captured by a portable camera. We printed characters on a sheet with a fixed print pitch and segmented each character by this pitch information. The size of the segmented characters was normalized for use as training data and input data.

3.1   Creating Training Data

The target characters for recognition are:

- Printed characters.
- Upper and lower cases of the alphabet and the Arabic numerals.
- Characters whose images are bigger than 6×6 pixels.

The training data consisted of printed characters captured by a portable camera. We used multi-frame images from a sequence of motion images for training data because they contain many variations of the same character. Since the size of characters was unknown beforehand, we prepared training data captured at

Fig. 3. Excerpt from the training data "A".

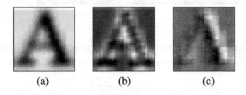

| (a) | (b) | (c) |

Fig. 4. Picturized eigenvector of "A". (a): the first eigenvector. (b): the second eigenvector. (c): the third eigenvector.

various resolutions by changing the distance between the camera and the sheet. Figure 3 is an excerpt from the training data.

3.2   Construction of the Subspace from the Training Data

First, our method found the orthogonal bases of the training data for each category. Each i-th learning data image was converted to a unit vector whose average was 0 (normalization). The normalized vector is represented by

$$\boldsymbol{x}_i = [x_1, x_2, \cdots, x_N]^T,$$

where N is the number of pixels. Next, matrix $\boldsymbol{X}$ is defined as

$$\boldsymbol{X} = [\boldsymbol{x}_1, \boldsymbol{x}_2, \cdots, \boldsymbol{x}_k],$$

where k is the amount of learning data for this category. Then, we calculated an autocorrelation matrix $\boldsymbol{Q}$ for the category using matrix $\boldsymbol{X}$:

$$\boldsymbol{Q} = \boldsymbol{X}\boldsymbol{X}^T.$$

We constructed the subspace for each category using R eigenvectors that corresponded to the largest R eigenvalues. A set of eigenvectors was represented by,

$$\{\boldsymbol{e}_1^{(c)}, \boldsymbol{e}_2^{(c)}, \cdots, \boldsymbol{e}_R^{(c)}\},$$

Figure 4 shows an example of eigenvectors that were computed and picturized implying that the blurred characters at several resolutions are included.

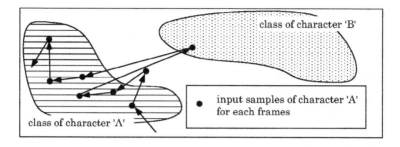

Fig. 5. Advantage of multi-frame input. This figure shows input multi-frame samples projected in subspace.

Fig. 6. Set of target characters (Font: Century).

3.3 Recognition

Each character is segmented from an input video and normalized. Each character was segmented from an input video and normalized. A set of vectors for the character was constructed from multi-frame images and represented by

$$\{a_1, a_2, \cdots, a_M\},$$

where M is the number of input frames. The similarity between category c and the input images is defined as

$$L^{(c)}(\boldsymbol{a}) = \frac{1}{M} \sum_{m=1}^{M} \sum_{r=1}^{R} (\boldsymbol{a}_m, \boldsymbol{e}_r^{(c)})^2$$

where $(\boldsymbol{x}, \boldsymbol{y})$ denotes an inner product. Then the category of input images was determined to maximize the above equation. If one sample is input which was closer to an incorrect class than a correct class, integration of multi-frame samples should enable correct category output (see Fig. 5).

4 Experiments

We verified the capability of this method experimentally by capturing a sequence of printed characters with either a portable digital camera or a phone camera. An alphanumeric "Century" font was used in the experiments on a total of characters in 62 categories, as shown in Fig. 6.

4.1   Recognition Rate Versus Number of Input Frames

To verify the performance of our method when applied to very low-resolution characters, we evaluated recognition rates by changing the number of frames and the size of characters. The data used for this experiment are as follows:

Training Data

- Captured with a DV camera.
- Character size controlled by changing the distance between the camera and the sheet on which the characters were printed.
  - Distance: less than $70cm$.
  - Average character size : 16×16, 11×11, 8×8, 7×7, or 6×6 pixels.
- Multi-frames of each character for a total of 50 frames per character.

Dictionary Data

- Ten eigenvectors that corresponded to the ten largest eigenvalues.

Test Data

- Captured with the same DV camera
- Different from the training data.
- Two test sample sets for character size controlled by changing the distance between the camera and a sheet.
  - **small:** $70cm$ (approximately 6×6 pixels).
  - **medium:** $60cm$ (approximately 7×7 pixels).
- Number of input samples: 30 sets for each character for a total of 1,860 sets.

The results are shown in Fig. 7. Recognition rates increased as the number of input frames increased until reaching a saturation point at around 15 frames. In the *medium* size, the recognition rate almost reached 100%, indicating that our method improves recognition accuracy by inputting multi-frame images.

4.2   Lighting Conditions Versus Recognition Rate

Since changes in light conditions are a serious problem for most computer vision systems, we checked the relationship between light conditions and recognition rate.

Training data were captured in "bright" light conditions. The remaining conditions of the training data and the dictionary data are identical to Section 4.1.

Test Data

- Captured with a DV camera.
- Character size: *small*.
- Lighting conditions: "bright", "middle", or "dark".
- Number of frames: 20.
- Number of input samples: 30 sets for each character for a total of 1,860.

The results in Table 1 show that our method is generally independent of light conditions. We also found that normalization (in Section 3.2) was effective.

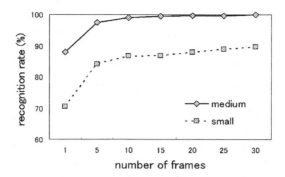

Fig. 7. Recognition rate vs. number of input frames.

Table 1. Recognition rates for change in light conditions. The character size is *small*.

Light condition	Recognition rate(%)
bright	88.1
middle	82.8
dark	85.4

4.3   Using Different Types of Cameras

For a character recognition system to be practical for use, its algorithm must be applicable to any type of camera. Therefore, we tried using image sequences taken by a phone camera in addition to the previous experiment. The image quality of this camera was worse than the DV camera used in the training stage. The specifications of this phone camera and test samples are as follows:

- Actual number of pixels of the CCD: 0.31 mega pixels.
- Captured image size: 164 × 220 pixels.
- Frame rate: 7.5 fps.
- Character size: *medium*.
- Distance between the camera and the printed sheet: approximately 20*cm*.
- Number of frames: 20.
- Number of input samples: 30 sets for each character for a total of 1,860 sets.

In the experimental results, the 92.0% recognition rate when using a phone camera is slightly lower than the 99.9% when using a DV camera because the image quality of the phone camera is inferior to the DV camera. The dictionary data for both cases were constructed from the data captured by a DV camera.

5   Conclusion

In this paper, we proposed a new framework based on a subspace method for recognizing low-quality, especially low-resolution, characters. We used various resolutions of image sequences to construct the subspace in the training step. Experimental results show that a recognition rate of 99.9% is obtained for low-resolution alphanumeric characters about 7×7 pixels in size. Our method performs well even when devices or light conditions are changed. We conclude that our method is useful in recognizing very low-resolution characters captured by a portable digital camera. Although slight shift and rotation of camera are absorbed in the training data set, the method can not cope with a large tilt or rotation.

Future work includes adding such figures as Japanese characters and different fonts. When we recognize a character from document images, it is difficult to segment characters from low-resolution sentence images. Since we used printed, pre-segmented character images in this research, in the future we must apply this algorithm to words and sentences and explore the ramifications.

Acknowledgments. The authors thank their colleagues for useful suggestions and discussion. Parts of this research were supported by the Grant-In-Aid for Scientific Research (16300054) and the 21st century COE program from the Ministry of Education, Culture, Sports, Science and Technology.

References

1. S. Mori, K. Yamamoto, and M. Yasuda, "Research on machine recognition of hand-printed characters," Trans. PAMI, vol.PAMI-6, no.4, pp.386-405, July 1984
2. P. Cheeseman, B. Kanefsky, R. Hanson, and J. Stutuz, "Super-resolved surface reconstruction from multiple images," Technical Report FA-94-12, NASA Ames Research Center, Artificial Intelligence Branch, October 1994
3. E. Oja, "Subspace methods of pattern recognition," Hertfordshire, UK: Research Studies, 1983.
4. H. Murase, H. Kimura, M. Yoshimura, and Y. Miyake, "An improvement of the auto-correlation matrix in the pattern matching method and its application to handprinted "HIRAGANA" recognition," IECE Trans., vol.J64-D, no.3, pp.276-283, March 1981
5. H. Murase and S. K. Nayar, "Visual learning and recognition of 3-D objects from appearance," International Journal of Computer Vision, vol.14, pp.5-24, 1995
6. S. Omachi, and H. Aso, "A qualitative adaptation of subspace method for character recognition," IEICE Trans., vol.J82-D-II, no.11, pp.1930-1939, November 1999
7. S. Uchida and H. Sakoe, "Handwritten character recognition using elastic matching based on a class-dependent deformation model," Proc. ICDAR, vol.1 of 2, pp.163-167, August 2003
8. M. Sawaguchi, K. Yamamoto, and K. Kato, "A proposal of character recognition method for low resolution images by using cellular phone," Technical Report of IEICE, PRMU2002-247, March 2003
9. A.J.Elms, S.Procter, and J. Illingworth, "The advantage of using an HMM-based approach for faxed word recognition," IJDAR, vol.1, no.1, pp.18-36, 1998
10. Paul D. Thouin and Chein-I Chang, "A method for restoration of low-resolution document images," IJDAR, vol.2, no.4, pp.200-210, 2000

An Effective Anchorperson Shot Extraction Method Robust to False Alarms

Sang-Kyun Kim, Doo Sun Hwang, Ji-Yeun Kim, and Yang-Seock Seo

Computing Lab, Digital Research Center, Samsung A.I.T.,
San 14-1, Nongseo-ri Giheung-up Yongin-si S.Korea
{skkim77, doosun.hwang, jiyeun.kim, ysseo}@samsung.com

Abstract. A new method to improve the performance of the anchorperson shot extraction from news programs is proposed in this paper. The anchorperson voice information is used for the verification of anchorperson shot candidates extracted by visual information. The algorithm starts with the anchorperson voice shot extraction using time and silence condition. The anchorperson voice models are created after segregating anchorperson voice shots containing 2 or more voices. The anchorperson voice model verifies the anchorperson shot candidates obtained from visual information. 720 minutes of news programs are tested and experimental results are demonstrated.

1 Introduction

Both the deluge of the video contents though media such as digital broadcasting, Internet and the emerging industry involving PVR, EPG, and large-size storage, are changing a paradigm on method of watching TV. For example, Tivo and ReplayTV are already changing the life style such that viewers can watch any contents in anytime in favor of the viewer's intention. The nutshell of this trend is viewers can record any broadcasting contents through EPG and watch them in a digested format. Since sports and news programs have some formatted structures and take much time to watch after recording, viewers need to see some highlights or storyboards for a quick browsing. In the case of the news program, viewers can see the main topics and their reports with a storyboard and quickly select what they want to indulge. The anchorperson shot detection has been a fundamental research issue to compose such a news storyboard.

There have been active research efforts going on the anchorperson shot detection. The template based search and match method [1], [2], [3] is good for the formatted news structure but has a weakness on structure or format changes. The occurrence frequency and time constraint of the anchorperson shot were used for the anchorperson shot candidate extraction in [4]. The motion information was used for the false alarm (e.g. interview shot and report shot) removal. The Graph-Theoretical Clustering method [5] was proposed for the similar anchorperson shot clustering in an unsupervised and model-free manner. Multi-feature information such as motion, color, face, cloth, and caption was used in [6]. This

K. Aizawa, Y. Nakamura, and S. Satoh (Eds.): PCM 2004, LNCS 3331, pp. 255–262, 2004.
© Springer-Verlag Berlin Heidelberg 2004

extracts faces in DC domain and uses luminance variation in the cloth area to confirm the anchorperson shot.

The purpose of this paper is to enhance the extraction performance of anchorperson shots using color and audio, especially using anchorperson's voice information. The entire anchorperson shot extraction process proposed is described in section 2. The section 3 shows the experimental results followed by discussion and conclusions in section 4.

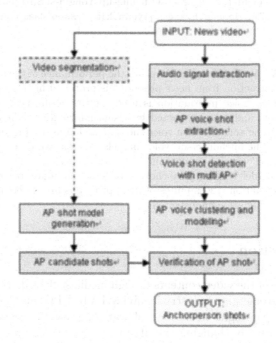

Fig. 1. The flow chart of anchorperson shot extraction

2   Anchorperson Shot Extraction Process

The objective of this research is to precisely extract anchorperson shots in news videos using a combination of visual and audio information; especially, using the anchorperson's voice information. The overall process flow is shown in Fig. 1. The video (e.g. mv1) and audio (e.g. wav) signals are extracted from the input news video. The shot detection algorithm is then applied to the video signal and the video shot boundaries are preserved for further processes. The audio signal is down-sampled to save the computational cost. The video shots longer than a predefined length are selected and the length of the silence frames is measured from the rear part of each shot selected. If the length of the silence frames of the rear part in the shot is longer then a predefined length, the shot is concerned as a shot containing anchorperson's voice. Among the detected shots with anchorperson voices, we can segregate shots containing more than or equal to 2 persons' voices. The remaining anchorperson voice shots except 2 or more anchorperson voice shots detected are used to make the anchorperson voice clusters and generate anchorperson voice models. The anchorperson shot candidates are extracted by using background color, face, and cloths information from key frames. Finally, the voice information in the anchorperson shot candidates are compared to the voice models created from the previous step in order to validate the anchorperson shots. Details are explained in the following sub-clauses.

2.1   Audio Signal Extraction

The audio signal can be separated from the input news video in MPEG-1/2. Even though the audio signal in MPEG-1/2 is usually 48kHz or 44.1kHz, which corresponds to CD sound quality, the result PCM data would be too large to analyze. In order to save computation, we down-sampled the input audio signal into 8kHz. The 8kHz signal retains enough voice/audio characteristics that correspond to the mobile phone sound quality. This signal is proven to be enough for our experiment.

2.2   Anchorperson Voice Shot Extraction

This step extracts shots containing anchorperson's voice. One thing should be noted is that the purpose in this step is not of extracting all of the shots with anchorperson voices but of finding a subset of the shots that explicitly contains anchorperson voices. In order to find news shots with anchorperson's voice, we assume two ground conditions based on the long observation on news programs. The first condition is that the length of the anchorperson shot is usually longer than 10 seconds. The second one is that the boundary between an anchorperson shot and the following news report shot contains substantial amount of a silent period. In other words, the news anchorperson shot contains a substantial silence in the vicinity of the end of the shot. In Fig. 2, the red boxes indicate the anchorperson shots and the yellow ellipses indicate the silence area of each anchorperson shot. These two ground conditions are combined to detect the shots containing anchorperson voices. The shots longer than a predefined length are selected as candidate shots containing anchorperson voices. In order to find the length of the silent period, the energy of the audio signal is calculated from each shot frame. An audio frame covers $25ms$ so that a frame contains 200 audio samples. The following equation is how to calculate an audio energy of a frame:

$$Energy_i = \frac{\sqrt{\sum_{n=1}^{200} pcm_n{}^2}}{200} \tag{1}$$

After calculating the energy from all of the audio frames, we can deduce a threshold for silence frames. Since news programs from different stations have different magnitude of silence, the threshold for silence should be adaptively derived from the audio energy information obtained from each input news program. This can

Fig. 2. Examples of the silence region in the real part of the anchorperson shot

Fig. 3. Key frames from anchorperson voice shots

be done by quantizing the energy values, counting the number of frames for each energy value, and finally taking a silence threshold from a low energy level (e.g. low 20%). This way of detecting silence threshold was proven to be effective through the experiment.

After determining the silence threshold, we can count the number of silent frames from each anchorperson voice shot candidate. The method is to count the frames having less energy than the silence threshold from the end of the candidate shot. Once we know the number of silent frames from each candidate shot, we can select shots retaining more than a predefined number of frames (e.g. 34 frames = 0.85s). The result shots are defined as the anchorperson voice shots. Fig. 3 demonstrates an example of key frames of the anchorperson voice shots detected. We have extracted the silent sections of anchorperson voice shots from 12 different news programs. There are no false alarms detected using this shot length and silent section constraint.

2.3   Voice Shot Detection with Multiple Anchorperson

The goal of extracting anchorperson voice shots is to cluster and model each anchorperson's voice presented in the news program. In order to do so, we should find voice shots including 2 or more anchorperson voices and exclude them from the voice clustering and modeling process.

From the audio information in the anchorperson voice shots extracted, we can now calculate Zero Crossing Rate (ZCR) per audio frame. The ZCR is of counting the number of sign changes in audio PCM data. The high ZCR means high frequency characteristics in the audio signal. The human's voice is composed of consonants and vowels. The vowels especially contain the fundamental frequency of the human voice. The ZCR can be used to classify audio frames as either a consonant or a vowel. The following equation is how to calculate the ZCR from an audio frame:

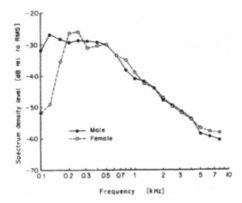

Fig. 4. Long-time average speech spectrum calculated for utterances made by 80 speakers [8]

$$ZCR_i = \frac{\# \text{ of sign changes in PCM (DB)}}{200} \qquad (2)$$

The next step is to calculate Mel-Frequency Cepstral Coefficient (MFCC) from an audio frame. The MFCC is proven to be effective in a speech recognition task which is composed of 13 coefficients. In order to compare voices in an anchorperson voice shot, we first need to get rid of silent frames in the shot. We use the energy information obtained from the previous step described in section 2.2. The next step is to remove consonant frames from the shot. We can get rid of the consonant frames by using the average ZCR in the shot. If a ZCR of an audio frame is as twice larger than the average ZCR of the shot, the audio frame is considered as a consonant frame.

Another important feature to distinguish between male voices and female voices is the power spectrum between 100Hz and 150Hz [7]. Fig. 4 demonstrates the average long-time speech spectrum between male/female voices. The spectrum shows big difference between 100Hz and 150Hz. Besides the fundamental frequency between male and female has a distinctive difference. Since the fundamental frequency is difficult to calculate, we instead divide the shot into windows and calculate the average spectrum in the window. The spectrum is then converted to decibel so that the decibel values between neighbor windows are compared to discover the existence of both male and female anchorperson in a shot. We can move a 3s window with 1s difference through the shot, and calculate average MFCC (i.e. average of 7th, 8th, 9th, 10th, 11th, and 12th coefficient) and average decibel between 100Hz and 150Hz. The two features are combined to determine a distance between windows. If this distance is larger than a predefined threshold, the shot is considered as a shot with more than or equal to 2 voices. The shots detected in this step are used for confirming news anchorperson shots in the later step.

$$\textbf{Diff} = W * \textbf{diff\_Avg\_MFCC} + (1 - W) * \textbf{diff\_Avg\_Decibel} \qquad (3)$$

Fig. 5. Anchorperson voice shot clustering

2.4   Anchorperson Voice Clustering and Modeling

After detecting shots containing two or more voices, the next step is to make voice models presented in the news program. The MFCC coefficient and the decibel value between 100Hz and 150Hz obtained in the previous step are used again for clustering the anchorperson voice shots. First, the closest two shots in the average MFCC are selected. Then, their decibel values between 100Hz and 150Hz are compared. If they are far apart, the two shots are not merged and flagged not to be merged later.

The merging is proceeded until every shot is merged into one of the clusters or there are not two shots left in a predefined MFCC distance. The voice shots containing more than or equal to 2 voices are added to compose the voice models. Each model contains the average MFCC and the average spectrum decibel value. Finally, for the short anchorperson shot detection (e.g. less than 6s), we provide a separate model for each anchorperson voice cluster from the first 4 seconds. Fig. 5 shows an example of key frames after clustering.

2.5   Anchorperson Shot Candidate Extraction

We can create a set of anchorperson shot visual models using face detection, background color comparison, and anchorperson shot occurrence constraint [4]. The anchorperson shot candidates are selected by comparing these models with key frames in the entire news program. Both the anchorperson visual models and the key frames are divided into NxN blocks for the comparison. The algorithm returns the anchorperson shot candidates with begin/end time and the block color differences between anchorperson shot model and anchorperson shot candidates. The block color difference is calculated using normalized value after applying Grey World algorithm in order to be robust to illumination change.

2.6   Anchorperson Shot Confirmation Using Multimodal

From the time information of the anchorperson shot candidates, we can get the corresponding audio signal and extract the average MFCC and the spectrum decibel values. We can calculate the voice difference between anchorperson voice

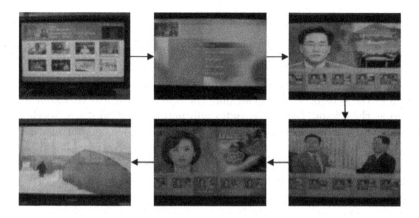

Fig. 6. An example of news storyboard

models and voices from the anchorperson shot candidates. The multi-modal difference could be obtained by combining this voice difference information with block color difference information. If this multi-modal distance is larger than a predefined threshold, the corresponding anchorperson shot candidate is considered as a false alarm (i.e. a shot with no anchorperson voice) and removed from the candidate list. The remaining shots are confirmed as final anchorperson shots in the input news program.

$$\mathbf{MM\_dist} = W2 * \mathbf{Block\_Color\_Diff} + (1 - W2) * \mathbf{Voice\_Diff} \qquad (4)$$

3   Experimental Results

We used 5 different news programs from 3 different Korean broadcast station, KBS, MBC, and SBS. 6 news programs corresponding to around 360 minutes were tested for selecting main parameters and optimization. Other 6 news programs corresponding to around 360 minutes were tested for the verification of the proposed algorithm. Without confirming with multimodal information, the original algorithm (section 2.5) returns 98.94% of recall and 93.36% of precision from the 12 news programs tested. After applying the anchorperson voice model mingled with the block color difference information, we could achieve 99.32% of recall and 100% of precision with the first set of news program. With the second set for verification, we have got 97.83% of recall and 100% of precision. The averaged performance is 98.58% of recall and 100% of precision. Compare to the original algorithm, the precision is substantially improved while the recall drops a bit. This proves that the proposed method is very effective for the false alarm detection and removal.

4 Discussion and Conclusions

The proposed algorithm has been applied to realize the news storyboard interface in DVR-EPG application. As shown in Fig. 6, viewers can easily select a news segment using the remote controller and the storyboard interface displayed at the bottom of the screen. Viewers can play the selected segment to watch in detail or stop as they want. Using the audio information may do many goods for the contents analysis. For example, we can derive anchorperson shot visual models described in section 2.5 directly from analyzing audio features. It will save the computation time of handling visual features in SD/HD quality programs. We will proceed this as a future work.

In conclusion, we have shown that anchorperson's voice information combined with some simple audio features is very effective tool for the verification of anchorperson shot candidates. Most of the false alarms that are visually similar to the anchorperson shot are removed by this method.

References

1. HongJiang Zhang, Yihong Gong, Smoliar, S.W., Shuang Yeo Tan, "Automatic parsing of news video," Multimedia Computing and Systems, Proceedings of the International Conference on, 45–54, 1994
2. Hanjalic, A., Lagensijk, R.L., Biemond, J., "Template-based Detection of Anchorperson Shots in News Program," Image Processing, ICIP 98. Proceedings. 1998 International Conference on, Vol 3, 148–152, 1998
3. JinWoun Choi, DongSeok Jeong, "Storyboard construction using segmentation of MPEG encoded news video," Circuits and Systems, Proceedings of the 43rd IEEE Midwest Symposium on, Vol 2, 758–761, 2000
4. Bertini, M., Del Bimbo, A., Pala, P., "Content based indexing and retrieval of TV news," Pattern Recognition Letter, Vol 22, 503–516, 2001
5. Xinbo Gao, Jie Li, Bing Yang, "A Graph-Theoretical Clustering based Anchorperson Shot Detection for news Video Indexing", ICCIMA, 2003
6. Nakajima, Y., Yamaguchi, D., Kato, H., Yanagihara, H., Hatori, Y., "Automatic anchorperson detection from an MPEG coded TV program," Consumer Electronics, ICCE. 2002 Digest of Technical Papers. International Conference on, 122–123, 2002
7. Irii, H., Itoh, K., and Kitawaki, N., "Multi-lingual speech database for speech quality measurements and its statistic characteristic," Trans. Committee on Speech Research, Acoust. Soc. Jap., S87–69, 1987
8. Sadaoki Furui, "Digital Speech Processing, Synthesis, and Recognition," Marcel Dekker, 1989

A Region Based Image Matching Method with Regularized SAR Model[*]

Yaowei Wang[1,2], Weiqiang Wang[1], and Yanfei Wang[3,4]

[1] Institute of Computing Technology, Chinese Academy of Sciences, Beijing, China
[2] Graduate School of Chinese Academy of Sciences, Beijing, China
{ywwang,wqwang}@jdl.ac.cn
[3] National Key Laboratory on Remote Sensing Science, Institute of Remote Sensing Applications, Chinese Academy of Sciences
yfwang@irsa.ac.cn
[4] Department of Mathematics, University of Central Florida, FL 32816, USA

Abstract. In this paper, we propose a new region-based image matching method to find the user defined regions in other images. We use color histogram and SAR (simultaneous autoregressive) model parameters as matching features. We characterize the spatial structure of image region with its block features, and we match the image region in target images with spatial constraints. SAR model was usually used to characterize the spatial interactions among neighboring pixels. But the spectrum of the transition matrix G in the SAR model is not well distributed. Therefore in this paper, we use a regularized SAR model to characterize the spatial interactions among neighboring image blocks, which is based on the solution of a penalized LSE (Least Squares Estimation) for computing SAR model parameters. The experimental results show that our method is effective.

1 Introduction

Image matching is usually defined as the establishment of the correspondence between various images. Image matching belongs to the class of inverse problems, which are known to be ill-posed [Heipke 1996]. There are two categories of image matching method: area based matching (ABM) and feature based matching (FBM) [Heipke 1996]. In ABM [Hannah 1989] [Ackermann 1984] [William 1995], each point to be matched is the center of a small window, and the window is statistically compared with equally sized windows in target images. In FBM, the image feature is extracted in the first place and then the feature is used to match. Features are usually some local operators [Moravec 1979] [Schimid 1997] [Gouet 2002]or edge features (Sobel, Canny, Laplacian, etc.). The matching problem is an ill-posed problem, some constraints are usually used to make it to be well-posed. These constraints include epipolar constraint, continuity constraint, order constraint, uniqueness constraint, photometry constraint and so on.

---

[*] Authors are supported by 863(2003AA142140)

K. Aizawa, Y. Nakamura, and S. Satoh (Eds.): PCM 2004, LNCS 3331, pp. 263–270, 2004.
© Springer-Verlag Berlin Heidelberg 2004

The concept of content-based image retrieval (CBIR) can be traced back to the early of 1990s. Recently, more and more researchers have realized that the complete automatic CBIR is too difficult to implement. Therefore, human's involvement is emphasized [Rui 1999][Nozha 2003]. In [Nozha 2003], the author has pointed out two ways that human participate in the system loop. One way is to allow the user to select the region of interest, the other is to allow the user to react on the system retrieval results. The latter method is commonly called relevance feedback, and the former is region based image retrieval.

There are mainly four kinds of methods in region based image retrieval. The first is based on image segmentation. In [Fauqueur 2002], image was segmented by using the LDQC feature, and then the segment results were taken as regions. This kind of method depends on the segment results. If the segment results are unacceptable, the method does not work. Another way is to divide the image into small blocks. In [Moghaddam 1999], an image was divided into blocks with 16×16 pixels. It utilizes the blocks' color, texture and edge features to describe the image region. The method is easy to implement and seems to be effective. The third way is to generate image regions from interest points extracted by local operator [Schimid 1997] [Gouet 2002]. They extract interest point and use its neighboring area as features. There are two questions concerning this method. First, can the point extracted by the local operator exactly describe the region? Second, is it necessary that all points extracted by the local operator can be used as feature points? The last one depends on vision clues. [Itti 1998] considered that the contrast of foreground and background attracted most of the attention of people. So the contrast was used as feature. But [Claudio 2000] claims that man's perception of image is a top-down and contextual process of eye focus motion. This kind of method is usually complex, and not easy to be implemented as the formers. In sum, more local features are used and more different constraints are taken into account than before.

Our contribution in this paper is that we propose a new region-based image matching method to find the user defined regions in other images and a stable solution method for reducing instability in parameters estimation when solving SAR model. In our method we use color histogram and SAR model parameters as matching features. We characterize the spatial structure of image region with its block features and match the image region in target images with spatial constraints.

The rest of the paper is organized as follows. There are two parts in section 2. In section 2.1, we introduce the SAR Model for parameter estimation and give analysis of the proposed penalized LSE method. In section 2.2, we present a realistic region-based image matching method. In section 3, we give some experimental results to show the effectiveness of our method. Finally in section 4, some concluding remarks are given.

2   Our Methods

The problem we will solve is to find the user defined region in other images. We do not concern what the user defined region is. In other words, the user can define any image region as his region of interest. To simplify the problem in our system, we assume that:

1. The user defined region is a rectangle region, and the region size could not be smaller than a specified size. We consider that a rectangle image region is representative and easy to be implemented. And if a region is too small, we can not get useful spatial structural information of the region.

2. The user can only define one interest region in one image. This assumption is just to simplify the problem.

Our method consists of three steps. First, we define the region of interest in an image. Then, we extract region features in both the original region and the image regions in target images. Finally, we match the image regions. We use color histogram and regularized SAR model parameters as the matching features. We characterize the spatial structure of the image region with its block features and match the image region in target images with spatial constraints. We will give an interpretation of the matching method in section 2.2.

The parameters of SAR model can be estimated by using the least square estimation technique, which is known to be simple, easy to perform and less time-consuming [Mao 1992]. However this method may be unstable due to the rank-deficient, ill-conditioning of the input data or the observations, or due to the data containing too much noise. It seems that this problem has not been paid too much attention in the previous research works. Therefore, to increase the stability in parameter estimation we propose a PLSE method in section 2.1, which is a regularization of LSE.

2.1   Regularization by Penalized LSE (PLSE)

The basic SAR model for texture images is usually in the form (1)

$$\sum_{r \in I} \theta(r)g(s+r) + \mu + \varepsilon(s) = g(s), \tag{1}$$

where $g(s)$ is the gray level of a pixel at site $s = (s_1, s_2)$ in an $m \times m$ textured image, $s_1, s_2 = 1, 2, \cdots, m$. I is the set of neighbors of pixel at site s, $\varepsilon(s)$ is an independent Gaussian random variable with zero mean and variance σ^2, $\theta(r)$, $r \in I$ are the model parameters characterizing the dependence of a pixel to its neighbors, and μ is the bias which is dependent on the mean gray value of the image. All parameters μ, σ and $\theta(r)$, $r \in I$ can be estimated by using the least squares estimation technique, which is known to be simple, easy to perform and less time-consuming. The parameters $\theta(r)$ are usually used for classification and segmentation of textured features. (1) can be written in the following simple form

$$\sum_{r \in I} g(s+r)\theta(r) = g_\varepsilon(s) - \mu, \tag{2}$$

where $g_\varepsilon(s) = g(s) - \varepsilon(s)$, ε is random variable and $\varepsilon \sim N(0, \sigma^2)$. For different r and s, (2) can be written as a linear equation

$$G\theta^r = g_\varepsilon^\mu, \tag{3}$$

with $G = (g^{ij})$ the matrix, θ^r, g_ε^μ the corresponding vectors, where $g_\varepsilon^\mu = g_\varepsilon(s) - \mu$.

In theory, we can estimate the parameters θ^r by solving the above equations. But we must keep in mind that, the matrix G is very ill-conditioning, hence the solution will be unstable. In [Wang 2003], we have shown that the LSE method is unstable, and apply standard regularization technique to overcome this problem, i.e., we solve the minimization problem

$$\min J(\theta^r) = \frac{1}{2}\|G\theta^r - g_\varepsilon^\mu\|_{l_2}^2 + \frac{\alpha}{2}\|\theta^r\|_{l_2}^2, \tag{4}$$

where $\|\theta^r\|_{l_2}^2$ serves as the stabilizer, $\alpha > 0$ is the parameter to balance the bias between the original and the new problem. However, this formulation is conservative. No priori information is applied on the solution. If so, it is in fact an identity operator E, i.e., $\|\theta^r\|_{l_2}^2 = \|E\theta^r\|_{l_2}^2$. If the solution has highly oscillatory part, then it can not be suppressed by the above standard regularization. To robustly solve for θ^r, we introduce the penalty technique, which is to say the solution is penalized in an a-priori way. Denote the penalty operator as P, the penalized LSE method [Wang 2002] is described as

$$\min \hat{J}(\theta^r) = \frac{1}{2}\|G\theta^r - g_\varepsilon^\mu\|_{l_2}^2 + \frac{\alpha}{2}(P\theta^r, \theta^r), \tag{5}$$

where P is a symmetric, positive semi-definite or positive definite matrix. The parameter $\alpha > 0$ can be chosen by users, hence the coefficient matrix $G^t G + \alpha P$ can be positive definite. The new problem (5) can also be considered as the least squares problem with nonnegative constraints [Wang 2002]. Numerically, Cholesky decomposition can be employed to get the solution

$$G^t G + \alpha E = LDL^t, \tag{6}$$

where L is the lower triangular matrix with the diagonal elements all ones and D is the diagonal matrix. With such configuration, the parameters θ^r are solved through the following systems:

$$v = L^{-1} G^t g_\varepsilon^\mu, \quad \theta^r = L^{-t} D^{-1} v. \tag{7}$$

Note that L is the triangular matrix, the cost of computation of the above two linear system is very small. For our problem, the parameters are determined by the choice of the neighborhood I and the choice of the window. Using different neighbor sets we can fit different resolution SAR model to the given image. Here, for convenience, we choose a simple second-order neighborhood. The choice of the parameter is an a priori. In this paper, we choose $\alpha = 0.01$. Note that α can not be too large or too small. For most of the time, α is chosen between 0 and

1. The penalty matrix P is a discrete non-negative Laplacian with homogeneous Neumann boundary conditions [Wang 2002]. The size of P is the same as G, which is in the following form

$$P = \begin{bmatrix} 1 & -1 & 0 & 0 & \cdots & 0 & 0 & 0 \\ -1 & 2 & -1 & 0 & \cdots & 0 & 0 & 0 \\ 0 & -1 & 2 & -1 & \cdots & 0 & 0 & 0 \\ \vdots & \vdots & \vdots & \vdots & \cdots & \vdots & \vdots & \vdots \\ 0 & 0 & 0 & 0 & \cdots & -1 & 2 & -1 \\ 0 & 0 & 0 & 0 & \cdots & 0 & -1 & 1 \end{bmatrix}.$$

2.2   Image Matching Method

Our goal is to find the user defined region in other images. To simplify the problem, we consider the target region has the same size with the original region. If the original region size is $M_0 \times N_0$, we use a $M_0 \times N_0$ window moving in the target image to match. At each position, the corresponding features are extracted. Let X and Y denote the feature vectors, we compute the feature similarity by the following equation

$$R = \sum_{i=1}^{n} X_i Y_i / (\sqrt{\sum_{i=1}^{n} X_i^2} \sqrt{\sum_{i=1}^{n} Y_i^2}), \ n \in \mathbf{Z}^+, \ R \in [0, 1]. \tag{8}$$

First of all, we separate an image region into small blocks (see Fig.1.(a)). In general, we let the number of blocks be $m_b \times n_b$. To ensure that each block contains enough information, we enlarge the block size to be $M_{\min} \times N_{\min}$ if the block size is smaller than $M_{\min} \times N_{\min}$.

In the system, color histogram and SAR model parameters are combined to characterize the content of regions. They are applied in different ways to reflect the information in different levels. When the SAR model is used to character the interactions among neighboring image blocks in one region, we regard each image block as a "pixel" and its gray value is the mean gray value of the blocks' pixels. Therefore, we can compute the **region's** SAR features. After that, the image blocks' features are computed, which include color histogram and SAR features. For the original region, we do not compute all blocks' features. We consider that the blocks in the main diagonal (see Fig.1.(a)) can characterize the region's spatial structure. Hence, only blocks in diagonal are processed.

In matching process, we have two thresholds T_{color} and T_{PLSE} to make decision, which are obtained by statistical method. The matching process consists of three main steps.

Step 1, we examine the global color distribution and the whole region's SAR feature. If the similarity of color histogram between the query region and the current window is lower than T_{color}, the current window will be declared to fail to match. Otherwise, further check based on PLSE model parameters of the window will go on. If SAR features' similarity is lower than T_{PLSE}, the region in the current window will be rejected.

Step 2, we check the remaining regions by spatial constraints. The matching process is shown in Fig.1(b). We denote the continuous image blocks in the diagonal of the original region by b_1, b_2, b_3, $\cdots$, b_m and call these blocks the key blocks. First, we match b_1 in the target region. It should be pointed out that the matching block can be any block in current window. In other words, the matching block in target region is not restricted to the diagonal ones of the region. If there is no matching block, we match the next block. Once we got the matching block of b_i (the grid block in Fig.1(b)), we match the next block b_{i+1} in its down right corner's four blocks (the blocks with parallel lines in Fig.1(b)). We use these blocks to confirm the continuous spatial relationships between the neighboring blocks, and to hold some image distortions at the same time. Thus, we can get a matching sequence which maps onto a sequence of key blocks. The sequence of key blocks is denoted by $b_i b_{i+1} \cdots b_{i+n-1}$, where $1 \leq i \leq m - n + 1$. If $n \geq N$, we add current region into a matching region's queue. Here N is also a threshold, and we choose $N = 5$ in our experiments. If $n < N$, we match b_{i+1} in the whole region and repeat the process.

Step 3, a matching region's queue is constructed after step 2. The result is the region which has the longest matching sequence in the queue.

Clearly our method can not work directly in the condition that the image region has some scale and rotation operations. But we can solve the problem by using a series of windows (with different scale and angular) to match in the target image.

3   Experimental Results

We choose examples from Brodatz album [Brodatz 1966] to compare the behavior of LSE and PLSE for computing the SAR features. We use the norm of the extracted SAR features as a quantity of the feature's stability. A large norm value means that the results are far away from the true value, which also means that the texture of the image may be very coarse or contains too much noise and hence that the corresponding method is unstable. Small norm values mean that the results are better and the corresponding method is stable. The norm of the SAR feature values is denoted by $Norm$. Fig.2 is a plot of the stability comparison of LSE and PLSE. The axis X denotes the number of images, and the axis Y denotes the norm distribution by $\log_{10} Norm$; the '*' line (the upper) is the results obtained by LSE and the '+' one (the lower) is the results by PLSE. From the figure, we can see the PLSE is much more stable than the LSE method. It deserves to point out that the choice of the parameter α is a delicate matter. In our tests, the choice of α as 0.01 is not optimal. The best value of should be matched with the error due to noise and machine precision. But this is difficult to realize.

We use about 7000 Corel Images and some video frames as test data for image region matching. We choose Corel images to test whether the spatial

Table 1. The image matching results

	Precision	Recall
Video Frames Of Advertisement 1	90.0%	85.3%
Video Frames Of Advertisement 2	86.5%	90.0%
Video Frames Of Golf	90.2%	85.6%
Pet Images	82.4%	80.1%
Flower Images	81.0%	79.3%
Mean Value	**86.0%**	**84.1%**

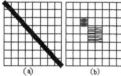

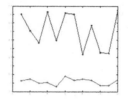

Fig. 1. (a) The description of image region; (b) the matching process of blocks with spatial constraints

Fig. 2. Stability comparison of LSE and PLSE. The top '*' line denotes the SAR model solved by LSE and the bottom '+' line denotes the SAR model solved by PLSE

Fig. 3. Matching results of a Golf video

constraints is effective or not. Most of Corel images from the same class have similar global color distribution. Also many image retrieval systems use Corel images as image database. We choose video frames to test the matching method with the distortion among continuous I frames. Note that most of continuous I frames have similar contents. Table 1 lists some results of our experiments. We do not have a quantitative standard to say whether the result is better or not. So, we use the similar way as was done by other researchers. The data we use is a mean result of 15 different people. We get a mean precision 86% and a mean 84.1%. Fig.3 is a plot of the matching example on Golf video frames. The top image gives the user defined region in the image, the lower three rows list some matching results. We can see clearly in fig.3 that the matching region does hold distortions. Though the matching region is not exactly the same as the defined region, it is very similar to the defined region. The experimental result is consistent with the analysis in section 2.2. Hence we say our method is effective.

4   Conclusion

In this paper, we propose a new region-based image matching method to find the user defined region in other images and a stable method PLSE for reducing instability in parameter estimation of SAR model. From the computation, we find that, for the matching method, by using the extracted features from SAR model solved by PLSE , we have a high precision and a high recall. Hence we conclude that our methods are effective.

References

[Ackermann 1984] Ackermann F., *Digital image correlation-performance and potential application in photogrammetry.* Photogrammetry Record, Vol. 11, No.64, pp.429-439, 1984

[Claudio 2000] Claudio M. Privotera and Lawrence W. Stack, *Algorithm for Defining Visual Region-of-Interest: Comparison with Eye Fixations.* IEEE Transaction on Pattern Analysis and Machine Intelligence, Vol.22, No. 9, 2000

[Fauqueur 2002] J. Fauqueur and N. Boujemaa, *Region-based Retrieval: Coarse Segmentation with Fine Signature.* in IEEE International Conference on Image Processing (ICIP) 2002

[Gouet 2002] Valerie Gouet, *About optimal use of color points of interest for content-based image retrieval.* INRIA RR-No.4439, Apr. 2002

[Hannah 1989] Hannah M.J., *A System for Digital Stereo Image Matching.* PERS(55)12, pp.1765-1770, 1989

[Heipke 1996] Heipke C., *Overview of Image Matching Techniques.* Proceeding of 16th OEEPE Workshop on Application of Digital Photogrammetric Workstation, Lausanne, March, 1996

[Itti 1998] L. Itti, C. Koth, E. Niebur. *A model of saliency-based visual attention for rapid scene analysis.* IEEE Transaction on Pattern Analysis and Machine Intelligence, Vol.20, No.11, 1998

[Mao 1992] J Mao and A K Jain, *Texture classification and segmentation using multi-resolution simultaneous autoregressive models.* Pattern Recognition, Vol.25, No.2, pp.173-188, 1992.

[Moghaddam 1999] B. Moghaddam, H. Biermann, and D. Margaritis. *Defining image content with multiple regions-of- interest.* IEEE Workshop on Content-Based Access of Image and Video Libraries. June 1999

[Moravec 1979] Moravec H.P., Visual Mapping by a Robot Rover, Proc. Of 6th International Joint Conference of Artificial Intelligence, Tokyo, Japan, 1979

[Nozha 2003] Nozha Boujemaa, Julien Fsauqueur, Valerie Gouet. *What's beyond query by Exmaple?*, INRIA RR-5068, Dec. 2003

[Rui 1999] Y Rui, T S Huang, and S F Chang. *Image Retrieval: Current Techniques, Promising Directions, and Open Issues.* J. Visual Comm. and Image Representation, Vol.10, No.1, pp.39-62, 1999

[Schimid 1997] C. Schmid and R. Mohr. *Local grayvalue invariants for image retrieval.* IEEE Transactions on Pattern Analysis and Machine Intelligence, Vol.19, No.5, 1997

[Wang 2002] Yanfei Wang, Ph D thesis, *On the Optimization and Regularization Algorithms for Inverse Problems,* Academy of Mathematics and System Sciences, Chinese Academy of Sciences, June, 2002

[Wang 2003] Yaowei Wang, Yanfei Wang, Wen Gao, Yong Xue. *A Regularized Simultaneous Autoregressive Model for Texture Classification.* The 2003 IEEE International Symposium on Circuits and Systems, ISCAS2003, Bangkok,Thailand, May 25-28, 2003, ppIV/105- ppIV/108

[William 1995] William J. Rukclidge, *Locating Objects Using the Huasdorff Distance,* ICCV1995

Shot Classification and Scene Segmentation Based on MPEG Compressed Movie Analysis

Masaru Sugano[1], Masanori Furuya[2], Yasuyuki Nakajima[1], and
Hiromasa Yanagihara[1]

[1] Multimedia Communications Laboratory, KDDI R&D Laboratories Inc.
2-1-15 Ohara, Kamifukuoka, Saitama 356-8502, Japan
[2] Department of Electrical Engineering, Science University of Tokyo
1-3 Kagurazaka, Shinjuku, Tokyo 162-8601, Japan

Abstract. This paper proposes shot classification and scene bound-ary/genre identification for MPEG compressed movies. Through statistical analysis of audio-visual features on compressed domain, the proposed method achieves subjectively accurate shot classification within the movies into a predefined genre set, as well as scene segmentation based on the shot classification results. By feeding subjectively evaluated feature vectors for each genre into the decision tree classifier, each shot is classified at very low computational cost. Then a sequence of shots belonging to the same genre is determined as a scene. The experimental results show that most of the shots in the movies are classified into subjectively accurate genres, and also that the scene segmentation results are more accurate and robust than the conventional approach.

1 Introduction

The metadata description such as MPEG-7 standard [1] allows us to easily search, retrieve and browse audio-visual contents. To achieve efficient metadata generation, both *structural* indexing and *semantic* indexing are important; the former is performed automatically while the latter is now often performed manually. As one of the semantic indexing technologies, determining shot genre is useful because the shot genre can represent fairly high semantic information. This information can be used for searching, filtering and describing the contents in terms of genre. On the other hand, scene segmentation is even more effective than shot segmentation since scene generally includes semantic meaning to some extent and enables efficient navigation, as seen in the DVD chapter.

In this paper, we propose a shot classification and scene boundary/genre identification algorithm for MPEG compressed movies. This method utilizes low-level and mid-level audio-visual features which can be directly obtained in the compressed domain, and statistically analyzes the feature vectors according to genre properties. The LMDT classifier is used for the actual classification task and accurate classification at very low computational cost can be achieved. In addition, shot classification results are further used for the scene segmentation

K. Aizawa, Y. Nakamura, and S. Satoh (Eds.): PCM 2004, LNCS 3331, pp. 271–279, 2004.
© Springer-Verlag Berlin Heidelberg 2004

task, which defines the higher semantic structures of movies. Unlike the previous approaches, the proposed method is able to determine a scene genre.

This paper is organized as follows. In Section 2, previous studies on classification and scene segmentation tasks are briefly discussed. Section 3 and Section 4 describe the proposed shot classification method and scene segmentation method, respectively. Then, the experimental results are shown in Section 5.

2   Previous Work

In the context of higher level semantic extraction, such as scene genre extraction, several methods have been reported using audio and/or visual features. In the audio feature approaches [2], more than 10 audio low-level features are exploited. In the case of visual features [3][4], shot length and other low-level features such as color and motion are used. As for integrating audio-visual features [5][6], shot length and some audio/visual low-level features such as spectrum, energy, motion and color mainly on baseband domain are utilized. Many of the successful classification methods adopt the HMM classifier. In terms of classification tasks, [2][3][5] classify TV programs into several categories such as news, sports, commercials, etc., and [4][6] classify movie previews into movie genres such as action, romance, etc. Most of these works focus on the classification of relatively large units such as the whole movie or TV programs. Recently, a rule-based approach has been proposed [7], where a model with at most two actors involved in a dialogue or action scene is exploited. As for scene segmentation, many algorithms have also been proposed, for example, as a low-level feature approach, constructing a sequence of shots into a group based on a color histogram and its difference [8], while as a low-/mid-level feature approach, dialog and setting are determined based on face detection and color/orientation, respectively [9]. Another approach focuses on segmenting movies into a Logical Story Unit, based on rather complicated visual feature investigation [10]. In our previous literature, we proposed a non rule-based, more simplified, and efficient classification method for MPEG compressed movies [11]. Though successful results were obtained in several movies, further refinement of the classification accuracy is required. In this paper, we improve the previously proposed shot classification algorithm, and also apply the classification results to scene segmentation, also effective semantic indexing technique for audio-visual contents.

3   Proposed Shot Classification Algorithm

The processing flow of the proposed algorithm is shown in Fig 1. In the previous paper, we proposed a basic algorithm for shot classification [11]. This paper aims to enhance the classification accuracy and apply the classification results to scene segmentation. The incoming MPEG compressed movie is first segmented into shots by the compressed domain shot detection algorithm [12], and then low-level features (motion intensity, consistency of motion direction and audio power) and mid-level features (shot length and audio class) are extracted from each shot. After feature data normalization, the classifier determines the genre of each shot by analyzing the feature set.

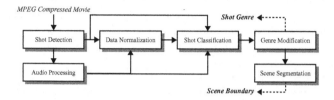

Fig. 1. Proposed shot classification and scene segmentation algorithm flow

3.1 Genre Set Definition

Before discussing the proposed classification algorithm, we need to define a shot genre set. In *Film Grammar* [13], the rules pertaining to the specific genre of a movie in the film literature [6], the following basic three types of scenes constitute the basic sentences of a movie [7]:

1. Dialogues without action
2. Dialogues with action
3. Actions without dialogue

In this paper, four shot genres are defined; *action, conversation, scenery* and *generic*. An *action* shot belongs to 3 and a *conversation* shot belongs to 1 or 2, hence the above three basic scene types are covered. A *scenery* shot is often inserted at the beginning of a scene and mainly used for the scene segmentation purpose described in Section 4. The other shots fall into *generic* class.

Action usually contains much dynamics in both audio and video in terms of audio volume and motion. In the case of semantic context, there could be destruction, fights, car chases, explosions, and so forth.
Conversation consists of some entity exchanging information by verbal communication to another entity, e.g. a human speaking to another. In terms of audio and visual dynamics, the conversation shot is almost static.
Scenery captures a scenery view with a slow, consistent camera operation such as zoom, pan, and tilt. This shot genre often appears in order to describe the changes in situations such as location.
Generic corresponds to a shot that does not fit into the above three genres.

3.2 Features Set Used for Classification

Selecting and determining a feature set is the most important element of shot classification, since the features are the interface to the underlying semantics.

The ultimate shot classification would be based on specific rule-based scene understanding, but it is still a very difficult task to achieve. Here, we use a composite, in a semantic context, low- and mid-level feature approach. The low-level features, which represents signal based characteristics, include motion intensity, consistency of motion direction, and audio power. The mid-level features, which can be obtained by analyzing and/or processing low-level features, include shot length and audio class. In the following, these features are further described.

Motion Intensity. An *Intensity* attribute of *MotionActivity* is defined in the MPEG-7 Visual [14]. Typical static shots such as *scenery* and *conversation* shots have very low motion intensity, whereas *action* shots such as car chase or fighting shots have quite high motion intensity, for example. Here, *Intensity* is calculated as the standard deviation of the motion vectors in a P picture, expressed by an integer value from 1 (lowest) to 5 (highest), and averaged in each shot. When discriminating among action, scenery and conversation shots, *Intensity* can provide important clues describing the amount of motion in that sequence.

Consistency of Motion Direction. Consistency of Motion Direction is mainly used for determining a scenery shot where a consistent camera motion such as zoom and pan is involved. MPEG-7 Visual specifies another aspect of *MotionActivity*, a *DominantDirection* attribute, which indicates dominant directions among 8 directions in a picture. Though capturing the characteristics of the above camera motions, *DominantDirection* is not appropriate for differentiating shot genres, because this attribute takes the averaged angle value which covers 0, 45, 90, 135, 180, 225, 270, and 315. Therefore, we employ the following criteria, where motion vectors are calculated using all the P pictures in each shot:

$$Consistency\,of\,Motion\,Direction = \frac{Number\,of\,MVs\,with\,dominant\,direction}{Number\,of\,total\,MVs}$$

$$(1)$$

Audio Power. Audio power is also used to differentiate shot genres. For example, in action shots the audio power is usually high due to sound effects and/or music, while in conversation and scenery shots the audio level is usually moderate or low. Here, we use the subband values of MPEG compressed audio to calculate audio power. RMS for j-th audio frame is then calculated as follows [15], where Sb is the number of subbands, $S_t[i]$ are the Sb-dimensional subband vectors, i is a subband number, and N is the number of samples in each subband:

$$RMS[j] = \sqrt{\frac{\sum_{i=1}^{Sb} M[i]^2}{Sb}}, \quad M[i] = \sqrt{\frac{\sum_{t=1}^{N} S_t[i]^2}{N}}, i = 1 \ldots Sb \qquad (2)$$

Shot Length. The video shot length is a powerful discriminant feature. According to our preliminary experiment, the shot length of action shots is usually shorter than those of scenery shots. Conversation shots with the actor/actress close-up may last relatively long, while other conversation shots may be short. The shot length is obtained by the shot boundary detection algorithm [12].

Audio Class. The shot genres are also correlated with audio classes (silence, speech, sound, etc.), for example, the conversation shot can be determined by exploiting speech segments. The audio classification algorithm [16] are used for classifying MPEG audio into four classes; silence, speech, music and applause. The number of occurrences of each audio class within a shot is normalized.

3.3   Feature Vectors Normalization

Feature vectors directly extracted from MPEG stream may be influenced by the encoding conditions such as recording audio volume and motion estimation accuracy. In some cases, audio volume in action shots of a certain movie may be smaller than that in conversation shots of another movie. Thus in our approach, shot length, motion intensity and audio power are normalized by dividing each value by a sequence averaged value, which absorbs these fluctuations.

3.4   Classifier

To associate independent feature vectors with a specific set of classes, many machine learning methods are available, such as neural networks, decision trees, SVM, and so forth. In a recent performance survey [17], several public-domain classifiers are benchmarked. The Linear Machine Decision Tree (LMDT) classifier [18] is proved to be advantageous in terms of classification accuracy and processing load. Therefore, the LMDT was chosen for the classification task in our proposed method.

4   Proposed Scene Segmentation Algorithm

As already described, the conventional scene segmentation methods focus on the changes of characterizations of low-level feature space. Here, we propose a scene segmentation algorithm using the shot classification results mentioned above. In this method, scene segmentation is performed based on the following two assumptions: 1) a scene generally consists of a group of shots belonging to the same genre, and 2) a single *scenery* shot locates a scene boundary. As for 1), before merging a sequence of shots, the misclassified shots are modified according to the adjacent shot genres. The modification strategies follow, which are also illustrated in Fig. 4, where $Genre(i)$ indicates the shot genre of the i-th shot:

- If $Genre(i) \neq Genre(i-1)$ and $Genre(i-1) = Genre(i+1)$, then $Genre(i)$ is modified to $Genre(i-1)$. Exceptionally a single scenery shot is regarded as a scene boundary.
- Otherwise, if $Genre(i) \neq Genre(i-1)$ and $Genre(i) \neq Genre(i+1)$, $Genre(i)$ is modified to $Genre(i-1)$.

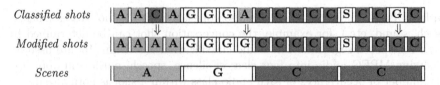

Fig. 2. Processing overview of shot genre modification and scene segmentation

Table 1. Shot classification results

(a) *Lord of the Rings*

	Gen.	Scen.	Conv.	Act.	Rec. [%]
Gen.	12	2	28	28	17.1
Scen.	0	6	0	0	100
Conv.	4	3	101	3	91.0
Act.	4	0	2	50	89.3
Prec. [%]	60.0	54.5	77.1	61.7	–

(b) *Spider Man*

	Gen.	Scen.	Conv.	Act.	Rec. [%]
Gen.	4	4	14	34	7.1
Scen.	0	10	0	1	90.9
Conv.	1	2	160	5	95.2
Act.	1	2	2	168	97.1
Prec. [%]	66.7	55.6	90.9	80.8	–

5   Experimental Results

Experiments were conducted to evaluate the proposed algorithms. In the experiments, portions of five kinds of MPEG-1 coded movies were used: 20 minutes from *Lord of the Rings* (2001), *Spider Man* (2002), *Pearl Harbor* (2001), and 10 minutes from *Back to the Future 3* (1990), and *Independence Day* (1996). 200 shots were selected among them (10 shots for each genre from each movie) and the LMDT tree was trained using the 8-dimensional feature vectors: 1) Motion intensity, 2) consistency of motion direction, 3) audio power, 4) shot length, and normalized occurrences of 5) silence, 6) speech, 7) music and 8) applause classes. The number of tree nodes was 4, after pruning the tree. When the training was finished, the feature vectors of 1101 shots were fed into the LMDT classifier.

5.1   Shot Classification Result

Table 1 shows the classification results for *Lord of the Rings* and *Spider Man*, where each row and column indicates a manually and an automatically classified genre, respectively. Each value indicates the number of shots. These results show that scenery, conversation and action genres are classified at a high recall rate, while generic has a very low recall value. Similar results were obtained in the other three movies. Based on our observations, the classification errors mainly occur from the following misinterpretations:

- *Shot length*; since shot boundaries between dark shots may be missed, shot length becomes longer. These shots are classified into conversation or scenery.
- *Audio*; since conversation shots with an ambient noise and/or background music may have large audio volume and they may be classified into applause or music instead of speech, which causes misclassification into action.
- *Consistency of motion direction*; in action shots with large camera motion, this value becomes large. Thus these shots may be classified into scenery.

Table 2. Scene segmentation results (number of scene genre boundaries)

(a) *Lord of the Rings*

	Gen.	Scen.	Conv.	Act.
Total	4	8	18	12
Detected	0	8	14	11
Undetected	4	0	4	1
Misdetection	0	2	11	9
Prec. [%]	–	80.0	56.0	55.0
Rec. [%]	0	100	77.8	91.7

(b) *Spider Man*

	Gen.	Scen.	Conv.	Act.
Total	4	4	16	8
Detected	0	2	14	8
Undetected	4	2	2	0
Misdetection	0	2	7	9
Prec. [%]	–	50.0	66.7	47.1
Rec. [%]	0	50.0	87.5	100

Table 3. Comparison of scene segmentation results (number of scene boundaries)

(a) *Lord of the Rings*

	Conventional	Proposed
Total	25	
Detected	6	21
Undetected	19	4
Misdetection	9	9
Precision [%]	70.0	40.0
Recall [%]	24.0	84.0

(b) *Spider Man*

	Conventional	Proposed
Total	20	
Detected	9	16
Undetected	11	4
Misdetection	7	10
Precision [%]	56.3	61.5
Recall [%]	55.0	80.0

– *Genre definition*; most generic shots are determined as either of the other, instead of generic; e.g. narrative shots are often classified into conversation.

Therefore, it is necessary to analyze the features in more detail or to incorporate other features. Defining new genres within generic shots is also promising since these errors are due to ambiguity in its definition. As for the computational cost, all the above mentioned classification task are performed more than 24 times faster than realtime playback on Pentium 4 2GHz PC.

5.2   Scene Segmentation Results

Table 2 shows the number of scene genre boundaries (beginning and end) for *Lord of the Rings* and *Spider Man*. Scenery scenes are successfully detected, and conversation and action scenes also result in high recall. In most cases, a scenery shot can contribute to correct scene boundary determination. Our method is also advantageous in terms of discriminating the scene genre derived from shot genres, which is difficult for the low-level feature approaches described in Section 2. On the other hand, no generic scene is detected since its classification accuracy is low as shown in 5.1. Therefore shot classification results, especially for generic shot, need to be improved. As described in 5.1, one of the solutions is to derive new genres currently involved in a generic class. The misdetections are mainly caused where a scene boundary and a shot genre change are not synchronized due to misclassifications of shot genre and where a scene changes to another without a scenery shot, especially conversation scenes.

Table 3 shows the resulting number of scene boundaries for the conventional method [8] and the proposed method. Only the number of scene boundaries is evaluated since the conventional method cannot identify the scene genre. As seen in the table, the proposed method achieves higher precision and recall. Though the conventional method well performs for scene changes accompanied by location change, i.e. conversation scenes outdoors and indoors, it is not robust for scene changes with different context and visually intense changes. The proposed method is more stable and robust since it employs several audio-visual features together and incorporates a scenery shot for scene segmentation purposes. For example, the proposed method successfully determines scene boundaries where a scene event changes from conversation to action at the same location.

6   Conclusions

This paper proposes shot classification and scene segmentation algorithms of MPEG compressed movies. We use only low- and mid-level features extracted on compressed domain, which greatly reduces the computational cost. Experimental results show that most of the shots are classified into subjectively appropriate genres, and that the proposed scene boundary/genre identification works successfully and outperforms the conventional method. The authors thank Dr. T. Asami, Dr. S. Matsumoto and Dr. M. Wada for their continuous supports.

References

1. ISO/IEC 15938-5: Information Technology – Multimedia Content Description Interface – Part 5: Multimedia Description Schemes. July 2003.
2. Z. Liu, J. Huang, and Y. Wang: Classification of TV Programs Based on Audio Information using Hidden Markov Model. IEEE Workshop on Multimedia Signal Processing, pp. 27-32, December 1998.
3. B.T. Truong, et al.: Automatic Genre Identification for Content-Based Video Categorization. IEEE ICPR 2000, Vol. IV, pp. 230-233, September 2000.
4. N. Vasconcelos and A. Lippman: Towards Semantically Meaningful Feature Spaces for the Characterization of Video Content. IEEE ICIP97, Vol. I, pp. 25-28, 1997.
5. S. Fischer, et al.: Automatic Recognition of Film Genres. ACM Multimedia 95, pp. 295-304, November 1995.
6. Z. Rasheed and M. Shah: Movie Genre Classification by Exploiting Audio-Visual Features of Previews. IEEE ICPR 2002, August 2002.
7. L. Chen and M. Tamer Özsu: Rule-based Scene Extraction from Video. IEEE ICIP2002, Vol. II, pp. 737-740, Sept. 2002.
8. Y. Rui, T.S. Huang, and S. Mehrotra: Exploring Video Structure beyond the Shots. IEEE ICMCS98, pp. 237-240, June 1998.
9. R. Lienhart, S. Pfeiffer, and W. Effelsberg: Scene Determination based on Video and Audio Features. IEEE ICMCS99, pp. 685-690, June 1999.
10. A. Hanjalic, et al.: Automatically Segmenting Movies into Logical Story Units. Visual Information and Information Systems, LNCS 1614, pp. 229-236, June 1999.
11. M. Sugano, R. Isaksson, et al.: Shot Genre Classification using Compressed Audio-visual Features. IEEE ICIP 2003, Vol. II, pp. 17-20, September 2003.

12. Y. Nakajima, et al.: Universal Scene Change Detection on MPEG Coded Data Domain. IEEE VCIP 97, Vol. 3024, pp. 992-1003, February 1997.
13. D. Arijon: Grammar of the Film Language. Focal Press, 1976
14. ISO/IEC 15938-3: Information Technology – Multimedia Content Description Interface – Part 3: Visual. July 2002.
15. G. Tzanetakis and P. Cook: Sound Analysis using MPEG Compressed Audio. IEEE ICASSP 2000, Vol. II, pp. 761-764, June 2000.
16. Y. Nakajima, Y. Lu, et al.: A Fast Audio Classification from MPEG Coded Data. IEEE ICASSP99, Vol. VI, pp. 3005-3008, March 1999.
17. P. W. Eklund: A performance survey of public domain supervised machine learning algorithms. Technical Report, University of Queensland St., 2002
18. P. E. Utgoff, et al.: Linear Machine Decision Trees. COINS Technical Report 91-10, Department of Computer Science, University of Massachusetts, January 1991.

Moving Object Segmentation: A Block-Based Moving Region Detection Approach

Wei Zeng[1] and Qingming Huang[2]

[1] Dept. of Compt. Sci. & Eng., Harbin Inst. of Technol., P.R.China
[2] Grad. Sch. of Chinese Acad. of Sci., P.R. China
{wzeng, qmhuang}@jdl.ac.cn

Abstract. This paper presents a novel block-based moving region detection algorithm to segment objects. The frame is first partitioned into homogeneous regions. Moving region is then determined by a voting procedure of pixels within the region. To exploit the local features, we divide the frame into $n \times n$ blocks and perform block analysis for moving object segmentation. An iterative motion re-estimation technique is developed to obtain reliable block motion parameters. The block eigen value is used to measure the block texture. Block location corresponding to the region partition is also considered as a clue. Based on motion, texture and location information, moving regions are classified. Experimental results show that our approach is robust and achieves remarkable performance.

1 Introduction

Moving object segmentation plays an important role in computer vision. Many applications, such as video surveillance, video coding, video indexing, etc., benefit from the reliable and robust object segmentation techniques. Many algorithms and techniques have been developed for the object segmentation task in the past decade. The techniques presented in [1-3] extract moving objects relied on motion information. However, most physical objects usually exhibit non-rigid motion and cannot be characterized by a parametric model, thus motion-based moving object segmentation techniques usually result in a finer partition than actually requirement.

To incorporate motion and object boundary, region-based segmentation algorithms introduce image partition to obtain accurate segmentation results. Original frame is first partitioned into homogeneous regions by image segmentation algorithms. Moving objects are then segmented by combining the motion information and the spatial partition. In [4], the first frame in a sequence is segmented into homogeneous regions based on pixel intensities. After spatial partition, regions are merged into objects based on the region motion similarity. On the other hand, human interaction can be introduced to obtain accurate object definition in the frame partition process. This leads to the semi-automatic object segmentation techniques [5, 6]. To employ the interaction of adjacent regions, Markov random filed model is adopted to guide object segmentation under the unified MRF-MAP framework [7-10].

K. Aizawa, Y. Nakamura, and S. Satoh (Eds.): PCM 2004, LNCS 3331, pp. 280–287, 2004.

However, local areas may have variant uncertainty in motion computation. For example, a very smooth block often fails in motion estimation and may obtain the false motion parameters. It poses a serious problem in moving object segmentation, because smooth foreground region will be miss-classified as background. To exploit local features of block, we design a block-based moving region detection algorithm to extract objects. The reference frame is first divided into nn blocks. Each block is imposed on an affine motion model estimated by a motion re-estimation scheme. Blocks are then classified into different types according to the block motion, texture and location information. Pixels within different types of blocks are assigned with different weights corresponding to the block types. Consequently moving regions are detected by the weighted pixel voting process. Moving objects are segmented by combination of the detected moving regions finally.

2   Block Motion Estimation

The reference image is divided into overlapped $2n \times 2n$ blocks ($n = 8$ in our experiments), where adjacent blocks are overlapped with each other by half of the block size. We adopt the six-parameter affine model as the block motion model. Suppose a pixel locates in the position (x, y). Under affine motion, the new location (x', y') is computed as

$$x' = a_1 x + a_2 y + a_3$$
$$y' = a_4 x + a_5 y + a_6, \tag{1}$$

where a_1 to a_6 are the motion model parameters. The robust regression for parametric motion estimation technique is used to estimate motion parameters [11]. The parameters are estimated by a coarse-to-fine gradient-based method, and solved by minimization the following error function

$$E_D(a) = \sum_R \rho((\nabla I)^T u(a) + I_t, \sigma), \tag{2}$$

where σ is a control parameter and R is the image region. The function ρ is the Geman-McClure norm in the implementation.

Sometimes motion estimation may fail to obtain true motion parameters due to large image warping, multiple motion, noise, occlusion, aperture problem, etc. Inaccurate motion estimation leads to unstable segmentation. To tackle the problem, we design a motion re-estimation technique that uses adjacent block motion as the parameter initialization in motion estimation. The idea underlying the approach is that motion parameters among adjacent blocks will have small difference, and can be used as a good initialization for the cost function minimization. From the up left corner of the image, block motion is re-estimated using the motion parameters of its four neighbor blocks as the initialization. If the new motion parameters are better than the old, we replace the motion parameters for the block. This step is repeated until no new motion model is assigned to any block. How to define the superior motion parameters is an interesting issue and outside the scope of this paper. We simple use the following rule to compare two motion models:

$$a(k) = \begin{cases} a(j) & if \quad N(a(i), a(j)) > S_b \cdot Th \\ a(k) & otherwise, \end{cases} \qquad (3)$$

where S_b is block size. $N(a(j), a(k))$ is the number of pixels whose DFD (displaced frame difference) under the motion parameters $a(j)$ is lower than the pixel under the motion parameters $a(k)$. Block j is a neighbor block of block k. Threshold Th is determined by image noise and set to 0.6 in our implementation.

As the block motion is estimated on overlapped $2n \times 2n$ blocks, an $n \times n$ block has four motion models covering the same block. Therefore, we assign the nn block with an optimal motion model by comparing the four motion models using Eq. (3). The advantage of the method is that the nn block motion is induced from larger blocks and reduces the over-fitting effect. Fig. 1 shows the comparison results between the proposed approach and the traditional block motion estimation technique without re-estimation. Two differences are computed between the traditional technique and our approach. The first is the difference of the average DFD between the corresponding blocks. The second is the difference of the summed block motion vector difference, which is computed between the block and its four neighbor blocks. Block motion vector is computed as the average of pixel-displaced vectors under the block motion. The experiments are carried out on the 53rd and 54th frame in the *Stefan* sequence. As shown in Fig. 1, the proposed approach has lower matching errors and smoother motion parameter space.

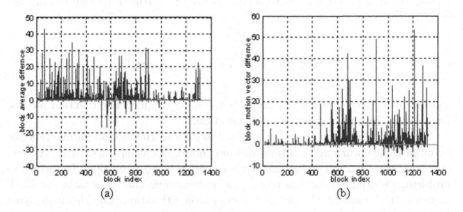

(a)   (b)

Fig. 1. Comparison between the proposed approach and the traditional block motion estimation.

3   Moving Region Detection

Each $n \times n$ block has variant motion, texture, and location information. Different types of blocks may provide different information in moving object segmentation. Therefore, block different block types provide different information for the moving region detection.

3.1   Block Motion Classification

According to the motion information, a block can be classified as one of the four motion types: background block (BB), moving block (MB), outlier block (O_uB), and occlusion block (O_cB). Suppose the background motion is well approximated by the dominant motion, moving block can be classified as outlier to the background. Let denote the DFD between frame I_k and I_{k+1}. Under the hypothesis that only background pixel is at location (x, y), the related difference d_k obeys a zero mean Gaussian distribution

$$p(d_k(x, y)) = \frac{1}{\sqrt{2\pi\sigma^2}} exp[-\frac{-d_k(x, y)^2}{2\sigma^2}], \tag{4}$$

where variance σ^2 is determined by the image noise. From the statistic theory, there are more than 95% pixels whose DFDs will drop into the close region $[-2\sigma, +2\sigma]$. Therefore, if a pixel's DFD is out of the range $[-2\sigma, +2\sigma]$, the pixel can be classified as an outlier. A block can be classified as the moving block, if the block has sufficient outliers. A moving block is defined as the block that has more than 20% outliers to the background motion; otherwise, the block is defined as the background block.

However, occlusion blocks are often classified as moving blocks because pixels in the occluded blocks have no matched pixels in frame I_{k+1}. An occluded background block will be classified as the moving block in the outlier detection. To tackle the problem, we develop a motion validation scheme to detect occlusion blocks. As the affine motion model is imposed on each block, we can validate the estimated block motion and detect outlier blocks to the block motion model. A moving block that fails in block motion estimation can be classified as an outlier block. If an outlier block locates on the boundaries of moving regions, the block is most probable an occlusion block. The outlier block within a moving region is probably caused by the object-to-object occlusion. Sometimes, the occlusion block is not outlier block, if the block has very similar texture to adjacent background. To find this type of occlusion blocks, we develop an overlapping area detection method. If a moving block and the background are both matched in the same target area of the frame I_{k+1} (the size of target area should be bigger than a predefined threshold), we compare the two motion models using Eq. (3). If the background motion model is better than the block motion model, the block is classified as an occlusion block. The idea underlying the approach is that the occluded block will partly match a background area in the frame I_{k+1} and has major matching errors.

3.2   Block Texture and Region Type Classification

Motion parameters for a sufficiently textured block are usually reliably estimated and thus the block texture can reflect the block reliability in motion estimation. Shi and Tomasi have proposed the block eigen value to represent the confidence of motion estimation [12]. Based on block eigen value, we classify blocks into two types: texture block (TB) and smooth block (SB). A texture block has sufficient texture and may have reliable motion parameters, while a smooth block may have false motion parameters. If a block's eigen value is above a predefined threshold, the block is classified as a texture block; otherwise it is a smooth block.

The reference frame is partitioned into homogeneous regions by an intensity-based watershed algorithm. A block locating in different position of a region may contribute variant information. For example, a smooth block within a region may provide less information than the block locating on the region boundaries. It is because region boundaries often suggest object boundary and provide relative high confidence in moving region detection. If a block has more than 80% pixels in the same region, the block is classified as an inner block (IB); otherwise the block is an edge block (EB).

4   Moving Region Detection

Moving objects can be considered to consist of moving regions. Moving region is determined by the types of blocks covering the region. If a region has majority of moving blocks, the region is classified as the moving region. However, a region may have several types of blocks simultaneously. Different types of blocks contribute different information in moving region classification. To make the moving region detection computation feasible, we assign each type of block with a weight. All pixels in a block have the same weight according to the block type. Consequently, the moving region $(MR(k) = 1)$ is classified by the sum of pixel weights as the following rule

$$MR(k) = \begin{cases} 1 & if \sum_{j \in R} W_j > 0 \\ 0 & otherwise. \end{cases} \tag{5}$$

In our weight assignment scheme, a moving block has positive weight, and a background block has negative weight. An outlier block has the small positive weight, while an occlusion block has zero weight. A smooth texture block has a scaled weight corresponding to the block motion type. If a smooth block is an inner block, the block weight is assigned to zero. The weight assignment rule is represented as

$$W_j = \begin{cases} \alpha \cdot s & j \in MB \\ \gamma & j \in O_u B \\ 0 & j \in O_c B \ or \ j \in SB \\ -\beta \cdot s & j \in BB. \end{cases} \tag{6}$$

where s is the scalar factor between 0 and 1. α, β and γ are constants determined by the relative weight to each block type.

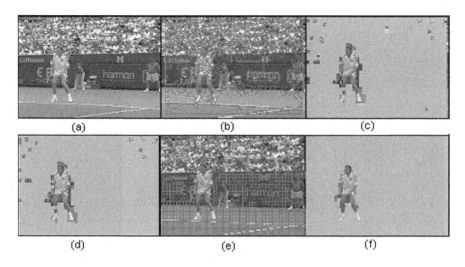

(a)   (b)   (c)

(d)   (e)   (f)

Fig. 2. Segmentation process of the proposed algorithm.

5   Experimental Results

The performance of the proposed algorithm was evaluated on several MPEG test sequences. The first is the *Stefan* sequence, which exhibits a moving camera and the man is presenting a non-rigid motion. The second is the *ETRI_A* sequence that is captured in an outdoor environment with a middle focal length. The two sequences are both SIF (352×240) sequences. The third is the *Hall* sequence, which is a typical videoconference sequence with QCF (176×144) format. The sequence displays slow motion over the stationary background.

Fig. 2 illustrates the segmentation process for the *Stefan* sequence between 50th and 51st frame. Fig. 2 (a) shows the original 51st frame. The result of spatial region partition is given in Fig. 2 (b). Although there are some fragments, most homogeneous regions are segmented out by the watershed algorithm and keep the region boundaries. After block motion type classification, moving blocks are found as outliers to the background motion. Because the real background motion cannot be completely approximated by the dominant motion model, some background blocks are miss-classified as shown in Fig. 2(c). Sometimes, smooth blocks in foreground region are also miss-classified as background blocks, e.g. the part of the man's right leg. The proposed overlapping area validation approach can successfully detect non-outlier occlusion blocks as displayed in Fig. 2(d). From Fig. 2(f), it can be clearly seen that our algorithm can efficiently segment moving objects by the block-based moving region detection approach though there are many smooth texture blocks in the frame (shown in Fig. 2(e)).

Fig. 3 shows the segmentation results for the *Stefan*, *ETRI_A* and *Hall* sequence. The segmented objects are displayed in Fig. 3 (c, f, i). Fig. 3 (a-c) demonstrate the segmentation results between 3rd and 4th frame for the *Stefan* sequence. In the scene of the *Stefan* sequence, background is panning left while

Fig. 3. Segmentation results of the proposed algorithm.

the man is standing in the center of frame. The spatial partition is performed on the 3rd frame. From Fig. 3 (c), the body of the man is entirely segmented from the moving background, but some background pixels are included in the object mask. It is because the partitioned region has inaccurate boundary and contains some background pixels. Fig. 3 (d-f) show the segmentation results of 66th and 67th frame for the *ETRI_A* sequence. The two men are moving from the left to right. The segmented object masks are given in Fig. 3 (f). The third line of Fig. 3 illustrates the results between 43th and 45th frame for the *Hall* sequence. Although a foreground block is miss-classified in the position of the suitcase (see Fig. 3(h)), the object is successfully segmented as well.

Our algorithm achieves satisfactory results in most cases. A bit of pixels are miss-classified in the object mask. It is because the spatial region partition cannot always coincide with the object boundary. From our experiments, the more accurate the region partition is, and the more precise the segmented results are. On the other hand, large size regions will have reliable segmentation results.

6   Conclusions

In this paper, we propose a novel moving object segmentation algorithm based on the block-based moving region detection. Block motion is reliably estimated by the proposed motion re-estimation scheme. Moving regions are efficient detected according to the types of blocks by the voting process. Moving objects are successfully segmented from the detected moving regions. As accurate spatial partition can improve the segmentation precision, future work will focus on developing more sophisticated spatial partition algorithms.

Acknowledgement. The work is supported by the NEC-JDL sports video analysis project and the One Hundred Talents Plan of Chinese Academy of Science.

References

1. Wang, J. and Adelson, E.: Representing Moving Images with Layer. IEEE Trans. Image Proc. **3** (1994) 625-638
2. Chang, M.M., Tekalp, A.M., Sezan, M.I.: Simultaneous Motion Estimation and Segmenta-tion. IEEE Trans. Image Proc. **6** (1997) 1326-1333
3. Wang, H.Y., and Ma, K.K.: Automatic Video Object Segmentation via 3D Structure Tensor. Proc. IEEE Int. Conf. Image Processing, Vol. 1. Barcelona, Spain (2003) 153-156
4. Wang, D.: Unsupervised Video Segmentation Based on Watersheds and Temporal Tracking. IEEE Trans. Circuits Syst. for Video Technol. **8** (1998) 539-546
5. Gu, C. and Lee, M.C.: Semiautomatic Segmentation and Tracking of Semantic Video Ob-jects. IEEE Trans. Circuits Syst. for Video Technol. **8** (1998) 572-584
6. Sun, S., Haynor, D.R., and Kim, Y.: Semiautomatic Video Object Segmentation using Vsnakes. IEEE Trans. Circuits Syst. for Video Technol. **13** (2003) 75-82
7. Gelgon, M. and Bouthemy, P.: A Region-Level Motion Based Graph Labeling Approach to Motion-Based Segmentation. Proc. IEEE Int. Conf. Computer Vision and Pattern Recognition. San Juan Puerto Rico (1997) 514-519
8. Tsaig, Y. and Averbuch, A.: Automatic Segmentation of Moving Objects in Video Se-quences: A Region Labeling Approach. IEEE Trans. Circuits Syst. for Video Technol. **12** (2002) 597-612
9. Cucchiara, R., Prati, A., and Vezzani, R.: Object Segmentation in Videos from Moving Camera with MRFs on Color and Motion Features. Proc. IEEE Int. Conf. Computer Vision and Pattern Recognition, Vol. 1. Madison, Wisconsin (2003) 405-410
10. Zeng, W. and Gao, W.: Unsupervised Segmentation of Moving Object by Region-based MRF Model and Occlusion Detection. Proc. The Fourth Pacific-Rim Conference on Multi-media. Singapore (2003)
11. Black, M.J. and Anandan, P.: The Robust Estimation of Multiple Motions: Parametric and Piecewise-Smooth Flow Fields. Computer Vision and Image Understanding. **63** (1996) 75-104
12. Shi, J. and Tomasi, C.: Good Features to Track. Proc. IEEE Conf. Computer Vision and Pattern Recognition. Seattle, WA USA (1994) 593-600

A Multi-view Camera Tracking for Modeling of Indoor Environment

Kiyoung Kim and Woontack Woo

GIST U-VR Lab.
Gwangju 500-712, S.Korea
{kkim,wwoo}@gist.ac.kr

Abstract. In this paper, we propose a method to track a multi-view camera for modeling indoor environment without calibration patterns. A multi-view camera is more convenient for modeling background or objects in speed and usage than expensive 3D scanner. However it requires a good initial pose and motion of a multi-view camera because the initial pose has an effect on overall accuracy. Thus, we use structural constraints of a multi-view camera and coplanar calibration pattern to provide a good initial poses. Then, we estimate camera motion by calculating rigid-body transformation between corresponding 3D points in each point clouds set. Finally we perform bundle adjustment in order to optimize all poses of the camera. Since it gives absolute camera motion in a room without scene constraints, the proposed technique is more useful than conventional pose estimation for modeling indoor environment. The proposed method can be used to accurately augment virtual objects.

1   Introduction

Camera calibration is the process that determines the relation between a world coordinate system and a camera coordinate system [1]. The relation is represented by camera parameters, and enables us to rectify images and reconstruct 3D background [2]. Especially, the pose of a camera including position and orientation plays an important role in registering initial point clouds for modeling indoor environment with a multi-view camera [3].

Many researchers have proposed various camera calibration algorithms in order to obtain camera parameters accurately. Tsai proposed two-step optimization algorithm that exploits an accurate non-coplanar pattern called Tsai's grid [1]. It is known as the first algorithm to consider radial coefficient of a lens distortion. However, a precise right angle pattern is required to get the correct results. Zhang [4], Sturm [5], etc., overcame this constraint by using homograpies of several images (more than three). Zhang proposed a flexible calibration method with a coplanar pattern for a desktop vision system (DVS) [4]. Calibration can be done by capturing feature points in a coplanar pattern at different positions. However, it requires several images in order to obtain accurate results [4].

The process of obtaining extrinsic parameters, which determine pose of a camera, with calibration patterns is inconvenient in modeling of indoor environment. The accuracy of camera poses largely depends on how precise calibration

K. Aizawa, Y. Nakamura, and S. Satoh (Eds.): PCM 2004, LNCS 3331, pp. 288–297, 2004.
© Springer-Verlag Berlin Heidelberg 2004

pattern is. Practically, it is difficult to make a calibration pattern with the required precision. In fact, it is more difficult than camera calibration because it uses only one image [6].

In this paper, we propose a method to track a multi-view camera for modeling of indoor environment without calibration patterns. Since the initial pose of a multi-view camera has an effect on overall accuracy, we use structural constraints of a multi-view camera to iteratively optimize an initial pose of a camera with known calibration pattern. This gives the absolute camera position in the indoor environment. Based on the initial position, we estimate camera motion by calculating rigid-body transformation between corresponding 3D points in each point clouds set. Finally, we apply bundle adjustment in order to optimize all poses of the camera. Thus, we can know the absolute motion of the camera in a room.

The proposed method provides a good initial pose with respect to a user-defined orientation in indoor environment. Since it only uses point clouds, it does not need calibration pattern to track a multi-view camera. It is useful for registration in an indoor environment object modeling, and it can be used to accurately augment virtual objects.

This paper is organized as follows: Camera model and the rigid-body transformation are introduced in Chapter 2. The method to find the initial pose and estimate motion by using 3D homographies is explained in Chapter 3. Then we show the experimental results of a proposed method in Chapter 4. We present the conclusion and future work in Chapter 5.

2   Camera Model and Rigid-Body Transformation

In a world coordinate system, a point, $M = [X, Y, Z]^T$, is projected onto $m = [u, v]^T$ in image plane by projection matrix P following simple pinhole camera model. Projection matrix consists of the product between intrinsic parameters and extrinsic parameters [2]. It is 3×4 matrix which has 11 degree of freedom.

$$\alpha \begin{bmatrix} u \\ v \\ 1 \end{bmatrix} = P \begin{bmatrix} X \\ Y \\ Z \\ 1 \end{bmatrix}, P = A \begin{bmatrix} R\,t \end{bmatrix} \tag{1}$$

where, α is an arbitrary scale factor, R is a 3×3 rotation matrix and $t = [t_x, t_y, t_z]^T$ is 3×1 translation matrix. $[Rt]$ is a transformation matrix between a world coordinate system to a camera coordinate system. A is a special matrix composed of intrinsic parameters which shape is as follows.

$$A = \begin{bmatrix} -fk_u & fk_u \coth\theta & u_0 \\ 0 & \frac{-fk_v}{\sin\theta} & v_0 \\ 0 & 0 & 1 \end{bmatrix} \tag{2}$$

where, f is a focal length, k_u and k_v are horizontal and vertical scale factors, respectively. (u_o, v_o) is a principal point where z axis meets image plane. θ

represents the angle between X and Y axis in retinal plane. In practice, θ is almost 90 degree, thus $fk_u \cot\theta$ becomes 0 and $\sin\theta$ has 1 value, ideally. In the 3D space, camera motion can be represented as sequential transformations. Change of coordinate system in the 3D space can be rigid-body transformation, 4×4 homography. Its homogeneous representation is shown in equation (3).

$$L_j = H_{i \to j} L_i = \begin{bmatrix} R_{i \to j} & t_{i \to j} \\ 0 & 1 \end{bmatrix} L_i \qquad (3)$$

where, $H_{i \to j}$ indicates a homography including rotation and translation matrices which transform L_i coordinate system to L_j coordinate system.

3   Pose Optimization and Motion Estimation

3.1   Initial Pose Optimization

We introduce the pose optimization method of a multi-view camera. The proposed method uses structure constraints of a multi-view camera. Coplanar pattern is used in determining orientation of a world coordinate system. Practically, the pose estimation with general calibration algorithm using coplanar pattern makes considerable errors. We found that the reconstructed shape of a multi-view camera with general camera calibration methods is much different from its original one shown in Fig. 1 (a), (b). We propose the optimization algorithm reducing those errors and overall procedure is shown in Fig. 1 (c). A multi-view camera is an extension of a general stereo camera. It has more than 2 lenses in one camera body. Generally, the poses of those lenses are determined with a small displacement error through lens alignment process in the factory. Initial

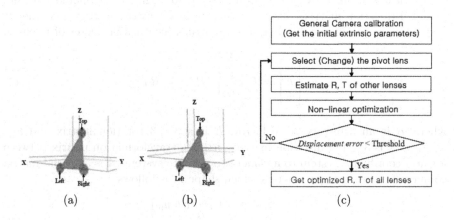

(a)   (b)   (c)

Fig. 1. Calibration error and overall procedure for optimizing poses of inner lenses (a) original shape of camera (3 lenses: top, left, right) (b) reconstructed shape of camera by general camera calibration (c) overall procedure for reducing calibration errors

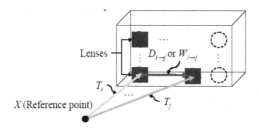

Fig. 2. Multi-view camera structure and displacement of inner lenses

displacements, then, were tested by using several calibration algorithms. Finally, manufacturers provide optimal intrinsic parameters and baselines so that it is possible to give disparity map. The important thing we focus on is that the distance among lenses are preserved whenever the camera is moving. We use displacement error including translation and rotation error as a cost function shown in equation (4).

$$R_{error} = \sum_{i=0, i \neq j}^{L-1} \|r_{i,j} - R_{i,j}\|, T_{error} = \sum_{i=0, i \neq j}^{L-1} \|G_{i,j} - S_{i,j}\|$$
$$E = R_{error} + \alpha T_{error}$$
(4)

where, L denotes combination number between lenses. α is a scale factor. $G_{i,j}$ and $R_{i,j}$ are ideal translation and rotation matrix between i_{th} lens and j_{th} lens, respectively. $S_{i,j}$ and $r_{i,j}$ is experimental translation and rotation matrix obtained by camera calibration between i_{th} lens and j_{th} lens. R_{error} is quaternion operation.

Fig. 2 shows a displacement of a multi-view camera. T_i and T_j is extrinsic parameters matrix of i_{th} and j_{th} lenses, respectively. And, $D_{i \rightarrow j}$ is transformation matrix between each lens in a camera coordinate system. $W_{i \rightarrow j}$ is transformation matrix between each lens in a world coordinate system.

Since the displacement of each lens is preserved in a world coordinate system, we can estimate extrinsic parameters of other lenses if we know the extrinsic parameter of a reference lens.

$$\begin{bmatrix} \acute{L}_j = W_{i \rightarrow j} \acute{L}_i \\ \widetilde{T}_j = T_i W_{i \rightarrow j} \end{bmatrix}, W_{i \rightarrow j} = \begin{bmatrix} R_i^T & -R_i^T t_i \\ 0 & 1 \end{bmatrix} D_{i \rightarrow j}$$
(5)

where, $D_{i \rightarrow j}$ is ideal transformation including $[Rt]$ in a camera coordinate system. $[R_i t_i]$ is extrinsic parameters matrix of i_{th} lens. We define the homography between i_{th} lens and j_{th} lens as $W_{i \rightarrow j}$.

When all lenses are located on the same plane and their Z-axis directions are parallel, $D_{i \rightarrow j}$ can be represented as the simple form which has only translation values.

$$W_{i \to j} = \begin{bmatrix} R_i^T & -R_i^T t_i \\ 0 & 1 \end{bmatrix} D_{i \to j} = \begin{bmatrix} R_i^T & -R_i^T t_i \\ 0 & 1 \end{bmatrix} \begin{bmatrix} I_{3 \times 3} & -I_{3 \times 3}^T t_{i \to j} \\ 0 & 1 \end{bmatrix} \qquad (6)$$

After estimating extrinsic parameters of other lenses, an overall optimization which minimizes calibration error must be performed. A cost function used in here is shown in equation (7).

$$\widetilde{E} = \sum_{i=0}^{L-1} \|T_i W_i X - T_j X\|, Optimize T_i = \begin{bmatrix} R_i & t_i \\ 0 & 1 \end{bmatrix} \qquad (7)$$

where, T_j is the transformation matrix of j_{th} lens obtained by general camera calibration. $T_i W_i$ represents estimated T_j, and X is the feature point in a world coordinate system. The proposed method is especially robust when the distance between the calibration pattern and a camera is far.

3.2   Direct Computation of Motion

The motion of a multi-view camera can be represented by rigid-body transformation. We calculate 4×4 homographies, called rigid-body transformation matrix, by using corresponding points of each point clouds without any calibration pattern. Overall flow of algorithm is shown in Fig. 3. In Fig. 3, A_i and B_i are the 2D corresponding points in each image. We can get depth values of A_i and B_i because we have several lenses. Since a multi-view camera cannot guarantee a perfect disparity map, we need the process to eliminate invalid points from the corresponding point set. Then, we get full 3D corresponding points from two images. Using these matched points, we can calculate rigid-body transformation. We exploit direct technique proposed by $K.Arun$ to calculate homography [7].

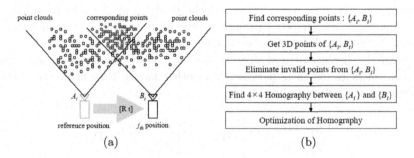

Fig. 3. Overall procedure to obtain 4×4 homography

We exploit direct technique proposed by $K.Arun$ to calculate homography [7]. Given two point clouds $\{a_i, b_i\}$ in 3D, 4×4 homography including rotation matrix and translation vector between each point cloud can be achieved through following steps. We use $Levenberg - Marquat$ non-linear optimization method to refine the results.

Step 1. Compute centers of each point cloud and vectors.

$$\bar{a}_i = \frac{1}{N} \sum_{i=0}^{N} a_i, \tilde{a}_i = a_i - \bar{a}_i, \bar{b}_i = \frac{1}{N} \sum_{i=0}^{N} b_i, \tilde{b}_i = b_i - \bar{b}_i \tag{8}$$

Step 2. Compute H matrix.

$$H = \sum_{i} \begin{bmatrix} \tilde{a}_{i,x}\tilde{b}_{i,x} & \tilde{a}_{i,x}\tilde{b}_{i,y} & \tilde{a}_{i,x}\tilde{b}_{i,z} \\ \tilde{a}_{i,y}\tilde{b}_{i,x} & \tilde{a}_{i,y}\tilde{b}_{i,y} & \tilde{a}_{i,y}\tilde{b}_{i,z} \\ \tilde{a}_{i,z}\tilde{b}_{i,x} & \tilde{a}_{i,z}\tilde{b}_{i,y} & \tilde{a}_{i,z}\tilde{b}_{i,z} \end{bmatrix} \tag{9}$$

Step 3. Compute the SVD(Singular Value Decomposition) of $H = USV^T$.
Step 4. Find $R = VU^T$ and Compute $Det(R) = 1$.
Step 5. Find $t = (b - R \cdot \tilde{a})$.
Step 6. Minimize R and t by using $Levenberg - Marquat$

$$Error = \|(R \cdot a_i + t) - b_i\|^2 \tag{10}$$

We obtain the $[Rt]$ matrix through above procedure without calibration patterns. The last step is called bundle adjustment [10]. In this step, we optimize all poses of cameras using the cost function defined in equation (11).

$$\tilde{E} = \sum_{i=0}^{L-1} \|T_i W_i X - T_j X\|, Optimize T_i = \begin{bmatrix} R_i & t_i \\ 0 & 1 \end{bmatrix} \tag{11}$$

where, M is the total number of images taken from a multi-view camera, $a_{j,i}, b_{j,i}$ is corresponding points between i_{th} and j_{th} point clouds.

4   Experimental Results and Analysis

We use $digiclops$, $IEEE1394$ multi-view camera, to obtain images and point clouds. $Digiclops$ exploits CCD sensor, $ICX084AK$, and its focal length is $6mm$ [8]. Especially, it has 3 lenses on the same plane, shown in Fig. 4(a), and its Z axis direction is parallel. Initially, we perform a Tsai's camera calibration with the non-coplanar pattern to achieve intrinsic parameters of each lens exactly. Fig. 4 shows the structure of $digiclops$ and the calibration pattern. The calibration pattern gives orientation of a world coordinate system and feature points.

The displacement error function of $digiclops$ defined in Chapter 3.1 is shown in (12). If we get optimized extrinsic parameters, then error is almost 0.

$$\begin{cases} T_{error} = \|S_{r,t} - G_{r,t}\| + \|S_{t,l} - G_{t,l}\| + \|S_{r,l} - G_{r,l}\| \\ R_{error} = \|R_t - R_r\| + \|R_r - R_l\| + \|R_l - R_t\| \end{cases} \tag{12}$$

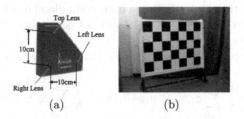

(a)   (b)

Fig. 4. Experimental setup (a) *digiclops* (b) calibration pattern

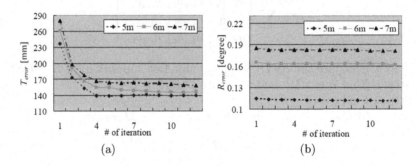

(a)   (b)

Fig. 5. Results of optimizing pose with increasing distance (a) T_{error} (b) R_{error}

where, R_{error} is quaternion operation. $G_{r,l}$ is ideal values related to the distance between *left* lens and *right* lens shown in Fig. 4. $S_{r,l}$ is experimental values related to the distance between *left* lens and *right* lens calculated by Tsai's camera calibration. Experimental results are shown in Fig. 5. Proposed method reduces calibration error effectively.

In order to measure an accuracy of camera motion, we perform experiments using synthetic data implemented in *OpenGL* space. Equation (13) is errors we measure.

$$Error = \sum_{i=0}^{M} \|(R \cdot a_i + t) - b_i\|^2, NormalizedError(NE) = \frac{Error}{M} \quad (13)$$

where, *Error* is the sum of all pixel errors which are differences between destination points $\{b_i\}$ and transformed source points $\{R \cdot a_i + t\}$. *NormalizedError(NE)* is the mean error of each pixel. The simulation results are shown in Fig. 6. Fig. 6 (a) shows initial two point clouds. Fig. 6 (b) shows the results after applying $[Rt]$ to source points. *Error* is under $0.001mm$. Fig. 6 (c) shows *Error* and *NE* when the number of points is increasing.

We also apply our algorithm to real environment. We use well-known *RANSAC* (Random Sample Consensus) method to find out 2D corresponding points from two images [9].

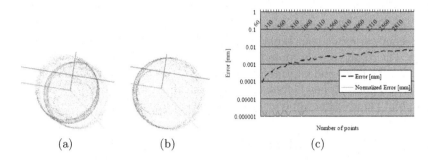

(a)   (b)   (c)

Fig. 6. Accuracy of rigid-body transformation (a) initial two point clouds (b) after fitting (c) errors as number of points is increasing

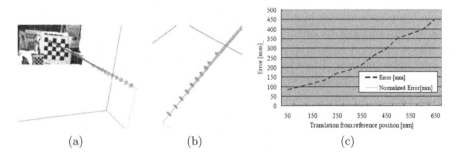

(a)   (b)   (c)

Fig. 7. Camera moving along Z axis (a) scene with cameras and point cloud (b) top view of motion (c) errors with translation along Z-axis from reference position

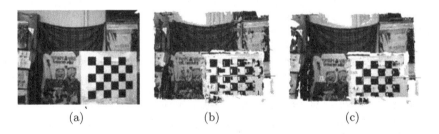

(a)   (b)   (c)

Fig. 8. Real scene experiment (a) original 2D image (b) before fitting two point clouds (c) after fitting two point clouds by obtained transformation

First, we move a multi-view camera along Z-axis (back-ward movement) by using accurate cart that enables us to move the camera along Z-axis exactly. We check a camera position per 50 mm movement. Fig. 7 (a), (b) show the camera motion in 3D space. Virtual cameras are represented as a circle. As expected, the motion follows Z axis. And the *Error* and NE are shown in Fig. 7(c). In this case, M is 120 points and NE is below 50 mm.

Second, we extend our experiment which estimates an arbitrary camera movement. The results are shown in Fig. 8. Fig. 8 (a) shows a starting scene. We move a camera by hand and capture point clouds at two different positions. Fig. 8 (b) shows two point clouds before applying transformation matrix. Fig. 8 (c) shows two point clouds after applying transformation matrix.

5   Conclusions and Future Work

We proposed a method to optimize camera poses with coplanar pattern and estimate motion for modeling indoor environment. The proposed method provides optimal starting position of a multi-view camera by using structural constraints. And camera motion is obtained by calculating homography between the corresponding points of each point clouds. In the experiment, we showed the simulation results and motion estimation results in the real environment. According to results, we can get registered point clouds of whole room environment by moving a multi-view camera. In order to improve accuracy, it is necessary to guarantee robust dense disparity estimation algorithm and obtain more corresponding points exactly. As future works, we consider full modeling of rooms or objects by using proposed method. The proposed technique can be extended to Augmented Reality, for accurately augmenting virtual objects, or Robot Vision.

Acknowledgements. This work was supported in part by the Ministry of Information and Communication (MIC) through the Realistic Broadcasting Research Center at GIST, and in part by MIC through Next Generation PC Project at GIST.

References

1. R. Tsai, "A versatile camera calibration technique for high-accuracy 3d machine vision metrology using off-the-shelf tv cameras and lenses," IEEE Journal of Robotics and Auto-mation, vol. 3, no. 4, pp. 323-344, 1987.
2. Richard Hartley and Andrew Zisserman, "Multiple View Geometry in computer vision", 2003.
3. S. Kim, E. Chang, C. Ahn and W. Woo, "Image-based Panoramic 3D Virtual Environment using Rotating Two Multi-view Cameras," IEEE Proc. ICIP2003, vol. 1, pp. 917-920, 2003.
4. Z. Zhang, "Flexible camera calibration by viewing a plane from unknown orientations," ICCV99, vol. 1, pp. 666-673, 1999.
5. Peter Sturm, Steve Maybank, "On Plane-Based Camera Calibration: A General Algorithm, Singularities, Applications", Proceedings of the IEEE Conference on Computer Vision and Pattern Recognition, Fort Collins, USA, pp. 432-437 June, 1999. 6.
6. P. Sturm, "Algorithms for Plan-Based Pose Estimation", Proc. Computer Vision and Pattern Recognition, vol.1, pp.706-711, 2002.

7. K.S. Arun, T. S. Huang, and S. D. Blostein, "Least-squares fitting of two 3-D point sets," IEEE Trans. Pattern Anal. Machine Intell., vol. PAMI-9, no. 5, pp.698-700, 1987.
8. Point Grey Research Inc., http://www.ptgrey.com, 2002.
9. M. Fischler and R. Bolles, "Random Sample Consensus: a Paradigm for Model Fitting with Application to Image Analysis and Automated Cartography", Commun. Assoc. Comp. Mach., 24:381-395, 1981.
10. B. Triggs, P. McLauchlan, R. Hartley and A. Fitzgibbon, "Bundle Adjustment - a Modern Synthesis", Springer Lecture Notes on Computer Science, Springer Verlag, 1883:298-375, 2000.

Image Registration Using Triangular Mesh

Ben Yip[1] and Jesse S. Jin[2]

[1] School of Information Technologies, the University of Sydney, NSW 2006, Australia,
benyip@it.usyd.edu.au,
http://www.it.usyd.edu.au/~benyip
[2] School of Design, Communication & Information Technologies, the University of
Newcastle, Callaghan, NSW 2308, Australia,
jesse.jin@newcastle.edu.au

Abstract. Image registration is a fundamental problem in the area of
computer vision and has been extensively researched. Different image
registration algorithm has its pros and cons. Unlike most of the algorithms, our approach defines a set of feature points uniformly distributed
on the image. The feature points are linked up as nodes in a triangular
mesh. The image registration in our approach seeks the corresponding
points in the other image, while maintaining the triangular mesh. This
approach guarantees the mapped result is smooth, and hence it is ideal
for smooth objects. Our approach is also relatively good for images that
do not have distinctive features.

1 Introduction

Image registration is a fundamental problem in the area of computer vision. Since
the publication by Marr and Piggio (1977) [12] of an algorithm for the stereo
matching, this area has been extensively researched. [1] Image registration is
commonly needed in two applications areas, motion tracking in video sequence
and binocular stereo matching.

In the application of motion tracking, images acquired from the same viewpoint at different time are compared to find the feature correspondence. Ishikawa
and Jermyn (2001) [7] assumed the series of images in time is the third dimension of the multiple 2D regions, and it uses an energy minimization approach
to select the 3D region, and hence the selected region in each image are corresponded. Wang and Duncan (1996) [15], Crossley, et al (1998) [2] suggested
algorithms for temporal matching while also taking advantage of the binocular
stereo cameras. There are some researches on mesh-based motion estimation and
Wang (2002) [16] introduced a good mesh-based framework. Nosratinia (2001)
[13]utilized the block matching algorithm motion vectors with a warping kernel
to achieve a mesh-based motion estimation.

In the application of binocular stereo, two images are acquired from two
known viewpoints at the same time. Grimson [4]-[6] is one of the better known
researchers in this area in since 1980s. Dehne and Guimarges (1997) [3] took
a subset of points and found the corresponding mapping of that subset based

K. Aizawa, Y. Nakamura, and S. Satoh (Eds.): PCM 2004, LNCS 3331, pp. 298–303, 2004.
© Springer-Verlag Berlin Heidelberg 2004

on analyzing a connected sub-graph. Pilu (1997) [14] solved the correspondence problem based on singular value decomposition. Maciel and Costeira (2002) [10]-[11] formulated the mapping problem into an integer optimization problem with a concave minimization function.

In general, there are two schools of approaches of image registration. One way, is separately find the feature points in each of the images and then match them up [3] [14]. Another way, which this paper adopts, is to find the feature points in one of the images first, and then seeks the corresponding points in the other image.

1.1 Our Approach

Feature point finding is an important initial process of image registration. However, algorithms on the feature point extractions are not reliable in general, and hence contribute inaccuracy to the mapping process. Our approach takes feature points uniformly from the input image. The feature points are linked up by a triangular mesh. We first find the best match of each feature point within its search space. Then, by sorting the matching result, we recalculate the mappings that are inconsistence with their neighboring feature points in the triangular mesh. Our approach naturally produces a smooth mapping, and hence is ideal for smooth objects. The results are evaluated with synthetic data and real data.

2 The Algorithm

2.1 Feature Points and Regular Triangular Mesh

If the computational time is not an issue, it is always possible to consider every pixel of the image is a feature point, and applies a mapping algorithm on each of the pixels. However, this is not practical and hence we need to find a subset of pixels as the feature points to which we apply the mapping algorithm with.

There are many ways to determine a feature in a given image, most commonly it is obtained from edge detection. [4] Our approach defines the nodes of a regular triangular mesh uniformly laid on the input image as the feature points. It is used because it eliminates the inaccuracy caused by wrongly detected feature points and it also guarantees an even distribution of feature points around the image.

Figure 1 depicts a sample of regular triangular mesh with 49 (7 x 7) feature points. In the examples of this paper, we used a 15 x 15 regular triangular mesh on the image registration. Theoretically, higher the dimensions of the regular triangular mesh, better the image registration result it could obtain.

Feature Space and Search Space. The feature space used in this algorithm is a 9 x 9 block of RGB color, with the feature point in the middle. The search space used in this algorithm is a 79 x 79 block of RGB color, with the expected position of the feature point in the middle of the search space.

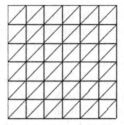

Fig. 1. A sample of a regular triangular mesh with 49 feature points.

Search Strategy. The examples in this paper contains no additional information on the input images, hence we assumed the expected positions of the feature points are the same as the positions of the feature point in the original image. In the situation of binocular stereo mapping or motion tracking, we could have an estimation of the ex-pected position based on the epipolar geometry or the motion vector in the video en-coding.

Similarity Metric. The similarity basically is defined as the average color difference for each of the pixel in the feature space, i.e. smaller the similarity value, better the match is found. Let F_{ij} be the pixel at the (i, j) position of the feature block, with (0,0) equals the feature point fp. Let S_{ij} be the pixel at the (i, j) position of the search block with (0, 0) equals the searching point sp. Let R(p1, p2) denotes the absolute difference of the red channel for pixel p1 and pixel p2. G(p1, p2) and B(p1, p2) are similarly defined for color green and blue. The similarity is defined as:

$$s = \lambda \sum \sum \frac{R(F_{ij}, S_{ij}) + G(F_{ij}, S_{ij}) + B(F_{ij}, S_{ij})}{3\|F\|} \tag{1}$$

where $\| F \|$ is the size of the feature space, which is 81 (9 x 9 block) in our example. λ is a scalar, ranges between 1 and 3, to panelize points further away from the expected position. It is based on the block distance from the search position to the feature point position, and is defined as:

$$\lambda = (1 + \frac{|sp.x - fp.x|}{maxX} + \frac{|sp.y - fp.y|}{maxY}) \tag{2}$$

where $maxX$ and $maxY$ are the furthest point away from the feature point, which both have the value of 39 (79 x 79 block of search space) in our example. Our experiments show that when the expected position is unknown, λ should be set to 1, i.e. ignoring the distance penalty variable, in order to give a better result.

Other than the matching position is found, the process of image registration also outputs the similarity values, which is used in the secondary feature point mapping later on.

Fig. 2. The pair of image used to test the algorithm. A RGB color picker image (left) is warped to generate the second image (right).

2.2 Secondary Feature Point Mapping

Finding the best match position for each feature point is a local process, and there is no consideration on the matching results of its neighbor feature points. It is possible that the resulting mesh after the primary feature point mapping may have crossings in the triangular mesh. This could be caused by the fact that there is an occlusion, or it is a mismatch. Our approach targets for a smooth mapping, and hence the resulted tri-angular mesh should not have crossings. Interested readers about occlusion may refer to Laurent, el al. [8]-[9]

Our approach first sort each of the feature points by their similarity scores in ascending order. Then, we add each of the sorted feature points into the output triangular mesh. If the newly added feature point generates a crossing, then this feature point needs to be re-mapped. The re-mapping process is the same as the primary feature point mapping described above, except that the search space is now bounded by the quadrangle form by the top, left, bottom, right neighbors of the feature point.

3   Evaluation

3.1   Synthetic Images

A pair of synthetic images with 256 x 256 pixel of RGB color is generated to test the algorithm. The first image is shown in Figure 2 (left) and the second image is generated by applying an image warping of the first image, and is depicted in Figure 2 (right). A 15 x 15 triangular mesh is used in this example as shown in Figure 3 (left). The same warping operation is applied to it and the result is shown in Figure 3 (middle). The output triangular mesh, as shown in Figure 3 (right), is close enough to the correct solution.

3.2   Real Images

A pair of 256 x 256 RGB images is captured from a video stream. Two frames of one second apart are captured and shown in Figure 4. Again, we use the same 15 x 15 triangular mesh as in the synthetic testing. The resulted triangular mesh is

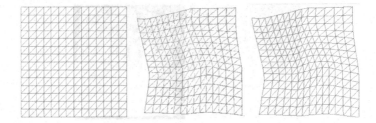

Fig. 3. This shows the result of our synthetic data testing. The initial 15 x 15 triangular mesh (right). The triangular mesh is applied with the same warping operation. (middle) The resulted triangular mesh (right) shows the algorithm has performed well as expected.

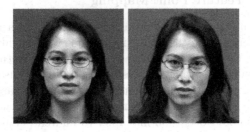

Fig. 4. Two frames from a video shot of one second apart are the input of our algorithm.

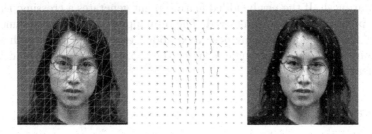

Fig. 5. The output triangular mesh of our algorithm (left) could be used to calculate the optical flow (middle) and it is superimposed on top of the input image (right).

shown in Figure 5 (left). The movement of the feature points, the optical flow, is drawn in Figure 5 (right). It is clear that the optical flow shows the head movement correctly.

4   Conclusion

There are many image registration algorithm researched in the literature, earlier ones could be dated back in 1970s. Our approach is unique in a way that it uses triangular mesh with image registration and having uniformly distributed feature points. Our approach is not designed for images with distinctive feature points, or images with occluded objects. It is designed for images of objects with smooth depth. It performs well relatively on images that do not have distinctive feature points. In addition, it is not uncommon that the result of image registration is used for the purpose of 3D re-construction. Our approach of using triangular mesh is the convenient to perform 3D modeling and rendering in the later stage of the whole process. [17]

References

1. Brown, L.G.: A survey of image registration techniques. ACM Computing Surveys (CSUR) **24** 4 (1992)
2. Crossley, S., Thacker, N.A., Seed, N. L.: Benchmarking of Bootstrap Temporal Stereo using Statistical and Physical Scene Modelling. BMVC (1998) 346-355
3. Dehne, F., Guimarges, K: Exact and approximate computational geometry solutions of an unrestricted point set matching problem. Information Processing Letters **64** (1997) 107-114
4. Grimson, W. E. L.: A Computer Implementation of a Theory of Human Stereo Vision. Philosophical Transactions of the Royal Society of London, Series B, 292, (1981) 217- 253
5. Grimson, W. E. L.: Computing Shape using a Theory of Human Stereo Vision. IEEE Computer Society's Fifth Int. Comp. Software and Applications Conf., Chicago, (1981) 209-210
6. Grimson, W. E. L.: Computational Experiments with a Feature-Based Stereo Algorithm. IEEE Pattern Analysis and Machine Intelligence, **7**(1) (1985) 17-34
7. Ishikawa, H., Jermyn, I. H.: Region extraction from multiple images. Proc. 8th IEEE Int'l Conf. Comp. Vis.. Vancouver, Canada (2001)
8. Laurent, N., Lechat, P., Sanson, H.: Limitation of triangles overlapping in mesh-based motion estimation using augmented Lagrangian. In Proc. International Conference Image Processing (ICIP98), Oct 1998, **2**, 223-227
9. Laurent, N., Lechat, P., Sanson, H.: Hierarchical mesh-based global motion estimation, including occlusion areas detection. In Proc. International Conference on Image Processing (ICIP 2000), Sept 2000, **3**, 620-623
10. Maciel, J., Costeira, J.: Robust Point Correspondence by Concave Mininization. Image and Vision Computing, Special Issue BMVC'00, Oct. 2002 (2000)
11. Maciel, J., Costeira, J.: Towards a Global Solution of the Correspondence Problem. IEEE Trans. PAMI (IN PRESS). (2003)
12. Marr, D., Poggio, T.: A Theory of Human Stereo Vision. Technical Report: AIM-451, MIT, USA. (1977)
13. Nosratinia, A.: New kernels for fast mesh-based motion estimation. IEEE Transactions on Circuits and Systems for Video Technology, **11**(1), Jan 2001, 40-51
14. Pilu, M: A direct method for stereo correspondence based on singular value decomposition. In Proc. IEEE Computer Society Conference on Computer Vision and Pat-tern Recognition, San Juan, Puerto Rico. (1997)
15. Wang, W., Duncan J.H.: Recovering the Three Dimensional Motion and Structure of Multiple Moving Objects from Binocular Image Flows. Computer Vision and Image Understanding, **63**, No. 3, (1996) 430-446
16. Wang, Y., Ostermann, J., Zhang, Y-Q,.: Video Processing and Communications, Prentice Hall, section 6.6. (2002) p169-176
17. Yip, B., Jin, J.S.: 3D reconstruction of a human face with monocular camera based on head movement. In Proc. VIP 2003 conference, Sydney, Australia (IN PRESS)

Online Learning Objectionable Image Filter Based on SVM

Yang Liu, Wei Zeng, and Hongxun Yao

School of Computer Science and Technology, Harbin Institute of Technology, Harbin, 150001, China
{yliu,wzeng}@jdl.ac.cn; yhx@vilab.hit.edu.cn

Abstract. In this paper we propose an on-line learning system for objectionable image filtering. Firstly, the system applies a robust skin detector to generate skin mask image, then features of color, skin texture and shape are extracted. Secondly these features are inputted into an on-line incremental learning module, which derives from support vector machine. The most difference between this method and other online SVM is that the new algorithm preserves not only support vectors but also the cases with longest distance from the decision surface, because the more representative patterns are the farthest examples away from the hyperplane. Our system is tested on about 70000 images download from the Internet. Experimental results demonstrate the good performance when compared with other on-line learning method.

1 Introduction

With the rapid development of internet, more and more digital information can be acquired from the world-wide web. Although the new tool bring us convenience for digital communication, it also makes it more easy for young persons to browse contents on adult web site. This side effects of internet has brought increasing severe social problems, such as sexy crime. It is urgent for us to set up effective safety net between internet and personal computer.

Some schemes have been implemented to solve the problem. All these methods can be divided into two types. One is to collect IP addresses within which adult contents exist. Once the web server finds these web sites are being accessed, it will block this behavior. The other is to stop the links through text semantic analysis. Some search engines clean the sexy web sites by this method. Although these two methods are effective partially, they face a lot of problems, since much more new sexy web sites are set up every day and text semantic analysis is difficult, even more, some famous search engine does not take measures, such as Google.

The two mentioned approaches both use net tools to avoid adult web site being accessed. In order to more effectively screen these objectionable images, a new method is being developed in which image content analysis technology is used. Forsyth's research group has done the pioneer work[1]. They designed and implemented a system that can tell whether an image contain warm description

K. Aizawa, Y. Nakamura, and S. Satoh (Eds.): PCM 2004, LNCS 3331, pp. 304–311, 2004.

content. In their scheme, skin detection and shape processing were combined to detect human body. Wang et al. presented a system of screening objection images for practical applications [2]. Wang's method employed a combination of an icon filter, a graph-photo detector, a color histogram filter, a texture filter and a wavelet-based shape matching algorithm. The image that passed histogram analysis, texture analysis and shape matching was classified as objectionable image. In [3] Jones and Rehg used statistical method for skin detection and artificial neural network to classify.

As our system is designed for gateway to identify objectionable image, system with on-line learning capacity are necessary. Meanwhile, through our analysis, objectionable image filtering system is unlike other two classes pattern recognition problem, because the class correspond to benign images is an open field. It is difficult to select the negative cases, if objectionable images are regarded as positive class. What type and how many images are selected? All the problems urge us to develop an on-line learning system for filtering objectionable images.

In this paper, we propose a new method for incremental learning support vector machine. In our algorithm, not only the support vectors but also the cases farthest from decision surface are reserved for the next learning step. Our method is different from the approaches in [4], [5], in which only the support vectors are preserved. Experimental results show that the proposed method has better performance.

2   Incremental Learning Support Vector Machine

In this section support vector machine will be introduced briefly, then we will give our new incremental learning support vector machine.

2.1   Support Vector Machine

Support vector machine is derived from Vapnik's work on statistic learning theory[6],[7], in which he regard the procedure of searching a decision rule as a functional problem. The goal is to find a function that can minimize the expected risk, described as (1).

$$R(u) = \int \int L\left(y, f\left(X\right)\right) \ dp(y|X) \ dp(X). \tag{1}$$

where $p(X)$, $p(y|X)$ are the distribution of the examples and their classification respectively. Unfortunately, these two functions can not be known in general and SVM has to estimate them from example set $(X_i, y_i), i \in N$. Instead of computing formula (1), SVM converts this problem into finding a hyperplane that maximize the minimal distance between example and the plane. The decision function can be written as $f(X) = sign(\sum_i^N \lambda_i K(X_i, X) + b)$, where all λ_i are calculated through the optimization process. The examples with non-zero λ_i are called support vectors and K is a kernel function that can convert non-linear problem into linear problem.

2.2   Incremental Support Vector Machine

Support vectors have an important property, that if SVM is trained only on support vectors, the same result will be acquired as the one trained on the whole data set. However it does not mean that the support vectors can represent the whole data set in all directions, since support vectors are only description of the decision boundary between the two classes examples, but not of the examples distribution. Well then, how can we select a small part of examples which can represents the complete data set more effectively? What are the more representative ones except for the support vectors? In our experiments, we found that some support vectors are ambiguous ones that can be classified into either class. Are such examples representative? In people's intuitive opinion, the more "classic" ones are the more representative. What are the "classic" ones in support vector machine in our objectionable image filtering system? It is observed that most of the examples with largest absolute value of decision function are easier to be "classified" since they are clear semantically. It means that these examples are more representative than support vectors for complete data set. This property motivates us to reserve these farthest examples for the next learning step in incremental SVM.

The second reason that we do like this is of concept inconsistent. In online learning process learning machines have to face the problem of drifting concept, because the distribution of the incremental data given to the machine in continuous learning steps may be different. Only the support vectors are not sufficient in this situation. We may ask, what if the farthest examples are put into incremental data set? Thus, support vectors depict one margin of the distribution of previous training data, while these farthest ones depict the other margin.

The upper mentioned reason drive us to update the SVM's optimization object as (2).

$$Min : \Phi(W, \xi) = \frac{1}{2}(W \bullet W) + C(\sum_{i=1}^{N} \xi_i + \sum_{i \in S} \xi_i + \sum_{i \in F} \xi_i)$$

$$subject \quad to : y_i(W^T X_i + b) \leq 1 - \xi_i, i = 1, \cdots, N$$

$$\xi_i \geq 0, i = 1, \cdots, N \qquad (2)$$

Where S and F are support vectors set and farthest cases set respectively. In comparison with SV incremental support vector machine, our new incremental support vector machine preserves not only the support vectors but also the vectors with the longest distance far from the decision surface for next learning step. Although the optimization function is different only in the last term $\sum_{i \in F} \xi_i$ from Stefan's method, the idea has proceeded. The farthest examples incorporate new meanings.

As described in [5], we also make the preserved examples have more punishment when an error occurs on them than an error on new incremental training data. Thus, the formula (2) is rewritten as (3).

$$\Phi(W,\xi) = \frac{1}{2}(W \bullet W) + C(\sum_{i=1}^{N} \xi_i + L\sum_{i \in S} \xi_i + L\sum_{i \in F} \xi_i),\tag{3}$$

where L is defined as:

$$L = \frac{\#All\_Trainning\_Examples}{\#SV + \#Farthest\_Examples}$$

3 Skin Detection and Feature Extraction

3.1 Skin Detection

Generally, objectionable images have much area of skin, so we decide to extract features from skin mask image, in which skin pixels are labeled as 1, and non-skin pixels as 0. Then, skin detection process can be treated as a two class classifying problem.

As described in [11], a skin color detector with the same performance can always be found no matter what color space is chosen, if there exists an invertible transformation between the color spaces. Since, statistical histogram of skin can describe the skin distribution accurately, the non-parametric method is adopted. Experiments show that it can acquire better performance than that of Gauss Mixture Model (GMM). Due to the space limitation, the result is not given out. According to the theory of Bayesian classification, the classifier for skin detection can be described as formula(4).

$$P(skin|rgb) = \frac{[P(rgb|skin)P(skin)]}{[P(rgb|skin)P(skin) + P(rgb|!skin)P(!skin)]}.\tag{4}$$

Where $P(skin|rgb)$ represents the probability of the pixel with the value rgb being skin. When the probability is larger than a threshold, then the pixel is regarded as pixel. Varying the threshold, we can acquire the ROC (receiver operating characteristic) curve. In order to save space, the ROC curve is not depicted. At last, the threshold corresponding to the rate of correct detection is 0.841 and the error rate 0.143 is adopted. All these results are tested on one hundred million skin pixels.

Because the reflection of the skin, some skin pixels are desaturated. Those skin pixels will be classified as non-skin pixel. Some pixels in shadow region will also be miss-classified because the color is very close black. These two types errors will produce many skin holes in the detected skin regions. Therefore, we apply a region analysis to eliminate the small holes. If the small region is surround by skin color and its color is closed to white or black. The region is marked as skin region.

At the same time, some pixels that belong to the background are detected as skin region. It produces some small skin regions in the background. To remove these small skin regions, we count the size of the connected small skin region. If connecting small skin area is less than 0.05 of the whole detected skin pixel number, the region is classified as background. The median filter is used to filter out the noise at the last step. Figure 1 gives some detection results.

Fig. 1. The results of skin detection

3.2   Feature Extraction

Following the output of skin detection process, feature extraction module is performed. To represent the objectionable images effectively, three kind of features are selected, including color feature, texture feature and shape feature. Details are described as the following.

Color feature: Such as mean of skin color probability, variance of skin color probability; The mean and variance of skin probability reflect the distribution of skin in the skin probability space. The two measures are calculated by (5)and(6).

$$P_{mean} = \frac{1}{N}\Sigma_{j \in skin}P_j(skin|rgb),\tag{5}$$

$$P_{var} = \frac{1}{N}\Sigma_{j \in skin}P_j(skin|rgb) - P_{mean},\tag{6}$$

where the N is the number of detected skin pixels.

Texture feature: Include texture contrast, texture coarseness. The texture contrast is defined as (7)

$$T_{con} = \frac{\sigma}{(\alpha_4)^4},\tag{7}$$

where $\alpha_4 = \mu_4/\sigma^4$ is kurtosis. μ_4 is the forth order moment and σ^2 is variance; And the texture coarseness is formulated as (8).

$$T_{crs} = \frac{1}{m \times n}\sum_{i=1}^{m}\sum_{j=1}^{n}S_{best}(i,j), S_{best}(i,j) = 2^k.\tag{8}$$

where m and n is the size of the window used to detect skin region. More details can be found in [12].

Shape feature: Include skin region area, region edge intensity, zernike moment.The area feature describes the proportion of skin pixel to the image. The compactness feature is calculated by (9).

$$C = \frac{(region\_border\_length)^2}{area}.\tag{9}$$

The zernike moment descriptor is represented by a set of ART (Angular Radial Transform) coefficients, and the definition can be formularized as (10).

$$F_{nm} = \langle V_{nm}(\rho,\theta), f(\rho,\theta) \rangle = \int_0^{2\pi}\int_0^1 V_{nm}^*(\rho,\theta)f(\rho,\theta)\rho d\rho\theta d\theta,\tag{10}$$

where F_{nm} is an ART coefficient of order n and m, $f(\rho, \theta)$ is an image function in polar coordinates, and $V_{nm}(\rho, \theta)$ is the ART basis function that are separable along the angular and radial directions. [13] describes more details.

The three type features involve low level and high level features. The former two are low level, and the latter is high level.

The third module is the classifier. There are two available incremental learning algorithms for us: incremental decision tree [10] and incremental support vector machine. For the sake of implementing the incremental learning capacity, decision tree has to maintain an information list for every node that stores prior classification info. It is very difficult to deal with the list, because it will cost so much memory when the data set is large. While incremental learning support vector machine has not this shortcoming. In the filtering system our incremental support vector machine is adopted.

4   Experiments

4.1   Experiment Design

In our experiment, we downloaded 70,406 nature images from the Internet and classified them into 11,349 objectionable images and 59,057 benign images by hand. For convenience, the objectionable images set is called positive case set, while the other one is called negative case set. The three kinds of features comprise a vector containing 49 components. Before training, every dimension attribute is scaled to expectancy 0 and variance 1.

To check the performance of our incremental learning support vector machine, all collected images are divided into six groups uniformly. Every group contains 1891 objectionable images and 9842 benign images. The former 5 groups are used for incremental training data set and the last group used for the test set. In order to eliminate contingency factor, all the following results are obtained on six test processes. Every group is used as test set rotatively and other groups are used as training data for five incremental learning steps. Before training the SVM in the new learning step, we incorporate all support vectors and five percent of farthest examples into the incremental training data set. Radial basis function is used as kernel with gama=0.01.

4.2   Experimental Results and Analysis

In this section the accuracy, precision and recall are defined as the followings respectively.

$$Accuracy = \frac{Num(o) + Num(n)}{N},$$

where $Num(0)$ is the number of truly classified objectionable images and $Num(n)$ is the number of truly classified non-objectionable images. The other two terms are defined as followings,

$$recall = \frac{a}{N_1}, \quad precision = \frac{a}{N_2}.$$

Table 1. Accuracy of the three earning algorithm (Method 1 is batch SVM, method 2 is our method and method 3 is the method in [5])

Test number	Method 1	Method 2	Method 3
1	91.52 %	91.52%	91.52%
2	91.73 %	91.01%	89.27%
3	91.40 %	91.40%	90.05%
4	91.65 %	91.00%	88.85%
5	91.50 %	90.85%	88.50%

Table 2. Precision of the three methods (Method 1 is batch SVM, method 2 is our method and method 3 is the method in [5])

Test number	Method 1	Method 2	Method 3
1	75.66 %	75.66%	75.66%
2	74.10 %	70.28%	63.35%
3	72.62 %	73.14%	67.72%
4	74.17 %	70.66%	63.09%
5	71.88 %	70.60%	61.82%

In these two formulas a is the number of truly classified objectionable images, N_1 is the number of all the objectionable images, and N_2 is the number of images that are classified as objectionable images.

Table 1 illustrates the accuracy of the two different incremental support vector machines and the batch SVM on objectionable images filtering system. From the test result, we find that the accuracy of incremental learning only with support vectors drops as the learning process continues. Our new method's accuracy has drops and rises, but it is always better than SV-incremental SVM.

Table 2 and 3 describe the precision and recall of the three methods. The same as the accurate our new methods has better performance than only support vector incremental learning algorithm.

Table 3. Recall of the three methods (Method 1 is batch SVM, method 2 is our method and method 3 is the method in [5])

Test number	Method 1	Method 2	Method 3
1	69.85 %	69.85%	69.85%
2	74.87 %	74.00%	73.21%
3	74.87 %	73.72%	73.09%
4	76.33 %	75.45%	74.20%
5	77.59 %	76.53%	74.90%

All the results tell us our incremental learning SVM has similar performance to that of batch SVM, But it is faster than batch SVM in learning process since it need little examples to be trained

5 Conclusion and Future Work

Our system makes a profitable attempt at to filter objectionable images through image contents analysis, although we are facing a lot of problems, for instance, how to make skin detection more robust in variant light condition and to extract more helpful visual feature? Our new incremental support vector machine has better performance than the traditional incremental learning method.

In a word, the proposed filtering system is effective and efficient. The most difference from other system is that it realizes on-line learning.

References

1. Margaret Fleck, David A. Forsyth, Chris Bregler: Find Naked People. Pro. 4th European Conf. on Computer Vision, UK, vol. 2, pp. 593-602, 1996.
2. James Z. Wang, Jia Li, Gio Wiederhold, Oscar Firschein: System for screening objectionable images. Computer Communications, vol. 21, no. 15, pp. 1355-1360, Elsevier, 1998.
3. Michael J. Jones, James M. Rehg: Statistical Color Models with Applications to Skin Detection. Technical report of the Cambridge Research Laboratory, No. 98-11, Dec, 1998.
4. N.A. Syed, H. Liu and K.K. Sung: Incremental Learning with Support Vector Machines. inProc. Int. Joint Conf. on Artificial Intelligence (IJCAI-99), 1999.
5. Stefan Ruping: Incremental Learning with Support Vector Machines. ICDM 2001.
6. V. Vapnik: The nature of statistical learning theory. Springer, New York, 1995.
7. V. Vapnik: Statistical learning theory. John Wiley and Sons, inc., 1998.
8. Joachims, T.: Making large-scale SVM learning practical. In B. Schölkopf, C. Burges & A. Smola, Advances in kernel methods-Support vector learning, Cambridge, MA, MIT Press.
9. Qixiang Ye, Wen Gao, Wei Zeng, Tao Zhang, Weiqiang Wang, Yang Liu: Objectional image detection on compression domain. International Conference on Intelligence Data Engineering and Automatic Learning, 2003, HongKong.
10. P. E. Utgoff: Incremental induction of decision tree. Machine Learning, 4:161–186, 1989.
11. Alberto Albiolt, Luis Torres, Edward J. Delp. Optimum: Color Spaces For Skin Detection. in Proceedins of ICIP2001.
12. Hideyuki Tamura, Shunji Mori, and Yamawaki: Textural Features Corresponding to Visual Perception. IEEE Trans. on Systems, Man, and Sybernetics, vol. SMC-8, no. 6, June 1978.
13. Rafael C. Gonzalez, Richard E. Woods: Digital Image Processing. Prentice Hall, 2002.

Motion Objects Segmentation Using a New Level Set Based Method

Hongqiang Bao[1] and Zhaoyang Zhang[2]

[1] School of Communication and Information Engineering, Shanghai University,
Shanghai 200072, China
bhq05@yahoo.com.cn
[2] Key Laboratory of Advanced Displays and System Application, Ministry of
Education, Shanghai 200072, China

Abstract. Segmentation of moving object in a video sequence is one of the difficult problems in video processing. Moreover, multiple objects segmenting and extracting is more challenging task due to the complexity of multiple motion. This paper presents a novel multiple object segmentation approach based on spatial-temporal curve evolution. First, According to the characteristic of the intra-frame and inter-frame (spatial and temporal) information, a joint energy model is proposed with global and local features, thus, a curve evolution equation could be achieved based on the method of level set. Then, after an initial object model is achieved with a simplified method using the difference between two successive frames, multiple object are tracked and extracted with spatio-temporal curve evolution. Finally, while the occlusion is emerged due to multiple object overlapping motion, the covered/uncovered object could be segmented using motion field template matching. The experiment results show that the approach is effective.

1 Introduction

Motion object segmentation of a video sequence belongs to the most difficult and important problems in video processing such as video compression(MPEG-4), object-based video database querying(MPEG-7), and computer vision (scene analysis). To date, a variety of approaches have been addressed to solve the problem. However, most of them only consider single object segmentation, and a great deal of sequences include several objects with complexity motion. Multiple objects, which simultaneity appear in a scene of sequence, could not only exist independent motion, but also occur mutual motions such as: connecting or separating, emerging or exiting, and overlapping or occluding. Therefore, segmentation of the multiple objects is quite complicated and ill-posed task. The approaches of multiple motion segmentation are approximately classified into two classes: 1)motion estimation and clustering based on Markov random field(MRF), and 2) curve evolution with level sets. The first utilize maximum a posteriori (MAP) estimation of the motion and segment field. Each field is considered as a MRF and is estimated in the energy minimization process. The

K. Aizawa, Y. Nakamura, and S. Satoh (Eds.): PCM 2004, LNCS 3331, pp. 312–318, 2004.

second utilize curve evolution based on level set to track and segment multiple objects. These methods can segment multiple objects, but only utilizing motion information, the boundary of the objects is not enough accurate to some high requirement, and can not process occlusion between two objects. Therefore, it is necessary to develop and study a method of accurately segmenting multiple objects. In this paper, we addressed a novel multiple objects segmentation method based on spatio-temporal curve evolution of level sets. Level set, a numerical analysis tool that originated in physics for the computation of propagating interfaces, have recently been applied to image segmentation, where they replace active contours as the descriptors of segment boundaries. The key features of a level set representation, as compared to active contours are: the ability to handle variations in the topology of segmentation, the numerical stability and the explicit definition of pixel memberships (a region is represented by the support of the positive part of a level set function). Level set have also been used in the context of motion. Recently, some algorithm for multiple motion segmentation, detection and tracking have been proposed[1][2][3], however these methods only utilized the partial information of the objects in a sequences. The effect is limited to some complexity motion. So we proposed a method which utilizes both the temporal and the spatial information, and could deal with various video object motion the occlusion. The paper is organized as follows: Section 2 introduces spatio-temporal energy model and a curve evolution equation, In section 3, a initial contour is derived using two frames difference. In section 4 the occlusion problem is dealt with. Finally, the experimental results and conclusions are sketched in Sections 5 and 6 respectively.

2   Description of the Basic Model

In a sequence, we can utilize the spatial and temporal information to segment and extract motion object segmentation. To facilitate curve evolution, these information is formularized as two kinds of energy in this paper.

2.1   Spatio-temporal Energy Model

Our basic idea is to evolve curves using inter-frame and intra-frame energy for segmentation multiple motion objects in a given sequence. The spatio-temporal energy functional can be expressed as:

$$E_{total} = E_{temproal} + E_{spatial} \tag{1}$$

where $E_{temporal}$ and $E_{spatial}$ respectively stand for the inter-frame and intra-frame energy. Chan and Vese proposed an energy model based active contours without edges[4]:

$$E(m_1, m_2, C) = E_1 + E_2 \tag{2}$$

$$E_1 = \mu \cdot Length(C) + \nu \cdot Area(inside(C)) \tag{3}$$

$$E_2 = \lambda_1 \int_{inside(C)} |I(x,y) - m_1|^2 dxdy + \lambda_2 \int_{outside(C)} |I(x,y) - m_2|^2 dxdy \quad (4)$$

where $I(x,y)$ is a given image, C is a evolving curve in the region of image, m_1, m_2 are the mean of inside and outside C, $\mu \geq 0, \nu \geq 0, \lambda_1, \lambda_2 > 0$ are fixed parameters. The first two term control the smoothness of the contour, while the last two terms attract the contour toward the object boundary where the energies inside and outside C will keep a balance, Observe that, by minimizing the energy (2), the curve which is utilize to segment and track objects will stop on the desired boundary at points of energy minimize. The energy model is adapt to the image in which m_1 is obviously different from m_2. The difference image between two consecutive frames is satisfied with this characteristic. therefore, we can define a temporal energy term:

$$E_{temporal} = E_3 + E_4 \quad (5)$$

$$E_3 = \sum_i \mu \cdot Length(C_i) \quad (6)$$

$$E_4 = \sum_i [\lambda_1 \int_{inside(C_i)} |d_n(x,y) - m_1|^2 dxdy + \lambda_2 \int_{outside(C_i)} |d_n(x,y)|^2 dxdy] \quad (7)$$

where $d_n(x,y)$ is the frame difference image, In almost all our numerical calculations, the mean m_2 outside C is considered as zero, and the parameter is fixed to zero.

The different image is mostly inaccurate due to the occlusion and not enough texture. Therefore the curve should be evolved in the intra-frame image, and the object edge is a main information which can be utilized. The typical snake method of curve evolution is also mainly dependant on objects edge. So we define a simplified curve evolution model in spatial image as follow[5]:

$$E_{spatial} = \sum_i \int_o^L g(|\nabla I(C_i(p)||C_i^{'}(p)| dp \quad (8)$$

where p is the point of evolving curve, L is the length of evolving curve, g is a monotonically decreasing function such that $g(0) = 1, \lim_{r \to 0} g(r) = 0$. Obviously, the curve is attracted towards the object spatial contour. In here we regard the spatial energy as an equivalent to the snake energy.

It is obvious that C , the boundary of the object, is the minimizer of the total energy term E_{total}. Therefore, we consider the minimization problem: inf $E_{total}(c)$.

2.2   Level Set Representation

In problems of curve evolution, the level set methods have been used extensively, because it allows for cusps, corners, and automatic topological changes. Moreover, the discretization of the problem is made on a fixed rectangular grid.

The evolving curve C is implicitly represented by zero level set. To facilitate observing, the level set can be described as follow:

$$\phi(x,y) = \pm dist[(x,y), C] \quad (x,y) \in \Omega \tag{9}$$

where the function $dist$ is the distance from arbitrary point in the region of image to the curve C. Thus, the problem of curve evolution is represented by the function ϕ that is dependent on the time variable t .

$$\phi(x,y,t) = \pm dist[(x,y), C, t] \quad (x,y) \in \Omega \tag{10}$$

we replace the unknown variable C by the unknown variable ϕ , and minimize E_{total} with respect to ϕ , we deduce the associated Euler-Lagrange equation for ϕ . Parameterizing the descent direction by an artificial time t , the equation, defining the initial contour, is:

$$\partial\phi/\partial t = \delta(\phi)[\mu \cdot div(\nabla(\phi)/|\nabla(\phi)| - \lambda_1(d_n(x,y) - m_1)^2 + \lambda_2 d_n(x,y)^2] \tag{11}$$

$$\partial\phi/\partial t = \delta(\phi)[\mu \cdot div(\nabla(\phi)/|\nabla(\phi)|g(\nabla(I)] \tag{12}$$

where $\delta(\phi)$ is a defined value Dirac function , $div(\nabla(\phi)/|\nabla(\phi)|)$is the curvature of the evolving curve. The equation (11)and (12) are defined in different region, (11) with respect to the temporal inter-frame image $d_n(x,y)$ is utilized to track the object, and (12) with respect to the spatial intra-frame image is applied to refine the objects edge. The task of the second term in (12) is boundary smoothness. Since the spatial curve have been smooth after the temporal curve evolution, this term can be omitted.

3   Initial Contour

The initial contour should be achieved before segmentation with spatio-temporal curve. The method proposed by Paragios define the initial contour to the rectangle box which is the similar size with the frame[1]. The initial contour could include all objects, but the complexity of curve evolution is increased. We propose a simplified method to achieve initial contour with the frames different image:

Step 1. Change detection mask (CDM) is computed by applying a decision rule(thresholding) on the intensity differences between successive frames. The significance test technique is used to obtain the threshold value[7].

Step 2. From the former step, we have obtained a CDM that roughly describe the moving object to be extracted. A post processing is used to eliminate noise regions and to filter out the ragged boundary. The morphological operators (open and close) can be adopted according to different situations. The structuring element is round to get the smooth boundary.

Step 3. Refined contour with spatial the equation (9), achieved an accurate contour.

4   Occlusion Handling

Sometimes, multiple motion objects may overlap, and one of them could partly or globally be not viewed. The phenomena is considered as occlusion. The object, which is completely observed is uncovered object, and the other is covered object. While the occlusion occur, many segmentation methods is non-effective. The spatio-temporal curve methods can track the multiple objects with topology variations,but not handle occlusion. Developing a generic algorithm for all kinds of the occlusion segmentation is not optimistic at present due to its complexity. So we narrow down the problem scope to the rigid object(not deforming while the occlusion occurs). Thus we propose a method of segmenting the covered/uncovered using motion template matching:

Step 1: Judge if the occlusion emerge or not. The number of the objects and their pixels is counted. If the objects number have decreased, and the pixels number of correspond object area have immensely increased, the occlusion is considered to be occurred.

Step 2: Decide the covered object and uncovered object. While the occlusion start to emerge, the object area, in front frame where the occlusion did not occur, is utilized to estimate motion field in current frame. If motion field is complete in the overlapping region, the correspond object is judged to be as an uncovered object, otherwise, it is a covered object.

Step 3: Estimate motion template matching of uncovered object and segment overlapping objects. After deciding covered/uncovered object, the motion template of uncovered is estimated with motion field matching, and the uncovered object is separated from occlusion region, the others part is covered object.

5   Experimental Results

In this section, we validate the method on several MPEG-4 sequences. The result of both sequences Children and Hall monitor are showed. There are four video objects in Children sequence: the first object is left child, the second object is right child, the third is a ball in right child hands, the fourth is a motion rectangle. The rectangle is emerged from the forth frame, and moving from right side to left side. The four objects motion is complicated, not only including independent motion, but also multiple motion join/disjoin, occlusion and so on. In our experiments, we generally choose the parameters as follows: $\mu = 1, \lambda_1 = 1, \lambda_2 = 1, m_i = 1$. the curve evolution step $\partial t(\triangle t) = 1$ is 0.5, the function $\delta(\phi) = 1/(1 + \phi^2)$, $g(r) = 1/(1 + r^2)$. Figure 1 and Figure 2 show the segmentation results of the 7th frame of Children sequences and the 100th frame of Hall monitor, respectively. The objects are accurately tracking and segmenting. Figure 3 show the occlusion segmentation results of the 13th frame of Children sequences. Since the covered object is a rectangle moving from right to left, it can be regarded as a rigid object. The uncovered object, the right child, is accurately segment with motion field matching. The result show that the proposed approach is effective.

(a) The result of curve evolution (b) The 1st object   (c) The 2nd object

Fig. 1. The 7th frame segmentation of children sequence

(a) The result of curve evolution   (b) The 1st object   (c) The 2nd object

Fig. 2. The segmentation results of the 100th frame of Hall monitor

(a) The result of curve evolution   (b) The 1st object   (c) The 2nd object

(d) The uncovered object   (e) The covered object

Fig. 3. Results of the occlusion segmentation of the 13h frame of Children

6   Conclusions

We proposed a new approach based on level set for segmenting and tracking multiple objects in a video sequence. Moreover the approach can process various complexity object motion and solve the problem of the covered/uncovered identification. The temporal and spatial energy model are utilized to evolve the level set curves. The initial curve is achieved by the difference image between two frames, which degrades the complexity of the curve evolution. The method of the motion field matching can solve the occlusion problem to some rigid objects. Experimental results indicate that the method provides a accurate segmentation. However, since the temporal curve evolution is based the frame difference image, the main drawback is the requirement that moving objects must have enough texture. The occlusion handling utilize the method of motion field matching, so unable to process deforming object while occlusion occurs. To incorporate such objects with the motion estimating and clustering is the next aspect of our work.

Acknowledgments. This work was supported by the National Natural Science Foundation of China under Grant 60172020.

References

1. Paragios, N., Deriche, R.: Geodesic active contours and level sets for the detection and tracking of moving objects. IEEE Trans. PAMI, vol..22 (2000) 266-280.
2. Masouri, A-R, Konrad, J.: Multiple motion segmentation with level sets. IEEE Trans. IP, vol.12 (2002) 1-19.
3. Paragios, N. and Deriche, R.: Detection of moving objects: A level set approach. In Proceedings of SIRS'97, Stockholm, Sweden, July 1997.
4. Chan T. F., Vese L.A.: Active contours without edge. IEEE Trans. IP, vol.10. (2001) 266-277.
5. Vicent Caselles: Geometric model for active contours. Proc. of the Int. Conf. Image Processing vol.10 (1995) 9-12.
6. S. Osher , J.A. Sethian: Fronts propagating with curvature-dependent speed: lgorithms based on Hamilton-Jacobi Formulation. J. Comput. Phys. Vol.79 (1988) 12-49.
7. Roland Mech, Michael Wollborn: A noise robust method for 2D shape estimation of moving objects in video sequences considering a moving camera. Signal Processing, vol.66 (1998) 203-217.

3-D Shape Analysis of Anatomical Structures Based on an Interactive Multiresolution Approach

Soo-Mi Choi[1], Jeong-Sik Kim[1], Yong-Guk Kim[1], and Joo-Young Park[2]

[1] School of Computer Engineering, Sejong University, Seoul, Korea
{smchoi, jskim, ykim}@sejong.ac.kr
[2] Dept. of Computer Science and Engineering, Ewha Womans University,
Seoul, Korea
jooypark@ewha.ac.kr

Abstract. 3-D shape comparison of anatomical objects is essential task in distinguishing between abnormal and normal organs. Such discrimination is also necessary in following up patients for the evaluation of treatments. This paper presents an efficient representation and analysis method for 3-D shape comparison based on a multiresolution approach. Initially, we reconstruct anatomical objects by adapting a multiresolution deformable surface model to the image pyramid with a coarse-to-fine fashion in order to avoid false surface. Then we interactively compare the reconstructed objects by multiresolution analysis based on an Octree structure. The partial comparison at specific location helps to focus on a region of interest within an anatomical structure and to detect local shape changes easily. We present some results of applying our method to the extracted brain cortical surfaces from MR images.

1 Introduction

As 3-D anatomical models reconstructed from medical images (e.g. CT and MRI) are becoming useful in medical areas, the issue of comparing two 3-D models or searching for a similar shape model in the local storage media becomes a practical problem [1,2]. Automatic shape comparison is essential in many diagnostic and patient monitoring applications, such as the experimental evaluation of drugs and treatments, precise monitoring of disease progression, and early disease diagnosis. High-speed shape comparison is also necessary in searching a specific anatomical object within a large database.

The early studies on similarity measure for 3-D shape models include Extended Gaussian Images [3] and harmonic shape images [4]. In these methods, it is assumed that the 3-D model is represented with surface mesh or explicit volume, but surface does not contain any topological faults. Other approach is to represent a 3-D model based upon special data structure. In these approaches, shape similarity between models is measured based on the topological relationship or the difference of feature values. The typical examples are generalized

K. Aizawa, Y. Nakamura, and S. Satoh (Eds.): PCM 2004, LNCS 3331, pp. 319–326, 2004.
© Springer-Verlag Berlin Heidelberg 2004

cylinders, shock graphs [5], medial axes [6] and skeletons [7]. However, it usually takes a lot of time in calculating the similarity because 2-D skeleton is extended into 3-D one. Recently, matching between two models or similarity measure is performed according to the geometrical or topological characteristics of 3-D models, such as topology matching [8] and shape distribution [9]. Other researches focus on how to improve robustness against different shape representations, and to reduce the computation time in measuring the global similarity between the models.

Although global morphologic assessments by volume measurements are practically used for many medical applications, it is necessary to have a certain way by which the user is able to access to the specific area within the anatomical organ with an interactive method by changing the resolution of the image.

We present here an efficient representation and analysis method for 3-D shape comparison based on an interactive multiresolution approach. This method is robust against the position and rotation variation. As it also allows user to compare 3-D shape by changing the level-of-detail, it is possible to analyze the structural changes at a specific location within the anatomical model.

The rest of this paper is organized as follows. Section 2 describes a multiresolution representation of anatomical objects and Section 3 describes multiresolution analysis for 3-D shape comparison. Experimental results and discussion are given in Section 4 and some conclusions and future works are given in Section 5.

2   Multiresolution Representation of Anatomical Structures

In this section, we describe how to represent the multiresolution shapes of an anatomical structure using an adaptive deformable surface model [10].

The 3-D shape of an anatomical structure can be reconstructed by fitting surface primitives (e.g. triangles) to the boundary extracted approximately from medical volume images. However, false surface can be often generated due to noise, artifacts and spurious edge features (not associated with the true boundary of the structure) in the images.

To avoid this problem, we use a multi-scale approach based on a volume image pyramid. As shown in Fig. 1, the image pyramid is a hierarchical structure of multiresolution volume images $I_0, I_1, \ldots, I_m$. The image at level $h + 1$ is generated from the image of level h by applying 3-D isotropic smoothing convolution operator [11]. We then reconstruct the shape of the anatomical structure by adapting a multiresolution deformable surface model to the image pyramid in a coarse-to-fine fashion as illustrated in Fig.1. The deformable model, initialized as coarse triangulated meshes, is first applied to the image of the lowest resolution in the pyramid. Once the coarse triangulated meshes fit rough shape, we proceed to the next finer level of the pyramid. Finer shape is reconstructed using refined triangulated meshes at the next level.

At each level, the model adapts its shape to the boundary of an anatomical structure by iterating two steps: deformation based on its force formulation and

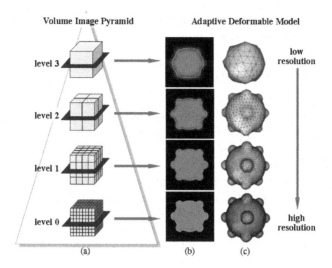

Fig. 1. Multiresolution shape reconstruction using adaptive deformable model based on volume image pyramid: (a) The pyramid structure of multiresolution volume images; (b) Slice images from the reconstructed shapes; (c) 3-D shapes reconstructed by adaptive deformable model

adaptive remeshing. The force formulation is composed of internal, external, and non-self-intersection forces applied to every model node i :

$$m\mathbf{a}_i + \gamma\mathbf{v}_i + \mathbf{f}_{int,i} + \mathbf{f}_{nsi,i} = \mathbf{f}_{ext,i} \qquad (1)$$

where $\mathbf{v}_i$, $\mathbf{a}_i$, m and γ are velocity, acceleration, mass and damping coefficient of node i. Internal force $\mathbf{f}_{int,i}$ provides flexible connections between model elements and external force $\mathbf{f}_{ext,i}$ attracts the model towards image features such as edges or boundaries. Non-self-intersection force $\mathbf{f}_{nsi,i}$ prevents the formation of non-simple structures due to self-intersection. Adaptive remeshing is to match the resolution of the model to the resolution of the volume image at each level of the pyramid and to regularize the size of the triangulated meshes.

This multi-scale approach helps to ensure that a good solution can be quickly and efficiently computed by hiding noise and artifacts until the model gets near a rough boundary approximation.

3   3-D Shape Analysis Based on an Interactive Multiresolution Approach

In this section, we describe how to analyze the shape of anatomical objects based on an interactive multiresolution approach. Given a pair of reconstructed objects, each object has to be placed into a canonical coordinate frame, where the position, orientation and scaling are normalized. Then we measure similarity among a pair of feature vectors by the L_2 Norm and Hausdorff distance based on the octree structure. The result of shape comparison is displayed on the surface of the target object using color-coding.

3.1 Canonical Coordinate Frame

By pose normalization, we assume finding a canonical position, orientation, and scaling, or briefly a canonical coordinate frame.

Let $P=\{\mathbf{p}_1,\ldots,\mathbf{p}_n\}$ ($\mathbf{p}_i = (x_i, y_i, z_i) \in \mathbb{R}^3$) be the set of vertices. The translation invariance is accomplished by finding the center of mass of a model $\mathbf{c} = (c_x, c_y, c_z)$ and forming the point set $P'=\{\mathbf{u} = (u_x, u_y, u_z)|\mathbf{u} = \mathbf{p} - \mathbf{c}, \mathbf{p} \in P\}$.

In order to secure the rotation invariance, we apply the Principal Component Analysis (PCA) on the set P'. PCA is a technique for linear feature extraction and dimensionality reduction and identify the most informative directions (i.e., those with the largest variance) of a given multivariate distribution. These directions are called the principal components of the distribution and are given by the eigenvectors of its covariance matrix.

The covariance matrix is a symmetric real matrix, therefore, its eigenvalues are positive real numbers. Then, we sort the eigenvalues in the non-increasing order and find the corresponding eigenvectors. The eigenvectors are scaled to the Euclidean unit length and we form the rotation matrix R, which has the scaled eigenvectors as rows. We rotate all the points of P' and form the new point set by $P'' = \{\mathbf{w} = (w_x, w_y, w_z)|\mathbf{w} = R \cdot \mathbf{u}, \mathbf{u} \in P'\}$.

The reflection invariance is obtained using the matrix F. The scaling invariance is provided by the scaling factor $s = \sqrt{(s_x^2 + s_y^2 + s_z^2)/3}$, where s_x, s_y, s_z represent average distance of points $\mathbf{w} \in P''$ from the origin along $\mathbf{x}$, $\mathbf{y}$, and $\mathbf{z}$ axes, respectively. These distances are computed by Eq. (3). The canonical coordinates are obtained by applying the affine map τ to the initial point set P.

$$F = \begin{bmatrix} sign(f_x) & 0 & 0 \\ 0 & sign(f_y) & 0 \\ 0 & 0 & sign(f_z) \end{bmatrix} \tag{2}$$

$$\text{where } f_x = \frac{1}{n}\sum_{i=1}^{n} sign(w_{xi})w_{xi}^2 \qquad (f_y, f_z \text{ analogously})$$

$$s_x = \frac{1}{n}\sum_{i=1}^{n} |w_{xi}| \qquad (s_y, s_z \text{ analogously}) \tag{3}$$

$$\tau(\mathbf{p}) = s^{-1} \cdot F \cdot R \cdot (\mathbf{p} - \mathbf{c}) \tag{4}$$

3.2 Similarity Measurement Based on the Octree Structure

For interactive partial comparison, we use the octree structure [12]. As illustrated in Fig. 2, an octree is a data structure to represent object in 3-D space, automatically grouping them hierarchically and avoiding the representation of empty portions of the space. In order to create an octree structure, we calculate the bounding box surrounding the 3-D model. It is defined to be the box

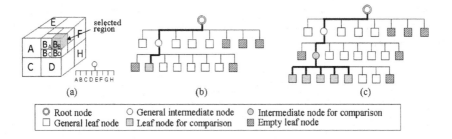

Fig. 2. Partial shape comparison based on the octree structure: (a) space partitioning (b) octree data structure of the reference model; (c) octree data structure of the target model

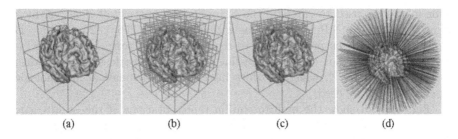

Fig. 3. Space partitioning (a - c) with multiresolution and its octree data structure (d) with feature vectors

in the canonical coordinate frame that encloses the model, with the center in the origin and the edges parallel to the coordinate axes. Then all vertices of the model are entered into an octree structure. Intermediate nodes of the octree represent subdivisions of the object space along the x, y, and z directions. The octree is successively refined by further subdivision of leaf nodes when entering new vertices until one vertex is placed in each sub-volume exactly.

Fig. 2 shows how to compare the reconstructed reference model to the target model based upon the octree structure. Suppose that one wants to compare the local shape located within B_B region using the octree data structure as illustrated in Fig. 2(a). First, the user chooses the B area within the octree node using a mouse-picking interface, and then he/she goes into the B_B region within the B area in the hierarchical fashion. Here, notice that it is possible to reduce the computation time in comparing two 3-D shapes by localizing a certain node from the remaining nodes. The thick lines in Fig. 2(b) are the reference and those of the Fig. 2(c) are the target.

The feature vectors are computed for each sampled meshes by shooting the rays fired from the bounding sphere. As the similarity metric, we used L_2 Norm and Hausdorff distance. The L_2 Norm is the metric to compute the distance between two 3-D points by equation (5), where x and y represents the centers of gravity of corresponding sample meshes. Hausdorff distance measures the extent to which each point of the reference model lies near some point of the target model as defined in equation (6), in which $h(A,B)$ is the directed Hausdorff distance from shape A to shape B.

$$L_2(x,y) = \left(\sum_{i=0}^{k} |x_i - y_i|^2 \right)^{\frac{1}{2}} \tag{5}$$

$$H(A,B) = \max\left(h(A,B), h(B,A)\right) \tag{6}$$

where $A = \{a_1, \ldots, a_m\}$, $B = \{b_1, \ldots, b_n\}$, $h(A,B) = \max_{a \in A} \min_{b \in B} \|a - b\|$

4   Results and Discussion

Our method is used to compare the brain cortical surfaces that are extracted from a volumetric MR brain images with dimensions $256 \times 256 \times 136$. The brain image has been preprocessed to remove the skin, bone, fat and other extracranial tissues. For the preprocessing, a semi-automatic software package, such as BrainSuite™, which provides interactive mathematical morphological operations, can be used.

Fig. 4(a - c) show the multiresolution representations of the brain cortical surface at different levels: level 3 (1,208 triangles), level 2 (6,870 triangles), and level 1 (36,920 triangles). The level 3 depicts the overall shape in a simple way, whereas the level 1 the detail of the cortical surface. The computation time of global similarity measure using L_2 Norm for three different levels (level 1, level 2 and level 3) was 0.24, 1.3 and 5.2 sec, respectively.

Fig. 4(d) shows how to choose a specific region within the reference model. In other words, the inner bounding box (blue) is selected by choosing Node A within an octree structure. Fig. 4(e) is a magnified image of the local region A in Fig. 4(d). Fig. 4(f - h) show three target models that will be compared to the reference model shown in Fig. 4(e). Two arrows within each target model indicate the deformed areas. Table 1 catalogs the result of shape differences by comparing the 3-D shapes between the reference model (REF) and three targets 1, 2 and 3 (T1, T2, and T3), respectively. Notice that similarity error at deformed region (Node A) is higher than that at other regions. In this fashion, we are able to distinguish a certain shape difference at a specific local region in a hierarchical fashion.

Table 1. Result of shape comparison based on the octree structure

	Node A	Node B	Node C	Node D	Node E	Node F	Node G	Node H
REF:T1	0.406	0.046	0.048	0.045	0.056	0.049	0.040	0.048
REF:T2	0.641	0.107	0.105	0.121	0.174	0.117	0.119	0.131
REF:T3	0.930	0.225	0.248	0.282	0.137	0.268	0.270	0.294

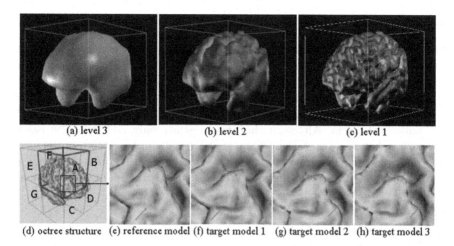

(a) level 3   (b) level 2   (c) level 1

(d) octree structure (e) reference model (f) target model 1   (g) target model 2 (h) target model 3

Fig. 4. Brain cortical surfaces extracted at each level of a MR volume image pyramid (a - c) and its octree structure (d), and reference model at level 1 (e) and deformed target models 1- 3 (f - h)

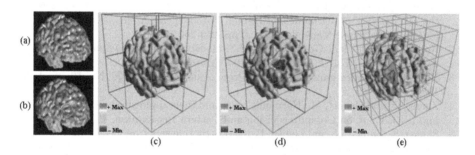

Fig. 5. Brain cortical surfaces are color-coded by the magnitude of similarity error

Suppose that a user wants to quantify the magnitude of shape difference between two local regions of the brain indicated as red circles in Fig. 5(a) and (b). For instance, the brain surface of Fig. 5(c) is color-coded by the magnitude of similarity error, which is obtained by calculating the difference from the reference model of Fig. 5(a) to the target model of Fig. 5(b). Fig. 5(d) shows the similarity measurement by exchanging the reference and the target models. The red area indicates the target surface is extruded from the reference surface, whereas the blue area the target surface is intruded from the reference surface.

Fig. 5(e) illustrates that it is also possible to analyze the more detail region by expanding the resolution of the octree, since it has a hierarchical structure. Such partial comparison based on the local similarity could help medical doctors to localize a certain pathological areas. Moreover, the octree hierarchical structure saves the computation time in searching a deformed region within the brain.

5   Conclusions and Future Works

The multiresolution approaches presented in this study allow us to compare 3-D models with a coarse-to-fine style. Because of that nature, the present method can save computation time for the shape comparison. The interactive partial comparison has an advantage in analyzing the specific part of the object using octree structure by allowing us to focus on a specific region of interest within an anatomical organ. Although the present study only addresses the issue of comparison between two 3-D anatomical objects, it can be extend, in the future, to a multiple comparison case, where it is possible to categorize abnormal and normal organs into several distinct groups using a multiple classifier such as Support Vector Machine.

Acknowledgements. This work was supported by grant No.(R04-2003-000-10017-0) from the Basic Research Program of the Korea Science and Engineering Foundation.

References

1. Crudele, M., Clapworthy, G. J., Krokos, M. A., et al.: A Distributed Database on the INTERNET of 3D Models of Human Pathological Organs. IEEE Symposium on Computer Based Medical Systems, pp. 256-260, 1997.
2. Keim, D. A.: Efficient Geometry-based Similarity Search of 3D Spatial Databases. ACM SIGMOD, Vol. 28, No. 2, pp. 419-430, 1999.
3. Horn, B.: Extended gaussian images. Proc. of the IEEE, Vol. 72, No. 12, pp. 1671-1686, 1984.
4. Zhang, D. and Hebert, M.: Harmonic maps and their applications in surface matching. IEEE Conf. on Computer Vision and Pattern Recognition, 1999.
5. Skiena, S., Smith, W. and Lemke, P.:Reconstructing sets from interpoint distances. Proc. of Sixth Annual Symp. on Computational Geometry, pp. 332-339, 1990.
6. Bardinet, E., Vidal, S. F., Arroyo, S. D., et al.: Structural object matching. TR-DECSAI-000303, Dept. of Computer Science and AI, University of Granada, Spain, Feb. 2000.
7. Bloomenthal, J. and Lim, C.:Skeletal methods of shape manipulation. Shape Modeling and Applications, pp. 44-47, 1999.
8. Hilaga, M., Shinagawa, Y., Kohmura, T. and Kunii, T. L.: Topology Matching for Fully Automatic Similarity Estimation of 3D Shapes. The proceeding of SIGGRAPH 2001, pp. 203-212, 2001.
9. Osada, R., Funkhouser, T., Chazelle, B. and Dobkin, D.: Matching 3D Models with Shape Distribution. Proc. Shape Modeling Int'l, 2001.
10. Park, J-Y., McInerney, T., Terzopoulos, D. and Kim, M-H.: A Non-self-intersecting Adaptive Deformable Surface for Complex Boundary Extraction from Volumetric Images. Computers and Graphics, Vol. 25, No. 3, pp. 421-440, 2001.
11. Lachaud, J.-O. and Montanvert, A.: Deformable meshes with automated topology changes for coarse-to-fine three-dimensional surface extraction. Medical Image Analysis, Vol. 3, No. 1, pp. 1-21, 1999.
12. Wilhems, J. and Van Gelder, A.: Octrees for Faster Isosurface generation. ACM Transactions on Graphics, Vol. 11, No. 2, pp. 201-227, 1992.

Integrating Color, Texture, and Spatial Features for Image Interpretation

Hui-Yu Huang[1], Yung-Sheng Chen[2], and Wen-Hsing Hsu[3,4]

[1] Department of Computer Science and Information Engineering,
Chaoyang University of Technology, Wufong, Taichung 413, Taiwan, R.O.C.
`hyhuang@mail.cyut.edu.tw`
[2] Department of Electrical Engineering, Yuan Ze University, Taoyuan 320, Taiwan,
R.O.C.
`eeyschen@ee.yzu.edu.tw`
[3] Department of Electrical Engineering, National Tsing Hua University, Hsinchu 300,
Taiwan, R.O.C.
[4] Institute of Information Science, Academia Sinica, Taipei 115, Taiwan, R.O.C.
`whhsu@ee.nthu.edu.tw`

Abstract. In this paper, we present an approach to achieve the region-based image semantic interpretation and recall process in color image from image database. This system includes feature extraction of region, indexing process, linguistic inference rules construction, as well as a semantic description of region image. Based on these features, each of human labeled regions in an image can be described by a corresponding linguistic meaning. The main procedure consists of two parts: procedure 1 (*forward*) and 2 (*recall*) processes. The forward process primarily presents the linguistic meaning description of a region image based on feature definitions, inference rules, and indexing process. In recall process, it mainly reconstructs the region image which performs the rough mental image of human memory retrieval according to the semantic meaning by means of a specified or the pre-staged result. Experiments confirm that our approach is reasonable and feasible.

1 Introduction

Natural image analysis may be made up the relevant researches involving computer vision and artificial intelligence. Recently, many researchers have considered the human vision mechanism in image processing schemes.

When human beings look at an image, some interesting regions are observed at a glance and reflected in eyes. After performing more complicated physiology operations via human vision cortex, the mechanism can quickly to decide the meaningful objects and further to interpret the linguistic meanings for an image. Some literature [1,2] proposed based on linguistic specification to achieve image understanding. Generally, as for natural image understanding, its aim is usually focused on recognizing and localizing the significant image objects in the scene and that of distinguishing the relative object relationships. In addition

K. Aizawa, Y. Nakamura, and S. Satoh (Eds.): PCM 2004, LNCS 3331, pp. 327–334, 2004.
© Springer-Verlag Berlin Heidelberg 2004

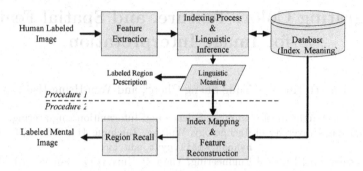

Fig. 1. System flowchart.

to interpretation and cognition of object, it is being still a very important and interesting topic.

Based on the fundamental characteristics of fuzzy set theory, the meaningful information of an image can be translated into a fuzzy number (or a membership function) to construct a knowledge base such as human knowledge and experiences [1,2]. Hence, useful data information can be presented by the fuzzy number, and this number can be parameterized to simplify the fuzzy computation. Owing to the mechanism of indexing process and fuzzy set theory which can simplify data amount, therefore, in this paper, we propose an approach to perform a human-based image interpretation by means of these technologies. This system is composed of image features, linguistic inference rule decision, and indexing process to interpret semantic meaning for specified image region.

2 Proposed Method

The major concept in color image interpretation is to describe the semantic meaning of a region based on color, texture, and spatial features. The system flowchart is illustrated in Fig. 1.

2.1 Feature Extraction of Region

Color, texture, and spatial information are three principal features adopted in our method. The color feature (color space) contains three components: Hue(H), Value(V), and Chroma(C). Directionality and contrast characteristics are used as the texture features. Rectangle bounding and spatial position of a region image represent as the spatial features. The corresponding schemes for feature extraction are described in the following.

2.1.1 Color Features
In HVC color space [3,4], each of three components can serve as an individual feature and use to analyze the characteristic of human labeled image region.

First, we perform the color histogram of each selected image region to obtain the three color histograms. Let $R(i)$ be one region for an image denoted by a three-element color vector $(h(i), v(i), c(i))^T$, where i denotes the ith region. Each element represents the corresponding color histogram. To efficiently specify color features, a 6-parameterized fuzzy number (named 6-PFN) is adopted to modeling the histogram.

After performing the 6-PFN process, each element within the three-element color vector is rewritten as the $(a_2(i), a_1(i), A(i), B(i), b_1(i), b_2(i))$ data format. If the image has n segmented regions, we can obtain n color features having 3×6 matrix size. One advantage of using 6-PFN fuzzy numbers is that can keep the principal information and properties of objects/regions in an image. In addition, based on the principles of fuzzy operation, the color features will take to the fuzzy max-min composition to obtain the corresponding membership grades.

2.1.2 Texture Features

A wide variety of texture features have been described in the machine vision literature. We chose texture features based on the modified versions of directionality and contrast features proposed in [5]. Owing to the natural images, some objects possess the regular directionality feature, such as "tree", it usually possess the feature of vertical orientation. Hence, in this paper the directionality characteristic is an important feature and used to obtain the edge's four orientations of region: 0^0, 45^0, 90^0, and 135^0. Here the edge points are obtained by using the compass gradient operators.

Generally, the variance α^2 about the gray-levels histogram distribution is more preferable as contrast. To perform the polarization of the distribution of block and white on the gray-level histogram, the well known *kurtosis* α_4 is adopted and defined as [5]

$$\alpha_4 = \frac{\mu_4}{\sigma^4},$$
(1)

where μ_4 is the fourth moment about the mean and σ^2 is the variance. This measure is normalized with respect to the range so that it can have the minimum value of one in case of twin peaks. Consequently, combining σ and α_4 for the second-step measure of contrast, it may be expressed as

$$F_{con} = \frac{\sigma}{(\alpha_4)^n},$$
(2)

where n is a positive number. In our experiments, n is set to $1/4$ and here the decision of this number is based on the empirical value according to our data.

2.1.3 Spatial Information

The spatial location of a region is also used in our system; it can provide the spatial information to construct the indexing process and spatial linguistic meaning definition, such as *left-up*, *left-bottom*, and so on. In order to facilitate spatial constraints, the approach organizes the location information of each region as part of its metadata. The spatial location of each region is represented by two parameters: the region centroid $C_{xy} = (x_c, y_c)$, and the coordinates of its minimum bounding rectangle (x_l, x_r, y_t, y_b), where subscript l, r, t, and b denote the (*left*,

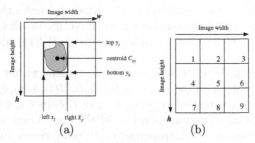

Fig. 2. (a) The spatial location of image region. (b) Indexing process of spatial location for an image.

right, top, bottom). The minimum bounding rectangle is the smallest vertically aligned box which contains the region completely as shown in Fig. 2(a). Hence, in our experiments, we noticed that the region is more intuitive and effective for catching the spatial information.

2.2   Indexing Process

According to the defined features, number of features is divided into five categories containing six elements: hue, value, chroma, edge, contrast, and spatial position. In color features, these have three color elements. The color attributes of each region of an image can be presented by the 6-PFN fuzzy number from those of histograms. First, we construct a set of reference 6-PFNs by using training process for all regions in image database. Based on the pre-clustered objects by human experiences, the same objects are further computed by those of color features. We take the average for the relative element of six parameters to obtain a set of reference 6-PFNs. Figure 3 shows the reference fuzzy number of h, v, and c. After performing the fuzzy max-min composition between each region and reference fuzzy numbers, the corresponding index value can be obtained. In our experiments, reference h, v, and c fuzzy numbers are divided into seven, three, and three classes, respectively. Table 1 shows the membership grade and the relative value for each region for Fig. 4(a).

As for texture features, the directionality and contrast are addressed in our system. For directionality feature, the maximum within number of edge points of four orientations for each region is computed and assigned to a relative index value. For example, if the number of edge points of 0^0 is greater than others, then this index value is labeled to number 1. Hence, based on this design, four categories are used to represent the directionality feature. As for contrast, we quantize it into eight levels, and thus it is labeled into eight indices.

As for spatial information, a standard position index and the corresponding coordinates of its minimum bounding rectangle (x_l, x_r, y_t, y_b), are first defined. Based on Fig. 2(b), we define 36 kinds of spatial positions and spatial linguistic meaning descriptions. After computing the closest spatial distance between each specified region and each of 36 regions in standard definitions, each of specified

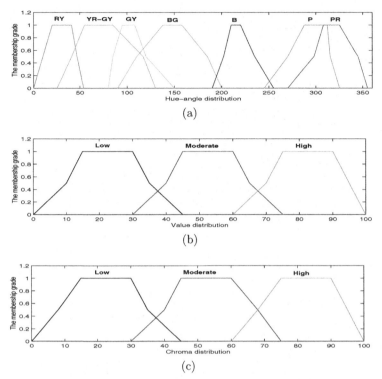

Fig. 3. Reference 6-PFN fuzzy number of color features (a)hue, (b)value, and (c)chroma.

regions for the image will be denoted its index value to further represent position and corresponding to a linguistic meaning.

2.3   Region-Based Semantic Description

After performing of indexing process, a linguistic database may be constructed by means of *if-then* rules based on human knowledge and experiences. The inference rules are defined as

$$if\,HueIndex \;=\; A_1 \text{ and } ValueIndex \;=\; B_1 \text{ and } ChromaIndex \;=\; C_1$$
$$\text{and } EdgeIndex \;=\; D_1 \text{ and } ContrastIndex \;=\; E_1 \quad then\,Output \;=\; F_1,$$
$$\cdots$$
$$if\,HueIndex \;=\; A_n \text{ and } ValueIndex \;=\; B_n \text{ and } ChromaIndex \;=\; C_n$$
$$\text{and } EdgeIndex \;=\; D_n \text{ and } ContrastIndex \;=\; E_n \quad then\,Output \;=\; F_n,$$

$$(3)$$

where $A_i \sim E_i$ denote the index value corresponding to the features computed by indexing process. Variable F_i is defined as index corresponding to the semantic meaning description of object.

Seven objects are defined in our system, i.e., we assign number 1 to 7 denoted to "sky", "building", " flower", " grass", "tree", "ground", and "sunset", respectively.

Table 1. The membership grade and relative index value of Hue component corresponding to each region of Fig. 4(a).

Fig. 4(a)	Hue categories							*Hue*
	R (I=1)	YR-GY (I=2)	GY (I=3)	BG (I=4)	B (I=5)	P (I=6)	PR (I=7)	*Index*
Reg. 1	0.00	0.00	0.00	0.086	1.00	0.00	0.00	5
Reg. 2	0.00	0.00	0.00	0.00	0.00	1.00	1.00	6/7

Fig. 4(a)	Value categories			*ValueIndex*
	Low(I=1)	Moderate(I=2)	High(I=3)	
Reg. 1	0.00	0.00	1.00	3
Reg. 2	0.60	1.00	0.00	2

Fig. 4(a)	Chroma categories			*ChromaIndex*
	Low(I=1)	Moderate(I=2)	High(I=3)	
Reg. 1	1.00	0.00	0.00	1
Reg. 2	1.00	0.00	0.00	1

Table 2. Results of the selected rule corresponding to each of the semantic descriptions and MOA value.

Region Semantic Description	Color Index			Results of MOA process
	Hue	Value	Chroma	$(Hue, Value, Chroma)$
sky	5	3	3	$(220.75, 86.25, 87.25)$
building	1	2	1	$(37.5, 57.25, 28.5)$
flower	6	3	2	$(293.5, 86.25, 59.0)$
grass	3	2	2	$(118.25, 57.5, 59.0)$
tree	4	1	3	$(153.5, 27.5, 87.25)$
ground	2	2	1	$(96.75, 57.5, 28.5)$
sunset	7	3	3	$(318.0, 86.25, 87.25)$

Table 3. Training and testing data for seven semantic objects.

	Sky	Building	Flower	Grass	Tree	Ground	Sunset	Overall
Total # regions	133	45	42	47	49	48	60	424
# training regions	20	20	20	20	20	20	20	140
# test regions	113	25	22	27	29	28	40	284

2.4   Recall Process

According to the previous result, the semantic description and feature definitions will be utilized again and regarded as input data. The recall process can automatically catch the object semantic index and the spatial index corresponding to features in database to represent the mental image. That is, using color features and spatial information, we can obtain the rough mental image based on the semantic description. In our approach, color features have been represented as a set of 6-PFNs, which have also applied for the reference fuzzy numbers of (H, V, C) complements. In order to obtain a set of color values (H, V, C) to specify the object color, a mean of area method (MOA) is used to export the

Table 4. The semantic description for each region corresponding to Fig. 4, respectively. Symbol * presents the error description for this region.

Figure 4	Semantic Description
(a) Reg. 1	This region is a **Sky** and located in the **Up-Horizontal** of image.
Reg. 2	This region is a **Flowers** and located in the **Bottom-Biased-Right** of image.
(b) Reg. 1	⋆ This region is a **Sunset** and located in the **Biased-Up** of image.
Reg. 2	This region is a **Building** and located in the **Center-Biased-Right** of image.
Reg. 3	This region is a **Trees** and located in the **Biased-Bottom** of image.

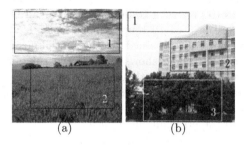

Fig. 4. Testing images

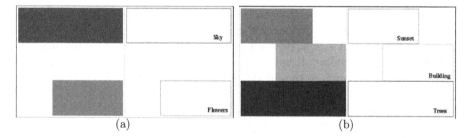

Fig. 5. Recall result and corresponding to linguistic meaning for Fig. 4, respectively.

reference fuzzy numbers and expressed as

$$z^* = a_2 + \frac{1}{2} \times w_2 \times (a_1 - a_2) + \frac{1}{2} \times w_2 \times (b_2 - b_1)$$
$$+ \frac{(w_2 + w_3) \times (A - a_1)}{2} + \frac{(w_2 + w_3) \times (b_1 - B)}{2}$$
$$+ w_3 \times (B - A), \tag{4}$$

where $(a_2, a_1, A, B, b_1, b_2)$ are six parameters for parameterized fuzzy number, and z^* is output value. Weight values, w_1, w_2, and w_3, are 0.0, 0.5, and 1.0, respectively. The typical 6-PFN fuzzy number is shown in Fig. 3. After computing the MOA method, the value of the exported reference fuzzy numbers with *hue* component is obtained as $(37.25, 96.75, 118.25, 153.5, 220.75, 293.5, 318.0)$, and the value of the exported reference fuzzy numbers with *value* and *chroma* components is presented as $(27.5, 57.5, 86.25)$ and $(28.5, 59.0, 87.25)$, respectively. Table 2 shows the fixed (H, V, C) values corresponding to the color index.

3   Experimental Results

The experimental data are obtained from a stock photo library. 424 image regions from the image source belonging to seven semantic classes are adopted. We divided these regions into no overlapping training and testing sets as shown in Table 3. Figure 4 shows the testing images. Based on our linguistic rule database, we select one of rules to present a common rule in recall process. The result of MOA for color feature is used to represent the color features of each region, and the spatial information is obtained via the spatial position of each specified region within an image. Table 2 shows the selected rule and fixed color values corresponding to each of the semantic descriptions. Figure 5 displays the recall and the relative linguistic meaning results. The semantic interpretations are shown in Table 4 corresponding to Fig. 4. In Table 4, there exists some regions which were expressed the error linguistic meaning.

4   Conclusions

This purpose of this approach is to interpret the primary semantic description of human specified region for a color image, and to represent the rough mental image such as human vision. However, some problems still exist in this proposed system. As for procedure 1, some objects may be interpreted to the mistake linguistic meaning because the inference rules in the current database are finite and cannot include the whole rules, in addition to the training images may be insufficient. Since only used color and spatial information to construct the mental image, it cannot make and represent the real object image. In the future, we will be to further improve the proposed system and to research the human visual perception on scene understanding.

Acknowledgement. This work war supported in part by the National Science Council of Republic of China under Grant No. NSC 93-2213-E-324-011.

References

1. Akrivas, G., Stamou, B. G., and Kollias, S.:Semantic association of multimedia document descriptions through fuzzy relational algebra and fuzzy reasoning. IEEE Trans. on Systems, Man, and Cybernetics, part A. **34** (2004) 190–196
2. Lu, Y., Zhang, H., Liu, W. and Hu, C.:Joint semantics and feature based image retrieval using relevance feedback. IEEE Trans. on Multimedia. **5** (2003) 339–347
3. Hunt, R. W. G.: Measuring Color. John Wiley and Sons. 1st Ed. (1989)
4. Huang, H. Y., Chen, Y. S., and Hsu, W. H.:Color image segmentation using self-organizing map algorithm. Journal of Electronic Imaging. **11** (2002) 136–148
5. Tamura, H., Mori, S., and Yamawaki, T.:Texture features corresponding to visual perception. IEEE Trans. Systems, Man, and Cybernetics. **SMC-8** (1978) 460–473

Automatic Video Genre Detection for Content-Based Authoring

Sung Ho Jin, Tae Meon Bae, and Yong Man Ro

IVY Lab., Information and Communications University (ICU) 119, Munjiro,
Yuseong-gu, Deajeon, 305-714, Korea
{wh966, heartles, yro}@icu.ac.kr

Abstract. In this paper, we propose a new video genre detection using semantic classification with multi-modal features. MPEG-7 audio-visual descriptors are used as multi-modal features. From the low-level multi-modal features, genre as high-level semantic meaning is detected by using GINI index in Classification And Regression Tree (CART) algorithm. Experimental results show that the proposed method is useful to detect video genre automatically with a high detection rate.

1 Introduction

The number of broadcasting channels and contents is increasing in digital broadcasting. Automatic video genre detection is known to be useful for authoring, retrieving or categorizing video contents from enormous video database. In advanced digital broadcasting environment, content providers should have content-based authoring tools to generate video skims (*i.e.*, summarized video clips) or metadata to provide personal oriented services. For the content-based authoring, automatic video genre detection is needed, that is to say, more accurate video skims can be obtained if video genre is known. Especially, for a large number of broadcasting contents, the automatic video genre detection is essential in terms of authoring efficiency while conventionally genre has been detected manually in the authoring process [1].

To extract semantic meanings like genre from video, several works have been studied such as video genre or scene detection methods with audio or visual information [2,3]. Ba Tu Truong et al. [2] showed about 83.1 % detection rate using C4.5 decision tree classifier and visual information from 60 second long video clips. Zhu Liu et al. [3] used audio information and 5-staste HMM with 28 symbols in their method. Their result described the accuracy of about 84.7 % with 10 minutes long audio clips. Recently, some methods were proposed to use multi-modal features [1,4]. These methods have shown better performance than those with uni-modal features. The classification result by J. Huang et al. [4] was 91.40 % in average. Their method uses audio-visual features and Product HMM with 10 minutes long video clips. However, the methods with multi-modal features take more processing time for video analysis, which could be crucial problem in video authoring with large amount of database. Nonetheless, only few works focus on the processing time.

K. Aizawa, Y. Nakamura, and S. Satoh (Eds.): PCM 2004, LNCS 3331, pp. 335–343, 2004.
© Springer-Verlag Berlin Heidelberg 2004

In this paper, we propose a video genre detection method using MPEG-7 audio-visual descriptors [5]. The paper focuses on three points of view: how reliable is the detection performance? How much does it reduce the detection time with high detection rate? What kinds of multi-modal features are proper in the method? To prove the usefulness of the method, we perform experiments with various genres.

2   Proposed Video Genre Detection Method

The overall procedure of the proposed method is shown in Fig. 1. First, video is segmented into short video clips, which are 60 seconds long for fast processing. After that, a shot detection algorithm is applied to extract the number of shots, which is one of low-level features. Further, MPEG-7 audio-visual features are extracted from the detected shots in the segmented video clip.

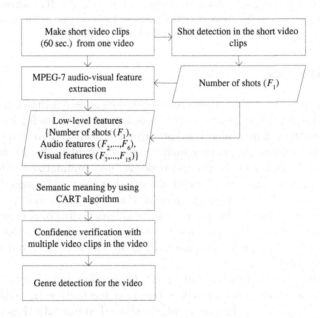

Fig. 1. Overall procedure of the proposed video genre detection method

The HSV color features for measuring color variation are calculated from every 10 frames of the video clip while other features are obtained within a shot duration. As seen in Fig. 1, the semantic meaning of genre is inferred by decision tree classifier using CART algorithm with the low-level features. Finally, the genre of video is decided by considering the probability of classified genre for multiple video clips. In the next section, the details of low-level features used in this paper and the semantic classification of genres from the features are explained.

2.1 Shot Detection in Short Video Clips and Finding the Number of Shots

The number of shots in the short video clip is one of low-level features used in this paper. It shows video tempo [3]. While most music videos have short shot durations due to various editing effects, sports and news videos have relatively long shots by tracking of one camera, for example. To detect shots from the video clip, visual features such as Homogeneous Texture (HT), Scalable Color (SC), and Edge Histogram (EH) descriptors are used. To detect transition, frame difference in terms of three visual features is calculated. The frame difference at i^{th} frame ($FrameDiff_i$) can be obtained from

$$FrameDiff_i = Diff\_SC_i + Diff\_EH_i + Diff\_HT_i, \tag{1}$$

where

$$Diff\_SC_i = (SC\_frame_{i-p} - SC\_frame_i)^2 / Max\_Diff\_SC, \tag{2}$$

$$Diff\_EH_i = (EH\_frame_{i-p} - EH\_frame_i)^2 / Max\_Diff\_EH, \tag{3}$$

$$Diff\_HT_i = (HT\_frame_{i-p} - HT\_frame_i)^2 / Max\_Diff\_HT. \tag{4}$$

In Eq. (1) to (4), $Diff\_SC_i$, $Diff\_EH_i$, and $Diff\_HT_i$ are the normalized difference values of the three visual features between the $(i-p)^{th}$ and the ith frame, respectively. In the difference calculation, p frame duration is used to detect gradual shot changes such as fade-in/out, dissolve, and wipe. SC_frame_i, EH_frame_i, and HT_frame_i denote the feature values of the three visual features, respectively. Max_Diff_SC, Max_Diff_EH, Max_Diff_HT are the maximum values of $Diff\_SC_i$, $Diff\_EH_i$, and $Diff\_HT_i$ for entire frames in the short video clip.

Using the frame difference, shot transition can be found as,

$$Shot\_Trans_i = \begin{cases} True, \ If \ FrameDiff_i > Th\_frame \ and \ |FrameDiff_{i-1}| > Th\_diff \\ False, \ Otherwise \end{cases}. \tag{5}$$

where Th_frame and Th_diff are empirical threshold. If $Shot\_Trans_i$ has a True value, then shot transition is detected at i^{th} frame.

After obtaining shot transitions, the number of shots denoted as F_1, is calculated by measuring the frequency of the shot transitions in the short video clip (with 60 second length in this paper).

2.2 Low-Level Multi-modal Features

As the standard of multimedia description, MPEG-7 provides proved audio-visual descriptors to characterize multimedia contents. We used MPEG-7 audio-visual descriptors as the multi-modal features.

Audio features. Generally, video genre has its unique audio characteristics. For example, a dialog scene in drama has low audio power, flat audio spectrum, and a low harmonic centroid value, etc. [5]. Audio features, therefore, could be the key components to measure the characteristics of video genre. The audio features of the MPEG-7 descriptors used in this paper are as follows:

- AudioPower: A music video has higher audio power than the other genres due to background music or a singer song. In contrast, a sports genre carries lower audio power [5]. The mean of the AudioPower descriptor in a video clip is denoted as F_2.
- FundamentalFrequency: Fundamental frequency is basic information of an audio signal which is a good predictor of musical pitch and speech intonation. Compared with other genres, the mean of the FundamentalFrequency descriptor denoted as F_3, is higher in a music video but lower in a news genre.
- HarmonicSpectralCentroid: Using harmonic information of an audio signal, one can distinguish sounds with a harmonic spectrum (musical sounds, voiced speech, etc.) from those with a non-harmonic spectrum (noise, unvoiced speech, etc.) [5]. The mean of this descriptor denoted as F_4 can distinguish an instrumental sound of a music video from anchor's speech of a news video.
- HarmonicSpectralDeviation: The mean of HarmonicSpectral-Deviation is denoted as F_5. Generally, it is high in a music video with high variation among several musical sounds. On the contrary, drama or news videos show low values since human voices have little gap between the amplitude of the harmonic peak and the local spectral envelope around the harmonic peak. The others form the middle class of the 3 classes.
- AudioSpectrumFlatness: This descriptor represents the deviation of the signal's power spectrum over frequency from a flat shape (corresponding to a noise-like or an impulse-like signal) [5]. The mean of the AudioSpectrum-Flatness denoted as F_6, could discriminate between a sport and a cartoon video.

Visual features. The visual characteristics in a video include several visual changes, *e.g.*, the amount of motion, the variation of color information, the motion of camera viewpoint, etc. [5]. The visual features used in this paper are as follows:

- Motion Activity: This descriptor is useful in distinguishing a sports or a music video with high actions from a drama video with relatively low actions. TemporalParameter and shot's activity histogram are used to detect motion information within a shot. The mean of a centroid value of this histogram denoted as F_7, indicates motion intensity in the video clip.
- Camera Motion: The Camera Motion descriptor describes 3-D camera motion parameters [5]. Some of the parameters including fixed, panning, tilting, and zooming are used. Especially, panning is good to identify a sport video

in the video database. But, a cartoon video has little panning camera motion. The average values of panning, tilting, zooming, and fixed parameters in the video clip are denoted as F_8, F_9, F_{10}, and F_{11}, respectively. F_{12} is denoted as the sum of F_8, F_9, and F_{10}.

- Color information in HSV coordinates: The color feature helps to detect dominant color or color variation in video. Usually, average brightness in cartoon video is much higher than those of other video genres and average saturation in sports video is much higher in comparison with drama and news videos. Especially, music videos show high variation of color flow due to various editing effects. The means of Hue, Saturation, and Value in the Scalable Color descriptor are denoted as F_{13}, F_{14}, and F_{15}.

2.3   Semantic Classification with Multi-modal Features for Genre Detection

As mentioned previously, the segmentation of the entire video into short video clips make video analysis fast and efficient. However, there are a large number of semantic patterns in the structures of the short video clips. For example, news video has various patterns within a short video clip: **A** (an anchor part), **N** (an article part), and mixed structures such as **A+N** (an anchor part + an article part), **N+A**, **A+N+A**, **N+A+N**, etc., even though its structure is relatively simple. Due to the variations of the structures, it is difficult to find out the unique rules to explain the short videos semantically. In this paper, low-level feature distributions in the short videos are analyzed statistically so that they lead to classify the video genres semantically.

The main advantage of decision tree classifier is that it reduces problem complexity by approximating the global decision regions using simpler local decision regions at each level of the tree [6]. Namely, a feature set of the proposed method with multi-dimension can be effectively divided into several clusters by the binary split approach of the decision tree classifier. This is helpful in making stable and fast prediction for huge video database. Also, because its methodology is characterized by a reliable pruning strategy, a powerful binary split search approach, and automatic self validation [7], CART algorithm provides an unique combination of automated solutions for classifying the genres. Therefore, the decision tree classifier is suitable to classify video genres with multi-dimensional low-level audio-visual features.

As a splitting criterion, we use GINI index which looks for the largest genre class in a feature set and strives to isolate it from all other genre classes. When a node p is split into k children, the quality of split is computed as,

$$GINI_{split} = \sum_{i=1}^{k} \frac{n_i}{n} GINI(i), \qquad (6)$$

where

$$GINI(i) = 1 - \sum_{j}[p(j|i)]^2. \qquad (7)$$

In Eq. (6), n_i is the number of features at child i and n is the number of features at node p. The classifier uses the splitting variables which make the index to be lowest in all of them. In Eq. (7), $p(j|i)$ is the relative frequency of genre j at node i.

In the training of the classifier, we choose and utilize the architecture of the tree classifier with stable performance by iterated calculation with 15 cross-validations which are applied to prune the architectures in order to maintain the performance and reduce the cost.

When the multi-modal features are fed into the CART, it selects a main splitter among the features to form a main tree in each node. With the multi-modal feature set, the main tree forms 10 nodes and 11 terminal nodes. F_1 (the number of shots) splits input data mainly in node 1. It means that the number of shots is the most important factor in the classification. F_7, Motion Activity, plays a role as a main splitter in node 2 and F_5, HarmonicSpectralDeviation, affects significantly to divide the data into several classes in node 3. Figure 2 shows the distribution of the video genres in the 3 main splitters' coordinates. Except the drama videos, the video genres are segmented into several clusters in the coordinates.

3   Experimental Results

The experiment has been conducted with MPEG-7 audio-visual descriptors as low-level features and the five video genres database. Each genre has 72 video clips with 60 seconds length and 352 x 240 size, in which 47 clips are used for training the classifier, and the others for measuring the classification performance. Cartoon, drama, music video, and news video clips are extracted from 9, 10, 30, and 6 different source videos respectively. Sports clips are taken from 12 different videos such as soccer, basketball, golf, running, etc. To extract audio features, we take audio samples with 16 KHz rate and use the hop sizes and window sizes recommended in MPEG-7.

To compare the usefulness of the proposed multi-modal features in the genre detection, we evaluated the classification performances of three cases: one case with audio features, another case with visual features, and the other with audio-visual features. Table 1 shows the classification results about three cases.

Using audio features and the number of shots, i.e., $F\_set_{audio} = \{F_1, F_2, F_3, F_4, F_5, F_6\}$, the average recall rate was 72.8 % and the average precision rate was about 75.6 %. The audio features have shown good performance for music video, news, and sports genres. These genres are related with audio characteristics: the musical sound with high audio frequency and power, the continuous human voice with a flat spectrum and low audio power, the audience shouting with high audio power and frequency, etc. On the contrary, cartoon and drama videos have audio sound mixed with a human voice, music or other sounds.

The average recall rate of 72.0 % and the average precision rate of 73.2 % were shown for visual features and feature of the number of shots, i.e., $F\_set_{visual} = \{F_1, F_7, F_8, F_9, F_{10}, F_{11}, F_{12}, F_{13}, F_{14}, F_{15}\}$. Visual information was useful to

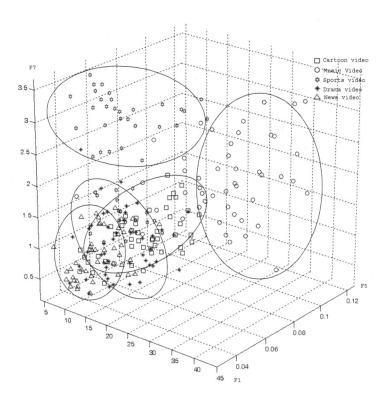

Fig. 2. Distribution of video genres in 3 main splitters' coordinates (F_1, F_5, and F_7)

Table 1. Genre classification results for the single video clip

Genre	$F\_set_{audio}(\%)$		$F\_set_{visual}(\%)$		$F\_set_{multi-modal}(\%)$	
	Recall	Prec.	Recall	Prec.	Recall	Prec.
Cartoon	56.0	60.9	76.0	65.5	92.0	88.5
Drama	64.0	69.6	56.0	53.8	76.0	95.0
Music video	80.0	83.3	92.0	88.5	96.0	88.9
News	84.0	80.8	60.0	78.9	88.0	91.7
Sports	80.0	83.3	76.0	79.2	92.0	92.0
Average	72.8	75.6	72.0	73.2	88.8	91.2

retrieve a music video and showed good possibilities to recognize a cartoon and a sports genre. The shot tempo of music video is faster than those of the others and the change of color is a key factor to classify cartoon videos. High motion activity and camera motion lead to distinguish a sports video from others. But, as seen in the table, it is difficult to discriminate drama and news genre by using only visual information because they have complex structures including several scenes with various motions and video tempos: running, dialog, article scenes, etc.

For the experiment with audio-visual features, nine multi-modal features, i.e., $F\_set_{multi-modal} = \{F_1, F_2, F_3, F_4, F_5, F_7, F_{13}, F_{14}, F_{15}\}$, were selected by iterative training to consider dependency among features. The average recall rate was 88.8 % and the average precision rate was 91.2 %. As shown in the table, the classification result of the drama genre is lower than those of the other genres because it has the most complex structure in which various scenes are combined: dialogs, songs, exercises scenes, etc.

The classification rate with a single video clip was 89 % in average in the experiment. The final genre detection of the video is performed with multiple video clips. Namely, we can select multiple short video clips from the entire video. Then we see that more than half of video clips are classified into one genre dominantly. If so, the video is assigned to the genre. To do that, we randomly tried to choose multiple video clips in the entire video. Table 2 shows the genre detection ratio. As is seen, the more the number of video clips increases, the higher the detection rate is obtained. Final genre detection rate is obtained by

$$Genre\_detection\_rate = \sum_{i=r}^{M} \binom{M}{i} P_g^i (1 - P_g)^{(M-i)}, \tag{8}$$

where

$$r = Round(M/2), M = 1, 3, 5, \ldots (odd\ numbers). \tag{9}$$

In Eq. (8), M is the number of video clips chosen from a video and P_g is the probability to classify one genre for single video clip.

We have calculated the genre detection time for the case with the multi-modal feature set. It takes about 102 seconds to detect genre about single video clip with PC (Pentium IV, 2.4 GHz CPU). Because the proposed genre detection is performed with unit of short video clip, the detection time is not affected by the length of entire video.

Table 2. Genre detection ratio obtained by the proposed method

Genre	Recall about a single clip from Table (%)	More than 2 out of 3 clips (%)	More than 3 out of 5 clips (%)
Cartoon	92.0	98.2	99.5
Drama	76.0	85.5	90.7
Music video	96.0	99.5	99.9
News	88.0	96.0	98.6
Sports	92.0	98.2	99.5
Processing time	102 sec.	306 sec.	510 sec.

4   Conclusion

This paper proposes new automatic video genre detection with multi-modal features and decision tree classifier. Our goal is to recognize video genre as a preprocessing technique of content-based authoring. We have analyzed statistical characteristics of audio-visual features. Based on that, low-level features are organized and applied to decision tree classifier that uses CART algorithm. To prove the usefulness of the proposed method, the experiments were performed to evaluate the detection performance with several video genres. The experimental results show that the proposed method to detect video genres gives high detection rate and reasonable processing time. As further works, we will extend the number of genres and reduce the processing time by reducing features.

References

1. Li, Y., Kuo, C.C.J.: Video Content Analysis using Multimodal Information. Kluwer Academic Publishers (2003)
2. Truong, B.T., Dorai, C.: Automatic genre identification for content-based video categorization. 15th International Con. on Pattern Recognition **4** (2000) 230–233
3. Liu, Z., Huang, J., Wang, Y.: Classification of tv programs based on audio information using hidden marcov model. IEEE Workshop on Multimedia Signal Processing (1998) 27–32
4. Huang, J., Liu, Z., Wang, Y., Chen, Y., Wong, E.K.: Integration of multimodal features for video scene classification based on hmm. IEEE Workshop on Multimedia Signal Processing (1999) 53–58
5. Jin, S.H., Bae, T.M., Choo, J.H., Ro, Y.M.: Video genre classification using multi-modal features. SPIE2004 **5307** (2003) 307–318
6. Safavian, S.R., Landgrebe, D.: A survey of decision tree classifier methodology. IEEE Trans. Systems, Man and Cybernetics **21** (1991) 660–674
7. Breiman, L., Friedman, J., Olshen, R.A., Stone, C.: Classification and Regression Trees. Chapman & Hall (1984)

Face Appeal Model Based on Statistics[*]

Bi Song[1], Mingjing Li[2], Zhiwei Li[2], Hong-Jiang Zhang[2], and Zhengkai Liu[1]

[1] University of Science and Technology of China Hefei 230026, China
bisong@mail.ustc.edu.cn
zhengkai@ustc.edu.cn
[2] Microsoft Research Asia, 49 Zhichun Road, Beijing 100080, China
{mjli, i-zli, hjzhang}@microsoft.com

Abstract. Human appearance plays an important role in image appeal ranking for efficient management of digital photographs. Considering that face is the most salient character of human beings, we propose a face appeal model in this paper. The model is based on the statistics of a large number of data, and can be used as a component in general image appeal evaluation.

1 Introduction

The rapid development of digital cameras and other imaging devices results in the increasing demand for efficient management of digital photographs. Image quality assessment is a useful technique for this purpose. Based on image quality measures, the low-quality images may be detected and potentially be removed from the photograph album.

A number of image quality measurements are proposed. However, most of them measure fidelity instead of quality. Such metrics assume that a 'reference' images is available and the difference between the reference and processed image is used as the criterion of the image quality. As to photographs, their reference images usually do not exist. Moreover, those metrics mainly focus on objective attributes of image quality, while subjective attributes, which can be referred to as image appeal [1], are more important in the measurement of photograph quality.

In a study of image appeal evaluation in consumer photography, a list of both positive and negative influences in picture ranking was compiled based on human estimation experiments [2]. Their results indicate that the most important attributions for image selection are related to people in the picture. Especially in family album, human is the main topic that people capture in their photos. As the most salient character of human beings, face always attracts the viewer's attention. In this paper, we focus on how to measure the image appeal based on the face information.

To automatically measure the face appeal in images, face detection must be performed at first. Over past few decades, face detection has been studied

---

[*] This work was performed at Microsoft Research Asia.

K. Aizawa, Y. Nakamura, and S. Satoh (Eds.): PCM 2004, LNCS 3331, pp. 344–351, 2004.
© Springer-Verlag Berlin Heidelberg 2004

extensively by numerous researchers in computer vision. As a result, efficient and robust face detection algorithms have become available [3][4]. Although the face detection technology has a broad field of application, there has been very little effort devoted toward the evaluation of face appeal in images. Ma et al. proposed a face model based on the sum of relative face sizes weighted by their positions [5]. Although this model is reasonable, it is too simple and has not been evaluated by large data set.

To address this issue, a new face appeal model is provided in this paper. The model is constructed on the distribution of large data set. Precise mathematic formulas are given, using which the rank of face appeal can be easily calculated.

The rest of this paper is organized as follows. Section 2 introduces the data basis on which the face appeal model is built. Section 3 describes the details of this model construction. Section 4 gives the experimental results. Thereafter, concluding remarks are given in Sect.5.

2   Face Distribution Analysis

2.1   Data Set

We have built up a database which contains 134,300 faces detected from images. The information of those faces was obtained by a multi-view face detector [3], including the number of faces, their positions and sizes. Fig.1 gives an example of face detection result in image.

Fig. 1. Face detection result

The size and position of a face usually reflect the importance of the face. Hence, the essential problem in developing a face importance index can be formulated as follows: given the information (size and position) of a face in an image only, how can the appeal of this image be computed? To solve the problem, we assume that the distribution face information (size and position) on large database reflects the ground truth of people's preference of face importance.

2.2 Face Position Analysis

We normalize the face position to the range of [-1, 1] on both horizontal and vertical orientation. A position histogram is the distribution of face position in the 2-dimention Euclidean space. We uniformly quantize face position into 25*25 bins. The histogram of the face position is illustrated in Fig.2(a).

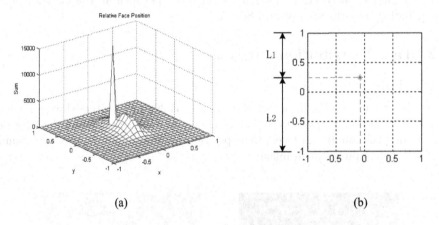

(a)   (b)

Fig. 2. (a)Face position histogram (b) Peak location of face position

It has been shown that the positions do not fall randomly in a plane, but form a specific distribution. This observation also verifies our assumption that people really have preference of face position. We have found that there is a high and sharp peak in the position histogram. This peak locates near the point (-0.08, 0.24), its height is 11.6%, i.e. about 15,000 faces are set around this position. Fig.2(b) shows on which location this peak exactly is.

In horizontal axis, this point is almost in the center with a little bit left offset. In vertical axis, this point divides the position range [-1 1] into two parts, the ratio of the two parts' length is $\frac{L_1}{L_2} = \frac{(1-0.24)}{0.24-(-1)} = 0.613$.

This ratio is very close to the golden ratio. How well this distribution coincides with people's aesthetic perception!

2.3 Face Size Analysis

First we normalize the faces' size: $size = SIZE_{face}/SIZE_{image}$. Fig.3(a) is the histogram of normalized face size (uniformly quantized into 100 bins). As we

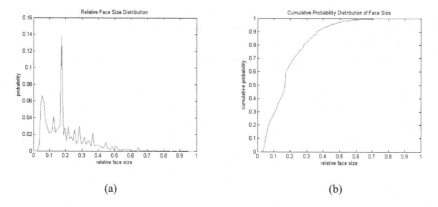

Fig. 3. Face size histogram. (a) Probability distribution (b) Cumulative probability

$$M_{face} = \sum_{k=1}^{N} \frac{A_k}{A_{image}} \times \frac{w_{pos}^i}{8}$$

	1/3	1/3	1/3	
1	2	1	3/12
4	8	4	4/12
1	2	1	5/12

Fig. 4. Face appeal model proposed in [5]

know, larger face should be more important. So instead of face size probability distribution, we use cumulative probability to represent the face size appeal, which is showed in Fig.3(b).

3   Face Appeal Model

3.1   Previous Face Appeal Model

A face attention model has been proposed in [5]. In this model, face size and position are used to evaluate the face importance in a picture. Their metric is as follows.

In this modal, A_k denotes the size of kth face in an image, A_{image} denote the area of image, w_{pos}^i is the weight of position defined in Fig.4.

From Fig.2(a), it's clear that most faces lie in the center block and they are all assigned the same weight in this model. But in fact, the distribution of face position in this block varies most. So we need a more accurate model to describe the face appeal.

3.2   Appeal Model Representation

Generally speaking, we can consider that several photographic styles are used most often in practice. For example, the peak of face position distribution described in Sect.2.2 stands for a most common style. We assume that those ranges of positions are approximately Gaussian in nature. So we choose the Gaussian mixture model (GMM) to represent the joint intensity distribution while each Gaussian in the mixture may correspond roughly to one type of photographic style.

Thus, for a given face, its position appeal is reflected by the probability that the face occurs in this position. This probability is a combination of K Gaussian densities:

$$f(X;\theta) = \sum_{k=1}^{K} p_k g(X; m_k, \Sigma_k) \qquad (1)$$

where

$$g(X; m_k, \Sigma_k) = \frac{1}{(2\pi)^{d/2} |\Sigma_k|^{1/2}} \exp(-\frac{1}{2}(X - m_k)^T \Sigma_k^{-1}(X - m_k)) \qquad (2)$$

and

$$\sum_{k=1}^{K} p_k = 1 \qquad (3)$$

The parameters of this model are $p_k, m_k, \Sigma_k | k \in K$

We would like to estimate the parameters of the Gaussian mixture density using a maximum likelihood estimator. Fortunately, maximum likelihood parameter estimation for a GMM can be solved using the EM algorithm [6].

Given an initial estimate $p_k^{(0)}, m_k^{(0)}, \Sigma_k^{(0)}$, EM iterates the following computations until convergence to a local maximum of the likelihood function:

E Step:

$$p^{(i)}(k|n) = \frac{p_k^{(i)} g(X_n; m_k^{(i)}, \Sigma_k^{(i)})}{\sum_{k'=1}^{K} p_{k'}^{(i)} g(X_n; m_{k'}^{(i)}, \Sigma_{k'}^{(i)})} \qquad (4)$$

M Step:

$$m_k^{(i+1)} = \frac{\sum_{n=1}^{N} X_n p^{(i)}(k|n)}{\sum_{n=1}^{N} p^i(k|n)} \qquad (5)$$

$$\Sigma_k^{(i+1)} = \frac{\sum_{n=1}^{N} p^{(i)}(k|n)(X_n - m_k^{(i+1)})(X_n - m_k^{(i+1)})^T}{\sum_{n=1}^{N} p^{(i)}(k|n)} \qquad (6)$$

$$p_k^{(i+1)} = \frac{1}{N} \sum_{n=1}^{N} p^{(i)}(k|n) \qquad (7)$$

In this model, the only parameter that should be set manually is the number of Gaussian components, which is denoted as K in (1). Due to the high and sharp peak exiting, it is obvious that $K \geq 2$. Indeed, if an arbitrary number of Gaussian function components are allowed, any density function can be approximated to any desired accuracy. Of cause, the complexity of the model will be high as the number of component increase. There is a trade-off between complexity and accuracy.

According to Fig.3(b), it is natural to fit face size appeal by polynomial and its coefficients are easy to get by solving a least-squares problem.

As a result, giving a face, its position appeal and size appeal are defined as follows:

$$Appeal_{pos} = \sum_{k=1}^{Kpos} p_k g(X; m_k, \Sigma_k) \tag{8}$$

$$Appeal_{size} = \sum_{m=1}^{Msize} a_m X^m \tag{9}$$

where $Msize$ is the degree of face size polynomial.

As proposed in [5], they are combined to form the face appeal of image by:

$$Appeal_{face} = \sum_{n=1}^{N} Appeal_{pos}^n \times Appeal_{size}^n \tag{10}$$

where N denotes the face number in the image.

4   Experimental Results

4.1   Peak Number Detection

In order to choose a proper number of Gaussian components for face position appeal model, we use Jeffrey-Divergence (JD) to measure the similarity of two distributions [7]. For binned histograms, it is:

$$D_{JD}(q, p) = \sum_{j=1}^{N} \sum_{l=0}^{L-1} [q_j(l) \log \frac{2q_j(l)}{q_j(l) + p_j(l)} + p_j(l) \log \frac{2p_j(l)}{q_j(l) + p_j(l)}] \tag{11}$$

where L is the number of bins and N is the dimension of distribution. We can select a proper K according to the JD.

We tried $Kpos$ from 2 to 6. Table 1 gives the Jeffrey-Divergence of the face position distribution in our database and GMM with different K. It can be observed that when $Kpos > 3$, the accuracy of GMM only increases a little. So we choose $Kpos = 3$. Table 2 gives corresponding parameters. And Fig.5(a) illustrates the result.

To determine the degree of polynomial in face size model, we tired $Msize$ from 5 to 11. Table 3 gives the Jeffrey-Divergence of the face size cumulative probability distribution in our database and polynomial with different degree. We observe that the first local minimum of JD occurs when $Msize = 8$. So

Table 1. JD of the face position distribution in our database and GMM with different component number

Kpos	2	3	4	5	6
JD	0.0765	0.0405	0.0364	0.0356	0.0347

Table 2. Parameters of Face Position Appeal Model. This model is a a combination of three 2-D Gaussian functions

k	p_k	m_k	Σ_k
1	0.3564	$\begin{bmatrix} 0.0181 \\ -0.0325 \end{bmatrix}$	$\begin{bmatrix} 0.0100 & 0.0006 \\ 0.0006 & 0.0290 \end{bmatrix}$
2	0.5368	$\begin{bmatrix} 0.0121 \\ 0.1532 \end{bmatrix}$	$\begin{bmatrix} 0.0828 & 0.0004 \\ 0.0004 & 0.0734 \end{bmatrix}$
3	0.1068	$\begin{bmatrix} -0.1059 \\ 0.2658 \end{bmatrix}$	$1e-26 * \begin{bmatrix} 0.2749 & 0.0486 \\ 0.0486 & 0.0086 \end{bmatrix}$

Table 3. JD of the face size cumulative probability distribution in our database and polynomial with different degree

Msize	5	6	7	8	9	10	11
JD	0.0649	0.0585	0.0532	0.0499	0.0522	0.0513	0.0484

Table 4. Parameters of Face Size Appeal Model. This model is represented by a polynomial of degree 8

a_8	a_7	a_6	a_5	a_4	a_3	a_2	a_1	a_0
106.9	-514.9	1040.7	-1141.1	728.8	-265.5	45.8	0.3	0.0

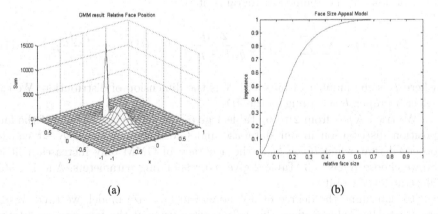

(a)   (b)

Fig. 5. Result of face appeal model. (a)Face position appeal model (b)Face size appeal model

we choose $Msize = 8$. Table 4 gives corresponding parameters. And Fig.5(b) illustrates the result.

In summary, we give the expression of face appeal model as follows:

$$Appeal_{face} =$$
$$\sum_{n=1}^{N}(\sum_{k=1}^{3} p_k \frac{1}{(2\pi)|\Sigma_k|^{1/2}} \exp(-\frac{1}{2}(X - m_k)^T \Sigma_k^{-1}(X - m_k)) \times \sum_{m=0}^{8} a_m X^m)_n \tag{12}$$

All parameters are given in Table 2 and Table 4.

5 Conclusion

In this paper, we have presented a model for determining the appeal of an image based on human face information. As far as we are aware, this is the first attempt to design a precise model for evaluating the face appeal. We use the distribution of face information of large data set as the basis of our model. The position appeal model is represented by GMM and its parameters are estimated with EM, while the size appeal model is represented by a polynomial. The face appeal of an image can be obtained by combining these two models together.

Our experiment results show that those models fit the original distributions fairly well. As the parameters have been given, the model can be used easily with low computation.

References

[1] Winkler, S.: Visually fidelity and perceived quality: Towards comprehensive metrics. Proc. SPIE Human Vision and Electronic Imaging **4299** (2001) 114-125
[2] Savakis, S.E., Etz, S.P., and Loui, A.C.: Evaluation of image appeal in consumer photography. Proc. of Human Vision and Electronic Imaging (2000)
[3] Xiao, R., Li, M., and Zhang, H.J.: Robust multi-pose face detection in images. IEEE Trans. on CSVT Special Issue on Biometrics (2003)
[4] Yang, M.H., Kriegman, D.J., and Ahuja, N.: Detecting faces in images: A survey. IEEE Trans. on PAMI **24(1)** (2002) 34-58
[5] Ma, Y.F., Lu, L., Zhang, H.J., and Li, M.: A user attention model for video summarization. Proc. of ACM Multimedia (2002)
[6] Bilmes, J.A.: A gentle tutorial of the EM algorithm and its application to parameter estimation for Gaussian mixture and hidden Markov models. U.C.Berkeley TR-97-021 (1998)
[7] Ojala, T., Pietikainen, M., and Harwood, D.: A comparative study of texture measures with classification based feature distributions. Pattern Recognition **29(1)** (1996) 51-59

A Novel Gabor-LDA Based Face Recognition Method

Yanwei Pang[2]*, Lei Zhang[1], Mingjing Li[1], Zhengkai Liu[2], and Weiying Ma[1]

[1] Microsoft Research Asia, Beijing 100080, China
{Leizhang,Mjli,Wyma}@microsoft.com
[2] Information Processing Center, University of Science and Technology of China,
Hefei 230027, China
{pyw,Zhengkai}@ustc.edu.cn

Abstract. In this paper, a novel face recognition method based on Gabor-wavelet and linear discriminant analysis (LDA) is proposed. Given training face images, discriminant vectors are computed using LDA. The function of the discriminant vectors is two-fold. First, discriminant vectors are used as a transform matrix, and LDA features are extracted by projecting original intensity images onto discriminant vectors. Second, discriminant vectors are used to select *discriminant* pixels, the number of which is much less than that of a whole image. Gabor features are extracted only on these *discriminant* pixels. Then, applying LDA on the Gabor features, one can obtain the Gabor-LDA features. Finally, a combined classifier is formed based on these two types of LDA features. Experimental results show that the proposed method performs better than traditional approaches in terms of both efficiency and accuracy.

1 Introduction

Face recognition has been an active research topic in the past few decades due to its scientific challenges and potential applications. In general, there are two main ap-proaches to face recognition, geometric feature-based and template-based [1]. Geometric feature-based methods analyze explicit local features (such as eyes, mouth and nose) and their geometric relationships. Representative works include Hidden Markov Model (HMM) proposed by Samaria [2], elastic bunch graph matching algorithm proposed by Wiskott et al. [3], and Local Feature Analysis (LFA) proposed by Penev et al. [4]. Template-based (or appearance-based) methods match faces using the holistic features of face images. The current state-of-the art of such methods is characterized by a family of subspace methods originated by "eigenface" [5]. Peter et al. switched from "eigenface" to "fisherface" [6]. Moghaddam et al. proposed to estimate density in high-dimensional spaces using eigenspace decomposition [7] and then derived a probabilistic similarity measure based on Bayesian analysis of image differences [8]. Wang et al. further

---

* This work was performed at Microsoft Research Asia.

K. Aizawa, Y. Nakamura, and S. Satoh (Eds.): PCM 2004, LNCS 3331, pp. 352–358, 2004.
© Springer-Verlag Berlin Heidelberg 2004

developed a unified analysis method that uses three subspace dimensions, i.e. intrinsic difference, transform difference and noise, and achieved better recognition performance than the standard subspace methods [9].

However, although many of the published algorithms have demonstrated excellent recognition results, there are still many open problems. The face recognition vender test (FRVT) 2002 [10] reports that recognition under illumination and pose variations still remain challenging. To obtain good features robust to such variations, many methods applied Gabor-wavelet transform which can capture the properties of orientation selectivity and spatial frequency selectivity [11]. PCA and LDA were employed on Gabor-filtered images instead of the original grey-level ones in [12] [13] respectively. Usually, 40 Gabor kernels (5 different scales and 8 orientations) are used. As a result, the dimension of the filtered vectors is up to $40 \times d$, where d equals the product of the width w and the height h of the image (i.e. $d = w \times h$). When the size of original image is 100×100, the dimension of the filtered vector can be as large as 400,000. Such a high dimensional vector will lead to expensive computation and storage cost.

To alleviate such problem and make the algorithm robust to pose variations, Gabor-wavelet features were extracted on fiducial points in [3]. The major disadvantage would be that only the areas which can be reliably located are used for recognition purposes. Another work in [13] employed simple down-sampling trick to alleviate the computational burden.

Motivated by [14], in this paper, we propose a method which can automatically select discriminant pixels using the discriminant vectors of LDA. Computational benefit is thus obtained when the number of selected *discriminant* pixels is smaller than that of the whole image. The experimental results show that discriminant pixels are related to local features such as eyes, nose and mouth, which coincide with intuitions. Finally, these local features and global features are combined to form the final classifier and improved face recognition accuracy is obtained. This paper does not describe the details of LDA and Gabor-wavelet. See Ref. [6] and [3] for details in-stead.

2   Overview of the Proposed Method

Fig. 1 illustrates the process of feature extraction and the design of the classifier. Note that discriminant vectors obtained by LDA are used to determine discriminant pixels which are related to intuitive local features. Since the number of discriminant pixels is much less than that of the whole image, the amount of computed Gabor-wavelet coefficient is decreased. Furthermore, local features and global features are combined to form the final classifier. Specifically, we describe our method as follows:

Given training images, discriminant vectors are computed using LDA. The function of the discriminant vectors is two-fold. First, discriminant vectors are used as a transform matrix, and LDA features are extracted by projecting gray-level images onto discriminant vectors. Second, discriminant vectors are used to select *discriminant* pixels, the number of which is much less than that of

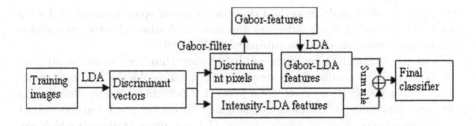

Fig. 1. The process of feature extraction and the design of final classifer. Sum rule is adopted to combine the similarity scores of local features (Gabor-LDA features) and global features (Intensity-LDA features). For simplicity, the feature extraction process for testing images is omitted since it is similar to that for training images.

a whole image. Gabor features are extracted only on these *discriminant* pixels. Then, applying LDA on the Gabor features, one can obtain reduced Gabor-LDA features. Finally, a combined classifier is formed based on these two types of LDA features.

3   The Selection of Discriminant Pixels

3.1   Principle

As stated in Section 1, an image has $d = w \times h$ pixels. But different pixels are of different importance for classification. If only important (discriminant) pixels are focused on, computational cost can be decreased and classification performance might be improved as well. Inspired by [14], we propose to use the values of the discriminant vectors $\mathbf{W} = [\mathbf{w}_1, \mathbf{w}_2, \mathbf{w}_m]$ computed by LDA to select discriminant pixels. We can only compute Gabor coefficients on those discriminant pixels to avoid high computational cost.

In [14], Peng et al. use linear SVM to search for a linear classifier: $f(\mathbf{x}) = \mathbf{w} \bullet \mathbf{x} + b$. The normal $\mathbf{w}$ is perpendicular to the separating hyperplane. Projected onto the direction $\mathbf{w}$, data can be separated with the largest margin. It is readily to induce that any direction, Θ, whose dot product with $\mathbf{w}$ is large, also carries discriminant information. In particular, when is restricted to the feature axes, i.e. $\Theta \in \{\mathbf{e}_1, ..., \mathbf{e}_d\}$, where $\mathbf{e}_i$ is a unit vector. Thus the dot product becomes $w_i = \mathbf{w} \bullet \mathbf{e}_i$. So $|w_i > w_j|$ implies that axis $\mathbf{e}_i$ carries more discriminant information than $\mathbf{e}_j$. As illustrated in Fig.2, data projected onto discriminant vector $\mathbf{w}$ can be separated reliably. Because the angle between y axis and vector $\mathbf{w}$ is smaller than that between $\mathbf{x}$ axis and $\mathbf{w}$, so it is safe to say that $\mathbf{y}$ axis carries more discriminant information than $\mathbf{x}$ axis.

3.2   Selection Procedure

Keep in mind that each pixel in an image corresponds to a dimension (axis) in the high dimensional space. If dimension i carries discriminant information, it

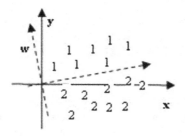

Fig. 2. Find the most discriminant axis in 2D space. There are two classes.

also means that pixel i carries discriminant information. Thus, one can use $|w_i|$ to measure the importance level of pixel i. Now we switch from SVM to LDA.

In LDA, a transformation matrix from a d-dimensional space to an m-dimensional space is determined such that the Fisher criterion of between-class scatter over within-class scatter is maximized. In LDA, C-1 discriminant vectors can be derived where C represents the number of total classes. These discriminant vectors jointly form a linear transform matrix $\mathbf{W} = [\mathbf{w}_1, \mathbf{w}_2, ... \mathbf{w}_m]$. Therefore, we combine them together to determine discriminant pixels as follows.

Because the dimension of each discriminant vector $\mathbf{w}_i$ is d, $\mathbf{w}_i$ can be expressed as $\mathbf{w}_i = [w_{i1}, w_{i2}, ..., w_{id}]^T$. Firstly, a new vector $\mathbf{w}'$ is defined as

$$\mathbf{w}' = \sum_{i=1}^{m} |\mathbf{w}_i| \tag{1}$$

Secondly, sort the elements of $\mathbf{w}' = [w'_1, w'_2, ..., w'_d]^T$ and denote the result vector by $\mathbf{v} = [v_1, v_2, ..., v_{r-1}, v_r, v_{r+1}, .., v_{d-1}, v_d]^T$ with $v_1 \geq ... \geq v_{d}$,. Thirdly, according to a predefined threshold t 1, tune r such that $r/d \approx t$. Then the elements of $\mathbf{w}'$ are binarized based on the threshold v_r. Consequently, a mask vector $\mathbf{w}^{mask}$ is achieved with $w_i^{mask}=1$ if $w'_i \geq v_r$ and $w_i^{mask}=0$ otherwise. The value of w_i^{mask} indicates whether or not the pixel i is a discriminant pixel. If $w_i^{mask}=1$, pixel i is treated to be a discriminant pixel, indicating that Gabor-filters will be applied on this pixel, otherwise it is not treated to be a discriminant one, indicating that this pixel needs not to be filtered. Notice that t=1 (thus r=d) means that Gabor-filters are applied on the whole image. Therefore, the computational load and storage cost will be high if t is big. On the other hand, if t is too small, useful information might be lost. As a tradeoff, t is empirically selected to be 0.2 in our experiments.

We have conducted experiments on a subset of FERET database [15] the details of which will be described later. Fig. 3 (b) visualizes $\mathbf{w}'$ and $\mathbf{w}^{mask}$, which will be analyzed in section 4.

4   Fusion of Local Features and Global Features

It can be seen from Fig. 3 (b) that local features are emphasized. Discriminant pixels are just around salient facial components such as eyes, nose and mouth.

Fig. 3. (a) Shows example FERET images used in our experiments. Four images are used as training images and the other two are used as testing images. The left image in (b) visualizes $\mathbf{w}'$ defined in Eq. (1) and the right image shows $\mathbf{w}^{mask}$

It is noted that few discriminant pixels lie around chin. Furthermore, there are many discriminant pixels along the contour of the face image. So the features extracted on the discriminant pixels can be considered as local features while those features extracted on the whole original image can be regarded as global features. According to [1], both local and global features are useful for face recognition. That's why in our proposed method local features and global features are combined to form the final classifier. Fig. 1 illustrates how local features and global features are fused. Intensity-LDA features in Fig. 1 are global features which are calculated directly on the original intensity images using LDA, while Gabor-LDA features are local features because they are extracted only from discriminant pixels.

Suppose that the feature vectors of a training (gallery) sample and a testing (probe) sample are denoted by $\mathbf{y}_{ij}$ and $\mathbf{z}$ respectively. The similarity scores of local features, global features, and the combined score are respectively given by

$$S_{ij}^{local} = \cos(\mathbf{y}_{ij}^{local}, \mathbf{z}^{local}) = (\mathbf{y}_{ij}^{local} \cdot \mathbf{z}^{local})/(\|\mathbf{y}_{ij}^{local}\| \times \|\mathbf{z}^{local}\|) \qquad (2)$$

$$S_{ij}^{global} = \cos(\mathbf{y}_{ij}^{global}, \mathbf{z}^{global}) = (\mathbf{y}_{ij}^{global} \cdot \mathbf{z}^{global})/(\|\mathbf{y}_{ij}^{global}\| \times \|\mathbf{z}^{global}\|) \qquad (3)$$

$$S_{ij} = \alpha S_{ij}^{global} + \beta S_{ij}^{local}, \qquad \alpha + \beta = 1 \qquad 0 \le \alpha, \beta \le 1 \qquad (4)$$

where $'\bullet'$ denotes dot product and (α, β) are the mixture parameters. The probe $\mathbf{z}$ is assigned to class label c according to:

$$S_{cj} = \max_{i=1,\ldots,C;j=1,\ldots,N_i} \{S_{ij}\} .$$

We denote our method IGLDA (both intensity and Gabor-filtered images are used), and denote face recognition method GLDA when the first item on the right side of equation (4) is ignored (i.e. $\alpha = 0, \beta = 1$). If $\alpha=1$ and $\beta = 0$, it is reduced to the conventional LDA method. Experiment results show that the proposed algorithm IGLDA works well when $\alpha = \beta = 0.5$.

5   Experimental Results

We randomly select 70 individuals from the FERET database [15]. Each individual has 6 frontal face images from which 4 images are selected as training images and the remained 2 images are used for testing. There are total 15 ways to select 4 images from the 6 images. In our experiments, 6 selection ways are randomly chosen. So there are 6 training sets and 6 testing sets correspondingly. For each training set and the corresponding testing set a recognition rate is recorded. The final recognition rate is the average of 6 recognition rates. The positions of two eye centers in each image are labeled manually. Then, all images are cropped and aligned according to these positions and normalized to the same size. Finally, the images are preprocessed by histogram equalization. Fig. 3 (a) shows example images used in our experiments.

For comparison, we implemented the following four methods: the PCA method [5], the LDA method [6], the GLDA and the proposed IGLDA. The later two methods have been stated in section 5. Here PCA plus LDA trick is utilized to perform LDA [6]. The principal component number of PCA is 100, which reserves 98% energies of eigenvalues.

Table 1. Comparison of different methods in term of recognition rate

Method	PCA	LDA	GLDA	IGLDA
Result (%)	88.92	92.50	95.11	97.01

Table 1 lists the results obtained by four methods, using the rank one match. PCA gets the lowest recognition rate. The recognition rate of LDA is higher than that of PCA, because LDA utilizes class-specific information [6] and the most discriminant features instead of the most expressive features are obtained [5]. The performance of GLDA further supersedes LDA. We can explain this from two aspects. First, in GLDA Gabor features are used which are more robust than original intensity features. Second, GLDA utilizes local features which tend to be invariant to expression, illumination and occlusion. Among four methods, IGLDA achieves the highest recognition rate. As IGLDA actually combines GLDA and LDA, thus both local features and global features are integrated to form the final classification decision. Consequently, IGLDA takes advantages of the merits of Gabor wavelet, local features and global features.

6   Conclusion

In this paper, a novel face recognition method, IGLDA, based on Gabor-wavelet and LDA has been presented. A major contribution of the method is that discriminant vectors obtained by LDA are used to determine salient local features, the positions of which are specified by discriminant pixels. Because the number of discriminant pixels is much less than that of the whole image, the amount of Gabor-wavelet coefficients is decreased. Another contribution is that local features and global features are combined to form the final classifier. IGLDA efficiently utilizes Gabor wavelet, local features and global features, and thus results in superior performance in the experiments.

References

1. Zhao, W., Chellappa, R., Rosenfeld, A., Phillips, J.: Face recognition: A Literature Survey. ACM Computing Surveys, Vol. 12, (2003) 399-458.
2. Samaria, F.S.: Face Recognition Using Hidden Markov Models. PhD thesis, University of Cambridge, 1994.
3. Wiskott, L., Fellous J., Kruger, N., Malsburg, C.: Face Recognition by Elastic Bunch Graph Matching. IEEE PAMI, Vol. 19, No. 7, (1997) 775-779.
4. Penev, P.S.: Local Feature Analysis: a General Statistical Theory for Object Repentation. Network: Computation in Neural Systems, Vol. 7, (1996) 477-500.
5. Turk, M., Pentland, A.: Face Recognition Using Eigenfaces. Proc. IEEE Conf. On Com-puter Vision and Pattern Recognition, (1991) 586-591.
6. Peter, N.B., Joao, P.H., David, J.K.: Eigenfaces vs. Fisherfaces: Recognition Using Class Specific Linear Projection, Vol. 19, No. 7, (1997) 711-720.
7. Moghaddam, B., Pentland, A.: Probabilistc Visual Learning For Object Reprentation. IEEE PAMI, Vol. 19, No.7, (1997) 696-710.
8. Moghaddam, B, Jebara, B., Pentland, A.: Bayesian Face Recognition. Pattern Recognition, Vol. 33, (2000) 1771-1782.
9. Wang, X., Tang, X.: Unified Subspace Analysis for Face Recognition. In Proc. IEEE Conference on Computer Vision, 2003.
10. Phillips P.J.: Face Recognition Vendor Test 2002 Evaluation Report, http://www.frvt.org/FRVT2002/Default.htm, 2003.
11. Lee, T.S.: Image Representation Using 2D Gabor Wavelets, IEEE PAMI, Vol. 18, No. 10, (1996) 859-970
12. Chung, K.C., Kee S.C., Kim S.R.: Face Recognition Using Principal Component Analysis of Gabor Filter Respones, International Workshop on Recognition, Analysis and Tracking of Faces and Gestures in Real-Time Systems, 1999.
13. Liu, C., Wechsler, H.: Gabor Feature Based Classification Using the Enhanced Fisher Linear Discriminant Model for Face Recognition. IEEE PAMI, Vol. 11, No. 4, (2002) 467-476.
14. Peng, J., Heisterkamp, D.R., and Dai, H.K.: LDA/SVM Driven Nearest Neighbor Classi-fication, IEEE Trans. on Neural Networks, Vol. 14, No. 4, (2003) 940-942.
15. Phillips, P.J., Moon, H., Rivzi, S., and Rauss, P.: The FERET evaluation methodology for face-recognition algorithms. IEEE PAMI, Vol. 22, (2000) 1090-1104.

Gesture-Based User Interfaces for Handheld Devices Using Accelerometer

Ikjin Jang and Wonbae Park

Dept. of Information and Communications, Kyungpook National University,
Daegu 702-701, Republic of Korea
frog30@korea.com

Abstract. This paper is about how to treat the signals of accelerometers to recognize user gestures from detected signals from accelerometers after applying small accelerometers to handheld devices, and about how to precisely recognize gestures to detect user gestures. To use handheld devices in recognizing gestures, overheads arising from the process of recognizing gestures should be little and gestures should be effectively recognized in real operational environments. Therefore, signals detected from accelerometers were treated after classifying them "static acceleration" and "dynamic acceleration", and signal patterns of accelerometers about simple gestures were analyzed. In addition, a device control module was created and evaluated the usability of gestures recognition. The result was that because gesture-based control is easy to use and can reduce preparation process to control for rapid system reaction, it is a proper user interface for handheld devices primarily used in mobile environments.

1 Introduction

For mobile convenience, handheld devices don't provide user interfaces such as a keyboard or a mouse used for notebooks. They use a keypad, a stylus pen and/or an input-panel as an input device, and use a small LCD device to output several text lines or simple images. Therefore, when using input devices such as a stylus pen or a key-pad to manipulate handheld devices, it consumes much time and is difficult to use because the small buttons on its display must be manipulated several times. There have been many researches about new input/output methods to solve this problem; voice recognition and gesture recognition are representative cases[1][2][4][5]. Proper sensors are necessary to detect user actions or to recognize gestures in the case of handheld devices, and the processing capacity and mobile convenience should be considered when applying sensors. Small accelerometers are the proper sensors for this purpose. Because accelerometers can measure the mobility and actions through acceleration, the size and moving directions detected from sensors can be used to classify simple user gestures. Therefore, in this paper, small accelerometers were applied to handheld devices, and gesture-based interactions to substitute a keypad or a stylus pen operation are described.

K. Aizawa, Y. Nakamura, and S. Satoh (Eds.): PCM 2004, LNCS 3331, pp. 359–368, 2004.

2   Related Works

Accelerometers are used in various fields and there are many study cases about utilizing them in gesture recognition. In particular, Ken Hinckley studied how to recognize various user gestures using several sensors altogether (Tilt Sensor, Touch Sensor and Proximity Sensor)[3]. In addition, some of the gesture recognition cases using accelerometers are a pointing device, which detect the movement of fingers after attaching accelerometers on the finger parts and hand of a glove [7], and Handwriting-recognition recognizes pen movement after attaching a pair of accelerometers on a pen [6]. When applying these study cases to the user interfaces of handheld devices, the operational environment and capacity of handheld devices should be considered and overheads due to increased accelerometers should be minimized. If the number of sensors is large enough, the precision of gesture recognition can increase, but system overheads in the signal processing of sensors also increase. Therefore, it is necessary to study how to recognize simple gestures efficiently and how to minimize the number of accelerometers as well. In this paper, signal patterns make for gestures easily ex-pressed in a real operational environment, and its usability be evaluated by simple examples.

3   Signal Processing of the Accelerometer for Gesture Awareness

3.1   Static Acceleration (e.g., Gravity)

Accelerometer can detect gesture changes for horizontal status. When accelerometer is in perfect horizontal status and there is no movement at all, detected values for dual axis are all zeros.

If the position is changed to a specific direction, detected value is different from that of horizontal status even if there is no movement at all, and this value sustains until horizontal status is recovered. Fig. 1 shows the signal type de-

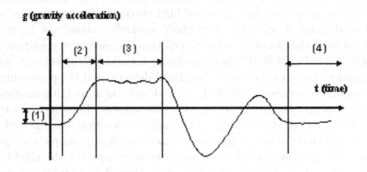

Fig. 1. Signal type of static acceleration

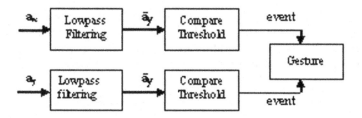

Fig. 2. The steps to recognize gestures from static acceleration (ax : static gesture' signals(x-axis))

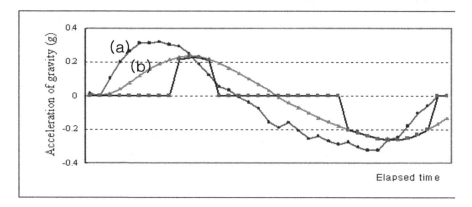

Fig. 3. Signal processing about Static gesture((a) : Static Gesture' Signal, (b) : Low-pass filter's output signals, (c) : Threshold and Compare's output signals)

tected when accelerometer changes its position, and shows signals for one-axis. At Fig. 1, differences in section (1) means that signals detected at accelerometer are different from those at horizontal status because the display of handheld devices used is tilted in the user direction. Signals in section (2) are signals when the position of handheld devices is changing and those in section (3) are detected when a specific position is sustained for a while. Signals in section (4) are those detected when the position returns to its original position. Static Acceleration can detect position changes from its early status and decide which direction the position is changed to compared to its original position if changed status is sustained for a while. The steps shown in Fig. 2 are necessary to recognize gestures from static acceleration signals detected at accelerometer. Signals detected from accelerometer are processed for each dual-axis as shown by Fig. 2, to grasp the case of the position of accelerometer being changed into one direction or two directions. The processes performed at the each step of Fig. 2 are outlined below.

Low pass filtering. It's a process to make signal changes consecutive by processing trivial movement. First order butterworth filter was used because using a simple filter was desirable considering the capacity of handheld devices. There-fore, it used 1st-order butterworth filter in this research. The pole-zero position and a amplitude quality of the filter are shown in Fig. 4. The transfer function and recurrence equation of the highpass filter are as follows.

$$H\left(z = e^{jw}\right) = A\frac{1 + z^{-1}}{1 - pz^{-1}}, A = \frac{1 - p}{2}$$

$$a_f[n] = pa_f[n - 1] + A\left(a[n] + a[n - 1]\right)$$

Fig. 3 shows output signals at each step in signal processing. In Fig. 3, (a) shows signals detected at accelerometer and (b) shows the output signals of the lowpass filter.

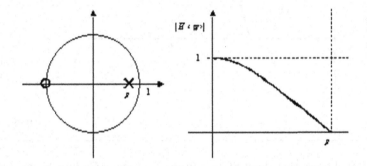

Fig. 4. 1-st order Butterworth filter (p = 0.8)

Thresholding and Comparing. If detected signals are lower than a threshold value, then such signals are ignored not to reflect them. In Fig. 3, (c) shows the status of trivial movements being eliminated at the Threshold and Comparing step (ignoring signals of which gravity acceleration is smaller than 0.2g)

3.2   Dynamic Acceleration (e.g., Vibration)

Dynamic acceleration happens when a sudden movement or a short shock is transmit-ted to accelerometer. Peaks existing for a short while are shown from detected signals. These kinds of signals happen when user gestures are not con-secutive or when there are slight knocking or sudden shocks. Fig. 5 show a representative dynamic acceleration, signals from knocking gestures.

At Fig. 5, section (1) shows several peaks generated by one knocking gesture. Though knocking gestures can happen from various places (bag, pocket or hand etc.), peak duration is normally within 100 ms (milliseconds). Therefore, the problem of 'multiple peak' can be solved if debouncing is realized by setting section (1) as 'dead period' because users are difficult to generate knocking gestures at the interval of 100 ms. If knocking gestures happen while a user

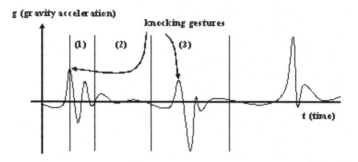

Fig. 5. Knocking Gesture's signal form

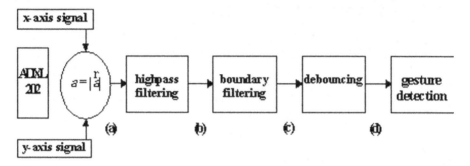

Fig. 6. Dynamic Acceleration's signal processing step

is moving, both multiple peak and consecutive vibrations happen altogether. Therefore, a silent period marked section (2) should be set to identify regular knocking signals different from vibration due to user movements. In addition, the next signal should be detected some time after one signal is detected. That is, another knocking gesture should exist in section (3) to be effective. Fig. 6 shows processes necessary to recognize user gestures using dynamic acceleration signals, and the output signals of each step ((a)-(d)) are shown in Fig. 7.

The first step marked as a circle shown in Fig. 6 is a process to obtain amplitude from dual-axis signals, and the content of each step is outlined below.

Highpass Filtering. When handheld devices are not used horizontally, accelerometer is under the influence of gravity acceleration. Therefore, changing the position of accelerometer also changes detected signals. Fig. 7 (a) shows a signal detected from accelerometer when knocking gestures happen, seizing a handheld device. Because this signal is detected under accelerometer being tilted in a random direction, x-axis signal and y-axis signal sustain random values. Therefore, considering various operational environments, DC components should be eliminated first of all to process detected signals in the same way regardless of the tilt direction of accelerometer. Therefore, it used 1st-order but-

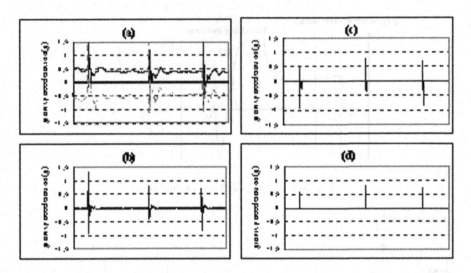

Fig. 7. Output signals about Fig.6 (Dynamic Acceleration's processing step) (a) ADXL202's output signals, (b) Highpass Filter's output signals, (c) Boundary Filter's output signals, (d) Debouncing's output signals

terworth filter in this research. Fig. 7 (b) shows signals after eliminating DC components from highpass filter. The transfer function and recurrence equation of the high-pass filter as follows and the pole-zero position and a amplitude quality of the filter are shown in Fig. 8.

$$H\left(z = e^{jw}\right) = A\frac{1 - z^{-1}}{1 - pz^{-1}}, A = \frac{1 + p}{2}$$

$$a_f[n] = pa_f[n - 1] + A\left(a[n] + a[n - 1]\right)$$

Boundary Filtering. It's a process to eliminate trivial signals to prevent unwanted gestures arising from slight vibration or movements to be transmitted. Fig. 7 (c) shows the output signal of the boundary-filtering step.

Debouncing. This is a process not to recognize several peaks, generated by one gesture, as gestures. It ignores multiple peaks shown in Fig. 5' (1). Fig. 7 (d) shows eliminating multiple peaks through debouncing.

4   Examples of Gesture-Based Control

4.1   Example 1: Bell and Sound Control

It is the function of stopping bell using knocking gestures without withdrawing hand-held devices when it bells. When bell control is difficult at places such

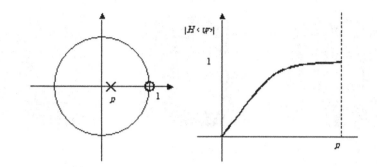

Fig. 8. 1-st order Butterworth filter (p = 0.2)

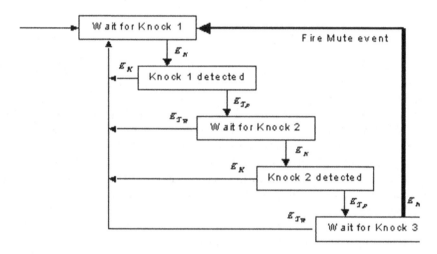

Fig. 9. State machine for knocking gesture awareness (Ek: Knock Event, Etp Etw: Timer Event, Tp: Minimum interval between two knocking events, Tw: Maximum waiting interval for a knocking event)

as convention halls or public rooms, rapid control through gestures is possible. To control bells using knocking gestures, users' other gestures should not be wrongfully recognized. Therefore, regular knocking gestures more than 3 times are necessary, and state ma-chines to detect regular knocking gestures more than 3 times are shown in Fig. 9.

To detect knocking gestures effectively, it is important to select Tp and Tw properly. In this experiment, Tp was applied 200 milliseconds, and Tw was applied 500 milliseconds. It should be adjustable by users. Fig 10 is a Bell Control example using knocking gestures. The example shows the process of recognizing knocking gestures step by step.

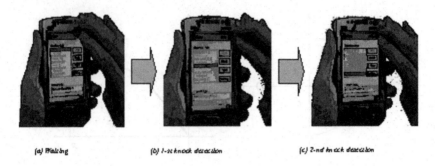

(a) Pticking   (b) 1-st knock detection   (c) 2-nd knock detection

Fig. 10. Bell Control Example

4.2   Example 2: Scrolling

To scroll handheld devices, a small button should be clicked using a stylus pen. How-ever, it's not easy to click the scroll button on a small display panel. To scroll through gestures, information about the direction of user gestures should be included. An ex-ample of gestures including information about user direction is the tilt method. In the case of accelerometer, if a one-axis signal is changed, then there is a tilt to the related direction, and if both dual axes change, then there is a complex tilt in two directions. Using tilting gestures to scroll, there can be slight movement or vibration because handheld devices are not fixed. Therefore, dead zone should be set, and signals from the dead zone should not be reflected to scrolling. Through experiments, the dead zone was applied 0.2g. Because there is no signal larger than 2g from tilting gestures, any signal larger than 2g was ignored. Fig. 11 shows a Tilt and Scroll example.

4.3   Example 3: Display Mode Alteration (Pivot)

Handheld devices use rectangular display panels, and display modes should be changed according to content and user preference. Sensors detection axis-rotation is necessary to change display modes, but signals detected from dual axes are not changed if there is axis-rotation during accelerometer being in horizontal status. How-ever, if a display status tilted to its user direction is set as its original status, then whether there is display rotation can be easily determined because signals detected from dual axes are different from its early signals if when axis-rotation happens. Fig. 12 shows an example realizing 'display mode alteration' by detecting axis-rotation at handheld devices.

5   Conclusions

The use of a keyboard or mouse as a user interface for handheld devices is awk-ward and impractical, therefore, the current study designed and realized a system

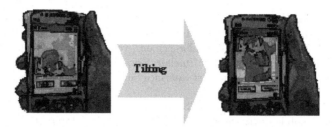

Fig. 11. Scrolling Example

Fig. 12. Display Mode Alteration

that uses gesture-based interactions as user interfaces after applying accelerometers to handheld devices. As such, the signal features of accelerometers towards gestures that can easily be used in the real operational environments of handheld devices were surveyed, plus the signals detected from accelerometers were processed after classifying them ac-cording to the kind of gesture. To recognize the signals detected from accelerometers as user gestures, the signal pattern of each gesture was analyzed and recognized as a valid gesture only when a signal pattern matched a gesture pattern. In addition, simple applications necessary for mobile environments were realized to verify the usability of gesture-based interactions, and the performance steps of each function compared. When using gesture-based interactions, the preparation steps of various functions, such as bell control, can be omitted, plus scrolling is possible without using both hands when moving or driving. In the current research, only one accelerometer was used based on the capacity of handheld devices and their mobile convenience. In addition, simple filters were used for the signal-processing step. Further research on using multiple sensors, designing precise filters, and algorithms that can exactly distinguish various gestures is necessary to identify various user gestures.

References

1. Bartlett, J.F.: Rock and Scroll Is Here to Stay, IEEE Computer Graphics and Applications, 2000.

2. Ehreumann, M.; Lutticke, T.; Dillmann, R.: Dynamic gestures as an input device for direct-ing a mobile platform, Robotics and Automation, 2001. Proceedings 2001 ICRA. IEEE In-ternational Conference on , vol.3 , 2001, pp: 2596 -2601

3. Ken Hinckley; Jeff Pierce; Mike Sinclair; Eric Horvitz: Sensing techniques for mobile interaction, Symposium on User Interface Software and Technology, CHI Letters 2, 2000, pp:91-100.

4. Mantyla, V-M,; Mantyjarvi, J.; Seppanen, T.; Tuulari, E.: Hand gesture recogni-tion of a mobile device user, ICME 2000. 2000 IEEE International Conference on Multimedia and Expo, 2000. vol.1 , 2000, pp: 281 -284

5. Matthieu, B.; Hedvig, S.; Jan-Olof, E.,: Recognition of gestures in the context of speech, Pattern Recognition, 2002. Proceedings. 16th International Conference on , vol.1 , 2002 ,pp: 356 -359.

6. Milner, B.: Handwriting recognition using acceleration-based motion detection, IEE Col-loquium on Document Image Processing and Multimedia, 1999.

7. Perng, J. K.; Fisher, B.; Hollar, S.; Pister, K. S. J.: Acceleration sensing glove(ASG), The Third International Symposium on Wearable Computers, 1999, pp: 178 - 180.

Face and Gesture Recognition Using Subspace Method for Human-Robot Interaction

Md. Hasanuzzaman[1], T. Zhang[1], V. Ampornaramveth[1], M.A. Bhuiyan[3], Y. Shirai[2], and H. Ueno[1]

[1] Intelligent System Research Division, National Institute of Informatics, 2-1-2 Hitotsubashi, Chiyoda-ku, Tokyo 101-8430, Japan.
hzamancsdu@yahoo.com
[2] Department of Computer Controlled Mechanical Systems, Osaka University, Suita, 565-0871 Japan.
[3] Jahangirnagor University, Dhaka-1343, Bangladesh.

Abstract. This paper presents a vision-based face and gesture recognition system for human-robot interaction. By using subspace method, face and predefined hand poses are detected from the three largest skin-like regions that are segmented using YIQ color representation system. In this subspace method we consider separate eigenspaces for each class or pose. Gesture is recognized using the rule-based approach whenever the combination of three skin-like regions at a particular image frame matches with the predefined gesture. These gesture commands are sent to robot through TCP/IP network for human-robot interaction. Using subspace method pose invariant face recognition has also been addressed. The effectiveness of this method has been demonstrated by interacting with an entertainment robot named AIBO.

1 Introduction

Rapid developments of computer hardware, robotics and vision system influence young researchers to work on gesture based human robot interaction system. Vision based technique does not require wearing any of contact devices with human body part, but uses a set of video cameras and computer vision techniques to interpret gestures. Gestures are expressive, meaningful body motions, i.e., physical movements of the head, face, fingers, hands or body with the intent to convey information or interact with the environment. Gestures can be static, where the user assumes a certain pose or configuration, or dynamic, defined by movement. Static gesture, or pose can be accomplished by using template matching, geometric feature classification, neural network and other standard pattern recognition techniques to classify pose. Dynamic gesture recognition is accomplished by using time-compressing templates, dynamic time warping, Hidden Markov Models (HMMs), etc.

There are significant amount of research on hand, arm and facial gesture recognition to control robot or intelligence machine in recent years. Takahiro

K. Aizawa, Y. Nakamura, and S. Satoh (Eds.): PCM 2004, LNCS 3331, pp. 369–376, 2004.
© Springer-Verlag Berlin Heidelberg 2004

Watanabe et. al. [1] used eigenspaces from multi-input image sequences for recognizing gesture. They have used single eigenspaces for different poses and consider only two directions. To achieve more accuracy we have used in our subspace method separate eigenspaces for each class or each pose and for face detection and recognition used five directions and five separate eigenspaces. Chao Hu et. al. [2] has proposed a hand gesture recognition for human-machine interface of robot teleoperation using edge features matching. Gerhard Rigoll et. al [3] used HMM-based approach for real-time gesture recognition. They extracted features from the differences between two consecutive images. They consider that the target image is always in the center of the input images. But practically it is difficult to maintain such condition. Akira Utsumi et. al. [4] detected hand using hand shape model and tracked hand or face using extracted color and motion. They proposed multiple cameras for data acquisition to reduce occlusion problem. But in this process there incurs complexity in computations. However, all these papers [7-15] did not consider face and two hands at the same time that we have considered here.

In this paper we present a method for recognizing face and gestures in real time using skin-color segmentation and subspace methods based patterns matching technique. In this method the three largest skin like regions are segmented from the input images using skin color information from YIQ color space, assuming that face and two hands may present in the images at the same time. Segmented regions are filtered and normalized to remove noises and to form fixed size images as training images. Subspace method is used for detecting hand poses and face from three skin-like regions. If the combinations of three skin-like regions at a particular image frame match with predefined gesture then corresponding gesture command is generated. In this experiment we have recognized eight gestures as shown in Fig. 2. Gesture commands are being sent to robot through TCP/IP network and robot actions are being accomplished according to users predefined actions for those gestures. This paper has also addressed rotated face recognition system using subspace method. We have prepared training images in different illuminations to adapt our system with illumination variation. As an application of our method, we have implemented a real-time human robot interaction system using a pet robot named AIBO.

This paper is organized as follows. In section 2, we briefly describe skin-like regions segmentation, filtering and normalization techniques. Section 3, focuses on subspace method for face and hand poses detection. Section 4, presents gestures recognition and pose invariant face recognition method. Section 5 presents our experimental results and discussions. In section 6 we conclude this paper.

2   Skin Color Segmentation, Filtering, and Normalization

From color images this system first segmented three larger skin-like regions by using skin-color information assuming that two hands and one face may present in the image. YIQ (Y is luminance of the color and I, Q are chrominance of the color) color representation system is used for skin like region segmentation, since

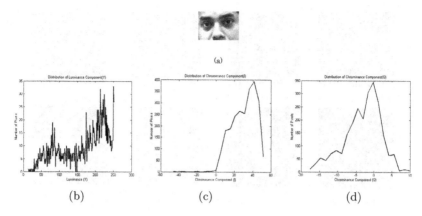

Fig. 1. a) sample skin region, b), c) and d). Y, I, Q distributions respectively

it is typically used in video coding and provides an effective use of chrominance information for modeling the human skin color. The RGB image is taken by video camera is converted to YIQ color representation system and threshold it by the skin color range [5]. Fig. 1, shows sample skin region and corresponding Y, I, Q distributions for every pixels. Chrominance component I, play an important role to distinguish skin like regions from non-skin regions, because it is always positive for skin regions. Values of Y and I increases for more white people and decreases for black people. We have included an off line program to adjust the threshold values for Y, I, Q, if the person color or light intensity variation affect segmentation output. For that reason a user need to manually select small skin region and non-skin region and run the threshold evaluation program, that will represent graphical view of Y, I, Q distributions. From those distinguishable graphs user can adjust threshold values for Y, I, Q.

Locations of the probable hands and face are determined from the image with three larger connected regions of skin-colored pixels. In this experiment, 8-pixels neighborhood connectivity is employed. In order to remove the false regions from the isolated blocks, smaller connected regions are assigned by the values of black color. Noise and holes are filtered by morphological dilation and erosion operations. Sample output of our skin color segmentation and filtering algorithm is shown in Fig. 2. Normalization is done to scale the image so that it match with the size of training images and convert the scaled images to gray images.

3   Hand Poses and Face Detection Using Subspace Method

Subspace method offer an economical representation and very fast classification for vectors with a high number of components only the statistically most relevant features of a class are retained in the subspace representation. The subspace method is based on the extraction of the most conspicuous properties of each

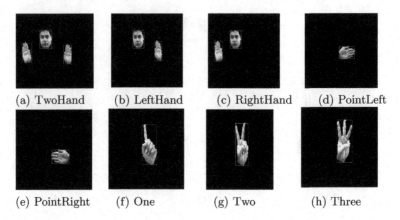

(a) TwoHand   (b) LeftHand   (c) RightHand   (d) PointLeft

(e) PointRight   (f) One   (g) Two   (h) Three

Fig. 2. Sample output of skin color segmentation and filtering

class separately as represented by a set of prototype sample. The main idea of the subspace method is similar to principal component analysis, is to find the vectors that best account for the distribution of target images within the entire image space. In normal PCA methods eigenvectors are calculated from training images that include all the poses. In subspaces methods training images are grouped according to poses (classes) and calculated eigenvectors for each class separately. In this methods known images are projected on corresponding subspace or eigenspace and input image is projected on all the subspaces. In subspace methods similarity measure is based on pose so that separation capability is better than normal PCA methods.

The approach of face and hand pose detection using subspace method includes following operations:

(I) Prepare noise free version of face and different hand poses corresponding to each class as training images $T_j^{(i)}$ ($N \times N$), where j is number training images of ith class and $j = 1, 2, \cdots, M$.

(II) For each class, calculate eigenvectors ($u_m^{(i)}$) using Matthew Truk and Alex Pet-land technique [6] and select k-number of eigenvectors ($u_k^{(i)}$) corresponding to the highest eigenvalues to form principal components for that class. These vectors for each class define the subspace of that class images.

(III) For each pose or class prepare a group of known images.

(IV) Calculate corresponding distribution in k-dimensional weight space for the known images, by projecting them onto the subspaces (eigenspaces) of the corresponding class and determined weight vectors ($\Omega_l^{(i)}$), using equations (1) and (2).

$$\omega_k^{(i)} = (u_k^{(i)})^T (s_l^{(i)} - \Phi_i)) \tag{1}$$

$$\Omega_l^{(i)} = [\omega_1^{(i)}, \omega_2^{(i)}, ..., \omega_k^{(i)}] \tag{2}$$

Where, average image of ith class $\Phi_i = 1/M \sum_{n=1}^{M} T_n$ and $s_l^{(i)}(N \times N)$ is l^{th} known images of ith class.

(V) Each segmented region is treated as individual input image and transformed each into eigenimage components and calculated a set of weight vectors (Ω) by projecting the input image onto each of the subspace as equations (1) and (2).

(VI) Determine if the image is face or other predefined hand poses based on minimum Euclidean distance among weight vectors using equation (3) and (4),

$$\epsilon_i = ||\Omega - \Omega_l^{(i)}|| \tag{3}$$

$$\epsilon = [\epsilon_1, \epsilon_2, ..., \epsilon_i] \tag{4}$$

If min $\{\epsilon\}$ is lower than predefined threshold then its corresponding class or pose is identified. For exact matching ϵ should be zero but for practical purposes we have used a threshold value through experiment, considering optimal separation among the classes.

4   Face and Gesture Recognition

4.1   Gesture Recognition

Gesture recognition is the process by which gestures made by the user are known to the system. Gestures are recognized using rule-based system according to predefined model with the combination of the detected results of three segments at a particular time. For examples: if two hands and one face are present in the input image then recognized it as "TwoHand" gesture. If one face and left hand open palm are present in the input image frame then recognized it as "LeftHand" gesture. Similarly others gestures (shown in Fig. 2) are recognized. According to recognized gestures, corresponding gesture commands are generated and sent to robot through TCP/IP network.

4.2   Face Recognition

Face recognition is important for human robot secure interaction and person dependent gesture command generation, i.e., gesture is same but different interpretations for different persons. If any segment (skin-like region) is detected as a face in pose detection stage (section-3), then it needs to classify the pattern, whether it belongs to a known person or not. In face recognition section we use five face classes: normal face (fc1), left rotate face (fc2), more left rotate face (fc3), right rotate face (fc4) and more right rotate face (fc5). For each class we have formed subspaces or eigenspaces. Known person images and detected face image are projected on those subspaces using equation (1) and (2) to form weight vectors. Determine minimum Euclidean distance between weight vectors

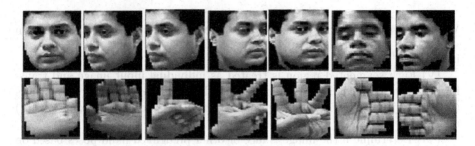

Fig. 3. Example template images

of known images and detected face images using equation (3) and (4). If minimum distance is lower than the predefined threshold then corresponding person is identified other wise result is unknown person. We have used face recognition output for human robot greeting application. For example, if the person is known then robot say ("Hi, person name, How are you?") but for unknown person robot say ("I do not know you").

5   Experimental Results and Discussions

This section describes experimental procedures, as well as experimental results of the face and gestures recognition system for human-robot interaction. This system uses a standard video camera for data acquisition. Each capture image is digitized into a matrix of 320×240 pixels with 24-bit color. First we prepare training images for 12 classes (five face classes and seven hand classes). All the training images are 60×60 pixels gray images. The training images consist of 480 (40 for each class) images. Fig. 3 shows the example training images. We have tested our system for real time input images. The sample output of our gesture recognition system is shown in Fig. 4(a). This shows gesture command at the bottom text box corresponding to matched gesture ("One"), in case of no match it shows "no matching found". We have considered for human-robot interaction that gesture command will be effective until robot finishes corresponding action for that gesture.

Accuracy of the gesture recognition system depends on the accuracy of the pose detection system. For example: in some cases two hands and one face were present in the image but pose detection method failed to detect one hand due to variation of orientation and output gesture is then either "LeftHand" or "RightHand". We use two standard parameters to define accuracy: precision and recall for pose detection system. In this system, the average precision of the pose detection system is around 90 percent and recall rate is about 84 percent. Wrong detection is occurred due to orientation and intensity variation. For face recognition the precision is 92 percent and recall rate is 80 percent. If we decrease the threshold value then precision also increases but decreases the recognition rate.

In this part we have explained a real time human-robot interaction system using gestures. We have run this application on a client PC (not in robot) as

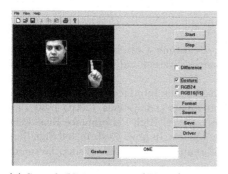

(a) Sample Vision output ("One")   (b) AIBO STAND-UP for Gesture "One"

Fig. 4. Sample output of gesture based human-robot interaction system

shown in Fig. 4(b). We have considered robot as a server and our PC as a client. Communication link has been established through TCP/IP protocol. Initially, we connected the client PC with robot server and then gestures recognition program was run in the client PC. As a result of gestures recognition program, client PC sends gesture commands to robot. After getting gesture command robot acted according to users predefined actions. Our approach has been implemented on a pet robot named AIBO. The actions of AIBO are: STAND, WALK FORWARD, WALK BACKWARD, TURN LEFT, TURN RIGHT, KICK (by right leg), SIT and LIE in accordance with gesture "One", "Two", "Three", "PointLeft", "PointRight" "RightHand" "TwoHand", and "LeftHand" respectively.

6   Conclusions

This paper describes a real-time face and hand gesture recognition system using skin color segmentation and subspaces methods based pattern matching technique. This paper also successfully implemented gesture based human-robot interaction system using a robot named AIBO. We have used separate principal components and a group of known images for each pose or class. So it is more reliable than any single feature based template-matching techniques or normal PCA based method. One of the major constrain of this system is that the background should be non-skin color substrate. If we use infrared camera then it is possible to overcome this problem just by a minor modification of our segmentation module and other module will remain the same.

Face recognition with gesture recognition will help us in future to develop person adaptable and secure human robot interface. Our next approach is to make the pose detecting system more robust and to recognize more facial and hand gestures for interaction with different robots such as AIBO, ROBOVIE, SCOUT, etc. Our ultimate goal is to establish a symbiotic society for all of the distributed autonomous intelligent components so that they share their resources and work cooperatively with human beings.

References

1. Takahiro Watanabe, Masahiko Yachida: Real-time Gesture Recognition Using Eigenspace from Multi-Input Image sequences. System and Computers in Japan, J81-D-II, (1998) 810–821
2. Chao Hu: Gesture Recognition for Human-Machine Interface of Robot Teleoperation. International conference on intelligent robots and systems, (2003) 1560–1565
3. Gerhard Rigoll, Andreas Kosmala, Stefan Eickeler: High Performance Real-Time Gesture Recognition Using Hidden Markov Models. In proc. Gesture and Sign Language in Human Computer Interaction, International Gesture Workshop, Germany (1997) 69-80
4. Akira Utsumi, Nobuji Tetsutani and Seiji Igi: Hand Detection and Tracking using Pixel Value Distribution Model for Multiple Camera-Based Gesture Interactions. Proc. of the IEEE workshop on knowledge Media Networking, (2002) 31-36
5. Md. Al-Amin Bhuiyan, Vuthichai Ampornaramveth, Shin Yo Muto, Haruki Ueno: Face Detection and Facial Feature Localization for Human-machine Interface. NII Journal (5), (2003) 25-39
6. Matthew Turk and Alex Pentland: Eigenface for Recognition. Journal of Cognitive Neuro-science, Vol. 3(1), (1991) 71-86
7. Yu Huang, Thomas S. Huang, Heinrich Niemann: Two-Hand Gesture Tracking Incorporating Template Warping With Static Segmentation. IEEE AFGR'02, (2002) 260-265
8. Lars Bretzner, Ivan Laptev, Tony Lindeberg: Hand Gesture Recognition using Multi-Scale Colour Features, Hierarchical Models and Particle Filtering. IEEE AFGR'02, (2002) 423-428
9. M.A. Bhuiyan, V. Ampornaramveth, S. Muto, and H. Ueno: On Tracking of Eye For Human-Robot Interface. International Journal of Robotics and Automation, Vol. 19(1), (2004) 42-54
10. Nobutaka Shimada, Yoshiaki Shirai: 3-D Hand Pose Estimation and Shape Model Refinement from a Monocular Image Sequence. Proc. of VSMM'96 in GIFU, (1996) 23-428
11. Radek Grzeszczuk, Gray Bradski, Michael H Chu, Jean-Yves Bouguet: Stereo Based Gesture Recognition Invariant to 3D pose and lighting. Proc. of the IEEE Conference on Computer Vision and pattern Recognition, (2000) 1826-1833
12. Yunato Cui and John J. Weng: Hand Segmentation Using Learning-Based prediction and verification for hand Sign Recognition. Proc. of the IEEE Conference on Computer Vision and pattern Recognition, (1996) 88-93
13. Yoichi Sato, Yoshinori Kobayashi, Hideki Koike: Fast Tracking of hands and Fingertips in Infrared Images for Augmented Desk Interface. IEEE AFGR'00, (2000) 462-467
14. Charles J. Cohen, Glenn Beach, Gene Foulk: A Basic Hand Gesture Control System for PC Applications. Proc. of the 30th IEEE Applied Imagery Pattern Recognition Workshop, (2001) 74-79
15. Dong, Guo, Yonghua Yan and M. Xie: Vision-Based Hand Gesture Recognition for Human-Vehicle Interaction. Proc. of the International conference on Control, Automation and Computer Vision, Vol. 1 (1998) 151-155.

Spatial Histogram Features for Face Detection in Color Images

Hongming Zhang and Debin Zhao

Department of Computer Science and Engineering, Harbin Institute of Technology,
Harbin, 150001, China
{hmzhang,dbzhao}@jdl.ac.cn

Abstract. This paper presents a novel face detection approach in color images. We employ spatial histograms as robust features for face detection. The spatial histograms consist of marginal distribution of color image information. Facial texture and shape are preserved by the spatial histogram representation. A hierarchical classifier combining histogram matching and support vector machine is utilized to identify face and non-face. The experiments show that this approach performs an excellent capability for face detection, and it is robust to lighting changes.

1 Introduction

Automatic localization of human faces is significant in many applications, such as human-computer interaction, face animating, face recognition, expression recognition and content-based image retrieval. Face detection is still a challenge because of variability in face orientations, face sizes, face locations, facial expression, partial occlusions, and lighting conditions. A comprehensive survey on face detection in images can be found in [1].

Many approaches have been proposed for face detection in still images. Generally speaking, these approaches can be classified as two categories: model-based technique and feature-based technique. The first one assumes that a face can be represented as a whole unit. Several statistical learning mechanisms are explored to characterize face patterns, such as neural network [2], probabilistic distribution [3], support vector machines [4], principal components analysis [5], naive Bayes classifier [6], and boosting algorithms [7,8]. The second method treats a face as a collection of components. Important facial features (eyes, nose and mouth) are first extracted, and by using their locations and relationships, the faces are detected [9,10].

Skin color is a powerful and fundamental cue that can be used as the first step in the face detection process. Many researchers utilize skin color models to locate potential face areas, then examine the locations of faces by analyzing each face candidate's shape and local geometric information [11,12].

What features are stable and scalable for face detection is still an open problem. Previous works have used many representations for facial feature extraction, such as edges, wavelets, and rectangle features [13,14,7].

K. Aizawa, Y. Nakamura, and S. Satoh (Eds.): PCM 2004, LNCS 3331, pp. 377–384, 2004.

In this paper, we propose a face detection method in color images. Spatial histograms are calculated on color measurements. Based on the spatial histogram representation, discriminating features are extracted for face detection. A hierarchical classifier combining histogram matching algorithm and support vector machine is utilized to identify face and non-face.

The structure of this paper is as follows. In Section 2, we propose the spatial histogram for face representation. A discriminating analysis of spatial histogram is given in Section 3. In Section 4, we describe a face detection system using hierarchical classification. Experimental results are provided in Section 5. At last, we give conclusions in Section 6.

2   Spatial Histogram Features for Face Representation

Human face patterns have much information including skin color cues and facial components configurations. In this section, we describe a new face pattern representation combining color cues and face spatial structures. Basically, we model face regions by their histograms, or marginal distribution, over the face color measurements.

Histogram is a global representation of one image pattern, which is translation invariant. However, for some non-face images and face images, their histogram can be very close or even identical, making the histogram not sufficient for object detection.

In order to overcome this limitation of histogram, we enlarge discrimination information by two ways. First, we adopt color information as measurements of face pattern. Second, we introduce spatial histograms to extract face shape information.

2.1   Color Measurements and Histogram Based Representation

Color information is often effective in image segmentation. For any color, its hue keeps almost constant under different lighting conditions. We consider YUV color space as the interesting color space because it is compatible to human color perception. We first convert the RGB color information to YUV color information:

$$\begin{cases} Y = 0.299R + 0.587G + 0.114B \\ U = -0.147R - 0.289G + 0.436B. \\ V = 0.615R - 0.515G - 0.100B \end{cases} \tag{1}$$

Hue is defined as the angle of vector in YUV color space, given by

$$\theta = \arctan(V/U). \tag{2}$$

We define a pattern as a 32x32 color image with RGB values, and its representation constitutes of five measures: Y, R, G, B and θ. We denote the five measurements by $m(i), i = 1, 2, 3, 4, 5$.

We compute histogram-based pattern representation as follows. First we extract the five measurements from original color images, next we apply histogram normalization on these measurements respectively, and then we use Basic Local Binary Pattern operator(LBP) [15,17] to transform the obtained measures, finally we compute histograms of the processed measurements as representation. We employ LBP opeator since it is invariant against any monotonic transformation of the gray scale or color measure. Fig.1 shows two gray image samples, their LBP images and histograms.

Fig. 1. Image samples, LBP images and LBP histograms

2.2   Spatial Histogram

Human face is a near-regular texture pattern generated by facial components and their configuration. We use 23 different spatial templates to preserve shape of face patterns. These spatial templates are shown in fig.2. Each template is a 32x32 mask. It has a white rectangle, and each white pixel has value 1 and each black pixel has value 0. We denote each template by $rect(x, y, w, h)$, where (x, y) is location and (w, h) is size of the white part in template. The spatial template set is simply denoted by $\{rect(1), rect(2), ..., rect(23)\}$.

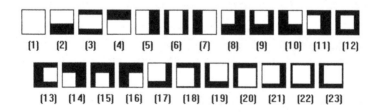

Fig. 2. Spatial templates

For a single spatial template $rect(x, y, w, h)$ and a given measurement $m(i)$, we model image window by histogram. First we convolve the whole preprocessed measurement window with the mask, and then we compute histogram, or marginal distribution, from the resulting measurement. We call this histogram as *spatial histogram*. Given an image P, one spatial histogram is denoted by $SH_{m(i)}^{rect(x,y,w,h)}(P)$.

There are many methods of measuring similarity between two histograms. We adopt histogram intersection measure since it is stable and computational inexpensive. According to [16], the intersection match of two histograms is defined as:

$$D(SH_1, SH_2) = \sum_{i=1}^{k} \min(SH_1^i, SH_2^i), \tag{3}$$

where SH_1 and SH_2 are two histograms, and K is the number of bins in the histograms.

3   Discriminant Analysis of Spatial Histogram

Spatial histogram representation is introduced in last section. In this section, we analysis each spatial histogram's discriminating ability and construct compact feature vectors for face detection.

To train and evaluate our system, we collect 11400 32x32 color face samples as positive training set. 3000 color images contained no face patterns are used as negative training set.

Histogram matching is a direct approach for object recognition. In this approach, we apply histogram intersection as distance measure to object recognition. Given a database with n face samples, we represent each face spatial histogram type by the average spatial histogram of face training samples, defined as

$$SH_{m(i)}^{rect(x,y,w,h)}(face) = \frac{1}{n}\sum_{j=1}^{n} SH_{m(i)}^{rect(x,y,w,h)}(P_j), \tag{4}$$

where P_j is a face training sample, $m(i)$ is the measurement and $rect(x, y, w, h)$ is the spatial template. For any sample P, we define its *histogram-matching feature* as the distance to the average face histogram, given by

$$f_{m(i)}^{rect(x,y,w,h)}(P) = D(SH_{m(i)}^{rect(x,y,w,h)}(P), SH_{m(i)}^{rect(x,y,w,h)}(face)). \tag{5}$$

Each type of spatial histogram has the discriminating ability between face and non-face pattern. To demonstrate this property, we take the gray histogram of the first template as an example. $SH_{m(1)}^{rect(0,0,32,32)}(face)$ is the average model of the positive train samples. Here we adopt histogram-matching feature

$$f_{m(1)}^{rect(0,0,32,32)}(P) = D(SH_{m(1)}^{rect(0,0,32,32)}, SH_{m(1)}^{rect(0,0,32,32)}(face))$$

as one feature. Fig.3 shows its positive and negative distribution over the training set. On this feature, we use threshold to classify face and non-face. By setting the threshold to 0.7, we retain 99.6% face detection rate with false alarm rate 30.2%.

We combine all kinds of histogram-matching features to obtain a compact and discriminating feature vector, given by

$$F = [f_{m(1)}^{rect(1)}, ..., f_{m(1)}^{rect(23)}, ..., f_{m(5)}^{rect(1)}, ..., f_{m(5)}^{rect(23)}]. \tag{6}$$

We call this feature vector as *Joint Spatial Histogram-Matching feature*(JSHM feature). The total set of spatial histogram types has size 23x5=115. Therefore,the JSHM feature is 115 dimensional.

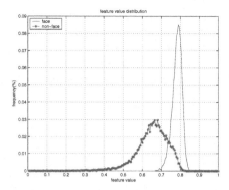

Fig. 3. Feature distribution of face and non-face on gray histogram of the first template

4   Hierarchical Classification for Face Detection System

We apply a hierarchical classification scheme for face detection, shown in Fig 4. First, we use histogram matching as coarse detection stage. In the second stage, a Support Vector Machine is used for fine face detection.

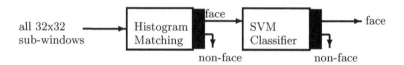

Fig. 4. Hierarchical classification for face detection system

4.1   Histogram Matching

As demonstrated in section 3, each type spatial histogram-matching feature has the ability to identify face and non-face. In practice, we specify three gray spatial histograms, $\{rect(1), rect(2), rect(6)\}$, to detect face pattern jointly. The decision rule is as follows:

$$H(P) = \begin{cases} 1 \text{ face} & \text{if}(f_{m(1)}^{rect(1)}(P) \geq T_1 \text{and} f_{m(1)}^{rect(2)}(P) \geq T_2 \text{and} f_{m(1)}^{rect(6)}(P) \geq T_6) \\ 0 \text{ nonface} & \text{otherwise} \end{cases},$$

$$(7)$$

where T_1, T_2, and T_6 are thresholds for matching. In our experiments, the three thresholds are all set to be 0.7.

4.2   Support Vector Machine

Given the JSHM feature and training sets of positive and negative image samples, face detection is regarded as a two-class pattern classification problem. A

SVM classifier[18] performs pattern recognition for a two-class problem by determining the separating hyper plane that maximum distance to the closest points of training set. These closet points are called support vectors.

Using JSHM feature and bootstrap technique, we train a non-linear SVM for face detection on the train data sets. The kernel adopted is a RBF kernel.

5   Experiments

We implement the proposed approach and conduct experiments to evaluate its effectiveness. Many face databases commonly used by researchers, including FERET face recognition dataset and CMU face detection dataset, contain gray-scale images only. Therefore, we have built a large-scale color face image database. This database set is consisted by images from different sources: news photos, movie video pictures, personal digital images and surveillance images. These images contain multiple faces under complex backgrounds and different lighting conditions. In total, 251 color images are collected. There are 356 frontal faces with variations in color, position, size and expression.

Our system can detect frontal faces under complex backgrounds. In Fig.5, some face detection examples are given. The examples demonstrate that our approach can handle multiple faces with different colors and sizes. Also our approach can detect dark skin-tone and bright skin-tone faces under complex lighting conditions.

Fig. 5. Face detection results

On the color image dataset, the system correctly detected 334 faces and produced 30 false alarms. The testing result is listed in Table.1. The correct detection rate is 93.8% and the precision is 91.7%, which prove that the proposed approach is effective in detecting faces. Note that precision is defined as the ratio of the number of positive detected faces to the sum of positive detected faces and negative detected faces.

Table 1. Testing results

Number of faces	Positive detected faces	Detection rate	Negative detected faces	Precision
356	334	93.8%	30	334/(334+30)=91.7%

As shown in Fig.6, the proposed method sometimes fails to detect real faces or detects false faces. Some faces are far smaller than 32x32, so they are often missing detected. Some false detected faces are similar to face patterns in color and shape. How to overcome these limitations is one of our future works.

Fig. 6. Face detection examples with missing and false detection

6   Conclusions and Future Work

In this paper, we propose a novel face detection approach in color images. We apply spatial histogram as pattern representation and extract histogram-matching features for face detection. We use a hierarchical scheme combining a histogram matching algorithm and a support vector machine for classification. Experiments show that the proposed approach performs an excellent capability for face detection in color images and it is robust to illumination changes. We will extend this approach to other objects recognition tasks, such as cars, and texts et al.

Acknowledgements. This research is partially supported by National Nature Science Foundation of China (No. 60332010), and ISVISION Technologies Co. Ltd. Thanks to Yuemin Li for her help on SVM code.

References

1. M.H. Yang, D.J. Kriegman, N. Ahuja: Detecting Faces in Images: A Survey. IEEE Translations on Pattern Analysis And Machine Intelligence, 24(1): 34-58, 2002.
2. H.A. Rowley, S. Baluja, T. Kanade: Neural Network-Based Face Detection. IEEE Translations on Pattern Analysis And Machine Intelligence, 20(1): 29-38,1998.
3. K.K. Sung, T. Poggio: Example-Based Learning for View-Based Human Face Detection. IEEE Translations on Pattern Analysis And Machine Intelligence, 20(1): 39-50,1998.
4. E. Osuna, R. Freund, F. Girosi: Training Support Vector Machines: an Application to Face Detection. Proceedings of CVPR, 130-136, 1997.
5. B. Menser, F. Muller: Face detection in color images using principal component analysis. Proceedings of 7th International Congress on Image Processing and its Applications, 13-15, 1999.
6. H. Schneiderman, T. Kanade: A Statistical Method for 3D Object Detection Applied to Faces and Cars. IEEE Conference on Computer Vision and Pattern Recognition, 2000.
7. P. Viola, M. Jones: Robust Real Time Object Detection. IEEE ICCV Workshop on Statistical and Computational Theories of Vison, 2001.
8. S.Z. Li, et al.: Statistical Learning of Multi-View Face Detection. Proc. of the 7th European Conf. on Computer Vision, 2002.
9. K.C. Yow, R. Cipolla: Feature-Based Human Face Detection. CUED/F-INFENG/TR 249, August 1996.
10. J. Miao, B.C. Yin, K.Q. Wang, L.S. Shen, and X.C. Chen: A hierarchical multiscale and multiangle system for human face detection in a complex background using gravity-center template. Pattern Recognition, 32(7): 1237-1248, 1999.
11. K. Sobottka, I. Pitas: A novel method for automatic face segmentation, facial feature extraction and tracking. Signal Processing: Image Communication, 12(3): 263-281, 1998.
12. Q.B. Sun, W.M. Huang, and J.K. Wu: Face detection based on color and local symmetry information. Proceedings of Third IEEE International Conference on Automatic Face and Gesture Recognition, 130-135, 1998.
13. F. Bernhard, K. Christian: Real-Time Face Detection using Edge-Orientation Matching.Audio and Video-based Biometric Person Authentication (AVBPA'2001), 78-83, 2001.
14. C. Garcia, G. Tziritas: Face Detection Using Quantized Skin Color Regions Merging and Wavelet Packet Analysis. IEEE Transactions on Multimedia, 1(3): 264-277, 1999.
15. M. Pietikäinen, T. Ojala, and Z. Xu: Rotation-invariant texture classification using feature distributions. Pattern Recognition, 33(1):43-52, 2000.
16. M. Swain, D. Ballard: Color indexing. Int. J. Computer Vision, 7(1): 11-32,1991.
17. T. Ojala, M. Pietikäinen, T. Mäenpää: Multiresolution gray-scale and rotation invariant texture classification with local binary patterns. IEEE Transactions on Pattern Analysis and Macine Intelligence, 24(7): 971-987, 2002.
18. V. Vapnik: Statistical Learning Theory. Wiley, New York, 1998.

Correlation Filters for Facial Recognition Login Access Control

Daniel E. Riedel, Wanquan Liu, and Ronny Tjahyadi

Department of Computing, Curtin University of Technology, GPO Box U1987 Perth,
Western Australia 6845
{riedelde,wanquan,tjahyadi}@cs.curtin.edu.au

Abstract. In this paper we utilise the minimum average correlation energy (MACE) and unconstrained minimum average correlation energy (UMACE) filters in conjunction with two correlation plane performance measures, max peak value and peak-to-sidelobe ratio, to illustrate the effectiveness of correlation filters in facial recognition login systems. A new technique for determining performance thresholds with the individual filters derived from the AMP and Biodm facial databases, was successfully developed producing high recall rates (67-94%) with 100% precision. A comparison of the precision and recall statistics obtained from the two different correlation plane measures, further demonstrated that max peak value is the better performance measure for use with MACE and UMACE filters for facial recognition login access control.

1 Introduction

Facial recognition is a popular biometric approach to login access control due to the uniqueness of the human face, ease of collecting facial images and good acceptability as a result of the techniques unobtrusiveness [1]. Typically, most current operating systems use password verification for the establishment of a users identity with the requested service being access to the system. However, these systems are vulnerable to password cracking, password sniffing and acquisition of passwords through simplistic means. Facial recognition attempts to minimise these inherent vulnerabilities by controlling the port of entry into a system via utilising ones own facial signature. Currently, we have developed a Linux biometric login system (Biodm) which employs facial recognition for login access control. In comparison to other applications of facial recognition, login access control requires systems to exhibit and maintain 100% precision for all users. This is necessary to prevent unauthorised users from being incorrectly accessed to a system and secondly, to prevent authorised persons from being incorrectly identified as other valid users. In addition, systems must also have a high recall to allow valid users access to a system when they present for authentication.

Correlation filtering, a relatively new approach to facial recognition, was initially applied in pattern recognition tasks, such as automatic target recognition, through the use of matched spatial filters (MSF) generated from a single training

K. Aizawa, Y. Nakamura, and S. Satoh (Eds.): PCM 2004, LNCS 3331, pp. 385–393, 2004.

image [2]. Unfortunately, MSFs demonstrated distortion variance, poor generalisation and poor localisation properties due to the use of a single training image and the broad correlation peak generated. To address these short-comings, the synthetic discriminant function (SDF) was introduced that linearly combined a set of training images into the one filter and further allowed one to constrain the filter output at the origin of the correlation plane [3]. By incorporating training images that best represented the expected distortions of an object, the SDF filter provided some degree of distortion invariance, yet like MSFs they did exhibit broad correlation peaks, making localisation difficult. To maximise peak sharpness for better object localisation and detection, the minimum average correlation energy (MACE) [3] and unconstrained MACE (UMACE) filters [4] were developed.

Prior research has demonstrated that MACE and UMACE correlation filters are effective at facial recognition, producing identification rates of 99.1-100% and verification rates of 93.5-100% with the AMP and PIE facial databases [5,6,7, 8]. Furthermore, MACE and UMACE filters have been shown to exhibit limited built-in tolerance to illumination variation [6], which is attractive for login access control in dynamic environments.

Facial recognition with correlation filters is performed by correlating a lexicographically ordered test image (transformed into the frequency domain via a Discrete Fast Fourier transform) with a synthesized, lexicographically ordered filter also in the frequency domain. The output correlation is subjected to an Inverse Fast Fourier transform and reordered into the dimensions of the original training image, prior to being phase shifted to the center of the frequency square. The resulting correlation plane is then quantified using a performance measure, typically the peak-to-sidelobe (PSR) ratio [7].

This paper investigates the use of an alternate correlation plane quantification metric (max peak value) to determine its effect on precision and recall rates in comparison to the standard PSR measure. In addition, an empirical method for deriving filter classification thresholds, is also introduced to avoid current *ad hoc* methods of threshold selection. Threshold selection is an important issue in login access control in order to maximise recall or usability, whilst maintaining 100% precision.

1.1   Minimum Average Correlation Energy Filters

MACE filters function to increase the peak sharpness by minimising the average correlation energy over a set of training images, whilst constraining the correlation peak height at the origin to a user-defined value. This in turn produces sharp peaks at the origin of the correlation plane, whilst producing values close to zero over the rest of the plane. The optimal solution to the MACE filter H is found using Lagrange multipliers in the frequency domain and is given by (1).

$$H = D^{-1}X(X^+D^{-1}X)^{-1}u \ . \tag{1}$$

where D is a diagonal matrix of size $d \times d$, (d is the number of pixels in the image) containing the average correlation energies of the training images across its diagonals. X is a matrix of size $n \times d$ where n is the number of training images and $+$ is the complex conjugate. The columns of X represent the Discrete Fourier coefficients for a particular training image X_i, where $1 \leq i \leq n$. The column vector u of size n contains the correlation peak constraint values for a series of training images, which are normally set to 1.0 for images of the same class [3,7].

The UMACE filter like the MACE filter minimises the average correlation energy over a set of training images, but without constraint (u), thereby maximising the peak height at the origin of the correlation plane. The UMACE filter expression H is given by (2).

$$H = D^{-1}X .\tag{2}$$

where D is a diagonal matrix of size $d \times d$ containing the average correlation energies of the training images and X is a column vector of size d, containing the average Fourier coefficients of the training images [4]. Computationally, UMACE filters are more attractive than their MACE counterparts as they require only the inversion of a single diagonal matrix. Furthermore, UMACE filters have been shown to perform similar to MACE filters in facial recognition [6].

1.2   Correlation Plane Performance Measures

Correlation plane performance measures are used to quantify the correlation between a filter and test image. In the context of facial recognition, the correlation plane is gauged with a performance metric in conjunction with a threshold, in order to classify a test image as belonging to a true or false class. Previous research with correlation filters and facial recognition has used the peak-to-sidelobe ratio (PSR) [5,6,7,8] as a performance index, primarily as it explicitly measures peak sharpness and is invariant to uniform changes in illumination [6]. PSR can be calculated according to (3).

$$PSR = \frac{peak - mean}{\sigma} .\tag{3}$$

where $peak$ is the maximum peak value in the correlation plane, $mean$ is the average of the sidelobe region surrounding the peak (20×20 pixels for a 64×64 pixel image, with a 5×5 excluded zone around the peak) and σ is the standard deviation of the sidelobe region values. More details on this technique can be found in [6,7,9].

In this study, we introduce an alternate simplistic measure, using just the maximum peak value, for measuring correlation planes in the context of facial recognition login access control. The maximum peak value is defined as the maximum correlation peak over a correlation plane and is equivalent to the peak parameter in (3). This performance metric measures only the strength of a match without taking into account sidelobe regions and is therefore more susceptible to misclassifications with high signal noise. However, in relation to true class matches, it is believed that the max peak value metric should yield an equal or higher percentage of true class matches in comparison to PSR, as good correlations produce strong correlation peaks irrespective of the quantity and magnitude of the noise in the sidelobe regions. Unfortunately, max peak value, unlike PSR, is susceptible to to uniform changes in illumination and changes in image dimension.

1.3   Facial Databases

Experimentation was carried out using the Advanced Multimedia Processing (AMP) facial expression [7] and the Biodm facial databases[1]. As much of the correlation filtering research in facial recognition has utilised the AMP facial database (13 subjects, 75 images per subject), it serves as a good experimental benchmark.

Comparative studies were also carried out with the Biodm facial database. Images of this database were captured in the Department of Computing, Curtin University of Technology, with a real-time Linux biometric login system, incorporating facial recognition with a Logitech® Quickcam Express Webcam. Histogram equalisation was performed on all captured images, which were obtained over several sessions. The Biodm database comprises 11 subjects with 14 images each and of size 150×200 pixels in PGM greyscale format.

1.4   Threshold Derivation

To determine the effectiveness of MACE and UMACE filters for facial recognition login access control, a threshold is required for each authentication decision. Typically, the same threshold is applied globally across a facial database and in the context of correlation filtering, is applied to all synthesized filters. In some facial recognition approaches, a separate threshold maybe applied for authenticating each individual in a facial database, however, in practice individual thresholds do not perform any better than their global counterparts and furthermore require added complexity for system implementation.

During the initial stages of experimentation, global thresholds were applied across the correlation filters of a facial database with both performance measures and filter types but resulted in low recognition performance. Consequently, a new approach was developed using individual upper and lower filter threshold ranges with a common pseudo-global threshold. The purpose of the approach was to find a filter threshold range to enable "better" threshold selection and to allow one to easily set a common pseudo-global threshold across all the filter threshold ranges of a facial database.

Firstly, upper and lower thresholds were determined for each of the n individuals, where the upper threshold represented the minimum quantised value of the true class correlations and the lower threshold refered to the maximum value of the false class correlations. Using the training set images of the facial database, the upper and lower thresholds were derived for each filter, according to the algorithm in Fig. 1.

---

[1] http://www.cs.curtin.edu.au/~riedelde/biodm.html

1. Filter H_i is synthesized using training images X_i (of size m), where $X_i \subseteq X$, $X = \{X_1 X_2 ... X_n\}$ and n is the number of individuals comprising the training set.

2. True class correlations α_i are performed in the frequency domain with filter H_i and the training images X_i. The corresponding correlation planes are quantified (β_i) using an appropriate correlation plane measure and the m values of β_i are then sorted in increasing order. The θ_{upper} threshold is then set to the minimum of the of the β_i values. ($*$ is the complex conjugate)

$$\text{FOR } j \leftarrow 1 \text{ TO } m \text{ DO}$$
$$\alpha_i^j \leftarrow H_i^* X_i^j$$
$$\beta_i^j \leftarrow CORRELATION\_MEASURE(\alpha_i^j)$$
$$\text{END}$$

$$\omega \leftarrow 1 \qquad\qquad\qquad // \text{ index of the current minimum } \theta_{upper} \text{ value in } \beta_i$$
$$SORT(\beta_i)$$
$$\theta_{upper} \leftarrow \beta_i^\omega$$

3. False class correlations γ_i are performed with the filter H_i and the training images Y_i, where $Y_i \subseteq X$ and $Y_i \not\subseteq X_i$. The corresponding correlation planes are quantified (δ_i) using the same correlation plane measure as in Step (2) and the θ_{lower} threshold is set to the maximum of the δ_i values.

$$\text{FOR } j \leftarrow 1 \text{ TO } m \times (n-1) \text{ DO}$$
$$\gamma_i^j \leftarrow H_i^* Y_i^j$$
$$\delta_i^j \leftarrow CORRELATION\_MEASURE(\gamma_i^j)$$
$$\text{END}$$

$$\theta_{lower} \leftarrow MAX(\delta_i)$$

4. IF $\theta_{lower} \geq \theta_{upper}$ AND $\omega \leq m$ THEN
$$\omega = \omega + 1$$
$$\theta_{upper} = \beta_i^\omega \qquad\qquad // \text{ increase upper threshold value}$$
$$\text{REPEAT Step (4)}$$
ELSE
$$\text{OUTPUT } \theta_{lower} \text{ and } \theta_{upper} \text{ (STOP)}$$
END

Fig. 1. Upper (θ_{upper}) and Lower (θ_{lower}) threshold derivation algorithm for a single filter i.

Login access control systems require 100% precision to prevent invalid authentication, with a high recall rate for good usability. To maintain this constraint, the training images, correlation filters and their corresponding lower and upper threshold values were used to empirically determine a θ_{global} threshold that produced 100% precision, whilst maximising recall. The θ_{global} threshold ratio was found using ϵ segments (10 was seen to be adequate) between the upper and lower thresholds of the filters and originating at the upper thresholds of the filters until the lower threshold. For each decrement, the training images and filters were cross-correlated and the number of false positives (FP) and true positives (TP) ascertained. If an FP of zero was obtained for a particular threshold, the threshold was lowered to the next decrement and the FP and TP re-evaluated. If an FP greater than zero was obtained for the filters, the algorithm stopped and the θ_{global} based on the previous threshold was output. In the event that the FP was greater than zero at the upper threshold of the filters or the FP was equal to zero at the lower threshold, the θ_{global} was set to the upper filter threshold or lower filter thresholds, respectively. The θ_{global} threshold derivation algorithm is shown in Fig. 2.

1. ϵ is used to quantise the space lying between the θ_{upper} and θ_{lower} of the n filters, producing ϵ possible thresholds. For each of the possible ϵ thresholds, starting at the upper threshold, the algorithm continues calculating the TP and FP statistics for the cross-correlations of the n filters and $m \times n$ training images until a threshold is reached that has greater than zero FP or the lower threshold is reached with zero FP.

```
ε ← 10                                      // number of threshold ratios to utilise
CurrentDecrement ← 0                        // current threshold decrement
TP ← FP ← 0

FOR i ← 1 TO ε DO                           // for each threshold ratio
    FOR j ← 1 TO m×n DO                     // for each image in the training set
        p ←((j-1) mod m)+1                  // determine image number within a class
        q ←((j-1) div m)+1                  // determine the image class
        FOR k ← 1 TO n DO                   // for each filter
            φⱼᵏ←Hₖ*Xq^p
            λⱼᵏ←CORRELATION_MEASURE(φⱼᵏ)
        END
        MaxValue←MAX(λⱼ)                    // find the maximum performance value
        r←FIND(MaxValue, λⱼ)               // find which filter had the max value
        CurrentThreshold ← θ^r_upper-(θ^r_upper-θ^r_lower)× CurrentDecrement/ε
        IF MaxValue>CurrentThreshold THEN   // if max value found > filters threshold
            IF r = q THEN                   // if training image belongs to its correct class
                TP←TP+1
            ELSE                            // training image belongs to a false class
                FP←FP+1
            END
        END
    END
END

IF FP > 0 THEN            // if any false positives found for the current threshold
    IF i ≠ 1 THEN         // if current threshold decrement is NOT the upper threshold
        CurrentDecrement←CurrentDecrement-1     // use previous threshold
    END
    OUTPUT CurrentDecrement/ε (STOP)            // θ_global
ELSE                      // no false positives so decrease threshold
    IF i = ε THEN         // if current threshold decrement is at the lower threshold
        OUTPUT CurrentDecrement/ε (STOP)        // θ_global
    ELSE                  // current threshold decrement is between upper and lower threshold
        CurrentDecrement←CurrentDecrement+1     // go to the next decrement
    END
END
```

2. The optimal threshold ratio between the θ_{lower} and θ_{upper} obtained in Step (1), occurs where the TP is maximum and the FP is zero. This value is set as the θ_{global} for the facial database and can be used for a filter s as follows:
$$OptimalThreshold_s \leftarrow \theta^s_{upper}-(\theta^s_{upper}-\theta^s_{lower}) \times \theta_{global}$$

Fig. 2. Pseudo-Global threshold (θ_{global}) derivation algorithm for a facial database of n persons.

2   Testing Methodology

Prior to experimentation, the AMP and Biodm facial database images were segmented into two data sets: the training set and the testing set. MACE and UMACE filters were synthesized for the individuals comprising the uniformly distributed training set images, whilst the testing set was used to measure the precision and recall statistics of the approach over a range of pseudo-global thresholds. The testing set also contained 2 persons who were not part of the

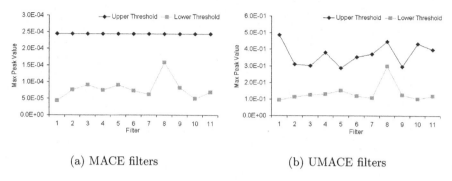

(a) MACE filters   (b) UMACE filters

Fig. 3. Upper and lower max peak value thresholds for the AMP facial database.

training set and thus should not be recognised. This particular approach of using testing images of persons not in the training set allows for a more accurate interpretation of the recognition results, by taking into account the ability of the system to reject external persons.

The training set for the AMP database consisted of the first 11 of 13 individuals comprising the database, with 5 training images per person (images 1,15,30,45 and 60). The corresponding testing set consisted of 40 uniformly selected images not present in the training set. Training sets for the Biodm facial database utilised the first 9 of the 11 subjects in the database, with 7 images selected per subject (images 1,3,5,7,9,11,13). The corresponding testing sets contained the remaining 7 images in the database for each of the 11 subjects (images 2,4,6,8,10,12,14).

To quantify the recognition performance of the filters and the performance metrics with the testing sets, precision and recall statistics were in turn calculated. Precision allows one to measure the ability of the technique to correctly classify, whilst recall measures the completeness of a techniques classification, that is the proportion of the true class test cases that were identified [10].

3   Experimental Results

Upper and lower thresholds were derived for MACE and UMACE filters with the AMP and Biodm facial databases, using the max peak value and PSR performance measures, however, we only show AMP database results in the figures. The thresholds in Figures 3-4 were obtained using the algorithm in Fig. 1.

Constant upper threshold values were observed for MACE filters using the max peak value metric in Fig. 3a, in contrast to the variable upper threshold values obtained with PSR in Fig. 4a. The max peak value upper thresholds observed with MACE filter correlations were consistent with both facial databases and can be explained by the MACE filter constraining the peak height at the origin of the correlation plane, with u in (1), to a user-defined value. Furthermore, the MACE filters utilising the max peak value metric in Fig. 3a, demonstrate

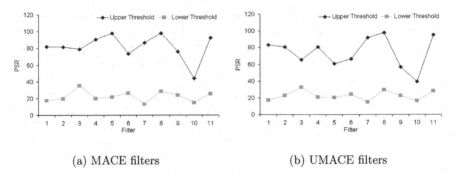

(a) MACE filters   (b) UMACE filters

Fig. 4. Upper and lower PSR thresholds for the AMP facial database.

Table 1. Recall rates for 100% precision thresholds with MACE and UMACE filters.

Performance Metric	Facial Database			
	AMP		Biodm	
	MACE	UMACE	MACE	UMACE
Max peak value	92.7%	94.1%	87.3%	66.7%
PSR	79.3%	80.2%	42.9%	34.9%

good separation between upper and lower thresholds, unlike PSR in Fig. 4a. The observed good separation between upper and lower thresholds could allow utilisation of a global threshold across the facial database, in turn producing high recall rates with 100% precision.

UMACE filter training set correlations in Fig. 3b and Fig. 4b consistently produced variable upper and lower thresholds for both performance measures. The variability in the observed thresholds for the UMACE filters are due to UMACE maximising the peak height at the origin *without* constraint, as evident in (2). Large threshold variability shown with UMACE filters and both performance measures indicates an unsuitability of this filter type with a global threshold, due to the high number of misclassifications which would be generated in order to maintain an adequate recall rate.

Following θ_{global} threshold derivation, the recognition performance of the MACE and UMACE filters was determined using testing set correlations. Derived correlation planes were quantified using the respective performance metrics, and precision and recall statistics were calculated as shown in Table 1. The application of the θ_{global} thresholds in Table 1 illustrates that quantification with max peak value produces larger recall rates with the filters, under the constraint of 100% precision. This result was found to be consistent with both filter types and facial databases. We attribute this observation to the max peak value metric measuring only the strength of the match without taking into account the average size and spread of signal noise about the peak, as per the PSR metric. Increases in signal noise about the maximum peak consequently decreases PSR but does not effect the magnitude of the maximum peak value and thus the authentication decision. Therefore, in the context of facial recognition login access control with correlation filters, max peak value is the more appropriate metric for quantifying correlation planes.

As shown in Table 1, the recognition performance of the MACE and UMACE filters also appears to be data dependent as the UMACE filters performed better with the AMP database, yet worse with the Biodm database.

4 Conclusion

This paper has provided a performance overview of two correlation plane performance measures with MACE and UMACE correlation filters as well as a mechanism with which to derive a threshold selection range and pseudo-global threshold for correlation filters. In this study, it was found that the max peak value performance measure outperformed the standard PSR measure in the context of login access control. In addition, the upper and lower filter threshold derivation technique, in conjunction with the pseudo-global threshold derivation procedure, were shown to be suitable for obtaining 100% precision filter thresholds, in turn generating high recall rates. We are currently endeavouring to verify these findings with larger facial databases, such as the PIE and BANCA databases.

References

1. Jain, A., Hong, L., Pankanti, S.: Biometric identification. Communications of the ACM **43** (2000) 91–98
2. Vanderlugt, A.: Signal detection by complex matched spatial filtering. IEEE Trans. Inf. Theory **IT-10** (1964) 139–145
3. Mahalanobis, A., B.V.K. Vijaya Kumar, Casasent, D.: Minimum average correlation energy filters. Applied Optics **26** (1987) 3633–3640
4. Mahalanobis, A., B.V.K. Vijaya Kumar, Song, S., Sims, S., Epperson, J.: Unconstrained correlation filters. Applied Optics **33** (1994) 3751–3759
5. Savvides, M., Venkataramani, K., B.V.K. Vijaya Kumar: Incremental updating of advanced correlation filters for biometric authentication systems. In: Proc. Of the IEEE Int. Conf. on Multimedia and Expo. Volume 3. (2003) 229–232
6. Savvides, M., B.V.K. Vijaya Kumar: Efficient design of advanced correlation filters for robust distortion-tolerant face recognition. In: Proc. Of the IEEE Conf. on Adv. Video and Signal Based Surveillance. (2003) 45–52
7. Savvides, M., B.V.K. Vijaya Kumar, Khosla, P.: Face verification using correlation filters. In: Proc. Of the Third IEEE Auto. Ident. Adv. Technologies. (2002) 56–61
8. B.V.K. Vijaya Kumar, Savvides, M., Venkataramani, K., Xie, C.: Spatial frequency domain image processing for biometric recognition. In: Proc. Of the IEEE Int. Conf. on Image Processing. Volume 1. (2002) I–53–I–56
9. B.V.K. Vijaya Kumar, Hassebrook, L.: Performance measures for correlation filters. Applied Optics **29** (1990) 2997–3006
10. Vijay, V., Bollmann, B., Jung, G.: A critical investigation of recall and precision as measures of retrieval system performance. ACM Trans. Info. Sys. **7** (2003) 205–229

Easy and Convincing Ear Modeling for Virtual Human

Hui Zhang[1] and In Kyu Park[2]

[1] Computing Laboratory, Samsung Advanced Institute of Technology,
YONGIN 449-712, KOREA
hui.zhang@samsung.com
[2] School of Information and Communication Engineering, INHA University,
INCHEON 402-751, KOREA
pik@ieee.org

Abstract. In this paper, we describe the human ear creation in a system for 3-D photorealistic face modeling from frontal and profile images taken by an un-calibrated handheld digital camera. The ear part is segmented in profile facial image with a boundary detection algorithm, and then mapped to the created face model. Our ear modeling procedure has several advantages. (1) A highly automatic detection algorithm is proposed to locate profile ear boundary accurately and robustly despite of a variety of illumination, hair shape, gender and race. (2) Deliberately designed shape deformation algorithm is proposed to stitch the ear and head smoothly. (3) Synthesized texture is utilized and merged with input images to compensate occluded ear-nearby areas and create realistic results. Experimental results show that the created ear is smooth and convincing, improving the face appearance dramatically.

1 Introduction

A large quantities of features in facial images under different view angles are analyzed for face detection, recognition and modeling [1][2][3][4]. However, ear analysis has been received little attention although it is significant feature, especially in profile image. Ears also affect the photorealistic appearance of a 3-D head model significantly.

In [5], some parts of profile ear boundary were used to create 3-D head models. However, only the boundary between hair and ear was detected by manual operation. In fact, the automatic and robust detection of complete ear boundary is quite difficult to achieve because: (1) the ear has large shape variation for different individuals; (2) the local contrast between ear and skin parts is very weak in many cases; (3) the appearance in nearby area varies dramatically because of hair and illumination.

The generation of ear shape and texture also needs special attention because: (1) the ear shape is too complex to be modeled accurately from image information with easy user interaction; (2) obvious occlusion occurs in ear-nearby area so that some compensation is needed to create convincing texture. However, existing face modeling system [6][7][8][9][10] paid little attention to these issues and resulted with ugly ears, which weaken the realism of the created models significantly.

In this paper, we propose algorithms for creating accurate ear models easily for the user of our face modeling system. The main contribution of our work includes:

K. Aizawa, Y. Nakamura, and S. Satoh (Eds.): PCM 2004, LNCS 3331, pp. 394–401, 2004.
© Springer-Verlag Berlin Heidelberg 2004

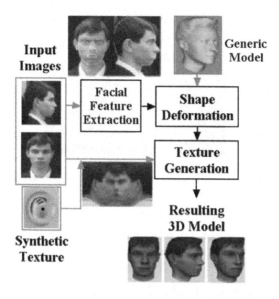

Fig. 1. Overview of the face modeling system.

- Presenting a robust and highly automatic algorithm to detect profile ear. This is achieved by exploring the different image information such as skin color and edge, and enforcing a priori knowledge about human ears with a template
- Presenting an automatic shape deformation algorithm to stitch ear and head smoothly
- Utilizing synthesized texture to compensate the occluded head areas, and combining it smoothly with the input image

The paper is organized as follows. In Section 2, the face modeling system is described briefly. Then Section 3, Section 4, and Section 5 are devoted to ear detection, ear shape deformation and ear texture generation, respectively. Finally, conclusive remarks are given in Section 6.

2   Overview of the Face Modeling System

We have proposed a system focusing on creating a highly automated procedure of a high-quality facial model generation from frontal and profile images without imposing strict conditions on picture taking conditions [11], thus to make photorealistic human head models very easily for a common PC user. As shown in Fig. 1, it takes two photos of a person (frontal and profile) and a generic head model as the inputs to produce a textured VRML model of the person's head. Two types of data are carefully combined: frontal and profile facial features. The recognition part of the system extracts the facial features robustly. A few algorithms have been developed to detect individual facial parts including eye, nose, mouth, ear, chin, and cheek. The generic head model is deformed to coincide with the detected facial features by employing Radial-Basis Functions (RBF)

Fig. 2. Scale and orientation normalization for ear detection. Normalized image, calibration points and ear search area are shown.

interpolation [12]. The model texture is created by blending frontal and profile face photos, together with some synthesized texture.

3   Ear Detection in the Profile Image

The ear detection can be divided into two steps: profile image pre-processing, and boundary detection. They will be described in following subsections.

3.1   Profile Image Pre-processing

In this step some normalization operation is performed to facilitate the further ear detection. Two fiducial points, the nose bridge top and the chin point, are detected in profile image, and utilized as calibration points to determine the normalization. The original image is rotated to make the segment connecting them to be vertical, then scaled to make the distance between them to be a predefined value. In this stage, we also define a rectangle as the search area for the ear by statistical analysis on the relative positions between ears and the calibration points in our test images. In Fig. 2, the normalized image, the calibration points (the two white crossing points), and the search area (the rectangle with black border line) are all shown.

These two points are selected because they can be robustly detected, and they are distant enough so that the normalization is less sensitive to the detection errors. In order to detect them automatically, we first rely on skin color classification results to detect profile facial curves. Afterwards the local curvature properties of profile curve pixels are analyzed to locate profile fiducial feature points such as nose tip, nose bridge top, mouth and chin points. The algorithm is similar to that in [13].

3.2   Ear Boundary Detection

Since the local low-level clues are usually weak and erroneous in the area nearby the ear, a curve template, which represents the priori knowledge about human ears, is utilized to detect the ear boundary. The template is first matched with ear image to be translated to an initial position, and then refined by deform it to match the accurate ear boundary.

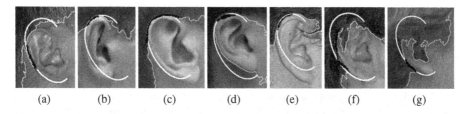

(a)   (b)   (c)   (d)   (e)   (f)   (g)

Fig. 3. Ear initialization results with skin color boundary. The translated template (white smooth curve), the skin color boundary (long, irregular-shaped grey curve), and the matched partial segments (dark partial segments) are shown.

Note that the purpose of previous pre-processing step is to compensate different scale and orientation for template matching. In our implementation, the template is a 5-degree polynomial, as shown in Fig. 3 (the smooth curve with the same shape on all photos).

The 'skin color boundary' (the boundary of the face region detected with skin color classification) is used for ear initialization because it coincides with the ear boundary at some partial segment in most cases, as shown in Fig. 3. Then the problem is to find the corresponding partial segment between the template and the skin color boundary inside the search area. After the scale and orientation normalization, it can be solved with a simple curve-matching algorithm based on the similarity of curve gradient. In more detail, the two curves are preprocessed to be 4-connected, avoiding local duplication. We denote the resultant point sets as $\{q_i \in \mathbf{R}^2|_{1 \le i \le N}\}$ for the template, and $\{p_j \in \mathbf{R}^2|_{1 \le j \le M}\}$ for the skin color boundary. Next, two displacement arrays are constructed as $\{VQ_s = q_{a(s+1)} - q_{as}\}$ and $\{VP_t = p_{a(t+1)} - p_{at}\}$, where a is a coefficient for sampling step. Now we evaluate $l(s,t)$ as the maximum integer l that satisfies

$$\sum_{m=1}^{l} \|VQ_{s+m} - VP_{t+m}\| \le \delta, \tag{1}$$

where δ is a threshold to measure the similarity of the tangential direction at $q_{a \cdot s}$ and $p_{a \cdot t}$. The position (s_m, t_m) where $l(s,t)$ is maximum is found to give the match result as $\{q_i|_{a s_m \le i \le a(s_m + l_m)}\}$ and $\{p_j|_{a t_m \le j \le a(t_m + l_m)}\}$. Finally, the template is translated based on the partial segment match. Such a simple method performs very well in our experiments, as shown in Fig. 3.

Based on the initialized ear template and the matched segment on the image ear boundary, we perform contour following to deform the template to match with the whole ear boundary in the image. In more detail, we approximate the template with line segments, using an adaptive polyline fitting algorithm. Then, the line segment that has its vertex on the ear boundary is selected as the starting position of contour following. We denote this vertex as $Cont_n$, and the next vertex along the polyline as $Cont_{next}$. Afterwards the segment is rotated to a new position that gives the best match evaluation, which is defined by combining local edge strength across the ear boundary with the segment similarity along it. All the following segments after $Cont_n$ along the polyline are rotated with respective to $Cont_n$, as illustrated in Fig. 4. Finally letting $n = next$, we perform this operation iteratively to deform the whole template. This procedure is employed twice for both directions of the polyline. The fully automatic boundary detection performs very well for significant variety of illumination, hair shape, gender, and race, as shown in Fig. 5. Even in the only one failure case (Fig. 5 (l)), the initialization and contour following are successful, but the determination of ear bottom point fails due to the earring.

In order to have a complete ear we also need to determine another half ear boundary, *i.e.* the open part of the detected curve. The completing curve part is detected semi-automatically. The user needs to manually specify the top and bottom points of internal ear boundary. Then an automatic algorithm is developed to connect them with a curve, by solving a minimal-path graph optimization problem, following the idea in [14]. Finally this inside curve is connected with outside ear boundary to form a complete ear contour. The gap between them is automatically filled by linear interpolation of ear vertices in the generic model.

4   Ear Shape Deformation

The ear shape can be determined automatically during the shape deformation stage shown in Fig. 1. That is, ear vertices are deformed together with other head vertices (Please refer to [11] for more details about head shape deformation). However, this usually gives un-satisfactory results. In fact, ear vertices are too far away from the head center, and the RBF interpolation determined by all facial feature points (eyes, nose, mouth, ears and profile fiducial points) sometime generates strange shapes for them due to extrapolation. Furthermore, the ear shape is so complex that its smoothness after RBF deformation is not ensured, and it is also difficult to be modeled accurately from image information. In our system a fixed ear shape from the generic model is used in created individual models. It is scaled to fit the specific ear size, and combined smoothly with the created heads. Such a simple strategy avoids ugly ear shape.

A key issue of this strategy is the smooth shape combination between the scaled generic ear and the deformed head model. This is solved with RBF data interpolation. We manually specify two boundaries on the ear patch. The outside boundary is the blending boundary between the deformed head model and the ear patch, while the inside boundary separates the ear patch into a facial part and a stitching-out one. The idea is to deform the facial-part ear patch to generate seamless effect across the blending boundary, while

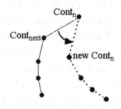

Fig. 4. The template segments before (solid line) and after (dashed line) rotation, during ear contour following.

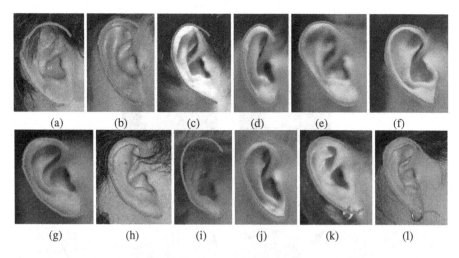

(a)   (b)   (c)   (d)   (e)   (f)

(g)   (h)   (i)   (j)   (k)   (l)

Fig. 5. Profile ear detection results.

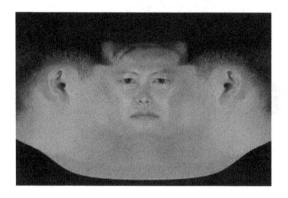

Fig. 6. Resulting face and ear texture.

keeping the shape of stitching-out ear part. Thus the combined model will be smooth around ear area.

In more detail, we first perform a global scale transform on the generic ear patch, to make the length of the blending boundary on it match with the counterpart on a deformed head. it is also translated so that the center of blending boundary vertices coincides to that of the deformed head model. Afterwards a RBF interpolation is performed for all ear-patch vertices, utilizing the two boundaries as constrained points. The blending boundary vertices are displaced to their corresponding positions on the deformed head, while the inside boundary vertices are remained at their original positions. Finally, the stitching out part can be scaled to match with the image ear size. This fully automatic algorithm creates smooth blending results in our experiment.

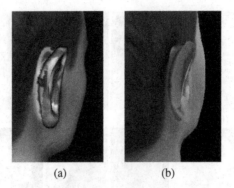

(a)   (b)

Fig. 7. Improved appearance with the proposed algorithm.

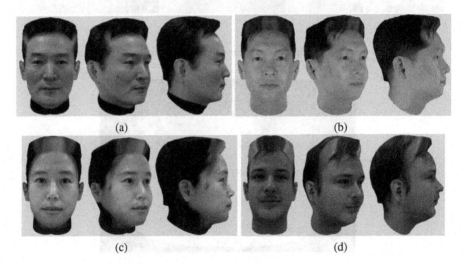

(a)   (b)

(c)   (d)

Fig. 8. Face and ear models generated by the proposed modeling system.

5   Ear Texture Generation

Special attention on ear is paid during face texture generation. First, during creating texture coordinates for all model vertices, we unfolded ear patches to create a non-overlap 2-D plane. Second, synthetic ear texture, as shown in Fig. 1, is combined with the profile image to compensate the occluded ear area, utilizing a multi-resolution spline algorithm [15]. Note that synthetic texture is first color aligned to ensure the smooth combination with input images, with an algorithm introduced in [16]. Experiments show non-overlap, realistic texture is generated, as shown in Fig. 6. The appearance improvement with the customized ear modeling algorithms can be obviously observed in Fig. 7. Final textured individual head models are shown in Fig. 8. It is observed that the ear part shows quite natural 3-D shape and matches well with the overall head model.

6   Conclusion

The image-based ear modeling issues, including ear detection in profile image, ear shape deformation and ear texture generation, are described. The detection algorithm is highly automatic, and achieves robust and accurate results for a variety of illumination, hair shape, gender and race. Both smooth shape and non-overlap, realistic texture is created for human ears, based on the detected ear boundary. The ear modeling part is integrated into a face modeling system, and improves the appearance of created face models dramatically.

References

1. Yang, M.H., Kriegman, D., Ahuja, N.: Detecting faces in images: a survey. IEEE Trans. on Pattern Analysis and Machine Intelligence **24** (2002) 34–58
2. Hjelmas, E., Low, B.: Face detection: A survey. Computer Vision and Image Understanding, **83** (2001) 236–274
3. Brunelli, R., Poggio, T.: Face recognition: Features versus templates. IEEE Trans. on Pattern Analysis and Machine Intelligence **15** (2003) 1042–1052
4. Goto, T., Lee, W., Thalmann, N.: Facial feature extraction for quick 3d face modeling. Signal Processing: Image Communication **17** (2002) 243–259
5. Lee, W., Kalra, P., Thalmann, N.: Model based face reconstruction for animation. Proc. of Multimedia Modeling (1997) 323–338
6. Pighin, F., Hecker, J., Lischinski, D., Szeliski, R., Salesin, D.: Perceptual 3d shape descriptor: Result of core experiment. Proc. of SIGGRAPH (1998) 75–84
7. Blanz, V., Vetter, T.: A morphable model for the synthesis of 3-d faces. Proc. of SIGGRAPH (1999) 187–191
8. Shan, Y., Liu, Z., Zhang, Z.: Model-based bundle adjustment with application to face modeling. Proc. of IEEE International Conference on Computer Vision (2001)
9. Fua, P.: Regularized bundle-adjustment to model heads from image sequences without calibration data. International Journal of Computer Vision **38** (2000) 153–171
10. Sarris, N., Grammalidis, N., Strintzis, M.: Building three dimensional head models. Graphical Models **63** (2001) 333–368
11. Park, I.K., Zhang, H., Vezhnevets, V., Choh, H.K.: Image-based photorealistic 3-d face modeling. Proc. of Sixth IEEE International Conference on Automatic Face and Gesture Recognition (2004) 49–54
12. Carr, J., Beaton, R., Cherrie, J., Mitchell, T., Fright, W., McCallum, B., Evans., T.: Reconstruction and representation of 3-d objects with radial basis functions. Proc. of SIGGRAPH (2001)
13. Akimoto, T., Suenaga, Y., Wallace, R.: Automatic creation of 3d facial models. IEEE Computer Graphics and Applications **13** (1993) 16–22
14. Mortensen, E., Barrett, W.: Intelligent scissors for image composition. Prof. of SIGGRAPH (1995) 191–198
15. Burt, P., Adelson, E.: The earth mover's distance as a metric for image retrieval. ACM Trans. on Graphic **2** (1983) 217–236
16. Reinhard, E., Ashikhmin, M., Gooch, B., Shirley, P.: Color transfer between images. IEEE Computer Graphics and Applications **21** (2001) 34–41

A Polyhedral Object Recognition Algorithm for Augmented Reality

Dong-Joong Kang[1], Jong-Eun Ha[1], and Muh-Ho Jeong[2]

[1] Tongmyong University of Information Technology
{djkang,jeha}@tit.ac.kr
[2] Korea Institute of Science and Technology
mhjeong@kist.re.kr

Abstract. Registration between cameras and objects is a central element for augmented reality applications and required to combine real and rendered scenes. In this paper, we present a new approach to solve the problem of estimating the camera 3-D location and orientation from a matched set of 3-D model and 2-D image features. An iterative least-square method is used to solve both rotation and translation simultaneously. We derive an error equation using roll-pitch-yaw angle to present the rotation matrix. From the modeling of an error equation, we analytically extract the partial derivates for estimation parameters from the nonlinear error equation. To minimize the error equation, Levenberg-Marquardt algorithm is introduced with uniform sampling strategy of rotation space to avoid stuck in local minimum.

Keywords: Nonlinear optimization, pose estimation, polyhedral object recognition, augmented reality, computer vision

1 Introduction

Main elements for initialization of polyhedral objects in augmented reality applications are feature detection, correspondence analysis, and pose estimation. This paper describes an algorithm that provides new solution for the problem of estimating cam-era location and orientation for pose determination from a set of recognized lines appearing in the image. If the correspondence is given from the relation between 3-D model lines and 2-D lines found in image, the goal of the 3-D object recognition is to find the rotation and translation matrices which map the world coordinate system to the camera coordinate system. There have been several approaches to solve these problems. For more de-tailed review, refer to [1]. The 3-D pose algorithm proposed in this paper is an extension of [2] method for 3-D pose decision. [2] proposed a point correspondence method to decide camera parameters and pose detection. We extended the algorithm to line correspondence from the point algorithm. Because using roll-pitch-yaw angle to present rotation is very simple and intuitive, we derive an error equation based on the roll-pitch-yaw angles as a nonlinear function. The error equation minimizes a point-to-plane distance that is defined as the dot product of unit normal to the

K. Aizawa, Y. Nakamura, and S. Satoh (Eds.): PCM 2004, LNCS 3331, pp. 402–409, 2004.

projected plane of image line and a 3-D point on the model line transformed to camera coordinates. We directly extract the partial derivable for the estimation parameters from the nonlinear error equation. The least-squares techniques to minimize the nonlinear function, are iterative in nature, and require an initial estimate. Because it is very difficult to provide good initial estimates avoiding local minimums without any additional information about object pose, we propose a simple uniform sampling strategy where the values uniformly sampled from three rotation angles of roll-pitch-yaw are provided to the initial estimates. To handle the correspondence problem between 3-D model lines and 2-D image lines, we first extract junctions formed by two lines in the input image, and then find an optimal relation between the extracted junctions, by comparing them with previously constructed model relations. Junction detection acts as a line filter to extract salient line groups in the input image and then the relations between the extracted groups are searched to form a more complex group in an energy minimization frame-work [3]. After solving the correspondence between two respective line sets, Leven-berg-Marquardt technique is applied to minimize the defined error function. Partial derivatives for the error equation are analytically derived to form Jacobian matrices providing linearized form of the non-linear equation. Experimental results using real image of a 3-D polyhedral object are presented.

2   Extraction of Polyhedral Objects

We assume that the edges as an image feature are extracted well and the line junction made from the edges is used for extraction of polyhedral objects. For the relational representation for junctions, it is possible to build a connected chain of the junctions in an energy minimization framework [3]. Figure 1(a) presents a schematic of lines consisting of an object. Figure 1(b) and (c) show the binary relations of sequentially connected junctions for description of polyhedral object. Each junction has the unary relation given as junction quality factor by two lines constituting of a single junction. The junction quality factor could be used to control the number of junctions extracted from image. The binary relation representing combination of two junctions defines a topological constraint between two junctions. For example, the followings describe the binary relations in Figure 1: (1) Two lines 1 and 4 should be approximately parallel (parallelism); (2) Two lines 2 and 3 must be a col-linear pair. That is, two junctions are combined by the collinear constraint; (3) Two connected junctions can share a common line between the two junctions; (4) Line ordering for two junctions and in Figure 1(b) should be maintained such as clockwise or counter-clockwise, as the order of line 1, line 2, line 3, and line 4. The relation defined by the connected two junctions includes all three perceptual organization groups that [4] used in SCERPO. The local relations can be selectively imposed and expanded to build bigger and more meaningful polyhedral objects. A bottom-up optimization strategy such as dynamic programming can provide the minimal energy combination of connected junction chains without increase of computing time in junction search.

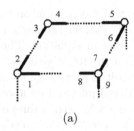

(a)

(b)   (c)

Fig. 1. Binary relations made from any two connected junctions: (a) Line segments on a polyhedral object; and (b), (c) Combination of junctions by perceptual constraints, such as proximity, collinearity, and parallelism.

Suppose that the global energy can be decomposed into the following form:

$$E(f_1, ..., f_M) = E_1(f_1, f_2) + E_2(f_2, f_3) + ... + E_{M-1}(f_{M-1}, f_M) \qquad (1)$$

$$E_i(f_I, f_{I+1}) = \alpha q(f_I) + \beta r(f_I, f_{I+1}) \qquad (2)$$

in which M is the number of the model nodes such as lines or junctions, and f_I is a scene label that can be assigned to the model node I. The unary equation $q(f_I)$ in (2) presents the quality factor of each junction and binary equation $r(f_I, f_{I+1})$ means compatibility factor of binary relation which presents the linking suitability of two connected junctions. The weighting coefficients α and β of the energy potential are experimentally given by considering the variance factor of the line perturbation for image noise. Hence a polyhedral object by using a pre-description about a known object shape can be found through combinatorial search of junctions given in image. For more details of polyhedral object extraction, refer to [3].

3   Pose Estimation

Perspective projection between a camera and 3-dimentional objects defines a plane in 3-D space that is formed from a line in an image and the focal point of the camera. If no errors with perfect 3-D models were introduced in during image feature extraction, then model lines in 3-D space projecting onto this line in the image would exactly lie in this plane. This observation is the basis for the fit measure used in a few previous works [1] [2]. We propose a pose decision method solving rigid transformation, which minimizes the sum-of-squared distances between points on 3-D model lines and the plane.

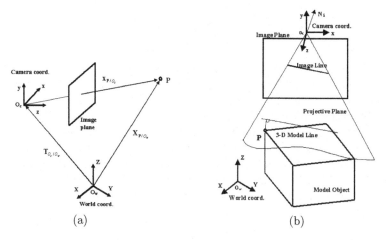

Fig. 2. Geometrical configurations. (a) The relationship between two coordinate systems (b) The perpendicular distance by point-to-plane fit measure

First of all, we describe the relationship between two coordinate systems. Camera and world coordinate systems are $O_c - xyz$, $O_w - XYZ$, respectively. Figure 2(a) shows the two coordinate systems where X_w, Y_w, and Z_w and, x_C, y_C, and z_C, represent the axes of the world and camera coordinates system, respectively. The relationship between the two coordinate systems is given by the following vector-matrix equation:

$$\begin{pmatrix} x_P/O_c \\ y_P/O_c \\ z_P/O_c \end{pmatrix} = \mathbf{R}^t \cdot \begin{pmatrix} X_{P/O_W} - t_{1/O_W} \\ Y_{P/O_W} - t_{2/O_W} \\ Z_{P/O_W} - t_{3/O_W} \end{pmatrix} \tag{3}$$

where $\mathbf{R}$ is rotation matrix from the world coordinate system to the camera coordinate system and $\mathbf{T}_{O_c/O_w} = (t_1 t_2 t_3)^t$ is translation vector from O_w point to O_c point. Upper index t presents transpose of a matrix. A point in 3-D space is represented by 3-D vector $\mathbf{P}$. We could use roll-pitch-yaw angles to represent the rotation matrix $\mathbf{R}$. Each of the three rotations takes place about an axis in the fixed reference frame:

$$\mathbf{R} = \mathbf{R}_Z(\gamma)\mathbf{R}_Y(\beta)\mathbf{R}_X(\alpha) \tag{4}$$

$$= \begin{pmatrix} \cos\gamma & -\sin\gamma & 0 \\ \sin\gamma & \cos\gamma & 0 \\ 0 & 0 & 1 \end{pmatrix} \begin{pmatrix} \cos\beta & 0 & \sin\beta \\ 0 & 1 & 0 \\ -\sin\beta & 0 & \cos\beta \end{pmatrix} \begin{pmatrix} 1 & 0 & 0 \\ 0 & \cos\alpha & -\sin\alpha \\ 0 & \sin\alpha & \cos\alpha \end{pmatrix}$$

Due to noise for extracting image lines, the segments usually will not lie exactly in the projection plane as shown in Figure 2(b). The point-to-plane distance may be defined as the dot product of the unit normal to the plane and a 3-D point on the model line transformed to camera coordinates. It is possible to provide an error equation denoting the sum of squared perpendicular distances for line segments:

$$e = \sum \sum e_{ij}^2 = \sum_{i=1}^{l} \sum_{j=1}^{m} (\mathbf{N}_i \cdot (\mathbf{R}^t(\mathbf{P}_{ij} - \mathbf{T}))^2. \tag{5}$$

The summation is over l pairs of corresponding 3-D and 2-D line segments. A point $\mathbf{P}$ on the 3-D model line in 2(b) might be one among two endpoints and center point of the line. The index m is the number of points selected on the 3-D line. $\mathbf{N}_i$ is the unit normal vector to the plane formed by each 2-D segment. The pose of the 3-D segments relative to 2-D segments is expressed as a rotation $\mathbf{R}$ and translation $\mathbf{T}$ applied to the 3-D points. The best-fit 3-D pose for a set of corresponding 3-D and 2-D line segments is defined by the rotation $\mathbf{R}^*$ and translation $\mathbf{T}^*$ which minimize (5). Solving for $\mathbf{R}^*$ and $\mathbf{T}^*$ is a non-linear optimization problem. The (5) for a specific point P on the 3-D model line is rewritten as:

$$e_{ij} = \begin{pmatrix} n_1 & n_2 & n_3 \end{pmatrix} \begin{pmatrix} r_{11} & r_{21} & r_{31} \\ r_{12} & r_{22} & r_{32} \\ r_{13} & r_{23} & r_{33} \end{pmatrix} \begin{pmatrix} X_{ij} - t_1 \\ Y_{ij} - t_2 \\ Z_{ij} - t_3 \end{pmatrix} \tag{6}$$

where $\mathbf{n}_i$ is normal vector components of the plane obtained from a corresponding 2-D image line and 3-D model line. The $\mathbf{P}_{ij}$ in relative to world coordinate system is $(X_{ij}, Y_{ij}, Z_{ij})^t$ and translation vector $\mathbf{T}$ between two coordinate systems from O_w to O_c is given as $(t_1, t_2, t_3)^t$. The number of unknown parameters in (6) is six for both of translation (t_1, t_2, t_3) and $(\alpha\beta\gamma)$ of rotation. From (6), we can create an equation that expresses this error as the sum of the products of its partial derivatives:

$$\frac{\partial e}{\partial t_1}\delta t_1 + \frac{\partial e}{\partial t_2}\delta t_2 + \frac{\partial e}{\partial t_3}\delta t_3 + \frac{\partial e}{\partial \alpha}\delta\alpha + \frac{\partial e}{\partial \beta}\delta\beta + \frac{\partial e}{\partial \gamma}\delta\gamma = \delta e. \tag{7}$$

For example, we can obtain six equations for three lines using two end points of a line and hence produce a complete linear system, which can be solved for all six cam-era-model corrections. In conventional cases, several line segments could give an over-constrained linear equation. Levenberg-Marquardt method provides a solution for linearized form of the non-linear equation [6]. The small displacement vector $\delta\mathbf{x}$ including δt_1, δt_2, δt_3, $\delta\alpha$, $\delta\beta$, and $\delta\gamma$ represent errors of each parameter and define the Jacobian matrix $\mathbf{J}$. The partial derivatives of e with respect to each of the six parameters are analytically derived. Therefore, Jacobian matrix is

$$\mathbf{J} = [\frac{\partial e}{\partial \alpha} \frac{\partial e}{\partial \beta} \frac{\partial e}{\partial \gamma} \frac{\partial e}{\partial t_1} \frac{\partial e}{\partial t_t} \frac{\partial e}{\partial t_3}]^t \tag{8}$$

4   Experiments

Experiments show that there is rapid convergence even with significant errors in the initial estimates. Several iterations are enough to obtain convergence of the parameters.

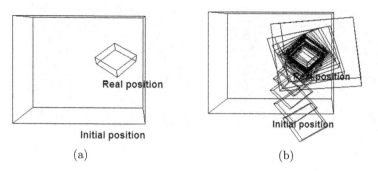

(a)   (b)

Fig. 3. Change of object pose viewed from camera coordinate during iterations. (a) Initial and true object poses viewed by initial and true camera locations; (b) Intermediate poses during iteration.

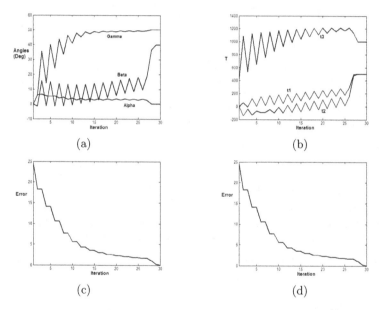

Fig. 4. Estimation of camera position. (a) Three rotation angles α, β, and γ values are shown during iteration; (b) Convergence of translation distance (c) Change of error values during iteration indicates successive convergence of the proposed algorithm (d) Error value in the case of 10 percent noise added to line data

Figure 3 in an experiment using synthetic image shows intermediate object positions that a false pose viewed from initial camera position converges to the exact object position with update of camera position during iteration. Figure 4 (a) and (b) show estimation of camera position parameters for above synthetic image. Three rotation angles and translational vector are exactly solved from the proposed pose estimation algorithm. Figure 4(c) and (d) show change of error value during iteration. Specifically, Figure 4(d) shows the error value

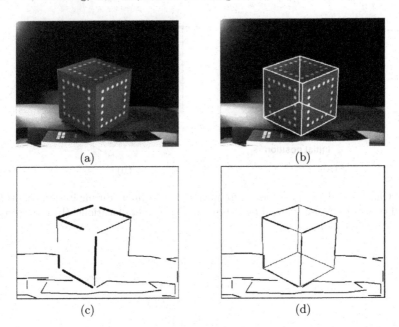

Fig. 5. Three dimensional object recognition for real image. (a) Original image (b) Model is overlapped to real image from the hypotheses (c) Line extraction with the found topological group (d) Model overlapped to line segments

when we added 10 percent perturbation noises to line data. Figure 5 shows an experiment using real image. Figure 5(a) shows the original image to be tested. After discarding the shorter lines, Figure 5(c) presents the extracted lines with the topological line groups matched for correspondence as described in [3]. The thick lines present an extraction of the line group.

Figure 5(b) shows the model overlapped from the 3-D pose determination algorithm of Section 3. The camera intrinsic parameters were solved previously by using the calibration box shown in the Figure 5(a). The thick lines matched in Figure 5(c) are enough to guide an initial hypothesis for 3-D object recognition. In this experiment, we set m=3 corresponding to two endpoints and a center point for a model line. And arbitrary three translation values and uniformly sampled rotation values in angle space are selected for initial values of six-pose parameters. In a few iteration steps, the con-vergence is reached. If the error function (5) for any initial values of six pose parameters is not reduced during a few iterations, the initial candidates are discarded and next initial values are tried from uniformly sampled angles. Convergence is very fast as within 1 sec in Pentium-4 desktop computer and we can reach the stable convergence if there is a solution.

5   Conclusion

This paper presents a new method to estimate the camera 3-D location and orientation from a matched set of 3-D model and 2-D image lines. If the correspondence is given from the relation between 3D model lines and 2D lines found in image, a key step of the 3-D object recognition is to find the rotation and translation matrices that map the world coordinate system to the camera coordinate system. We propose a method using roll-pitch-yaw angle to present rotation. We derive a nonlinear error equation based on the roll-pitch-yaw angles. The error equation is designed to minimize a point-to-plane distance that is defined as the dot product of unit normal to the projected plane of image line and a 3-D point on the model line transformed to camera coordinates. Levenberg-Marquardt method minimizes the error equation with uniform sampling strategy of rotation space to avoid stuck in local minimum. From experiments using real images, the proposed method is proved to be stable to initial values of estimating parameters. From corresponding line sets between 3-D model and 2-D real images, the method converses to good pose solutions in only a few iterations.

Acknowledgement. Dr. Kang is now a visiting research staff in Computational Synthesis Lab. of Cornell Univ., USA This work was supported by the Post-doctoral Fellowship Program of Korea Science and Engineering Foundation (KOSEF).

References

1. Kumar, R. & Hanson, A.R.: Robust methods for Estimating Pose and a Sensitivity Analysis. CVGIP: Image Understanding, **60** (1994) 313-342
2. Ishii, M., Sakane, S., Kakikura, M., Mikami, Y.: A 3-D Sensor system for Teaching Robot Paths and Environments. Int. J. Robotics Research, **6** (1987) 45-59
3. Kang, D.J., Ha, J.E., & Kweon, I.S.: Fast Object Recognition using Dynamic Programming from Combination of Salient Line Groups. Pattern Recognition, **36** (2003) 79-90
4. Lowe, D.G.: Three-Dimensional Object Recognition from Single Two-Dimensional Images. Artificial Intelligence **31** (1987) 355-395
5. Craig, J.J.: Introduction to Robotics: Mechanics and Control. Second Ed., Addison-Wesley Publishing (1989)
6. Press, W.H., Teukolsky, S.A., Vetterling, W.T., & Flannery, B.P.: Numerical Recipes in C, Cambridge Press (1992)

Spectral Coding of Three-Dimensional Mesh Geometry Information Using Dual Graph

Sung-Yeol Kim, Seung-Uk Yoon, and Yo-Sung Ho

Gwangju Institute of Science and Technology (GIST)
1 Oryong-dong, Buk-gu, Gwangju, 500-712, Korea
{sykim75, suyoon, hoyo}@gist.ac.kr

Abstract. In this paper, we propose a new scheme for the geometry coding of three-dimensional (3-D) mesh models using a dual graph. In order to compress the mesh geometry information, we generate a fixed spectral basis using the dual graph derived from the mesh topology. After we partition a 3-D mesh model into several independent submeshes to reduce coding complexity, each submesh geometry is projected onto the generated orthonormal basis for the spectral coding. We encode two initial vertices and the dual graph information of the mesh geometry and prove the reversibility between the dual graph and the mesh geometry. The proposed scheme overcomes difficulty of generating a fixed spectral basis, and it provides multi-resolution representation of 3-D mesh models.

Keywords: Spectral coding, fixed spectral basis, dual graph

1 Introduction

As the demand for high quality visual services has increased from consumers and the interest of three-dimensional (3-D) meshes has grown rapidly, it is essential to develop efficient 3-D mesh data coding methods. In general, a mesh model is simply a set of planar polygons in the 3-D Euclidean space. In order to represent a mesh surface, we can assume that the 3-D model consists of triangular faces. Basically, there are three types of information to describe the mesh surfaces: geometry, connectivity, and photometry information. In this paper, we focus on coding of the mesh geometry information.

Mesh geometry coding methods can largely be divided into two categories: spatial prediction methods and spectral methods. Deering [1] and Taubin *et al.* [2] traversed all the vertices according to the connectivity information, and then coded the vertices using a simple linear predictor in the spatial domain. Similarly, the mesh coding scheme by Touma and Gotsman [3] encoded the topology information as a traversal of the vertices in the spatial domain, and the vertex coordinates were coded by predicting them along the traversal order using a parallelogram scheme. Finally, the prediction errors were entropy-coded. On the other hand, Karni and Gotsman [4] proposed the spectral method for the 3-D mesh geometry coding. Karni and Gotsman projected the mesh geometry

K. Aizawa, Y. Nakamura, and S. Satoh (Eds.): PCM 2004, LNCS 3331, pp. 410–417, 2004.

onto the basis vectors that are the eigenvectors of the mesh Laplacian matrix. Although Karni and Gotsman obtained good results with the spectral method, there are some critical problems, such as difficulty of fixed spectral basis generation and tremendous coding complexity. In this paper, we are concerned about the mesh geometry coding using the spectral method and try to solve the problem of fixed spectral basis generation.

This paper is organized as follows. Section 2 explains previous works, and Section 3 describes the proposed spectral coding method of the mesh geometry. After we provide experimental results in Section 4, we conclude in Section 5.

2 Spectral Coding of Mesh Geometry

Karni and Gotsman showed us how to extend the classical Fourier analysis to 3-D mesh data [4]. We consider a simple 3-D mesh model that is composed of n vertices. The adjacency matrix of the model is represented by the circular n x n matrix, and the diagonal matrix is represented by the n x n matrix. Finally, we can obtain the so-called Laplacian matrix from the adjacency matrix and the diagonal matrix. The Laplacian matrix describes the analog of the second spatial derivative conceptually.

The Fourier basis functions for 2-D signals are obtained as the eigenvectors of the Laplacian matrix of the graph with the topology of a 2-D grid. Karni and Gotsman extended the 2-D spectral transformation to the 3-D mesh topologies, and they performed the spectral coding by projecting the geometry data onto the eigenvectors of the Laplacian matrix. We should note that the eigenvectors are not fixed since valences of the vertices can be different. In other words, the spectral bases are different according to the mesh topology. Karni and Gotsman tried to solve the problem by mapping an arbitrary mesh topology into a regular mesh topology [5]. However, serious deformation has occurred when the arbitrary mesh is mapped into a regular mesh, as we can see in Fig. 1. In this paper, we propose a new algorithm to generate the fixed spectral basis.

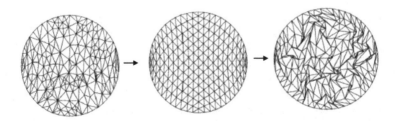

Fig. 1. Deformation problem

3   Spectral Coding Using Dual Graph

3.1   Spectral Coding Method

In order to compress the geometry information of 3-D mesh models, we propose a spectral coding using a fixed spectral basis. In the proposed scheme, we generate a fixed spectral basis from the dual graph derived from the mesh topology. In essence, we try to extend the popular 2-D transform coding approach based on the fixed spectral basis into 3-D mesh coding.

Fig. 2 shows the entire block diagram for the proposed scheme. After we analyze the input mesh model into the three types of information, we partition the mesh into several submeshes to reduce coding complexity. During the mesh partitioning operation, we obtain a dual graph from the connectivity information for each submesh. Then, we find a fixed spectral basis from the property of the dual graph. Finally, the mesh geometry is projected onto the generated fixed spectral basis, and the transformed coefficients are coded by a quantizer and a variable length coder.

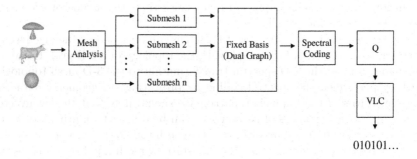

Fig. 2. Block diagram of mesh geometry spectral coding

3.2   Mesh Partitioning

Mesh partitioning is used to divide a 3-D mesh model into several independent pieces, called as submeshes. When submeshes are transmitted separately, instead of the whole 3-D mesh model, we can send the 3-D model more robustly to the receiver side since transmission errors may affect only some submeshes, not the entire model. However, the main reason that we perform the mesh partitioning in this paper is to decrease coding complexity of the spectral coding.

We apply a multi-seed traversal algorithm that is a well-known partitioning technique [6]. In the mesh partitioning, we should carefully select the initial vertices that are the starting points of the partitioning process. In this paper, we adopt the k-means clustering algorithm for initial vertex selection. When we partition a given 3-D mesh model into n submeshes, we select n vertices arbitrarily as the initial center vertices of the submeshes. Then, the initial center vertices are convergent to new center vertices by the k-means clustering algorithm. Finally, the convergent center vertices are selected as the initial vertices. Since the selected vertices are optimal positions, the mesh partitioning from these initial vertices can be performed in an optimal manner.

On the contrary, the k-means clustering algorithm needs more computation time than other algorithms, such as the maximum-distance algorithm. However, we do not require a real-time partitioning technique since the submeshes will be stored in a data storage through an off-line process. Fig. 3(a) and Fig. 3(b) show selections of the initial vertices by the maximum-distance algorithm and the K-means clustering algorithm, respectively, when the number of submeshes is three. As shown in Fig. 3, we can notice that the initial vertex positions, selected by the k-means clustering algorithm, are more optimal than those selected by the maximum-distance algorithm.

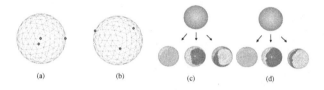

Fig. 3. Initial vertex selection (a) maximum-distance algorithm, (b) k-means algorithm, (c) the result of (a), (d) the result of (b)

3.3   Generation of the Fixed Basis Using the Dual Graph

Given a planar graph G, its geometric dual graph G* is constructed by placing a vertex in each region of G. The dual graph G* of a polyhedral graph G has dual graph vertices, each of which corresponds to a face of G and each of whose faces corresponds to a graph vertex of G [7]. Fig. 4 shows an example of a dual graph for the simple planar graph.

In this paper, we employ the dual graph to generate a fixed spectral basis. After obtaining submeshes from mesh partitioning, we generate their dual graphes by connecting the centers of gravity of triangle faces for each submesh such that we should be able to regenerate the mesh geometry from its dual graph.

As shown in Fig. 5, we should know the two initial vertices of the original mesh in order to regenerate the mesh geometry. We can construct a triangle face from two vertices, v_1 and v_2, of the original mesh and the one vertex d_1 of the dual graph. The third vertex v_3 of a triangle face is located on the defined plane. When we calculate the midpoint t_1 from v_1 and v_2, we can notice that the third vertex v_3 is located on the line from d_1 and t_1. Finally, we can find the third vertex v_3 by advancing two times of the distance between d_1 and t_1 from d_1. With this procedure, we regenerate the mesh geometry properly. In other

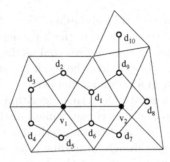

Fig. 4. Polyhedral graph and its dual graph

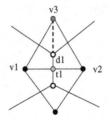

Fig. 5. Regeneration of mesh geometry with its dual graph

words, we can replace the mesh geometry with the first two initial vertices of the original mesh geometry and its dual graph information. Therefore, we encode the dual graph information, instead of the original mesh geometry.

The main problem of generating a fixed spectral basis is the irregularity of the mesh. We solve the problem by using the duality between the mesh topology and its dual graph. Since the 3-D mesh model is composed of triangular faces, valences of most vertices in a dual graph vertices are 3. This property is the key idea to generate a fixed spectral basis.

As shown in Fig. 4, the valence of each vertex in the dual graph is 3 when the triangle face is the inner face in the 3-D mesh model. When the triangle face is located on the boundary of the model and is not an ear, the valence of each vertex in the dual graph is 2. In case the triangle face is an ear, we can assume that the valence of each vertex in the dual graph is 1. With the assumption, we can generate the fixed spectral basis by analyzing each submesh topology.

In general, we can extract the boundary information at the decoder side since the topology information is transmitted prior to the mesh geometry information. As a result, we can generate the spectral basis with the extracted boundary information and the number of inner triangles.

3.4   Spectral Coding of Mesh Geometry

After the dual graph vertices are projected onto the generated basis, the spectral coefficients are coded by a quantizer and a variable length coder. In general, the spectral coefficients are uniformly quantized using between 10 bits and 16 bits. Finally, the quantized coefficients are entropy coded using a Huffman or arithmetic coder. We can provide the progressive transmission and multi-resolution representation of 3-D meshes by selecting the spectral coefficients to be sent.

4   Experimental Results and Analysis

We have evaluated the proposed algorithm with the COW model. It consists of 2903 vertices and 5804 faces. We partitioned the COW model into 20 submeshes. We used the Hausdroff distance [8], which is the common measure of 3-D model deformation, to compare performances of the proposed algorithm and other algorithms.

Fig. 6. 19th submesh of the COW model

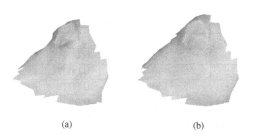

(a)   (b)

Fig. 7. Result of the 19th submesh (a) basis generation using a regular mesh, (b) basis generation using a dual graph

Fig. 6 shows the 19th submesh of the COW model, and Fig. 7 shows the result of spectral coding. We generated 196 fixed spectral bases for the 19th submesh. In our experiment, we coded 150 spectral coefficients of 196 spectral coefficients.As shown in Fig. 7, we had some deformations in both algorithms. However, our

Fig. 8. 4th submesh of the COW model

(a)   (b)

Fig. 9. Result of the 4th submesh (a) basis generation using a regular mesh, (b) basis generation using a dual graph

Table 1. Comparison of Hausdroff distances

Submesh	Vertices	Coded Coefficients	Regular mesh	Proposed Scheme
1st	182	130	0.0055	0.0059
2nd	156	130	0.0079	0.0062
3rd	158	130	0.0069	0.0059
4th	186	150	0.0104	0.0118
5th	187	150	0.0072	0.0068
6th	182	150	0.0058	0.0051
7th	152	130	0.0046	0.0049
8th	177	130	0.0102	0.0093
9th	174	150	0.0046	0.0039
10th	159	130	0.0064	0.0048
11th	185	150	0.0088	0.0075
12th	159	130	0.0041	0.0036
13th	172	150	0.0047	0.0039
14th	198	150	0.0072	0.0071
15th	188	150	0.0042	0.0049
16th	164	130	0.0051	0.0045
17th	161	130	0.0027	0.0031
18th	174	130	0.0045	0.0041
19th	170	150	0.0058	0.0035
20th	173	150	0.0069	0.0052

proposed algorithm had less deformation than the previous algorithm in the left eye region of the COW model, because there was mismatching between the original mesh and a regular mesh in the previous algorithm.

Fig. 8 shows the 4th submesh of the COW model, and Fig. 9 shows the results of the 4th submesh. As we can see in Fig. 8, valances of the 4th submesh vertices are all 6. As a result, the previous algorithm worked better than ours. Our algorithm had an error propagation problem when we regenerated the mesh geometry from the dual graph. We can overcome the problem by inserting a original mesh geometry information at the encoder side randomly to refresh the propagated errors. Table 1 shows the Hausdroff distance for other submeshes.

5   Conclusions

In this paper, we proposed a new algorithm for 3- D mesh geometry coding. We generated the fixed spectral basis from the dual graph derived from the mesh topology. After we generated the fixed spectral basis, we projected the mesh geometry onto the basis. Then, we coded the spectral coefficients using a quantizer and a variable length coder. The proposed algorithm can reduce the deformation after spectral coding and minimize coding complexity using mesh partitioning. The proposed algorithm can be used for progressive transmission and multi-representation of 3-D mesh models.

Acknowledgements. This work was supported in part by Gwangju Institute of Science and Technology (GIST), in part by the Ministry of Information and Communication (MIC) through the Realistic Broadcasting Research Center at GIST(RBRC), and in part by the Ministry of Education (MOE) through the Brain Korea 21 (BK21) project.

References

1. Deering, M.: Geometry Compression. Proceedings of SIGGRAPH (1995) 13-20
2. Taubin, G., Rossignac, J.: Geometric Compression through Topological Surgery. ACM Transactions on Graphics (1998) Vol. 17 84-115
3. Touma, C., Gotsman, C.: Triangle Mesh Compression. Proceedings of Graphics Interface (1998) 26-34
4. Karni, Z., Gotsman, C.: Spectral Compression of Mesh Geometry. Proceedings of SIGGRAPH (2000) 279-286
5. Karni, Z., Gotsman, C.: 3D Mesh Compression using Fixed Spectral Basis. Proceedings of Graphics Interface (2001) 1-8
6. Yan, Z., Kumar, S., Li, J., Kuo, C-C.J.: Robust Coding of 3D Graphics Models using Mesh Segmentation and Data Partitioning. Proceedings of IEEE International Conference on Image Processing (1999) 25-28
7. Joseph O.:Computational Geometry in C, Cambridge University Press (1998)
8. Chang, E.Y., Ho, Y.S.: Three-dimensional Mesh Simplification by Subdivided Edge Classification. Proceedings of IEEE Region 10 Annual Conference (2001) 1-4

Real-Time Free-Viewpoint Video Generation
Using Multiple Cameras and a PC-Cluster

Megumu Ueda, Daisaku Arita, and Rin-ichiro Taniguchi

Department of Intelligent Systems, Kyushu University
6-1, Kasuga-koen, Kasuga, Fukuoka 816-8580 Japan
TEL:+81-92-583-7618, FAX:+81-92-583-1338
{ueda, arita, rin}@limu.is.kyushu-u.ac.jp

Abstract. In this paper, we propose a system generating free-viewpoint video using multiple cameras and a PC-cluster in real-time. Our system firstly reconstructs a shape model of objects by the visual cone intersection method, secondly transforms the shape model represented in terms of a voxel form into a triangular patch form, thirdly colors vertexes of triangular patches, lastly displays the shape-color model from the virtual viewpoint directed by a user. We describe details of our system and show some experimental results.

Keywords: Image-based rendering, Shape and color reconstruction, Real-time computer vision, Parallel computer vision

1 Introduction

Currently, televisions are used for real-time, or live distribution of scenes in the world. In television, however, a video captured by a camera are displayed on a screen and the viewpoint is chosen only among camera positions, not among arbitrary positions. On the other hand, computer graphics techniques can generate a free-viewpoint video, in which a viewer can changed the viewpoint to arbitrary positions. However, computer graphics require a structure and motion model of objects and it is time consuming to construct such a model in advance. Then, we aim to construct a computer graphics model by computer vision techniques in real-time for generating live free-viewpoint videos.

Several researches have been done for generating free-viewpoint videos using multiple cameras since Kanade et al.[1] had proposed the concept of "Virtualized Reality". We can classify such researches into two approaches. The first approach reconstructs 3D shapes of objects and the second one does not reconstruct them. We select the first approach because it has more applications such as motion analysis, reflectance analysis and so on. As the first approach, Matsuyama et al.[2] and Carranza et al.[3] have developed systems which generate a computer graphics model from multiple camera videos. However, they cannot generate the model in real-time since precise shape reconstruction and model coloring from multiple images consume a lot of time. In comparison with these systems, our system cannot reconstruct a shape model precisely. However, our system can generate free-viewpoint video in real-time because of a new model coloring method proposed in this paper. Our system can be used for live videos from arbitrary viewpoints.

K. Aizawa, Y. Nakamura, and S. Satoh (Eds.): PCM 2004, LNCS 3331, pp. 418–425, 2004.

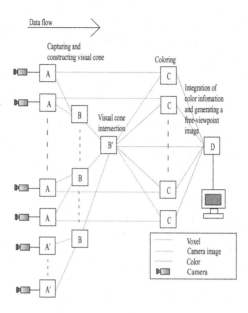

Fig. 1. System configuration

2   Free-Viewpoint Video Construction

Our system realizes real-time free-viewpoint video generation using a PC-cluster and RPV[4] which is a programming environment for real-time image processing on a distributed parallel computer such as a PC-cluster. Multiple cameras synchronized by an external trigger are placed in a convergent setup around the center of the scene. Each camera is connected to a PC.

The processes for generating free-viewpoint videos in real-time are as follows.

1. Reconstructing a shape model of objects by the visual cone intersection method[5].
2. Transforming the shape model represented in terms of a voxel form into a triangular patch form by the discrete marching cubes method[6].
3. Coloring vertexes of triangular patches varying with the position relation between the virtual viewpoint directed by a user and the viewpoints of cameras.
4. Displaying the shape-color model from the virtual viewpoint with painting triangular patches by interpolating among vertexes.

These processes are distributed to PCs shown in Fig. 1 and executed in pipeline parallel.

2.1   Node-A

First, each node-A extracts object silhouettes from video frames captured by a camera by background subtraction and noise reduction. Secondly, each node-A constructs visual cones. A visual cone is defined as a cone whose apex is the viewpoint and whose cross section coincides with the silhouette of the object. Visual cones are represented in terms of a voxel space. Lastly, each node-A sends the visual cones to a node-B and sends the colored silhouette image to a node-C.

Each node-A' has same functions as a node-A without sending the colored silhouette image. This means that a node-A' does not works for model coloring but only for shape model reconstruction. Shape model reconstruction requires as many cameras as possible. On the other hand, model coloring needs large processing time, and then it is difficult to use many cameras. The number of node-A's is determined based on the balance between model coloring precision and processing power.

2.2   Node-B

Each node-B gathers and intersects visual cones from multiple viewpoints to construct a shape model of the objects represented in terms of a voxel space. Since this process is time consuming, it is distributed to multiple node-Bs hierarchically. Node-B', the last node of node-Bs, transforms the finale shape model represented in terms of a voxel space into that in terms of triangular patches by the discrete marching cubes method. However, node-B' sends the voxel space and its corresponding patterns of the discrete marching cubes method instead of triangular patches since the triangular patch form is not efficient from the viewpoint of data size.

2.3   Node-C

First each node-C transforms the shape model represented in terms of a voxel space into those of triangular patches by the discrete marching cubes method using patterns sent from node-B'. Secondly, each node-C colors visible vertexes of the shape model based on one camera image. At this time, each triangular patch is divided into six triangular patches as shown in Fig. 2 since increasing the number of vertexes makes coloring resolution higher without lengthening processing time for shape reconstruction. Lastly, each node-C sends color information of all vertexes of the shape model.

For coloring vertexes in real-time, it is necessary to quickly judge whether each vertex is visible from the camera or not. Conservative visibility check method has to check whether each vertex is occluded by each triangular patch. That computation amount is $O(N^2)$, where N is the number of vertexes. So we propose a new method based on the Z-buffer method, whose computation amount is $O(N)$. Our method consists of two steps (See Fig. 3). At the first step, node-C searches for the object surface which faces against the viewpoint and which is nearest to the viewpoint in each pixel p. This step is realize by the Z-buffer method altered to taking account of not all surfaces but only surfaces facing against the viewpoint. Then, node-C lets d_p be the distance between the viewpoint and the nearest surface. At the second step, node-C colors all vertexes which faces toward the viewpoint and which is nearer to the viewpoint than d_p in each pixel p. The color of the vertexes is that of pixel p.

2.4   Node-D

First node-D receives the position of the virtual viewpoint directed by a user.

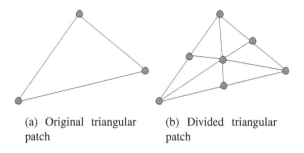

(a) Original triangular patch

(b) Divided triangular patch

Fig. 2. Dividing triangular patch

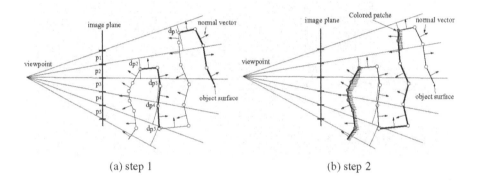

(a) step 1

(b) step 2

Fig. 3. Coloring vertexes

Secondly node-D transforms the shape model represented in terms of a voxel space into those of triangular patches by the discrete marching cube method in the same way as node-C. There are two reasons why shape model transformation is made on both node-C and node-D. The first one is because the data size of triangular patches is very large and the time to transport triangular patches is too long. The second one is because processing times of node-B, node-C and node-D are balanced best.

Thirdly, node-D integrates color information of all cameras. The integrated color value for each vertex is weighted mean of color value from node-C. The weight W_n of camera n is calculated by the following expression;

$$W_n = \frac{(cos\theta_n + 1)^\alpha}{\sum\limits_{x=0}^{N}(cos\theta_x + 1)^\alpha} \tag{1}$$

where N is the number of cameras visible the vertex, θ_n is the angle between the vector from the virtual viewpoint to the vertex and that from the camera viewpoint to the vertex

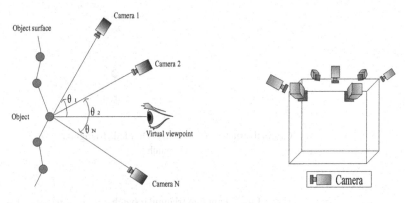

Fig. 4. Angle between camera and virtual viewpoint   **Fig. 5.** Camera arrangement

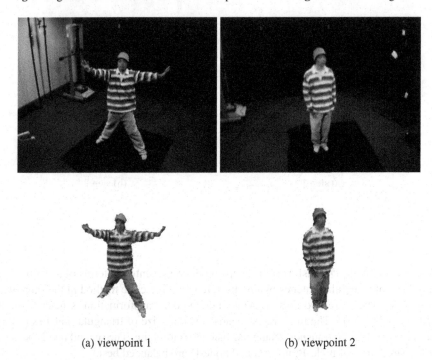

(a) viewpoint 1   (b) viewpoint 2

Fig. 6. Camera images(upper) and generated images(lower)

(See Fig 4). In this experiment, we let α be 1. Color value of a vertex visible from no camera is let be same as the mean value of neighbor vertexes.

Lastly, node-D generates an image from the directed viewpoint. Each triangular patch is painted by interpolating among vertexes acceleratedly on a state-of-the-art consumer-grade graphics card.

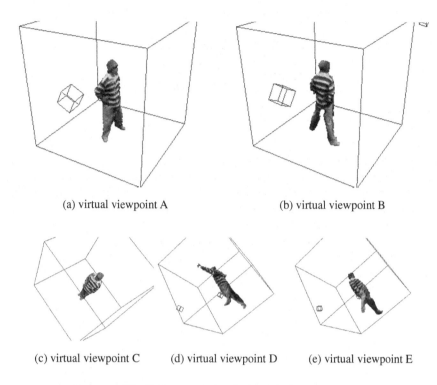

(a) virtual viewpoint A   (b) virtual viewpoint B

(c) virtual viewpoint C   (d) virtual viewpoint D   (e) virtual viewpoint E

Fig. 7. Generated virtual-viewpoint images

3 Experiments

Using our proposed system, we generate free-viewpoint video in real-time to evaluate
the precision of generated images, processing time of each node, latency, and the amount
of data transfer. We use 17 PCs (six node-As, one node-A', two node-Bs, one node-B',
six node-Cs, one node-D), each of which has an Intel Pentium4 (3GHz), 1GB memory
and NVidia GeForce FX. PCs are connected by Myrinet, which is a kind of Gigabit network. And we use seven IEEE1394-based digital cameras, whose resolution is
320×240, arranged as shown in Fig. 5. The ceiling camera is connected to the node-A'.
All cameras are calibrated in advance by Tsai's method[7]. Voxel space resolution is
$128 \times 128 \times 128$ and the size of a voxel is 2cm.

Fig. 6 shows two pairs of a camera image and a generated image whose viewpoints
are same. And Fig. 7 shows five generated images from virtual viewpoints. Each image
is well-generated.

Fig. 8 shows the sum of root mean square errors between a camera image and a
generated image with a same viewpoint. This may be caused by
– shape reconstruction error,
– camera calibration error,
– re-sampling error from image pixels to triangular patch vertexes, and
– color integration error.

Table 1. Amount of data sending from each node

Node	Average (Kbyte)
A (Image)	93.5 (variable)
A and B (voxel)	256.0 (constant)
B'	28.6 (variable)
C	92.0 (variable)

Fig. 9 shows the mean of processing time of each node in case that there is one person in the experimental space and the latency of the system is 200ms. Table. 1 shows the amount of data sending from each node. Node-D receives the largest amount of data, 600KB/frame, of all nodes. This data size requires 4.8ms for receiving via Myrinet. And the actual throughput of the system is about 20fps and 13fps in case of one person and two persons respectively. This means that the actual throughput is lower than the theoretical one calculated by adding the longest processing time (node-D) and the longest data-sending time (to node-D) owing to the overhead of OS such as process switching. However enough performance is realized by using a PC-cluster.

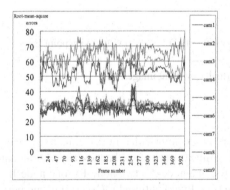

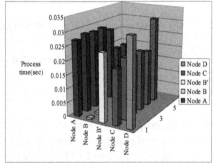

Fig. 8. Error: Cam 7 is ceiling camera unused for model coloring. Cam 8 and cam 9 are cameras unused for shape reconstruction and model coloring

Fig. 9. Processing time from each node

4   Conclusion

In this paper, we propose a system generating free-viewpoint videos using multiple cameras and a PC-cluster in real-time. And we make some experiments to show the performance and the precision of our system.

Future works are as follows.

Reduction of latency. The latency of the current system is 200ms. That value is not small. We think that streaming processing and data compression is effective for reduction of latency. Streaming processing is introduced only from node-A to node-B' on the current system. So we will introduce streaming processing to all nodes.

Algorithm stable against object size. The throughput of our system is not stable since the number of voxels and the number of triangular patches depends on the size and the shape of objects. We think that variable resolution of the voxel space depending on the position of the virtual camera makes the throughput stable.

Precision of shape reconstruction. The precision of shape reconstruction much effects naturalness of free-viewpoint videos. Higher resolution of the voxel space, shape refinement after visual cone intersection and better object extraction from a camera image are planed to make.

References

1. P. J. Narayanan T. Kanade, P. W. Rander, "Concepts and early results," *IEEE Workshop on the Representation of Visual Scenes*, pp. 69–76, June. 1995.
2. Takashi Matsuyama, Xiaojun Wu, Takeshi Takai, and Shohei Nobuhara, "Real-time generation and high fidelity visualization of 3d video," in *Proc. of MIRAGE2003*, Mar. 2003, pp. 1–10.
3. Joel Carranza, Christian Theobalt, Marcus A. Magnor, and Hans-Peter Seidel, "Free-viewpoint video of human actors," *ACM Trans. on Graphics*, vol. 22, no. 3, pp. 569–577, Jul. 2003.
4. Daisaku Arita and Rin-ichiro Taniguchi, "RPV-II: A stream-based real-time parallel vision system and its application to real-time volume reconstruction," in *Proc. of Second International Workshop on Computer Vision System*, Jul. 2001, pp. 174–189.
5. W. N. Martin and J. K. Aggarwal, "Volumetric description of objects from multiple views," *IEEE Trans. on Pattern Analysis and Machine Intelligence*, vol. 5, no. 2, pp. 150–158, 1983.
6. Yukiko Kenmochi, Kazunori Kotani, and Atsushi Imiya, "Marching cubes method with connectivity," in *Proc. on International Conference on Image Processing*, Oct. 1999, vol. 4, pp. 361–365.
7. Roger Y. Tsai, "A versatile camera calibration technique for high-accuracy 3d machine vision metrology using off-the-shelf tv cameras and lenses," *IEEE Trans. on Robotics and Automation*, vol. 3, no. 4, pp. 323–344, 1987.

Framework for Smooth Optical Interaction Using Adaptive Subdivision in Virtual Production

Seung Man Kim, Naveen Dachuri, and Kwan H. Lee

Gwangju Institute Science and Technology (GIST),
Intelligent Design and Graphics laboratory, Department of Mechatronics,
1 Oryong-dong, Buk-gu, Gwangju, 500-712, Korea
{sman, naveend, lee}@kyebek.kjist.ac.kr
http://kyebek9.kjist.ac.kr

Abstract. 3D descriptions of real scene are widely used for virtual studios and special effects in virtual production. There is an increasing demand for the use 3D models in realistic broadcasting applications. However, due to the limitation of system resources, densely captured 3D models should be simplified into a small size of meshes. Virtual CG(Computer Graphic) objects or real scenes can be considered as collections of rough 3D models. When CG objects are synthesized in these real scenes, smooth rendered scene due to optical interactions, such as lighting reflections and shadows, may not be produced. Although rough 3D models are used for optical interactions, smooth rendering can be achieved by using adaptive subdivision techniques. In this paper, we propose a procedure to get smooth optical interactions by applying composite subdivision method to synthesized 3D scene.

1 Introduction

3D models in broadcast applications have been used at the moment in virtual studios and special effects. In virtual productions, the main issue is the composition of virtual CG objects and real scene elements that are reconstructed 3D models from real world. For the realistic composition, several optical phenomena such as camera perspective, occlusions, depth perception, shadows, and light reflections, should be considered. In order to generate a full and realistic looking optical interaction, a 3D description of the real and virtual scene must be available for rendering the synthetic image[1].

In recent years many research activities have been carried out on 3D scene reconstruction from captured multiple 3D images or depth images. With the technological advancement of 3D depth sensors, especially 3D color scanners, scanned models are being widely used for several areas such as in computer graphics, geometric modeling, etc. Recently, a depth camera(e.g., Z-CAM from 3DV Systems) can capture a moving 3D scene at normal video frame rate[2]. However the complexity of reconstructed 3D models has increased much higher than that of graphics hardware techniques. Because of hardware limitations, it

K. Aizawa, Y. Nakamura, and S. Satoh (Eds.): PCM 2004, LNCS 3331, pp. 426–433, 2004.
© Springer-Verlag Berlin Heidelberg 2004

is necessary to reduce the amount of data by applying simplification methods in order to display 3D models in real time.

When simplified models are applied in optical interactions, rough models may produce non-smooth rendering results, since they have distinct normal vectors and distances which increase the difference of reflections between consecutive vertices. Normal vector interpolation approaches using graphics hardware such as vertex shader or pixel shader are generally used to solve this kind of rendering problem. However it is difficult to implement adaptive interpolation of normal vectors since neighborhood searching process is necessary to determine where to densely interpolate based on optical interactions. GPU(Graphics Processing Unit) does not support a high level of mesh data structure such as half-edge or quad-edge data structure. However, those data structures are available in the application stage of graphics rendering pipeline that consists of three conceptual stages such as application, geometry, and rasterizer stage. The application stage is driven by the application and implemented in software. Adaptive subdivision techniques in application stage can be used to improve the smoothness of the rendering results, even though rough models are used.

Uniform subdivision methods for surfaces are firstly introduced by Doo-Sabin[3] and Catmull-Clack[4]. Doo-Sabin developed subdivision method for bi-quadratic B-spline surface, whereas Catmull-Clack used a bi-cubic B-spline surface. Loop proposed a smooth subdivision method based on triangular meshes[5]. Loop's algorithm is based on the quadratic uniform box spline surface and therefore a triangular mesh is used. Most of subdivision techniques apply a refinement process and then produce a smooth shape of the surface. However uniform subdivision methods highly increase the number of vertices. In order not to generate unnecessary dense data in 3D models, adaptive subdivision methods have been used. Many adaptive subdivision algorithms are based on only geometric conditions such as curvatures or face areas. However, in this paper, we will consider optical interactions, especially lighting conditions of synthesized CG objects, as the refinement metric for smooth rendering.

2   Complete 3D Shape Generation from a Real Scene

Fig. 1 shows a 3D color scanner equipped by an active 3D sensor that uses active illumination technique. The system can capture 3D data of a million points in 0.7 second. In order to create a full and complete 3D description, real scenes are captured multiple times in different directions as shown in fig. 2(a). All data are then integrated into a unified 3D coordinate system. Fig. 2(b) shows a registered 3D model containing 307,348 faces.

3   Compact Shape Description

Since the captured model is very dense, it is not suitable for real-time broadcasting applications. Therefore simplification process is necessary to reduce the size of data. Mesh simplification is an important stage after 3D model reconstruction

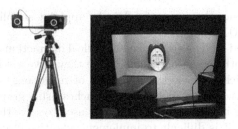

Fig. 1. Complete 3D shape generation.

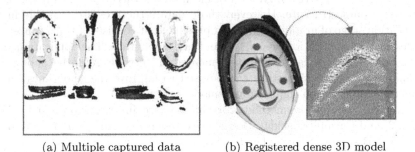

(a) Multiple captured data   (b) Registered dense 3D model

Fig. 2. Composition of virtual object into a 3D real scene

since the constructed models can contain a large number of faces that make them difficult to manipulate. Schroeder et al.[6] proposed a network filter to reduce the number of meshes based on the distance of each vertex to the average plane. Garland et al.[7] proposed a mesh decimation method based on QEM(quadric error metric). In our approach, QEM techniques are used and additionally color information at each vertex is applied to simplify dense 3D models. Fig. 3 shows simplified models. Since the simplification process takes color information into account, generated rough 3D models maintain a reasonably good original look although the number of faces is highly decreased.

4   Synthesize CG Objects to 3D Real Scene

Composition of 3D images using real scene and virtual objects are emerging technologies for virtual production. Many researchers have developed different image composition systems such as chroma-keying techniques[8] where foreground objects are placed in front of a screen of constant reference blue color. The chroma-key has the advantages of being simple to comprehend and yields a very good quality images. However, if the depth information is captured by a 3D depth sensor, we can synthesize virtual objects into any positions in real scene. Furthermore, once we created rough 3D model of real scene objects, optical interactions can be realistically performed. Fig. 4(a) shows synthesized a virtual

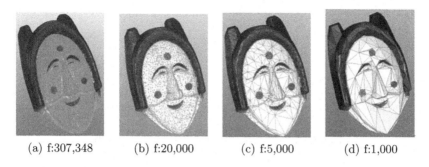

(a) f:307,348   (b) f:20,000   (c) f:5,000   (d) f:1,000

Fig. 3. Composition of virtual object into a 3D real scene

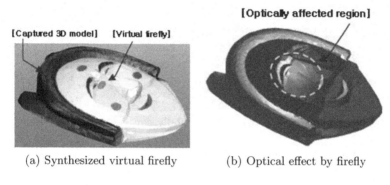

(a) Synthesized virtual firefly   (b) Optical effect by firefly

Fig. 4. Composition of virtual object into a 3D real scene

firefly model into a real 3D scene. If the firefly emits lights, some regions of 3D objects are affected by luminance as shown in fig. 4(b).

5 Adaptive Subdivision Considering Optical Interactions

5.1 Adaptive Subdivision

In order to get smooth optical interaction, we applied composite adaptive subdivision operators designed by [9],[10] as a sequence of atomic splitting and averaging rules. The API of adaptive subdivision enables the refinement of mesh face by using half-edge data structure enhanced by additional temporary information of the refinement level. Fig. 5 shows the adaptive mesh refinement process. Vertices and faces store corresponding refinement level and neighboring information. Fig. 5(d) shows the assignment of states for three rule sequences. The vertex at the center has been raised to state 3 since three rules such as face split, vertex averaging and face averaging are applied to an original mesh.

In case of uniform subdivision in fig. 6(b), the number of unnecessary vertices exceedingly increases as subdividing iteration proceeds. However, the adaptive

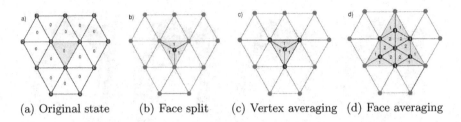

(a) Original state   (b) Face split   (c) Vertex averaging   (d) Face averaging

Fig. 5. Adaptive mesh refinement process[[9],[10]]

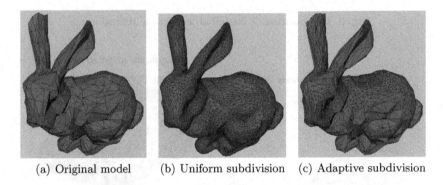

(a) Original model   (b) Uniform subdivision   (c) Adaptive subdivision

Fig. 6. Uniform subdivision vs. adaptive subdivision methods

subdivision method can produce reasonable number of meshes selectively. Since this operator applies low-pass filter to the vertex positions, it produce smooth meshes locally as shown in fig. 6(c). In our approach, lighting conditions are considered as criteria for subdivision, i.e., highly affected region by lights will be adaptively subdivided.

5.2   Simple Optical Interaction Test

Fig. 7(a) shows a simply tested model containing 85 vertices and 144 faces. The virtual CG object such as a firefly is placed above the model. When some objects are synthesized into a real 3D scene, they optically affect surrounding objects in types of interfered lights. In that sense, we assume that the synthesized firefly is a single point light source. The optical interaction is then formulized into an equation of irradiance E_i as follows.

$$E_i = \frac{I(n_i \cdot l_i)}{r_i^2} \tag{1}$$

Where I is the intensity of a point light source and n_i represents a normal vector at each vertex, l_i is the unit directional vector from vertex p_i to the point light source, and r_i is the distance between a vertex and a light source. Some

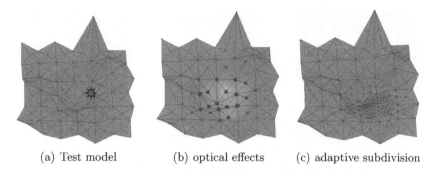

(a) Test model   (b) optical effects   (c) adaptive subdivision

Fig. 7. Adaptive subdivision based on optical interaction effect

vertices are highly affected by the irradiance from the point light source and are displayed with squared dots that correspond to the effect of applied conditions as shown in fig. 7(b). Based on calculated effects of optical interactions, we can decide the region in which dense meshes should be distributed for the smooth optical interaction as shown in fig. 7(c).

5.3   Applications

We assume that the captured 3D models act like 3D real scenes in our approach, i.e., arbitrary 3D scenery from real world also can be applied. The optical effects are directly calculated when firefly moves around the 3D scene model containing 5,000 faces. Fig. 8 shows the moving path of a synthesized firefly.

Fig. 8. CG object moves around the 3D model of real scene.

The firefly has lighting effects on particular region on the 3D real scene, and the interfered region is usually highlighted by viewers. Therefore, by selectively refining the affected region, optical interactions are smoothly enhanced. Fig. 9 shows adaptively subdivided 3D real scenes based on the effects of a synthesized CG object. Fig. 10 shows lighting effects of original dense model, simplified model, and refined model. Adaptively refined model in Fig. 10(c) shows much better rendering effects than simplified meshes given in Fig. 10(b).

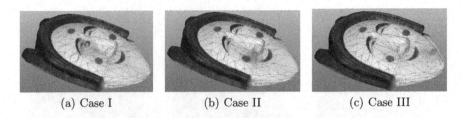

(a) Case I   (b) Case II   (c) Case III

Fig. 9. Adaptive subdivision based on optical interaction effect

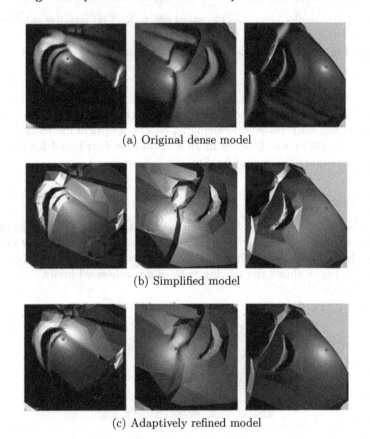

(a) Original dense model

(b) Simplified model

(c) Adaptively refined model

Fig. 10. Comparison of lighting effects for Case I, II, III

6   Conclusion

In this paper, we propose the framework of getting smooth optical interactions by generating adaptively subdivided 3D real scenes in the field of virtual production. We define new criteria of optical interactions for 3D model refinement. When CG objects are synthesized into a real-scene containing simplified 3D models, 3D real scenes are effectively improved based on optically interfered effects of synthesized objects by using adaptive subdivision methods. Experimental results demonstrate that optical interactions can be smoothly achieved without using dense 3D models. Since rough 3D models are refined adaptively, the increased number of vertices is proper for limited system resources of broadcasting applications. Recently 3D color scanners are widely used, but shape and color information can not be captured in real time. In the future we will consider 3D models reconstructed from depth images that is captured in video frame rate.

Acknowledgements. This work was supported in part by the Ministry of Information and Communication (MIC) through the Realistic Broadcasting Research Center at GIST.

References

1. Oliver, G., Marc, P., Graham, A.T.: Use of 3d techniques for virtual production. Proc. of SPIE, Conference Proc. of Videometrics and Optical Methods for 3D Shape Measurement, Vol. 4309. (2001)
2. www.3dvsystems.com
3. Doo, D., Sabin, M.: Behavior of recursive division surfaces near extraordinary points. Computer Aided Design, Vol. 10. No. 6. (1978) 356-360
4. Catmull, E., Clark, J.: Reursively generated B-spline surfaces on arbitrary topological meshes. Computer Aided Design, Vol. 10. No. 6. (1978) 350-355
5. Loop, C.: Smooth subdivision surfaces based on triangles. Master's thesis. University of Utah. Department of Mathematics. (1987)
6. Schroeder, W.J., Zarge, J., Lorensen, W.E.: Decimation of triangle meshes. SIGGRAPH 98 proceeding. (1998)
7. Garland, M., Heckbert, P.S.: Surface simplification using quadric error metrics. SIGGRAPH 97 proceeding.(1997)
8. Fukui, K., Hayashi, M., Yamanouchi, Y.: A virtual studio system for TV program production. CSMPTE Journal. (1994)
9. Sovakar, A., von Studnitz, A., Kobbelt, L.: API Design for adaptive subdivision schemes. OpenSG Symposium. (2003)
10. Oswald, P., Schroder, P.: Composite Primal/Dual root(3) Subdivision Schemes. Computer Aided Geometric Design,Vol.20. No.3. (2003) 135-164

Projection-Based Registration Using Color and Texture Information for Virtual Environment Generation

Sehwan Kim, Kiyoung Kim, and Woontack Woo

GIST U-VR Lab.
Gwangju 500-712, S.Korea
{skim,kkim,wwoo}@gist.ac.kr

Abstract. In this paper, we propose a registration method for 3D data which uses color and texture data acquired from a multi-view camera for virtual environment generation. In general, most registration methods depend on 3D data acquired by precise optical sensors. However, as for a multi-view camera, depth errors are relatively large and depths in homogeneous areas are not measurable. We propose a projection-based registration method to cope with these limitations. First, we perform *initial registration* by establishing relationship between multi-view cameras through inter-camera calibration. Then, by applying color and texture descriptors to projected images, *fine registration* is accomplished. Finally, by exploiting adaptive search ranges, *color selection* is attained. Even if the accuracy of 3D data is relatively low, the proposed method can effectively register 3D data. In addition, an effective color selection can be done by setting up adaptive search ranges based on depth. Through this method, we can generate a virtual environment that supports user interaction or navigation.

1 Introduction

Modeling of real environment plays a vital role in various virtual reality applications. Image-based virtual reality systems (IBVR) are gaining popularity in computer graphics as well as computer vision communities. The reason is that they provide more realism by using photo-realistic images and modeling procedure is rather simple. For generating realistic models, accurate registration of acquired 3D data is essential.

Until now, various methods for object modeling have been proposed. ICP (Iterative Closest Point) algorithm has been widely used [1]. Johnson proposed Color ICP to reconstruct indoor environment [2]. On the other hand, Levoy et al. registered 3D data of several statues, obtained from range scanners, by utilizing a volumetric approach [3]. A registration method for multiple range images using an M-estimator was also proposed [4]. Pulli proposed a projective registration method that employs planar perspective warping [5] [6]. Invariant features were used to improve ICP [7]. On the other hand, Fisher applied projective ICP to Augmented Reality (AR) applications [8]. However, most methods

K. Aizawa, Y. Nakamura, and S. Satoh (Eds.): PCM 2004, LNCS 3331, pp. 434–443, 2004.
© Springer-Verlag Berlin Heidelberg 2004

depend on expensive equipment, and require substantial time for generating 3D models. Cameras are usually used for modeling small objects in a short distance. Furthermore, effective registration is very difficult when 3D depth data includes relatively large errors.

In this paper, to remedy the above-mentioned problems, we propose a registration method based on color and texture information acquired from a multi-view camera for virtual environment generation. First, in *initial registration step*, we get initial pose relationship between cameras by inter-camera calibration. Second, in *fine registration step*, we project 3D data acquired from each camera onto a destination camera. Then, we find an optimized transformation matrix based on color and texture information by exploiting Levenberg-Marquardt algorithm. Finally, we determine adaptive search ranges in a *color selection step* and select the most suitable color.

In general, registration methods depend on very precise range scanners. However, it is expected that off-the-shelf multi-view cameras will soon be popular. The proposed method employs multi-view cameras whose depth errors are relatively large for a middle-range distance. However, we can generate a virtual environment conveniently by moving multi-view cameras. Furthermore, adaptive search ranges enable effective color selection. Although it has a disadvantage in terms of higher computational complexity than ICP, it provides better visual quality.

The paper is organized as follows. In chapter 2, we explain the projection-based registration method for VE generation. After experimental results are analyzed in chapter 3, conclusions and future work are presented in chapter 4.

2   Projection-Based Registration for Virtual Environment

The conventional ICP, based on the shortest distance, is not appropriate for registration of 3D data acquired from a multi-view camera due to its inherent depth errors. Thus, we propose a projection-based registration to carry out a pairing process effectively. Fig. 1 shows a flowchart of the proposed method. Fig. 1(a) depicts the overall procedure, and Fig. 1(b) illustrates only the projection-based registration process.

2.1   Preprocessing for Noise Removal

We assume that surface of the whole scene is Lambertian. However, we observe that some parts have very large variations in depth values even in a static scene. Thus, we must exclude unstable parts. In disparity map of a static scene, the variations of disparity values are modeled as Gaussian distributions. Thus, the threshold value for pixel i is determined by function of standard deviation of each pixel for excluding the unstable areas. A pixel is excluded if the following condition is satisfied.

$$Th_i(d) > \lambda \sigma_i(d) \tag{1}$$

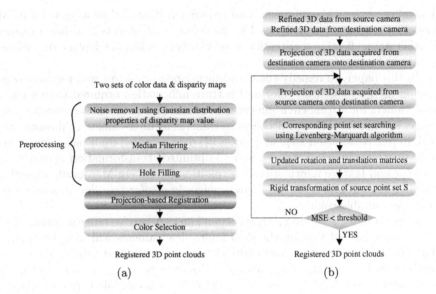

Fig. 1. Flowchart for projection-based registration (a) overall procedure for projection-based registration (b) projection-based registration part of overall procedure

where d denotes disparity and $\sigma_i(d)$ represents standard deviation. Scale factor λ must be decided empirically. $Th_i(d)$ is the threshold value for pixel i. Then, Median filter is applied to remove spot noises.

As a final step, hole filling is required on homogeneous areas or holes generated in the above step. We fill in the holes by only using valid depth values as follows.

$$
\begin{aligned}
x_c &= ((1-u)x_l + ux_r + (1-v)x_t + vx_b)/2 \\
y_c &= ((1-u)y_l + uy_r + (1-v)y_t + vy_b)/2 \\
z_c &= ((1-u)z_l + uz_r + (1-v)z_t + vz_b)/2
\end{aligned}
\tag{2}
$$

where (x_c, y_c, z_c) are 3D coordinates of the current pixel (within a hole) in an image. We can reach 4 valid points in horizontal and vertical directions starting from the current position. The corresponding 3D coordinates to these 4 points are (x_t, y_t, z_t), (x_b, y_b, z_b), (x_l, y_l, z_l) and (x_r, y_r, z_r). Here, u and v denote the ratios for horizontal and vertical directions.

However, this procedure generates errors if depth difference between adjacent pixels is large. To avoid this, we do not apply this procedure if depth discontinuity is larger than the threshold Th_{dd}, e.g at boundary of an object. After examining 3D coordinates of each of the 4 directions, we apply this procedure only to holes which are small enough to be considered a plane.

2.2 Initial Registration Using Inter-camera Calibration

In *initial registration step*, we calculate initial pose relationship between multi-view cameras by ICP-based inter-camera calibration [1] [9]. We estimate rotation and translation matrices, (R_S, T_S) and (R_D, T_D) using Tsai's algorithm [10]. S and D denote source and destination point sets, respectively. Each camera is a generalized multi-view camera with several lenses in horizontal and vertical directions.

However, back-projected 3D coordinates from each camera cannot be matched in VE due to inherent calibration errors. Thus, the inter-camera calibration is employed to find (R_S, T_S) and (R_D, T_D) by minimizing the distance between 3D grid points of a calibration pattern through an optimization process. Accurate geometric relationship between two cameras can be found by minimizing this distance. (The complete quaternion-based ICP algorithm can be found, e.g. in [1])

2.3 Fine Registration Using Color and Texture Descriptors

In *fine registration step*, we employ color and texture descriptors to obtain correct pairing. Fig. 2(a) shows the projection of 3D point cloud, acquired from a destination multi-view camera, onto 2D image plane. Fig. 2(b) is an image of 3D point cloud, from a source camera, projected onto a destination camera. Note that self-occlusion should be removed. Theoretically, Fig. 2(b) should exactly overlap with Fig. 2(a). However, discrepancies exist due to the errors in disparity estimation, camera calibration, etc. Therefore, based on the projection matrix P_S of a source camera, which minimizes errors in the overlapped area, we can register two sets of 3D point clouds.

 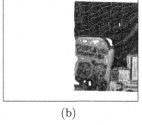

(a)   (b)

Fig. 2. Projection of 3D point cloud onto 2D image plane (a) projection of 3D point cloud of a destination camera onto its own image plane (b) projection of 3D point cloud of a source camera onto the image plane of the destination camera

We adopt color and texture information to define a cost function. That is, we split the whole image into blocks, and extract features by applying color and texture descriptors to source and destination images. Fig. 3 explains the process for extracting color and texture features from a single block.

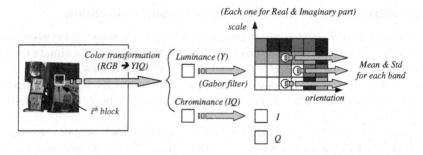

Fig. 3. Color and texture descriptors for a single block

Unlike luminance, shading does not have a significant influence on chrominance. Thus, a selection of a color space that reflects this property is essential for finding corresponding points between images. We decrease the influence of shading by separating chrominance from luminance in YIQ color space.

$$
\begin{pmatrix} Y \\ I \\ Q \end{pmatrix} = \begin{pmatrix} 0.299 & 0.587 & 0.114 \\ 0.596 & -0.275 & -0.321 \\ 0.212 & -0.523 & 0.311 \end{pmatrix} \begin{pmatrix} R \\ G \\ B \end{pmatrix} \tag{3}
$$

We define a cost function based on the color descriptor that takes account of only chrominance, as follows.

$$
ColorDiff = \sqrt{(I_S - I_D)^2 + (Q_S - Q_D)^2} \tag{4}
$$

We use a Gabor wavelet filter as a texture descriptor. Scale (frequency) and orientation tunable property of Gabor filter enables effective texture analysis [11]. Therefore, by applying Gabor filter (M scales and N orientations) to each block of an image, $M \times N$ filtered images are obtained for real and imaginary parts, respectively. We employ mean and standard deviation as features of each filtered image, and define the following cost function.

$$
TextureDiff = \sqrt{(\mu_S - \mu_D)^2 + (\sigma_S - \sigma_D)^2} \tag{5}
$$

where μ and σ denote mean and standard deviation, respectively, for each band of every block in source and destination images. Discrimination is very difficult in the shoulder of a bear or the upper central part in Fig. 3 because the color is similar. However, texture descriptor enables us to distinguish those blocks. The total cost function is defined as follows.

$$
TotalDiff = (ColorDiff) + \alpha(TextureDiff) \tag{6}
$$

where α is used as a weighting factor between color and texture information, and is determined experimentally.

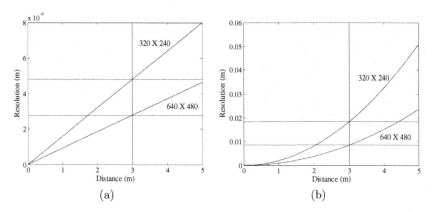

Fig. 4. Distance from camera vs. Resolution (a) Δx or Δy (b) Δz

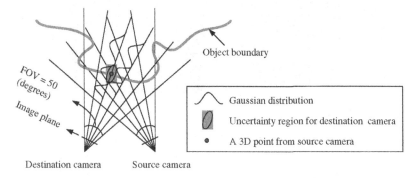

Fig. 5. An adaptive search range. When a point from a source camera is given, the corresponding point for a destination camera occupies an oval-shaped uncertainty region in 3D space

2.4   Color Selection Using Adaptive Search Ranges

After registration, for color composition between corresponding points in 3D space, we define adaptive search ranges that change with the distance between camera and object. That is, we use oval-shaped adaptive search ranges for color selection in overlapped areas. The multi-view camera has a correlation error m in disparity estimation and a calibration error p. Using 3D coordinates x, y and z, we can determine tolerance for each axis as follows.

$$\Delta x = \frac{pz}{f}; \Delta y = \frac{pz}{f}; \Delta z = \frac{fB}{d-m} - \frac{fB}{d} \qquad (7)$$

where d denotes disparity. B represents baseline and f means focal length.

Fig. 4 depicts the tolerances of Eq. (7). These values have Gaussian distributions for each coordinate axis, and correspond to standard deviations. We can apply the above description onto a pair of multi-view cameras as shown in Fig. 5.

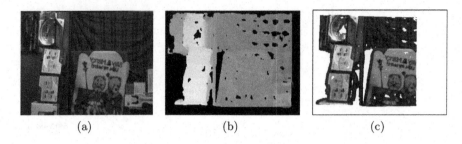

(a)   (b)   (c)

Fig. 6. Data from a source camera (a) original image (b) corresponding disparity map (c) 3D point cloud

(a)   (b)

Fig. 7. Preprocessing results (a) 3D point cloud (b) corresponding disparity map

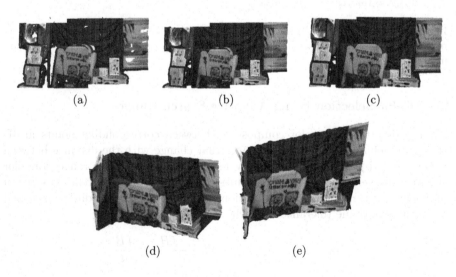

Fig. 8. Registration results (a) combined 3D point cloud (b) combined 3D point cloud after preprocessing (c) registered 3D point cloud (d) reconstructed mesh model (view 1) (e) reconstructed mesh model (view 2)

Table 1. Performance comparison among methods

Methods	Conventional ICP	Color ICP (YIQ)	Proposed method		
			$\alpha = 6.0$	$\alpha = 7.0$	$\alpha = 8.0$
PSNR(dB)	27.33097	27.36363	28.24907	28.25096	27.10863

(a)   (b)

Fig. 9. The comparison of visual quality (a) conventional ICP algorithm (b) proposed method (α=7.0)

That is, we can get Gaussian distribution linearly increasing with the distance along x and y axes; and Gaussian distribution increasing with distance along z axis. Therefore, we should consider oval-shaped adaptive search ranges, which change with the distance, to find corresponding points in D for 3D points in S.

3   Experimental Results and Analysis

The experiments were carried out under a normal illumination condition of general indoor environment. We used Digiclops which is a multi-view camera for image acquisition, and a Xeon 2.8 GHz CPU computer [12]. We employed a planar pattern with 7×5 grid points for initial registration. Distance between two consecutive points is 10.6 cm.

Fig. 6 shows original image, disparity map and corresponding 3D point cloud acquired from a source camera. Fig. 7 demonstrates preprocessing results. We can see that holes are filled only in small areas whose disparity difference is very small.

On the other hand, Fig. 8 illustrates registration results. Fig. 8(a) combines two 3D data. Fig. 8(b) and Fig. 8(c) show the results after preprocessing and registration. Fig. 8(d) and Fig. 8(e) show reconstructed mesh models adopting our algorithm.

In Table 1, performances of several methods are compared after 64 iterations. From the table, we can see that performance of the proposed method changes depending on the weighting factor α. Nevertheless, Fig. 9 explains that the visual quality of the proposed method is better than that of ICP algorithm. Fig. 9(a) and Fig. 9(b) show the results of conventional ICP and the proposed method, respectively. Actually, total error is larger than the conventional ICP in terms of the closest distance. However, we observed that the visual quality of the proposed method is much better than that of the conventional ICP. The reason is that the conventional ICP only considers the closest distance instead of data themselves. For performance comparison, we used *PSNR* as follows.

$$PSNR = 20log_{10}\frac{255}{\sqrt{\frac{1}{N}\sum_{n=0}^{N-1}(Y_{S,n} - Y_{D,n})^2}}(dB) \tag{8}$$

where N is the number of points which are valid for both images.

4   Conclusions and Future Work

We proposed a novel registration method that employs multi-view cameras for image-based virtual environment generation using color and texture information. The proposed method can be used for modeling an indoor environment even when we cannot get accurate depth information. Furthermore, it enables a user to navigate through the generated VE by wearing a stereoscopic HMD. The proposed method not only lessens the real-time rendering burden but also provides the user with more realism and immersion as compared to model-based VE. There are still several remaining challenges. Global registration should be optimized and the time required for registration should be reduced. A natural composition between virtual objects and VE requires light source estimation and analysis to match illumination conditions of the VE.

Acknowledgements. This work was supported by the Ministry of Information and Communication (MIC) through the Realistic Broadcasting Research Center at GIST.

References

1. P. J. Besl and N. D. McKay, "A Method for Registration of 3-D Shapes," IEEE Trans. on PAMI, vol. 14, no. 2, pp. 239-256, 1992.
2. A. Johnson and S. Kang, "Registration and Integration of Textured 3-D Data," Tech. report CRL96/4, Cambridge Research Lab, 1996.
3. M. Levoy, K. Pulli, B.Curless, S. Rusinkiewicz, D. Koller, L. Pereira, M. Ginzton, S. Anderson, J. Davis, J. Ginsberg, J. Shade, and D. Fulk. The digital Michelangelo project: 3D scanning of large statues. SIGGRAPH'00, pp. 131-144, July 2000.
4. K. Nishino and K. Ikeuchi, "Robust Simultaneous Registration of Multiple Range Images Comprising A Large Number of Points," ACCV2002, 2002.
5. Kari Pulli, Surface Reconstruction and Display from Range and Color Data, Ph.D. dissertation, University of Washington, 1997.
6. R. Szeliski and H.-Y. Shum. "Creating full view panoramic image mosaics and environment maps," SIGGRAPH '97, pp. 251-258, 1997.

7. G. C. Sharp, S. W. Lee and D. K. Wehe, "Invariant Features and the Registration of Rigid Bodies," IEEE Int'l Conf., on Robotics and Automation, pp. 932-937, 1999.
8. R. Fisher, "Projective ICP and Stabilizing Architectural Augmented Reality Overlays," Int. Symp. on Virtual and Augmented Architecture (VAA01), pp 69-80, 2001.
9. S. Kim, E. Chang, C. Ahn and W. Woo, "Image-based Panoramic 3D Virtual Environment using Rotating Two Multi-view Cameras," IEEE Proc. ICIP2003, vol. 1, pp. 917-920, 2003.
10. Z. Zhang, "Flexible camera calibration by viewing a plane from unknown orientations," Proc. of the Seventh IEEE Int'l Conf., vol. 1, pp. 666-673, 1999H.
11. B. S. Manjunath and W. Y. Ma. "Texture features for browsing and retrieval of large image data" IEEE Trans on PAMI, Vol. 18 (8), pp. 837-842, 1996.
12. Point Grey Research Inc., http://www.ptgrey.com, 2002.

Enhanced Synergistic Image Creator: An NPR Method with Natural Curly Brushstrokes

Atsushi Kasao[1] and Kazunori Miyata[2]

[1] Tokyo Polytechnic University, Department of Design, Faculty of Arts,
2-19-3 Honchou, Nakanoku Tokyo, Japan
kasao@dsn.t-kougei.ac.jp
[2] Japan Advanced Institute of Science and Technology, Center for Knowledge Science
1-1 Asahidai, Tastunokuchi, Ishikawa, Japan
miyatak@acm.org

Abstract. This paper proposes a non-photorealistic rendering (NPR) method for image creation which can produce various styles of painting. To create an expressive painting from a photograph, it is important to add artistic expression onto appropriate regions and to give viewers a natural impression. The proposed method introduces curly brushstroke generation for producing natural impression, and a new image merging technique for finding the appropriate regions in which to add artistic expressions.

1 Introduction

Non-photorealistic rendering (NPR) methods pursue the communication and stylization of visual images. Recent image processing studies also have been concerned with methods for generating artistic impressions, which involve using specific processing techniques such as the use of special image filters. These studies can be applied to promote novel artistic expression, and also to implement a tool which helps people without actual painting skill create artistically expressive images. This paper proposes a novel NPR method, called the "enhanced Synergistic Image Creator (E-SIC)", which can create new type of image rendering using natural curly brushstrokes.

2 Background

"Synergistic Image Creator (SIC)" [1] is the basic scheme underlying the proposed method. This section describes other related works and indicates their relationship to our method, and also gives an overview of SIC.

2.1 Related Works

Several NPR methods have been proposed for creating images automatically according to a specific artistic form [2,3,4,5]. In these examples, however, one

K. Aizawa, Y. Nakamura, and S. Satoh (Eds.): PCM 2004, LNCS 3331, pp. 444–452, 2004.
© Springer-Verlag Berlin Heidelberg 2004

special technique has been devised to create each specific expression. Therefore, the expression of each new style of painting requires the creation of yet another algorithm. Our method, on the other hand, codes an image, and applies the algorithms of various expressions to those codes in order to create an artistic picture. Therefore, within our framework the user can easily customize an algorithm for various types of expression.

Herzmann et al. have reported a framework for image processing by example, which generalizes texture synthesis for two corresponding image pairs [6]. However, their method only treats the features at pixel level, which makes it difficult to express painterly characteristics, such as artistic touches, in large homogenous areas and in highly contrastive areas. With E-SIC, these areas are extracted from a source image, and expressed in appropriate painting styles.

DeCarlo and Santella have devised an abstracted image stylization method based on human processing of visual information [7]. Their method represents images as hierarchical structures, relating meaningful image contents across image scales. Data obtained from an eye-tracker is used to predict the important parts of the image. The output image is then abstracted by pruning the structure with the obtained prediction data. E-SIC also represents an image as a hierarchical structure. The contents of the hierarchical structure in DeCarlo's method are mainly regional data, but E-SIC contains vectorized brushstrokes. By changing the characteristics of vectorized brushstrokes, the appearance of the image is easily varied.

2.2   Overview of SIC

We have adopted SIC as the framework, because our new method must have the ability to give an image various appearances. SIC takes the painting process into consideration [8]; it consists of the following three main procedures.

Image segmentation: This process divides the source image into segments, using color and edge information from the source image.

Vectorization: Each segment's shape, size, position and color is calculated and defined as vector data.

Brush Stroke Creation and Rendering Process: Each   vectorized   segment is transferred into a brushstroke. An image is rendered by painting all pixels in brushstrokes in an appropriate color.

Our new method adds to SIC the ability to obtain and classify the structure of the source image, and to create natural curved brushstrokes with that data.

2.3   Objectives

SIC is a promising NPR technique for automatically drawing natural and creative paintings. However, its brushstrokes are expressed only by linear formulas and it can not add expression individually according to the position of the pixel. Figure 1(a) shows a portrait expressed with lines. A stiff impression is created because every line is straight and holes in the image are filled by similar lines. It would be

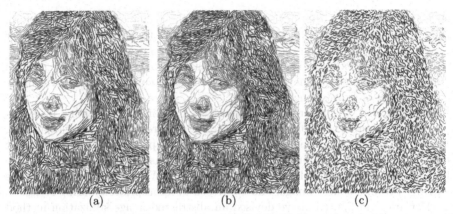

(a)   (b)   (c)

Fig. 1. (a) Picture created by conventional SIC; (b) and (c) were created by new curved brushstrokes with $A_{user}=2$ and $A_{user}=8$, respectively.

better if the drawing lines expressed natural curves and only important regions were drawn. The main objectives of this paper are as follows; 1) To create natural curly brushstrokes, and 2) find appropriate regions in which to add expressions.

3   Algorithm

This section describes the algorithm we devised to generate artistic paintings.

3.1   Brushstroke Creation

Brushstrokes are created from the arranged vectorized segments and classified segment information.

Legacy brushstrokes in original SIC: For reference, this section describes the method used to create legacy brushstrokes in the original SIC. Basically, brushstrokes are created by deciding which pixel belongs to which segment, as shown in Figure 2(a).

The distance function affects the shape of the brushstroke. Euclidean distance is not suitable for making a natural brushstroke, because it defines circular strokes, so it is necessary to define another distance function to make ellipsoidal brushstrokes. The distance $L_{j,n}$ is given by Equation (1) to make a natural brushstroke.

$$L_{j,n}^2 = x_n^2 + y_n^2 \tag{1}$$

$$x_n = (X_n - X_j)(D_{j,n} \cdot F_j)/N_j^{1/2} \tag{2}$$

$$y_n = (Y_n - Y_j)(D_{j,n} \cdot F_j)/N_j^{1/2} \tag{3}$$

$$D_{j,n} = |(tan^{-1}((X_n - X_j)/(Y_n - Y_j)))/\pi - D_j| \tag{4}$$

$$D_{j,n} = 1 - |(tan^{-1}((X_n - X_j)/(Y_n - Y_j)))/\pi - D_j|, if D_{j,n} \geq 0.5 \tag{5}$$

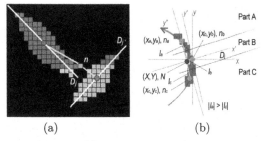

(a)   (b)

Fig. 2. Brushstroke creation. (a) The current processing pixel, n, belongs to the brush-stroke that has the shortest distance function in the brushstroke creation process. (b) Notation of curved segment.

where

(X_n, Y_n) : Coordinate of current pixel n
(X_j, Y_j) : Centroid of segment j
N_j : Number of pixels included in segment j
D_j : Direction of segment j
F_j : Thinness of segment j

When pixel n takes the position shown in Figure 2(a), and $L_{j,n} < L_{j',n}$, then pixel n is included in brushstroke j instead of brushstroke j', which is nearer pixel n in Euclidean space. Consequently, the shape of brushstroke j will be stretched along the long axis. Modifying Equation (1) changes the shape of the brushstrokes. Suppose that every segment is an ellipse. Note that this assumption does not mean that the actually created brushstrokes will be ellipses or symmetrical shapes [8].

Enhanced brushstrokes – Curly brushstrokes: In most paintings every segment is curved to some extent. Accordingly, defining the brushstroke with curvature parameters makes it appear to be more natural. A curly brushstroke is created by introducing curved coordinates. In this method, only the y-coordinate is deformed by a quadratic curve, as shown in Figure 2(b). It is not necessary to use a rectangular coordinate system, because we only need to define the distance from the origin of each arranged segment to the current pixel.

In the case of a legacy brushstroke, the origin of the coordinate is the centroid of the segment. On the other hand, in the case of a curly brushstroke, it is reasonable that the centroid of Part B is chosen as the origin of the coordinate system. Accordingly, the center of a curved arranged segment is shifted from the centroid of the whole segment to the centroid of Part B. Then, the axis of the coordinate is rotated by D_j. The new coordinate (x', y') is given by Equations (6) and (7).

$$x' = cos(D_j)(x - x_b) + sin(D_j)(y - y_b) \tag{6}$$

$$y' = -sin(D_j)(x - x_b) + cos(D_j)(y - y_b) \tag{7}$$

The final coordinate (x'', y'') is given by Equations (8) and (9).

$$x'' = x' + Ay'^2 \tag{8}$$

$$y'' = y' \tag{9}$$

where

$$A = A_{user}(l_b/l_a) \quad when \ 0 \le D_j < \pi, x_a y_b \times x_b y_a > 0, \tag{10}$$

$$A = -A_{user}(l_b/l_a) \quad when \ 0 \le D_j < \pi, x_a y_b \times x_b y_a \le 0, \tag{11}$$

$$A = A_{user}(l_c/l_a) \quad when \ \pi < D_j \le 2\pi, x_a y_b \times x_b y_a < 0, \tag{12}$$

$$A = -A_{user}(l_c/l_a) \quad when \ \pi < D_j \le 2\pi, x_a y_b \times x_b y_a \ge 0 \tag{13}$$

A_{user} is a positive constant controlling the curvature of the brushstroke. The generated artwork is faithful to the source image by setting 1 to A_{user}. A variety of expressions can be given to the artwork by controlling this constant. The distance $L''_{j,n}$ is given by Equation (14).

$$L''_{j,n} = \sqrt{x''^2 + y''^2} \tag{14}$$

A final curved brushstroke is created by choosing the region that has the minimum $L''_{j,n}$ for all pixels. Figure 1(b) and (c) shows the results according to A_{user} = 2 and 8.

3.2   A Method of Segment Merging

One of the most meaningful applications of E-SIC is to create artistic portraits. Creating an appropriate portrait requires not only holding the facial features, but also expressing an artistic style. Accordingly, in E-SIC a merged image segment is classified into one of three types: type 1 and type 3 segments are important for representing a source image; type 2 segments are used to vary the amout of brushstrokes.

Type 1: Contours and feature lines: A narrow segment, whose thickness F_j is greater than 0.95, is not merged and remains as it is.

Type 2: Large and homogeneous areas: First, neighbors for each image segment are listed. Next, a segment (dark green region in Figure 3) is identified, and the color differences, ΔC, between that region and its neighbors are calculated. The segments whose ΔC is within the color threshold value, T_c, are marked. After that, each marked segment (light green region in Figure 3) is identified, and the same process is performed again. This procedure is repeated recursively for each segment until there are no regions left to be marked, and all the marked segments are merged into one. This procedure is performed for n-th segment merging, by setting the threshold value to nT_c. The greater the color threshold value, the larger the merged segment.

A merged segment is fixed and classified as a type 2 area, if the following two conditions are satisfied: where, $N_{j,n}$ is the number of segments to be merged into j-th merged segment in the n-th merging process, and N_{all} is the number of all segments.

$$\begin{cases} N_{j,n}/N_{j,n-1} < 0.1 & (c1) \\ N_{j,n}/N_{all} > 1/60n & (c2) \end{cases}$$

In general, the merged segment that has a large area and that was merged under a lower T_c value is most valuable when creating an artistic painting. The value of T_c is given by Equation (15).

$$T_c = (C_{max} - C_{min})/T_a \qquad (15)$$

where,

C_{max} : Color of pixel having the highest intensity in all segments
C_{min} : Color of pixel having the lowest intensity in all segments
T_a : User defined constant (default: 80)

Type 3: Highly contrastive areas: The highly contrastive area is conspicuous if the number of segments to be merged is small. The merged segment is registered as type 3 if the following conditions are satisfied: the number of segments to be merged is less than 5, and will not be changed, and the color difference with neighbors is greater than $10T_c$ Figure 4 (a) visualizes an example of classified segments: the black segments are edges (type 1), white ones are highly contrastive areas (type 3), and those colored in another unique color, such as light blue and dark red, are homogeneous areas (type 2). This classified segment information will be used in the following processes.

Fig. 3. Segment merging: The region marked with green dot is the segment whose color difference is within T_c, and the segment marked with black dot is not.

3.3   Results of Image Segment Merging

In the process of segment merging, condition c1 is important for acquiring an appropriately merged segment. In general, it is hard to merge gradational areas into one. However, some gradational areas, such as a blue sky, are better classified into almost one area because sky is usually painted with the same touch. From now on, condition c1 will be called the adaptive condition. Figure 4 shows the effect of the adaptive condition. The figures in the upper row, Figure 4 (b) and (c) show results satisfying only c2. The figures in the lower row, (d), (e), and (f), show results satisfying both conditions c1 and c2.

(a) classified segments (b) $T_a=80$ (c) $T_a=160$

(d) $T_a=80$ (e) $T_a=160$ (f) $T_a=240$

Fig. 4. Results of image segment merging.

(a)

(b)

Fig. 5. Source photo.

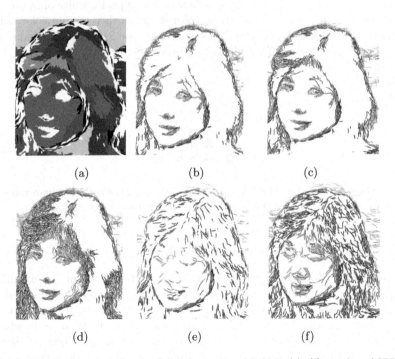

(a)   (b)   (c)

(d)   (e)   (f)

Fig. 6. (a) Classified segments, (b)–(d) results of E-SIC, (e)–(f) results of SIC.

In Figure 4 (b) and (c), the areas in the sky are merged incorrectly, but in (d), (e), and (f), the segments in the blue sky are merged into one. This is because condition c1 does not terminate the merging process while there still are remaining segments to be merged. On the other hand, target segments in (a), (b), and (c) are forced to merge incorrectly with region whose color does not match, under condition c2 alone. This fault also creates inappropriately merged segments in the facial area in (a), (b), and (c).

3.4 Rendering

Fig. 5 (a) is a source photo image and (b) is an enlarged image of a facial area in (a). Fig. 6 (a) shows the classified image segments of the photo in Fig. 5. Colored areas, black areas, and white areas are classified into type 2, type 1, and type 3, respectively. Type 1 and type 3 areas are the most important parts to draw. Fig. 6 (b) is the artwork created by drawing only the type 1 and 3 areas. Fig. 6 (c) shows the artwork with the addition of type2 areas classified at the 9th and 10th iterations into (b), and Fig. 6(d) is created by adding the 7th to 10th iterations. Fig. 6(e) and (f) are drawn by conventional SIC; they are drawn with only thin segments, which have a large F_j value, because the shapes of the segments on the edges are thought to be quite thin. Fig. 6 (b), (c) and (d) are clearly better than (e) or (f) because the eyes have not been drawn in (e) and (f). The ability to change the number of drawing parts without deterioration of drawing quality is one of the strong points of our E-SIC method.

4   Conclusion

We have presented a method for classifying the parts of a source image according to their importance to expression, and a technique for drawing parts with natural curved brushstrokes in order of importance. The proposed method can be extended to a rendering system to produce more than one painting style. Within this framework a user can easily design a desired painting style by customizing an algorithm to define the shape of the brushstrokes. In the future, we would like to pursue the development of a rich, expressive NPR method based on E-SIC.

References

1. Kasao, A., and Nakajima M., "Synergistic image creator - A picture generation system with consideration of the painting process," Systems and Computers in Japan, Vol.30, No.10, pp.13-21, 1999.
2. Gooch, A., et.al., "A non-photorealistic lighting model for automatic technical illustration," Proc. of ACM SIGGRAPH 1998, pp.447-452, 1998.
3. Hertzmann, A., "Painterly rendering with curved brush strokes of multiple sizes," Proc. of ACM SIGGRAPH 98, pp.453-460, 1998.
4. Shiraishi, M., and Yamaguchi, Y., "An algorithm for automatic painterly rendering based on local source image approximation," Proc. of the First International Symposium on Non-photorealistic Animation and Rendering, pp.53-58, 2000.

5. Hertzmann, A., and Zolin, D., "Illustrating smooth surfaces," Proc. of ACM SIG-GRAPH 2000, pp.517- 526, 2000.
6. Hertzmann, A., et.al., "Image analogies," Proc. of ACM SIGGRAPH 2001, pp.327-340, 2001.
7. DeCarlo D., and Santella A., "Stylization and Abstraction of Photographs," ACM Transaction on Graphics, Vol.21, No.3, pp.769-776, 2002.
8. Kasao, A., and Nakajima M., "A Resolution Independent Nonrealistic Imaging System for Artistic Use," Proc. of the International Conference on IEEE Multimedia Computing and Systems, pp.358-367, 1998.

An XMT Authoring System Supporting Various Presentation Environments*

Heesun Kim

Division of Computer & Multimedia Engineering, Uiduk University,
780-713, 525 Yugeom, Gangdong, Gyongju, Korea
kimhs@mail.uiduk.ac.kr

Abstract. MPEG-4 is a multimedia specification that can represent scenes composed of multimedia objects by unit of content. The MPEG-4 system requires the MPEG-4 scene information to be stored in the BIFS binary format. It also defines the XMT text syntax to facilitate easy authoring, distributing, and altering. Since XMT(eXtensible MPEG-4 Textual format) is constructed in XML format, it is easy to analyze the information on scene composition. Using XSLT, it is also possible to convert it into a different multimedia language, such as VRML/X3D of the Web3D consortium and SMIL of the W3C consortium. This paper presents an XMT authoring tool that generates the scene information in XMT, converts the XMT into other multimedia languages such as BIFS of MPEG-4 or SMIL, and supports various multimedia-playing environments.

1 Introduction

XMT is a specification document that represents the MPEG-4 scene description in text format[1]. The MPEG-4 scene description is defined in XMT format as one that enables an exchange of content among various environments. For example, the content written in XMT format can be easily parsed and then played in an SMIL[2] player, VRML[3] player, or MPEG-4[4] player. XMT provides two types of abstract languages: one is XMT-A, which has a structure of one-to-one mapping between the binary syntax of BIFS and XML, and the other is XMT-Ω, a higher-level description language based on SMIL. Therefore, the content information written in XMT can be easily converted into BIFS, VRML, and SMIL.

Studies on authoring tools and players for MPEG-4 are currently under way, although a few MPEG-4 BIFS authoring tools, such as MPEG-Pro[5] and Harmonia[6], have been developed. XMT conversion tools include HotMedia[7] from IBM, XMT-A reference software, Mp4Tool, and MPEG-4 Authoring Tools from GMD/Optibase[8]. Nonetheless, studies on those tools all focus on the conversion between BIFS and XMT and on the MP4 file generation. Since the organization

---

* This work was supported by grant No.(R04-2002-000-20026-0) from the Basic Research Program of the Korea Science & Engineering Foundation.

K. Aizawa, Y. Nakamura, and S. Satoh (Eds.): PCM 2004, LNCS 3331, pp. 453–460, 2004.

of the node is mostly a one-to-one correspondence, XMT conversion between two formats is relatively easy.

In this paper, an XMT authoring tool that is capable of generating the XMT file and supporting MPEG-4 BIFS and SMIL in a web environment has been developed in order to provide exchangeability between various multimedia languages, which is the ultimate goal of XMT. This authoring tool provides a visual authoring environment for novice users to generate XMT without requiring expertise in XMT scene description language. The authoring tool presented in this study can generate alpha and omega text files in XMT format as a basic functionality and convert the text files into SMIL and BIFS of MPEG-4.

Various playing environments and characteristics of different multimedia description languages are explained in Section 2. The structure of the MPEG-4 authoring tool and file generating method are explained in Section 3. The implementation and evaluation of the tool are presented in Section 4. Finally, Section 5 presents the conclusion.

2   Various Multimedia Descriptions

XMT is a profile that is based on XML and SMIL, which makes it convertible into SMIL, VRML, BIFS of MPEG-4, etc. Converted multimedia documents can be played in their own playing devices. In order to support various playing environments, the authoring tools need a common interface that supports two types of profiles in XMT. The scene description tree should be designed to include all necessary information. In addition, the authoring tools must be capable of converting generated XMT-A and XMT-Ω profiles into other multimedia description languages.

XMT-A is a low-level format that defines the binary MPEG-4 BIFS in XML style texts, whereas XMT-Ω is a high-level abstraction of MPEG-4 features that has a design based on SMIL. Due to the one-to-one mapping between XMT-A and each node of BIFS, conversion between the two is readily available. Although it is based on SMIL, the XMT-Ω has a number of tags that are not defined by SMIL. SMIL defines objects as audio, video, text, animation, etc., although it does not include the definition of two-dimensional geometrical objects that could be found in XMT-Ω. In order to represent two-dimensional objects, SVG[9], a two-dimensional vector graphic representation language, is used.

3   XMT Authoring Tool for Various Playing Environments

The authoring system proposed in this paper provides a visual authoring environment for XMT and helps users author XMT nodes easily and intuitively.

3.1   System Structure

The XMT authoring system consists of authoring interface, scene description tree manager, XMT file generator, and multimedia file converter. Figure 1 depicts

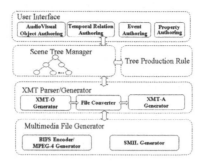

Fig. 1. Structure of the XMT Authoring Tool

the structure of the XMT authoring tool. The user interface provides a tool box for the efficient authoring of media objects such as two-dimensional geometrical objects, images, video, audio, text, animation, etc. It also provides authoring environments for event information and for time-space relation-ships between objects that form scenes. The tree manger generates and maintains the objects, the event information, and the attributes generated from the authoring interface in the form of a scene description tree. The XMT file-generating module gener-ates XMT-A and XMT-Ω, which are the two file formats of XMT specification. The files are generated according to the selected mode setting. The multimedia file generator is in charge of converting XMT into other multimedia file formats, and the authoring tool referred to in this paper converts XMT-A into MPEG-4 BIFS and XMT-Ω into SMIL to support various playing environments.

3.2   Scene Description Tree Manager

As a data structure with which the authoring tool manages the authoring objects internally, the tree manager provides the functionality of generating, deleting, inserting, and approaching the tree. Scene trees consist of scene information, object information, and event information. Nodes are specifically designed to enable scene trees to include the information of the two profiles regardless of the structure of a given profile. For the scene composition tree suggested in this paper, the event node, temporal relation node, and audio-visual node can be a child object of a group object with the group object as its root. If the temporal relation between audio-visual objects is not established, the audio-visual object is connected to the group object. The audio-visual object again has an attribute object. Figure 2 is an example of a scene composition tree with temporal relation and events. The audio-visual object, if written on a screen, is inserted as a child node of the root node with an attribute node as its child node. In figure 2, Video1 has location information, material, color, and time attributes as its child node.

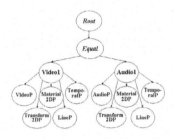

Fig. 2. Example of a scene tree

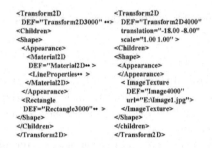

Fig. 3. Sample Generation of XMT-A

3.3   XMT File Generator

The file generator generates XMT-A and Ω files, and the parser parses the two files to generate the scene description tree. The file generator receives the scene description tree as input and performs a depth first search on the tree before generating the XMT text file. Rules for generating each XMT-A and Ω files are defined internally, and the text files are generated according to the rules.

(1)XMT-A Generation. The generating rules for XMT-A and BIFS are the same. All the elements defined in XMT-A are defined as the nodes of BIFS, and the attribute of each is identical. Although the file generating methods are different, XMT-A and BIFS can therefore be processed in the same module. Figure 3 shows an example of generating the rules of a basic object of XMT-A. As shown in the example, XMT-A is a method that describes the information of position(Transform2D)and shape(Appearance) prior to the description of the object(Rectangle). In the authoring tool shown in this paper, the scene description tree has a structure in which an object may have children nodes that hold the information about the object. Therefore, a module is constructed to search the scene tree in the order of the description of the XMT-A file. By putting all modules (that describe each object) together, a group is formed. Since a group

```
<rectangle ID="rectangle_3000" •• >
<transformation ID="transformation_3000" •• >
   <material ID="material_3000" color="#c0c0c0" •• >
   <outline ID="outline_3000" color="#000000" </rectangle>
<image ID="image_4000" src="E:\Image1.jpg" begin="1s" end="46s">
<transformation ID="transformation_4000" translation="-18 -8"
scale="1.00 1.00"></transformation></image>
```

Fig. 4. XMT-Ω Generation Sample

may not only have geometric objects but also another group for its children elements, the overall structure of the file is hierarchical.

(2) XMT-Ω Generator. Since all the elements in XMT-Ω are based on SMIL, the implementation method of the XMT-Ω generator is far easier than that of the XMT-A. Likewise, the file description method is similar to the scene description tree provided in this authoring tool. Figure 4 shows an example of XMT-Ω description. As shown in the example, an object is described first in the file before the information about the object is described later. Therefore, it is sufficient to describe the objects in the order of the search. Likewise, in the case of XMT-Ω, each object is processed as a module. Since an object can be a child element of a certain group, and a group can have other groups as its child element, the structure of a file is hierarchical.

3.4 Multimedia File Generator

The conversion from XMT-A into BIFS is easy due to the one-to-one correspondence in their structure. In this paper, XSLT is used to convert the XMT-Ω file into an SMIL file. The scene information generated in XMT-Ω is converted into SMIL, using The inputs to the converter are XMT-Ω generated from the XSL and the XSLT engine. The XSLT engine is predefined for conversion. The XSL file used in this case is based on the SMIL 2.0 schema, which refers to the conversion rule. The conver-sion process for the style sheet application is shown in Figure 5. authoring system, and XSL file for SMIL conversion. These two files are parsed to DOM trees by MSXML4. SMIL files are obtained by applying the DOM tree to the conversion engine. The XSL file is the language

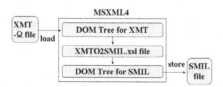

Fig. 5. File Conversion using XSLT

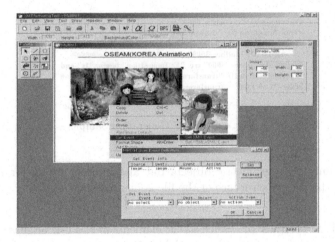

Fig. 6. Example of Authoring a Multimedia Scene

that describes the conversion method from XMT-Ω into SMIL. The XSL file is largely divided into two parts: one that describes the head of SMIL, and the other that describes the body. The head part mainly describes the information on the size and back-ground color of the scene, layout information on the output position of each object, transition information, meta information, and information process methods for switch. The body part describes the conversion rule for the information about objects that must come out as output. The composed XSL file consists of a number of templates. By applying the template to each corresponding media starting from the root template, it can be converted either into a unit of object or module.

4   Development and Evaluation

The authoring system presented in this paper stores the scene composition for playing multimedia as XLT, i.e., one of the MPEG-4 scene description language and outputs, using the two types of XMT in various multimedia formats including SMIL and MPEG-4. Figure 6 shows an authoring example of a multimedia scene as proposed in this paper. An MS-Windows operating system is used as the test environment for this authoring tool, and an interface was developed using Visual C++ 6.0. MSXML 4.0 SP1 is used for XSLT application. The media to be used in the scene can be added by selecting the icons located at the left hand side of the screen. The basic information about each media is displayed in the attribute window located at the right hand side of the screen. On the interface screen, the corresponding objects are positioned in the form of icons within the authoring space, and the playing time information for each object can be entered. The attribute of each object and each event information can be set up using the pop-up menu of the object, and the output sequence adjusted. Based on the searched information, the scene information is generated

Fig. 7. Presentation Example in SMIL Player

Table 1. Comparison of XMT Generation and File Conversion of Authoring Tools

Comparison items	MP4 tool	IBM HotMedia	GMD/ Optibase	Proposed Authoring Tool
XMT authoring interface	-	O	-	O
XMT file generation	-	O	-	O
XMT-A conversion of BIFS	O	-	-	-
BIFS conversion of XMT-A	O	O	O	O
MP4 conversion of XMT	O	O	O	O
XMT-A conversion of XMT-Ω	-	O	-	O
XMT-Ω conversion of XMT-A	-	-	-	-
VRML conversion of XMT-A	-	-	O	-
SMIL conversion of XMT- Ω	-	-	-	O

in the form of an XMT file to comply with the XMT schema, converted into BIFS or SMIL form, and played. An XMT file generated in this authoring tool was converted into SMIL and played by an SMIL player as shown in Figure 7. There are various SMIL players available, such as RealOne player from RealNetworks, QuickTime from Apple, or GRiNS from Oratrix Development VB. This paper chose RealOne Ver. 2.0 in order to use SVG as the output mechanism for two-dimensional geometrical objects. Since the time base authoring of XMT-Ω follows the basic framework of SMIL, it can be played as intended. In order to analyze the performance of the proposed authoring tool, MPEG-4 authoring tools that are either already commercialized or being used for developmental purposes are compared in Table 1. Since the proposed system is based on the language conversion of different multimedia, only those items that are related to the XMT generation and conversion are compared.

5   Conclusion

In this paper, an MPEG-4 authoring system that generates XMT was developed, and the method of converting the generated XMT file into BIFS and SMIL proposed. The authoring tool is capable of not only storing the scene information in the form of XMT but also producing them in MPEG-4 and SMIL, which fulfills the intended goal of supporting playing environments. To support various playing environments, this study focuses on the conversion of XMT into SMIL, which is the web environment, as well as the conversion into BIFS. Although it is based on SMIL, however, the conversion of XMT-Ω is not easy because a number of tags are not defined in SMIL. In order to represent the two-dimensional geometrical object that is not defined in SMIL, SVG, which is a language capable of representing two-dimensional vector graphic, was used. The XMT profile is generated using the scene tree information and converted into various multimedia languages. This authoring tool therefore increases the reusability of content and provides various forms of content that are suitable to the users' playing environments.

References

1. ISO/IEC JTC1/SC29/WG11, Working Draft 2.0 of ISO/IEC 14496-1/AMD3, N3385, June 2000.
2. Synchronized Multimedia Integration Language (SMIL) 1.0 Specification, W3C Recommendation, http://www.w3.org/TR/ REC-smil, 1998.
3. VRML 97, ISO/IEC DIS 14772-1, 1997.
4. ISO/IEC FCD 14496-1, Part 1: Systems, ISO/IEC JTC1/SC29/WG11 N2201, Approved at the 43rd Meeting, 1998.
5. S. Boughoufalah, J. Dufourd and F. Bouihaguet, "MPEG-Pro, an Authoring System for MPEG-4 with Temporal Constraints and Template Guided Editing," Proceedings of the 2000 IEEE International Conference on Multimedia and Expo, 2000.
6. Boughoufalah, S., Brelot, M., Bouihaguet, F. and Dufourd, J., "A Template-guided authoring environment to produce MPEG-4 content for the web, " Proceedings of MediaFutures 2001.
7. http://www.alphaworks.ibm.com/tech/tk4mpeg4/
8. http://www.fokus.gmd.de/research/cc/magic
9. Scalable Vector Graphics (SVG) 1.1 Specification, W3C Recommendation, http://www.w3.org/TR/SVG11/REC-smil, 2003.

An Adaptive Scene Compositor Model in MPEG-4 Player for Mobile Device

Hyunju Lee and Sangwook Kim

Computer Science Department, Kyungpook National University
1370 Sankyuk-dong Buk-gu, Daegu, 702-701, Korea
{hyunju, swkim}@cs.knu.ac.kr

Abstract. MPEG-4 supports dynamic scene composition through various interactions such as adding/removing/replacing objects and changing object's properties. MPEG-4 content can express rich meanings through various dynamic scene composition by object-based, and can be played to mobile or desktop environment. Therefore, the MPEG-4 player must effectively play according authoring purpose and meaning, and compose dynamic scene in any device. This paper proposes an adaptive scene compositor model. It is optimized for dynamic scene composition of MPEG-4 content in mobile device. This model supports exact analysis of the scene description, core information extraction for rendering through extraction rule table and object-based information management for object's reusability and flexibility.

1 Introduction

MPEG-4(Moving Picture Experts Group, ISO/IEC 14496)[1] is an international standard, comprehensive multimedia content standard that covers the coded representation and composition of media objects, interaction between objects, interaction between user and object, scene description, delivery and synchronization of media data. The MPEG-4 defines a multimedia system for interoperable communication of complex scenes containing various audiovisual objects.

The MPEG-4 player must play audiovisual scene that consists of various media objects, which change scene dynamically and also support various network environment. Other existing MPEG-4 players for mobile environment focus on transmitting and playing the limited number of multimedia data according to MPEG-4 standard. Therefore, it is insufficient for characteristic of MPEG-4 such as playback of various objects and playback of dynamic scene composition in any device environment.

In general, the MPEG-4 player's content playback is as follows. The MPEG-4 file formatter analyzes the header of an MPEG-4 file, which separates several media data that are included in a file, and delivers it to the system decoder. The system decoder reads media data in decoder buffer, and decodes according to decoding time. The audiovisual data is stored to composition buffer. The scene compositor analyzes the scene description, and arranges data of composition buffer on a screen. The player receives various user interactions.

K. Aizawa, Y. Nakamura, and S. Satoh (Eds.): PCM 2004, LNCS 3331, pp. 461–469, 2004.
© Springer-Verlag Berlin Heidelberg 2004

For effective scene composition of dynamic MPEG-4 content in mobile device, we propose an adaptive scene compositor in MPEG-4 player. This scene compositor supports object information of scene description sufficiently. In order to improve content's playback efficiency in mobile device, the scene compositor provides module optimization from scene description's parsing to scene rendering. The scene compositor supports three core components: the content analyzer for analyzing/applying the scene description, the information manager for object-based management and the presenter for composition/rendering the scene.

This paper is organized as follows. Section 2 describes the scene compositor in the MPEG-4 player. Section 3 shows implementation result and evaluations. Finally, section 4 presents conclusions.

2   The Scene Compositor

The adaptive scene compositor module is composed of three major processing parts. These are the content analyzer for scene description's analyzing, the information manager for independent management of object information according to object's properties and the presenter for composition and rendering the scene. In order to expand module easily, this each module in scene compositor is managed independently.

Figure 1 shows the processing step of the scene compositor in the MPEG-4 player.

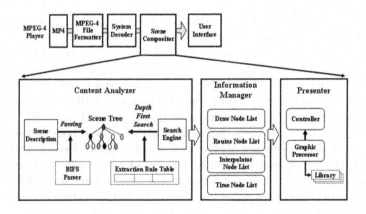

Fig. 1. The processing step of the scene compositor in the MPEG-4 player

After parsing the scene description, the scene tree is created. The search engine traverses a scene tree and extracts necessary information. To improve rendering efficiency, we redefined the information manager in order to object-based media management. We are going to explain in detail in next section.

2.1   The Content Analyzer

The content analyzer analyzes exactly the scene description of MPEG-4 content, searches and extracts the core information of objects that need to rendering. It consists of the BIFS parser, the search engine and the extraction rule table.

The MPEG-4 describes the composition of a complex scene relies on the concept of both BIFS and OD. The BIFS(BInary Format for Scenes) describes the spatial-temporal composition of objects in a scene and provides this data to the presentation layer of the MPEG-4 terminal. The OD(Object Descriptor)[2]-[4] identifies and describes elementary streams and associates these streams with corresponding audiovisual scene data. It is used to connect BIFS and media stream resources. The MPEG-4 describes objects and their behavior in hierarchical models. The MPEG-4 uses the concept of a scene tree with object nodes. The scene tree can be obtained through BIFS parsing, and is a data structure used to hierarchically organize and manage the content of spatially oriented scene data. The multimedia information that is defined in scene tree can extract the necessary information through various search mechanism and can manage data from the user's point of view. To support sufficiently object's interactive information that is defined in tree, the MPEG-4 player needs to search the tree fast and exactly. It is important to MPEG-4 player's performance evaluation.

In this paper, we use a top-down method and DFS(Depth First Search) mechanism for object-based search. The search engine receives a tree's header, searches an object node and judges whether searched object node can draw. Now, current playback time and drawing order are considered. When the search engine searches an object, we extract object information according to extraction rules. The extracted object information is stored in the information manager.

Figure 2 shows the extraction rule table's contents.

Object	Field	Field Type	Object	Field	Field Type
Video Audio Image	url	mpeg4_url(char)	Text	whichChoice	mpeg4_int32 (short)
	whichChoice	mpeg4_int32 (short)		center	mpeg4_vec2f(float x, y)
	center	mpeg4_vec2f(float x, y)		scale	mpeg4_vec2f(float x, y)
	scale	mpeg4_vec2f(float x, y)		drawingOrder	mpeg4_float (float)
	drawingOrder	mpeg4_float (float)		translation	mpeg4_vec2f(float x, y)
	translation	mpeg4_vec2f(float x, y)		diffuseColor	mpeg4_color(float r, g, b)

Object	Field	Field Type			filled	mpeg4_bool (char)
Circle Rectangle Line	whichChoice	mpeg4_int32 (short)			transparency	mpeg4_float (float)
	center	mpeg4_vec2f(float x, y)			lineColor	mpeg4_color(float r, g, b)
	scale	mpeg4_vec2f(float x, y)			width	mpeg4_float (float)
	drawingOrder	mpeg4_float (float)			string	mpeg4_string (char)
	translation	mpeg4_vec2f(float x, y)			length	mpeg4_float(float)
	diffuseColor	mpeg4_color(float r, g, b)			family	mpeg4_string (char)
	filled	mpeg4_bool (char)			horizontal	mpeg4_bool (char)
	transparency	mpeg4_float (float)			justify	mpeg4_string (char)
	lineColor	mpeg4_color(float r, g, b)			size	mpeg4_float (float)
	width	mpeg4_float (float)			spacing	mpeg4_float (float)
					style	mpeg4_string (char)

Fig. 2. The extraction rule table

The extraction rule table is basis of search engine and information manager. In extraction rule table, object and object's main property field are defined. This is objects and object's properties that can do playback in mobile device, and is possible to extend according to playback environment. For example, if search engine searches a video object, the scene compositor extracts property information such as url, whichChoice, center, scale, drawingOrder, translation that is defined to extraction rule table. We can do optimization of search through core information in extraction rule table.

2.2   The Information Manager

The BIFS parser[5] creates interiorly the scene tree through scene description parsing. We applied the optimized search technique of scene tree to the MPEG-4 player. However, a tree is only possible hierarchic management of all object information that is included in MPEG-4 content. For reusability and flexibility of object-based, we propose the information manager that manages object information efficiently. It consists of five data structure and is designed adaptively for rendering.

The main characteristic of MPEG-4 is the object-based coding and representation of an audiovisual scene. For rendering object management, we create the DNL(Draw Node List). The DNL consists of head and sub. It is a structure that is added to the head and subs whenever an object is searched, searching is continued to last node of scene tree. The head contains object ID, the sub contains several property nodes. Whenever user event happens, the DNL is real-time updated. Several field's values of target object in the DNL are changed. The presenter again renders after recomposing the DNL.

The MPEG-4 BIFS's ROUTEs mechanism describes interactivity and behavior of objects. The event model of MPEG-4 uses ROUTEs to propagate events between scene elements. ROUTEs are comprised of connections that assign the value of one field to another field in the tree interiorly. It is information that processes dynamic user events that are defined in the MPEG-4 standard. ROUTEs combined with interpolators can cause animation in a scene. We create the RNL(Routes Node List) for interaction processing. The RNL consists of source object ID, event type, target object ID, the property field, and modification values. We extract interactive information after scene description's ROUTEs definition part parsing.

The MPEG-4 scenes can display a wide range of complicated dynamical behavior. The MPEG-4 provides stream animation to the scene with the BIFS-Animation tool. BIFS-Animation is a dynamic scene composition framework that enables optimal compression of the animation of all parameters of a scene. We compose two INLs (Interpolator Node List) for interpolator processing. If an object includes interpolator node when the search engine searches a scene tree, the search engine divides whether interpolator information is color or position, and store it in each List (CINL: Color Interpolator Node List, PINL: Position Interpolator Node List). The interpolator information consists of key and key-

Value. The INL consists of object ID, key(time value) and keyValue(changing value according to key).

The MPEG-4's another mechanism for dynamic scene composition is time-related interaction. In this paper, we create the TNL(Time Node List) for time-related interaction. An object needs playback start time and end time. The MPEG-4 player sets the system timer and processes the content's time information. The TNL consists of object ID, time value(start time or end time) and property value. The property value is activity or inactivity information of object. The time information is defined in the scene description's last part. The MPEG-4 can give playback time in object when content created. The MPEG-4 player preferentially processes time information than other user events. Each object of the first screen is played according to time information that is defined to the TNL, and receives other user events in addition.

Figure 3 shows five data structure of the information manager.

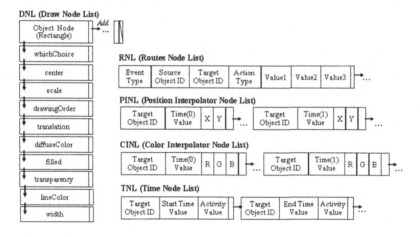

Fig. 3. Five data structure in the information manager

The information manager manages rendering and interaction processing by object-based, and reduces tree recomposition and frequent search of object information. Therefore, the new data structure reduces the load of system-side for additional scene update processing. Whenever scene is updated, it can offer high-level quality of scene to user through object's reusability.

2.3   The Presenter

In MPEG-4 Systems, scene rendering uses various frameworks. For scene rendering, the presenter consists of two components: the graphic processor and the controller.

The graphic processor consists of various graphic libraries to render various audiovisual object types. These graphic libraries consist of video/audio/image library for rendering, and support various data formats such as MP4v/H.264 video format, MPEG-4 AAC/G.723 audio format and JPEG/GIF/BMP image format. In order to expand easily scope of audiovisual data types by adding various kinds of graphic library, the library is independently managed from the presenter. Therefore, the presenter can support different audiovisual data types as well as various kinds of graphic libraries.

The controller connects media streams in scene compositor with media's graphic library in presenter. For example, if media object is mp4v format video object, the controller connects to video format library. If media object is JPEG format image object, the controller connects to JPEG format library. The controller is also independent module.

3   Implementation and Evaluation

The scene compositor supports Complete2D profile of the MPEG-4 standard. Additionally, the scene compositor can manage the MPEG-4 content that consists of various media objects. The scene compositor can be included in desktop's MPEG-4 player as well as mobile(PDA) device's MPEG-4 player. It is difficult that mobile device's MPEG-4 player plays various media objects at the same time due to resource limitations. Therefore, content's playback quality is inferior in case of desktop's player. This proposed scene compositor model is optimized to be applied on mobile-based player and desktop-based player. This scene compositor's development uses C/C++ in MS-Windows 2000/XP and Linux environment.

Figure 4 shows an execution example of MPEG-4 content in CLM MPEG-4 player. The CLM player contains our scene compositor model fully.

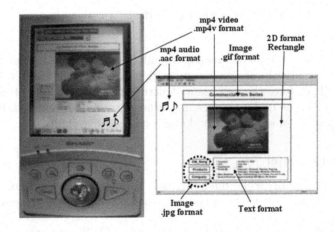

Fig. 4. An execution of MPEG-4 content in MPEG-4 player for PDA and desktop

In figure 4, an MPEG-4 content consists of an MPEG-4 video object(PDA: QCIF size 176x144 pixels, Desktop: CIF size 352x288 pixels), an MPEG-4 audio object(AAC mono, 64Kbps), several GIF/JPEG format images, and a geometric object. The image object receives click event. This MPEG-4 content is manufactured as commercial film and made from the MPEG-4 Authoring System[6]. We made two contents because playback environment is different. Object's sizes in contents are different but content's purpose and meaning are same.

Fig. 5. An MPEG-4 content's playback example

In figure 5, the CLM player is PDA-based. The MPEG-4 content supports several user interactions.

The MPEG-4 scene's action scenario is as follows.

(a) The first scene is composed of two image objects, a front image object receives user's click event.

(b) If event happens, second scene runs. The second scene is composed of a title of image format, an MPEG-4 video object, three image icons and a rectangle object of background. All objects excepting video are defined time-related event. All objects are played after video playback 5 seconds.

(c) The video object is presented, the three icon images receive click event and presents a text. Video object is played during 4 minutes. While video object is played, user can give event in image object.

(d) If MPEG-4 video object ends, then the scene is ended.

To evaluate scene compositor's object information management and scene composition capability, we compared our scene compositor model with KNU player(ver 1.0) and IM1-2D player(ver 5.0).

The KNU player[7] and IM1-2D player are MPEG-4 content player of Windows-based. Specially, the IM1-2D player is an open architecture. Our scene compositor model is included in the CLM player. The CLM player is two versions that have different O/S and device environment, and included the proposed scene compositor in these two players. One is Linux-based for PDA, another is Windows-based for Desktop. Three players focused on the Systems part of the MPEG-4 standard and applied highly player's components modularization.

Table 1 shows the comparison of scene compositor's several capabilities in each player.

Table 1. The comparison of scene compositor's several capabilities in each player

Requirement	Scene Compositor in KNU player	Scene Compositor in IM1-2D player	Scene Compositor in CLM player
Audiovisual object information management	Supported (through various data structure and media libraries)	Supported (through the core class and rendering functions)	Supported (through various data structure and media libraries)
Spatial and temporal composition	2D composition of simple scene	2D composition of simple and complex scenes	2D composition of simple and complex scenes
Object-based Interactivity	Supported (limited: user interaction)	Supported (limited: user interaction and time-based in object)	Supported (limited: user interaction and time-based in object)
Independent management of module	Supported (limited)	Module dependency on the lower part in the player	Fully supported
Adaptability with other environment (platform independency)	Not supported (O/S dependency)	Not supported (O/S dependency)	Supported (Linux-based PDA and Windows-based Desktop)
Profile	2D Complete	2D Complete	2D Complete
Module extensity	Supported	Supported (complexity)	Supported (more ease through modularization
Module optimization for mobile environment	Not supported	Not supported	Fully supported

Several core comparison items are compositor's information management capabilities and adaptability with players of different environment(O/S, Device). The proposed scene compositor can improve player's performance through optimization, and play MPEG-4 content of same purpose to player of different environment through adaptability.

4   Conclusions

In order to compose a dynamic scene in MPEG-4 player for mobile device, research about scalability of the scene description and object-based data management are very important.

In this paper, we proposed the scene compositor model that is optimized for effective searching of scene composition information and management of the extracted information. The scene compositor consists of the content analyzer, the information manager and the presenter. For effective extracting of object and object's properties field value, we defined the extraction rule table. For extracted information management, we defined the information manager. The information manager improves reusability and flexibility by object-based that is MPEG-4 scene's characteristic. The presenter renders efficiently according to the information manager. It consists of the graphic processor for media objects of various formats and the controller for connection of the scene compositor and the presenter. This scene compositor model is designed to be adapted to any player regardless of O/S and device environment through module optimization.

In the future, to support sufficiently spatial-temporal relationships of content for mobile device, we will improve the scene compositor's composition capability, processing the various events and playback quality in MPEG-4 player that requires high QoS.

Acknowledgment. This work was supported by Korea Research Foundation Grant (KRF-2003-002-D00304).

References

1. R. Koenen, "MPEG-4 Overview," ISO/IEC JTC/SC29/WG11/N4668, March 2002, http://www.m4if.org/resources/Overview.pdf
2. A. Puri and T. Chen, Multimedia Systems, Standards, and Networks, Marcel Dekker, New York, USA, March 2000.
3. A.E. Walsh and M. Bourges-Sevenier, MPEG-4 Jump-Start, Prentice Hall, Upper Saddle River, NJ, USA, December 2001.
4. F. Bouilhaguet, J-C. Dugourd, S. Boughoufalah and C. Havet. "Interactive Broadcast Digital Television. The OpenTV Platform versus the MPEG-4 Standard Framework," IEEE International Symposium on Circuits and Systems, Vol. 3, pp. 626-629, Geneva, Switzeland, May 2000.
5. H. Lee and S. Kim, "An Effective Management Technique of MPEG-4 Scene Description," Proceedings of the 13th Joint Conference on Communications and Information, pp. I-A-2.1-4, Anmyeondo, Korea, April 2003.
6. K. Cha, H. Kim and S. Kim "The Design and Development of MPEG-4 Contents Authoring System," Journal of the Korea Information Science Society, vol. 7, No. 4, pp. 309-315, August 2001.
7. H. Lee, Y. Lim and S. Kim, "An MPEG-4 System supporting XMT Scene Description," Proceedings of the 14th Joint Conference on Communications and Information, pp. II-D-2.1-4, Chungmu, Korea, April 2004.

JPEG2000 Image Adaptation for MPEG-21 Digital Items

Yiqun Hu, Liang-Tien Chia, and Deepu Rajan

Center for Multimedia and Network Technology
School of Computer Engineering
Nanyang Technological University, Singapore 639798
{p030070, asltchia, asdrajan}@ntu.edu.sg

Abstract. MPEG-21 user cases bring out a scenario of Universal Multimedia Access which is becoming the reality: people use different devices such as desktop PC, personal digital assistant as well as smartphone to access multimedia information. Viewing images on mobile devices is more and more popular than before. However, due to the screen size limitation, the experience of viewing large image on small screen devices is awkward. In this paper, an enhanced JPEG2000 image adaptation system is proposed for MPEG-21 digital item adaptation. The image is adapted considering both visual attentive region(s) of image and terminal screen size. Through the subjective testing, the system has been approved to be a solution of efficiently displaying large images in different devices.

Keywords: MPEG-21 Digital Item Adaptation, JPEG2000, Image Adaptation

1 Introduction

MPEG-21 multimedia framework aims to provide universal multimedia access and experience for users with different devices. The most vital limitation of device terminal is the screen size. Viewing images especially large images on the small device is awkward. Many inconvenient scrolling operations are required when viewing the large images in its original size on small screens. On the contrary, if the image is directly down-scaled to the screen size, users can not see them efficiently. The ideal solution is to make the best of screen by only cropping the region which attracts human visual attention and fitting to the screen size. New JPEG2000 image compression standard provides flexible scalability for transmission as well as adaptation. With its scalability, different image related applications are becoming efficient such as scalable coding and progressive transmission. MPEG-21 Standard Part 7 Digital Item Adaptation [1] describes a standardized framework to adapt format-dependent and format-independent multimedia resources according to terminal capability. Both of these two factors motivate our work of JPEG2000 image adaptation using standard MPEG-21 digital item adaptation. In this paper, visual attention analysis is integrated into the

K. Aizawa, Y. Nakamura, and S. Satoh (Eds.): PCM 2004, LNCS 3331, pp. 470–477, 2004.

MPEG-21 digital item adaptation framework for JPEG2000 image adaptation. Using our image adaptation system, different devices will display different views of the same JPEG200 image while reserving most attentive information. The whole adaptation is performed on JPEG2000 bitstream level and transparent to users.

The rest of this paper is organized as follows. We begin in Section 2 by briefly review related work for visual attention and introduce the attentive region extraction procedure. In Section 3, the JPEG2000 adaptation engine using the enhanced visual attention model and MPEG21 digital item adaptation is introduced. Experiment evaluations are given in Section 4 and we conclude our paper in Section 5.

2   Visual Attention Model

General speaking, when human visually view an image, some particular regions attract visual attention more than others. This visual attention mechanism is useful in displaying large images on the devices with different screen size. Through cropping and downsizing operation, a possible best solution which both reduces the number of awkward scrolling operation and reserves important information can be achieved with the attentive region information. In this section, we discussed the techniques for attentive image region detection and our attentive region extraction method.

2.1   Review of Visual Attention Model

Selective attention mechanism in human visual system has been studied and applied in the literature of active vision. Designing computational model for visual attention is the key challenge to simulate human vision. Several visual attention models have been proposed from different assumptions of saliency. Itti and Koch [2] [3] proposed a computational model to compute the saliency map for images. They used contrast as the cue for visual attention. In their method, pyramid technology was used to compute three feature maps for three low level features: color, intensity and orientation. For each feature, saliency is measured by the cross scale contrast in the neighboring location (1).

$$C_{i,j} = F_c(i,j) \ominus F_s(i,j) \tag{1}$$

Where $C_{i,j}$ is the saliency at the location (i,j), $F_x(i,j)$ is the low-level feature (color, intensity and orientation) at the location (i,j) of the scale x. Finally saliency map is generated by combining all feature maps. To shift among different salient points, a "inhibition of return" mechanism is performed iteratively.

Using the same cue of contrast, Ma et al. [4] provided another attention model which only considered the color contrast. They divide the total image into small perception units. Color contrast is calculated in each of the perception units using (2).

$$C_{i,j} = \sum_{q \in \Theta} d(p_{i,j}, q) \tag{2}$$

where Θ is the neighborhood of (i, j) whose size controls the sensitivity of perceive field. $p_{i,j}$ and q denote the color features in the neighboring pixel and center pixel. d is the gaussian distance of color in LUV space.

Another saliency measure is based on the information loss along fine-to-coarse scale space which is proposed by Ferraro et al. [5]. They measured the saliency using the density of entropy production (3) which is loss of information at a given pixel for unit scale.

$$\sigma = (\frac{\nabla f(x,y,t)}{f(x,y,t)})^2 \tag{3}$$

Where ∇ is gradient operator, (x,y) is spatial coordinates and t is scale parameter. Chen et al. [6] also proposed a semantic attention model combining visual attention, face attention as well as text attention and different applications using this attention model have also been proposed such as image navigation [7] and thumbnail cropping [8].

In our system, our objective is to provide a general solution of efficient displaying images on the devices with different screen size. Hence we currently use Itti's model [2] because of its generality.

2.2   Attentive Region Extraction

It is assumed that small object at the edges of an image is unlikely to be the main attention region and the attention region closer to the center of the image is perceptually more important in human vision. We assign a weight to each pixel in the image. Without additive restriction, we assume the surface of the weights of the image satisfies the gaussian distribution along both horizontal and vertical directions ((4), (5)) and the total weight is the arithmetic mean of two directions.

$$\mathcal{N}(\mu_x, \sigma_x^2) = \frac{1}{\sqrt{2\pi}\sigma_x} \exp[-\frac{1}{2}(\frac{x - \mu_x}{\sigma_x})^2] \tag{4}$$

$$\mathcal{N}(\mu_y, \sigma_y^2) = \frac{1}{\sqrt{2\pi}\sigma_y} \exp[-\frac{1}{2}(\frac{y - \mu_y}{\sigma_y})^2] \tag{5}$$

Both gaussian curves are centered at the center point of the image by setting μ_x the half of the width (Width / 2) and μ_y the half of the height (Height / 2). The σ_x and σ_y are fixed to 10 so that the gaussian curve is smooth, avoiding sharpness which only considers the small center region of the image. These weights are used to modify the saliency map as (6).

$$\bar{S}_{x,y} = S_{x,y} * (\frac{\mathcal{N}(\mu_x, \sigma_x^2) + \mathcal{N}(\mu_y, \sigma_y^2)}{2}). \tag{6}$$

$\bar{S}_{x,y}$ is the weighted value of the saliency map at location (x,y). Weighting the saliency map differently according to the position in the image, if there are tiny attention points in the edges of the image, we will skip them and keep our focus on the most important attention region. Our experiment result shows that this simple factor has a good effect on noise reduction. The modified saliency map will

Fig. 1. Same image displayed on Desktop PC and PDA

now assign different value for each point according to their topology attention. In our image adaptation model, a simple region growing algorithm whose similarity threshold is defined as 30% of the gray level range in the saliency map is used to generate the smallest bounding rectangle that includes the identified attention area(s). Firstly, we take the pixels with maximum value (one or multiple) as the seeds and execute the region growing algorithm. In each growing step, the 4-neighbour points are examined, if the difference between the point and the current seed is smaller than a threshold (30% of the range of gray-level value), the point will be added into the seed queue and will be grown later. The algorithm will continue until the seed queue is empty. Finally, the output are one or several separate regions and we generate a smallest rectangle to include these regions.

3   JPEG2000 Image Adaptation Engine

Different from current image engine, the proposed image adaptation server provides a transparent resolution adaptation for JPEG2000 images in the standard way: MPEG-21 Digital Item Adaptation [9]. JPEG2000 image bitstream and its *Bitstream Syntax Description (BSD)* [10] compose of digital item. BSD describes the high-level structure of JPEG2000 bitstream and adaptation is performed on the bitstream according to BSD. The adapted image is directly generated from JPEG2000 bitstream according to both attentive region information and terminal screen size. In our system, accessing image through different devices will obtain different views of the original image each of which deliveries the best experience using limited screen space. Figure 1 shows the view of accessing image through desktop PC as well as the view through the PDA. We can see only most attentive information is displayed on the small screen to avoid over down-scaling the image or additional scrolling operations. Our standard image adaptation engine automatically detects the visual attentive region(s) and adapts JPEG2000 image in bitstream level using standard digital item adaptation mechanism which differs itself from other similar wok. The advantage of our intelligent resolution adaptation engine is to preserve, as much as possible, the most attentive (important) information of the original image while satisfying terminal screen constraints.

The engine utilizes the Structured Scalable Meta-formats (SSM) for Fully Content Agnostic Adaptation [11] proposed as a MPEG-21 reference software module by HP Research Labs. The SSM module adapts JPEG2000 images resolution according to their ROIs and the terminal screen constraints of the viewers. BSD description of the JPEG2000 image is generated by BSDL module [10]. The attentive region is automatically detected using our enhanced visual attention model and adaptation operation is dynamically decided by considering both attentive region and terminal screen size constraint. We change the resolution of JPEG2000 image by directly adapting JPEG2000 bitstream in compressed domain. The whole adaptation procedure is described as follows. The BSD description and attentive region information are combined with image itself as a digital item. When the user requests the image, its terminal constraint is sent to server as a context description (XDI). Then combining XDI, BSD descrption and attentive region information, the Adaptation Decision-Taking Engine decide on the adaptation process for the image [11]. Finally, the new adapted image, its corresponding BSD description will be generated by the BSD Resource Adaptation Engine [10]. Description can be updated to support multiple step adaptation. A snapshot of BSD digital item adaptation is shown in Figure 2.

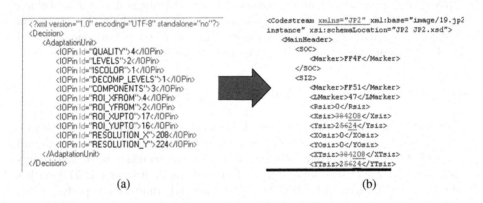

(a)   (b)

Fig. 2. Example of Digital Item BSD Adaptation; (a) Adaptation Decision Description; (b) JPEG2000 BSD Adaptation (Green - Original BSD, Blue - Adapted BSD).

The intelligent attentive region adaptation is decided according to the relationship between image size (I_{size}), attentive region size (AR_{size}) and the terminal screen size C_{size}.

- If $C_{size} > I_{size}$: No adaptation, the original image is sent to the user directly.
- If $AR_{size} < C_{size} < I_{size}$: Crop the attentive region according to the result of visual attention analysis, removing non-attention areas.

Fig. 3. Example of good intelligent adaptation; (a) Original Image; (b) Saliency Map; (c) Adapted Image on PDA; (d) Directly down-scaling Image on PDA

- If $C_{size} < AR_{size}$: Crop the attentive region first and reduce the region resolution to terminal screen size. (another adaptation can be performed by the adaptation engine)

4   Experiment Evaluations

600 images were selected from different categories of the standard Corel Photo Library as data set. The system was implemented as a web server application. Users can view the image through desktop PC as well as PDA. Several output examples of our intelligent visual attention based adaptation are shown in Figure 3 and Figure 4. Notice that the most interest information are reserved on small screen to achieve possible better user experience. Compared with directly downsizing image, it provides a better solution of viewing images on small devices. Due to the subjectivity of visual attention perspective, we applied the

(a)   (b)   (c)

Fig. 4. Example of bad and failed intelligent adaptation; (a) Original Image; (b) Saliency Map; (c) Cropped Image.

Table 1. User Study Evaluation - percentage of images in each category

Category	Failed	Bad	Acceptable	Medium	Good
Animal	0.02	0.09	0.22	0.33	0.34
People	0.01	0.11	0.22	0.30	0.36
Scenery	0.03	0.13	0.22	0.40	0.22
Others	0.01	0.10	0.26	0.41	0.22
Average	0.017	0.108	0.23	0.38	0.29

user study experiment in [4] to test the effectiveness of the proposed algorithm. 8 human subjects were invited to assign a score to each output of our adaptation for 4 different topics. The users were asked to grade the adapted images from 1 (failed) to 5 (good).

From the evaluation result shown in Table 1, we found that for different categories of images, an average of close to 87% cases are acceptable including 67% are better than acceptable. Only 10% are bad and 1% are failed. Results are bad mainly because not the whole visual object is included in the cropped images (eg. the legs of a animal) and 1% failure rate is due to either wrong visual object identified as the attention region or images like scenery shots where there may not be specific visual objects. The framework works reasonably well for a general set of natural images. Among the 8 testers, all of them agree that visual attention based adaptation improves the experience of viewing images on small devices.

5   Conclusion

In this paper, we design a JPEG2000 image adaptation engine for efficiently displaying images on different devices. The engine intelligently analyzes visual attentive region of images and provides different views of the image for different devices which makes the best of terminal screen to provide most interest information. The advantages of this engine over others is its capability of attentive region automatic detection and because using standard MPEG-21 digital item adaptation mechanism as well as JPEG2000 format, it is interoperable and extensible in future. Larger image test set and more extensive subjective test will be done in future to validate its efficiency.

References

1. Vetro, A., Timmerer, C.: Iso/iec 21000-7 fcd - part 7: Digital item adaptation. In: ISO/IEC JTC 1/SC 29/WG 11/N5845. (2003)
2. Itti, L., Koch, C., Niebur, E.: A model of saliency based visual attention for rapid scene analysis. IEEE Tran on Pattern Analysis and Machine Intelligence **20** (1998)
3. Itti, L., Koch, C.: A comparison of feature combination strategies for saliency-based visual attention systems. In: Proc. SPIE Human Vision and Electronic Imaging IV (HVEI'99), San Jose, CA. Volume 3644. (1999) 473–482
4. Ma, Y., Zhang, H.: Contrast-based image attention analysis by using fuzzy growing. In: Proc. ACM Multimedia, Berkeley, CA USA (2003)
5. Ferraro, M., Boccignone, G., Caelli, T.: On the representation of image structures via scale space entropy conditions. IEEE Tran on Pattern Analysis and Machine Intelligence **21** (1999)
6. Chen, L., Xie, X., Fan, X., Ma, W., Zhang, H., Zhou, H.: A visual attention model for adapting images on small displays. ACM Multimedia Systems Journal (2003)
7. Liu, H., Xie, X., Ma, W.Y., Zhang, H.J.: Automatic browsing of large pictures on mobile devices. In: Proceedings of the eleventh ACM international conference on Multimedia. (2003) 148–155
8. Suh, B., Ling, H., Bederson, B.B., Jacobs, D.W.: Automatic thumbnail cropping and its effectiveness. In: Proceedings of ACM symposium on user interface software and technology, Vancouver, Canada (2003)
9. Bormans, J., Hill, K.: Mpeg-21 overview v.5. In: ISO/IEC JTC1/SC29/WG11/ N5231. (2002)
10. Panis, G., Hutter, A., Heuer, J., Hellwagner, H., Kosch, H., Timmerer, C., Devillers, S., Amielh, M.: Bitstream syntax description: a tool for multimedia resource adaptation within mpeg-21. Singal Processing: Image Communication, EURASIP **18** (2003)
11. Mukherjee, D., Kuo, G., Liu, S., Beretta, G.:   Motivation and use cases for decision-wise bsdlink, and a proposal for usage environment descriptor-adaptationqoslinking. In: ISO/IEC JTC 1/SC 29/WG 11, Hewlett Packard Laboratories. (2003)

An Annotation Method and Application for Video Contents Based on a Semantic Graph

Tomohisa Akafuji[1,3], Kaname Harumoto[2], Keishi Kandori[3], Kôiti Hasida[4], and Shinji Shimojo[5]

[1] Graduate School of Information Science and Technology, Osaka University,
5-1 Mihogaoka, Ibaragi, Osaka, 567-0047, Japan ,
aka@ais.cmc.osaka-u.ac.jp
[2] Graduate School of Engineering, Osaka University, Osaka, Japan
[3] Information Technology Center, Asahi Broadcasting Corporation, Osaka, Japan
[4] Cyber Assist Research Center, National Institute of Advanced Industrial Science and Technology; CREST, Japan Science and Technology Agency, Tokyo, Japan
[5] Cybermedia Center, Osaka University, Osaka, Japan

Abstract. The progress of digitization at broadcasting stations enables the intellectual production of high-quality contents from video materials. Metadata plays an important role in describing the semantics of multimedia contents by aiding in the semantic structuralization of video material. In this paper, we propose an annotation method for video contents based on the concept of a semantic graph, which allows semantic queries on video contents. This method incorporates three ideas: an annotation for metadata on video scenes; time-series links between video scenes; and semantic links to external data. In the proposed annotation method, metadata are provided as human annotations practical for TV productions. We also present the application of a semantic graph to real baseball game contents and evaluate this application to show the usefulness of the proposed annotation method.

Keywords: Metadata, semantics, video contents, retrieval

1 Introduction

The digitization of video material in broadcasting stations makes storing and processing video contents by computer easy. In addition, both the reuse of contents and the production of high-quality contents can be expected. Metadata is essential for realizing video archiving with an intelligent video retrieval function, which aids in the production of high-quality contents. Many video materials are needed for high-quality contents, and some retrieval system is many important factor as an editing support.

In this paper, we propose an annotation method including an input support, in which the concept of a semantic graph is introduced. Moreover, broadcasting stations often have valuable external data already attached to video contents. Our annotation method can utilize the external data for annotation support or as the complement of semantically structured annotation data.

K. Aizawa, Y. Nakamura, and S. Satoh (Eds.): PCM 2004, LNCS 3331, pp. 478–486, 2004.

We have implemented a video search system and an annotation system based on the semantic structure of baseball contents, as an application example of the proposed method. The implemented systems were operated using video materials of real baseball games held in High School Baseball tournaments in Japan. In this paper, we describe the knowledge and evaluation obtained through the experience of implementation and operation.

2   Semantic-Based Structuralization for Video Contents

2.1   Necessary Requirements for Production in Broadcasting Stations

Video editing in broadcasting stations is not based on definitive standards or clear rules, and will be performed by experience and sensitivity. The director generally maintains consistency of the edited video by a trial and error process.

In order to select scenes that match the director's intentions from many video materials, a considerable amount of work is required. For example, in the case of video materials of the high-school baseball tournament games, which were used for demonstrating the proposed method in this paper, neither the players' names nor the peculiar information of the games remains clearly in our memory in many cases. Many games include preliminary matches that are performed in a short period, and the details of the game in the tournament are often difficult to recall. Thus, we need a mechanism that can efficiently retrieve video scenes that match the director's intention, even if s/he does not know the details of the games.

In creating the digest of a game, typical retrieval queries for video materials such as in Table 1 can be considered. In order to realize a video search system that can handle such ambiguous queries, the semantic-based structuralization of video materials is needed. This paper is based on the use of annotation in which human intervention is a realistic choice in the link between video contents and their semantics.

2.2   The Proposed Method by Annotation and Semantic Graph

The semantic-based structuralization method in this paper is based on a semantic graph. The semantic graph models video scenes as labeled nodes. The node

Table 1. Typical Query of Video Retrieval for Baseball Contents

Situation	Typical query
Pitcher's duel	Double play after hit; Back to back strikeouts
Run scene	Back to back hits; Two-run or Three-run homer
The close game	An inning with a miss-hit and a strikeout

label represents a human annotation attached to the video scene. Furthermore, the external data are modeled as external nodes. The node label of the external node represents the external data itself. The semantic graph has two kinds of edges; one represents time precedence relationships between video nodes, and the other represents a link between a video node and an external node.

The retrieval method in this paper has the distinctive feature of utilizing not only keywords, as in the traditional retrieval methods, but also in utilizing semantic structure for retrieval. Specifically, a query is also dealt with as a graph with labeled nodes, and the query processing is performed as a graph-matching problem.

2.3   Formal Definition of the Semantic Graph

A semantic graph G is represented by nodes and edges.

$$G = (V, E)$$

V is a set of nodes and E is a set of edges. The set of nodes V consists of a set of video nodes V^c and a set of external nodes V^s, which are defined as follows:

$$V = V^c \cup V^s, \; V^c \cap V^s = \phi, \; V^c = \{v^c{}_i \mid 1 \leq i \leq n\}, \; V^s = \{v^s{}_i \mid 1 \leq i \leq m\}$$

where $v^c{}_i$ is a video node is and $v^s{}_i$ is an external node. For each node, a set of labels $L(v)$ is defined. For a video node, $L(v^c{}_i)$ represents human annotations for the video scene, and for an external node, $L(v^s{}_i)$ represents the external data associated with the node.

For each video node $v^c{}_i$, an in-point $in(v^c{}_i)$ and an out-point $out(v^c{}_i)$ are defined. The in-point and out-point identifies the video scene in the video material. We assume the following equation holds: $out(v^c{}_i) \leq in(v^c{}_{i+1}), 1 \leq i < n$

The set of edges E consists of a set of time-series edges E^c and a set of external edges E^s, which are defined as follows:

$$E = E^c \cup E^s, \; E^c \cap E^s = \phi$$
$$E^c = \{(v^c{}_i, v^c{}_{i+1}) \mid 1 \leq i < n\}, \; E^s = \{(v^c{}_i, v^s{}_k) \mid C_0(v^c{}_i, v^s{}_k)\}$$

Here, C_0 is a predicate representing the link condition. C_0 is true if there exists a link between a video node $v^c{}_i$ and an external node $v^s{}_k$, otherwise C_0 is false.

An extended label set $L^s(v^c{}_i)$ is defined as follows for each video node $v^c{}_i$.

$$L^s(v^c{}_i) = \bigcup_{(v^c{}_i, v^s{}_k) \in E^s} L(v^s{}_k)$$

The conceptual illustration of the semantic graph is shown in Fig. 1.

2.4   Retrieval Based on the Semantic Graph

A query Q is expressed by a directed graph which consists of any number of nodes l as follows:

$$Q = (V', E'), \; V' = (v'_i \mid 1 \leq i \leq l), \; E' = \{(v'_i, v'_{i+1}) \mid 1 \leq i < l\}$$

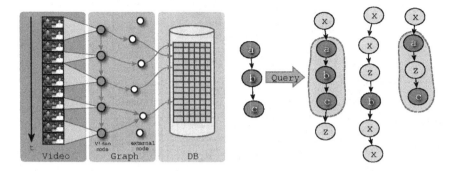

Fig. 1. Graph of Video Contents

Fig. 2. Basic Concept of Video Retrieval by Semantic Graph

Each node in the query graph has a label set $L(v_i')$. Intuitively, the query graph represents a query that retrieves a series of video scenes such that the ith scene includes the label set $L(v_i')$.

The solution of a query is also represented as a directed graph, the nodes and edges of which are defined as follows:

$$V_1(G,Q) = \{v^c{}_i \mid \exists j, \forall k (1 \leq k \leq l), L(v_k') \subseteq L(v^c{}_{j+k-1}) \cup L^s(v^c{}_{j+k-1}),$$
$$j \leq i \leq j + l - 1\}$$
$$E_1(G,Q) = \{(v^c{}_i, v^c{}_{i+1}) \mid (v^c{}_i, v^c{}_{i+1}) \in E^c, j \leq i < j + l - 1\}$$

However, there are cases where we want to retrieve a series of video scenes more ambiguously. To allow ambiguous query to perform, we define another type of solution as follows:

$$V_2(G,Q) = \{v^c{}_i \mid \exists j, k, \ L(v_1') \subseteq L(v^c{}_j) \cup L^s(v^c{}_j) \wedge L(v_l') \subseteq L(v^c{}_k) \cup L^s(v^c{}_k)$$
$$\wedge out(v^c{}_j) \leq in(v^c{}_k), j \leq i \leq k\}$$
$$E_2(G,Q) = \{(v^c{}_i, v^c{}_{i+1}) \mid (v^c{}_i, v^c{}_{i+1}) \in E^c, j \leq i < k\}$$

This solution represents a series of video scenes, the first scene of which includes a label set of the start-node of the query, and the last scene of which includes a label set of the end-node of the query. That is, the intermediate nodes of the query are ignored and only the end-points of the query are used for matching. Because start-node can be considered to be the cause and end-node can be considered to be a result, and image of editor corresponds to them.

This kind of solution is useful especially when we want to retrieve video scenes, contents of which are not certain. In this case, we can evaluate manually the accuracy by the number of nodes of the query included in the solution. A conceptual illustration of the retrieval based on a semantic graph is shown in Fig. 2.

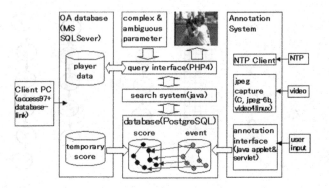

Fig. 3. Implemented System of Annotation and Video Retrieval

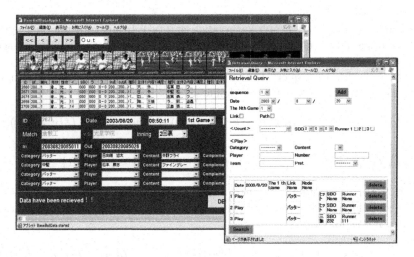

Fig. 4. Annotation Tool and Retrieval Tool

3   Implemented System

For the actual demonstration of the proposal method, an annotation system and a retrieval system have been implemented and evaluated using the video contents of the 85th National High School Baseball Championship in Japan.

The input support plays an important role in human annotation. We utilized the external database used for broadcasting. The database stores the information about players' names, the batting lineup, and defense positions. The annotation system dynamically changes the list of possible annotations according to the inning and the player's name. The annotator can annotate a video scene simply by choosing an annotation from the list, and manual text data input is basically not required. The in-point and the out-point of an event can be specified simply by clicking an appropriate thumbnail image which is updated every second.

Table 2. Label of Video Node

In-point,Out-point	YYYYMMDDhhmmss
The N th game	{1-4}
Inning	{top/bottom} of {1-15}
Player's name	first name, last name
Attribute	{batter,pitcher,first c}
Event	{hit,two base,error, c}

Table 3. Label of Score Node

Game date	YYYYMMDDhhmmss
The N th game	{1-4}
Inning	{top/bottom} of {1-15}
SBO	{0-2}{0-3}{0-2}
Runner	{0,1}{0,1}{0,1}

The data inputted on the annotation tool are the information on the event of the player in connection with a game. This information becomes the label of the video node on the semantic graph. The possible label values are shown in Table 2.

On the other hand, in the case of a sport, the information concerning a score, in addition to the information about a particular event of game, is also important. From the external database, which is updated for broadcasting once every few seconds, this score data is acquired automatically, and is stored to the database. The score data of this arbitrary time is dealt with as an external node. The possible label values are shown in Table 3. Since the video node and the score node are related on time-axis, these are liked automatically.

We have also developed a retrieval system with the query algorithms described in section 2.4. The client interface was developed as a web application. Query processing is performed at the server side. In this system, solutions for a query are limited to video scenes within the same inning.

This entire system is shown in Fig. 3. The images of annotation system and retrieval system are shown in Fig. 4. In the annotation system, many images located at the top of the screen are thumbnail view for identifying in-point and out-point of the event. And multiple select lists at middle of the screen is for inputting players' events. In the retrieval system, editors input consecutive events by selecting events lists in sequential order, and execute. In case only labels of nodes other than first node and end node are different from a query, those are highlighted as an incomplete solution in the result of a retrieval.

4   Evaluation

The implemented systems were evaluated as follows. The annotation work was performed for about 40 games out of all games. The annotator is a university student who is not a computer specialist. First, we evaluated the accuracy and efficiency of the annotation operation. The graph in Fig. 5 shows the error rate and the error correction count. The graph in Fig. 6 shows the average time and standard deviation for annotation per one record.

Errors of the annotation, which is to a batter's event, are incorrect input and lack of input data as compared with a scorebook. The horizontal axis of each graph represents experience (i.e., cumulative count of games) regarding the annotation. These graphs show that the implemented annotation system has a

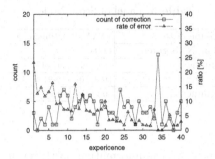

Fig. 5. The relation between experience and input error

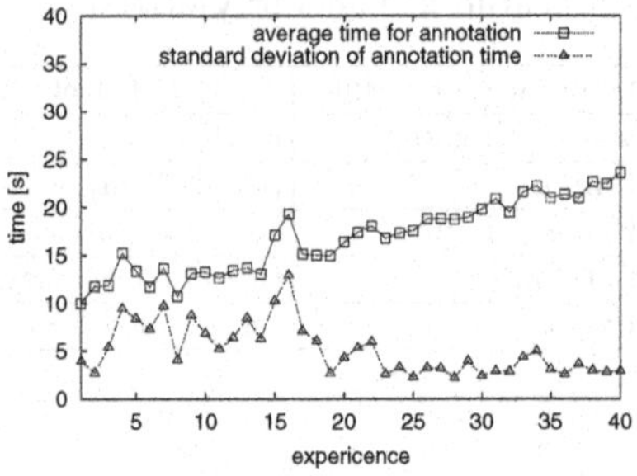

Fig. 6. The relation between experience and time for input data

Table 4. Retrieval Time by Traditional Means

	Homerun	Two-straight strikeouts
Editor A	120 s	250 s
Editor B	210 s	290 s

low error rate, costs little time, and has a low deviation time for inputting data as accumulated experience. These results indicate that our proposed annotation method using input support and linked external data is practical and efficient.

Secondly, we evaluated the time required to search a series of video scenes. We assumed two retrieval scenarios: one for retrieving a homerun scene, and the other for retrieving two straight strikeouts. We compared the retrieval times between the traditional method and the proposed method about particular scene selected in the certain game for evaluation. The traditional method is searched by viewing actually from the video data stored in the storage of an editing system. In the traditional method, the time needed for the search is shown in Table 4. On the other hand, the average time needed in the proposed method was less than 15 seconds. This result shows that our semantic-based annotation and retrieval are very effective.

5   Related Works

Various research for structuralization of retrieval and for the summary of video contents have been proposed.

Pradhan et al.[1] have suggested a method for acquiring an inclusive relation, which specifies as optimal solution dynamically. This method uses various joint operations uniquely defining the partial section of the solution for retrieval demands in the video contents. Since that research is an algebraic operation processing of a partial section containing a keyword, it corresponds to neither an ambiguous query nor a structural retrieval.

The retrieval method in the research of Zettsu et al.[2] extracts nodes with keywords contained in a query and extracts the semantics, from a minimum partial graph linked either manually or automatically based on the coincidence relation among words. However, since this method uses retrieval by a keyword set, the semantic structure of a query is not reflected in an algorithm and this method cannot search structural semantic contents. In addition, the cost and efficiency for manual input of sentence and link relation is not considered in this demonstrated annotation method.

In research of Okamoto et al.[3], the feature of the contents of a game is analyzed from the electronic scorebook of a baseball game, and a template of game classification and the selection of important events are performed. An explanatory text is created from those processings. Moreover, the video is synchronized, and a digest is generated. Although the digest created by the template has semantically organized contents, it does not correspond to a general-purpose retrieval query for editing.

In the semantic transcoding of Nagao[4], the semantics of the announcement comment and a semantic relation of contents are described using GDA[5]. Furthermore, this transcoding demonstrates the summary of a viewer-contents application based on situation dependence by linking video data.

Thus, in the conventional structuralization method, realizing a retrieval which takes the relevance of a series at the time of the video into consideration under ambiguous retrieval conditions is difficult. Therefore, an approach from the viewpoint of the semantic structure of video contents is needed.

6   Conclusion

The necessity of metadata for searching video materials from a huge storage of data and for creating intelligent contents is increasing dramatically. In this paper, we have proposed a semantic-based structuralization of video contents by a practical annotation method, and have implemented the application system and evaluated it using real baseball contents. The accuracy of metadata is most significant in broadcasting stations, because of the social impact of broadcasting. Therefore, the human input of data and the human confirmation of such data are required. It is considered consistent that those works are shifted to our proposed annotation, of which practicality have been demonstrated. For search and utilization of video contents including similar scenes like sports contents, the retrieval system for video scenes of a time-series with external data (e.g. score data) are generally needed. The method proposed in this paper is very efficient in these cases.

Acknowledgment. This work was supported in part by Research and Development Program of Ubiquitous Network Authentication and Agent (2003), The Ministry of Public Management, Home Affairs, Posts and Telecommunications (MPHPT), Japan.

References

1. Sujeet Pradhan, Keishi Tajima and Katsumi Tanaka: "A query model to synthesize answer intervals from indexed video units", IEEE Trans. on Knowledge and Data Engineering Vol. 13 No.5, pp.824-838, (Sep., 2001)
2. Koji Zettsu, Kuniaki Uehara and Katsumi Tanaka: "A time-stamped authoring graph for video databases", Proceeding of the 8th International Conference on Database and Expert Systems Applications (DEXA '97), LNCS 1308, Springer-Verlag, pp.192-201, (Sep., 1997)
3. Michiya Okamoto, Kazunori Ueda, Junzo Kamahara, Shinji Shimojo and Hideo Miyahara, "An architecture of personalized sports digest system with scenario templates", in Proceedings of 7th International Conference on Database Systems for Advanced Applications (DASFAA2001), pp. 170-171, (April, 2001)
4. Katashi Nagao: "Digital content annotation and transcoding", Artech House Publishers, Boston, (2003)
5. Kôiti Hasida: "Global Document Annotation (GDA)", http://www.i-content.org/GDA/

An Annotated-Objects Assist Method for Extraction of Ordinary-Objects in a Video Content Generation Support System

Wenli Zhang, Shunsuke Kamijyo, and Masao Sakauchi

Sakauchi Lab, the 3rd Department, Institute of Industrial Science, University of Tokyo

Abstract. In our previous work, we proposed a semantic video content generation support system, based on an interactive approach that maps low-level features to semantic concepts [11]. By consulting an ontological semantic object
model database, the main semantic objects in key frames of each video shot can
be extracted and annotated based on similarities in color, area, and position of
each region. This system has high potential for use in object-based interactive
multimedia applications. This paper extends our previous works [11][12], first
by showing system evaluation results, and then by proposing an object extraction assist method that aims at ordinary objects by combining low-level features and high-level concepts of annotated objects.

1 Introduction

In recent years, advances in video technology have provided the opportunity to access
huge amounts of video data. The introduction of digital broadcasting services such as
satellite broadcasting, CABLE TVS, and the Internet, make it possible for the user to
access video content interactively. Therefore, in order to deal with video content at a
semantic level, there is a need to build a multimedia system that includes new tools to
manage and manipulate video content more efficiently. Moreover, users require various application services based on such systems.

Currently available systems allow video content to be automatically extracted and
represented, based on low-level feature-based models [1], [2], [7]. Other systems such
as [3], [4], [5], [8], and [9] add textual annotation such as attributes or keywords,
either manually or semi-automatically, to represent the high-level concepts of a
video's content.

In our previous works, we have proposed a semantic video content generation support system based on an interactive approach that maps low-level features to semantic
concepts [11]. By consulting an ontological semantic object model database, the main
semantic objects in key frames of each video shot can be extracted and annotated
based on similarities in the color, area, and position of each region. This system has
high potential for use in object-based interactive multimedia applications. A web-
based application has also been implemented [11][12]. In this paper, to extend this
work, we first discuss the system evaluation results, and then propose an object ex-

K. Aizawa, Y. Nakamura, and S. Satoh (Eds.): PCM 2004, LNCS 3331, pp. 487–496, 2004.

traction assist method, which aims at ordinary objects by a combination of low-level features and high-level concepts from the object annotations.

The remainder of this paper is organized as follows: Section 2 presents an overview of the proposed system; Section 3 discusses the system evaluation. Section 4 discusses the proposed object extraction assist method that aims at general semantic objects. And Section 5 provides a summary and discusses future works.

2 An Overview of the Proposed System

The architecture of the proposed semantic video content generation support system [11] is shown in Fig.1.

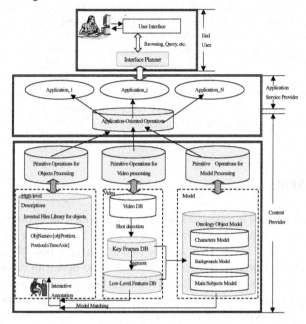

Fig. 1. The Architecture of the System

In this system, the raw video data is processed applying object recognition and video content data, whereby annotations of the semantic concepts, the position coordination, and temporal information of each object in the video are generated. Based on this system, various application-oriented operations can be produced. Corresponding to these operations, various object-based applications can be produced for different user purposes. DCPVS, which has been proposed in [11][12], serves as one of these applications in the semantic video content generation support system.

The main parts of establishing the system will be introduced briefly as follows.

✓ *Ontological Semantic Object Model*

A hierarchical structure is used for establishing a semantic object model from objects, matching salient regions to low-level features of each salient region. For example, a character model can be treated as a combination of hair, face and body regions. The same object may often be depicted in different ways in different videos/shots of same video. For example, in the case of a character model, the same person can appear in various movies or even in one movie as several different characters or as a character dressed in several different costumes. Therefore, we established the semantic object model database based on ontological theory. The models are classified based on a video's title, the date it was aired, and the objects.

✓ *Region-based Model Matching and object extraction*

In general, an object model is a template describing a specific object. During the matching process, each template is inspected to find the "closest" matches related to each object model. Model matching processing [10] is realized by comparing low-level features, including colors, area size, position, time and broadcasting date, between key frames and the object model. A key frame is considered as a final candidate of the object model if it contains the regions that are reasonably similar to that of the object model in terms of color, spatial relationship, area rate and broadcasting date. If a key frame is identified as the result, the position of matched regions makes up the semantic object and constitutes the object extraction.

✓ *Human-assisted Object Annotation Approach*

A semi-automatic object annotation approach [10][11] has been proposed to annotate objects that are extracted using the above region-based model matching approach. This object annotation approach can help us to bury the gap between low-level features and semantic concepts. We have implemented the model matching method to 10 drama videos. The highest precision rate we achieved was 51.9%; our highest recall rate reached 80.5%[11].

The content provider selects those frames that contain the true objects, ignoring any false ones via an interactive annotation interface. The high recall rate enables us to obtain mostly relevant results. Therefore, a higher quality video content database is obtained for further use.

Except for this necessary manual operation, all other annotation requirements are completed automatically. The annotated information on the selected true objects is stored in an inverted file. The inverted file represents the relationship between the description or keywords of the semantic concepts of an object and the set of frames that contain the object related to the description, the object's position, and the time information in those frames.

✓ *Application-oriented Operations*

Application-oriented operations are a combination of various primitive operations. They are used for generating more flexible semantic content for various applications. The application service provider can establish application-dependent services that are based on the output from the content provider layer.

Currently, operations that have been implemented include (1) the linkage of abstract concepts to video, (2) Q&A on an object, (3) Spatial relationship between objects, (4) Video content analysis/ classification (5) query of scene phase, and etc.

A web-based application, called DCPVS [11][12], which used Q&A on an object, one of the operations above, has been proposed.

3 System Evaluation

3.1 Evaluations

At present, video data for system implement have been compiled from television broadcasting. The system stores ten TV dramas, with a total of about 543 minutes. Details on the video database are shown as Tab.1.

Table 1. Video Database Size

Items	Number
Shot	12,893
Key frame	12,893
Region	309,593

Table 2. System Evaluations

	Process Name / one video	Average Time(minute)
Total : 487 minutes (76.3% of Total Time)	Shot & Key frame(automatic)	54.2
	Image Seg. (automatic)	323
	Feature Extraction(automatic)	107.8
	High-dimensional Tree(automatic)	2
15 minutes. For one model, Total 151 minutes (23.7% of Total time)	Model Creation(semi-automatic)	5 min./1model * 10 = 50
	Model Matching(automatic)	3-5 sec./model * 10 = max(0.83 min)
	Annotation(semi-automatic)	10 min./1model *10 = 100
	Total(one video with 10 models)	637.8 min.→ 10.63 hours

In order to increase model matching efficiency, all low-level features of regions are constructed into a 5-dimensial-tree structure [10].

The average processing time for providing semantic description to one video can be seen in Tab. 2

In order to annotate one 54.3minutes video with 10 models, 10.63 hours are needed.

✓ 76.3% of the total time is for automatic procedures including (1) shot detection and key frame extraction, (2) key frame segmentation, (3) features extraction, and (4) high-dimensional tree structure. All the procedure times can be improved with high-speed PC processing ability.

✓ The remaining 23.7% of the total time, 151 minutes, is for annotation of objects, which are matched to 10 models; a single model matching requires only 15 minutes on average. The semi-automatic procedures, i.e., model creation and annotation, require the most time. However, since content providers have individual differences, they can improve this time with experience and skill with model creation and object annotation.

3.2 Discussion

Supposing that automatic processing such as shot detection, etc. can be run at night; the 2.5-hours requirement for object extraction and annotation of a one-hour video should not be prohibitive. The results of system evaluation show the effectiveness of our system. The system will be useful if we limit our annotations to the main characters, background, and subjects, using the interactive approach. The main objects mean those that appear or those that have clarified features. However, it costs more and becomes ineffective when the focus is on ordinary objects, i.e., those that appear well but don't have clarified features.

In this paper, we propose an assist approach for querying ordinary objects by a combination of the object's low-level features and semantic concepts of one or more annotated objects. The details will be discussed in the next section.

4 Extraction of Ordinary-Objects

4.1 The Proposed Approach

In everyday life, we often witness conversations such as the following:
Q: Do you know Joe?
A: No, what is he like?
Q: Joe is the man who always wears a gray suit.
A: There are many such people in the company.
Q: The one who is together with Lily, who always had green dress on.
A: I know Lily, so the man who always dines with Lily, is Joe, right?

If we try to find "Joe" individually, a large number of candidate results, including both true and false results, would be returned because "the man who wears a gray suit" is such a popular feature in the video database. If all objects like "Joe" are annotated by the semi-automatic method, the workload will become overwhelming. Even if they are not annotated, just browsing and viewing them also takes time and effort. In this example, with the help of "Lily", a well-known or prominent girl in the company, we can specify "Joe", a man who is not prominent and can only be known by a particularly common feature.

Therefore, if a query contains one annotated object and one non-annotated object, the query accuracy will be higher than if both are non-annotated objects. The procedure is shown as Fig.2 (b).

As shown in Eq.1, Obj_{main} is the candidate key-frame set corresponding to an annotated object, with a high precision result because the results are from the inverted file [11]; Obj_{non} is the candidate key-frame set corresponding to a non-annotated ordinary object with lower precision because the results are from low-level feature matching. Thus, we propose a definition as follows.

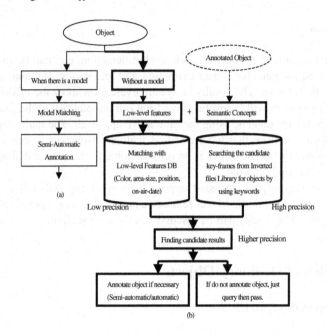

Fig. 2. The approach for query objects in video

◆ Definition: If the annotated object and the queried ordinary object exist together in the same key frame, this key frame becomes the true candidate result of the query.

Eq. 2 shows that the final result set $Obj_{ordinary}$ derived from the intersection set of Obj_{main} and $Obj_{non.}$ has a higher precision rate than if only the non-annotated ordinary object Obj_{non} were queried.

$$Obj_{main} = \{f_1, f_2, ..., f_N\}, Obj_{non} = \{f'_1, f'_2, ..., f'_M\} \quad \text{(Eq.1)}$$

$$Obj_{ordinary} = Obj_{main} \overset{f_i = f'_j}{\underset{i \in [1,N], j \in [1,M]}{\bigcap}} Obj_{non} \quad \text{(Eq.2)}$$

However, if an ordinary object has the case of independent existence it will be ignored as a special case in our system.

4.2 Implementation

We have implemented the proposed approach into our system. Two types of interface have been used.

(1) Sketch Interface (Fig. 3)

This is used when the user has only an ambiguous image to query: for example, "the person has this kind of hair color, this kind of face, this kind of dress color." The interface gives the three shape regions (rectangle, circle, and ellipse), and HSV color

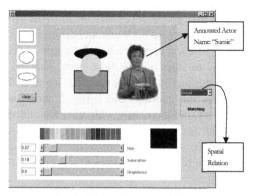

Fig. 3. Sketch Interface

Fig. 4. Real Scene Interface for select salient regions

bar so that user can draw his/her image freely. Then the region-based Model matching method [10] is used for matching low-level features DB to get candidate key frames containing objects similar to the user-drawn images.

In the same time, this interface also allows the user set an annotated object (i.e. "Sumie" has green dress in Fig.3), the spatial relationship (left, right, etc) also could be decided between the annotated object (i.e "Sumie") and the queried object (i.e the sketched gray-body person that is in the left of "Sumie").

The application-oriented operation for spatial-relation, such as "query the person like the sketch, who is in the left of "Sumie", can be run for getting candidate results.

(2) Real Scene Interface (Fig.4)

This interface helps the user find his/her query image from the real scene. While browsing the video content database, the user will have a question such as: "I want to know more about this man", or "Has this object appeared in other scenes?" The user is able to cut off the region of the object of interest from the real scene. Then the segmentation tool can be run to segment the cut sub-image and extraction features (color, area-rate, etc.). After selecting the silent regions, candidate key frames containing objects similar to the one that the user given are returned by running a region-based model matching tool [10].

◆   *Combination of the results of (1) or (2) with the inverted file.*

After procedure (1) or (2), there are both true and false objects in the candidate key frames. According to the proposed approach and definition in section 4.1, we use the records in the inverted file to filter out the false ones. That is, if the candidate key frame number is same as the one in the inverted file, we treat this key frame as the true candidate that includes the queried object. Fig. 5 shows a table of the rate at which a queried object exists simultaneously with other annotated objects.

If the use clicks any color part in the circle in Fig.5, the corresponding results will show out. For example, Fig.6 shows a part of results of "the queried man together with Misaki Sudoh" when the blue part in the circle was clicked.

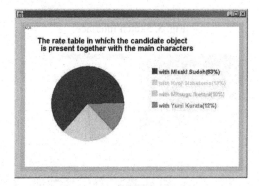

Fig. 5. The rate table of queried objects and others.

Fig. 6. Example results of "together with Misaki Sudoh".

In the above example, there are 244 candidate frames if we search the black-suit man in Fig.4 individually. It will be a costly work if we extract the objects from so many frames. However, by using the proposed method, we focus on about candidate 104 frames, which are filter into four items. With four different main annotated characters ("Misaki Sutoh", "Kyoji Nabetomo", "Mitsugu Iketani" and "Yumi Kurata"). Although there still are false results exist (i.e the ones without marks under frames in

Fig.6). The proposed method makes us extract ordinary objects more precisely and effectively than before.

The same query also can be realized, such as "query the scene of Joe is holding an red balling." "Query the scene of the criminal who rode and escaped on the red motorbike" and etc.

This function not only helps the user to obtain more precise results but also to discover potential phenomena and tendencies. It becomes possible to acquire more high-level semantic video content. For example, from Fig.5, we can know that the queried character (the man with black suit) usually exists (the rate is 63%) together with the character "Misaki Sudoh" and seldom appears simultaneously with the character "Mitsu Iketani(10%)".

5   Conclusion

In this paper, which extends our previous work [10][11][12], we have evaluated the proposed semantic video content generation support system. The evaluation data showed that the system is useful and effective. Moreover, we proposed a combination method to query ordinary objects in a video. We treat this approach as an efficient assist method. In future works, we will use this approach to develop general video content applications.

References

[1]   Shih-Fu Chang, William Chen, Horace J.Meng, Hari Sundaram, and Di Zhong, "A Fully Automated Content-based Video Search Engine Supporting Spatiotemporal Queries", IEEE Transactions on circuits and systems for video technology, Vol.8, No.5, Sep.1998.

[2]   M.Flickner, H.Sawhney, W.Niblack, J.Ashley, Q.Huang, B.Dom, M.Gorkani, J.Hafner, D.Lee, D.Petkovic, D.Steele, and P.Yanker,"Query by image and video content: The QBIC system", IEEE Comput., Mag., vol.28, pp.23-32,Sept.1995

[3]   M.-S Hacid, C.Decleir, and J. Kouloumdjian, "A Database Approach for Modeling and Query video Data", IEEE Trans. On Knowledge and Data Engineering, Vol.12, No.5, Spet/Oct. 2000.

[4]   S.Adali, K.S.Candan, S.-S Chen, K.Erol, and V.S.Subrahmanian, "Advanced Video Information System: Data Structures and Query Processing", ACM-Springer Multimedia Sys., vol.4, pp-172-186, 1996.

[5]   Duc A. Tran, Kien A. Hua, and Khanh Vu. "Semantic Reasoning based Video Database Systems". In Proc. of the 11th Int'l Conf. on Database and Expert Systems Applications, Sep. 4-8, 2000, pages 41-50.

[6]   A. Gupta and R.Jain, "Visual Information Retrieval", Comm. ACM, Vol.40, No.5, pp.71-79, 1997.

[7]   John R.Smith and Shih-Fu Chang, "VisualSEEk: a fully automated content-based image query system", ACM Multimedia 96, Boston, MA, November 20,1996.

[8]   E.Oomoto, K.Tanaka, OVID: Design and Implementation of a Video-Object Database System, IEEE Trans. Knowledge and Data Engineering, 5(4), 1993,62-643.

[9]   E.Ardizzone and M.L. Cascia. "Automatic video database indexing and retrieval", Multimedia Tools and Applications, 4(1), 1997.

[10]   Wenli Zhang*, Xiaomeng Wu, Shunsuke Kamijo, Yoshitomo Yaginuma, Masao Sakauchi. "Movie Content Retrieval and Semi-Automatic Annotation Based on Low-Level Descriptions", IEEE The Third Pacific-Rim Conference on Multimedia,Taiwan, Dec.15-19, 2002

[11]   Wenli Zhang*, Xiaomeng Wu, Shunsuke Kamijo, Masao Sakauchi. "A Proposal for a Video Content Generation Support System and its Applications", IEEE International Conference on Multimedia and Expo 2003 (ICME2003), Baltimore, Maryland, USA, July, 2003.

[12]   Xiaomeng Wu, Wenli Zhang*, Shunsuke Kamijo, Masao Sakauchi. "Construction of interactive video information system by applying results of object recognition", ACM Multimedia 2003, Berkeley, CA, USA, Nov.2-8, 2003.

Free-Viewpoint TV (FTV) System

Toshiaki Fujii and Masayuki Tanimoto

Graduate School of Engineering, Nagoya University, Japan
{fujii,tanimoto}@nuee.nagoya-u.ac.jp

1 Introduction

Free-viewpoint TeleVision (FTV) is a next generation television where users can move their viewpoints freely. FTV has many promising applications in wide areas such as personal, industrial, business, medical and social fields. It will open a new road to future broadcasting and communication systems.

We report a prototype system of FTV based on Ray-Space. The Ray-Space[1, 2,3] was originally introduced as a common data format for the "Integrated 3-D Visual Communication". In this framework, various types of 3-D images, such as stereo image, multi-view image and holographic image are converted to the "Ray-Space" data, and it is compressed, coded, stored and transmitted to the receiver. At the receiver, the corresponding 3-D images to the input format are extracted from the decoded data and displayed on various 3-D displays. Since the Ray-Space gives general representation for 3-D information, it is appropriate as a common data format for 3-D visual communications. We have been developing Ray-Space 3-D image processing techniques such as generation of free viewpoint images and variable-focused images without complicated analysis and rendering process.

The idea similar to Ray-Space has been proposed in computer graphics field, which is called "Light-Field Rendering[5]" or "Lumigraph[6]". These papers proposed an image rendering system using light-field concept. Now, this light-field rendering technique has been widely known as a photo-realistic image generating methods and it has been widely used to create photo-realistic virtual world.

Although the light field method has achieved a great success as a photo-realistic rendering method, the Ray-Space "communication" has been considered impractical as a real-time application. The main reason for that is the acquisition of the Ray-Space is difficult; most of the light field demos were performed as an off-line applications.

In this paper, we introduce a full real-time system based on the Ray-Space method. In the system, (1) Ray-Space data are acquired by multiple cameras, (2) Ray-Space is interpolated by adaptive filtering method, and then (3) arbitrary viewpoint image is displayed according to the viewpoint specified by a user. We call the system "Free-Viewpoint Television(FTV)".

K. Aizawa, Y. Nakamura, and S. Satoh (Eds.): PCM 2004, LNCS 3331, pp. 497–504, 2004.

2   Ray-Space Representation of 3-D Space

2.1   Definition of Ray-Space[1,2,3]

Let (x, y, z) be three space coordinates and θ, ϕ be the parameters of direction. A ray going through the space can be uniquely parameterized by its location (x, y, z) and the direction (θ, ϕ); in other words, a ray can be mapped to a point in this 5-D ray parameter space. In this ray parameter space, we introduce a function f whose value corresponds to an intensity of the specified ray. Thus, all the intensity data of rays can be expressed by

$$f(x, y, z; \theta, \phi). \tag{1}$$
$$-\pi \leq \theta < \pi, -\pi/2 \leq \phi < \pi/2.$$

We call this ray parameter space the "Ray-Space".

In the Ray-Space representation, a process of obtaining a view image is formulated as the following. We assume a pin-hole camera as an image acquisition device. A pin-hole camera is an equipment which records the intensity of rays which pass through the pin-hole. When we set a camera at (x_0, y_0, z_0), the intensity data of rays which go through the pin-hole are given by

$$f(x, y, z, \theta, \phi)|_{x=x_0, y=y_0, z=z_0}. \tag{2}$$

Note that the rays represented by Eq. 2 provide a 2-D image $I(i, j)$ viewed from the viewpoint (x_0, y_0, z_0). Although the 5-D Ray-Space mentioned above includes all the information viewed from any viewpoint, it is too redundant and impractical for real applications. In most of the 3-D image applications, the 4-D Ray-Space data is sufficient instead of the 5-D Ray-Space data. We can reduce 5-D Ray-Space to 4-D using an appropriate projection. Figure 1 shows an example of a definition of Ray-Space.

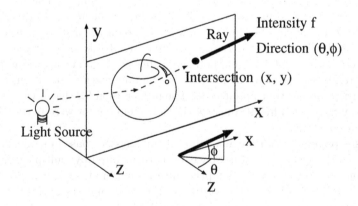

Fig. 1. Definition of Ray-Space.

2.2   Free-Viewpoint TV Based on Ray-Space

Here, we describe to generate free-viewpoint images from the Ray-Space. For simplicity, we consider a 2-D case. The 2-D case means that we neglect the vertical parallax ϕ and we consider only a cross section $y = $ const. Then, we obtain 2-D Ray-Space $f(x, \theta)$. Let the coordinate of a point P be (X, Z). The rays which pass through the point P form the following locus in the Ray-Space:

$$X = x + uZ \quad (u = \tan \theta) \tag{3}$$

From a standpoint of the Ray-Space concept, the acquisition is the process to sample the ray data in the real space by cameras and record them as a cross section data of the Ray-Space. A view image from a different viewpoint is recorded as another cross section of the Ray-Space. Thus, multiple view images are mapped to Ray-Space data, and the collection of multiple view images constructs the whole Ray-Space. The display process, on the other hand, is the process to "cut" the Ray-Space data and extract a cross section image. Figures 2 and 3 shows an acquisition and display process of free-viewpoint images. This elegant characteristic of Ray-Space enables us to generate free-viewpoint images without a complicated rendering process.

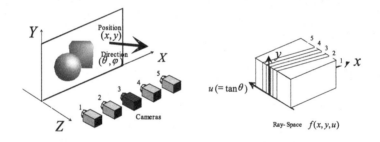

Fig. 2. Acquisition of the Ray-Space by multiple cameras.

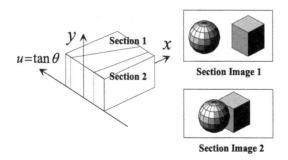

Fig. 3. Generation of free-viewpoint images from the Ray-Space.

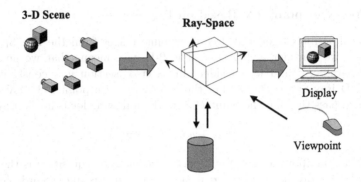

Fig. 4. Free-viewpoint TV system based on the Ray-Space concept.

Figure 4 shows our FTV system based on Ray-Space. First, many video cameras or some equivalent devices capture the dynamic 3-D scene. Then, geometrical calibration, intensity/color calibration, and view interpolation are carried out to the data, and the data is converted to the Ray-Space. Data compression and coding are applied to the Ray-Space data, if necessary, and the data is transmitted to the receiver. At the receiver side, a user determines a viewpoint, and the image from the viewpoint is generated by extracting 2-D subspace of the Ray-Space and displayed on a monitor.

3   Acquisition and Display System of FTV

To acquire the dynamic Ray-Space, it is a straightforward approach to use multiple video cameras. The acquisition system uses multiple video cameras capturing the same 3-D scene as shown in Fig. 5. Each camera is a conventional NTSC video camera and outputs composite video signal. To synchronize the multiple video signals, Gen-Lock signal is generated and distributed to each camera. To capture the multiple video streams, we used multiple PCs connected each other by network. Each PC is equipped with an image grabber board that digitizes the video signal and sends it to the main memory of the PC. All PCs are connected with high-speed network and can communicate each other at up to 1Gbps.

The output of multi-camera is then sent to processing unit. The first step of the processing is geometrical transformation. The Ray-Space is defined by ray parameters in the world coordinate. On the other hand, a pixel coordinate is based on the camera coordinate. Therefore, we need to convert the pixel coordinate into the ray parameter. This transformation is derived from the camera calibration. We used the strong calibration that uses a target pattern placed in the scene. The camera intrinsic parameters and extrinsic parameters are solved using the relationship between the world and camera coordinates. And then, the transformation matrix is derived and applied to the view image. Finally, all the view images are mapped to the Ray-Space. The second step is the interpola-

Fig. 5. Camera array for FTV data acquisition (left) and user-friendly display system(right).

tion of the Ray-Space. This is required because the distances between adjacent cameras are too large to obtain the dense Ray-Space data in the multi-camera system. (See Sec. 4 in more detail). The final step is to generate a free-view image. Since we have the dense Ray-Space after the previous two steps, a free-view image is easily generated by simply extracting a subspace of the Ray-Space.

Next, we focus on the display system of FTV. The problem we address here is how to specify a change of the viewpoint to the system. A human interface for FTV is desired to be as natural, human-friendly, easy-to-use, and intuitive as possible. From this viewpoint, we developed an FTV viewing system with a non-contact type head tracking system. Various kinds of human interfaces have been proposed and used in 3-D navigating system, especially in computer graphics and virtual reality. Typical human interface is a conventional joystick or mouse. These kinds of mechanical human interfaces are cost effective, and hence, they are widely used in games and consumer class PCs. More sophisticated human interface is a head tracking system. A position of user's head is detected by some means and it is used to change the viewpoint of the user. This type of interface is human-friendly and brings a sense of motion parallax to the user. We developed a display system for FTV shown in Fig. 5(Right).

4   Interpolation of Ray-Space

To apply the Ray-Space method to free-view generation, we need densely sampled Ray-Space. In real experimental systems, however, it is difficult to obtain dense Ray-Space data because physical size of cameras is too large to put cameras very closely. Therefore, the Ray-Space data obtained by a real camera setup is too sparse to apply the Ray-Space method. To solve this problem, it is a good solution to generate missing ray data, i.e., to "interpolate" Ray-Space data from sparsely sampled Ray-Space. This process is called the "interpolation of Ray-Space".

We proposed a Ray-Space interpolation scheme based on "adaptive filtering"[8]. Figure 6 illustrates the proposed interpolation scheme. First, we prepare a set of interpolation filters. Then the original sparse Ray-Space is up-sampled and sent to the interpolator. For a pixel to be interpolated, the neighborhood area of the pixel is analyzed and the selector determines the best interpolation filter based on the analysis. Then, the selected filter is convoluted to the up-sampled Ray-Space and interpolated Ray-Space is obtained. This process is carried out on pixel-by-pixel basis and repeated until all the missing pixels are interpolated.

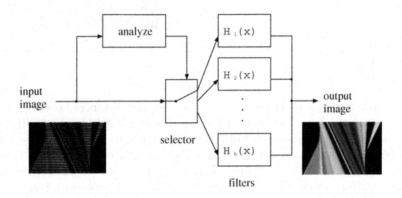

Fig. 6. Interpolation of Ray-Space by adaptive filter

5   Prototype System of FTV

We constructed a prototype of Free-viewpoint TV system. Figure 7 shows the overview of the system. This system consists of 16 video cameras, 16 Client PCs and one Host PC. All the Client PCs and Host PC are connected by Gigabit Ethernet. Each PC is general-purpose PC, which has Intel Pentium III 800MHz CPU. The image capturing board is mounted in a PCI bus in each client PC. 16 small CCD cameras (Toshiba IK-SM43) are arranged in 1-D arc. We used a fish tank and fishes as objects, because it is suitable to demonstrate FTV's capability to generate free-viewpoint images, where objects are difficult to be modeled. The arbitrary view images at 10 frames per second are generated in resolution 320x240. Figure 8 shows the generated free-viewpoint images.

Fig. 7. Overview of free-viewpoint TV system.

Fig. 8. Generated free-viewpoint images.

6 Conclusion

In this paper, we introduced Free-viewpoint Television(FTV) based on Ray-Space representation. The key technologies of this system are the acquisition and interpolation the Ray-Space data. We developed an interpolation method that is suitable for real-time processing. By integrating multi-camera acquisition system, a processing unit which consists of PC cluster, and human-friendly display system, we succeeded a real-time experiment of the FTV. Also, the function of FTV was successfully demonstrated by generating free-viewpoint images of the fish tank. Although there still remain problems to be solved, the results give us a positive view of realization of FTV.

Acknowledgement. This research is partly supported by "Grant-in-Aid for Scientific Research (A) No. 15206046, Japan Society for the Promotion of Science" and "Grant-in-Aid for Young Scientists (A) No. 16686025, The Ministry of Education, Culture, Sports, Science and Technology (MEXT)".

References

1. T. Fujii, "A Basic Study on the Integrated 3-D Visual Communication", Ph.D thesis of engineering, The University of Tokyo, 1994. (in Japanese)
2. T.Fujii, T.Kimoto, M.Tanimoto, "Ray Space Coding for 3D Visual Communication", Picture Coding Symposium '96, pp. 447–451, Mar. 1996.
3. T. Fujii, M. Kaneko, and H. Harashima, "Representation of 3-D Spatial Information by Rays and Its Application ",The Jounal of The Institute of Television Engineers of Japan , Vol.50, No.9, pp. 1312–1318. 1996.(In Japanese)
4. T. Naemura, M.Kaneko, and H. Harashima,"3-D Visual Data Compression Based on Ray-Space Projection", Proc. SPIE VCIP '97, pp. 413–424, 1997.
5. M. Levoy and P. Hanrahan,"Light Field Rendering", ACM SIGGRAPH '96, pp. 31–42, Aug. 1996.
6. S.J.Gortler, R.Grzesczuk, R.Szeliski, and M.F.Cohen,"The Lumigraph", ACM SIGGRAPH '96, pp.43–54, Aug. 1996.
7. T. Fujii, T. Kimoto, M. Tanimoto, "A New Flexible Acquisition System of Ray-Space data for Arbitrary Objects",IEEE Trans. on Circuits and Systems for Video Technology, Vol. 10, No. 2, pp.218-224, Mar. 2000.
8. T. Kobayashi, T. Fujii, T. Kimoto, M. Tanimoto, "Interpolation of Ray-Space Data by Adaptive Filtering", SPIE Electronic Imaging 2000, Vol. 3958, pp. 252–259, Jan. 2000.
9. M. Magnor and B.Girod, "Data Compression for Light-Field Rendering", IEEE Trans. on Circuits and Systems for Video Technology, vol. 10, no. 3, pp. 338–343, Apr.2000.
10. M. Tanimoto and T. Fujii, "FTV—Free Viewpoint Television", ISO/IEC JTC1/SC29/WG11 M8595, July 2002.
11. T. Fujii, M. Tanimoto, "Free-Viewpoint TV System Based on Ray-Space Representation", SPIE ITCom Vol. 4864-22, pp.175–189, Aug. 2002(invited).
12. T. Fujii, M. Tanimoto, "Real-Time Ray-Space Acquisition System", SPIE Electronic Imaging, Vol. 5291, pp. 179–187, Jan. 2004.
13. "Applications and Requirements for 3DAV", ISO/IEC JTC1/SC29/WG11 N5877, July 2003.
14. "Report on 3DAV Exploration", ISO/IEC JTC1/SC29/WG11 N5878, July 2003.
15. M. Droese, T. Fujii, M. Tanimoto, "Ray-Space Interpolation based on Filtering in Disparity Domain", 3D Image Conference 2004, pp. 213–216, July, 2004.

In-Car Speech Recognition Using Distributed Multiple Microphones

Weifeng Li[1], Takanori Nishino[1], Chiyomi Miyajima[1], Katsunobu Itou[1],
Kazuya Takeda[1], and Fumitada Itakura[2]

[1] Nagoya University, Nagoya, 464–8603 Japan
[2] Meijo University, Nagoya, 468-8502 Japan

Abstract. This paper describes a new multi-channel method of noisy speech recognition, which estimates the log spectrum of speech at a close-talking microphone based on the multiple regression of the log spectra (MRLS) of noisy signals captured by the distributed microphones. The advantages of the proposed method are as follows:
1) The method does not make any assumptions about the positions of the speaker and noise sources with respect to the microphones. Therefore, the system can be trained for various sitting positions of drivers.
2) The regression weights can be statistically optimized over a certain length of speech segments (e.g., sentences of speech) under particular road conditions. The performance of the proposed method is illustrated by speech recognition of real in-car dialogue data. In comparison to the nearest distant microphone and multi-microphone adaptive beamformer, the proposed approach obtains relative word error rate (WER) reductions of 9.8% and 3.6% respectively.

1 Introduction

Improving the accuracy of speech recognition in a noisy environment is one of the important issues in extending the application domain of speech recognition technology [1]. Among the various approaches previously proposed for noisy speech recognition, speech enhancement based on multi-channel data acquisition is currently under extensive research. The most fundamental and important multi-channel method is the microphone array beam-former method because the assumption that the target and the interfering signals are not spatially dispersed, and are apart from each other, is reasonable in many situations. In other words, the microphone array beam-former method is effective when the positions of the speaker and the noise sources are predetermined and the positions do not change during the signal acquisition process.

On the other hand, when the spatial configuration of the speaker and noise sources is unknown or changes continuously, it is not easy to steer the directivity adaptively toward the new environment. One of the most common approaches for adaptive microphone array systems is the *Generalized Sidelobe Canceller* (GSC) [2] and its modifications. However, these techniques usually assume that the desired source is slowly varying and at a known location, and are very sensitive

K. Aizawa, Y. Nakamura, and S. Satoh (Eds.): PCM 2004, LNCS 3331, pp. 505–513, 2004.
© Springer-Verlag Berlin Heidelberg 2004

to steering errors [3]. In-car speech recognition suffers from such problems when using beamformers because neither the speaker position nor the primary noise location is fixed. In such situations, changes of the target's and the interfering signal's locations may even aggravate the recognition performance due to the use of microphone-array-based signal processing. The tolerance of the multi-channel system to a change in the spatial configuration is an important issue for in-car speech recognition.

The authors have earlier proposed the *feature averaging* method for recognizing distant speech captured through distributed microphones. In [4], we experimentally confirmed that using the average cepstrum of the distant speech signals captured through distributed microphones improves the recognition accuracy of the distant speech by about 20%. In this paper, we extend the idea of *feature averaging* to multiple regression of the log spectrum (MRLS) of speech captured by multiple spatially distributed microphones so as to approximate the log spectrum of the speech of the close-talking microphone. The expected advantages of the proposed method are as follows: 1) The method does not make any assumptions about the positions of the speaker and noise sources with respect to the microphones. Therefore, the system can be trained for various sitting positions of drivers. 2) The regression weights can be statistically optimized over a certain length of speech segments (e.g., sentences of speech) under particular road conditions.

The aim of this paper is to describe the proposed method and evaluate the performance of the method for in-car speech recognition. In Section 2, we introduce the spectral regression method for speech enhancement. In Section 3, the in-car speech database that is used for the evaluation experiments is described. In Section 4, we present evaluation experiments, and Section 5 summarizes this paper.

2   Multiple Regression of Log Spectra (MRLS)

2.1   Two-Dimensional Taylor-Series Expansion of Log Spectrum

Assume that speech signal $x_i(t)$ at the ith microphone position is given by a mixture of the source speech $s(t)$ and the noise $n(t)$ convolved with transfer functions to the position, $h_i(t)$ and $g_i(t)$, i.e.,

$$x_i(t) = h_i(t) * s(t) + g_i(t) * n(t).$$

Assume also that the power spectrum of $x_i(t)$ is given by the 'power sum' of the filtered speech and noise, i.e.,

$$X_i(\omega) = |H_i(\omega)|^2 S(\omega) + |G_i(\omega)|^2 N(\omega),$$

where $S(\omega)$, $X_i(\omega)$ and $N(\omega)$ are the power spectra of the speech signal at its source position, the noisy speech signal at the ith microphone position and the noise signal at its source position, respectively. (The frequency index (ω) will be omitted in the remainder of this paper.) Consequently, the corresponding log power spectrum of the signals at the ith microphone position are given by

$$\log X_i = \log \left\{ |H_i|^2 S + |G_i|^2 N \right\}.$$

The derivative of $\log X_i$ can be calculated by

$$\Delta \log X_i = \frac{\partial \log X_i}{\partial \log S} \Delta \log S + \frac{\partial \log X_i}{\partial \log N} \Delta \log N$$
$$= a_i \Delta \log S + b_i \Delta \log N, \tag{1}$$

where a_i and b_i are given by

$$a_i = \frac{|H_i|^2 S}{|H_i|^2 S + |G_i|^2 N}$$
$$b_i = \frac{|G_i|^2 N}{|H_i|^2 S + |G_i|^2 N}. \tag{2}$$

Note that both a_i and b_i are functions of the ratio between signal and noise at their source positions, i.e., S/N. Small deviations in the log-power-spectrum of the signal at the ith microphone position can be approximated by a two-dimensional Taylor-series expansion around X_i^0, i.e.,

$$\log X_i - \log X_i^0 \approx a_i(\log S - \log S^0) + b_i(\log N - \log N^0), \tag{3}$$

where

$$\log X_i^0 = a_i \log S^0 + b_i \log N^0.$$

Using superscript $(\bullet)^{(d)}$ for the deviation from $(\bullet)^0$, e.g. $\log X_i^d = \log X_i - \log X_i^0$, the Taylor expansion can be rewritten as

$$\log X_i^{(d)} \approx a_i \log S^{(d)} + b_i \log N^{(d)}. \tag{4}$$

2.2 Multiple Regression of Multi-channel Signals

Approximation of $\log S^{(d)}$ by the multiple regression of $\log X_i^{(d)}$ has the form

$$\log S^{(d)} \approx \sum_{i=1}^{M} \lambda_i \log X_i^{(d)} \tag{5}$$

where M denotes the number of microphones and λ_i is the regression weight. By substituting this into equation (4), the regression error of the approximation, ϵ, can be calculated as follows.

$$\varepsilon = \left[\log S^{(d)} - \sum_{i=1}^{M} \lambda_i \log X_i^{(d)} \right]^2$$

$$
= \left[\log S^{(d)} - \sum_{i=1}^{M} \lambda_i \left\{ a_i \log S^{(d)} + b_i \log N^{(d)} \right\} \right]^2
$$

$$
= \left[\left(1 - \sum_{i=1}^{M} \lambda_i a_i \right) \log S^{(d)} - \sum_{i=1}^{M} \lambda_i b_i \log N^{(d)} \right]^2
$$

Assuming the orthogonality between $\log S^{(d)}$ and $\log N^{(d)}$, the expectation value of the regression error becomes

$$
E \left[\left(1 - \sum_{i=1}^{M} \lambda_i a_i \right)^2 \{ \log S^{(d)} \}^2 + \left\{ \sum_{i=1}^{M} \lambda_i b_i \right\}^2 \{ \log N^{(d)} \}^2 \right].
$$

The minimum regression error is then achieved when

$$
\sum_{i=1}^{M} E \{ a_i \} \lambda_i = 1, \quad \sum_{i=1}^{M} E \{ b_i \} \lambda_i = 0. \tag{6}
$$

Thus, the optimal $\{\lambda_i\}$ can be uniquely determined as a vector that is orthogonal to $\{b_i\}$ and its inner product with $\{a_i\}$ is equal to unity.

a_i and b_i correspond to the Signal-to-Noise and Noise-to-Signal ratios, respectively, at the microphone position, and the relationship

$$
a_i + b_i = 1
$$

holds for every microphone position. Therefore, once the Signal-to-Noise ratios at all microphone positions are given, λ_i can be uniquely determined. Multiple regression on the log power spectrum domain can be regarded as an implicit estimation of the local SNR at each microphone position.

2.3   Implementation

In our implementation, the optimal $\{\lambda_i\}$ is obtained by regression training using the log spectrum of the close-talking microphone and those of the five distant microphones simultaneously. In the recognition phase, the optimal weights are utilized to generate the estimated log spectrum using Equation (5), where the speech of close-talking is not required any more. The spectrum of the speech captured by the close-talking microphone, X_0, is used as the speech at the source position S. All log power spectrum $\log X_i$ values are normalized so that their means over an utterance become zero, i.e.,

$$
\log X_i^{(d)} \approx \log X_i - \overline{\log X_i}. \tag{7}
$$

Note that in this implementation, minimizing the regression error is equivalent to minimizing the MFCC distance between the approximated and the target spectra, due to the orthogonality of the discrete time cosine transform (DCT) matrix. Therefore, the MRLS has the same form as the maximum likelihood optimization of the filter-and-sum beamformer proposed in [5].

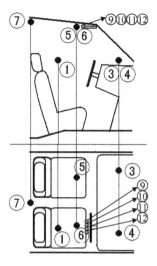

Fig. 1. Side view and top view of the arrangement of multiple spatially distributed microphones and the linear array in the data collection vehicle.

3   Experimental Evaluations

3.1   In-Car Speech Corpus

For data collection, we have devised a special Data Collection Vehicle (DCV) which supports synchronous recording of multi-channel audio data from 16 microphones. The corpus includes isolated word utterances, phonetically balanced sentences and dialogues recorded while driving. For dialogue corpus, about 1 terabytes of data has been collected by recording three sessions of spoken dialogue in about 60 minute of driving from each of 800 drivers.

Five spatially distributed microphones (#3 to #7) are placed around the driver's seat, as shown in Fig. 1, where top and side views of the driver's seat are depicted. Microphone positions are marked by the black dots. While microphones #3 and #4 are located on the dashboard; #5, #6 and #7 are attached to the ceiling. Microphone #6 is nearest to the speaker. In addition to these distributed microphones, the driver wears a headset with a close-talking microphone (#1). A four-element linear microphone array (#9 to #12) with an inter-element spacing of 5 cm is located at the visor position.

3.2   Adaptive Beamforming (ABF)

The adaptive beamforming approach has become attractive for speech enhancement and speech recognition. One of the most common approaches for adaptive microphone array systems is the *Generalized Sidelobe Canceller* (GSC) [2]. For comparison, we apply the *Generalized Sidelobe Canceller* (GSC) to our in-car

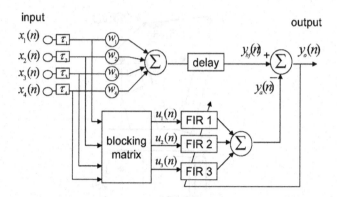

Fig. 2. Block diagram of Generalized Sidelobe Canceller.

speech recognition. Four linearly spaced microphones (#9 to #12 in Fig. 1) with an inter-element spacing of 5 cm at the visor position are used. The architecture of the GSC used is shown in Fig. 2. The three FIR filters are adapted sample-by-sample to generate replicas of the noise or interfering sources involved in the beamformed signal by using Normalized Least Mean Square (NLMS) method [6]. The number of taps and step-size of adaptation in the adaptive beamformer are set as 100 and 0.01 experimentally.

3.3   Recognition Experiments

Speech signals used in the experiments were digitized into 16 bits at the sampling frequency of 16 kHz. For the spectral analysis, a 24-channel mel-filter bank (MFB) analysis is performed by applying the triangular windows on the FFT spectrum of the 25-ms-long windowed speech with a frame shift of 10 ms. Spectral components lower than 250 Hz are filtered out since the spectra of the in-car noise signal is concentrated in the lower-frequency region. This basic analysis is realized through HTK standard MFB analysis [7]. The regression analysis is performed on the logarithm of MFB output to obtain the estimated feature vectors. Then 12 cepstral mean normalized mel-frequency cepstral coefficients (CMN-MFCC) are obtained.

The training data comprises a total of 7,000 phonetically balanced sentences (uttered by 202 male and 91 female speakers): 3,600 of them were collected in the idling condition and 3,400 of them while driving the DCV on the streets near Nagoya University. The structure of the HMM is fixed, i.e.,

1) three-state triphones based on 43 phonemes that share 1,000 states;

2) each state has 32-component mixture Gaussian distributions; and

3) the feature vector is a 25-dimensional vector (12 CMN-MFCC + 12 Δ CMN-MFCC + Δ log energy).

The test data for recognition includes 364 sentences, uttered by 21 speakers while talking to an ASR based restaurant guidance system while driving the DCV

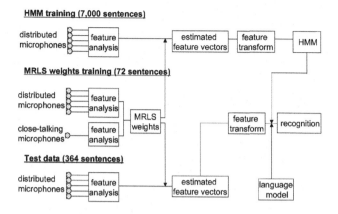

Fig. 3. Diagram of the MRLS-based HMM and speech recognition.

[8]. After MRLS weights are learned by the use of 12,569 frames as examples (from 72 sentences uttered by another 5 speakers), they are used to generate the 7,000 sentences for training HMM and the 364 sentences for testing. The diagram of the MRLS-based HMM and speech recognition is given in Fig. 3. For language models, forward bi-gram and backward tri-gram models with 2,000 word vocabulary are used. The decoder used is Julius 3.4.1 [9].

To evaluate of the performance of MRLS, we performed the following four recognition experiments:

CTK recognition of the close-talking microphone speech using the HMM trained by the close-talking microphone;

ABF recognition of adaptive beamforming output using the HMM trained by the adaptive beamformer's output;

MRLS recognition of MRLS output using MRLS HMM; and

DST recognition of the nearest distant microphone's (#6 in Fig. 1) speech by the corresponding HMM.

Fig. 4 shows averaged word accuracy scores. The word accuracy scores are defined as

$$Accuracy = \frac{N - S - D - I}{N} \times 100 \quad [\%] \tag{8}$$

where N, S, D and I denote the number of words, the number of substitutions, the number of deletions, and the number of insertions. This figure clearly shows the MRLS method outperforms the adaptive beamforming method. Compared to the use of the nearest distant microphone, recognition accuracy is improved by 4% with the proposed MRLS method. In comparison to the nearest distant microphone and multi-microphone adaptive beamformer, the proposed MRLS obtains a relative word error rate (WER) reduction of 9.8% and 3.6% respectively. This result indicates shows that approximation of the speech signals from

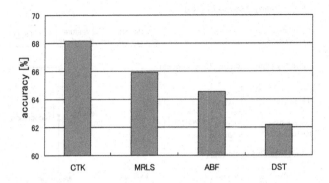

Fig. 4. Recognition performance of MLRS.

the close-talking microphone using MRLS is reasonable and practical for improving the recognition accuracy. In light of the computation cost, the proposed MRLS method is far superior to the adaptive beamforming approach.

The effectiveness of the approximation by regression is verified from the viewpoint of spectral distortion. The signal-to-deviation ratio (SDR) is given by

$$\text{SDR [dB]} = 10 \log_{10} \frac{\sum_{l=1}^{N} \left\| X^{(l)} \right\|^2}{\sum_{l=1}^{N} \left\| X^{(l)} - \hat{X}^{(l)} \right\|^2}$$

where $X^{(l)}$ is the log spectrum vector of the reference speech captured by the close-talking microphone, and $\hat{X}^{(l)}$ is the log spectrum vector to be evaluated. N denotes the number of frames during one utterance. Among the distributed distant microphones, the best SDR value is 19.3 dB, which is obtained by the nearest microphone, as we expected. The effectiveness of the spectrum regression is revealed from the result that the SDR of the approximated log spectrum is about 1.7 dB higher than that of microphone #6, whereas the adaptive beamformer contributes only a 0.3 dB improvement.

4   Summary

In this paper, we have proposed a new speech enhancement method for robust speech recognition in noisy car environments. The approach utilizes multiple spatially distributed microphones to perform multiple regression of the log spectra (MRLS), aiming at approximating the log spectra at a close-talking microphone. The method does not require a technically demanding microphone array infrastructure and makes no assumptions about the positions of speaker and noise sources with respect to the microphones. The results of our studies have shown that the proposed method can obtain good approximation to the speech of a close-talking microphone and can outperform the adaptive beamformer in terms of recognition performance while maintaining a low computation cost.

References

1. Junqua, C., Haton, P: Robustness in Automatic Speech Recognition. Kluwer Academic Publishers, 1996.
2. Griffiths, L. J., Jim, C. W: An Alternative Approach to Linearly Constrained Adaptive Beamforming, IEEE Trans. on Antennas and Propagation, vol. AP-30, no. 1, (1982) 27-34.
3. Brandstein, M, Ward, D: Microphone Arrays: Signal Processing Techniques and Applications, Springer-Verlag, 2001.
4. Shimizu, Y., Kajita, S., Takeda, K. and Itakura, F.: Speech Recognition Based on Space Diversity Using Distributed Multi-Microphone, Proc. IEEE ICASSP, Vol.III, (2000) 1747-1750.
5. Seltzer, M. L., Raj, B., and Stern, R. M: Speech Recognizer-based microphone array processing for robust hands-free speech recognition, Proc. IEEE ICASSP, Vol. I, (2002) 897-900.
6. Haykin, S.: Adaptive Filter theory, Prentice Hall, 2002.
7. http://htk.eng.cam.ac.uk
8. Fujimura, H., Itou, K., Takeda, K. and Itakura, F.: In-car speech recognition experiments using a large-scale multi-mode dialogue corpus, Proc. ICA, Vol. IV, (2004) 2583-2586.
9. http://julius.sourceforge.jp

Development of Advanced Image Processing Technology and Its Application to Computer Assisted Diagnosis and Surgery

Takayuki Kitasaka[1], Kensaku Mori[1], and Yasuhito Suenaga[1]

Graduate School of Information Science, Nagoya University,
Furo-cho, Chikusa-ku, Nagoya, Aichi, 464-8603, Japan
{kitasaka, kensaku, suenaga}@is.nagoya-u.ac.jp

Abstract. This paper describes our studies on medical image processing and its medical applications. We have developed systems of computer aided diagnosis (CAD) and computer assisted surgery (CAS) in our laboratory. The important features of CAD and CAS are (1) generation of anatomical maps based on image recognition and understanding technologies, (2) automated detection of abnormal regions, (3) guidance to specific areas, e.g., an abnormal region, (4) generation of additional assistant information that is not visible directly in practice, e.g., anatomical names, measurement values (diameter, volume, and so on.), results of surgical simulation, and organs existing beyond an organ's wall in an endoscopic view, and (5) visualization of such information. We briefly introduce medical image processing technologies and CAD/CAS systems that we have developed.

1 Introduction

From the early years of media processing, image recognition and understanding have attracted many researcher's attention. Many products based on image processing technology such as OCR and individual authentication systems have been commercialized. Medical images including X-ray CT, MR, and ultra sound images are also targets of media processing. Some products for assisting diagnosis using image processing techniques have been commercialized.

Information contained in medical images has significantly increased based on the development of devices such as multi-detector row X-ray CT and MRI scanners. Three dimensional (3D) CT image involves very precise information from inside a human body, and it enables a medical doctor to make a diagnosis from the image more accurately. However, such a large amount of information in the 3D CT image makes it harder for the doctor.

Therefore, assistant systems will play an important role in image diagnosis: e.g., automated detection of abnormal regions, navigation to suspicious regions, presentation of information that is not visible on a CT image such as anatomical names, measurement values (diameter, volume, etc.), and surrounding organs existing beyond the target organ's wall in an endoscopic view. Medical doctors

K. Aizawa, Y. Nakamura, and S. Satoh (Eds.): PCM 2004, LNCS 3331, pp. 514–521, 2004.
© Springer-Verlag Berlin Heidelberg 2004

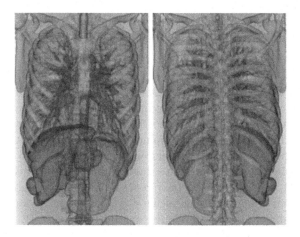

Fig. 1. Organ recognition results (left) viewed from front to back, and (right) from back to front

will most likely utilize such assistant systems, which are called computer aided diagnosis (CAD) and computer assisted surgery (CAS) systems.

Many researches on CAD and CAS systems have been reported[1,2]. Our laboratory has also been engaged in developing CAD and CAS systems[3]-[20]. The important features in CAD and CAS are (1) generation of anatomical maps based on image recognition and understanding technologies, (2) automated detection of abnormal regions, (3) guidance to specific areas, e.g., an abnormal region, (4) generation of additional assistant information that is not visible directly in practice, and (5) visualization of such information.

In this paper, we introduce some examples of medical image processing technologies and the applications for it that we have developed so far.

2   Medical Image Processing Technologies

2.1   Medical Image Recognition and Understanding

Organ Segmentation. Organ segmentation is an indispensable process in CAD and CAS systems. Each organ is segmented by extracting its characteristics e.g., shape and intensity distribution. The target organs are the lungs, bronchi, aorta, and pulmonary vessels in the chest, and the liver, spleen, kidneys, and colon in the abdomen[3,4,5,6,7]. Figure 1 shows examples of organ recognition results.

Organ analysis. Each organ has its own name, and each part of an organ also has its own unique name. For example, the bronchi form a tree structure starting from the trachea. The trachea ramifies the right and left main bronchi, the main bronchus bifurcates into lobe bronchial branches, and a lobe bronchus branches into segmental bronchi. We have developed a method for automated anatomical labeling of bronchial branches[8,9], and its labeling accuracy is more than 90 %[9].

Detection of abnormal regions. Detecting lung nodules, liver cancers, colorectal polyps, and other problems is important to prevent from oversights of abnormal regions and to reduce diagnostic time. Abnormal features of a shadow in CT images that medical doctors point out are quantified. Abnormal regions such as lung nodules and liver cancers are then classified into benign and malignant classes by measuring feature values (roundness, the mean and standard deviation of CT values, etc.)[10]. In colorectal polyp detection, a method based on curvature was reported because many colorectal polyps are observed as a round convex shape[11]. We developed a robust and adaptive method to the polyp size using a curve fitting technique[12]. Examples of polyp detection results are shown in Fig. 3.

2.2 Image Generation

Virtual Endoscopy. The virtual endoscopy system is a system that visualizes inside a human body using computer graphics technology, and it enables user to explore inside of the body freely as if he/she were in a real one[13]. The advantages of this system are, we can observe inside a human body (it is not animation!!), observe from an arbitrary viewpoint and view direction, and measure some features (the diameter of a bronchial branch, size of a polyp, etc.), and it is less invasive and applicable to almost all parts of a human body.

Image Deformation. Medical images are useful not only for an observation but also for generating deformed images that an organ is cut and stretched like as a medical doctor does during surgical operation. Image deformation consists of three major steps: (a) modeling an extracted organ by a node and spring model or a finite element model, (b) model deformation, and (c) reconstruction of the image from the deformed model. A virtual specimen and pneumoperitoneum mentioned next are good examples of applications of image deformation[14,15].

3   Practical Applications

3.1 Bronchoscope Navigation System

A bronchoscope navigation system has been designed for real-time navigation to a destination point of biopsy or an abnormal region and for a real-time presentation of various information obtained from a pre-operative CT image such as anatomical names of organs and measurement values (such as the length, diameter, and volume)[16].

   To achieve such a navigation, it is indispensable to track the actual endoscope position and orientation in the airway and to register them to the CT

Frame   20   40   70   90   100   140   220   250

RE

VE

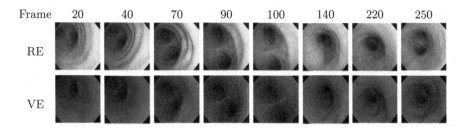

Fig. 2. Examples of endoscope motion tracking RE=Real Endoscope, VE=Virtual Endoscope

image taken before the inspection. Because the bronchoscope is a flexible and narrow instrument, it is physically impossible to detect them by using a magnetic positioning sensor. We therefore achieve the endoscope motion tracking by finding a time series of virtual endoscopic parameters (camera position and orientation) that generate the most similar virtual endoscopic view to a real endoscopic view, based on the image registration technique[17].

The tracking results of the endoscope motion are indicated in Fig. 2. As shown in Fig. 2, our endoscope motion tracking method works satisfactorily. Computation time is about 2 seconds per frame.

3.2   CAD System for Colorectal Polyps

The colon is a long and winding organ and has many haustra. Thus, automated detection of colorectal polyps and navigation to them are important functions in CAD systems. In addition, for reducing inspection time, generating an image that enables observing the entire colon efficiently is useful. An unfolding of the colon is a way to do that.

An outline of the CAD system we have developed for colorectal polyps[18] is illustrated in Fig. 4. This system consists of four functions: (1) preprocessing, (2) image generation, (3) control, and (4) medical support. A preprocessing function segments the colon region and generates a navigation path. The image generation function displays a virtual endoscopic view (VE view), virtual stretched view (VS view), and a CT slice. The viewpoints of these three views are synchronized, i.e., the corresponding part is displayed.

3.3   CAD System for Quantifying COPD

Chronic obstructive pulmonary disease (COPD)) is the fifth most common cause of death in the world (2.7 million, '02). Because it is an irreversible disease, early detection and treatment are vital. COPD regions are observed as dark gray regions on X-ray CT images. These dark areas are often called low attenuation areas (LAAs). A medical doctor diagnoses a COPD by perceiving LAAs on CT slices and reconstructing their 3D distribution in his/her mind. However, no

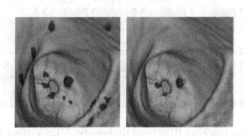 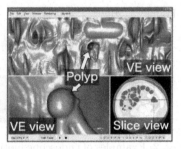

Fig. 3. Examples of polyp detection. (left) the previous method[11], (right) our method

Fig. 4. Outline of the CAD system for colorectal polyps

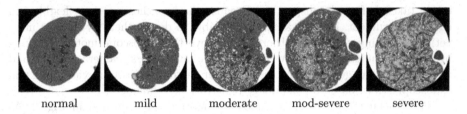

| normal | mild | moderate | mod-severe | severe |

Fig. 5. Examples of extracted LAAs and psuedo coloring display of the concentration index

objective or quantitative indices are available for the diagnosis. A CAD system for quantifying 3D distribution will likely be developed. We have developed a concentration index of the distribution of LAAs and have determined that the index has a high correlation with a medical doctor's diagnosis[19,20].

Figure 5 shows extracted LAAs and a pseudo-coloring display of the concentration index.

3.4   Virtual Specimen

For observing organs with a large cavity such as the stomach, unfolding (or projection of) the organ to a plane as like a pathological specimen of the stomach is more useful and efficient than observing them as they are. We have studies on a method for generating a stretched image of luminal organs by using the organ recognition and image deformation technologies[14]. An example of a virtually stretched stomach is shown in Fig. 7.

3.5   Virtual Pneumoperitoneum

In laparoscopic surgery for abdominal organs, the pneumoperitoneum which makes a work space by lifting the abdominal wall is performed. The laparoscopic surgery requires abundant experiments and high skill, because the viewable area

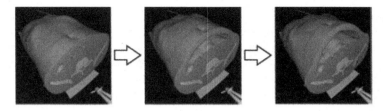

Fig. 6. Deformation process of the virtual pneumoperitoneum

of the laparoscope is very narrow. If a simulation of the pneumoperitoneum can be carried out, a medical doctor can grasp the pneumoperitoneum state before the operation. Therefore, a virtual pneumoperitoneum whould be a great help for him/her in planning the operation. Also, in intraoperation, it can provide intraoperative support because a doctor can recognize the location of an important organ such as the aorta, which is not visible.

We have been developing a virtual pneumoperitoneum by using segmentation of the abdominal wall and an image deformation technique[15]. The process of the virtual pneumoperitoneum is shown in Fig. 6. Lifting the abdominal wall is simulated well from the CT image taken before performing the pneumoperitonum. Figure 8 shows a super-imposed view of the liver, spleen, kidney, and aorta. As shown in Fig. 8, recognition of locations of each organ is very useful for preoperative or intraoperative support.

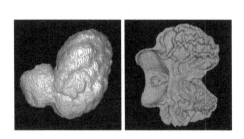

Fig. 7. Example of stretching the stomach

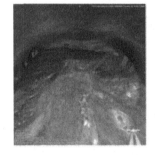

Fig. 8. Super-imposed view of the liver, spleen, kidney, and aorta

4   Conclusion

This paper introduced our studies on CAD and CAS systems based on image recognition, understanding, and generation technologies with some applications. The CAD and CAS systems require various technologies: (1) generation of anatomical maps based on image recognition and understanding technologies, (2) automated detection of abnormal regions, (3) guidance to specific areas, (4) generation of additional assistant information that is not visible directly in practice, and (5) visualization of such information. Applications we presented here are still in the middle of the development. We aim to develop more reliable and more highly intelligent technologies and CAD/CAS systems.

Acknowledgments. The authors thank Dr. S. Nawano of the National Cancer Center Hospital East Japan, Dr. H. Natori of the Sapporo Medical University, Dr. M. Mori of the Sapporo Kousei Hospital, Dr. H. Takabatake of the Minami-ichijyo Hospital, and Dr. M. Hashizume of the Center for Integration of Advanced Medicine and Innovative Technology, Kyushu University Hospital for providing CT images and for giving us useful advice. They also thank the members of our laboratory at Nagoya University for their collaboration. This work was supported in part by the Grant-In-Aid for Scientific Research for the Private University High-Tech Research Center and the 21st COE program provided by the Ministry of Education, Culture, Sports, Science and Technology of the Japanese government and the Grant-In-Aid for Cancer Research from the Ministry of Health, Welfare and Labor of the Japanese government.

References

1. B. van Ginneken, B. M. ter H. Romeny, and M. A. Viergever, "Computer-Aided Diagnosis in Chest Radiography: A Survey,", *IEEE trans. on Medical Imaging*, Vol.20, No.12, pp. 1228–1241, 2001.
2. K. Cleary and C. Nguyen, "State of the Art in Surgical Robotics: Clinical Application and Technology Challenges,", *Computer Aided Surgery*, Vol.6, No.6, pp. 312–328, 2001.
3. J. Hasegawa, K. Mori, J. Toriwaki et al., "Automated Extraction of Lung cancer lesions from multi-Slice Chest CT Images by Using Three-Dimensional Image Processing," IEICE D-II, Vol.J76-D-II, No.8, pp. 1587–1594, 1993 (in japanese).
4. T. Kitasaka, K. Mori, J. Hasegawa et al., "A Method for Extraction of Bronchus Regions from 3D Chest X-ray CT Images by Analyzing Structural Features of the Bronchus," *FORMA*, Vol.17, No.4, pp. 321–338, 2002.
5. T. Kitasaka, K. Mori, J. Hasegawa et al., "Automated Extraction of Aorta and Pulmonary Artery in Mediastinum from 3D Chest X-ray CT Images without Contrast Medium," *Proc. of SPIE*, Vol.4684, Part 3, pp. 1496–1507, 2002.
6. T. Yamaguchi, T. Kitasaka, K. Mori et al., "A preliminary study for automated recognition of branches of pulmonary artery and vein using anatomical positional relations from a 3-D chest X-ray CT image," *Proc. of the 16th International Congress and Exhibition on Computer Assisted Radiology and Surgery (CARS 2002)*, pp. 782–787, 2002.
7. Y. Hayashi, K. Mori, J. Hasegawa et al., "Quantitative evaluation of observation methods in virtual endoscopy based on the rate of undisplayed region," *Medical Image Computing and Computer-Assisted Intervention (MICCAI2002)*, pp. 631–638, 2002.

8. K. Mori, J. Hasegawa, Y. Suenaga et al., "Automated Anatomical Labeling of the Bronchial Branch and Its Application to the Virtual Bronchoscopy System," *IEEE Trans. on Medical Imaging*, pp. 103–114, 2000.

9. S. Ema, K. Mori, T. Kitasaka et al., "An improved method for automated anatomical labeling of bronchial branches extracted from 3-D CT images," *Proc. of the 18th International Congress and Exhibition on Computer Assisted Radiology and Surgery (CARS 2004)*, p.1358, 2004.

10. Y. Hirano, J. Hasegawa, and J. Toriwaki, "A feasibility study on computer classificaiton of benign and malignant tumors in lung cancer diagnosis from chest X-ray CT images," *Proc. of the 14th International Congress and Exhibition on Computer Assisted Radiology and Surgery (CARS 2000)*, pp. 773–778, 2000.

11. H. Yoshida and J. Nappi, "Three-Dimensional Computer Aided Diagnosis Scheme for Detection of Colonic Polyps," *IEEE Trans. on Medical Imaging*, Vol.20, No.12, pp. 1261-1274, 2001.

12. T. Kimura, Y. Hayashi, T. Kitasak et al., "A study on automated detection of colonic polyps from 3D abdominal CT images based on shape," *TECHNICAL REPOT OF IEICE*, MI2003-102, pp. 29–34, 2004 (in japanese).

13. K. Mori, J. Hasegawa, J. Toriwaki et al.," Automated extraction and visualization of bronchus from 3D CT images of lung," *Proc. of 1st International Conference on Computer Vision, Virtual Reality and Robotics in Medicine (CVRMed'95)*, pp. 542–548, 1995.

14. H. Oka, Y. Hayashi, K. Mori et al., "A Method for Generating Unfolded Views of Organ and Its Comparison With Virtual Endoscopy Based on Undisplayed Region Rate," *Proc. of SPIE*, vol.5031, pp. 99–101, 2003

15. K. Mori, Y. Hayashi, K. Ohta et al., "Virtual pneumoperitoneum for generating virtual laparoscopic images based on shape deformation," *Proc. of SPIE*, Vol.5639, pp. 178–188, 2004.

16. K. Mori, D. Deguchi, J. Sugiyama et al., "Tracking of a bronchoscope using epipolar geometry analysis and intensity-based image registration of real and virtual endoscopic images," *Medical Image Analysis*, No. 6, pp. 321–336, 2002.

17. K. Mori, T. Enjouji, D. Deguchi et al., "New image similarity measures for bronchoscope tracking based on image registration between virtual and real bronchoscopic images," *Proc. of SPIE*, Vol.5639, pp. 165–176, 2004.

18. M. Oda, Y. Hayashi, T. Kitasaka et al., "Development of Computer Aided Diagnosis System for Colorectal Cancer based on Navigation Diagnosis," *TECHNICAL REPORT OF IEICE*, MI2004-18, pp. 35–40, 2004.

19. J. Nagao, T. Aiguchi, K. Mori et al., "A CAD System for Quantifying COPD Based on 3-D CT Images," *Medical Image Computing and Computer Assisted Intervention - MICCAI 2003*, Lecture Notes in Computer Science, Vol.2878, pp. 730–737, 2003.

20. M. Mori, H. Takabatake, H. Natori et al., "Three-dimensional Display of Pulmonary Emphysema: Quantitative Analysis of Spatial Distributions," *Scientific Assembly and Annual Meeting Program, Radiological Society of North America (RSNA 2003)*, p. 805, 2003.

Discussion Mining:
Annotation-Based Knowledge Discovery from Real World Activities

Katashi Nagao[1], Katsuhiko Kaji[2], Daisuke Yamamoto[2], and Hironori Tomobe[4]

[1] EcoTopia Science Institute, Nagoya University
nagao@nuie.nagoya-u.ac.jp
[2] Department of Media Science, Graduate School of Information Science,
Nagoya University
{kaji,yamamoto}@nagao.nuie.nagoya-u.ac.jp
[3] 21st Century COE Program on Intelligent Media Integration,
Nagoya University
tomobe@nagao.nuie.nagoya-u.ac.jp

Abstract. We present *discussion mining* as a preliminary study of knowledge discovery from discussion content of offline meetings. Our system generates minutes for such meetings semi-automatically and links them with audio-visual data of discussion scenes. Then, not only retrieval of the discussion content, but also we are pursuing the method of searching for a similar discussion to an ongoing discussion from the past ones, and the method of generation of an answer to a certain question based on the accumulated discussion content. In terms of mailing lists and online discussion systems such as bulletin board systems, various studies have been done. However, what we think is greatly different from the previous works is that ours includes face-to-face offline meetings. We analyze meetings from diversified perspectives using audio and visual information. We also developed a tool for semantic annotation on discussion content. We consider this research not just data mining but a kind of real-world human activity mining.

1 Introduction

It will be very helpful that we can proceed to a discussion smoothly in a meeting or in a place for debating, and that we can retrieve and reuse the content such as minutes of these discussions. Generally speaking, however, unlike online discussions on bulletin boards on the Web, on offline ones at face-to-face meetings, making minutes reusable is difficult.

In this research, we propose a system that generates structured data on minutes semi-automatically and that displays them being visualized in real time. In addition, the data are registered in an XML database and in a relational database so that retrieval and summarization will be available. To apply this function, we made a trial system for supporting discussions.

K. Aizawa, Y. Nakamura, and S. Satoh (Eds.): PCM 2004, LNCS 3331, pp. 522–531, 2004.

One of the purposes of our research is to acquire knowledge from read world human activities such as conversations and discussions. Also, we are researching methods to annotate human activity records like meeting minutes with some semantic structures and to reuse them for supporting ongoing activities.

We have been developing some technologies which can record the sounds and the visions in meetings and generate multimedia minutes semi-automatically. Our technologies also include search and summarization methods for finding and browsing relevant and useful information.

In this paper, we focus on two technologies. One creates discussion content not just meeting minutes but also hypertext documents linked with video and audio. The discussion content also includes discussion graphs that visualize semantic/pragmatic structures of discussions. The other allows the users to annotate the discussion content with additional information about the structure of the discussion. The semantically-annotated discussion content is easily converted into more appropriate formats to be reused.

2   Creation of Discussion Content

There is a method mainly using video (image and sound) to make a discussion reusable. What we employed is a method that generates data on minutes primarily by text input through the forms in a Web document. The forms are subdivided and not only the content of the discussion but the information such as presenter, date, title and participants are inputted.

We especially focused on information about presentation slides in the trial system. In recent years people tend to use slides made by Microsoft Power-Point for meetings. We employed JACOB (A Java-COM Bridge) to handle COM (Component Object Model) with Java. Specified with Microsoft PowerPoint from the ones made in advance, the slide is converted to GIF format and is displayed on an input page of minutes. Simultaneously the information of characters in the slide is obtained and is added to the minutes. Then the minutes are structuralized by relating with the slide and a statement.

Furthermore the information of the statement is input after being categorized into three types, question, answer, and comment. We limited the types of statement to the three in order to avoid troubles when inputting its content in plain text. We assumed that the information of a discussion consisted of three kinds of statement, question, answer, and comment. So when a subject changes to another, we realized a system that enabled to show a new form for input.

Figure 1 shows a display screen of inputting minutes.

gIBIS [2] seems to represent groupware by structural approach. This can display the structure of a discussion graphically to turn into facilitating the grasp of the content of minutes and encouraging effective statements.

In this system, we visualized the structure of minutes by creating graphical display and edit mode of statements with the use of SVG (Scalable Vector Graphics) [6]. The graph was semi-automatically structuralized with the perti-

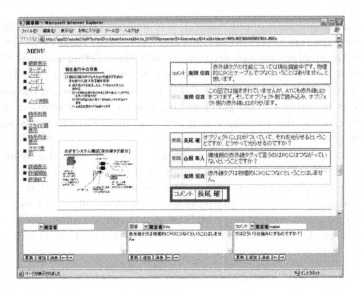

Fig. 1. Input of Minute

nent information and keyword on the statements and slide as shown in Figure 2. In result, it allows users to edit.

Minutes are mainly created from the inputted text and the presented slide. The format of minutes is XML (eXtensible Markup Language) and they are stored in an XML database and a relational database at a server machine with Java Servlet. On this study, we used Xindice [1] as the XML database and PostgreSQL as the relational database.

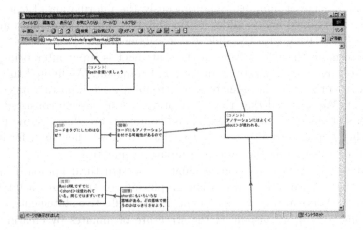

Fig. 2. Graph View of Minute

3   Reuse of Discussion Content

The users can access and retrieve only required minutes from the search form on the Web as shown in Figure 3. As the retrieval field is subdivided into several fields for title, date, a presenter and so on, we can easily access, retrieve and view the minutes that we want. As far as the retrieval, high-speed access will be available thanks to PostgreSQL.

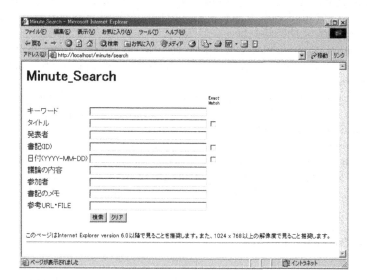

Fig. 3. Minute Search

The users can reedit and add the minutes, and correct their inputting errors through the Web browsers. When the users need to see the main points of the minutes, they can also see the summarized versions of the minutes in the order of importance. We utilize the structure of the statements at the time of inputting, the keyword of the statements, and the earned points for grades added to manually that are described later.

4   Semantic Annotation on Discussion Content

To utilize minutes more effectively, we add some semantic features to minute data such as linguistic structures, reference information to external content, and exact meanings of ambiguous words. We developed an authoring tool to create semantic annotation on minutes by linguistic analysis of text such as sentence parsing, anaphora resolution, and word sense disambiguation [5].

By using semantic information associated with mimutes, we can extract some important points in meetings and create summaries that include short history of discussions on the important topics.

Although annotation-based intelligent content processing is one of the major topics in some international research activities such as MPEG-7 [3] or Semantic Web [7], it has not obtained a definite result. We have already developed the system for interactive summarization and translation of Web content including multimedia data based on semi-automatically-created semantic annotation. Our annotation-based architecture is called "Semantic Transcoding" [5].

The annotation here includes the detailed language structure of the sentences in the document and the semantic segments of multimedia content which are generated semi-automatically. Each piece of the annotation is correctly associated with some part of the content.

The annotation enables Web audiences use the content more easily by using the semantic relationships among some media. For example, searching for videos using a keyword and summarization of videos connected with the summaries of voice transcript texts became possible because of the annotation. However, generation of the annotation costs very much. We need some methods to make this task more cost effective without making the annotation generation more complicated and inaccurate. One of our solutions captures some explicit hints or suggestions which are given by human who can easily understand the meaning of content and infers the semantic structure underlining the content. Our new user tools and software will make these processes simple and easy.

5   Discussion Mining

Discussion mining is a new research domain that aims at digitization of discussion content and discovery of knowledge from the content. Our developed system records audio-visual scenes of discussions in face-to-face meetings and visualizes discussion content in the form of Web documents linked with videos captured by several cameras and microphones.

We have done some preliminary studies and evaluations of the prototype systems for discussion capture and visualization. We have also implemented a minute editing tool that is capable of semantic annotation.

The meeting participants support the automatic generation of the minutes by transmitting their user IDs and types of their statements at the meeting via InfraRed signals by using a special device called "the discussion tag". Each participant has three types of the discussion tag colored green, yellow, and red, respectively. The green one is indicated to all participants when the participant wants to make a comment. The red one is used for asking a question. The yellow one is for answering it. All tags are also used for evaluation of whole discussion. Our system detects IR signals from each participant's discussion tag and generates a graph structure consist of each statement (some keywords included in the utterance are manually inputted by a meeting secretariat) as a node and each relation between statements (question-its answer, referred comment-referrer comment, etc.) as an arc. The nodes are also linked with the corresponding scenes in the recorded video and audio.

Figure 4 shows a scene of the discussion using the system, and Figure 5 shows a screen shot of a structured minute generated semi-automatically. The minute is visualized as a graphical structure of the discussion, and allows the users to retrieve the video related to specific scenes. Figure 6 illustrates the whole system configuration, and Figure 7 illustrates the discussion tag system. How to use the discussion tag is very simple and easy. A potential speaker will hold up the discussion tag just before beginning of a talk at the meeting. The tag automatically transmits the data to the system.

Fig. 4. Scene of Discussion

As mentioned earlier, the content of the minutes is represented in an XML data format and stored in the XML database. The audio-visual content is accumulated in the multimedia database. These databases are connected with the network and the XML data include the pointers to the multimedia data.

The minutes in the XML format enable keyword-based retrieval and summarization. The summarization method is based on importance values calculated by node importance (more linked modes are more important) and word importance (more salient words are more important). We evaluate each discussion by using discussion tags (the green, yellow, and red tag indicate "good", "soso", and "not good", respectively). We also evaluate each statement at a meeting by using a Web-based discussion annotation tool. These evaluations are also considered to calculate the importance of the discussion.

Not only visualization, retrieval and summarization of single minute content, we have also developed a mechanism of visualization of multiple minutes. Our system performs grouping of the accumulated minutes and linking between related minutes. A group of the minutes includes similar minutes and their corre-

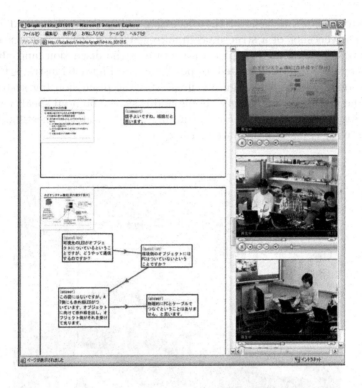

Fig. 5. Screen Shot of Structured Minute with Videos

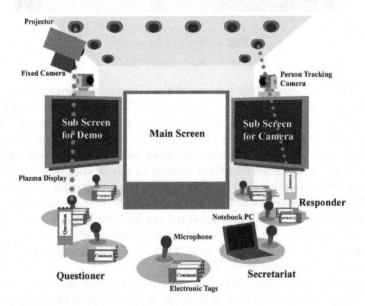

Fig. 6. Configuration of Discussion Mining

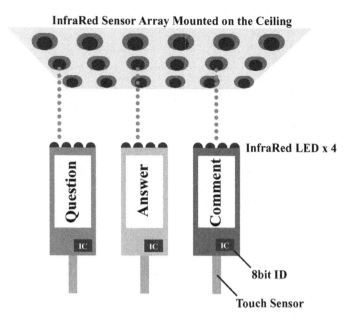

Fig. 7. Discussion Tag System

spondences. The groups of the minutes are visualized as a "minute map" which shows distances among the minutes as shown in Figure 8. The map supports the users to observe the whole discussions deeply and to discover knowledge. In order to make the map more informative, we have to create the annotation that indicates semantic relationships among the minutes. By using such annotation, we can discover more detail about discussion structures across several minutes such as some background information of an argument and its derivations.

From the minute map, we can also find the most important minute, the most significant statement and the most active speaker and questioner. Furthermore, we are analyzing the role of the sounds and the visions in meetings more deeply. We are also considering a new way of linking between multiple media related to human real-world activities such as conversations and discussions.

We should pursue some methods for not just capturing real world activities but also utilizing them for some meaningful tasks such as remembrance assistance and knowledge discovery.

6   Concluding Remarks

In this paper, we described the system of registering the minutes of meetings in database and reusing them. The following is the issues that we are planning to examine and to improve the system:

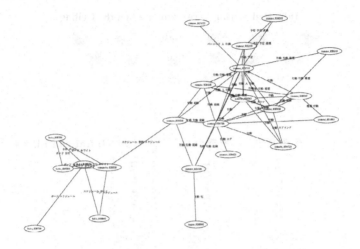

Fig. 8. Minute Map

1. Annotation over Multiple Discussions

   Minutes generated by this system are not related to the past ones, for they only refer to a certain meeting. The system should be improved to examine relevance to the past minutes semi-automatically from a keyword and to summarize covering multiple minutes. It will help to create annotations across multiple minutes.

2. Use of Voice Transcripts

   The use of voice will enable us to refer afterward to the information that cannot be contained in the minutes. Since the voice data is difficult to be searched as it is, using annotation can make it possible to largely reduce the problems like retrieval if speech recognition creates transcripts.

3. Use of Video Annotation

   Since video data is available, the system will be able to utilize hard-to-get data from other information like mood of meetings and gestures and facial expressions of the participants. We have also developed a video annotation editor to annotate visual objects in video frames with some notes and attributes and to edit scene descriptions and voice transcripts [4].

   In this research, we have shown one example of the knowledge discovery from the information in the real world, and the multiple media integration based on semantic annotation.

   Our annotation system will be a strong tool to associate some elements in the media data with the other media elements. For example, the image and the motion of the speakers' reference expressions such as finger pointings will be connected with the particular linguistic expressions such as deixis in the voice and the text data. The relationships among the multiple media will be pointed out clearly by using the semantic annotation, and contribute to finding out the rule of them.

Furthermore, the integration of other knowledge sources with the semantic annotation on the minutes makes it possible to search for and add to the information about speakers who made good arguments.

Semantic annotation is supposed to cost much in generally. However, involving human intervention effectively into the annotation task when the original content or the material of content is created improves cost performance very much. Needless to say, improving the quality of automatic analysis of the content such as vision and speech recognitions is able to facilitate the efforts for creation of the semantic annotation.

We also need more user-friendly tools that reduce the human labor as much as possible. For example, in addition to the discussion tags, a mechanical button on the desk will be useful during meetings. Just pressing it by each participant lets the system know which comment is important in the discussion and which action is meaningful in the physical event. Such simple mechanism will work for automatic annotation to the audio-visual data.

References

1. The Apache XML Project. Apache Xindice. http://xml.apache.org/xindice/. 2001.
2. Conklin, J. and Begeman, M.L. gIBIS: A Hypertext Tool for Exploratory Policy Discussion. Proc. of CSCW '88. pp. 140–152, 1988.
3. MPEG. MPEG-7 Overview. http://www.chiariglione.org/mpeg/standards/mpeg-7/mpeg-7.htm. 2002.
4. Nagao, K., Ohira, S., and Yoneoka, M. Annotation-Based Multimedia Annotation and Transcoding. in *Proceedings of the Nineteenth International Conference on Computational Linguistics (COLING 2002)*. pp. 702–708, 2002.
5. Nagao, K. *Digital Content Annotation and Transcoding*. Artech House Publishers. 2003.
6. W3C. Scalable Vector Graphics (SVG) 1.0 Specification. http://www.w3.org/TR/SVG/. 2001.
7. W3C. The Semantic Web Community Portal. http://www.semanticweb.org/. 2002.

Determining Correspondences Between Sensory and Motor Signals

Kento Nishibori, Jinji Chen, Yoshinori Takeuchi, Tetsuya Matsumoto,
Hiroaki Kudo, and Noboru Ohnishi

Graduate School of Information Science, Nagoya University,
Furo-cho, Chikusa-ku, 464-8603, Japan
{kent,chen,takeuchi,matumoto,kudo,ohnishi}@ohnishi.m.is.nagoya-u.ac.jp

Abstract. A human being understands the environment by integrating information obtained by the senses of sight, hearing and touch. To integrate information across different senses, a human being must find the correspondence of events observed by different senses. We obtain image, sound signals by the senses of sight and hearing from the external world as afferent signals, and the copy of efferent signals (a command to the motor system), which are the information of the internal world. In this paper, we propose a method for relating multiple audio-visual events to an efferent signal (motor command to hand) according to general laws without object-specific knowledge. As corresponding cues, we use Gestalt's grouping law; simultaneity of sound onsets and changes in movement, similarity of repetition between sound and movement. We conducted experiments in the real environment and obtained satisfactory results showing the effectiveness of the proposed method.

1 Introduction

Several-month-old infant can relate speech sound (audio information) to its mouth movement (visual information) and learn pronunciation and language by this ability [1]. Thus the ability of corresponding audio and visual events is necessary for human to understand the environment by integrating multimodal sensory information (sensor fusion) and to acquire the knowledge about objects in the environment without any supervisor. If a robot system has this ability, it can understand well the environment by sensor fusion and acquire several information about objects without teaching by humans.

Over last few years, a few studies of audio-visual fusion in machine learning have been reported [2]. Suyama et al. [3] developed a method for finding a face in images uttering speech based on the cue signal. The method uses multiple-microphones and relies on the relation between mouth movement and voice level. Mukai et al. [4] focused only on a periodic movement in the scene. Hayakawa et al. [5] extended Mukai's method to find the correspondence in the scene where one sound and multiple movements exist. But these two studies have a limitation of the number of movements and sounds. Chen et al. corresponded the multiple

K. Aizawa, Y. Nakamura, and S. Satoh (Eds.): PCM 2004, LNCS 3331, pp. 532–539, 2004.

audio-visual events, and treated the case of entire object movement or sound location change by using the spatiotemporal invariant (STI) [6].

While these papers focus on correspondences between audio and visual events, i.e. sensory signals, this paper focuses on correspondences between sensory and motor signals. Suppose that human grasps a toy rattle by a hand and shakes it. Then he/she can recognize the sound of the rattle even if other sounds exist. This means that among several sounds, human selects an appropriate sound (sensory signal) relating to hand motion (motor signal). Sensory signals are observed by the senses of sight and hearing, and convey the information about the external world. Motor signals are command ones which are sent to actuators in order to manipulate objects in the environment. They include the information about the internal world of robot itself.

In this paper, we propose a method for determining the sensory signal, among several signals, relating to robot hand motion. The method is based on Gestalt's similarity law. This paper is organized as follows. Clues of audio-visual correspondence are described in section 2. In section 3, we show how to find sensory-motor correspondence. In section 4, we describe several experiments as well as its results and discussion. Finally, we conclude this paper in section 5.

2   Clues of Audio-Visual Correspondence

In psychology, we tend to perceptually group elements in stimuli. This is known as the Gestaltist's perceptual organization (or perceptual grouping). Gestalists proposed the laws for perceptual grouping. The law of common fate and the law of similarity are typical ones of these laws. We tend to group stimuli with the same characteristics. This is the law of similarity. If the stimuli change or move together, we also tend to group these stimuli. This is the law of common fate. Though Gestalt's laws have been proposed only in one sensation, we extend this concept to correspond events among different types of sensation.

We summarized clues for relating visual and auditory information along with Gestalt's grouping factors corresponding to each clue [4]. In this paper, we only use two clues to determine the correspondence of audio-visual events. One is the simultaneity of change in movement and sound onset. This clue corresponds to the law of common fate. The instance of sound occurrence generally coincides with that of moving direction change. Another is similarity of repetition between sound and movement. This clue corresponds to the law of similarity. If a movement is repetitive, the corresponding sound has the same repetition as the movement.

3   How to Find Sensory-Motor Correspondence

3.1   Outline of Processing

This paper assumes that a robot operates an object in the environment (external world) and the robot observes the resultant events by its sensory system (microphone, camera). The processing is divided into three parts, audio information

Table 1. Clue of audio-visual correspondence.

	Visual information	Auditory information	Corresponding Gestalt's
Clue 1	Category, Material	Category, Sound tone	None
Clue 2	Size, Distance	Loudness	Common fate
Clue 3	Location	Direction	Similarity
Clue 4	Change in movement	Sound onset	Common fate
Clue 5	Repetition of movement	Repetition of sound	Similarity

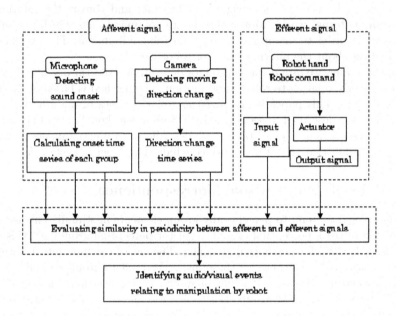

Fig. 1. Overview of signal processing.

processing, visual information processing, and correspondence between between afferent and efferent signal as shown in Fig. 1. The details of each part except for visual information processing are described above.

3.2 Audio Information Processing

Onset detection. Onset (the start part of sound) has two characteristics. One is that onset is not influenced by echo. Another is that only onset contains a single sound, when multiple sounds are not emitted at the same time. Multiple sounds rarely begin at the same time, so that it is possible to separate mixed sound signals at the onsets. Huang et al. [7] proposed the multivalue thresholding for onset detection. The period of silence is from t_1 to t_2, and the onset of the sound signal is from t_2 to t_3. Parameters a and b are amplitudes of the sound signal (see Fig. 2).

We assume the following: a robot (human) operates an object in the environment (external world), and observes the resultant changes by its sensors such as a camera and a microphone. The robot also can get the information of his operation (motor command) as an internal signal.

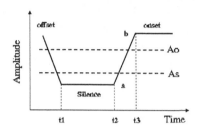

Fig. 2. Onset detection.

An onset is detected if the following conditions are satisfied.

1) The increase rate b/a of the amplitude between t_2 and t_3 exceeds one.

2) $t_2 - t_1 > T_s$ (T_s should be the minimum time, which is long enough to ignore former sound influence.)

3) $a < A_s$ (A_s is the maximum amplitude of silence, and exceeds the average level of the background noise.)

4) $b > A_o$ (A_o is the threshold value for detecting onset. It exceeds A_s and the maximum level of the background noise, and is smaller than the level of the signal sound.)

Separation of sound sources. Because it is very unlikely that different sources emit sound simultaneously, one onset corresponds to one sound source. We transform audio signals at each onset into the Time-Frequency space (TF space) by a short-term Fast Fourier Transform (FFT). If frequency components in different onsets are similar to each other, these onsets are related to the same sound source. Whether sounds in different onsets are from the same sound source or not is evaluated by the similarity of frequency components. We adopted the correlation coefficient $Cor(E_i, E_j)$ in Eq. (1) as a measure of the similarity.

$$Cor(E_i, E_j) = \frac{Cov(E_i, E_j)}{\sqrt{Var(E_i)Var(E_j)}} ,$$ (1)

where E_i and E_j are power spectra at onsets i and j, respectively, and E_i takes a value of power at each frequency. $Cor(E_i, E_j)$ is the correlation coefficient between power spectra E_i and E_j. If the value of $Cor(E_i, E_j)$ is near to 1, there is correlation between E_i and E_j, and the possibility that onset i and onset j are the same sound source is high. If the absolute value of $Cor(E_i, E_j)$ is near to 0, there is no correlation between E_i and E_j, and the possibility that onset i and

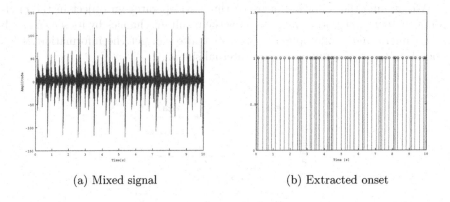

(a) Mixed signal   (b) Extracted onset

Fig. 3. Mixed signal and extracted onset.

onset j are the same sound source is low. Based on the values of the correlation coefficient, onsets are grouped by the max-min method.

Detection of sound onset series. For each separated sound source, we obtain time series of sound onsets. Thus represents the onset time of the jth sound source and is called sound onset series in this paper.

3.3 Determining the Correspondence Between Afferent and Efferent Signals

By the audio/visual information processing described above, we obtain a time series for sound onsets and/or motion-direction-change. In the final stage of the processing, we determine correspondences between time-series (of afferent signals) and efferent signals. In this paper, the correspondence is determined by the similarity of cycle times. That is, we select the time-series the cycle time of which is the most similar to that of the efferent signal. Thus the robot know the resultant sound or motion caused by its object manipulation.

4   Experiment and Discussion

4.1 Experiment

We conducted experiments for corresponding hand motion and observed sound. We used a robot which has a hand manipulator (Mitsubishi Electric, RV-1A) and a microphone (RION, UC-30). The robot grasps an object like a rattle and shakes it periodically. Then the objects emitts periodical sound. In the environment, there is another sound source (a metronome), whose cycle time is 0.2619[second]. The robot observed a scene for 10 seconds by a microphone.The sampling rate is

Table 2. Correlation of spectra between the first onset and other onsets.

	Onset1	Onset2	Onset3	Onset4	Onset5	Onset6	Onset7
Onset 1	**1.0000**	**0.6080**	**0.4996**	0.2075	**0.5958**	**0.5828**	**0.5956**

	Onset8	Onset9	Onset10	Onset11	Onset12	Onset13	Onset14
	0.3088	**0.6120**	**0.6218**	**0.5258**	0.1277	**0.7463**	**0.7125**

Table 3. Correlation of spectra between onset 12 and other onsets.

	Onset1	Onset2	Onset3	Onset4	Onset5	Onset6	Onset7
Onset 12	0.1277	0.1707	0.0896	**0.9047**	0.1531	0.1395	0.0705

	Onset8	Onset9	Onset10	Onset11	Onset12	Onset13	Onset14
	0.8328	0.0799	0.1335	0.1438	**1.0000**	0.1587	0.1512

Table 4. Cycle times.

Amplitude	14 deg.	20 deg.	30 deg.	40 deg.
Motion Cycle Time	0.2619	0.3050	0.3738	0.4288
Cycle Time of sound group 1(rattle)	0.2536	0.2734	0.3664	0.4665
Cycle Time of sound group 2(metronome)	0.9209	0.9308	0.9216	0.9149

16 kHz. Simultaneously the robot gets the internal signal, which is the command to the hand manipulator.

Figure 3(a) shows the measured sound signal which contains two sound signals: the object sound and metronome sound. Onsets (Fig. 3(b)) are extracted from the mixed signal. Onsets are classified into groups based on their spectral similarity. Table 2 shows correlation coefficients of spectra between the first onset and other onsets. The onset 12 with the least correlation is selected as a prototype of another sound source. Table 3 shows correlation coefficients of spectra between the onset 12 and other onsets. The onsets with the correlation of more than 0.5 in Tables 2 and 3 are grouped into sound group 1 and 2, respectively. Figure 4(c) and (d) show time series of sound onsets for the sound group 1 and 2, respectively.

Next, the robot determine the sound onset time series corresponding to hand motion. The averages of cycle time for two onset series are 0.2536 and 0.9209. Compared with the motion cycle time of 0.2619, sound group 1 is selected as the sound caused by the robot hand manipulation.

We also conducted experiments by changing the amplitude of periodic hand motion. Table 4 shows average cycle times for hand motion, sound group 1 and sound group 2. We know that according the similarity of cycle time, the robot can determine the sound corresponding to the robot motion.

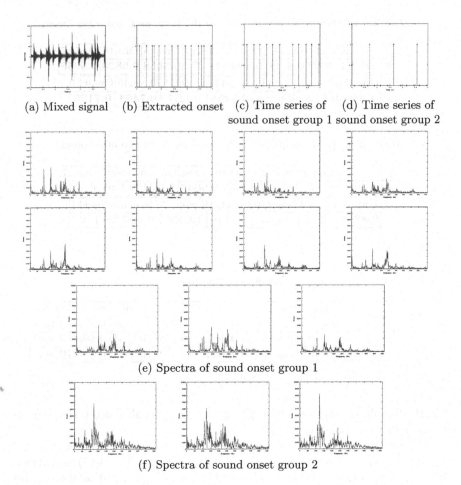

(a) Mixed signal   (b) Extracted onset   (c) Time series of   (d) Time series of
                                          sound onset group 1 sound onset group 2

(e) Spectra of sound onset group 1

(f) Spectra of sound onset group 2

Fig. 4. Separation of onsets in mixed signal (3 sec.).

4.2   Discussions

In the experiments, we succeeded in determining the sound relating to hand motion when another sound exists. This function is necessary for a robot to acquire information (the property of material, sound etc.) about objects in the environment by interacting with the environment. In the experiments, the number of sound sources is two and the sound is periodical. Then we have to conduct experiments under a complex situation; more than two sources and non-periodic sound.

5   Conclusion

We have proposed the method for determining the exteral signal (sound/image) relating to robot motion (internal signal) when other external signals exist. As a result of experiments in the real world, we obtained satisfactory results.

References

1. P.K. Kuhl and A.N. Meltozoff, "The Bimodal perception of Speech in Infancy", Science, Vol.218, pp.1138–1140, 1982.
2. Matthew J. Beal, Nebojsa Jojic, "A Graphical Model for Audiovisual Object Tracking", IEEE Transactions on Pattern Analysis and Machine Intelligence, Vol. 25, No.7, July 2003.
3. K. Suyama, K. Takahashi and H. Iwakura, "Multiple Sound Source Location Using Two-Stage Data Selection", IEICE A Vol.J79-A, No.6, pp.1127–1137, 1996 (in Japanese).
4. T. Mukai and N. Ohnishi, "Grouping Corresponding Parts in Vision and Audition Using Perceptual Grouping among Different Sensations", IEEE/RSJ Integration for Intelligent System, pp.713–718 (1996).
5. K. Hayakawa, R. Suzuki, T. Mukai and N. Ohnishi, "Finding Correspondence Between Vision and Audition Based On Physical Law", Technical Report of IEICE, EID98-147, IE98-138, pp.13–18 (1999) (in Japanese).
6. J. Chen, T. Mukai, Y. Takeuchi, T. Matsumoto, H. Kudo, T. Yamamura and N. Ohnishi, "Finding the Correspondence of Audio-Visual Events Caused by Multiple Movements", The Journal of The Institute of Image Information and Television Engineers, Vol.55, No.11, pp.1450–1459 (2001).
7. J. Huang, N. Ohnishi and N. Sugie, "A System for Multiple Sound Source Localization", The 5th International Symposium on Robotics in Construction (1988).

Architecture of Authentication Mechanism for Emerging T-commerce Environments

Sangkyun Kim[1], Hong Joo Lee[2], and Choon Seong Leem[2]

[1] Somansa, Woolim e-Biz center, 16, Yangpyeongdong 3-ga, Yeongdeungpogu, Seoul
150-103, Korea
[2] Department of Computer and Industrial Engineering, Yonsei University,
134, Shinchondong, Seodaemoongu, Seoul 129-749, Korea

Abstract. With the emergence of convergent information devices capable of delivering multimedia contents and providing an interactive communication with independence of location, new challenges about the implementation of secured environments for electronic business have arisen. Digital television (D-TV) uses the wire-network connections to provide interactive multimedia contents and value-added services such as electronic shopping. T-commerce (Digital Television Commerce) technologies make a dream of new business models an actuality, but these technologies lack in provision of the authentication architecture of users for the accountability, confidentiality and integrity of business contracts and personal preferences. This paper presents the architecture of authentication mechanism to deal with the specific challenges arising from these applications and to overcome the weakness of traditional architecture of the Internet commerce or m-commerce for the secured infrastructure of T-commerce business environments.

1 Introduction

With the convergence of digital communication networks and the Internet, the usage of digital commerce applications utilizing digital devices such as cellular phone and digital television has been increased. The digital television commerce, in short T-commerce, is a particular case of electronic commerce using the digital television and other devices in connection with it as an infrastructure of commerce. The users can acquire information, browse product catalogs, place orders for analog or digital goods, pay and contact customer support services using handheld devices. Even in real time, multi parties pricing negotiations such as online auctions have become feasible. As T-commerce is often coupled with novel business models, it also brings new challenges in provision of information security. Nowadays, the major problematic issue in T-Commerce is the matter of authentication.

In an electronic commerce using the Internet environments, the user possesses a public and private key pair of any encryption algorithm using public key mechanism, and maintains a certificate issued by a certification authority.

K. Aizawa, Y. Nakamura, and S. Satoh (Eds.): PCM 2004, LNCS 3331, pp. 540–547, 2004.

If an authentication is required, the user engages in an authentication protocol which is relying on a public-key infrastructure.

These days, the television sets tend to contain multimedia terminals or tend to be linked to set-top-boxes which do not only provide the Internet access, but also allow the users to buy products electronically during a television show. For example, during watching a TV drama or telecasting football game, a small sign might pop up at the upper right corner of the TV screen, indicating that the viewer might buy some of the objects currently shown on the screen. However, it is hard to imagine that every digital television set in the world can adopt a traditional public-key infrastructure.

In this paper, we propose the mechanism of authentication for T-commerce environments. The mechanism of authentication proposed in this paper includes: 1) Making orders using the remote controller of home TV, 2) The authentication of private orders using the personal mobile device, and 3) Making a charge based on the authentication result using the personal mobile device.

2   Digital Television

2.1   Key Characteristics of Digital Television

After the advent of color TV in 1945, there were many changes in telecast infrastructure. The convergence of telecast and communication infrastructure in the consequence of the development of information technology and the growth of digital telecast provide new waves of changes [1].

The digital TV has the key characteristics of digital representation, processing and transmission of the signal. The broadcasting of digital TV converts the images and sounds into digital codes. The digitization of images and sounds starts with a compression process which minimizes the capacity requirement of transmission channel. The transmission standard of digital TV adopts the digital processing and the compression to support a simultaneous transmission of various television programs or the reception of a single program at a quality of actual pictures that depends on the complexity of receiver. However, an analog TV closed captioning of current level can transport data at 960 bits per second, while a digital TV closed captioning under the new standard will work at 9600 bits per second [2].

2.2   High Definition Television

High Definition Television (HDTV) means a high-resolution, wide-screen, digital surround sound, and no artifacts. HDTV can display at least 1000 vertical measured lines in interlaced mode and has a 16:9 aspect ratio [3]. The table 1 describes the differences between analog TV and digital TV.

Table 1. Comparison of analog TV and digital TV

	Analog TV	SDTV	HDTV
Resolution	525	704*480	1902*1080
Sound	2 channel FM stereo	5.1 channel	5.1 channel
Ratio	4:3	4:3 or 16:9	16:9
Useful function	Data broadcasting	Home shopping, home banking, Internet access, interactive TV	

3   T-commerce Authentication Mechanism

3.1   Introduction to T-commerce

The fundamental application of T-commerce is similar to the following distributed applications delivering VOD (Video On Demand) services in digital television environments. The several contents providers offer digital contents of videos to customers who are registered as users of broadcast services offered by an infrastructure provider. The contents providers use the infrastructure of broadcast organizations to deliver their digital contents to the customers [4]. Customers can order products directly from the contents providers via the infrastructure of broadcaster. Within this situation, several problems of information security are arisen apparently. To process a purchasing order of customer according to the legal liabilities, the authentication between the customers and contents providers must be established. Furthermore, the control messages sent to all parties must be confidential, and no party should be able to alter identification information during transmission without any means of detection [5]. Both the customers and contents providers should not be able to deny their agreement unfaithfully on the purchasing conditions in later. Another requirement may be anonymity. Customers will not fully accept services that erode their privacy. For example, in digital television environments, the analysis of user's viewing habits is very simple and the customer profiles can be compiled for the purpose of direct marketing campaigns. The electronic commerce protocols also need to include a mechanism for copyright protection when digital products are sold electronically to guarantee an acceptance by content creators and thus ensure a wider range of qualified contents [6].

3.2   Security Requirements of T-commerce

Key Factors of T-Commerce Protocols. The design of T-commerce protocol is strongly influenced by the availability of hardware and its functions. For example, the hardware in set-top-boxes might contain special units which process multimedia streams, but lack in the provision of general purpose units which support a public key cryptosystem. The existence or absence of a traditional public-key infrastructure and the organizational constraints of contents providers and broadcasters such as the requirements of accounting between the contents provider and the broadcaster are also key factors of the design of T-commerce protocol.

Basis of Security Design. The electronic commerce applications partially operating with hardware-based security solutions are usually feasible in m-commerce and T-commerce. It may be assumed that every user is equipped with at least one information device that contains a unique string of identification called Hardware-ID. Furthermore, every user has a remote controller of digital television and unique code of customer ID. In these aspects, the problem of T-commerce security must be resolved on the basis of decentralized authentication mechanism. It is one of the major axioms to design information security that the system should provide security features in a transparent way so that a minimum amount of user interaction is required [7].

Security Requirements of e-Commerce. The following security requirements for e-commerce application should be addressed in T-commerce environments [8].

Confidentiality. Persons not involved in an electronic transaction should not be able to gain any information about the orders placed by a user at a content provider; thus, all messages sent in the protocol must be encrypted.

Authentication. As contracts must be legally binding, an authentication mechanism for both customers and content providers is required.

User Authentication. To prevent theft of mobile devices, the user has to authenticate himself or herself to the device before starting any transaction. However, the overhead of authentication must be as low as possible; otherwise the usability of the mobile device might be affected.

Integrity. Messages sent in the electronic commerce protocol should not be altered by any party not involved in the transaction.

Fairness. M-commerce protocols may include some kinds of copyright protection mechanism. Such mechanisms must be "fair" toward both the customer and contents provider, meaning that no false claims of infringements should occur. However, in case of an illegal copy, it must allow resolving the copyright situation clearly.

Non-repudiation. No party should be able to deny later their agreement to the conditions of any given transaction.

Partial anonymity. In order to provide privacy of the customers, anonymous transactions are necessary. However, since these are nearly impossible in reality, partial anonymity will be required, which distributes the relevant information in such a way that the creation of a complete customer profile by any participating party without any cooperation becomes unlikely.

Partial traceability. In case of the single enforcement of illegal actions, it must be possible to retrieve an identity of that person. This is complicated by the partial anonymity requirement, but possible in a similar fashion such as tracing of email: every party knows "someone" who is closer to knowing the real identity of a given party; by following these links, a party with authoritative information on a user's identity will be eventually found.

3.3   Authentication Mechanism of T-commerce

This paper suggests new authentication mechanism using mobile devices to overcome the limitation of traditional authentication mechanism using a remote controller of digital TV and set-top-box. This mechanism improves the level of security of user authentication. This model consists of thirteen steps which are described below.

Step 1. The customer browses products' catalogues using a remote controller of digital TV.

Step 2. The browsing information is transferred to shopping mall via digital set-top-box.

Step 3. The quantities in stock are verified.

Step 4. The information about products is transferred to customer via set-top-box.

Step 5. The customer places an order.

Step 6. The ordering information is transferred to the product supplier by way of shopping mall.

Step 7. The shopping mall requests a payment on customer's ordering.

Step 8. The first authentication is executed using the smart card which is embedded in set-top-box.

Step 9. The authentication agency sends an authentication code to customer's mobile device to execute second authentication.

Step 10. The customer inputs an authentication code provided by the authentication agency into a remote controller of digital TV.

Step 11. The shopping mall asks a payment on customer's ordering to payment gateway with the result of an authentication code.

Step 12. The shopping mall delivers the products ordered by the customer.

Step 13. The purchase process is terminated.

The mutual relationships and data processes are illustrated in figure 1.

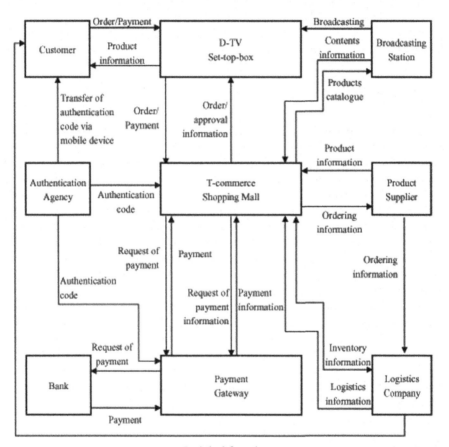

Fig. 1. Authentication mechanism for T-commerce environments

3.4   Significance of This Mechanism

The traditional interactive TV adopts CAS (Conditional Access System). The digital set-top-box has a smart card which records subscriber's information. The users are authenticated with the information recorded in smart card when the users try to use VOD services. That is to say, if users try to watch charged channels, he should be authenticated with the information recorded in smart card. If users are authenticated, the contents provider transfers the key which decrypt the scrambled data of charged channels [1]. So, the security risks of current mechanism of interactive TV include: 1) Theft or lost of smart card adhered to digital set-top-box, and 2) Breaches of the key transferred by the contents provider.

In this paper, we suggest enhanced mechanism of two steps authentication which provides personal authentication code using personal mobile device such as cellular phone and receives an authentication code that the user input by himself to solve these problems.

4   Conclusion

This paper provides new authentication mechanism using mobile devices to overcome the limitation of existing mechanism which only uses the smart card embedded in digital set-top-box. To protect the risks of breaches of private information and fraud or alteration of payment information, we suggest an authentication mechanism which has the characteristics: 1) First step of authentication is processed with the smart card embedded in digital set-top-box, 2) After the successful processing of first step of authentication using smart card, the authentication agency issues second authentication code via the mobile device that the user already has. The user inputs an authentication code by himself with a remote controller of digital TV, and 3) The authentication agency verifies user's credentials to grant a payment.

New authentication mechanism suggested in this paper may protect the security risks that the existing mechanism exposes, but it requires one more step using mobile device which makes the T-commerce users to suffer from difficulties. Furthermore, this mechanism cannot protect the whole risks related to smart card itself. So, further researches must provide: The easy of usage of secured authentication, and the protection mechanism of smart card adhered to digital set-top-box.

References

1. Kim, D.H.: Interactive TV. Nanam (2002)
2. Li, Z. and Nikolaos G. Bourbakis: Digital Video and Digital TV: A Comparison and the Future Directions. Academic Press (2001) 545–556
3. Evans, B.: Understanding Digital TV. IEEE Press (1995)
4. Kim, G.H. and Moon, M.N.: Strategy and Technology for T-Commerce. Sigma Insight (2002)
5. Lee, H.J.: A Study on Method Using Effectiveness Interaction TV. HCI Conference 2003, Korea (2003)

6. Tomsich, P. and Katzenbeisser, S.: Towards a Secure and De-centralized Digital Wartermarking Infrastructure for the Protection of Intellectual Property. Lecture Notes in Computer Science **1875** (2000) 38–47
7. Katzenbeisser, S. and Tomsich, P.: Applied Information Security for m-Commerce and Digital Television Environment,Lecture Notes In Computer Science **2115** (2001) 165–175
8. Tanh, D.V.: Security Issues in Mobile eCommerce. Lecture Notes in Computer Science **1875** (2000) 467–476

Threat Description for Developing Security Countermeasure

Seung-youn Lee[1], Myong-chul Shin[1], Jae-sang Cha[2], and Tai-hoon Kim[3]

[1] SungKyunKwan Univ., Department of Information & Communication Eng.,
Kyonggi-do, Korea
{syoun, mcshin}@ece.skku.ac.kr
[2] SeoKyeong Univ., Dept. of. Information & Communication Eng., Seoul, Korea
chajs@skuniv.ac.kr
[3] San 7, Geoyeou-dong, Songpa-gu, Seoul, Korea
taihoonn@empal.com

Abstract. Evaluation has been the traditional means of providing assurance and is the basis for prior evaluation criteria documents such as ITSEC. The Common Criteria (CC) defines a Protection Profile (PP) that defines the security environments and specifies the security requirements and protections of the product to be evaluated. The security environments consist of assumptions, threats, and organizational security policies, so the editor of the PP must describe the threats for the PP. This paper proposes a method for the description of the threats for developing PPs or countermeasures by introducing the concept of the assets protected by Target of Evaluations (TOE).

1 Introduction

The CC philosophy is to provide assurance based upon an evaluation of the IT product or system that is to be trusted. Evaluation has been the traditional means of providing assurance.

There are many evaluation criteria, and many countries have worked in close cooperation with the International Organization for Standard (IS) 15408 [1]. The CC is a standard for specifying and evaluating the security features of IT products and systems, and is intended to replace previous security criteria such as the TCSEC. This evaluation process establishes a level of confidence that the security functions of such products and systems, and the assurance measures applied to them, must meet.

The CC defines a PP that specifies the security requirements and protections of the product to be evaluated. If someone wants to select IT systems which meet his requirements for security, he can use the PP to express his security requirements.

Those who want to express their security requirements using the PP must first define the security environments which consist of assumptions, threats, and organizational security policies, and connect the security environments to the security objectives and security requirements in the CC. When the writing the threat phrases

K. Aizawa, Y. Nakamura, and S. Satoh (Eds.): PCM 2004, LNCS 3331, pp. 548–555, 2004.

for the PP, we use the production rule of multi-stage graph. But the assets and the attack methods increase rapidly, the count of the total threat phrases increases too and some new method for reducing these is needed.

In this paper, we introduce the concept of the 'assets protected by TOE' and propose a new method for reducing the count of the threat phrases by using that concept.

2 Threat Description for the PP

2.1 Protection Profile

A PP defines an implementation-independent set of IT security requirements for a category of TOEs. Such TOEs are intended to meet common consumer needs for IT security. Consumers can therefore construct or cite a PP to express their IT security needs without reference to any specific TOE.

The purpose of a PP is to state a security problem rigorously for a given collection of systems or products (known as the TOE) and to specify security requirements to address that problem without dictating how these requirements will be implemented. For this reason, a PP is said to provide an implementation-independent security description. A PP thus includes several related kinds of security information (See the Fig. 1).

A description of the TOE security environment which refines the statement of need with respect to the intended environment of use, producing the threats to be countered and the organisational security policies to be met in light of specific assumptions.

2.2 How Should Threats Be Identified?

A 'threat' is simply an undesirable event, which is characterized in terms of a threat agent, a presumed attack method, an identification of the asset under attack, and so on. In order to identify what the threats are, we therefore need to answer the following questions:

- What are the assets that require protection? The assets subject to the attack (e.g., sensitive data),
- Who or what are the threat agents? The threat agent (e.g., an authorized user of the TOE),
- What attack methods or undesirable events do the assets need to be protected from? The attack methods employed (e.g., impersonation of an authorized user of the TOE).

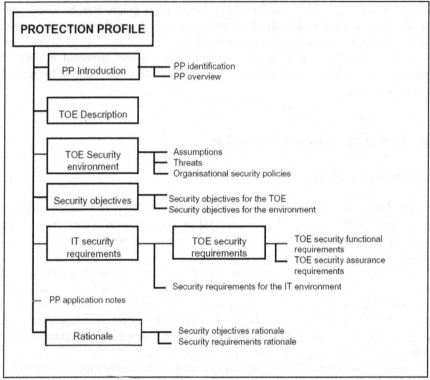

Fig. 1. Protection Profile content

3 How to Describe the Threats in the PP?

In the PP, in order to ensure we have a 'concise' statement of threats, the threat descriptions should be 'disjoint' as far as possible. In other words, there should be minimal overlap between different threats. This will help avoid potential confusion on the part of the reader of the PP as well as helping to simplify the PP rationale by avoiding needless repetition.

If we specify all threats at the same level of detail, the overlaps between threats can be more easily avoided. For example, it's not good that a threat description contains a detailed attack method against a specific asset if this is a specific attack scenario that is already associated with a more general threat stated elsewhere in the PP. Therefore, if we want to describe the threats for the PP, more considerations are needed.

Actually, all IT systems and communications channels face security threats that can compromise the systems themselves, the services they provide, the data stored on, and the data transmitted between them. For describing the threats for the PP, next items must be identified.

3.1 Identifying the Assets

In the case of writing threat phrases, it is very important to categorize the asset. When considering the assets of systems, we first think the factors threat agents want to compromise. Maybe we can use the next items as assets of the wireless systems.

− Wireless devices or systems.
− Service that wireless systems provide.
− Data stored on the wireless systems.
− Data transmitted between the wireless systems.
− Other network resources.

In fact, these are very simple categorization of asset. For example, let's consider a wireless phone. The device user has is an important asset and must be protected from unauthorised user. If the device provides a commerce service, the service is protected from misuse, abuse, and so on. And the phone numbers or keys or passwords stored in the device are critical things and if these data transmitted to other system, they must be checked for confidentiality and integrity.

3.2 Identifying the Threat Agents

Threat agents may either be human or non-human, and we can use the next items as threat agents of the wireless systems.

− Authorized users or owners of the wireless systems.
− Unauthorized users of the wireless systems.
− Attackers or intruders or hackers.
− IT entities.

When we consider the threats described in the PP, authorized users or owners of the wireless device is looked on as threat agent because they can commit abuse or unauthorized use.

In the field of requirement engineering, the concept of user is inclined to be restricted to human. But in the CC, the concept of user is extended to the IT entities and this may be correct thing because the malicious codes or viruses can be the user of the function.

3.3 Identifying the Attack Methods

Having identified the assets to be protected and the threat agents which may be the subject of attack, the next step is to identify the possible attack methods which could lead to a compromise of the assets.

This will be based on what is known regarding the TOE security environment. There is a very important thing must be considered. If we want to consider all attack methods already known, maybe it is impossible because the attack methods are too various and created or found everyday. Therefore, if we want to describe the threats about the TCP/IP, should use the phrase 'by using TCP/IP vulnerabilities already known' not dividing as like flooding, spoofing, DoS, and so on.

4 Description of Threat in the PP

After identifying the assets, threat agents, and attack method, we can describe the threats for the PP. For example, we can describe the threats concerned with the confidentiality of assets in the PP as like this:

- Threat agents may discover wireless networks by unauthorized methods,
- Threat agents may disclose the services provided by unauthorized methods,
- Threat agents may disclose the data stored by unauthorized methods,
- Threat agents may disclose the data transmitted by unauthorized methods,
- Threat agents may disclose the systems or network resources by unauthorized methods,
- Etc.

But if we describe the threats as like these, there can be too many threat phrases in the PP, so a new method defining the threat is needed. We did not consider various threat agents and the threat methods above. If we divide the threat agents as authorized user and unauthorized user, threats may be two times as above.

4.1 Identifying of the Threats Considered the Composition of the Assets, the Threat Agents, and the Attack Methods

Many cases, when we describe the threats in the PP, we can use the 'production rule of multi-stage graph' (See the Fig. 2). In other words, the threats can be described by the combination of the assets, the threat agents, the attack methods, and so on. (But the Fig. 2 is not complete form.) Therefore, there can be very many phrases for the threats, and these phrases are the headache of the editors of PP.

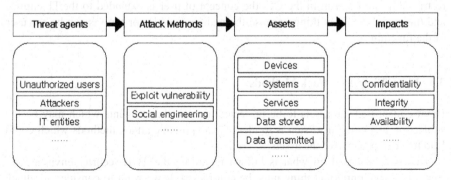

Fig. 2. Threat production rule of multi-stage graph (Example)

As you saw in the Fig. 2, the total numbers of the threat phrases are decided by the next numerical formula:

Total numbers of threats = Threat agent * Attack method * Asset * Impact * Etc.

Therefore, we must re-consider and minimize the terms of numerical formula mentioned above for the efficient writing of threat phrases. In many cases, we can solve this problem by adjusting the 'Assumption' and 'Organizational Security Policy (OSP)', but this method is 'minimizing the threat agent' or 'reducing the attack methods possible'. When developing the systems which consider the security, most functional requirements are implemented by the threats not assumption or OSP. If we describe the security environments with many assumptions and OSPs, many of the functional requirements can't be implemented correctly and these systems may not cover the real threats.

4.2 Assets Protected by TOE

We propose a method for minimizing the assets of IT systems including wireless systems to reduce the count of threat phrases. As mentioned earlier, maybe we can use the next items as assets of the wireless systems.

- Wireless devices or systems,
- Service that wireless systems provide,
- Data stored on the wireless systems,
- Data transmitted between the wireless systems,
- Other network resources

In the aspects of the security requirements and the evaluation of the IT systems, we can re-identify the assets as like;

- TOE (target of evaluation),
- Assets protected by TOE
  - Systems not included in the TOE
  - Services provided
  - Data stored
  - Data transmitted
  - etc.

This method for identifying of assets is available for the PP, because the identifying of the security environments is connected to the security functional requirements included in the CC. For example, let's describe the threat concerned with the confidentiality of assets (In this example, we didn't classify the threat agents and the attack methods, and applied 'the assets protected by TOE' to the description).

- Threat agents may compromise the confidentiality of the assets protected by TOE by unauthorized methods.

But this phrase is not sufficient because the threat agents and the attack methods are having the possibility to be divided. It's very important to keep in mind that many kinds of threat agents and attack methods may exist in the 'assets protected by TOE. Therefore, the threat agents and the attack methods must be considered to contain all cases. For example, the phrase 'by unauthorized methods' is not suitable in some cases, because the 'threat agents' can contain the 'authorized users' and the authorized users may comprise the confidentiality of the assets protected by TOE by accident. So we should remove the phrases 'by unauthorized methods' and 'Threat agents', because all types of users and attack methods must be considered. Now, we can use the threat description as like:

- The confidentiality of the assets protected by TOE may be compromised

As seen at the above phrase, in the case we use the concept of the 'assets protected by TOE', the descriptions for the threat are expressed as a kind of 'possibility' of attack. Some examples are like these:

- Malicious code may exist in the assets protected by TOE,
- Vulnerabilities may exist in the assets protected by TOE,
- Etc.

Systems, services, and others are included in the assets protected by TOE, and systems and services may consist of resources and source codes. Therefore, they may contain the malicious codes or vulnerabilities in the resources and codes.

4.3   Benefits

The benefits of this method we proposed are as like:

Simplicity: When describing the threat in the PP for security environments, many threat phrases which finally come to same security functional requirement are needed because the assets, attack methods, and the threat agents are different. Sometimes, it's possible to use the assumptions or OSPs to reduce the threats, it is not sufficient. If we use the concept 'the assets protected by TOE', we can reduce the count of the threat phrase because the reason of dividing threat may be removed.

Expandability: Because of the fast growth of technology, everyday we are faced to many new malicious codes, viruses, and security holes. If does the new asset is added in the operating environments? If does the new vulnerability is found in the source codes which consist of a service? In these cases, we can solve problems by adding a few phrases to the 'PP INTRODUCTION' part of the PP, or maybe, if we are lucky, nothing will be changed.

Comprehensiveness: In fact, the form we used does not help the reader to understand what the security need is, especially since it applies to any TOE. But this may be another benefit of the method we proposed. The method using the concept of the assets protected by TOE is applied to many security systems like as Intrusion Detection Systems (IDS), Firewall, Virtual Private Network (VPN), and so on. The assets of these systems can be divided by using same way we proposed in this paper.

It's very important to keep in mind that the method we proposed is applicable only to the assets must be protected by the TOE. The threat descriptions for the TOE should only refer to potential events which could 'directly' compromise the assets requiring protection.

5   Conclusions

Many kinds of PPs are developed already and they have strong theoretical rationale about the development process. But there is no consistent theory for describing the security environments especially threats. Therefore, when readers review the PPs developed by other person or company and developers write the PPs they are to use make many kinds of mistakes and feel complexity. In fact, when we develop the PPs, we can find that there are many similar things between secure systems because the IT systems which aim to protect something have the similar structures and characteristics.

In this paper, we proposed a method for dividing the assets and this method will be helpful to describe the threat phrase for the PP.

References

1. ISO. ISO/IEC 15408: Information technology - Security techniques - Evaluation criteria for IT security, 1999
2. KISA. Information Security Systems & Certification Guide, 2002
3. ISO. ISO/IEC WD 18045 Methodology for IT Security Evaluation
4. NSA. Virtual Private Network Boundary Gateway Protection Profile for Basic Robustness Environments, Version 0.6, 2001
5. NSA. Virtual Private Network Protection Profile for Unclassified Sensitive Environments R1.0, 2000

RPS: An Extension of Reference Monitor to Prevent Race-Attacks

Jongwoon Park[1], Gunhee Lee[1], Sangha Lee[2], and Dong-kyoo Kim[1]

[1] Graduate School of Information and Communication, Ajou University,
Suwon, Korea
`hizcool74@kornet.net`, {`icezzoco, dkkim`}`@ajou.ac.kr`
[2] Department of Information and Communication, Dong Seoul College,
Seongnam, Korea
`shyi@dsc.ac.kr`

Abstract. Most software involves some vulnerabilities because of various potential factors such as design flaw and program bug. Among them, a faulty assumption on file access results in a side-effect as known TOCT-TOU vulnerability. Race–attack is an attack using this vunerability. In this paper, we propose a novel mechanism to prevent race–attack, each process maintains status of related object at check step operation and compares the status of the use step with that of the check step. Since every process must pass through the reference monitor to use an object, it is the most suitable point to detect the attack and response to the attack.

1 Introduction

Generally, most software involves the vulnerability because of various potential factors such as design flaw and program bug. Among them, a faulty assumption on file access results in a side-effect as known TOCTTOU(Time of Check to Time of Use) vulnerability. A subject checks the specific characteristic of an object (Check Step), and then it takes some action that assumes the characteristic still holds (Use Step). When an object identifier is changed by the race condition attack using TOCTTOU vulnerability, there is an unwilled problem.

In this paper, we propose RPS(Race–attack Prevention System) to prevent these problems through an extension of reference monitor. For this, we define the semantic characteristics of race condition problems and the concept of pseudo transaction, and then propose a new mechanism to detect these problems. In the proposed mechanism, each process maintains status of the related object at check step, and then the system compares the status of an object at use step operation with it. Since every process must pass through the reference monitor to use an object, it is the most suitable point to detect race attack. Therefore we enhance the reference monitor to adopt the RPS component.

The rest of this paper is organized as follows. Section 2 describes the TOCT-TOU vulnerability, and section 3 shows some cases of the race condition attack. We explains the design of the proposed system in section 5. This is followed by the implementation and evaluations in section 6. Section 7 concludes.

K. Aizawa, Y. Nakamura, and S. Satoh (Eds.): PCM 2004, LNCS 3331, pp. 556–563, 2004.
© Springer-Verlag Berlin Heidelberg 2004

2   TOCTTOU Vulnerabilities

In order to perform an operation on a file object, a program should carry out following four steps.

1. A process acquires a reference for the object.
2. By the reference, the process obtains the status information of the object.
3. The process analyzes that the information is acceptable to perform operation.
4. If it is acceptable, the process performs the operation on the object.

An assumption should be kept through above four steps. the status information of the file object should be maintained consistently during the time interval between step 2 and step 4. However there is some possibilities of change on the the status of the object anywhere from step 2 to step 4. Therefore the assumption is faulty, and it results in TOCTTOU vulnerability.

As the vulnerability is considered as a significant security flaw of the software, there are many researches on it [2]. There are two approaches to solve the vulnerability as follows [3];

- *Minimizing the time interval between the step 2(check step) and the step 4(use step)*: This method increases the execution frequency of the step 2 or approaches the execution point of the step 2 to that of the step 4. As the time interval becomes small, the probability of change also does. However, there is no way to make the interval zero.
- *Maintaining consistency between the reference of the file object and the status information of the file through file access steps*: To do so, above four steps are considered as an atomic transaction or a consistent information, such as file descriptor, is used as the reference of a file object. However, since most software uses the file name as the reference of a file object, it is difficult to fully solve the TOCTTOU vulnerability by using this approach.

3   Demonstration of the Race-Attack

One of serious attack using the TOCTTOU vulnerability is race condition attack (race–attack). This attack includes all actions that result in an execution of unwilled operaltion by changing the reference of the file object between the check step and the use step. Fig. 1 shows the concept of race condition attack. Next, we will explain several cases of race condition attacks.

3.1   Filename Redirection

Bishop and Dilger introduce that the status information of certain file can be modified by an attacker between creating a file and granting the ownership to a user, where the file system uses the file name as reference of the file [4]. For example, a program creates the directory *filename*. Before it grants the ownership to a user, the attacker changes the reference of the directory *filename* to a security sensitive file such as */etc/passwd*. Therefore the attacker gains the ownership of the file */etc/passwd*.

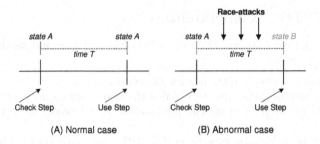

Fig. 1. Concept of race condition attack: there is no change of state in the (a), while the state is changed from state A to state B by the race–attacks in the (b).

3.2 SetUID Scripts

A script file is executed through two steps. The system reads the parameters and file paths, and then the interpreter executes the script line by line. Thus the script file is easily used to the race–attack [1]. Moreover, if the setuid bit of the victim script is true, the attacker gains all permissions of the owner of the file. After the *exec* system call executes the script *script_link*, the attacker changes the reference of the script to another script *malicious_script*. Thus the *malicious_script* is run with the permission of the *script_link*'s owner. If the owner is the root, the attacker runs the *malicious_script* with the permission of the root.

3.3 Relocated Subdirectory

Most of GNU utilities have some faulty assumption [1]. For example, 'rm' utility can remove the contents of directories recursively with '-r' option. When it moves up to parent directory after deleting a subdirectory, it uses the relative path '..'. The 'rm' assumes that there is no change in the path of the parent directory until it comes back to the parent directory. For example, when a program deletes a directory that has a subdirectory *child_dir*, an attacker changes the current directory from *child_dir* to */root* during the *rm* deletes the contents of the *child_dir*, and then the *rm* removes all contents of the '/' directory.

3.4 Temporary File Creation

Much software uses temporary files for their own purposes. To use the temporary file, there are two steps. One is checking existence of the file with *stat* system call, and another is using the temporary file with *open* system call. The time interval between these two steps results in the TOCTTOU vulnerability [6]. For example, before a program open a file *filename*, an attacker creates a symbolic link file that has the same name *filename*. If the link file is linked to */etc/passwd*, the program may overwrite the */etc/passwd*.

4   Existing Detection Approaches

TOCTTOU vulnerability detection methods are categorized into two approaches; one is the static analysis, the other is the dynamic analysis.

The *Static Analysis* scans the source code at compile time to detect the TOCTTOU vulnerabilities. It finds out the probability of race–attack by checking both the control dependencies and the data dependencies of the program. Bishop and Dilger introduced this approach [4]. Anguiano also uses this approach [5]. Various software vulnerability analysis tools, such as ITS4, Flawfinder, and RATS, employ this approach to prevent race–attacks.

However, this approach uses limited information provided at compile time. For example, if the relative path is used as the file path, the reference value of the file can not be acquired at compile time. Pointer aliasing problem also does. Therefore this approach has high false positive rate.

The *Dynamic Analysis* checks the operation of the process at run time. Each operation is observed whether it breaks the assumption. It has lower false positive rate than static analysis, but it is difficult to implement this method.

In Linux OpenWall project, the system limits the location and the condition when a process creates a link file [8]. However, this system does not practical, since all software already developed are altered to adopt the system. The Race-Guard defines some system calls that is used to the race–attack, and it checks those system call is occured in real time. This system is concerned about only the temporary file creation problem. It does not propose the general and formal method that describes the correlation between related events.

5   The Design of the Proposed System

In this paper, we propose a race–attack prevention system that employs the dynamic analysis. The proposed system uses the extended reference monitor analyzes the system call at kernel level. A program is executed as a process in the operating system and the process uses the system call to use the service of the operating system. Therefore the reference monitor that observes every system call is suitable to detect the race–attack.

5.1   Extension of the Reference Monitor

The existing reference monitor consists of three components such as the syscall wrapper that intercepts the system call, security server that enforces the security policies of the system, and object manager that binds the security attribute to the object and manage the object.

In this paper, we employ a new component RPS in the reference monitor. The RPS is located at between the syscall wrapper and the security server. It analyzes the patterns of the system call for every process in order to detect and response to the race–attacks. RPS cache stores the inode information of the related object by a process. Fig. 2 shows the architecture of the proposed system.

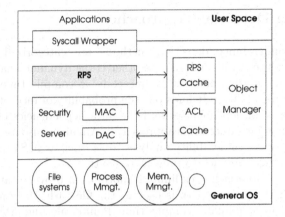

Fig. 2. The architecture of the proposed system

5.2   Pseudo Transactions

In order to keep the assumption, four characteristics should be satisfied as known ACID (Atomicity, Consistency, Isolation, and Durability). However, the system that does not support the concept of transaction is not able to guarantee these characteristics. In this paper, to solve this problem, we define the concept of the pseudo transaction. We identify the mutual dependent pair among events, and then we build each pair into a pseudo transaction so that it satisfies the consistency or isolation. The proposed system is able to detect the race–attack by check the consistency of the reference information during the pseudo transaction.

The (a) of Fig. 3 shows the structure of the pseudo transaction. It begins with the word PT and ends with the word END. Between these two phrases, the lists of system calls at check step and use step are stated. The (b) of Fig. 3 shows the example of the normal pseudo transaction profile.

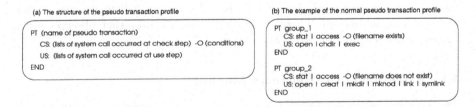

Fig. 3. The structure of the pseudo transaction profile

5.3   Detecting and Preventing the Race-Attacks

The RPS component detects the change of the status information during the pseudo transaction. To do so, the component checks the inode value of the re-

Fig. 4. The flowchart of the detection mechanism

ferred object, when the operation of the list in the pseudo transaction profile is caught by the syscall wrapper. Fig. 4 shows the flow of the detection sequence.

At check step, the system saves the reference information of the related object, and then it executes the simple heuristics that decides the existence of the object. According to the result of the simple heuristics, two different detection mechanisms are applied. If there exists the related object, the system verifies the consistency of the inode information using the function namei. Otherwise, it checks the consistency of the object name like as RaceGuard.

When the RPS detects a race condition attack, it returns the result of the operation at use step. This is able to minimize the damage, though it does not satisfy the concept of all–or–nothing like as the transaction. Moreover, the RPS component controls the access to the object using the ACL. It activates the allowed list of the process, the user/group list, and role to prohibit the abnormal access.

6   Implementation and Evaluations

6.1   Implementation

The prototype system was developed for the Linux operating system. The kernel version is 2.4.20. The system consists of a kernel module that intercepts and

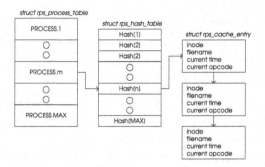

Fig. 5. The structure of the RPS cache

Table 1. The result of the performance tests

System Calls	mkdir	chown	exec	rm	chdir	stat	open	mv	symlink	unlink
RPS off (ms)	3.72	5.17	5.04	5.31	3.01	3.21	2.57	4.87	3.02	3.57
RPS on (ms)	3.85	6.91	5.17	5.51	4.31	3.30	4.13	6.13	4.82	5.27
Overhead (%)	3.5	33.7	2.6	3.8	43.2	2.8	60.7	25.9	59.6	47.6

checks a number of system calls. Using kernel module saves time writing and debugging the kernel code.

Security kernel that extends the reference monitor controls the operation from a process by checking each system call. In Linux system, the *interrupt 80* handler calls the run code that registered at the system call table (SYSENT) in order to execute a system call. Thus the security kernel changes the address of the run code registered at the SYSENT.

Intercepted system calls are mainly the file–system calls that accept pathnames as their parameters. If it is a member of the check step in the pseudo transaction profile, the module creates the RPS cache entry as shown in Fig. 5. The RPS cache is maintained by each process. Each entry is accessed by the PID value and the hash value of the inode. When the process is terminated, the related RPS cache entry is also deleted.

When a child process is created, the cache entry of the parent is inherited to the child. Thus RPS also detects the inconsistency problem between the parent and the child. In this case, the deletion of the cache entry is performed by the termination of the parent process.

6.2   Evaluation

Security Tests. To test the effectiveness of the proposed system, we developed four scenarios as we mentioned in section 3. These scenarios were carried out with the RPS (race–attack prevention system) being disabled and enabled. All the attacks were successfully detected and stopped. While all of the attacker processes are suspended by the RPS, the victim processes are continued to run.

Performance Tests. We measured the system performance by gauging the latency of a system call. This method measured how long does the system executes a system call. We used the system calls as shown in the examples (mkdir, chown, exec, rm, chdir, stat, open, mv, symlink, and unlink). Each system call was executed 10,000 times in a test. Each test was carried out 10 times, and then we calculated the average of the result. The overhead means the rate of the increased time in comparison with the test without RPS. The latencies are overall low. Since the security kernel should performs the race-attack detection process with the system call at use step, some system calls, such as *chdir, chown, open, mv, unlink, and symlink*, has large overhead with the RPS.

7   Conclusion

In this paper, we propose a race attack prevention system (RPS) that extends the reference monitor. The proposed system identifies the mutual dependent pair among events, and then we build each pair into pseudo transactions. With this, the system checks the consistency of the file reference during a pseudo transaction. Since it decides the occurrence of the attack with dynamic and real-time information, the detection accuracy is relatively high and it has low false positive rate.

In the future work, we will enhance the performance of the system by improving the RPS cache structure and optimizing the pseudo transaction profile.

References

1. Lowery, J.C.: A Tour of TOCTTOU, SANS GSEC practical v1.4b (2002)
2. Landwehr, Carl, E.: A Taxonomy of Computer Program Security Flaws, ACM Computing Surveys, Vol.26, No. 3. (1999) 211-254
3. Krause, M., Tipton, H. F.: Handbook of Information Security Management, CRC Press LLC (1998)
4. Bishop, M., Dilger, M.: Checking for Race Conditions in File Access, Computing Systems (1996) 131-152
5. Anguiano, R.: A Static Analysis Technique for the Detection of TOCTTOU Vulnerabilities, Master Thesis, University of California Davis (2001)
6. Cowan, C., Beattie, S., Wright, C., Kroah-Hartman, G.: RaceGuard: Kernel Protection From Temporary File Race Vulnerabilities, Proceedings of the 10th USENIX Security Symposium (2001)
7. Jose, N.: Source Code Scanners for Better Code, LinuxJournal.com (2002)
8. OpenWall Project: Linux Kernel Patch, URL:http://www.openwall.com/linux/

SITIS: Scalable Intrusion Tolerance Middleware for Internet Service Survivability

GangShin Lee[1], Chaetae Im[1], TaeJin Lee[1], HyungJong Kim[1], and Dong Hoon Lee[2]

[1] Korea Information Security Agency (KISA), Seoul, Korea
{kslee, chtim, tjlee, hjkim}@kisa.or.kr
[2] Center for Information Security Technologies (CIST), Korea University, Seoul, Korea
donghlee@korea.ac.kr

Abstract. In this paper, we present design and implementation of SITIS: a middleware for intrusion tolerance of internet service. SITIS is designed for scalable deployment of intrusion tolerant capability in essential internet services. SITIS has abnormal status monitoring and group management modules. The monitoring module gathers various system-information such as memory and processor usages, and group management module manage the server farm using several mechanism such as group leader selection, abnormal server isolation and joining of new server. Also, the voting mechanism is utilized in the group management to check the integrity of each member's service. In our work, we developed the web server's intrusion tolerance system using SITIS middleware and it is presented at the end of this paper.

Keywords: SITIS, Intrusion Tolerance, Group Management, Voting, Middleware

1 Introduction

Nowadays, since the human activity is strongly associated with the information and communication network, the discontinuity of network service makes people feel difficulty and causes big loss in their economic activity. Especially, there are services that are essential to support the normal operation of computer network such as DNS services, DHCP services and so on. If these services meet failures that are caused by external attack, internal fault or unexpected accident, it causes a kind of disaster in the human's daily life. So, in the security research area, the survivability related work is urgently required to preserve the continuity of essential services such as DNS, DHCP and so on. One of those works is the ITS (Intrusion Tolerant System) which enables client users to access the service though severe attack is appeared. Since ITS system's functions are against the attacks that cannot be handled by the IDS and Firewall's defense mechanism, it is almost impossible to apply the vulnerability related knowledge to the ITS system's monitoring rules.

In this paper, we present design and implementation of SITIS middleware for intrusion tolerance of internet service. SITIS is designed for scalable deployment of intrusion tolerant capability in essential internet services. SITIS has abnormal status monitoring and group management modules. The monitoring module gathers the

K. Aizawa, Y. Nakamura, and S. Satoh (Eds.): PCM 2004, LNCS 3331, pp. 564–571, 2004.

various system information such as memory and processor usages, and group management module manage the server farm using group leader selection, abnormal server isolation and joining of new server. Also, the voting mechanism is utilized in the group management to check the integrity of each member's service. In our work, we developed the web server's intrusion tolerance system using SITIS middleware.

In the section 2, the related work will be presented and the design of SITIS will be shown in section 3. Section 4 contains the implementation result and application of web service and we make our conclusion at section 5.

2 Related Work

Among the ITS related work, MAFTIA(Malicious and Accidental-Fault Tolerance for Internet Applications) [1,2] is representative research project which is conducted by EU's IST. MAFTIA's principle about the intrusion is that all intrusion cannot protect and some of them are inserted into the system, and system must prepare about those uncontrolled attacks. Based on this principle, middleware type ITS framework which contains five main modules is suggested such as intrusion detection, group communication protocol, encryption module, data fragmentation/scattering, and user access control. The goal of MAFTIA is to research the tolerance paradigm and support by proposing and developing the integrated tolerance architecture that many application programs have dependability.

The OASIS(The Organically Assured and Survivable Information Systems) project[3,4,6,7,8] that is carried out by DARPA proceeds 12 research projects which are categorized four research topics such as server architecture, application program, middleware, network fundamental technology. The OASIS program has goal to develop, experiment, and validate every elements such as architecture, tools, and techniques for survivability of the information systems. Some main concepts of the 12 project in OASIS are as follows. First, the diversity of application and OS platform enhances the availability of the service and system because usually the intrusions exploit vulnerabilities that exist in a specific system platform. Second, the system and service should be redundant and if there is intrusion or fault that cause problem in system or service, the redundant system or service do the work of main system and service during the restoring time. Third, there are some mechanisms to guarantee the integrity and availability of services, and those mechanisms cooperate with the security mechanisms such as intrusion prevention and detection. To enhance the availability, load-balancing facility is applied and to enhance the integrity of service, voting mechanism, service member isolation and restoration are used. The Fourth there are monitoring facility that used to see the abnormal status of services and systems. In the tolerant system, as the monitoring is done after the prevention and detection mechanism is applied, the monitoring factors should be specialized for intrusion tolerance.

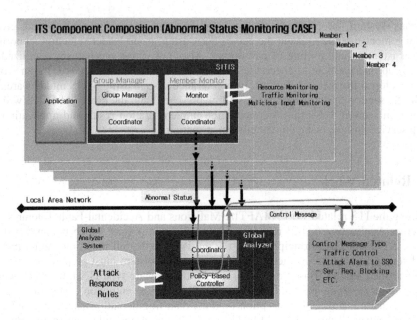

Fig. 1. Overall Procedure of the Intrusion Tolerant Service – Abnormal Status Monitoring

3 SITIS Middleware Design

3.1 Overall Structure

As shown in the Fig. 1, our proposed SITIS architecture is mainly composed of Group Manager, Member Monitor, and GAM (Global Analyzing Manager). Fig. 1 shows the message flow from monitor to global analyzer. Each member monitors in every parts of the system. For example, resource consumption, traffic status, malicious attack attempts, and so on. The monitored information is passed to the GAM and the GAM analyzes them to assess causes and damages. Based on intrusion tolerant policy, it responds with control message to settle down the problem. The control messages include commands for recovery such as traffic control, attack alarm, access control, and so on.

Group management module maintains the group and also checks each member's status periodically. To validate the service reply, it has the voter which selects the correct result by comparing service results from all members. Through group maintaining we can enhance the availability and through voting mechanism the integrity of target service can be guaranteed in a certain degree.

Member monitor module is for detecting abnormal events, analyzing them, and report to GAM. The monitoring module covers the factors that are related to the normal service provision. All monitored information is stored in database and is used for providing historical statistics and sophisticated analyzing. Some events should be handled as a group to analyze the causes and effects. In other cases, the GAM analyzes them and triggers the recovery process based on its policy.

GAM has two main roles for providing intrusion tolerant service. The one is to collect information of all events and analyze them. The other is to react against abnormal events. The reaction is recovery process that is based on the intrusion tolerant policy. All modules in SITIS have the coordinator which provides communication interface to exchange the messages one another.

In our work, one of contribution is the scalability of the intrusion tolerant facility that is preserved by the SITIS middleware. As you can see in Fig. 1 and Fig. 2, the extension of group member is done by just install the SITIS middleware in the new server system that is to be a member.

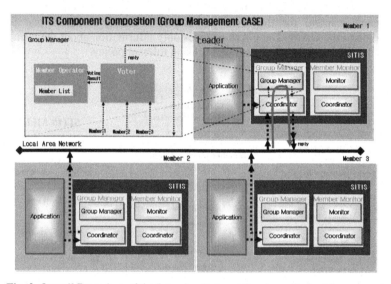

Fig. 2. Overall Procedure of the Intrusion Tolerant Service – Group Management

3.2 Group Management Module

In a group, there are leader and members. The leader has additional jobs such as transmitting heart beat request message, triggering recovery process. To select the leader in a group, group management module has the leader selection mechanism which is widely used in distributed environment. If a leader is corrupted, then the group selects a new leader by itself. To maintain the group, group reconfiguration that is joining new member or isolation of the corrupted member from the group is conducted when member's corruption is detected. The group management module also checks each member's status periodically by heart beat mechanism. Moreover, to validate the service result, the group management module has the voter which determines the correct result by comparing service results from all members. By such functions, group management module enhances the availability and integrity of the target service.

The Fig. 2 shows the voting flow. In the figure, the voter of the member 1 receives all service result from other members and compares them to determine the correct service result. Finally, the determined service result is returned to the client.

3.3 Member Monitoring Module

Member monitor has the role of collecting all events, analyzing them and reporting it to GAM. As described in Fig. 3, member monitor consists of monitoring controller and analyzer to collect all abnormal events and analyze them respectively. All monitored information is formatted as appropriate to analyzer in monitoring controller. Also, events are stored to provide historical statistics and sophisticated analyzing in GAM.

Occasionally, to clear the cause and damage some event's sequence is handled as one event. Also, GAM receives the event's sequence as a one event. However, if the group can't respond for the abnormal events, 'member monitor' just pass the information to the GAM. The GAM receives only information about the events and it triggers the restoring process based on intrusion tolerant policy.

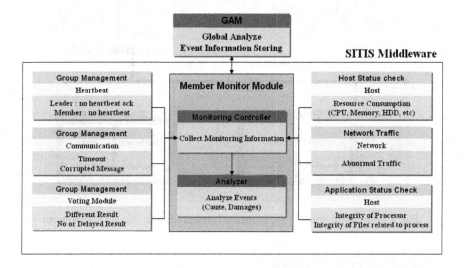

Fig. 3. Monitoring Factors in SITIS

Monitoring factors are shown in Fig. 3, such as system environment parameter, intrusion tolerant middleware, and service result. In the group management module, abnormal status can be detected by heartbeat exchange, and voting mechanisms. By heart beat mechanism, all members can detect each member's status periodically. The leader transmits the heart beat request which contains the group information, and the other members which receive the heart beat request send the heart beat reply. In voter, group management module checks whether the expected message is received in certain duration and whether the format of the message is proper. Also voter validates the service result before client receives it. If some results are different from majority, delay of them is over predefined duration, those events are notified to the monitor and passed to the GAM. Additionally, there are some sensors for checking host, application server, and network status. If the abnormal event occurred, those events are detected in 'monitor module' and it responds directly.

4 SITIS for Web Server

This section is for application of SITIS to intrusion tolerant web service. Since web service has visible requests and responses, it is easy to check the effectiveness of SITIS. Also, web service is widely used and has many trial of malicious attack. Through our experiments, we validate the service continuity with SITIS even if the malicious attacks which can fail the system occur.

We construct the test-bed, which can be explained as three parts. The first one is clients group in exterior of web servers' network, the group members can be a normal or malicious attacking system. Second one is clustering architecture of switches and routers which are linked with doubled lines to enhance the availability. The third part is the web server farm. The web servers are operated based on the SITIS middleware.

Table 1. Web service testing scenario

index	Attack Target			Attack Pattern
	Operating System	Web Server	SITIS Middleware	
1	O	X	X	Host Crash
2	X	O	X	Web Server Crash
3	X	O	X	Web Server Buffer Overflow
4	X	O	X	Incorrect Responses by Worm
5	X	X	O	Middleware Crash
6	O	O	O	Host DoS

We take into account the several scenarios as shown in Table 1. We categorized our scenario as six cases. First case, when each member recognize the failed member by heart beat exchange, elect the new leader if necessary and reconfigure group members. Second case, each middleware can recognize the web server status and if web server has no reply, the member's abnormal status is notified to the leader and it reconfigures group members. In third case, some members may be compromised by buffer overflow attack, but in this case, whole members do not fail about the single attack because of the diversity in our system design. Fourth case is web server's incorrect responses which are caused by worm such RAMEN. It can be detected by means of the voting mechanism. The fifth and sixth cases' pattern can be detected by heart beat.

Fig. 4 and Fig 5 shows the each member status, data flow and web service results. In left picture, each rectangle means the host, which consists of the web server, voter and middleware status. Through the member status view, we can monitor which member is compromised and see the group reconfiguration procedures. In Fig 5, we can see the each member's response and voting result. With those global monitoring tool, we check that SITIS works properly according to the scenarios.

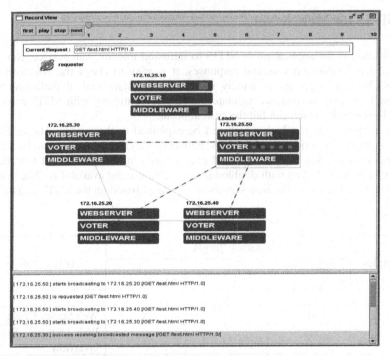

Fig. 4. Member Status View in SITIS based Web service

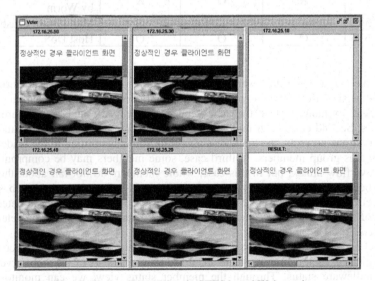

Fig. 5. Voting Status View in SITIS based Web service

5 Conclusion

In this work, we present design and implementation of SITIS middleware for intrusion tolerance of internet service. SITIS is designed for scalable deployment of intrusion tolerant capability in essential internet services. The SITIS monitoring module gathers various system information such as memory and processor usages. The SITIS group management module manages the server farm using group leader selection, abnormal server isolation and joining of new server. In our work, we developed the web server's intrusion tolerance system using SITIS middleware.

As a future work, we are developing a SITIS for DNS and DHCP intrusion tolerance system for the Windows and Linux platform. The result of our work will be applied to the ISP's DNS and DHCP servers to enhance the survivability of them.

References

1. A. Adelsbach, et. al, "Conceptual Model and Architecture of MAFTIA," Project MAFTIA IST-1999-11583 deliverable D21.
2. D. Powell, et. al "MAFTIA (Malicious and Accidental-Fault Tolerance for Internet Applications)," Supplement of the 2001 International Conference on Dependable Systems and Networks, June 2001.
3. James Reynolds, James Just, and Karl Levitt, "The design and implementation of an intrusion tolerant system," Supplement of the 2002 International Conference on Dependable Systems and Networks, June 2002.
4. Cukier, M., et. al, "Intrusion Tolerance Approches in ITUA", Supplement of the 2001 International Conference on Dependable Systems and Networks, June 2001
5. M. Castro, B. Liskov, "Practical Byzantine Fault Tolerance", Proceedings Of the 3rd Symposium on Operating System Design and Implementation February 1999.
6. Courtney Tod, Lyons James, et.al, Providing Intrusion Tolerance with ITUA, Proceedings of the ICDSN 2002, June 2002.
7. Feiyi wang, Fengmin Gong, and Chandramouli Sargor, "SITAR: A Scalable Intrusion-Tolerant Architecture for Distributed Services," Workshop on Information Assurance and Security, June 2001.
8. Adnan Agbaria, Roy Friedman, "Overcomming Byzantine Failures Using Checkpointing," University of Illinois at Urbana-Champaign Coordinated Science Laboratory technical report no. UILU-ENG-03-2228 (CRHC-03-14), December 2003.
9. G. Bracha and S. Toueg, "Asynchronous Consensus and Broadcast Protocols", Journal of the ACM Volume 32 , Issue 4, October 1985, Pages: 824 - 840

On Minimizing Distortion in Secure Data-Hiding for Binary Images

Yongsu Park and Yookun Cho

Department of Computer Science and Engineering, Seoul National University,
San 56-1 Shilim-Dong Gwanak-Ku, Seoul 151-742, Korea
{yspark,cho}@ssrnet.snu.ac.kr

Abstract. Numerous digital binary images are widely used today. Because modifying or forging digital images is not difficult, it is important to develop data-hiding methods to insert authentication data. In order to minimize distortion in secure data-hiding, there is an approach to reduce the number of flipped bits in the embedded image. The most recent method (Tseng-Chen-Pan's scheme) that appeared on IEEE Trans. on Comm. 2002, flips only 2 bits for hiding n bits in the embedded image of size 2^n bits. In this paper, we show that the problem of finding the lower bound on the minimum number of flipped bits in the 2^n bits embedded image to hide n bits data is closely related with finding the minimum dominating sets of the binary hypercube of dimension n. To the best of our knowledge, our work is a first approach to convert the data-hiding problem to the relatively well-known graph problem.

Keywords: Data hiding, binary image, authentication

1 Introduction

Today, numerous digital binary images are widely used in everyday life for scanned documents or faxed images, etc. Since modifying or forging digital images is not difficult, developing data-hiding methods to insert authentication data as well as to detect tampering is very important.

As for data-hiding techniques, there are two approaches to minimize the impairment of the embedded image. The first is to cheat human perception to reduce the visible artifacts by changing line/character spacing or modifying the thickness of strokes. However, These methods have shortcomings that they require special types of images or the amount of hidden data should be extremely restricted.

Another approach is to minimize the number of flipped bits in the embedded image to reduce distortion. The most recent method (Tseng-Chen-Pan's scheme) that appeared on IEEE Trans. on Comm. 2002 [9], flips only 2 bits for hiding n bits in the embedded image of size 2^n bits. However, to the best of our knowledge, there have been no research activities for finding general solutions or lower bounds on this problem.

K. Aizawa, Y. Nakamura, and S. Satoh (Eds.): PCM 2004, LNCS 3331, pp. 572–577, 2004.

In this paper, we show that the problem of finding the lower bound on the minimum number of flipped bits in the 2^n bits embedded image to hide n bits data is closely related with finding minimum dominating sets of the binary hypercube of dimension n. To the best of our knowledge, our work is a first approach to convert the data-hiding problem to the relatively well-known graph problem. We believe that our results can be helpful to find lower bounds or general solutions for data-hiding in binary images, color images or audio/video data.

The rest of this paper is organized as follows. In Section 2 we describe the previous work. In Section 3, we explain the relation between the data-hiding problem and the minimum dominating set problem in the binary hypercube. Finally, we offer some conclusions in Section 4.

2   Related Work

Related work can be classified into two groups [12]. The first [5,4,13,9] flips a white pixel to black or vice versa. The second [6] modifies thickness of lines or line spacing. In [6], Maxemchunk and Low proposed a method which changes the line spacing and character spacing. Since the latter has some demerits such as the amount of data to be hidden is limited [12], we chose the first approach.

The first one can be further classified into two. The first is to cheat human perception to reduce the visible artifacts by appropriately choosing the positions of flipped bits. In [5] Matsu *et al* modified dithering patterns to embed the secret information. To embed information, Koch *et al*'s algorithm [4] modifies the ratio of black and white pixels in each block to be larger/smaller than 1. In [13], Wu and Liu proposed an efficient scheme that uses flippability lookup table to minimize distortion. However, these methods have shortcomings that they require special types of images, or the amount of hidden data should be restricted.

Another approach is to minimize the number of flipped bits in the embedded image to reduce distortion. The most recent method (Tseng-Chen-Pan's scheme) that appeared on IEEE Trans. on Comm. 2002 [9], flips only 2 bits for hiding n bits in the embedded image of size 2^n bits. This scheme has a strong point in that quality degradation (or distortion) does not depend on the types of binary image or information to be hidden.

As for data hiding in color and gray-scale images, there have been many research activities [7,3,2,1,8,11,10,14]. Mainly they change pixel values by a small amount so that the majority people may not noticeable [13], which cannot be applied to data hiding in the binary image.

3   Our Work

In this section we first describe the data hiding method briefly. Then, we explain the minimum dominating set problem and show the relation between the data-hiding problem and the minimum dominating set problem in the binary hypercube.

3.1   Overview of Data Hiding Scheme

In this subsection, we describe the overview of the typical data hiding scheme. Data hiding scheme consists of 2 modules: encoding module and decoding module. The encoding module $E(B, K, I)$ takes an original image B, data to be hidden I and symmetric key K and outputs the embedded image C. Given C and K, the decoding module $D(C, K)$ restores I.

Note that $D()$ does not require the original image B to get I. In encoding process, K is used for scrambling the positions of the flipped bits and it is the outside of the scope of our paper.

[9]'s scheme changes at most two bits for embedding I in B where the size of I and that of B are n and 2^n, respectively. It is apparent that the smaller the number of flipped bits is, the less distortion of the original image is. Hence, to address the lower bound of this problem, we relate this problem to the relatively well-known problem in the graph.

3.2   Minimum Dominating Set Problem

In this subsection we describe the minimum dominating set problem. Let $G = (V, E)$ be an undirected graph, where V is a set of vertices and E is a set of edges. Two vertices x, y of G are *adjacent* or *neighbour* if there is an edge xy. For a vertex i, $N(i)$ denotes a set of the all neighbouring vertices of i.

A $S \subset V$ is a *dominating* set if $N(i) \cap S \neq \{\}$ for every $i \in V - S$. That is to say, every node in V is either a member of S or a neighbour of some member of S. A dominating set S is *minimal dominating* if no proper subset is dominating. Figure 1 shows an example of the minimal dominating set.

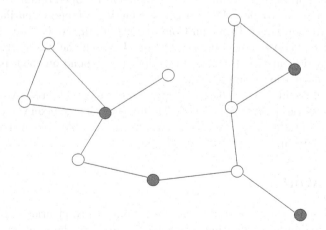

Fig. 1. An example of the minimal dominating set

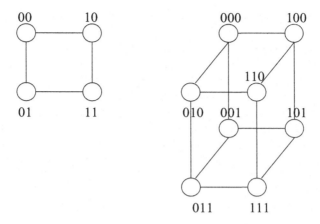

Fig. 2. Binary hypercubes $H(2,2)$ and $H(3,2)$

The number of vertices in the minimal dominating set is called the *dominance number* of G. In the above figure, the dominance number is 4.

3.3   Relation Between Data Hiding and Minimum Dominating Set Problem

In this subsection, we first define a group for representing the original image B. Then, we define subgroups each of which corresponds to the embedded image C that hides each possible data I. Then, we define a graph which represents a original image B and show that the subgroups are related to the dominating set in the graph.

Assume that there exists a group $\mathbb{G} = \{0,1\}^{2^n}$ that represents an original binary image B and suppose that the size of I is n bits. Then, for each possible value of I, we discuss the subgroup $\mathbb{S}_I \subset \mathbb{G}$ which represents C for all the possible original images B and the specific I.

Assume that the number of flipped bits is k. Then, $\mathbb{S}_I$ should have the following properties.

1. The subgroups are disjoint. If not, there is a possibility that for different I and I' the encoding scheme produces the same image C.
2. For each elements in $\mathbb{G}$, there exists at least one element in all the subgroup such that Hamming distance is at most k.

Note that we do not need that the sum of all the subgroups is $\mathbb{S}$. Moreover, the sizes of the subgroups can be different.

$\mathbb{S}_{min}$ denotes the subgroup whose size is the smallest. The size of $\mathbb{S}$ is 2^{2^n} and there are 2^n subgroups. If the size of $\mathbb{S}_{min}$ is bigger than $2^{2^n}/2^n$, by the pigeon-hole principle, the subgroup would not meet the Property 1.

Let us consider the simplest case where $k = 1$. The binary code $\mathbb{B}$ can be represented as a binary hypercube of dimension n (or equivalently, Hamming graph $H(n, 2)$). In this graph, each vertex means each code in $\mathbb{B}$ and the edge exists if and only if Hamming weight between the two nodes is at most 1. Figure 2 shows the binary hypercubes, $H(2, 2)$ and $H(3, 2)$.

If we find the dominating set in this graph, it meets all the properties for the subgroup. Note that the minimal dominating set has the smallest size among the dominating sets. Hence, If the size of the minimal dominating set is bigger than $2^{2^n}/2^n$, then we are unable to construct encoding/decoding routine for $k = 1$.

Although the size is less than $2^{2^n}/2^n$, it does not guarantee the existence of the encoding/decoding routine for $k = 1$. Since we have 2^n subgroups, if we show that the sum of the size of all the subgroups is not bigger than 2^{2^n}, then it guarantees the existence. In short, our method is a way for finding lower bound but not a tight lower bound.

Let us consider the case where $k > 1$. The binary code $\mathbb{B}$ can be represented as a graph G where each vertex means each code in $\mathbb{B}$ and the edge exists if and only if Hamming weight between two nodes are at most k.

4   Conclusion

To minimize distortion in secure data-hiding, there is an approach to reduce the number of flipped bits in the embedded image. The most recent method (Tseng-Chen-Pan's scheme) that appeared on IEEE Trans. on Comm. 2002, flips only 2 bits for hiding n bits in the embedded image of size 2^n bits. In this paper, we show that the problem of finding the lower bound on the minimum number of flipped bits in the 2^n bits embedded image to hide n bits data is closely related with finding minimum dominating sets of the binary hypercube of dimension n. To the best of our knowledge, our work is a first approach to convert data-hiding problems to relatively well-known graph problem. We believe that our results can be helpful to find lower bounds or general solutions for data-hiding in the binary image or audio/video data.

Acknowledgments. This work was supported by the Brain Korea 21 Project.

References

1. I. Cox, J. Kilian, T. Leighton, and T. Shamoon. Secure spread spectrum watermarking for multimedia. *IEEE Trans. Image Processing*, 6:1673–1687, 1997.
2. I. J. Cox, M. L. Miller, and J. A Boom. Digital Watermarking. *IEEE Trans. Image Processing*, San Mateo, CA: Morgan Kaufmann, 2001.
3. F. Hartung and M. Kutter. Multimedia watermarking techniques. In *IEEE, Vol. 87*, pages 1079–1107, 1999.
4. E. Koch and J. Zhao. Embedding robust labels into images for copyright protection. In *Int. Congr. Intellectual Property Rights for Specialized Information, Knowledge & New Technologies*, 1995.
5. K. Matsui and K. Tanaka. Video-steganography: how to secretly embed a signature in a picture. In *IMA Intellectual Propery Project, Vol. 1, No. 1*, 1994.

6. N. F. Maxemchunk and S. Low. Marking text documents. In *IEEE ICIP'97*, 1997.
7. F. A. P. Petitcolas, R. J. Anderson, and M. G. Kuhn. Information hiding–a survey. In *IEEE, Vol. 87*, pages 1062–1078, 1999.
8. C. Podilchuk and W. Zeng. Image adaptive watermarking using visual models. *IEEE J. Select. Areas Commun.*, 16:525–538, 1998.
9. Yu-Chee Tseng, Yu-Yuan Chen, and Hsiang-Kuang Pan. A Secure Data Hiding Scheme for Binary Images. *IEEE Transactions on Communication*, 50(8):1227–1231, 2002.
10. M. Wu and B. Liu. Watermarking for image authentication. In *IEEE Int. COnf. Image Processing (ICIP'98)*, volume 2, 1998.
11. M. Wu, H. Yu, and B. Liu. Data hiding in images and videos: Part II–Designas and applications. *IEEE Trans. Image Processing*, 12:606–705, 2003.
12. Min Wu. Multimedia Data Hiding. Ph.D. Dissertation, Princeton Univ., 2001.
13. Min Wu and Bede Liu. Data Hiding in Binary Image for Authentication and Annotation. *IEEE Transactions on Multimedia*, 6(4):528–538, 2004.
14. M. M. Yeung and F. Mintzer. An invisible watermarking technique for image verification. In *IEEE ICIP'97*, volume 2, pages 680–683, 1997.

Software Design Method Enhanced by Appended Security Requirements

Eun-ser Lee[1] and Sun-myoung Hwang[2]

[1] Chung-Ang University, 221, Huksuk-Dong, Dongjak-Gu, Seoul, Korea
eslee@object.cau.ac.kr

[2] Daejeon University, 96-3 Yongun-dong, Tong-gu, Taejon 300-716, South Korea
sunhwang@dju.ac.kr

Abstract. The IT products like as firewall, IDS (Intrusion Detection System) and VPN (Virtual Private Network) which made to perform special functions related to security are used to supply security characteristics. But the method using these products may be not the perfect solution. Therefore, when making some kinds of software products, security-related requirements must be considered. It is essential that not only the customer's requirements for software functionality should be satisfied but also the security requirements imposed on the software development should be effectively analyzed and implemented in contributing to the security objectives of customer's requirements. The customer's requirements must be implemented to software perfectly, but this is not sufficient. The secure software may be implemented by not only applying Firewall or IDS but also considering security requirement appended to customer's requirement. In this paper, we propose a security engineering based approach considering security when developing software.

1 Introduction

With the increasing reliance of society on information, the protection of that information and the systems contain that information is becoming important. In fact, many products, systems, and services are needed and used to protect information. The focus of security engineering has expanded from one primarily concerned with safeguarding classified government data to broader applications including financial transactions, contractual agreements, personal information, and the Internet. These trends have elevated the importance of security engineering [1].

When we are making some kinds of software products, ISO/IEC TR 15504 may provide a framework for the assessment of software processes, and this framework can be used by organizations involved in planning, monitoring, controlling, and improving the acquisition, supply, development, operation, evolution and support of software. But, in the ISO/IEC TR 15504, considerations for security are relatively poor to other security-related criteria such as ISO/IEC 21827, the Systems Security Engineering Capability Maturity Model (SSE-CMM), or ISO/IEC 15408, Common Criteria (CC) [2-4]. Security-related software development is concerned with many

K. Aizawa, Y. Nakamura, and S. Satoh (Eds.): PCM 2004, LNCS 3331, pp. 578–585, 2004.
© Springer-Verlag Berlin Heidelberg 2004

kinds of measures that may be applied to the development environment or developer to protect the confidentiality and integrity of the IT product or system developed.

In this paper, we will propose a concept of security requirements appended to customer's requirements.

2 Application of Security Engineering

A wide variety of organizations can apply security engineering to their work such as the development of computer programs, software and middleware of applications programs or the security policy of organizations. Appropriate approaches or methods and practices are therefore required by product developers, service providers, system integrators, system administrators, and even security specialists. Some of these organizations deal with high-level issues (e.g., ones dealing with operational use or system architecture), others focus on low-level issues (e.g., mechanism selection or design), and some do both.

The security engineering may be applied to all kinds of organizations. Use of the security engineering principle should not imply that one focus is better than another is or that any of these uses are required. An organization's business focus need not be biased by use of the security engineering.

Based on the focus of the organization, some, but not all, of approaches or methods of security engineering may be applied very well. In fact, generally, it is true that some of approaches or methods of security engineering can be applied to increase assurance level of software.

Next examples illustrate ways in which the security engineering may be applied to software, systems, facilities development and operation by a variety of different organizations.

Security service provider may use security engineering to measure the capability of an organization that performs risk assessments. During software or system development or integration, one would need to assess the organization with regard to its ability to determine and analyze security vulnerabilities and assess the operational impacts. In the operational case, one would need to assess the organization with regard to its ability to monitor the security posture of the system, identify and analyze security vulnerabilities, and assess the operational impacts.

Countermeasure Developers may use security engineering to address determining and analyzing security vulnerabilities, assessing operational impacts, and providing input and guidance to other groups involved (such as a software group).

Software or product developers may use security engineering to gain an understanding of the customer's security needs and append security requirements to the customer's requirements. Interaction with the customer is required to ascertain them. In the case of a product, the customer is generic as the product is developed a priori independent of a specific customer. When this is the case, the product marketing group or another group can be used as the hypothetical customer, if one is required.

As mentioned earlier, the main objective of application of security engineering is to provide assurance about the software or system to customer, and the assurance level of a software or system may be the critical factor has influence on deciding purchase. Therefore, the meaning of the application of security engineering to the software is the application of some assurance methods to the software development lifecycle phases.

Assurance methods are classified in Fig.1 according to the three assurance approach categories [1].

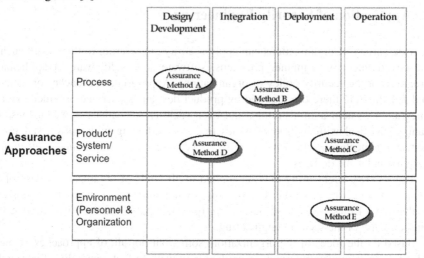

Fig.1. Categorization of existing assurance methods

3 Security Requirements for Software

3.1 General Software Development Process

There are many methodologies for software development, and security engineering does not mandate any specific development methodology or life cycle model. Fig.2 depicts underlying assumptions about the relationship between the customer's requirements and the implementation. The figure is used to provide a context for discussion and should not be construed as advocating a preference for one methodology (e.g. waterfall) over another (e.g. prototyping).

It is essential that the requirements imposed on the software development be effective in contributing to the objectives of consumers. Unless suitable requirements are established at the start of the development process, the resulting end product, however well engineered, may not meet the objectives of its anticipated consumers.

The process is based on the refinement of the customer's requirements into a software implementation. Each lower level of refinement represents a design decomposition with additional design detail. The least abstract representation is the software implementation itself.

In general, customer does not mandate a specific set of design representations. The requirement is that there should be sufficient design representations presented at a sufficient level of granularity to demonstrate where required:

a) that each refinement level is a complete instantiation of the higher levels (i.e. all functions, properties, and behaviors defined at the higher level of abstraction must be demonstrably present in the lower level);

b) that each refinement level is an accurate instantiation of the higher levels (i.e. there should be no functions, properties, and behaviors defined at the lower level of abstraction that are not required by the higher level).

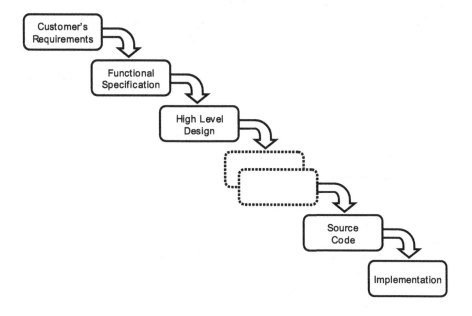

Fig. 2. The relationship between the customer's requirements and the implementation

3.2 Security Requirements

For the development of software, the first objective is the perfect implementation of customer's requirements. And this work may be done by very simple processes. However, if the software developed has some critical security holes, the whole network or systems that software installed and generated are very vulnerable.

Therefore, developers or analyzers must consider some security-related factors and append a few security-related requirements to the customer's requirements. Fig.3 depicts the idea about this concept.

The processes based on the refinement of the security-related requirements are considered with the processes of software implementation.

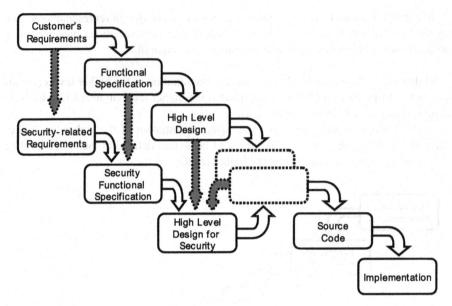

Fig. 3. Append security-related requirements

3.3 Strength of Security Requirements

Security Engineer should define the degree of robustness as the level of strength and assurance recommended for potential security mechanism(s). To determine this level for a given security service in a particular application, the customer and the information systems security engineer should consider the value of the information to be protected (in relation to the operational mission), and the perceived threat environment. Guidelines for determining these values May be provided in the IATF [8]. Once a determination has been made regarding the information value and threat environment, the security engineer may decide the robustness level by determining EALs (Evaluation Assurance Levels) and SML (Strength of Mechanism Levels).

The level of countermeasure is determined by robustness, and robustness should be considered in selecting security countermeasures. The robustness strategy provides the philosophy behind, and initial guidance for, selection of the strength of security mechanisms and the security assurance provisions that may be needed for a particular value of information and a potential threat level. The selection of mechanisms and the decision on the level of strength and assurance needed will be based on a Security Engineering activity that addresses the situation of a specific user, mission, and environment.

3.4 Implementation Example

For example, if the customer's requirement 'management by web' is specified, we can append some security-related requirements:

(1) Customer's requirement: We want to manage the program by web

(2) Level of robustness: By considering of assets protected and the attack potential to those assets, basic level is enough

(3) Appended requirements: Next lists are not perfect but general to all cases

(4) Grouping of security-related requirements

Requirements appended above can be classified in groups as below:

Grouping	Requirements
Identification and Authentication	-Requirements for identify mechanisms. -Requirements for authentication mechanisms. -Requirements for defining values for some number of unsuccessful authentication attempts and SF actions in cases of authentication attempt failures.
Access	-Requirements for the SF to provide the capability for SF-initiated and user initiated locking and unlocking of interactive sessions.
Cryptography	-Requirements for Cryptographic operations (Key generation and so on)
Trusted path/channels	-Requirements to establish and maintain trusted communication to or from users and the SF -Requirements for the creation of a trusted channel between the SF and other trusted IT products for the performance of security critical operations.
Auditing	- Requirements for recording the occurrence of security relevant events that take place under SF control. - Requirements for audit tools that should be available to authorized users to assist in the review of audit data.

(5) Characterizing and mapping to Security functional requirements in CC

Characterizing of requirements	Mapping to security class
- Identification - Authentication	FIA (Identification and Authentication)
- Access	FAU (Audit Review)
- Cryptographic operations	FCS (Cryptographic Support)
- Trusted path - Trusted channels	FTA (TOE access)
- Audit	FTP (Trusted path/channels)

(6) Selection of security family in the class

Security class	Mapping to security family
FIA	User authentication (FIA_UAU), User identification (FIA_UID), Authentication failures (FIA_AFL)
FAU	Security audit data generation (FAU_GEN), Security audit review (FAU_SAR), Security audit event selection (FAU_SEL), Security audit event storage (FAU_STG)
FCS	Cryptographic key management (FCS_CKM), Cryptographic operation (FCS_COP)
FTA	Limitation on multiple concurrent sessions (FTA_MCS), Session locking (FTA_SSL), TOE session establishment (FTA_TSE)
FTP	Inter-TSF trusted channel (FTP_ITC), Trusted path (FTP_TRP)

(7) Selection of security component in the family

Security family	Mapping to security component
FIA_UAU, FIA_UID, FIA_AFL	FIA_UAU.2 User authentication before any action, FIA_UAU.5 Multiple authentication mechanisms, FIA_UAU.7 Protected authentication feedback FIA_UID.2 User identification before any action FIA_AFL.1 Authentication failure handling
FAU_GEN, FAU_SAR, FAU_SEL, FAU_STG	FAU_GEN.1 Audit data generation, FAU_GEN.2 User identity association FAU_SAR.2 Restricted audit review, FAU_SAR.3 Selectable audit review FAU_SEL.1 Selective audit FAU_STG.1 Protected audit trail storage, FAU_STG.3 Action in case of possible audit data loss
FCS_CKM,	FCS_CKM.1 Cryptographic key generation, FCS_CKM.2 Cryptographic key distribution,

FCS_COP	FCS_CKM.3 Cryptographic key access, FCS_CKM.4 Cryptographic key destruction FCS_COP.1 Cryptographic operation
FTA_MCS,	FTA_MCS.2 Per user attribute limitation on multiple concurrent sessions
FTA_SSL,	FTA_SSL.1 TSF-initiated session locking, FTA_SSL.2 User-initiated locking
FTA_TSE	FTA_TSE.1 TOE session establishment
FTP_ITC,	FTP_ITC.1 Inter-TSF trusted channel
FTP_TRP	FTP_TRP.1 Trusted path

(8) Implementation of requirements to software, hardware or firmware.

4 Conclusions

In this paper, we proposed a method appending some security-related requirements to the customer's requirements by considering robustness level.

For the development of software, the first objective is the perfect implementation of customer's requirements. However, if the software developed has some critical security holes, the whole network or systems that software installed and generated may be very vulnerable.

Therefore, developers or analyzers must consider some security-related factors and append a few security-related requirements to the customer's requirements. The processes based on the refinement of the security-related requirements are considered with the processes of software implementation.

References

1. ISO. ISO/IEC 21827 Information technology – Systems Security Engineering Capability Maturity Model (SSE-CMM)
2. ISO. ISO/IEC 15408-1:1999 Information technology - Security techniques - Evaluation criteria for IT security - Part 1: Introduction and general model
3. ISO. ISO/IEC 15408-2:1999 Information technology - Security techniques - Evaluation criteria for IT security - Part 2: Security functional requirements
4. ISO. ISO/IEC 15408-3:1999 Information technology - Security techniques - Evaluation criteria for IT security - Part 3: Security assurance requirements
5. Tai-Hoon Kim, Byung-Gyu No, Dong-chun Lee, Threat Description for the PP by Using the Concept of the Assets Protected by TOE, ICCS 2003, LNCS 2660, Part 4, pp. 605-613
6. NSA, The Information Assurance Technical Framework, September, 2002

On the Disk Layout for Periodical Video Broadcast Services*

Meng-Huang Lee

Department of Information Management
Shih-Chien University, Taipei, Taiwan
meng@mail.usc.edu.tw

Abstract. In this paper, we base on region-based disk layout and propose a data placement technique and its associated disk scheduling policy for providing periodical video broadcast services. We present a quantitative study and design algorithms, while still maintain the quality of service, for (1) placing video data on disk, and (2) simultaneously serving of maximum number of broadcast channels with minimal data buffer. By an example evaluation, we demonstrate the advantage of our design.

1 Introduction

The goal of a true VOD service is to allow users to watch arbitrary video sequences at arbitrary time. To provide such flexibility in viewing time and choices of video, a true VOD service requires enormous amount of I/O, network bandwidth, and storage capacity. On the network bandwidth, serving 1,000 requests simultaneously needs in total 4Gbps (bits per second), when the video quality is MPEG-2(4Mbps bit rate). One approach to provide video services with efficiently utilizing system bandwidth is to distribute the so-called "hot" videos more efficiently. Broadcast is such a solution. It transfers each video according to a fixed schedule and consumes constant bandwidth regardless of the number of requests for that video. This approach aligns the incoming requests on predetermined temporal boundaries, and thereby significantly reduces the amount of bandwidth required to provide user requests.

Many studies show the benefit of bandwidth sharing of broadcast service from the view point of network bandwidth. But there are not many papers discuss about how the server design to provide such kind of service. Although [1] discusses the program data placement for providing the broadcast service, but the systematic design and analysis to exploit the efficient disk utilization are not discussed.

For a video server design, the most important design issue is to minimize the disk overhead. The disk overhead is incurred either by seek times (the time to reposition the head) or rotational delays (the time for the referenced data under the disk head). By minimizing the disk overhead, the disk system can

---

* This work has been supported in part by Shih-Chien University, Taiwan, under Grant USC 93-05-38804-035

K. Aizawa, Y. Nakamura, and S. Satoh (Eds.): PCM 2004, LNCS 3331, pp. 586–593, 2004.

provide a higher number of simultaneous VOD requests. In our previous works and other articles [3,5], region-based disk layout is proved to effectively eliminate disk overhead and improve disk utilization. For a video broadcast service, the video playback is highly time-predictable and the incoming requests are aligned on pre-determined temporal boundaries. Therefore, in this paper, we base on region-based disk layout scheme and time-predictable features of video data and design a disk system for video broadcast service. A model that relates disk device characteristics to maximizing the disk utilization is also developed. To simplify discussion, this paper assumes the system is configured with a single disk.

2   Data Placement Technique and Disk Scheduling Policy

In our data placement technique, we want to exploit the periodicity nature of broadcast services and the periodical access patterns. Take a 2-hour video program which periodically broadcasts at every 30 minutes for example (shown in Figure 1). This service requires 4 broadcast channels. Each channel playbacks the same video program but at different file blocks which are temporal related. In the case of Figure 1, at 09:30, channel D broadcasts the beginning file blocks of the video program, but channel C, B, A broadcast the file blocks indexed at 30, 60, 90 minutes past the beginning of the same video program, respectively. The goal of our data placement technique is to utilize the disk bandwidth with minimal data buffer by exploring this periodicity nature of broadcast service and temporal characteristics of video program. It is obvious that file blocks of a video program which are playbacked at the same time for different periodical broadcast channels should be placed together such that disk system can retrieve them in one disk access operation and improve disk utilization. Therefore, in the case of Figure 1, file blocks indexed at beginning, 30, 60, and 90 minutes past the beginning of the video program should be placed together, such that the disk can retrieve them at one disk access operation. Our proposed data placement technique is region-based and the disk is evenly partitioned into several regions. Then, the file blocks described above will be placed in a certain region of disk. During a service cycle, for every broadcast channel, one file block is retrieved in one disk access operation when the disk head scans across the partitioned region. Later in time, the disk head moves to next region and starts another disk access operation, and the buffered data in previous disk access operation will be broadcasted to user clients. If the end region of disk is accessed, the disk head will round trip back to disk beginning region and again start another sequence of disk access operations. Here, disk access round trip time is defined as the lump sum of time of disk access operations from the beginning region of the disk to the end region and round trip back to the disk beginning region. In this scheme, dual data buffers are assigned to each broadcast channel. And for uninterrupted video playback, the amount of retrieved and buffered data must be equal to or larger than the amount of data consuming of the video playback during the time of the service cycle. Each region is composed of a number of physically consecutive tracks and the basic storage unit is a disk track. A file

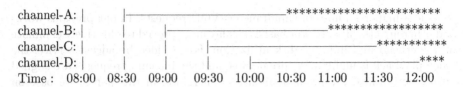

Fig. 1. An example of periodical video broadcast service. The video program duration is 2 hours, and it periodically broadcasts at every 30 minutes. The service requires 4 broadcast channels.

Table 1. The design example of Figure 1, with disk is partitioned into 10 regions and the disk access round trip time is assumed 10 minutes. Note: The number in each region denotes the file blocks indexed at the playing time past the beginning of the video program.

Region 0	0*,10**,20***,30*,40**,50***,60*,70**,80***,90*,100**,110***
Region 1	1*,11**,21***,31*,41**,51***,61*,71**,81***,91*,101**,111***
Region 2	2*,12**,22***,32*,42**,52***,62*,72**,82***,92*,102**,112***
Region 3	3*,13**,23***,33*,43**,53***,63*,73**,83***,93*,103**,113***
Region 4	4*,14**,24***,34*,44**,54***,64*,74**,84***,94*,104**,114***
Region 5	5*,15**,25***,35*,45**,55***,65*,75**,85***,95*,105**,115***
Region 6	6*,16**,26***,36*,46**,56***,66*,76**,86***,96*,106**,116***
Region 7	7*,17**,27***,37*,47**,57***,67*,77**,87***,97*,107**,117***
Region 8	8*,18**,28***,38*,48**,58***,68*,78**,88***,98*,108**,118***
Region 9	9*,19**,29***,39*,49**,59***,69*,79**,89***,99*,109**,119***

block (or retrieval unit) comprises one or more disk tracks. The reason behind adopting this practice is to eliminate rotation latency during disk access. If the disk features on-arrival read-ahead and file blocks always start and end at disk track boundaries, then disk rotation latency can be completely eliminated.

Table 1 depicts the above discussions with the disk access round trip time is 10 minutes and the disk is partitioned into 10 regions. The file blocks in a region are then grouped into 3 groups, which are marked up with *, **, and ***. The file blocks in a group are 30 minutes temporal separated in playing time. In one disk access operation, only one group is accessed and all file blocks in this group are retrieved.

For generalize our discussion, here, let us use the symbols listed below in the subsequent discussions.

- N: denotes the number of broadcast channels that the system can admit.
- R: denotes the number of regions into which the disk is partitioned.
- C: denotes the number of cylinders of the disk
- S_b : denotes the file block size of video program in the units of disk track size.
- S_r: denotes the disk region size in the units of disk track size.

- S_v: denotes the video program size in the units of disk track size.
- S_d: denotes the whole disk space in the units of disk track size
- $T_{seek}(d)$: denotes the seek time of disk head to scan $d$distance in number of cylinders in the disk.
- T_o: denotes the worst-case time of disk access operation for N broadcast channels. It is the time that disk head scans across one disk partitioned region and makes N file blocks' retrieval. T_o contains two major components. The first component is the worst-case lumped sum of seek time. The second component is the lumped sum of N file blocks' retrieval.
- T_{rot}: denotes the time of one disk revolution which is also the time to retrieve a disk track
- T_p: denotes the duration time of playing back one track size of video program.
- T_{bp} : denotes the broadcast period in seconds. It is the time interval between two beginnings of the video program broadcast service.

File blocks from a video program are interleaved and placed in the disk region system according the following rule (as shown in Table 2): *file blocks with index $(j \times R + k)$ are placed in region k.*

R is the number of regions into which the disk is partitioned, j is the integer runs form 0, and k is the index of the regions and runs from 0 to R-1.

Table 2. The general scheme of the proposed disk technique. File blocks of a program with index $j \times R + k$ are placed in region k, j is the integer runs form 0.

Region 0	0, R, 2R, 3R, ...$j \times R + 0$
Region 1	1, R+1, 2R+1, 3R+1,......$j \times R + 1$
....	....
Region R-1	R-1, R+(R-1), 2R+(R-1), 3R+(R-1), ...$j \times R + (R-1)$

A disk system is featured by its bandwidth and space capacity. For a disk system providing the broadcast service, the system not only considers the bandwidth issue but also the storage capacity issue. At first glance, the disk capacity should accommodate the whole video program and its bandwidth should larger than the service demand. Therefore, the following two inequalities are derived:

$S_v \leq S_d$...(1)

$N/T_p \leq 1/T_r$...(2)

Inequality (1) guarantees the video program can in a whole be stored in the disk system, while Inequality (2) guarantees the demand bandwidth.

Note here that, if the disk system desires to provide Nchannels broadcast service, this means that the system must afford the disk bandwidth for N video streaming. In inequality (2), the left hand side denotes the demand disk bandwidth for N channels broadcast service, and the right hand side denotes the disk sustained bandwidth. The sustained bandwidth is the bandwidth observed when the disk continuous to retrieve data out from consecutive tracks. But the performance of disk bandwidth very much depends on the data placement technique and disk scheduling policy. Without systematic data placement and disk scheduling, the sustained bandwidth can not be achieved. Therefore, the sustained bandwidth and the whole disk space in the inequalities are the best-case that the disk system can provide. System meets these criteria still can not guarantee the service quality be achieved. Our proposed data placement technique is region-based, therefore, the disk system should also meet the service demand criteria in a disk region. Then, the following two inequalities are derived:

$N \times S_b \leq S_r ...(3)$

$(N \times S_b \times T_{rot}) + (N+1) \times worst\_seek\_time\_overhead) \leq \{S_b \times T_p\}... (4)$

From [2], the *worst_seek_time_over_head* is equal to $T_{seek}((C/R)/N)$.

As described above, file blocks with index $j \times R + k$ are placed in region k. Assume a video program periodically starts at T_{bp} time interval, the file blocks of the kth region of the disk are grouped into $T_{bp}/(T_o \times R)$ groups. The the mth group of the kth region contains the $(i \times (T_{bp}/(T_o \times R)) \times R + (m \times R) + k)^{th}$ blocks of this video program, m is the integer from 0 to $T_{bp}/(T_o \times R)-1$ and i is the integer runs from 0 to $(S_v/(S_b \times R))/(T_{bp}/(T_o \times R))-1$. When disk scans and accesses the kth region, file blocks of a certain group are all retrieved at the same time.

From above discussions, the data placement technique, in no doubts, is determined by the broadcast period, T_{bp}. But the disk access round trip time is also a major design issue. It determines the grouping of file blocks in a disk region. In the above example, the broadcast period is 30 minutes and disk access round trip time is 10 minutes, then the file blocks in a disk region are grouped into 3 groups. Therefore, there are many alternatives in disk access round trip time issue to meet a certain broadcast period. And, the disk access round trip time is determined by number of region which the disk is to be partitioned into, i.e. R defined above. Which alternatives is the optimal needs systematic analysis as the following discussions.

From the disk modeling by Ruemmler and Wilkes[4], the disk seek overhead could be model by

$$\text{seek time}(d) = \begin{cases} c1 + c2\sqrt{d}, d \leq Cb \\ c3 + c4 \times d, d \geq Cb \end{cases}$$

where Cb is a constant defining the boundary of two formulas above and d is the distance of disk head movement in number of cylinders. Mathematically, it can be proved that the worst-case lumped seek time occurs when the N stops are evenly apart [2]. Accordingly, the designer derives the following formula for computing T_o:

$T_o = (N \times S_b \times T_{rot}) + (N+1) \times T_{seek}((C/R)/N)$ ...(5)

Given the above equation, the designer now needs to work out the value of R that guarantees uninterrupted service of video program (inequality (4)). Thus,

$T_{seek}((C/R)/N) \leq (S_b \times T_p - N \times S_b \times T_{rot})/ (N+1)$ ...(6)

Then, we apply Ruemmler and Wilkes[4]'s seek time model to (6),

$C/(N \times (((S_b \times T_p - N \times S_b \times T_{rot})/ (N+1)-c1)/c2)^2) \leq R$ ...(7-1)

and

$C/(N \times ((S_b \times T_p - N \times S_b \times T_{rot})/ (N+1))-c3/c4) \leq R$ ...(7-2)

From (7-1) and (7-2), we can derive the minimal value of R. Base on this result, we can design the disk system with maximal system utilization.

3 Design Example and Evaluation

In this section, we present an example to illustrate our disk system design. Table 3 shows the disk specifications of our design example which are from the disk modeling by Ruemmler and Wilkes[4]. The seek time of the disk is modeled by

$$\text{seek time}(d) = \begin{cases} 3.24 + 0.400\sqrt{d}, d \leq 383 \\ 8.00 + 0.008d, d \geq 383 \end{cases}$$

where d is the distance of disk head movement in number of cylinders and the unit of time is millisecond. Table 4 shows the video program specifications of our periodical video broadcast system.

In this section, we want to evaluate how many broadcast channels which the disk system specified in Table 3 can provide when the video program is specified in Table 4. At first view of specifications in Table 3 and Table 4, it seems that the disk system can provide about 10 broadcast channels, for the disk maximum sustained disk bandwidth is 2.17 Mbytes per second and the video bit rate is 1.5 Mbps. As discussed in previous sections, without data placement technique and disk scheduling, the disk system is hard to achieve this performance. Therefore, we will compare our proposed data placement technique and its associated disk scheduling policy with system design without any particular planning. That is, the video data is placed in the disk randomly and the disk accesses the video data by FCFS (first come, first serve) across the whole disk space. Also in our previous discussions, disk access round trip time, number of partitioned region and file block size are orthogonal and these factors make the tradeoff between disk bandwidth utilization and data buffer required. Therefore, in the following evaluations, we start with the maximal number of broadcast channels that disk system can provide by its best efforts (in our case, this number is 10) and discuss the effect of above factors to the system performance and data buffer required. The same evaluation will be continued by decreasing the number of broadcast channels the disk system desires to provide until the number that the disk system can provide without any particular design planning.

Table 3. Disk specifications from [4]

Rotation speed	4000rpm
No. of cylinders	1962
No. of sectors per track	72
Tracks per cylinder	19
No. of bytes per sector	512 bytes
Maximum sustained disk bandwidth	2.17Mbytes per second
Formatted capacity	1.3Gbytes

Table 4. The specifications of the video program

Media type	MPEG-1
Demand bandwidth per channel	1.5Mbps
Program duration	100 minutes

Table 5. Broadcast_period=10 minutes, number of broadcast channels=10

	Region-base placement	System without particular design and planning
Meet the continuity requirement	yes	no
File block size(tracks)	1	In any cases
No. of region	3728	
Region size(tracks)	10	

Table 6. Broadcast_period=12.5 minutes, number of channels=8

	Region-base placement	System without particular design and planning (III)	System without particular design and planning (II)	System without particular design and planning (I)
Meet the continuity requirement	yes	yes	no	no
File block size(tracks)	1	> 3	2	1
No. of region	> 26			
Region size(tracks)	< 1433			

Table 7. Broadcast_period=14.3 minutes, number of channels=7

	Region-base placement	System without particular design and planning (II)	System without particular design and planning (I)
Meet the continuity requirement	yes	yes	no
File block (tracks)	1	> 2	1
No. of region	> 3		
Region size(tracks)	< 12426		

Table 5 to Table 7 illustrate the evaluations. In Table 5, we discuss the case that the disk desires to provide 10 broadcast channels. At first, the file block size for each channel is assumed as one disk track (36kbytes in our design example). If the system design without any particular planning, the disk system requires 268.4 msec to retrieve 10 file blocks. But the playback time of the one file block data at 200kbytes/sec playback rate is 180 msec. This violates the continuity requirement. Although we adjust file block size to improve the disk utilization, but the system still violate the continuity requirement. But with 3728 partitioned regions and file block size is equal to one disk track (36kbytes), the system can provide 10 broadcast channels. Then, in Table 6, we discuss the case of 8 broadcast channels. System design without any particular planning also can not provide the service demand except the file block size is equal to or greater than 3 disk tracks. But with 26 partitioned regions (or more than this number) and file block size is as one disk track, the system can provide the service demand. By the same evaluation, if system is only demanded to provide 5 broadcast channels (i.e., the broadcast period is 20 minutes),we can observe that the system can provide the desired bandwidth without any particular design and planning. But when the system is demanded to provide 7 channels, from Table 7, we can see that without data placement technique, this demand can not be achieved except file block size is equal to or greater than 2 disk tracks.

The data buffer required for each channel is 2 times of the file block size evaluated in Table 5 to Table 7 (for the dual data buffer system is adopted). And, in our data placement technique, a file block (or retrieval unit) comprises one or more disk tracks (in order to eliminate rotation latency). Then the evaluation set that meet the service demand with file block size is one disk track will be our design alternatives. They not only meet the service demand but also with minimal data buffer.

References

1. Tzi-Cker Chiueh, "A periodic broadcast architecture for large-scale residential video-on-demand service" Proceedings of SPIE First International Symposium on Technologies and Systems for Voice, Video, and Data Communications, 2615-20, Philadelphia PA, October 1995.
2. Yen-Jen Oyang. "A tight upper bound of the lumped disk seek time for the scan disk scheduling policy" *Information Processing Letters*, 54, 1995
3. Yen-Jen Oyang, Meng-Huang Lee, Chun-Hung Wen, and Chih-Yuan Cheng, "Design of Multimedia Storage Systems for On-Demand Playback",Proceedings of the IEEE 11th International Conference on Data Engineering, Taipei, Taiwan, Mar. 1995.
4. Chris Ruemmler and John Wikles. "An Introduction to Disk Drive Modeling" *IEEE Computer*, Vol. 27, No 3, 1994
5. P. Bocheck, H. Meadows, and S. Chang, "Disk Partitioning Technique for Reducing Mulmedia Access Delay", In ISMM Distributed Systems and Multimedia Applications, August 1994

Paged Segment Striping Scheme for the Dynamic Scheduling of Continuous Media Servers*

KyungOh Lee, J.B. Lee, and Kee-Wook Rim

Sunmoon University, 336-840 ChungNam Asansi, Korea
leeko@sunmoon.ac.kr

Abstract. An innovative dynamic scheduling scheme is proposed to improve the efficiency of video-on-demand servers. We first introduce a paged segment striping model that makes dynamic scheduling possible. Based on this striping scheme, we propose a dynamic scheduling scheme that adapts to frequently changing workloads. In particular, we can change the round length without any additional disk access so that it can be adapted to changing request trends with a negligible cost in performance. This dynamic scheduling scheme always shows better performance than the static scheduling scheme in simulation. Although the dynamical scheme introduces additional scheduling overhead, it is very small when compared with the performance degradation in the static scheme.

1 Introduction

The optimal value of round length in continuous media servers may vary significantly if heterogeneous streams such as HDTV streams, MPEG-1 movies, and audio streams, are serviced and users' requesting patterns changes significantly [1,4]. That is, an optimal value in one situation may be far from optimal in other situations. If most streams have a low data rate (say, 1.5 M bps, as in MPEG-1), then a long round length will show better performance; on the other hand, if most of streams have a high data rate (say, 10 M bps, as in HDTV), then a short round length will show better performance. If changing the round length induces additional disk seeks, then the performance may become worse. Under our proposed Paged Segment Striping (PSS) scheme, we can increase or decrease the round length without any additional disk access. Through extensive simulation we have verified that an adaptive scheduling scheme always shows better performance than a static scheduling scheme. Furthermore, the additional scheduling overhead of the adaptive scheme is relatively small.

---

* This research was supported by University IT Research Center Project.

K. Aizawa, Y. Nakamura, and S. Satoh (Eds.): PCM 2004, LNCS 3331, pp. 594–601, 2004.

2   Striping Models

Since fine-grained striping schemes waste disk bandwidth due to an excessive number of disk seeks, they are typically outperformed by coarse-grained schemes [1]. Constant time length (CTL) schemes also show better performance than constant data length (CDL) schemes, since CDL schemes tend to require much more buffer space [2]. Accordingly, we adopted a coarse-grained CTL as our basic striping scheme. Reducing the number of seeks required to read the necessary data blocks is much more important in optimizing the throughput than reducing the seek time or the rotational latency. By making it possible for a stream to get enough data for one round from only one access to one disk, we can minimize the frequency of disk seeks.

2.1   RTL(Round Time Length Striping)

If we let DT, the playback time of a striping unit, be the same as the round length, T, then each stream needs to access exactly one disk in a round. A CDL striping scheme, however, may require two or more blocks from round to round, even if a similar configuration is adopted. Thus, we divide each multimedia object into segments that have the same playback duration, and these segments are striped along the disks. When placing the first segments of objects we apply a staggered striping scheme [1]. This reduces the possibility of load imbalance by storing more segments on one disk than on the others. This striping scheme is illustrated in figure 1 and we call the scheme RTL (Round Time Length) striping.

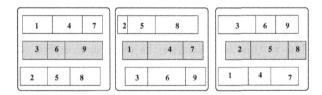

Fig. 1. RTL(Round Time Length) Striping

If k active streams are being serviced from disk i at the current service round, then these streams will be serviced from disk $(i + 1)$ mod n at the next round where n is the number of data disks in the disk array under the RTL striping model. If we assume that every disk in the disk array is identical[1], then it follows that if we have serviced a set of streams without any problems at round j, then there will be no problems at round $j + 1$.

---

[1] If there are many different kinds of disks, we can assume that every disk has the same characteristics as the slowest disk. Otherwise, we should make several disk arrays that have identical (or similar) disks.

If the worst case assumption (i.e., that each stream requires peak data rate, all the time) is used to prevent starvation or overflow, then resources are wasted. Instead of the peak data rate, we use the *maximum segment data rate* $(R(DT))$, which is much smaller than the peak data rate. Assume that we split a multimedia object i into segments that have equal playback time DT, and let $r_{i,j}$ be the average data rate of the jth segment of object i. We can then define the *maximum segment data rate* $R_i(DT)$ of object i, as follows.

$$R_i(DT) = MAX(r_{i,j}(DT) \ for \ all \ j) \qquad (1)$$

This equation is the same as the following equation.

$$Ri(DT) = MAX(Size\_of\_Segments)/playback \ time \ of \ a \ segment \qquad (2)$$

For example, if maximum segment size is 5M bit, and DT is 2 seconds, then $R(DT)$ becomes 2.5Mbps. In many cases, the worst-case assumption is used to prevent the hiccup or jitter. Yet, even though we use $R(DT)$ instead of the peak data rate for resource reservation, there will be neither starvation nor overflow since each segment is stored contiguously and retrieved segment by segment. If DT is the same as the playback time of a frame, then $R(DT)$ is the same as the peak data rate, but if DT is the same as the playback time of a whole video object, then $R(DT)$ is the same as the average data rate of that video object. Thus, $R(DT)$ becomes smaller as DT becomes larger, and the following equation holds globally.

$$R(DT_1) < R(DT_2) \ if \ DT_1 > DT_2 \qquad (3)$$

2.2   Paged Segment Striping(PSS)

As users' request trends vary, so does the optimal round length. Thus, in a multimedia server that serves heterogeneous streams, we should change the round length from time to time to maximize the performance. The change in round length should not, however, cause additional disk overhead as disk bandwidth is commonly the bottleneck of performance. For example, assume that we stripe the objects by RTL and the optimal round length is altered from DT to 1.5DT or 2 DT. We need only one disk access per stream with round length DT, but 2 accesses are required if we increase the round length to 1.5 DT or 2 DT. This means that it requires twice as much seek overhead, which is unacceptable.

To solve this problem, we propose the Paged Segment Striping (PSS) scheme. Each object is split into segments as in RTL and each segment is divided into the same number of pages with equal playback time. All the pages in a segment are stored contiguously on one disk. Figure 2 shows one case of PSS with 6 pages in each segment.

The optimal round length becomes maximum or minimum when 100% of the streams are supposed to be of lowest data rate streams or of highest data rate streams, respectively. Consequently, the optimal round length varies between these minimum and maximum values according to the workload situation. The size (say, playback time) of each segment is set to the maximum round length.

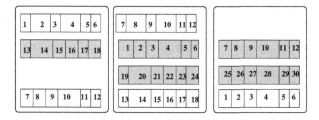

Fig. 2. Paged Segment Striping Scheme(Each segment has 6 pages in it)

Let n be the number of pages in a segment. We allocate from the 1st to the nth pages (first segment of an object) on the 1st disk contiguously and from the $(n + 1)$th to the $2n$th on the 2nd disk, and so on. We store each segment of an object on the disks in the round robin manner. In choosing n, we should take an integer which has many divisors, but is not too large.In particular, 6, 8, 12, 24, etc. are suitable candidates for n.

3   Dynamic Scheduling Scheme

A new stream can not be accepted if the server does not have enough resources, such as disk bandwidth or buffer space. If both these resources are inadequate, then the new stream has no more chance of being accepted, but if only one resource is inadequate, then there is still a chance. Let us suppose that we run out of disk bandwidth but have some buffer space left. By increasing the round length, we can use the disk bandwidth more effectively since it requires less disk seeks per unit time, but this increases the buffer space requirement at the same time. If we have enough buffer space to increase the round length, then the new stream may be accepted. On the other hand, let us suppose a new stream can not be accepted, since there is no buffer space left while there is still disk bandwidth left. In this case, reducing the round length may make the new stream acceptable.

Example 1. Let a segment have 6 pages and p be the playback time of a page. Then the possible round lengths which do not induce additional seeks are p, $2p$, $3p$, and $6p$. If the current round length is $2p$(or $3p$), then each stream accesses the same disk 3 times (resp. 2 times). After 3 (resp. 2) rounds, each stream starts to read data from the next disk in the array. Additional disk seeks are incurred in some cases, however, even if we change round length using the divisors. Assume that a stream reads page 3 and 4 in figure 2 in the current round and the server decides to change the round length from $2p$ to $3p$. Then, the stream needs to read page 5, 6 and 7 in the next round. This means this stream should access two disks to read sufficient data for one round and this results in doubling the disk seek frequency. However, if we change the round length after a round so that it will read pages 7, 8 and 9, then there will be no additional seeks. Therefore, if changing (increasing or decreasing) the round length causes additional overhead, then we should wait a few rounds so that reading a round is always aligned at the disk boundary. We call this postponement of the changing round *Segment Alignment* delay.

Assume that we stripe each object by PSS, each segment has n pages, and the playback time of a page is p. If we have to change the round length in some situation, then we change round length as $m \cdot p(m$ is one of the divisors of $n)$ so that no additional disk seek is induced, that is, *Segment Alignment* needs to be considered. As we have stated before, there are many choices for n. If n is a large integer which has many divisors, then fine-grained change of a round is possible but scheduling and admission control becomes more complex. For example, if n is 24, then the round can be one of p, $2p$, $3p$, $4p$, $6p$, $12p$, or, occasionally, $24p$, while if n is 6, then the round can be one of p, $2p$, $3p$, or $6p$. Initially, the round length is set to $2p$ or $3p$ if n is 6 and $4p$ or $6p$ if n is 24 so that the round length can be increased or decreased afterwards. Since 6 showed reasonably good performance in our experiments and scheduling is simple compared to other values, we adopt 6 as the number of pages in one segment.

4   Admission Control Algorithm

There are many constraints in admission control, but a buffer constraint (is there enough buffer to store necessary data even if a new stream is accepted?) and a disk constraint (is there enough disk bandwidth to read all the necessary data even if a new stream is accepted?) are the most important for a multimedia storage server. If the admission of a stream does not break either of these constraints, it can be accepted safely.

4.1   Buffer Constraint

We need to store the retrieved data in buffer before sending to clients. Let m be the number of streams to be serviced, $Avail\_Buf$ be the total buffer size, DT be the playback time of a segment. To accept a new stream, the following constraint should hold.

$$Total\_Amount\_of\_Data\_to\_be\_Stored \leq Available\_Buffer\_Size \quad (4)$$

$$2 \cdot \sum_{i=1}^{m} R_i(DT) \cdot T \leq Avail\_Buf \quad (5)$$

$$2 \cdot \sum_{i=1}^{m} R_i(DT) \cdot n \cdot DT \leq Avail\_Buf \quad (6)$$

If we assume $R_i(DT)$ is all the same as R(say, constant) for all streams, then we can simplify equation (6) as follows.

$$2 \cdot m \cdot R \cdot DT \leq Avail\_Buf \quad (7)$$

In equation (7), we can easily see m is inversely proportional to DT. However, since $R_i(DT)$ is a function of DT as in equation (3), we can not simplify $R_i(DT)$ as constant to get correct solution. But we can still guess m is generally in inverse proportion to DT in equation (5).

4.2   Disk Bandwidth Constraint

Disk service time consists of seek time, rotational latency, transfer time of data, and other latencies [4]. Let d be the number of disks in the array, m be the number of streams to be serviced, k be the number of segments to be retrieved from the most heavily loaded disk. If there are many active streams and many disks in the array, then we can approximate $k \simeq \lceil \frac{m}{d} \rceil$. If the service time to read k blocks from a disk is shorter than a round, we can service m streams without any starvation. In particular, if the following equations hold

$$Seek\_Time + Transfer\_Time + Rotational\_Latency + other\_overhead \leq T \quad (8)$$

$$Seek(k) + \sum_{i=1}^{k} \left(\frac{R_i(DT) \cdot DT}{Tranfer\_Rate} + Rotation\_Time + \epsilon \right) \leq DT \quad (9)$$

disk access rate will be adequate. In equation(9), we can guess that k is generally proportional to DT. Since m is proportional to k, we can say that m is generally proportional to DT.

4.3   Admission Control Algorithm Using PSS

Assume that m active streams are in the system, disk i has a service list queue $Q[i]$, and a new stream wants to be served from disk i (i.e., the first segment for that stream is stored on disk i). If a new stream passes both *Buffer_Test* and *Disk_Test*, then it is added to $Q[i]$, but if it fails in both tests, it is rejected. However, if it fails only in one test, it still has a chance. Let us suppose a new stream passes *Buffer_Test*(or *Disk_Test*) but fails in *Disk Test*(resp. *Buffer_Test*). In this case, we may accept the stream by increasing(resp. decreasing) the round length. Sometimes, it is impossible to change the round length since the round length is the same as the largest (resp. smallest) value, $n \cdot p$(resp. p) or for the *Segment Alignment*. Then, this stream can not be accepted. If a new stream can pass both of the tests only after changing the round length, then the round length is changed and the new stream is added to $Q[i]$.

$\quad$ *Disk_Test* and *Buffer_Test* are required in most admission control algorithms. One more *Disk_Test* or *Buffer_Test* may be issued in the dynamic scheme than in the static scheme, and there can be the overhead in changing the round length. However, since these kinds of overhead are required only when the characteristics of workloads vary significantly, the additional overhead is not much. In normal cases, the round length remains unchanged.

5   Experimental Results

We have conducted extensive simulations to compare the performance. In our experiment, we used 20 MPEG-1 traces from [3]. To simulate an environment of serving heterogeneous streams (the difference of data rates among streams are not negligible), we multiply the original traces by 10 to simulate MPEG-2 traces. We have carried out simulations with 20 high data rate objects (MPEG-2) and 20 low data rate objects (MPEG-1). In the simulation, we used the characteristics of an IBM-HDD3200 disk. The access patterns to each video depend on the popularity of the video. We use a Zipf distribution [5].

In figure 3, the performance of the adaptive scheduling scheme is compared with that of the static scheduling scheme that has no change of the round length. If users' trends are exactly the same as expected at the system design time and there is no change in the trends, then there is almost no performance difference between the two schemes. But, if users' requesting mode changes into a totally different pattern, then there is about 33% to 46% of performance degradation in the static scheme. In the adaptive scheme, however, the round length can be changed so there is almost no performance degradation.

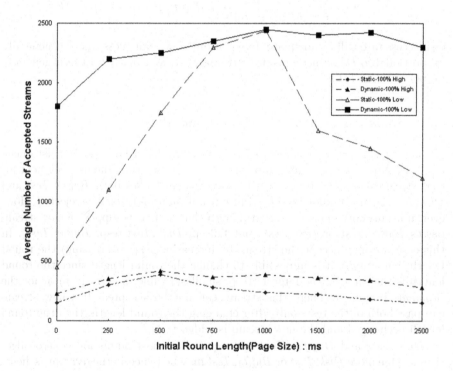

Fig. 3. Comparison of the dynamic scheme and the static scheme

6   Conclusion

In this paper, we have studied the problem of how to maximize the through-put of a contiguous-media system, given that the amounts of buffer space and disk bandwidth are both predetermined at design time. We have presented a new striping model (PSS) which makes it possible to change the round length dynamically without additional seek overhead. In the adaptive scheme, even a significant change in the users' trends induces only a small degradation of perfor-mance as the scheme adapts to trend variations by adjusting the round length. By building on the adaptive scheme's ability to self-adjust the round length we have increased the performance up to 46% with the same resources even if there is a severe change in the users' trends. Furthermore, since it requires little more calculation overhead than the static scheme, we are convinced that the adaptive scheduling scheme is better than the static scheme in most cases.

References

1. Scott A. Barnett and Gary J. Anido: Performability of disk-array-based video servers. ACM Multimedia Systems Journal, 6(1), January (1998) 60–74
2. Jin B. Kwon, Heon Y. Yeom: Generalized Data Retrieval for Pyramid-based Periodic Broadcasting of Videos, Future Generation Computer Systems,20(1) (2004) 157–170
3. Informatik MPEG-I traces:
   ftp://ftp-info3.informatik.uni-wuerzburg.de/pub/MPEG (1998)
4. KyungOh Lee and Heon Y. Yeom: An effective admission control mechanism for Variable-Bit-Rate video streams. ACM Multimedia Systems Journal, 7(4), July (1999) 305–311
5. Carlos M Urzua: A simple and efficient test for Zipf's Law, Economics Letters, v66, March (2000) 257–260

A Heuristic Packet Scheduling Algorithm for Media Streaming with Server Diversity

Yajie Liu, Wenhua Dou, and Heying Zhang

School of Computer Science,
National University of Defense Technology, ChangSha, 410073, China
liuyajie@nudt.edu.cn

Abstract. This paper studies the streaming of packetized media from multiple servers to a receiver over a lossy network with retransmissions. Considering these factors such as packet decoding interdependencies, decoding deadline requirements and diversified network/server conditions, we propose a receiver-driven heuristic packet scheduling algorithm to decide which packet(s) to be requested from which server(s) at each given request opportunity in order to minimize the end-to-end distortion while conforming to rate constraints on the paths that from the servers to the receiver. Simulation results demonstrate the benefit of exploiting server diversity with our proposed packet scheduling algorithm.

1 Introduction

Video streaming over best-effort, packet-switched Internet is challenging due to the following reasons: (i) Internet route paths have the characters such as constrained bandwidth, loss rate, delay jitter and so on. (ii) Each media packet has its decoding deadline by which it must arrive at the decoding buffer, or be too late to be usefully decoded. (iii) There exist interdependencies on media packets' decoding, and the losses of some packets (such as these packets contained in I type frames or these packets contained in base layer of layered encoding) have more severe impacts on qualities than the losses of others. As such, transport protocols such as TCP are not suitable for streaming applications, and many solutions have been proposed for video streaming. But in a traditional single-server system no matter how well the system is organized, the media service might still suffer from the inevitable intermittent congestions and server/link failures, which cause interruptions in the streamed media. One way to maintain an uninterrupted acceptable quality is to exploit the potential benefits of using multiple servers concurrently. Nevertheless, considering the above reasons, a media streaming protocol is needed for coordinately scheduling packets from multiple servers.

This paper addresses this issue and proposes a receiver-driven, retransmission-permitted, heuristic scheduling algorithm that at each request opportunity it just requests these packets with more importance for transmissions while conforming to the bandwidth constraints from diversified

K. Aizawa, Y. Nakamura, and S. Satoh (Eds.): PCM 2004, LNCS 3331, pp. 602–609, 2004.

servers to the receiver. Here we use the concept of *expected run-time distortion* to denote a packet's importance which takes into account packet interdependencies, timeline requirements and network/server conditions. This concept was first proposed by [1] in a single server, server-driven environment, here we extend its proposition and incorporate server diversity and bursty loss characters of paths in a receiver-driven system.

Real time media streaming with server diversity has only been proposed in recent years. In [2], an MD-FEC coding framework was utilized to achieve a target quality with minimum bandwidth usage. In [3] the author proposed a novel rate allocation scheme to be used with FEC in order to minimize the probability of packet loss in a bursty loss environment. To our knowledge, the most closely related work was proposed in [4], it proposed a receiver-driven rate-distortion optimal packet scheduling algorithm that decided which packet(s) to be requested from which server(s) at a given request opportunity, and the computational complexity of their proposed algorithm normally grew exponentially with the number of request opportunities. Our proposed heuristic algorithm reduces the computational complexity greatly with respect to [4] for it only grows linearly with the number of request opportunities.

2   System Model

Suppose there exist M servers which are located at different locations in the network and communicate with the receiver over independent network paths. The media is packetized into data packets and these packets are replicated at each server. During transmission any packet may be lost on any of the paths due to congestion or erasures. According to our proposed packet scheduling algorithm, the receiver is responsible for deciding which data packet(s) to be requested from which server(s), based on the feedback it receives from the servers. The servers merely respond to send data packet(s) as a response to request packet(s) that received.

To each packet l, let s_l denote its size, $t_{DTS,l}$ denote its decoding deadline, Δd_l denote its distortion or importance, a_l denote whether packet l is decodable in the playback, A_l denote l's parent packet set, B_l denote l's children packet set. Δd_l is a measurement of the amount by which the distortion decreases when the receiver decodes packet l. A_l is defined as the set of packets that has to be available in order to decode l. B_l is defined as the set of packets that cannot be decoded without the presence of l. The 0-1 variable a_l is assigned to 1 only if all the packets of A_l are available at the receiver side by the time $t_{DTS,l}$. Any packet that is received later than its decoding deadline will be discarded. To any data packet l, suppose there are N consecutive and discrete request opportunities $t_{0,l}, t_{1,l}, ..., t_{N-1,l}$ prior to l's decoding deadline, and at each request opportunity the receiver is permitted to send a request packet for l except that it has been received by the receiver. The time intervals among all request opportunities are equal, and the proposed packet scheduling algorithm is executed on the receiver side every this time interval. It can be seen that there may exist many data packets that have not been requested by the receiver or have been requested but not received at each request opportunity, and in the residual of this paper we will call these packets as *candidate requested packets* for they are permitted to be requested for transmission at each request opportunity. Let t_{cur} denote the current request opportunity, and let G_{cur} denoted the candidate requested packet set at t_{cur}.

Define the path from each server to the receiver and the path from the receiver to each server as forward and backward channels respectively, model each channel as a bursty loss channel using a K-state discrete Markov model [5,6]. The forward and the backward channels make state transitions independently of each other every T seconds with transition probability matrices $P_{(F)}$ and $P_{(B)}$ respectively. Let $\varepsilon_{F/B}^k$ denote the packet loss probability and $p_{F/B}^k$ denote the probability density of the transmission delay, on the forward and backward channels in state k, $k = 1, ..., K$. This means that if the server sends a data packet as a response to a request packet on the forward channel at time t, given that the forward channel is in state k at t, then the data packet is lost with probability ε_F^k. However, if the packet is not lost, then it arrives at the receiver at time t', where the forward trip time $FTT^k = t' - t$ is randomly drawn according to the probability density p_F^k. Therefore, we let $P\{FTT^k > \tau\} = \varepsilon_F^k + (1 - \varepsilon_F^k)\int_\tau^\infty p_F^k(t)dt$ denote the probability that a data packet transmitted by the server at time t, given that the forward channel is in state k at t, does not arrive at the receiver by time $t+\tau$, whether it is lost or simply delayed by more than τ. Similar expression can also be derived for a request packet on the backward channel. Now with the assumption that the transmission on the backward channel occurs immediately after the channel makes a state transition, we can derive the probability $P\{RTT^{kj} > \tau\}$ that the receiver does not receive the requested packet by the time $t + \tau$ for a request packet transmitted at time t, given the backward and the forward channels are respectively in states k and j at t, as follows

$$P\{RTT^{kj} > \tau\} = \sum_{l=0}^{\infty} P\{RTT^{kj} > \tau | lT < BTT^k \le (l+1)T\}P\{lT < BTT^k \le (l+1)T\}$$

$$= \sum_{l=0}^{Q-1} P\{RTT^{kj} > \tau | lT < BTT^k \le (l+1)T\}P\{lT < BTT^k \le (l+1)T\}+$$

$$P\{RTT^{kj} > \tau | QT < BTT^k \le \tau\}P\{QT < BTT^k \le \tau\} + P\{BTT^k > \tau\}$$

where $Q = \lfloor \tau/T \rfloor$. The first equality holds according to the total probability theorem, and the second equality holds since $P\{RTT^{kj} > \tau | BTT^k > \tau\}P\{BTT^k > \tau\} = P\{BTT^k > \tau\}$. Furthermore, as the state on the forward channel when the acknowledgement is sent can be any of the K states, hence we can compute the desired quantity as the expected value over all of them, i.e., $P\{RTT^{kj} > \tau | lT <$

$$BTT^k \le (l+1)T\} = \sum_{p=1}^{K} P_{jp(F)}^{(l)}P\{BTT^k + FTT^p > \tau | lT < BTT^k \le (l+1)T\}$$

where $P_{jp(F)}^{(l)}$ is the probability of making a transition from state j to state p in l transition intervals. These probabilities are obtained using matrix power, i.e., $P_{(F)}^{(l)} = P_{(F)}^l$.

3   Heuristic Packet Scheduling Algorithm

Suppose there are L data packets in the media presentation. The goal of the packet scheduling algorithm that to minimize the end-to-end distortion can be denoted as

$$Min \quad \sum_{l=1}^{L} \Delta d_l - \sum_{l=1}^{L} a_l \Delta d_l \qquad (1)$$

while conforming to the available bandwidth between each server and the receiver. As at current request opportunity the scheduling objects are only these packets that contained in the candidate requested packet set G_{cur}, assuming s is any request order on the candidate requested packets of G_{cur}, the scheduling goal of (1) can be approximately converted to

$$Min \quad \sum_{l \in G_{cur}} \Delta d_l - \sum_{l \in G_{cur}} (\prod_{i \in A_l} (1 - P_i(s))) \Delta d_l \qquad (2)$$

where $P_i(s)$ is the probability that packet i will be lost or delayed under the given scheduling police s. $\prod_{i \in A_l} (1 - P_i(s))$ is the probability that the packet l can be used for decoding. However, the minimization of (2) is still difficult for the packet decoding interdependencies, timeline requirements and diversified network conditions.

Here we propose a heuristic packet scheduling algorithm that at each request opportunity, it only requests these data packets that with more importance from the candidate requested packet set for transmission, and the number of the selected requested packets is limited by the available bandwidths from the servers to the receiver. In the next subsection we will introduce how to compute a candidate requested packet's expected run-time distortion which denotes this packet's importance.

3.1   Compute a Packet's Expected Run-Time Distortion with Server Diversity

Let P_l^H denote the probability that the data packet l can not be received by the receiver just based on its request history and its current status, that is, if l has been received, then P_l^H equals to 0; if l has not been requested for transmission, P_l^H equals to 1; if l has been requested in history but not received by current request opportunity t_{cur}, furthermore, if $t_{cur} \geq t_{DTS,l}$ then P_l^H equals to 1 since to any data packet that is received latter than its decoding deadline will be discarded by the receiver, otherwise, P_l^H can be calculated as follows: assume l's historical request opportunities are $t_{0,l}, t_{1,l}, ..., t_{j-1,l} (j \leq N)$, let the 0-1 variable $r_{im,l}$ denote whether the receiver has transmitted a request for l to the server m $(m = 0, 1, ..., M - 1)$ at request opportunity $t_{i,l} (0 \leq i \leq j - 1)$, if not then assigned to 0 otherwise assigned to 1; let

$S_B(t_{i,l}, m)$ and $S_F(t_{i,l}, m)$ denote the states on the backward and forward channels of path m at request opportunity $t_{i,l}$, respectively; thus P_l^H can be denoted as $\prod\limits_{i=0}^{j-1} \prod\limits_{m:\, r_{im,l}=1} P\{RTT^{S_B(t_{i,l},m)S_F(t_{i,l},m)} > t_{DST,l} - t_{i,l}\}$ in this case.

After the deduction of above probability, we can get a candidate requested packet l's *run-time distortion* $\Delta\hat{d}_l$ which captures the decoding interdependencies among packets. $\Delta\hat{d}_l$ is defined as follows:

$$\Delta\hat{d}_l = \Delta d_l \prod_{i \in A_l} (1 - P_i^H) + \sum_{i \in B_l} \Delta d_i (1 - P_i^H) \qquad (3)$$

where $\Delta d_l \prod\limits_{i \in A_l} (1 - P_i^H)$ indicates that the original distortion of a packet is weighted by the probability of receiving all its parent packets, and if l has no parent packet, then let $\prod\limits_{i \in A_l} (1 - P_i^H) = 1$; $\sum\limits_{i \in B_l} \Delta d_i (1 - P_i^H)$ indicates that a packet's importance increases if any of its children packets has been received, and if l has no children packet then let $\sum\limits_{i \in B_l} \Delta d_i (1 - P_i^H) = 0$. Equation (3) implies that only after request (at least once) of all its parents, does a packet's run-time distortion become non-zero (except that this packet has no parent packet), and it also increases if any children packet has been requested.

As to a candidate requested packet, the less the number of its remaining request opportunities, the greater chance that the packet to be requested for transmission should be, but from equation (3) we can see that the run-time distortion does not reflect this relationship for it only considers the historical request behaviors. The minimum probability of a candidate requested packet l that it can not be received by the receiver before its decoding deadline, just based on its possible request(s) at its remaining request opportunities, can reflect this relationship; let P_l^X denote this probability, suppose l's remaining request opportunities are $t_{j,l}, t_{j+1,l}, ..., t_{N-1,l}(j \geq 0)$, as there at most exists one request chance to l at each request opportunity, P_l^X can be defined as follows

$$P_l^X = \prod_{i=j}^{N-1} \left(\frac{1}{M} \sum_{m=1}^{M} P\{RTT^{S_B(t_{i,l},m)S_F(t_{i,l},m)} > t_{DTS,l} - t_{i,l}\} \right). \qquad (4)$$

The term $P\{RTT^{S_B(t_{i,l},m)S_F(t_{i,l},m)} > t_{DTS,l} - t_{i,l}\}$ in (4) denotes the probability that the receiver will not receive the requested packet l by the time $t_{DTS,l}$ for a requst packet of l transmitted at time $t_{i,l}$ to server m, given that the backward and forward channels of path m are respectively in states $S_B(t_{i,l}, m)$ and $S_F(t_{i,l}, m)$ at $t_{i,l}$. As we don't know which server the request of l will be transmitted to, so $\frac{1}{M} \sum\limits_{m=1}^{M} P\{RTT^{S_B(t_{i,l},m)S_F(t_{i,l},m)} > t_{DTS,l} - t_{i,l}\}$ can denote the average probability that the receiver will not receive l by the time $t_{DTS,l}$ for a requst packet of l transmitted at time $t_{i,l}$.

The value of $P\{RTT^{S_B(t_{i,l},m)S_F(t_{i,l},m)} > t_{DTS,l} - t_{i,l}\}$ can not be directly derived for we don't know the states on the backward and forward channels of path

m at the remaining request opportunities (except for the current request opportunity). As each state can be any of the K states, we can compute the desired value as the expected value over all of them, i.e., $P\{RTT^{S_B(t_{i,l},m)S_F(t_{i,l},m)} >$

$$t_{DTS,l} - t_{i,l}\} = \sum_{k=1}^{K}\sum_{g=1}^{K} P_{(B)}^{k}(m)P_{(F)}^{g}(m)P\{RTT^{kg} > t_{DTS,l} - t_{i,l}\} \quad \text{where}$$

$P_{(B)}^{k}(m)$ and $P_{(F)}^{k}(m)$ are the stationary probabilities that the states on the backward and forward channels of path m are k and g respectively. $P_{(B)}^{k}(m)$ can be deduced from the transition probability matrix $P_{(B)}$ of path m, and $P_{(F)}^{k}(m)$ can also be deduced from the transition probability matrix $P_{(F)}$ of path m.

Now we can get the expected run-time distortion $\Delta\tilde{d}_l$ of a candidate requested packet l as follows:

$$\Delta\tilde{d}_l = \Delta\hat{d}_l \times P_l^X. \tag{5}$$

Equation (5) indicates that the importance metric of $\Delta\tilde{d}_l$ has taken into account (i) the packet distortion (in $\Delta\hat{d}_l$), (ii) the packet interdependencies (in $\Delta\hat{d}_l$), (iii) the packet decoding deadlines (in$\Delta\hat{d}_l$ and P_l^X), (iv) the channel conditions such as loss rate, delay jitter, etc. (in $\Delta\hat{d}_l$ and P_l^X).

3.2   Heuristic Packet Scheduling Algorithm

The heuristic packet scheduling algorithm is described in Fig.1, where $S_{m(F)}$ is the size constraint of packets that permitted to be requested from server m at t_{cur}, ξ_m is the packet set that permitted to be requested from server m at t_{cur}. Labeling the request of l as transmitted to server m at t_{cur} (in line 7) is to realter the expected run-time distortion value of l's parent and children packets of G_{cur} in the subsequent computations of t_{cur}.

1. $\xi_m \leftarrow \Phi\ (0 \le m \le M - 1)$;
2. **For** $m \leftarrow 0$ to $M - 1$ **do**
3.   **while** $\sum_{l:l\in\xi_m} s_l < S_{m(F)}$ **do** /* size of packets in ξ_m is less than $S_{m(F)}$ */
4.   To each packet l of G_{cur}, compute its $\Delta\tilde{d}_l$;
5.   Select a packet with max. expected run-time distortion from G_{cur};
       /* suppose the selected candidate requested packet is l */
6. $\xi_m \leftarrow \xi_m \cup \{l\}$, $G_{cur} \leftarrow G_{cur} - \{l\}$;
7.   Label that a request packet of l transmitted to server m at t_{cur};
8.   **end while**
9.   To each packet of ξ_m, send a request of it to server m for transmission;
10. **end for**

Fig. 1. The heuristic packet scheduling algorithm

4   Simulation Results

In this section, we present simulation results to evaluate the performance of the proposed packet scheduling algorithm. The video sequence is FOREMAN which with 250 frames and CIF size. The codec we used is a MPEG-4 FGS software codec [7], the video sequence is encoded into a base layer and a SNR FGS enhancement layer with corresponding rates of 300Kbps and 1200Kbps. The packet size is 1000 bytes, the frame rate is 30 fps and the size of the Group of Picture (GOP) is 10 frames, consisting of an I frame followed by 9 consecutive P frames. We also modified this codec to generate the related statistical info of the media data packets, such as the packet_id (frame_id, layer_id), packet distortions, packet interdependencies (parent packet set, children packet set), decoding deadlines, etc. Performance is measured in terms of the luminance peak signal-to-noise ratio (Y-PSNR) in dB of the end-to-end distortion, averaged over the duration of the video clip, as a function of the overall bit rate available on the forward path(s) of the network path(s) between the server(s) and the receiver.

We employ a $K = 2$ state Markov model for each channel, and the model parameters keep unchanged over all paths which specified as follows: $\varepsilon_B^1 = \varepsilon_F^1 = 2\%$, $\varepsilon_B^2 = \varepsilon_F^2 = 30\%$, $P_{(B)} = P_{(F)} = \begin{pmatrix} 0.985 & 0.015 \\ 0.665 & 0.335 \end{pmatrix}$, the delay density is modeled using a shifted Gamma distribution [8] specified with rightward shift κ, parameter n and α, and the three parameter values are respectively (25, 1, 1/50) and (25, 1, 1/250) of the two states.

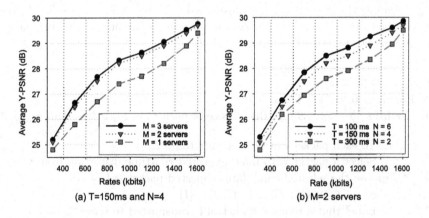

(a) T=150ms and N=4   (b) M=2 servers

Fig. 2. Performance of the proposed packet scheduling algorithm.

At first we use $T = 150$ms as the interval of request opportunities and $N = 4$ as the number of request opportunities, and study the performance of the proposed heuristic packet scheduling algorithm with different number of servers. It can be seen from Fig.2(a) that streaming FOREMAN from two servers can improve performance compared to the case of streaming from a single server and the improvement (up to 0.8dB) is observed over the whole range of available rates. The improved performance is due to that while the sing-server system suffers from the congestions, the two-server system is able to alleviate these effects by using the less-congested path. It can also be seen from Fig.2(a) that using further servers for streaming does not provide much additional gains in performance, this is because the probability that a data packet can't be delivered to the receiver on time is quite reduced for $M = 2$.

Next we study the performance of the proposed heuristic packet scheduling algorithm with different parameters of the request opportunities. From Fig.2(b) it can be seen that under same playback delay, the more the number of the request opportunities, the more improvement the heuristic packet scheduling algorithm gains. This is expected as these lost or delayed packets have more chances to be requested for transmission before their decoding deadlines with more request opportunities.

5   Conclusions

In this paper, we present a heuristic packet scheduling algorithm which results in unequal error protection provided to different portions of the media stream. Simulation results show that using our proposed packet scheduling algorithm with multiple servers, a receiver can obtain an improved performance over the case that with a single server. The algorithm's computational complexity is very low, it does not impose much overhead on the servers and the receiver.

Acknowledgements. We would like to thank Dr. Z. Miao of University of Southern California for his suggestions to the simulation.

References

1. Miao Z., Ortega A.: Expected run-time distortion based scheduling for delivery of scalable media. In Proc. PVW 2002, Pittsburgh, PA, Apr. 2002.
2. Majumdar A., Puri R., Ramchandran K.: Rate-distortion efficient video transmission from multiple servers. In IEEE ICME, 2002.
3. Nguyen T., Zakhor A.: Distributed video streaming with forward error correction. In Proc. Int'l Packet Video Workshop, Pittsburg, PA, Apr. 2002.
4. Begen Ali C., Altunbasak Y., Begen Mehmet A.: Rate-distortion optimized on-demand streaming with server diversity. In IEEE ICIP, Sept. 2003.
5. Yajnik M., Moon S., Kurose J., Towsley D.: Measurement and modeling of the temporal dependence in packet loss. In Proc. INFOCOM, vol. 1, 1999, pp.345-352.
6. Wenyu J., Schulzrinne H.: Modeling of packet loss and delay and their effects on real-time multimedia service quality. In ACM NOSSDAV, 2000.
7. Radha H., van der Schaar M., and Chen Y.: The MPEG-4 fine-grained scalable video coding method for multimedia streaming over IP. In IEEE Transaction Multimedia, vol. 3, no. 1, Mar. 2001.
8. Mukherjee A.: On the dynamics and significance of low frequency components of internet load. Internetworking: Res. Experience, 5:163-205, Dec. 1994.

Proxy Caching Scheme Based on the Characteristics of Streaming Media Contents on the Internet

Hyeonok Hong[1], Seungwon Lee[2], Seongho Park[3],
Yongju Kim[4], and Kidong Chung[2]

[1] Department of Computer Science, Dongeui Institute of Technology, Rep. of Korea
hohong@dit.ac.kr
[2] Department of Computer Science, Pusan National University, Rep. of Korea
{swlee, kdchung}@melon.cs.pusan.ac.kr
[3] Computer Center, Pusan National University, Rep. of Korea
shpark@pusan.ac.kr
[4] Department of Computer Engineering, Silla University, Rep. of Korea
yjkim@silla.ac.kr

Abstract. In this paper we analyzed the workloads based on the access logs from three media servers which have different characteristics. These servers deliver highly qualified contents such as movies, dramas, education contents and music videos throughout Korea on the web. We analyzed the workloads in terms of media file size, user access pattern and distribution of the user request arrival time. Then we applied these specific characteristics of analysis to the design of replacement algorithm for proxy caching scheme. The proposed proxy caching scheme shows $3 \sim 10$ % improvement of BHR and reduces the server workload by decreasing replacement amount.

1 Introduction

According to the recent research[1] results, 58% of Korean population use internet and 82% of Korean family retaining personal computer use broad bandwidth internet network such as ADSL, cable network. Home shopping enterprises and broadcasting stations service streaming media contents on the internet and contents with fee are increasing continuously. Delivering these high bandwidth contents over the internet presents a number of problems. Real-time nature of multimedia contents makes it sensitive to congestion conditions on the internet. Moreover, multimedia streams can consume significant bandwidths, and their large sizes require magnitude amount of storage at the media servers and proxy caches. Therefore understanding the nature of media server workloads is crucial to properly designing and provisioning current and future services[4].

In this paper we analyzed the workloads based on the access logs from three media servers which have different characteristics. The servers deliver highly qualified contents such as movies, dramas, education contents and music videos

K. Aizawa, Y. Nakamura, and S. Satoh (Eds.): PCM 2004, LNCS 3331, pp. 610–617, 2004.

to many people throughout Korea on the web. We analyzed the workloads in terms of media file size, user access pattern and distribution of the user request arrival time. Then we applied these specific characteristics of analysis to the design of replacement algorithm for proxy caching scheme.

The organization of this paper is as follows. Section 2 discusses related works and section 3 describes the respective specific characteristics of three media servers' workloads. Section 4 provides proxy caching policy in consideration of the characteristics presented in section 3 and examine the performance experimentally. Finally, section 5 presents conclusion.

2   Related Works

2.1   The Analysis of Multimedia Server Workload

[2] analyzed the media proxy workload at a university. The author presented the difference between characteristics of web server workload and characteristics of media server workload. The study[3] is based on two media servers in use at major public universities : eTeach and BIBS. The authors provide a detailed study of user session arrival process, time and space locality of frequency based on popularity using trace log data analysis, and the performance analysis of several multicast technologys to reduce server workload. One recent study[4] analyzed the enterprise media server workloads based on the access logs from two different media servers in Hewlett-Packard corporation. Both logs are collected over long period of time(2.5 years and 1 year 9 months). They propose two new metrics (new files impact, life span) to characterize the dynamics and evolution of the accesses, and the rate of change in the site access pattern.

2.2   Proxy Caching of Media Contents

[5] proposed the prefix proxy caching strategy where initial portions of achieved objects are cached so that their initial latency could be reduced and the burstiness of VBR streams could be smoothed. [6] proposed a caching policy based on the layered encoding technology so that caching could be done on the layer basis and thus transfer the stream adaptively depending on the available network bandwidth. The studies described above proposed several techniques for effective proxy server, but there have been relatively fewer papers written about proxy caching technique considering characteristics of streaming media contents on the internet.

3   The Characteristics of Streaming Media Contents

3.1   The Analysis Environment of Three Streaming Media Servers

We analyzed the log data collected from the servers of three well-known web sites which service streaming media contents. A server services drama, music and entertainment contents which were broadcasted by television. B server services education contents which were broadcasted by television also. C server which belongs to internet newspaper company services mainly music video and preview of movies. [Table 1] shows the analysis environment of three media servers respectively.

Table 1. The analysis environment of three media servers

Sites	A site	B site	C site
logging server	arbitrarily selected among 20	arbitrarily selected among 5	only one server
data collecting period	2001.5.12 - 2001.5.31(21 days)	2002.4.17 - 2002.4.25(9 days)	2002.2.13 - 2002.3.3 (19 days)
contents serviced mainly	drama, entertainment, news, etc.	courses of lectures, education, etc.	preview of movies, music videos, etc.

Table 2. Statistics about streaming media files of three media servers

sites	A site	B site	C site
Num. of files requested during surveying period	5,058	10,868	1,488
Surveying period (hour)	477	212	454
Total Num. of accesses	1,969,737	556,663	164,376
Num. of start access request	452,216	132,699	151,762
Num. of random access request	1,517,521	423,964	12,614
Avg. Num. of request per hour	4,129	2,626	362
Avg. length of contents(min)	38.4	30.2	3.1
Avg. size of contents(Mbyte)	21.3	35.5	3.5
Avg. bandwidth of contents(Kbps)	73.9	156.8	147.0
Avg. playback time(min) per access	3.4	3.2	0.7
Avg. transmitted amount(Mbyte) per access	1.3	4.7	1.4

3.2   The Characteristics of Streaming Media Files

[Table 2] shows the statistics of three streaming media servers respectively.

New media objects are created everyday regularly in A and B server. But new media objects are created irregularly in C server. The log data of window media server includes both start and random access requests. The start request is a request to playback from the beginning while the random access one is to choose the playback point arbitrarily at users' own will in the object. C server services shorter media files in comparison with A and B server, hence the playback time rate to request is higher than A and B server. There is the difference between average playback time rate of requested files and average transmitted amount rate of them because of the server and network workloads.

[Fig. 1] shows the distribution of file sizes in three servers respectively. The sizes of 98 % files in C server belong to between 1 Mbytes and 15 Mbytes, 95% in A server belong to between 2 Mbytes and 46 Mbytes and 97 % in B server belong to between 3 Mbytes and 82 Mbytes.

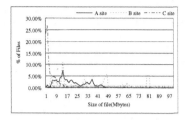

Fig. 1. Percent of files as a function of file size

3.3 The Characteristics of User Access Pattern

The distribution of users' requests to streaming media contents. [Fig. 2, 3, 4] show the percentage of files, requests, playback time and transmitted amount of data as a function of file size. The rate of requests is higher than files, and the rate of transmitted amount of data is higher than requests. This characteristic which is shown in the analysis of [2] also reflects the browsing nature of the web user access, and that users are looking for a specific fragment of content in a video interactively and are not interested in watching it completely.

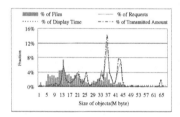

Fig. 2. Requests distribution of A site as a function of file size

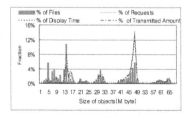

Fig. 3. Requests distribution of B site as a function of file size

The distribution of user access time. [Fig. 5] shows the distribution of user access time to the streaming media files during the period of measurement.

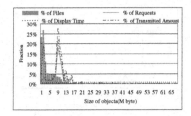

Fig. 4. Requests distribution of C site as a function of file size

The percentage of user accesses are higher than 3% between AM. 10 and AM. 2 next day, whereas lower than 3% between AM. 2 and AM. 10. The distribution graphs of A and C servers which service entertainment contents mainly show the similar pattern, but the graph of B server which services education contents shows a skewed pattern between PM. 6 and AM. 1 next day compared with A and B servers. Clearly, such knowledge about user access patterns can be beneficial when designing media caching schemes.

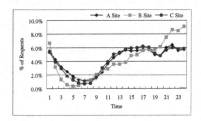

Fig. 5. Distributions of users' request time

4   Proxy Caching

In this section, we present the proxy caching scheme considering the characteristics of streaming media contents based on the analysis in section 3, and test our proposed algorithm through simulation

4.1   The Proxy Caching Configuration

We perform simulations on the assumption that the proxy caching configuration on the internet is like [Fig. 6]. A, B and C sites are placed at the different LAN respectively. The users and proxy server are placed at the same LAN. The proxy server caches the streaming media contents which are served by A, B and C servers and service them to users at the same LAN.

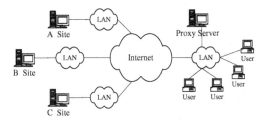

Fig. 6. Proxy caching configuration on the internet

4.2   Proxy Caching Scheme

In this paper, we propose the proxy caching scheme to improve the caching efficiency applying the respective characteristics of three sites. Caching streaming media objects at proxy server requires expensive cost for replacement because of the big file sizes and the tremendous bandwidth consumption. Therefore we also consider the popularity of contents in the latest period and cost for replacement in the design of this scheme.

$P(O_k)$: Popularity of k th streaming media content O_k during Δt.

$P_{min}(O_k)$: The content whose $P(O_k)$ value is the smallest among cached streaming media objects at proxy server.

$S(O_k)$: The file size of kth continuous media content O_k.

T : Constant for the distribution of user access time divided into two groups applying the result from 3.3.2 section: hot-zone($AM.10 \sim AM.1$ next day), cool-zone($AM.1 \sim AM.10$). If it is cool-zone, then $T = 1$, otherwise(hot-zone) the value of T is determined by experiment.

α : Constant for calculation of replacement cost. It is varied according to network bandwidth and workload of servers.

$C(O_k)$: The replacement cost of kth streaming media content O_k at time t.

[Fig. 7] shows the algorithm to decide on whether to cache the content O_m or not using the above parameters.

4.3   Performance Evaluation

In this section, we analyze the proposed algorithm based on the simulation for 48 hours.

We analyzed the performance of the proposed algorithm in comparison with LFU algorithm. [Fig 8, 9] show the BHR and replacement amount as a function of cache size of two algorithms. We set the interval for recalculating the value of replacement to 10 minutes.

T and α are determined experimentally. [Table 3] shows the value of constant obtained from experiment.

The proxy caching scheme proposed in this paper shows $3 \sim 10$ % improvement of BHR applying user access pattern to replacement algorithm. Especially, this algorithm reduces the server workload by decreasing replacement amount.

$R = \{\forall_q, q \in contents\ in\ Proxy\}$
RCS : Remained space of Proxy
while(true){
    if $(RCS \geq S(O_m))$ {
    do cache O_m
    return. }
    if$(R = \emptyset)$ {
    do not cache O_m
    return. }
    choice $P_{min}(O_q)$
    $C(O_k) = \frac{T}{\alpha} \times \frac{S(O_m)}{S(O_q)}$
    if$((P(O_m) + C(O_m))R > P_{min}(O_q))$ {
    $RCS+ = S(O_q)$
    selects O_q for replacement }
    $R \leftarrow R - \{q\}$
}

Fig. 7. The algorithm of selection object for replacement

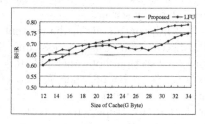

Fig. 8. Byte Hit Ratios

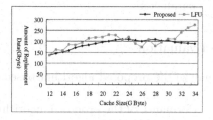

Fig. 9. Amount of Replacement

Table 3. Constants used in simulations

constants	T of cool-zone	T of hot-zone	α
value	1	1.5	0.9

5   Conclusion

We analyzed three media servers' workloads in terms of the media file size, user access pattern according to encoding bandwidth, access frequency to respective media contents and the distribution of the user request arrival time. Then we applied these specific characteristics of the workloads analysis to the design of replacement algorithm for proxy caching scheme. The proxy caching scheme proposed in this paper shows $3 \sim 10$ % improvement of BHR and reduces the server workload by decreasing replacement amount.

References

1. K. H Song, "A survey about users of internet", Korea Internet Information Center, http://www.nic.or.kr/index.html , 2002.
2. M. Chesire, A. Wolman, G. Voelker and H. Levy, "Measurement and Analysis of a Streaming Media Workload," Proc 3rd USENIX symp. on Internet Technologies and Systems, San Francisco. March 2001.
3. Jussara M. Almeida, Jeffrey Krueger, Derek L. Eager and Mary K. Vernon, "Analysis of educational media server workloads," 11th International workshop on Network and Operating Systems support for digital audio and video January 2001
4. Ludmila Cherkasova, Minaxi Gupta, "Analysis of Enterprise Media Server Workload: Access Patterns, Locality, Dynamics, and Rate of Change", ACM NOSSDAV 2002.
5. S. Sen, J. Rexford and D. Towsley, "Proxy Prefix Caching for Multimedia Streams," In Proc. IEEE Infocom, March 1999.
6. Reza Rejaie, Haobo Yu, Mark Handely, Deborah Estrin, "Multimedia Proxy Caching Mechanism for Quality Adaptive Streaming Applications in the Internet", In Proc. of IEEE Infocom'2000 , Tel-Aviv, Israel, March 2000

A Distributed VOD Server Based on VIA and Interval Cache*

Soo-Cheol Oh and Sang-Hwa Chung

School of Electrical and Computer Engineering, Pusan National University, Pusan,
609-735, Korea
{osc, shchung}@pusan.ac.kr

Abstract. This paper presents a PC cluster-based distributed VOD server that minimizes the load of an interconnection network by adopting the VIA communication protocol and the interval cache algorithm. VIA, which removes the overhead of TCP/IP, minimizes the time spent in transferring the data. The interval cache reduces traffic on the interconnection network by caching, in main memory, the video data transferred from disks of remote server nodes. Experiments using the distributed VOD server of this paper showed a maximum performance improvement of 21.3 % compared with a distributed VOD server without VIA and the interval cache, when used with a four-node PC cluster.

1 Introduction

As a cost-effective solution for video on demand (VOD) service, distributed VOD servers such as the Yima [1] and VoDKA [2] have been developed. In these servers, video data is distributed to the disks of the distributed VOD server and each server node receives data from disks through an interconnection network connecting all the server nodes, and sends the video data to clients. The distributed VOD server can service client requests in real time and resources are used efficiently. A disadvantage is that the load on the interconnection network increases because of the large video data transfers. It is therefore important to minimize the load of the interconnection network to improve performance of the distributed VOD server.

A distributed VOD server presented in this paper is based on a PC cluster system with a Gigabit Ethernet interconnection network, and adopts the virtual interface architecture (VIA) communication protocol [3] and an interval cache algorithm [4] to minimize the load of the interconnection network. Because TCP/IP, a representative communication protocol for Gigabit Ethernet, has many software overheads, user software cannot fully utilize the physical bandwidth of Gigabit Ethernet. To solve this problem, VIA that removes the overheads of TCP/IP was developed. In the VOD service, most client requests will be for videos with high popularity and the data for these will be transferred

---

* This work was supported by grant No.(R05-2003-000-10726-0) from the Korea Science and Engineering Foundation.

K. Aizawa, Y. Nakamura, and S. Satoh (Eds.): PCM 2004, LNCS 3331, pp. 618–625, 2004.

redundantly through the interconnection network. This paper proposes use of the interval cache, which caches the video data transferred from remote disks on main memory of each server node, to reduce the redundant traffic. By using VIA and the interval cache, the distributed VOD server can send more video streams simultaneously to clients.

2   Related Work

Much research have been performed to improve performance of distributed VOD servers from the viewpoint of the disks and the client network. Striping is the most popular strategy for storing video data, and weighted striping strategies [5, 6] have been developed to improve the performance of the striping. Different disks of one distributed VOD server can have different performance characteristics, because disks can be added or removed for maintenance or expansion. Weighted striping assigns higher priority to disks with higher performance and enables them to store more video data. Because this strategy considers the performance of each disk, load balancing to the disks is achieved and the performance of the disks is improved.

The strategies to reduce the traffic of the client network are proxies [7] and cooperative caches [8]. A proxy server exists on the client network and caches the video data transferred from the VOD server to clients. When other clients request the data cached on the proxy server, the proxy server sends it directly to the clients without accessing the VOD server. The proxy server can thus reduce the load of both the client network and the VOD server. Cooperative caching is a similar strategy to the proxy server, except that clients rather than proxy servers cache the video data. If other clients request cached video data, the clients forward data that they have cached.

As explained above, much research has been performed to improve the performance of the disks and the client network, but there has been relatively little research on the interconnection network. Therefore, this paper is intended to improve the performance of the interconnection network.

3   Distributed VOD Server

Figure 1 shows the structure of the distributed VOD server presented in this paper. It is based on a PC cluster system, and the server nodes are connected by Gigabit Ethernet. Each server node is a Pentium-based system with main memory, SCSI hard disks and two Gigabit Ethernet cards for the interconnection network and the client network. Video data is partitioned into blocks of a fixed size and the partitioned blocks are distributed to the disks of the distributed VOD server using a striping strategy. The video data can be transferred to any server node through the interconnection network. Each server node then merges the video data received and sends it to clients through the client network at a constant transfer rate using the server-push model, until a stop message arrives from the client. In this work, we use VIA and the interval cache to improve

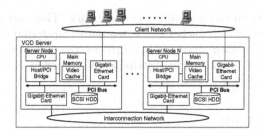

Fig. 1. Structure of the distributed VOD server

performance, as explained in the introduction. Thus, the distributed VOD server can send more video streams simultaneously to clients.

3.1   VIA

In our distributed VOD server, video data and control messages between server nodes are transferred using VIA [3]. TCP/IP's many overheads, including kernel intervention, multiple data copies and context switching from user level to kernel level, do not allow user software to utilize fully the physical bandwidth of Gigabit Ethernet. To solve this problem, VIA, a user-level communication protocol for PC cluster systems, was developed by Compaq, Intel and Microsoft. In VIA, the context switching overhead is removed by performing the communications tasks at the user level instead of the kernel level, and data is copied less frequently by simplifying protocol layers. Therefore, VIA removes the overheads of TCP/IP and allows the user software to fully utilize the physical bandwidth of the network. In this work, M-VIA [9], a representative software implementation of VIA, was chosen as the interconnection network protocol.

Figure 2 shows the organization of the VIA Architecture. VIA uses the Virtual Interfaces (VIs) to reduce the communication overhead. A VI for each node functions as a communication endpoint, and VIs generated between two nodes establish a virtual communication channel. VI Kernel Agent provides the necessary kernel services, which include connection management and memory registration, to establish VI connections between nodes. VI User Agent provides routines for data transfer, connection management, queue management, memory registration, and error handling. Each VI contains a Work Queue (WQ), which consists of a Send Queue and a Receive Queue. A send/receive transaction is initiated by posting a VI descriptor on the WQ, and the network adaptor is notified of the send/receive transaction using a doorbell mechanism. Each VI descriptor contains all the information the network adaptor needs to process the corresponding request, including control information and pointers to data buffers. Then, the network adaptor performs the actual data transfer using DMA without any interference from the kernel. The send/receive transaction is completed when the VI descriptor's done bit is set and the Completion Queue (CQ) is updated by setting the corresponding VI descriptor handle.

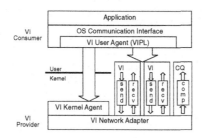

Fig. 2. VIA architecture

Fig. 3. Interval cache algorithm

3.2   Internal Cache

In this work, traffic on the interconnection network is reduced by caching the video data transferred from remote disks in a video cache, which is located in the main memory of each server node. Because video data is accessed sequentially and is very large, it is not appropriate to use cache strategies for general data in the video cache. Many cache algorithms for video data have been developed and we chose the interval cache algorithm [4], which has superior performance to other cache strategies. In the interval cache algorithm, when client requests for the same video data are generated consecutively, the video data corresponding to the time gap between these requests is cached. The interval cache algorithm considers video data with shorter time gaps between client requests as video data with higher popularity and assigns a higher priority to them. Then, the video data with higher priority is first cached on the video cache and the hit ratio of the video cache is improved.

For example, consider that S_{i1}, S_{i2} and S_{i3}, client requests for the same movie M_i, are generated consecutively, as shown in Fig. 3. If S_{i2} arrives at the distributed VOD server serving S_{i1}, consecutive client requests S_{i1} and S_{i2} form interval I_{i1}. Using the same method, S_{i2} and S_{i3} form interval I_{i2}. The video data read from the disks for S_{i1} is cached on the video cache for S_{i2} and S_{i2} reads the video data from the video cache without accessing the disks. S_{i2} also caches the video data for S_{i3}. When the video data read from the disks for S_{i1} is cached for S_{i2}, the memory requirement in the video cache is the number of video data blocks corresponding to interval I_{i1}. For example, if time gap of I_{i1} is three seconds and six video data blocks are necessary to play the video for three seconds, S_{i1} caches six video data blocks for S_{i2}. Video data blocks cached on the video cache are maintained using a circular queue, and S_{i1} and S_{i2} work as provider and consumer respectively of the circular queue.

4   Experimental Results

We performed experiments on a distributed VOD server with four nodes. Each node had a 1.4 GHZ Pentium III processor, 512 MB of main memory, a 20 GB SCSI hard disk and a 64 MHz/64 bit PCI bus. The operating system was based on Linux kernel 2.4.7. Intel 1000/Pro Gigabit Ethernet cards and a 3Com SuperStack3 4900 Gigabit Ethernet switch were used as the interconnection network. The video data for the VOD service is in MPEG 4 format, which has an average bit rate of 110 KB/s.

4.1   Performance Comparisons Between M-VIA and TCP/IP

The performance of the distributed VOD server with M-VIA and TCP/IP as the interconnection network protocols was measured, and the striping block size of the disks was varied from 64 KB to 512 KB to determine the best size. In this experiment, no client requests for the same video data were generated and the video cache did not operate. The client requests were generated every six seconds.

Figure 4 shows the maximum number of streams that the distributed VOD server can send simultaneously to clients. The version with M-VIA sends more streams, 314 for the four-node version, than the TCP/IP version's 282 streams, so the M-VIA version is 11.3 % superior to the TCP/IP version. As the number of nodes increases, the performance improvement of M-VIA over TCP/IP increases. This is mainly because M-VIA minimizes the overhead of the interconnection network, so that the time spent transferring video data through the interconnection network is reduced.

Figure 4 also shows that as the striping block size increases, the performance of the distributed VOD server increases. In this work, the striping block size and the packet size of M-VIA are the same. As the striping block size increases, the bandwidths of the disks and the interconnection network increase and the performance of the distributed VOD server increases. The best striping block size for this paper was chosen as 512 KB because the performance of the distributed VOD server saturates at 512 KB.

4.2   Performance of the Interval Cache

Performances of the distributed VOD server with video cache sizes of 50 MB, 100 MB and 150 MB were measured. M-VIA was adopted and the striping block size was 512 KB. To activate the video cache, consecutive client requests to the same video data were generated by assigning popularity to the video data using a Zipf distribution. The total number of videos in the VOD service is 20 and the client requests were generated every six seconds.

Figure 5 shows that as the size of the video cache increases, the performance of the distributed VOD servers with the video cache improves, and saturates with a video cache of 100 MB. As the number of nodes increases, the performance of the server with the video cache also increases proportionally up to four nodes.

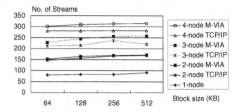

Fig. 4. Performance of the distributed VOD server with M-VIA and TCP/IP

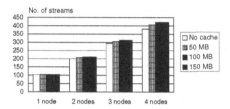

Fig. 5. Performance of the distributed VOD server with the video cache

With four nodes, the VOD server with the video cache sends 420 streams, which is 10 % superior to the VOD server without the video cache, which sent 382 streams. This is mainly because as the video cache size and the number of nodes increases, more video data is cached and the time spent in transferring the video data from the remote disks through the interconnection network therefore decreases.

4.3   Performance Effects of Time Gaps Between Client Requests

In the experiment of this section, the time gaps between the client requests were varied from 3 seconds to 18 seconds. This maximum gap was selected because in Section 4.2, the distributed VOD server sent 420 streams simultaneously. Consider that the average play time of each video is two hours, and that 420 client requests are generated over two hours. The average time gap between each request is thus 18 seconds. In two hours of generating client requests, the number of streams that the distributed VOD server sends simultaneously reaches 420. After that, the distributed VOD server always sends the maximum number of streams if the clients' stream requests are generated every 18 seconds.

Figure 6 shows that as the time gap increases, the performance of the distributed VOD server with a 100 MB video cache decreases. When the time gaps are 9, 12 and 18 seconds, if the sizes of the video cache are expanded up to 150 MB, 150 MB and 200 MB respectively, the distributed VOD server sends the maximum number of streams. As the time gap increases, the cache requirement

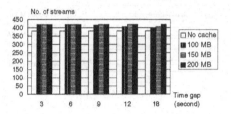

Fig. 6. Performance effect of time gaps

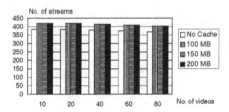

Fig. 7. Performance while varying the number of videos

for caching the video data corresponding to each interval increases and the number of intervals to be cached decreases. The main purpose of the interval cache algorithm is to improve the hit ratio of the video cache by caching more intervals. Therefore, as the time gap increases, the hit ratio of the video cache decreases and the performance of the distributed VOD server decreases. If the size of the video cache is expanded to 150 MB or 200 MB, the hit ratio of the video cache increases and the performance of the distributed VOD server increases.

4.4   Performance with a Varying Number of Videos

In Sections 4.2 and 4.3, the total number of videos for VOD service was 20. In this section, the number of videos was varied from 10 to 80. Client requests are still generated every six seconds. Figure 7 shows that as the number of videos increases, the performance of the distributed VOD server decreases a little. Although the size of the video cache is expanded to 200 MB, the performance of the distributed VOD server is not improved. As the number of the videos increase, each video is assigned a lower popularity according to the Zipf distribution and consecutive client requests for the same video data become less frequent. Therefore, the video cache caches less intervals and the hit ratio of the video cache decreases. Although the size of the video cache is expanded to 200 MB, the consecutive client requests for the same video data do not increase and the hit ratio of the video cache also does not increase.

As the number of videos increases, the performance of the server without the video cache also decreases. Linux supports a disk cache. As the number of the videos increases, a given block of video data is read less often from disk and the performance of the disk cache decreases. Consequently, Fig. 10 shows that the distributed VOD server with the video cache always shows about 10 % performance improvement over that without the video cache although the number of videos is varied.

5 Conclusions

It is important to minimize the load of the interconnection network in a distributed VOD server. We have presented a distributed VOD server that minimizes the load of the interconnection network by adopting VIA and an interval cache. VIA, which has less overhead than TCP/IP, minimized the time spent transferring video data through the interconnection network. The interval cache reduced traffic on the interconnection network by caching the video data transferred from the disks of remote server nodes in main memory. According to experiments with a four-node VOD server, our distributed VOD server of this paper showed performance improvement of 11.3 % and 10 % from VIA and the interval cache respectively, compared with the distributed VOD server that did not adopt VIA and the interval cache, for a total 21.3 % performance improvement. In addition, our distributed VOD server keeps the performance improvement although the number of videos and time gaps between client requests are varied.

References

1. Cyrus Shahabi, Roger Zimmermann, Kun Fu, and Shu-Yuen Didi Yao: Yima: a second-generation continuous media server. Computer, Vol. 35, Issue 6 (2002) 56–62
2. M. Barreiro, V. M. Gulias, J. L. Freire, and J. J. Sanchez.: An Erlang-based hierarchical distributed VoD. 7th International Erlang/OTP User Conference(EUC2001), Ericsson Utvecklings AB (2001)
3. D. Dunning et al.: The Virtual Interface Architecture. IEEE Micro, Vol. 18, No. 2 (1998) 66–76
4. A. Dan, D. Dias, R. Mukherjee, D. Sitaram and R. Tewari: Buffering and Caching in Large-Scale Video Server. In Proceeding COMPCON. IEEE (1995)
5. Yuewei Wang, David H. C. Du: Weighted Striping in Multimedia Servers. IEEE multimedia systems (1997) 102–109
6. You-Jung Ahn; Jong-Hoon Kim; Yoo-Hun Won: A placement policy to maximize the number of concurrent video streams supported in clustered video-on-demand servers. Proceedings of the IEEE Region 10 Conference (1999) 333–336
7. Chen-Lung Chan, Te-Chou Su, Shih-Yu Huang and Jia-Shung Wang: Cooperative proxy scheme for large-scale VoD systems. 9th International Conference on Parallel and Distributed Systems (2002) 404–409
8. Leonardo B. Pinho, Claudio L. Amor and Edison Ishikawa: GloVE: a distributed environment for low cost scalable VoD systems. 14th Symposium on Computer Architecture and High Performance Computing (2002) 117–12
9. "M-VIA", http://www.nersc.gov/research/FTG/via

Clustering of Video Packets Using Interactive Refinement by Relevance Feedback

Yukihiro Kinoshita, Naoko Nitta, and Noboru Babaguchi

Graduate School of Engineering, Osaka University
2-1 Yamadaoka, Suita, Osaka, 565–0871 Japan
{yukihiro,naoko,babaguchi}@nanase.comm.eng.osaka-u.ac.jp,

Abstract. Structuralization of the video stream is necessary for effective handling of video media. Especially, collecting similar scenes with sufficient accuracy contributes to the structuralization. In this paper, we propose a method of clustering with relevance feedback. First, fixed-length segments are clustered according to the feature of each segment. For the results of clustering, the user gives the feedback information whether each element is relevant to the cluster it belongs to. The accuracy can be improved by re-clustering based on the feedback information. Applying this method to a variety of video streams, we demonstrated the effectiveness of the relevance feedback.

Keywords: Video Packet, Tensor Histogram, Clustering, Relevance Feedback

1 Introduction

The amount of data offered through televisions or the Internet is increasing due to the recent progress of communication technology, and so is the time and effort required to retrieve particular video scenes from the video stream. In order to use the video media efficiently and effectively, the video stream should be structured. We try to realize structuralization by dividing the video stream into video segments and establishing links between them.

In this paper, we propose a method of clustering that collects video segments with similar content with sufficient accuracy. Usually, video segments of variable length, called shots, are used as a unit of video processing. Instead, in this method, fixed-length video segments called *video packets*[1] are used. Using video packets exempts the need for the perfect shot detection and helps us handle the variance of the video content in a single shot.

Let us mention related work. There is another clustering method where short continuous frame sequences called video scenelets[2] are used. Although their and our method are similar in terms of not taking shot changes into consideration, the features are different. H.Lu et al.[2] employed the HSV color histogram computed as the average of all the frame color histograms in the scenelet. On the other hand, we employ tensor histograms[3] to analyze spatio-temporal images. Ngo

K. Aizawa, Y. Nakamura, and S. Satoh (Eds.): PCM 2004, LNCS 3331, pp. 626–633, 2004.
© Springer-Verlag Berlin Heidelberg 2004

et al.[3] demonstrated that tensor histogram was effective for temporal slice analysis.

As a representative clustering method using the feedback information from the users, relevance feedback[4][5][6] is used in information and image retrieval. Relevance feedback is a tool where a system presents more suitable results based on the feedback information whether the results are relevant to the user's queries. Rui et al.[4] proposed a method of weight updating for feature vectors based on the user's feedback, and our method is deeply related with their method. While the conventional methods[4][5][6] applied feedback to the still images, our method applies feedback to the videos. In this paper, we propose a method of refining the clustering results through the interaction between a system and a user based on re-weighting of feature vectors with relevance feedback.

The rest of this paper is organized as follows. Section 2 discusses the outline of clustering and the relevance feedback. Section 3 discusses the details of clustering of video packets. In Section 4, experimental results and the examinations are given. Concluding remarks are given in Section 5.

2   Outline of the Proposed Method

Here, we define clustering of video segments. We classify video segments based on their feature vector. Our method uses fixed-length *video packets* instead of shots as a unit of video segments for clustering. The definitions of shots and video packets are shown below.

- shot $\cdots$ a consecutive image frames taken by a single camera
- video packet $\cdots$ a partial video stream of fixed length

The flow of clustering is shown in Fig. 1. First, we divide the video stream into the video packets. The spatio-temporal images are generated from each video packet and clustering is performed based on the feature vector calculated from each spatio-temporal image using tensor histograms[3]. When the results of clustering are shown to a user through the interface, the user specifies whether each video packet is relevant or irrelevant to the clusters to refine the elements that induced the incorrect clustering. The system is not able to evaluate the accuracy of the results of clustering since there is no objective ground truth. Therefore, we try to improve the clustering results by reflecting the information from the user to the system. Based on the feedback information from the user, the system updates the feature vectors and generates new feature vectors. The system performs re-clustering with the new feature vectors and presents the results of clustering to the user. We aim at improving the accuracy of clustering by repeating the operation above.

3   Clustering of Video Packets

In this section, we explain the details of each step of our method; feature extraction, clustering algorithm, and feature vector updating.

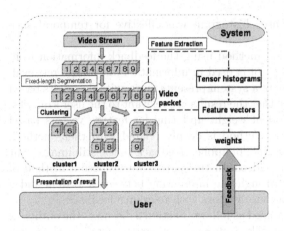

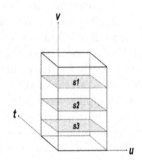

Fig. 1. The Flow of Clustering   **Fig. 2.** Spatio-Temporal Images

3.1   Feature Extraction from Spatio-temporal Image

In our method, features are extracted from spatio-temporal images as the features of video packets. Fig.2 shows a video packet, where v and u are the height and width of a frame respectively and t represents the time, and three spatio-temporal images are obtained horizontally with u and t. Since many types of camera work and movements of objects are horizontal, we apply three spatio-temporal images (s1, s2, and s3 in Fig.2). The feature of the spatio-temporal images is represented with tensor histograms. Tensor histograms encode the distribution of local orientation in spatio-temporal images. They are computed based on the structural tensor[7] to estimate the orientations of movement in images. This feature is often used for motion characterization and video segmentation.

The structural tensor Γ of an image H can be expressed as

$$\Gamma = \begin{bmatrix} J_{uu} & J_{ut} \\ J_{ut} & J_{tt} \end{bmatrix} \triangleq \begin{bmatrix} \sum_d H_u^2 & \sum_d H_u H_t \\ \sum_d H_u H_t & \sum_d H_t^2 \end{bmatrix} \tag{1}$$

where H_u and H_t are partial derivatives along the spatial and temporal dimensions, respectively. The window of w is set to 3×3. The rotation angle θ of Γ indicates the direction of gray level changes in w. Rotating the principle axes of Γ by θ, we have

$$R \begin{bmatrix} J_{uu} & J_{ut} \\ J_{ut} & J_{tt} \end{bmatrix} R^T = \begin{bmatrix} \lambda_u & 0 \\ 0 & \lambda_t \end{bmatrix} \tag{2}$$

where

$$R \triangleq \begin{bmatrix} \cos\theta & \sin\theta \\ -\sin\theta & \cos\theta \end{bmatrix}. \tag{3}$$

From (2), since we have three equations with three unknowns, θ can be solved and expressed as

$$\theta = \frac{1}{2}\tan^{-1}\frac{2J_{ut}}{J_{uu} - J_{tt}}. \tag{4}$$

It is useful to add in a certainty measure to describe how well θ approximates the local orientation of w. The certainty c is estimated as

$$c = \frac{(J_{uu} - J_{tt})^2 + 4J_{ut}^2}{(J_{uu} + J_{tt})^2} = \left(\frac{\lambda_u - \lambda_t}{\lambda_u + \lambda_t}\right)^2 \tag{5}$$

and $c = [0, 1]$. For an ideal local orientation, $c = 1$ when either $\lambda_u = 0$ or $\lambda_t = 0$. For an isotropic structure, i.e., $\lambda_u = \lambda_t$, $c = 0$.

The distribution of the local orientations across time inherently reflects the motion trajectories in an image volume. A 2-D tensor histogram $M(\theta, t)$, with the dimensions as a 1-D orientation histogram and time respectively, can be constructed to model the distribution. The histogram can be expressed as

$$M(\theta, t) = \sum_{u' s.t. \Gamma(u', t) = \theta} c(u', t) \tag{6}$$

which means that each pixel in images votes for $\text{bin}(\theta, t)$ with the certainty value c.

For motion retrieval, the 1-D tensor histogram $\mathcal{M}(k)$ is computed directly by

$$\mathcal{M}(k) = \frac{1}{n}\left\{\sum_{\theta'}\sum_{t} M(\theta', t)\right\}, \forall\theta'\{\mathcal{Q}(\theta') = k\} \tag{7}$$

where $\mathcal{Q}(\theta')$ is the quantization function and $k = \{1, 2, \cdots, 8\}$ represents the quantized level. Our method uses the tensor histograms $(\mathcal{M}_{s1}(k), \mathcal{M}_{s2}(k), \mathcal{M}_{s3}(k))$ of three horizontal slices (s1, s2, and s3 in Fig.2) for feature computation. As a result, the feature vector is expressed as

$$Y = (\mathcal{M}_{s1}(1), \cdots, \mathcal{M}_{s1}(8), \mathcal{M}_{s2}(1), \cdots, \mathcal{M}_{s2}(8), \mathcal{M}_{s3}(1), \cdots, \mathcal{M}_{s3}(8)). \tag{8}$$

3.2   Clustering with K-Means

K-means[8] is a method of un-hierarchical clustering that partitions the data into K clusters so that the sum of the distances of the data to the respective group centroids over all groups can be minimized. K-means clustering works as follows:

Step1. Pick k elements at random to represent the centroid of each cluster.
Step2. Assign every element to the clusters with the closest centroids.
Step3. Compute the new centroid of each cluster with the assigned elements.
Step4. Repeat step2 and step3 until convergence.

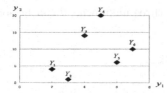

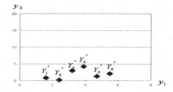

Fig. 3. Original feature vector distribution

Fig. 4. Updated feature vector distribution

3.3 Feature Vector Updating

The user gives the feedback whether each element is relevant or not to the cluster it belongs to after referring to the results of clustering presented by the system. The system updates the feature vectors based on the feedback and operates the clustering with the updated feature vectors. We describe the method of feature vectors updating based on the feedback information below.

For the set of feature vectors Y, the user specifies which elements are relevant or not. In the set of relevant feature vectors, when the standard deviation of the i-th ($1 \leq i \leq 24$) component of the feature vectors is large, the system recognizes that the user considers i-th component is not important and gives small weights w_i. On the contrary, the system gives large weights for the components whose standard deviations are small. Based on the idea above, the weight w_i is defined as $w_i = 1/\sigma_i(1 \leq i \leq 24)$ where σ_i is the standard deviation of i-th component. The system normalizes W_i with the sum of w_i. ($W_i = w_i/\sum w_i$) The system updates the feature vector with W_i. When the feature vector is $Y = (y_1, y_2, \cdots, y_{24})$, the updated feature vector is $Y' = (W_1 y_1, \cdots, W_{24} y_{24})$. Suppose that the feature vector is two dimentional, i.e. $Y = (y_1, y_2)$. Fig.3 shows the distribution of the feature vectors from Y_1 to Y_6. The feature y_1 with the small dispersion is more effective feature than the feature y_2 with the large dispersion. Fig.4 shows the distribution of the updated feature vectors from Y_1' to Y_6'. New feature vectors are generated by updating original feature vectors, and clustering is operated with the new feature vectors using K-means algorithm.

4 Experimental Results

In this section, we present experimental results with various kinds of videos. We also investigate how the accuracy changes according to the length of the packets.

4.1 Example of Operation

An example of the results when the user gives the feedback information which elements in a cluster are relevant or not is presented. The results were evaluated with the accuracy (= (the number of relevant packets)/(the number of all packets)). Fig.5 shows a cluster before the feedback is given. The video is 5-minute

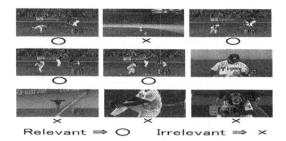

Relevant ⇒ ○   Irrelevant ⇒ ×

Fig. 5. Before clustering

Fig. 6. After re-clustering   **Fig. 7.** After ten times re-clustering

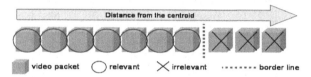

Fig. 8. Alternative way of feedback

long. The first frame of each video packet is presented as the representative image. Fig.5 also shows how the user gave the feedback to the cluster. Fig.6 shows the new cluster obtained by re-clustering based on the data according to the user's feedback. Fig.5 and Fig.6 show only parts of clusters since the sizes of both clusters were large. Fig.5 and Fig.6 indicate that the accuracy of clustering was improved with a single feedback operation. Furthermore, after ten times re-clustering, the new cluster was generated as shown in Fig.7. We demonstrated that interactive re-clustering was able to improve the performance.

Now, since the relevance feedback is given to all the packets, too much effort is required for large video libraries. To solve this problem, we also conducted the priliminary experiments of applying the relevance feedback only to a part of all the packets. We first applied the relevance feedback to the first five or ten packets from the closest one to the centroid of each cluster. However, the accuracy did not improve from the initial accuracy and stayed less than 60%. Alternatively, we determined a border line in each cluster as shown in Fig.8. A border line represents the threshold between relevant and irrelevant packets. The packets before the border line are considered as relevant packets. As a result, the accuracy was improved to about 80% and the effort to specify the relevance by the user was decreased by 90%. These experiments yielded promising results which show that our system will enable users to easily work with large video libraries.

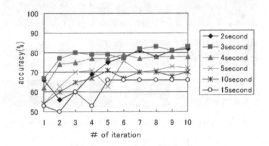

Fig. 9. Clustering accuracy for the length of packets

Table 1. Clustering accuracy for each video (packet length:3sec.)

video	kind of video	accuracy(%)		
		Initial	5times	10times
1	Baseball1	67	79	83
2	Baseball2	64	79	82
3	Baseball3	75	84	90
4	Sumo	64	85	88
5	Volleyball	46	70	88
6	Soccer	63	70	86
7	American football	46	62	92
8	Variety	56	63	81
9	Cooking	53	68	69
10	News	49	70	74
	average	58.3	73.0	83.0

4.2   Experiments About Length of Video Packets

We also conducted experiments to examine how the accuracy of clustering changed according to the length of the packets. Each video is composed of some categories. We determined categories for each video beforehand. The examples of the categories in baseball videos are the scenes of pitching, zooming up of a player, etc. This is done in order to avoid changes in the user's subjective evaluation scheme. The user specifies if each element in the clusters is relevant or irrelevant based on the pre-defined categories. The length of the packets was set to 2, 3, 4, 5, 10, and 15 seconds, and we investigated the accuracy of clustering with three 5-minute long baseball videos. The results are shown in Fig.9. Fig.9 shows that when the length of the packets was too long, the recursive feedback did not have any effect on the performance. We also applied our method to other types of videos (volleyball, news, drama, etc.) with setting the length of the packets to 2, 3, and 4 seconds. The results with the 3-second packets are shown in Table 1. For ten videos, the accuracy of clustering was 58% on average before operating the feedback. After 10-time feedbacks, the accuracy of clustering was improved to 83% on average.

When the length of the packets was set to 4 seconds, the final accuracies for video1, 2, 3, and 5 were not improved as much and they were about 10% less than the results with the 3-second packets. This is due to the camera work and shot changes in the videos. Since the packets with a shot change have different features from those without a shot change, the packets with a shot change can not be classified correctly. That is to say, if the length of the packets is too long, the number of the packets with a shot change increases and the accuracy cannot be improved. Therefore, the length of the packets should be set shorter for the videos with many shot changes. Investigating the relation between the appropriate length of packets and the video content will be one of our future work.

5   Conclusion

In this paper, we proposed a method to improve the accuracy of clustering of the fixed-length video packets with relevance feedback. Experiments with eight types of broadcasted videos showed that the accuracy was improved with 24.7% on average after ten times iterations. We also conducted the experiments of applying the relevance feedback only to a part of all the packets. As a result, the final accuracy was about 80% with 90% less effort.

As a future work, we will consider how to select the representative packets which can more effectively improve the accuracy. Furthermore, we will also apply the features related to colors and propose more appropriate methods of feature vector updating.

References

1. H. Okamoto, Y. Yasugi, N. Babaguchi, and T. Kitahashi, "Video Clustering Using Spatio-Temporal Image with Fixed Length," Proceedings of IEEE International Conference on Multimedia and Expo, Vol.1, pp.53–56, Aug.2002.
2. H. Lu and Y.P. Tan, "On Model-Based Clustering of Video Scenes Using Scenelets," IEEE International Conference on Multimedia and Expo, Vol.1, pp.301-304, Aug.2002
3. C.W. Ngo, T.C. Pong, and H.J. Zhang, "On Clustering and Retrieval of Video Shots Through Temporal Slice Analysis," IEEE Transactions on Multimedia, Vol.4, No4, pp.446–458, Dec.2002.
4. Y. Rui, T.S. Huang, M. Ortega, and S. Mehrotra, "Relevance Feedback: A Power Tool for Interactive Content-Based Image Retrieval," IEEE Transactions on Circuits and Systems for Video Technology, Vol.8, No.5, pp.644–655, Sept.1998.
5. N.D. Doulamis, A.D. Doulamis, and T.A. Varvarigou, "Adaptive Algorithms for Interactive Multimedia," IEEE Multimedia, Vol.10, No.4, pp.38-47, Oct.2003.
6. Y. Lu, H. Zhang, L. Wenyin, and C. Hu, "Joint Semantics and Feature Based Image Retrieval Using Relevance Feedback," IEEE Transactions on Multimedia, Vol.5, No3, pp.339–347, Sept.2003.
7. H. Knutsson, "Representing Local Structure Using Tensors," The 6th Scandinavian Conference on Image Analysis, pp.244-251, 1989.
8. T. Kanungo, D.M. Mount, N.S. Netanyahu, C.D. Piatko, R. Silverman, and A.Y. Wu, "An Efficient k-Means Clustering Algorithm: Analysis and Implementation," IEEE Transaction on Pattern Analysis and Machine Intelligence, Vol.24, No.7, pp.881-892, July.2002.

Semantic Video Indexing and Summarization Using Subtitles

Haoran Yi, Deepu Rajan, and Liang-Tien Chia

Center for Multimedia and Network Technology
School of Computer Engineering
Nanyang Technological University, Singapore 639798
{pg03763623, asdrajan, asltchia}@ntu.edu.sg

Abstract. How to build semantic index for multimedia data is an important and challenging problem for multimedia information systems. In this paper, we present a novel approach to build a semantic video index for digital videos by analyzing the subtitle files of DVD/DivX videos. The proposed approach for building semantic video index consists of 3 stages, viz., script extraction, script partition and script vector representation. First, the scripts are extracted from the subtitle files that are available in the DVD/DivX videos. Then, the extracted scripts are partitioned into segments. Finally, the partitioned script segments are converted into a *tfidf* vector based representation, which acts as the semantic index. The efficiency of the semantic index is demonstrated through video retrieval and summarization applications. Experimental results demonstrate that the proposed approach is very promising.

Keywords: Subtitles, retrieval, video summarization, script vector.

1 Introduction

As the size of multimedia databases increase, it becomes critical to develop methods for efficient and effective management and analysis of such data. The data include documents, audio-visual presentations, home made videos and professionally created contents such as sitcoms, TV shows and movies. Movies and TV shows constitute a large portion of the entertainment industry. Every year around 4,500 motion pictures are released around the world spanning approximate 9,000 hours of video [8]. With the development of digital video and networking technology, more and more multimedia content are being delivered live or on-demand over the Internet. Such a vast amount of content information calls for efficient and effective methods to analyze, index and organize multimedia data.

Most of the previous methods for video analysis and indexing are based on low level visual or motion information, such as color histogram [6] or motion activity [7]. However, when humans deal with multimedia data, they prefer to describe, query and browse the content of the multimedia in terms of semantic

K. Aizawa, Y. Nakamura, and S. Satoh (Eds.): PCM 2004, LNCS 3331, pp. 634–641, 2004.
© Springer-Verlag Berlin Heidelberg 2004

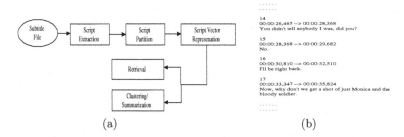

Fig. 1. (a) The proposed approach to building a semantic index (b) Example of a script file.

keywords rather than low level features. Thus, how to extract semantic information from digital multimedia is a very important, albeit a challenging task. The most popular method to extract semantic information is to combine human annotation with machine learning [3]. But such methods are semiautomatic and complex because the initial training set need to be labelled by human and the learned classifiers may also need to be tuned for different videos.

Subtitle files of a video provides direct access to the semantic aspect of the video content because the semantic information is captured very well in the subtitle files. Thus, it seems to be prudent to exploit this fact to extract semantic information in videos, instead of developing complex video processing algorithms. In this paper, we provide a new approach to building the semantic index for video content by analyzing the subtitle file. This approach is illustrated in Figure 1(a).

First, the scripts with time stamps are extracted from the subtitle file associated with the video. Such subtitle files are available in all DVD/DivX videos. The second step is to partition the scripts into segments. Each segment of the script is then converted into a vector based representation which is used as the semantic index. The vector based indexes can be used for retrieval and summarization.

The organization of the paper is as follows: Section 2 describes in detail the process of building a semantic index based on a script file. Section 3 describes two applications with the script vector representation - retrieval and summarization. Section 4 presents the experimental results and concluding remarks are given in Section 5.

2   Semantic Video Indexing

In this section, we describe in detail the 3 stages of the proposed technique to index video sequences based on semantic information extracted from a script file in a DVD/DivX video. The stages are script extraction, script partition and script to vector mapping.

2.1   Script Extraction

DVD/DivX videos come with separate subtitle or script files for each frame in the video sequence. There are two types of subtitle files - one in which the scripts are recorded as bitmap pictures which are drawn directly on the screen when the video plays and the other in which the scripts are recorded as strings in a text file. The text based subtitle files are much smaller and more flexible than those based on bitmaps. The advantage of using a text based subtitle file is that it is not only human-readable, but the user can easily change the appearance of the displayed text. However, bitmap pictures can be converted to text using readily available software such as 'VOBSUB'[1]. Hence, we focus on script extraction from the text base subtitle file. An example of a text based subtitle file is shown in Figure 1(b). Each script in the file consists of an index for the script, the time of appearance and disappearance of the script with respect to the beginning of the video and the text of the script. The subtitle file is parsed into *ScriptElements*, where each *ScriptElement* has the following three attributes: 'Start Time', 'End Time' and 'Text'. We use the information in the *ScriptElements* in order to partition them in the next step.

2.2   Script Partitioning

The objective of script partitioning is to group together those *ScriptElements* that have a common semantic thread running through them. Clearly, it is the temporally adjacent *ScriptElements* that are grouped together because they tend to convey a semantic notion when read together. At the same time, some *ScriptElements* may contain only a few words, which by themselves do not convey any semantic meaning. This leads us to the question of how to determine which *ScriptElements* should be grouped together to create a partitioning of the entire script.

We use the time gap between *ScriptElements* as the cue for script partition. This time gap, which we call the *ScriptElement* gap is defined as the time gap between the 'EndTime' of the previous *ScriptElement* and the *StartTime* of the current *ScriptElement*. In a video, when there is a dialogue or a long narration that extends to several frames, the *ScriptElement* gap is very small. Concurrently, it is evident that *ScriptElements* that constitute an extended narration will also have a high "semantic correlation" among themselves. Hence, it is seen that the *ScriptElement* gap is a useful parameter by which to group together semantically relevant *ScriptElements*, thereby creating a partition of the scripts. In the proposed method, the *ScriptElements* are partitioned by thresholding the *ScriptElement* gap. We call each partition as a *ScriptSegment*.

2.3   Script Vector Representation

After partitioning the scripts into *segments*, we build an index for each script segment. We adopt the *term-frequency inverse document frequency(tfidf)* vector space model [4], which is widely used for information retrieval, as the semantic index for the segments. The first step involves removal of stop words, e.g. "about", "I" etc. The Potter Stemming algorithm [5], is used to obtain the stem of each word, e.g., the stem for the word "families" is "family". The stems are collected into a dictionary, which are then used to construct the script vector for each segment. Just as the vector space model represents a document with a single column vector, we represent the script segment using the *tfidf* function [2] given by

$$tfidf(t_k, d_j) = \#(t_k, d_j) \cdot \log \frac{|S_s|}{\#S_s(t_k)} \tag{1}$$

where $\#(t_k, d_j)$ denotes the number of times that a word t_k occurs in segment d_j, $|S_s|$ is the cardinality of the set S_s of all segments, and $\#S_s(t_k)$ denotes the number of segments in which the word t_k occurs. This function states that (a) the more often a term occurs in a segment, the more it is representative of its content, and (b) the more segments a term occurs in, the less discriminating it is. The *tfidf* function for a particular segment is converted to a set of normalized weights for each word belonging to the segment according to

$$w_{k,j} = \frac{tfidf(t_k, d_j)}{\sqrt{(\sum_{i=1}^{T}(tfidf(t_i, d_j))^2)}}. \tag{2}$$

Here, $w_{k,j}$ is the weight of the word t_k in segment d_j and T is the total number of words in the dictionary. This is done to ensure that every segment extracted from the subtitle file has equal length and that the weights are in [0,1]. It is these weights that are collected together into a vector for a particular segment such that the vector acts as a semantic index to that segment. We call this vector as the "*tfidf* vector" in the following discussion.

3 Applications

We now illustrate two applications of the semantic index that has been extracted from the script files of DVD/DivX videos using the proposed method. In the first instance, we retrieve a video sequence using a keyword or a sentence as the query. The second application is video summarization wherein the semantic index is used to create a summary of the entire video - the summary can be expressed as a set of keywords or as a video.

3.1 Video Retrieval

In this subsection, we illustrate video retrieval with script vector based representation which acts as a semantic index. As described in the previous section, each script segment is represented as a *tfidf* vector. We collect all the column script vectors together into a matrix of order $T \times |S_s|$, called the script matrix.

The query can be in the form of a single word in which case the query vector (which has the same dimensions as the *tfidf* vector) will consist of a single non-zero element. For example, a query with the word "bride" will result in a query vector like $[0 \cdots 1 \cdots 0]$, where only the entry of the vector corresponding to the word "bride" is set to 1. The query can also take the form of a sentence like "The bride and groom are dancing"; here the query vector will look like $[0 \cdots 1/\sqrt{3} \cdots 1/\sqrt{3} \cdots]$. As we see, the word(s) that are present in the query will have higher values in the query vector. The result of the querying process is the return of script segments which are geometrically close to the query vector; here, we will use the cosine of the angle between the query vector and the columns of the script matrix using,

$$\cos\theta_j = \frac{\mathbf{a_j}^T \mathbf{q}}{||\mathbf{a_j}||_2||\mathbf{q}||_2} = \frac{\sum_{i=1}^{T} a_{ij}q_i}{\sqrt{\sum_{i=1}^{T} a_{ij}^2}\sqrt{\sum_{i=1}^{T} q_i^2}} \tag{3}$$

for $j = 1 \cdots |S_s|$, where $\mathbf{a_j}$ is a column vector from the script matrix, $\mathbf{q}$ is the query vector and T is the number of words. Those script vectors for which equation (3) exceed a certain threshold are considered relevant. Alternatively, we could sort the values of $\cos\theta_j$ to present the top n results.

We could also use other similarity/distance measures, such as the norm of the difference between the query vector and script vector. Since both the computations are monotonic, they will achieve the same result. In both cases, we have to normalize the vectors. We observe that the sparsity of the vectors, especially the query vector, is a key feature in the model. Consider what happens when we take the similarity of a very sparse query vector with a dense script vector. In order to compute the Euclidean distance between such vectors, we would have to subtract each entry of the query from each entry in the script vector, and then square and add each of them. Even precomputing the norms of the script vectors is not feasible since it is computationally expensive and, furthermore, large storage will be required to store the values when dealing with videos with thousands of script segments. However, using cosines, we can take advantage of the sparsity of the query vector, and only compute those multiplications (to get the numerator in the equation) in which the query entry is non-zero. The number of additions is also then limited. The time saved by taking advantage of sparsity would be significant when searching through long videos.

Another observation about the script matrix is that it is very sparse because many of its elements are zero. On the other hand, the dimensionality of the script vectors is very high. Hence, it is desirable to reduce the rank of the matrix. This is viable because if we assume that the most represented words in the script matrix are in many basis vectors, then deleting a few basis vectors will remove the least important information in the script matrix resulting in a more effective index and search.

We use the Singular Value Decomposition (SVD) to reduce the rank of the script matrix. SVD factors a $T \times |S_s|$ script matrix A into three matrices: (i) a $T \times T$ orthogonal matrix U with the left singular vectors of A in its columns, (ii) a $|S_s| \times |S_s|$ orthogonal matrix V with the right singular vectors of A as its columns, and (iii) a $T \times |S_s|$ diagonal matrix E having the singular values in descending order along its diagonal, i.e.$A = UEV^T$. If we retain only the largest k singular values in the diagonal matrix E, we get the kth rank matrix A_k, which is the best approximation of the original matrix A (in terms of Frobenius norm) [4]. Hence,

$$||A - A_k||_F = \min_{rank(X) \leq k} ||A - X|| = \sqrt{\sigma_{k+1}^2 + \cdots + \sigma_{r_A}^2}. \tag{4}$$

Here $A_k = U_k E_k V_k^t$, where U_k is a $T \times k$ matrix, V_k is a $|S_s| \times k$ matrix, and E_k is $k \times k$ diagonal matrix whose elements are the ordered k largest singular values of A. The σ's in the equation (4) are the singular values, or the diagonal entries in E.

Using the approximate k^{th} rank script matrix made by SVD, we can recompute equation (3) as [4]

$$\cos\theta_j = \frac{(A_k \mathbf{e_j})^T \mathbf{q}}{||(A_k \mathbf{e_j})||_2 ||\mathbf{q}||_2} = \frac{(U_k \Sigma_k V_k^t \mathbf{e_j})^T \mathbf{q}}{||(U_k \Sigma_k V_k^t \mathbf{e_j})||_2 ||\mathbf{q}||_2} = \frac{\mathbf{e_j}^T V_k \Sigma_k (U_k^T \mathbf{q})}{||\Sigma_k V_k^t \mathbf{e_j}||_2 ||\mathbf{q}||_2} \tag{5}$$

$$\cos\theta_j = \frac{\mathbf{s_j}^T (U_k^T \mathbf{q})}{||\mathbf{s_j}||_2 ||\mathbf{q}||_2}, \quad j = 1, \cdots, |S_s| \tag{6}$$

where $\mathbf{s_j} = E_k V_k^T \mathbf{e_j}$, and $\mathbf{e_j}$ is the jth canonical vector of dimension S_s. The SVD factorization of the script matrix will not only help to reduce the 'noise' of script matrix, but also improve the recall rate of retrieval.

3.2 Summarization

In this subsection, we propose a new video summarization method using the script matrix. Recall that the columns of the script matrix are the script vectors for the script segments. The script vectors can be viewed as points in a high dimension vector space. Principle Component Analysis(PCA) is used to reduce the dimensions of the script vector. The PCA used here has the same effect as the SVD used in the retrieval application on reducing the script vector representation. The script vectors are then clustered in the high dimension space using the K-means algorithm. After clustering, those script segments whose script vectors are geometrically closest to the centroids of the clusters are concatenated to form the video summary. Besides, the script text of the selected segments can be used as the text abstract of the videos. The number of clusters can be determined by the desired length of the video summary, e.g, if the desired length of the video summary is 5% of the original video, then the number of clusters should be one twentieth of the total number of the script segments.

4   Experimental Results

In this section, we present the experimental results to demonstrate the efficacy of the proposed semantic indexing method. Our test data consists of a single episode from the popular TV sitcom 'Friends'(season 8 episode 1).

Figure 2(a) shows the distribution of the time gap between *ScriptElements* for a total of 450 *ScriptElements*. In our implementation, we use 2 seconds as the threshold to partition the scripts into segments. With this threshold, the 450 *ScriptElements* are partitioned into 71 script segments. For each script segment, a script vector is extracted from the text as described in subsection 2.3.

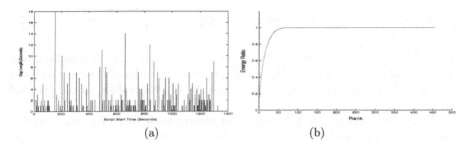

Fig. 2. (a) Time gap between the script element of 'friends' video. (b) Energy ratio VS Dimension of reduced script vector with PCA.

Several queries by keywords are performed on the script matrix to retrieve the corresponding script segment as described in subsection 3.1. The retrieval results using the keywords 'bride', 'dance', 'groom' and 'wedding' are shown in Figures 3 (a), (b), (c) and (d), respectively. As we can see, the proposed method has successfully retrieved the relevant scripts as well as the associated video sequences. Thus, a high level semantic notion like 'bride' can be easily modelled using the technique described in this paper.

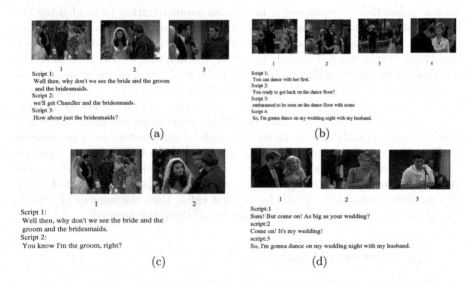

Fig. 3. Example retrieved results: (a) 'bride' query, (b) 'dance' query, (c) 'groom' query, (d) 'wedding' query

In order to illustrate the results for video summarization, we use Principal Component Analysis (PCA) to reduce the script vector from 454 to 50 dimensions. Figure 2(b) shows the plot of the percentage of the total energy of the script vectors when the dimension of the script vectors is reduced with PCA.

The first 50 dimensions capture more than 98% of the total energy. We extract 10 keywords from 5 principle components with the largest 5 eigenvalues. We examine the absolute value of each entry in those principle component vectors and pick out the largest two entries for each principle component vector as the key words. The extracted ten key words are 'happy', 'Chandler', 'marry', 'Joey', 'Monica', 'bride', 'husband', 'pregnant', 'baby' 'dance'. This episode talks about two friends 'Chandler' and 'Monica' getting 'married', Rachel getting 'pregnant' (with a 'baby') and Rose dancing with bridesmaids at the wedding party. We see that the extracted key words give a good summary of the content of this video.

We also extracted video summaries from the original video with the lengths of 5%, 10%, and 20% of the original video. We find that the video summaries capture most of the content of the video. We observe that the 10% video summary is the optimal one. While the 5% summary is too concise and a little difficult to understand, the 20% summary is quite a few redundancies (The result summary videos are available at ftp://user:123456@155.69.103.62/).

5   Conclusion and Future Work

In this paper, we provide a new approach to tackle the semantic video indexing problem. The semantic video index is extracted by analyzing the subtitle file in a DVD/DivX video and represented by the vector based model. Experimental results on video retrieval and summarization demonstrate the effectiveness of the proposed approach. In future, we would consider other Information Retrieval models and incorporate the extracted video summary into MPEG-7 standard representation.

References

1. http://www.doom9.org/dvobsub.htm.
2. M. W. Berry, Z. Drmavc, and E. R. Jessup. Matrices, vector spaces, and information retrieval. *SIAM Review*, 41(2):335–362, June 1999.
3. C.-Y. Lin, B. L. Tseng, and J. R. Smith. VideoAnnEx: IBM MPEG-7 annotation tool for multimedia indexing and concept learning. In *IEEE International Conference on Multimedia & Expo*, Baltimore, USA, July 2003.
4. M.W.Berry, S.T.Dumais, and G.W.O'Brien. Using linear algebra for intelligent information retrieval. *SIAM Review*, 37:301–328, 1995.
5. M. F. Porter. An algorithm for suffix stripping. *Program*, 14(3):130–137, July 1980.
6. S. Smoliar and H. Zhang. Content-based video indexing and retrieval. *IEEE Multimedia*, 1:62–72, 1994.
7. X. Sun, B. S. Manjunath, and A. Divakaran. Representation of motion activity in hierarchical levels for video indexing and filtering. In *IEEE International Conference on Image Processing*, volume 1, pages 149–152, September 2002.
8. H. D. Wactlar. The challanges of continuous capture, contemporaneous analysis and customized summarization of video content. *CMU*.

Audio Visual Cues for Video Indexing and Retrieval

Paisarn Muneesawang[1], Tahir Amin[2], and Ling Guan[2]

[1] Dept. of Electrical and Computer Engineering,
Naresuan University, Thailand
[2] Dept. of Electrical and Computer Engineering,
Ryerson University, Toronto, Canada
{pmuneesa, tamin, lguan}@ee.ryerson.ca

Abstract. This paper studies content-based video retrieval using the combination of audio and visual features. The visual feature is extracted by an adaptive video indexing technique that places a strong emphasis on accurate characterization of spatio-temporal information within video clips. Audio feature is extracted by a statistical time-frequency analysis method that applies Laplacian mixture models to wavelet coefficients. The proposed joint audio-visual retrieval framework is highly flexible and scalable, and can be effectively applied to various types of video databases.

1 Introduction

There are many challenges involved in content analysis and summary of video documents. Compared to a still image, the spatio-temporal information of video files contains a fusion of multimodality signal of the visual frame, music, caption text, and spoken words that can be deciphered from the audio track. When they are all used together, these modality signals are the most powerful features for an analysis of video content to convey meanings and semantic information as compared to any single modality. In a sport video, audiovisual joint analysis is effective to detect key episodes, such as a goal event scene, a touchdown sequence [1], and racket hits in a tennis game [2]. In television broadcasting, multimodality signals can be used to classify video into certain types of scenes such as a dialogue, story, and action [3]; weather forecasts, and commercials [4]. The multi-modality also plays an important role in combining content and context features for multimedia understanding. This understanding includes multimedia object detection and organization [5][6], which aims at supporting a better interface of high-level-concept queries.

In this paper, we present a work on joining visual and audio descriptors for effective video content indexing and retrieval. Unlike the previous works discussed, the proposed method retains its *scalability* and *flexibility* properties. Firstly, the scalability demonstrates that the current technique can be applied to a wide range of applications. As compared to the techniques in [1][2][3], the

K. Aizawa, Y. Nakamura, and S. Satoh (Eds.): PCM 2004, LNCS 3331, pp. 642–649, 2004.
© Springer-Verlag Berlin Heidelberg 2004

proposed method does not restrict itself either to specific video domains or pre-defined event and scene classes. Secondly, the proposed technique is flexible in that it can be applied to a longer portion of video clip, beyond the shot or key frames. We proposed to adopt an *adaptive video indexing* (AVI) technique demonstrated in [7] to characterize visual contents. AVI puts a strong emphasis on capturing spatio-temporal information, so that it can be effectively applied to video clips at various levels, such as shot, scene, and story [7].

As well as the visual domain, the proposed method for the characterization of audio content is flexible enough to apply to an audio clip that contains several applications of music, speech, or noise. We apply a statistical time-frequency analysis method to characterize an audio clip, where the method is independent of the pre-defined audio segments. The audio is regarded as a non-stationary signal, in which the signal characteristic can be changed dramatically within a given portion of audio clip. Unlike the audio classification techniques proposed by Wold [10] and Saunders [11], which emphasize a few pre-defined audio classes such as speech and music, the current method can attain features that address a high degree of flexibility in characterizing the comprehensive characteristics of the audio content.

Our main objective in this paper is to demonstrate the analytic techniques of visual and audio contents, and how these visual and audio features can be joined in an effective manner for video indexing and retrieval. Our simulation results show that the proposed audiovisual analytic techniques can be generalized and effectively applied for retrieval of various video types, including movie, music video, and commercial from a database of 6,000 video clips.

In the following discussion, Section 2 describes visual characterization, and Section 3 describes audio content characterization. Section 4 presents the combination of audio and visual descriptors, and Section 5 presents the experimental results.

2   Visual Modeling by Adaptive Video Indexing (AVI) Technique

Our motivation for using visual content characterization is based on the fact that video data is a sequence of images. Videos which have similar contents usually contained similar images. The degree of similarity between videos may depend on the degree of "overlapping", describing how often the videos refer to a similar set of images. Let D_{I_x} be a primary content descriptor for video interval I_x. In general, D_{I_x} can be defined by:

$$D_{I_x} = \{(X_i, f_i) \mid X_i \in \mathbb{R}^p, \ i = 1, 2, ..., N\} \tag{1}$$

where f_i denotes the i-th video frame within I_x; X_i is its feature vector, and N is the total number of frames. It is noted that the video interval I_x can be of any levels as defined by shot, scene, and story clips.

With the AVI model, a descriptor is defined by the probability of finding a frame model (or template) $\mathcal{M}_t$ in the input video, which is given simply by:

$$P(\mathcal{M}_t) = (N \times N_1)^{-1} \sum_{j=1}^{N \times N_1} I(\ell_j = \ell_{\mathcal{M}_t}) \tag{2}$$

where $\ell_{\mathcal{M}_t}$ is the label of the model vector $\mathcal{M}_t$, and $N \times N_1$ is the total number of labels used to index the input video (described in Eq. (3)). The function $I(\cdot)$ is equal to 1 if the argument is true, and 0 otherwise.

Let $\mathbf{M}$ be the set of models, $\mathbf{M} = [\mathcal{M}_1, ..., \mathcal{M}_t, ..., \mathcal{M}_T]$, $\mathcal{M}_t \in \mathbb{R}^p$, where T is the total number of models. These models are generated and optimized from the training vectors X_j, $j = 1, ..., J$, which are obtained from the primary descriptors of the entire videos in the database. Here, we shall assume that the number of model vectors is significantly smaller than the number of training vectors, i.e., $T << J$. In this work, the optimization process is attained by the application of the competitive learning algorithm [8] to the training set X_j, $j = 1, ..., J$. In addition, the space of X is characterized by a color histogram feature, using HSV color space and 48 bins.

To obtain video indexing, a secondary descriptor is generated to characterize spatio-temporal information. We generate a set of labels via a multiple-label-mapping function $F(X) : \mathbb{R}^{48} \to \mathbb{R}^{N_1}$, where each $X_i, i \in \{1, ..., N\}$ is mapped onto a Voronoi Space through:

$$X_i \Rightarrow \left\langle t^*, \mathcal{R}_{t^*}^{N_1} \right\rangle \Rightarrow \rho^{(X_i)}, \quad t^* = \arg\min_{t \in \{1, ..., T\}} (\|X_i - \mathcal{M}_t\|), \quad \mathcal{R}_{t^*}^{N_1} = \cup_{j=1}^{N_1} \mathcal{M}_{t^*,j} \tag{3}$$

where $\mathcal{R}_{t^*}^{N_1}$ is a region containing the wining node $\mathcal{M}_{t^*}$ and other $N_1 - 1$ Voronoi cells neighboring to the node $\mathcal{M}_{t^*}$. The set of labels, $\rho^{(X_i)} = \ell_{t^*,1}^{X_i}, \ell_{t^*,2}^{X_i}, ..., \ell_{t^*,N_1}^{X_i}$, contains the associated labels of the Voronoi cells in $\mathcal{R}_{t^*}^{N_1}$. In other words, all labels, $\ell_{t^*,j}^{X_i}$, $j = 1, .., N_1$, represent the top N_1 best match models which are most similar to the input vector X_i. This multiple-label mapping process allows the interpretation of the correlation information among the winning node and its neighbors. It also addresses the correlation information between video frames for better analysis, since these frames are usually highly correlated in the input video.

The mapping of all video frames results in the sets of labels, $\rho^{(X_i)}$, $i = 1, 2, .., N$, which are then concatenated into a single feature vector $W_{I_x} = [w_1, ..., w_t, ...w_T]$. According to Eq. (2), each w_t is obtained by:

$$w_t = P(\mathcal{M}_t) = (N \times N_1)^{-1} \sum_{i=1}^{N} \sum_{j=1}^{N_1} I(\ell_j^{X_i} = \ell_{\mathcal{M}_t}). \tag{4}$$

It is noted that only a few of w_t have a nonzero value since $T >> N$. Therefore, the resulting vector W_{I_x} is very sparse, which allows for efficient storage space and fast vector matching. This sparse vector can be formally defined as:

$$\hat{W}_{I_x} = [(\hat{t}, w_{\hat{t}})], \ \hat{t} \in \mathcal{X}, \ \mathcal{X} \subset \{1, 2, ..., T\}, \tag{5}$$

where $\mathcal{X}$ is a set of indexes t associated with the nonzero component w_t. By this way, the similarity matching between two video intervals, I_x and I_y can be computed by:

$$S_{xy}^{(v)} = 1 - \hat{W}_{I_x} \cdot \hat{W}_{I_y} \Big/ \left(||\hat{W}_{I_x}|| \times ||\hat{W}_{I_y}|| \right) \qquad (6)$$

where $S_{xy}^{(v)}$ denote the similarity score between I_x and I_y, and the second term in Eq. (6) is defined by the popular cosine measure.

3   Feature Extraction from Embedded Audio

In the previous section, visual information is used for video indexing. However, the users of the video data are often interested in certain action sequences that are easier to identify in the audio domain. While visual information may not yield useful indexes in this scenario, the audio information often reflects what is happening in the scenes. The existing techniques to classify audio or the embedded audio may not be very useful for application to video retrieval. In this type of application, music, speech, noise and crowd voices may be found together in the same video clip. Therefore, we need features that represent the global similarity of the audio content. A statistical approach based on wavelet transformation and Laplacian mixture models has been adopted here to analyze the audio data and extract the features for video indexing.

Wavelet coefficient distributions are very peaky in nature due to their energy packing property. This type of peaky distribution is non-Gaussian in nature. We can model any arbitrary shaped distribution using a finite mixture model [9]. Here we use a mixture of only two Laplacians for modeling the shape of the distribution. The model parameters of this mixture are used as features for indexing the video clips based on the audio information only.

3.1   Feature Extraction Algorithm

The proposed indexing scheme does not depend on the segmentation method. The video may be firstly segmented into clips using any existing algorithm. Audio is then separated from the video clips and the signals are re-sampled to a uniform sampling rate. Each audio segment is decomposed using a one-dimensional Discrete wavelet transformation (DWT). One-dimensional DWT decomposes the audio signals into 2 sub-bands at each wavelet scale; a low frequency sub-band and a high frequency sub-band. The wavelet decomposition scheme matches the models of sound octave-division for perceptual scales. Wavelet transformation also provides a multi-scale representation of sound information, so that we can build indexing structures based on this scale property. Moreover, audio signals are non-stationary signals whose frequency contents evolve with time. Wavelet transform provides both frequency and time information simultaneously. These properties of wavelet transformation for sound signal decomposition is the foundation of the proposed audio based video indexing and retrieval system.

An increase in the level of wavelet decomposition increases the number of features extracted for indexing. This improves the retrieval performance at the expense of more computational overhead. We now model the distribution of the wavelet coefficients in the high frequency sub-bands using a mixture of two Laplacians centered at 0. The parameters of this mixture model are used as features for indexing the audio content. It has been observed that the resulting features possess high discriminatory power for audio classification with the low dimensionality.

The model can be represented as:

$$p(w_i) = \alpha_1 p_1(w_i|b_1) + \alpha_2 p_2(w_i|b_2), \quad \alpha_1 + \alpha_2 = 1 \tag{7}$$

where α_1 and α_2 are the mixing probabilities of the two components p_1 and p_2; w_i are the wavelet coefficients; b_1 and b_2 are the parameters of the Laplacian distribution p_1 and p_2, respectively .The Laplacian component in Eg.(7) is defined as:

$$p_1(w_i|b_1) = \frac{1}{2b_1} \exp(-|w_i|/b_1) \tag{8}$$

The shape of the Laplacian distribution is determined by the single parameter b. We apply EM algorithm [12] to estimate the parameters of the model.

E-Step: For the n-th iterative cycle, the E-step computes two probabilities for each wavelet coefficient:

$$p_{1i}(n) = \frac{\alpha_1(n) p(w_i|b_1(n))}{\alpha_1(n) p(w_i|b_1(n)) + \alpha_2(n) p(w_i|b_2(n))}, \tag{9}$$

$$p_{2i}(n) = \frac{\alpha_2(n) p(w_i|b_2(n))}{\alpha_1(n) p(w_i|b_1(n)) + \alpha_2(n) p(w_i|b_2(n))} \tag{10}$$

M-Step: In the M-step, the parameters $[b_1, b_2]$ and *a priori* probabilities $[\alpha_1, \alpha_2]$ are updated.

$$\alpha_1(n+1) = \frac{1}{K}\sum_{i=1}^{K} p_{1i}(n), \quad \alpha_2(n+1) = \frac{1}{K}\sum_{i=1}^{K} p_{2i}(n), \tag{11}$$

$$b_1(n+1) = \frac{\sum_{i=1}^{K} |w_i| p_{1i}(n)}{K\alpha_1(n+1)}, \quad b_2(n+1) = \frac{\sum_{i=1}^{K} |w_i| p_{2i}(n)}{K\alpha_2(n+1)} \tag{12}$$

where K is the number of wavelet coefficients in the current subband.

The following components form the feature vector used for indexing the audio clips: (1) Mean and standard deviation of the wavelet coefficients in the Low frequency subband; (2) Model parameters $[\alpha_1, b_1, b_2]$ calculated for each of the high frequency subband.

For N-level decompositions, the above algorithm gives $(N \times 3) + 2$ feature components for characterized audio content in the input video clip.

The similarity function used for matching audio feature vectors is described by the Euclidean distance:

$$S_{xy}^{(a)} = \sqrt{\sum_{i=1}^{P} (F_x[i] - F_y[i])^2}, \tag{13}$$

where F_x and F_y are the audio feature vectors of the video clips I_x and I_y, respectively.

4   Audio and Visual Score Ranking

The audio and visual features may not be directly combined because they are different in both physical structure as well as their dimensions. Thus, the video ranking is obtained separately between audio and visual feature databases. These ranking results are then combined to obtain the final similarity ranking decision. Using the visual feature database, the similarity scores between the query interval I_q and other video intervals in the database are generated by Eq. (6). This results in $S_{qi}^{(v)}$, $i = 1, ..., M$, where M denotes the total number of video files in the database. These scores are sorted in increasing order, so that an video interval I_i can be associated with its ranking index, $Rank_{I_i}^{(v)}$. This way, $Rank_{I_i}^{(v)} < Rank_{I_j}^{(v)}$ if $S_{qi}^{(v)} < S_{qj}^{(v)}$, $\forall j \neq i$. Similarly, the ranking of audio feature database produces the similarity scores, $S_{qi}^{(a)}$, $i = 1, ..., M$, which are used to obtain ranking indexes, $Rank_{I_i}^{(a)}$, $i = 1, ..., M$. For the i-th video interval I_i, the resulting $Rank_{I_i}^{(v)}$ and $Rank_{I_i}^{(a)}$ are then combined to obtain a new similarity score as:

$$S_{qi}^{(v,a)} = Rank_{I_i}^{(v)} + \xi \times Rank_{I_i}^{(a)}, \tag{14}$$

where ξ is the scaling factor, which is set to $0 \leq \xi \leq 1$, so as to control the impact of audio-feature ranking outcomes. This combination produces a new set of similarity scores, $S_{qi}^{(v,a)}$, $i = 1, ..., M$ which are arranged to obtain the retrieval set. It is noted that the audio content may have less number of class than visual content, so that the parameter ξ can be used to weight audio feature to improve retrieval. In the current application, the value of ξ is determined experimentally.

5   Experimental Results

For our video database, we used 3 Hollywood movies, 15 music videos, and 6 commercial videos. These videos were segmented into 6,000 video clips, each of which contained one to three shots, and has length of approximately 30 seconds. For visual descriptor, we chosen a model set length of $T = 2000$, which was used to index video and obtain nonzero feature vector $\hat{W}_{I_i}$, $i = 1, ..., 6000$. The feature length of $\hat{W}$ was in a range between 5 and 159, with mean value ≈ 29. The system took approximately 6 seconds for indexing a single video clip. The audio feature extraction discussed in Section 3 was applied to the video database. The wavelet decomposition was taken up to 9 levels. Since the components of the feature vector represent different physical quantities and have different dynamic ranges, Gaussian normalization procedure discussed in [13] was employed to convert the dynamic range of the component feature to $[-1, 1]$.

Twenty five queries were generated from different high-level query concepts that include "fighting", "ship crashing", "love scene", "music video", and "dancing party". We used five queries for each concept, and measured retrieval precisions from the top 16 best matches. Figure 1 compares precision results obtained by using audio description, visual description, and audiovisual description. The results in this figure were obtained by averaging the precisions within the query concepts, as well as within the overall queries. This figure clearly reveals the benefits of combined audiovisual descriptions. Using the visual and audio features together yielded the highest retrieval accuracy at 94.8% of precision. Depending on the characteristic of the query, the retrieval results obtained by audio descriptor can be higher or lower than that of visual descriptor. In comparison, these results show that the benefits gained from the audio and visual cues are substantially insensitive to the query's characteristic. The audiovisual descriptor takes advantage of the dominant feature in each query concept, thereby exploring the benefit of multimodality approach.

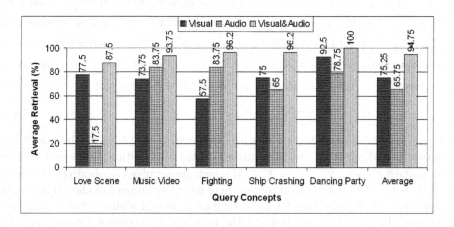

Fig. 1. Average Precision Rate (%) obtained by using audio, visual, and audiovisual descriptors, measured from five high-level query categories.

6   Conclusion

We have presented a framework on joining the audio and visual information for effective video retrieval. Since video data involves both audio and visual signals to convey semantic meanings, the application of audio-visual cues provides the most accurate tools for content analysis, compared to the method using either visual or audio feature alone. The adaptive video indexing technique, together with the statistic time-frequency analysis of audio contents, effectively address the spatio-temporal content information from video clips. This is confirmed by our simulation studies, where the proposed system successfully attained high retrieval precision from various types of video databases.

References

1. Y.-L. Chang, W. Zeng, I. Kamel, and R. Alonso, "Integrated image and speech analysis for content-based video indexing," *Proc. of IEEE Int. Conf. on Multimedia Computing and Systems*, pp. 306-313, 1996.
2. R. Dahyot, A. Kokaram, N. Rea, and H. Denman, "Joint audio visual retrieval for tennis broadcasts," *Proc. of IEEE Int. Conf. on Acoustics, Speech, and Signal Processing*, vol. 3, pp. 561-564.
3. C. Saraceno, "Video content extraction and representation using a joint audio and video processing," *Proc. of IEEE Int. Conf. on Acoustics, Speech, and Signal Processing*, vol. 6, pp. 3033-3036, 1999.
4. J. Huang, Z. Liu, Y. wang, Y. Chen, and E. K. Wong, "Integration of multimodal features for video scene classification based on HMM," *IEEE Workshop on Multimedia Signal Processing*, pp. 53-58, 1999.
5. R. S. Jasinschi, N. Dimitrova, T. McGee, L. Agnihotri, J. Zimmerman, D. Li, and J. Louie, "A probabilistic layered framework fro integrating multimedia content and context information," *Proc. of IEEE Int. Conf. on Acoustics, Speech, and Signal Processing*, vol. 2 , pp. 2057-2060, 2002.
6. M. R. Naphade and T. S. Huang, "Extracting semantics from audiovisual content: The final frontier in multimedia retrieval," *IEEE Trans. on Neural Networks*, vol. 13, no. 4, pp. 793-810, July 2002.
7. P. Muneesawang, and L. Guan, "Video retrieval using an adaptive video indexing technique and automatic relevance feedback," *IEEE Workshop on Multimedia Signal Processing*, pp. 220-223, 2003.
8. T. Kohonen, *Self-organising MAPS*, 2nd ed., Springer-Verlag, Berlin, 1997.
9. M.S. Crouse, R.D. Nowak, and R.G. Baraniuk: Wavelet-based statistical signal processing using hidden Markov models, *IEEE Transactions on Signal Processing*, Vol. 46 , Issue 4, pp. 886-902, April 1998.
10. E. Wold, T. Blum, D. Keislar and J. Wheaton, "Content-based classificaiton, search and retrieval of audio," *IEEE Multimedia*, vol. 3, no. 3, pp. 27-36, 1996.
11. J. Saunders, Real-Time Discrimination of Broadcast Speech /Music, *IEEE Int. Conf. on Acoustic, Speech, and Signal Processing,*, vol. 2, pp. 993-996, Atlanta, May 1996.
12. J. Bilmes, "A gentle tutorial on the EM algorithm and its application to parameter estimation for Gaussian mixture and hidden Markov models", *Technical Report ICSI-TR-97-021*, University of Berkeley, 1998.
13. Y. Rui, T.S. Huang, M. Ortega, and S. Mehrotra, "Relevance feedback: A power tool for interactive content-based image retrieval," *IEEE Trans. Circuits Syst. Video Tech.*, vol 8, no. 5, pp. 644-655, 1998.

Key Image Extraction from a News Video Archive for Visualizing Its Semantic Structure

Hiroshi Mo[1], Fuminori Yamagishi[2], Ichiro Ide[3], Norio Katayama[1],
Shin'ichi Satoh[1], and Masao Sakauchi[1]

[1] National Institute of Informatics
2-1-2 Hitotsubashi, Chiyoda-ku, Tokyo 101-8430, Japan
{mo, katayama, satoh, sakauchi}@nii.ac.jp
[2] Graduate School of Information Science and Technology, The University of Tokyo
fuminori@nii.ac.jp
[3] Graduate School of Information Science, Nagoya University
ide@is.nagoya-u.ac.jp

Abstract. Recently, it has become possible to handle a large amount
of video data with a video archive system. It is very important that
a video data is structured based on semantics for useful access to a
large video archive. Video data is consisted of images, sounds and texts.
Therefore video data should be structured by using their information in
multi-modality. In this paper, we introduce a method to extract the key
images for visualizing the semantic structure of news video archive by
analyzing semantic structure using both images and texts.

1 Introduction

Nowadays, we can access and collect many kinds of video data along with the
development of the storage device and the telecommunication technology. It has
become possible to handle a large amount of video data with a video archive
system. In order to utilize the large amount of video data effectively, it is very
important to structure the video data based on semantics by using contents
analysis and data-mining techniques.

Although many works have tried to extract the semantic structure of video
data, they were for intra-video structuring based on shot detection and scene
identification. However, it becomes more important to extract the relations between many videos for extraction of semantic information. In particular, we
have to analyze the structure between many videos such as continuity, merger
and branch of subjects in a topic for news videos.

Video data consist of images, sounds and texts. Therefore video data should
be structured by using these information in multi-modality, because it makes it
possible to analyze the data from a different or a complex viewpoint comple-
mentarily.

In this paper, we propose a method to extract key images for useful access to
a large news video archive by visualizing its semantic structure. The extraction
of key images is realized by analyzing the semantic structure based on a "topic"

K. Aizawa, Y. Nakamura, and S. Satoh (Eds.): PCM 2004, LNCS 3331, pp. 650–657, 2004.
© Springer-Verlag Berlin Heidelberg 2004

and an "identical video shot". The topic segmentation and topic threading are realized by using the relations between closed-caption texts. On the other hand, extraction of identical video shots is realized by using the similarity of images. The key images are extracted by selecting frequent images in a topic.

2   Semantic Structure in a News Video Archive

2.1   Semantic Structure Based on Text

There are two types of relational structure in a video archive, "intra-video structure" and "inter-video structure". In a news video archive, the semantic structure is based on a news topic. A news video consists of some news topics with different subjects. This structure is an intra-video structure. A news video broadcast every day consists of many subjects in the form of topics. Each topic in news videos has continuous or related subjects. Therefore, the topic relation is usually structured not from a single video but from two or more videos. This structure is an inter-video structure. Figure 1 (a) shows an example of a topic-based intra-/inter-video structure in the archive.

Here, the extraction of the boundary of topics is called "topic segmentation", the extraction of the related topics is called "topic tracking" and the extraction of the chain of related topics is called "topic threading". In this paper, these were analyzed by using closed-caption texts. A closed-caption text is a transcript of speech.

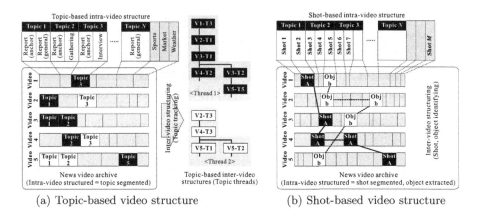

(a) Topic-based video structure   (b) Shot-based video structure

Fig. 1. Intra-/Inter-video structures in a news video archive

2.2   Semantic Structure Based on Image

The structure based on image is structured as a segment, an object, a frame, a shot and so on. Figure 1 (b) shows an example of a shot-based intra-/inter-video structure in the archive. Although a news video consists of various shots, the shots tend to be used repeatedly, because news videos contain related subjects continuously. An example of these shots is shown in Figure 2.

- Important shots
  These shots contain a big accident or a catastrophic disaster such as shots from the asylum seeker incident in Shenyang and the great earthquake in Kobe.
- Rare shots
  These shots cannot be taken frequently such as the shots of Mr. Kim Jong Il or Mr. Osama bin Ladin.
- Reference shots
  These shots contain specific contents such as ths shot of the Diet Building and the Metropolitan Police Department.
- Others
  These shots are limited to shots such as the opening and ending.

A building and a person appear in shots frequently, such as the Tokyo Tower, a politician and so on. It is possible to achieve a video structure based on shots and objects by associating these relations. If fixed form shots such as the opening, the ending, sports and weather reports are used, it becomes possible to extract program structures based on news topics. In this work, we use the information of same shots for structuring news videos.

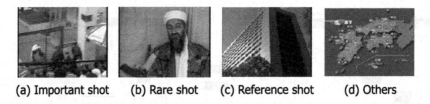

(a) Important shot   (b) Rare shot   (c) Reference shot   (d) Others

Fig. 2. Example of video shots which appear repeatedly

3   Extraction of Key Images from a News Video Archive

3.1   Framework of Key Images Extraction

The semantic structure of news videos can be expressed as a thread structure of topics. On the other hand, the image of a shot which appears in a video archive repeatedly becomes a candidate of the key image representing the contents of a topic, such as an important shot, a rare shot, or a reference shot.

In this work, we try to extract key images from a news video archive by analyzing the topic thread structures using closed-caption texts and analyzing identical video shots using video image. Here, "identical video shots" is a pair of shots which exists in two or more different places in a news video archive. That is, the identical video shots have same images. Concretely, key images representing a topic are extracted from identical video shots belonging to a topic class. A topic class consists of some topics related to the topic of interest. The visualization of a news video archive is realized by displaying its key images for each topic. The example of key image extraction based on topic threads and identical video shots is shown in Figure 3.

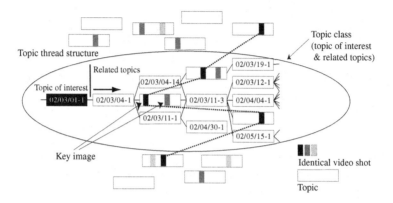

Fig. 3. Key image extraction based on topic threads and identical video shots

3.2 Extraction of the Topic Thread Structure

Extraction of the topic thread structure (topic chain) in a news video archive is executed by (1) topic segmentation and (2) topic tracking/threading [3].

The topic segmentation is performed based on the similarity of keyword vectors between the sentences in a closed-caption text. The topic tracking/threading are performed based on the semantic relevance and the time relevance by evaluating the similarity of keyword vectors of segmented topics. We use all the nouns in the closed-caption text as keywords.

Topic Segmentation. Topic segmentation is realized by applying the following procedure to closed-caption texts in Japanese.

1. Apply morphological analysis to each sentence of a closed-caption text to extract the compound nouns. For Japanese morphological analysis, JUMAN [1] was employed.
2. Apply semantic analysis to the compound nouns to generate a keyword frequency vector for each semantic class (general, personal, locational/organizational, or temporal) per sentence (k_g, k_p, k_l, k_t), which has frequencies as values. For semantic analysis, a suffix-based method [2] was employed.

3. Evaluate the similarity of keyword frequency vectors with w preceding and succeeding vectors to detect the boundary of topics. The similarity between sentences i and $i + 1$ is defined as follows:

$$R(i) = \sum_{S=\{g,p,l,t\}} a_S \max_w R_{S,w}(i). \tag{1}$$

$$R_{S,w}(i) = \frac{\sum_{m=i-w+1}^{i} \mathbf{k}_S(m) \cdot \sum_{n=i+1}^{i+w} \mathbf{k}_S(n)}{\left|\sum_{m=i-w+1}^{i} \mathbf{k}_S(m)\right| \left|\sum_{n=i+1}^{i+w} \mathbf{k}_S(n)\right|} \tag{2}$$

$$(i = w, w + 1, ..., i_{max} - w)$$

where, $S = \{g, p, l, t\}$ and i_{max} is the number of sentences in a program. We set $w = 1, 2, ..., 10$ in the experiment.

Multiple linear regression analysis was applied to manually segmented training data (consists of 39 daily closed-caption texts, with 384 boundaries), which resulted in obtaining the weights: $(a_g, a_p, a_l, a_t) = (0.23, 0.21, 0.48, 0.08)$.

4. Create a keyword vector $\mathbf{K}_S$ for each detected topic, and re-evaluate the relations between adjoining stories i and $j(= i+1)$ by the following function:

$$R(i, j) = \sum_{S=\{g,p,l,t\}} a_S \frac{\mathbf{K}_S(i) \cdot \mathbf{K}_S(j)}{|\mathbf{K}_S(i)| \, |\mathbf{K}_S(j)|}. \tag{3}$$

Topic Tracking/Threading. After topic segmentation, relations between all combinations of topics are evaluated for tracking by again adopting Equation 3. When the relation $R(i, j)$ between topics i and j exceeds a certain threshold θ_{trk}, i and j are considered as highly related and linked for tracking. Following the evaluation of relations comes topic threading. The purpose of the threading is to form a chain of related topics along time.

1. All the topics (children) relevant to a certain topic (parent) are associated.
2. If there is a topic related to a sibling of a certain child topic, it is re-associated as a child with the nearest time stamp.

We can retrieve information on a specific news topic easily by using the topic thread structure which is made by chaining relevant topics such as continuity/merger/branch. In this way, we can recognize the flow of topics easily by using the structure. In the case of using a video archive system, it became more important to extract the structure for useful access to a large amount of news videos, because it is very difficult to follow the flow of topics.

3.3   Extraction of Identical Video Shots

We call a pair of shots which exists in two or more different places in a news video archive "identical video shots". The identical video shots are extracted by detecting the same frames in image[4].

We define a pair of shots including almost the same frames in image as identical video shots. Here, the identical video shots are extracted by detecting the "same" but not "similar" frames. Since it is necessary to perform precise comparison in the "same" frame detection, we use the Normalized Cross Correlation (NCC) between frames for comparison. The NCC between the frames to compare is defined by the following:

$$NCC(a,b) = \frac{1}{n}\sum_i^n (a_i - \bar{a})(b_i - \bar{b}) \left/ \sqrt{\frac{1}{n}\sum_i^n (a_i - \bar{a})^2} \sqrt{\frac{1}{n}\sum_i^n (b_i - \bar{b})^2} \right. \quad (4)$$

where $\bar{a},\bar{b}$ are average intensities of each image, a_i,b_i are intensities of each pixel.

The NCC take a value from -1 to 1 and it becomes 1 when two identical images are evaluated. In this work, we define as same images when the NCC is very close to 1 (0.9 or more). As a result of verifying with actual images, the "same" image pairs were mostly detected.

3.4   Extraction of Key Images Representing Topic

As mentioned above, since it has a certain "important" meaning, the identical video shots are taken up two or more times in a news video archive. It is possible that identical video shots have a meaning as a key image representing a news topic in the archive. On the other hand, in a video archive, the contents of each news topic can be expressed by the topic thread structure where two or more topics merge/branch from in the sense of semantic and time relevance. A topic is defined as a topic class which consists of itself and related topics. Therefore, an image representing the contents of each topic is extracted as an image of the identical video shot, which belongs in the topic class derived from the topic.

$IVS_i (i = 1, \ldots, I)$ are the kinds of identical video shots, $VS_{ij} (j = 1, \ldots, J_i)$ are each shots belonging to an identical video shot IVS_i. $TPC_p (p = 1, \ldots, P)$ are the kinds of topic class, $TP_{pq} (q = 1, \ldots, Q_p)$ are topics belonging to a topic class TPC_p. Here, the identical video shots IVS_i will consist of two or more shots VS_{ij}, and the topic class TPC_p becomes a set which consists of one or more topics TP_{pq}. Therefore, a key image representing a topic class can be extracted as an image of each shot VS_{ij} belonging to an identical video shot IVS_i which has time overlaps with each topic TPC_p belonging to a topic class TPC_p.

Moreover, when shots belong to identical video shots IVS_i in shot VS_{ij}, let the number of shots belong to a topic class TPC_p be $M_{ip}(M_{ip} \leq J_i)$, an important factor $S(p,i)$ of the identical video shots IVS_i in the topic class TPC_p is defined by follows:

$$S(p,i) = M_{ip} \log(N_{IVS}/J_i). \quad (5)$$

It is possible to display the contents of a topic using key images by sorting them according to the $S(p,i)$ for each topic.

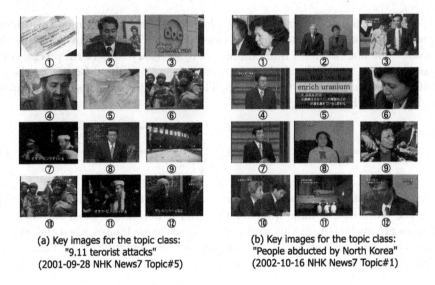

(a) Key images for the topic class: (b) Key images for the topic class:
"9.11 terorist attacks"   "People abducted by North Korea"
(2001-09-28 NHK News7 Topic#5)   (2002-10-16 NHK News7 Topic#1)

Fig. 4. Experimental results

4   Experiment of Key Image Extraction

4.1   Large-Scale Video Archiving System

We constructed a large-scale broadcast video archiving system, in order to analyze video data broadcast for a long period. This system captures broadcast
video data from 7 channels in the Tokyo area for 24 hours a day in MPEG-1
format. The system can store the video data for about one month. In addition,
in order to analyze long-term news video data, a daily news program "NHK
News7" broadcast from 7 p.m. every night is stored. Currently we have stored
more than 1,000 programs (approximately 500 hours) from the year 2001 till
present. We record the main/sub-voices, the closed-caption texts, and the EPG
(Electric Program Guide) data along with the video data. In this work, we use
the news video data stored by this system.

4.2   Experimental Result of Key Image Extraction

In a preliminary experiment, we extracted key images representing a topic class
from a news program "NHK News 7" since September 1, 2001 to February 5,
2003 by NHK. From the video data for 513 days, we found 1,547 kinds of identical
video shots which appeared in 2 to 46 places, except for the opening and the
ending shots.

The 12 key images, which were extracted from a topic class made from topics
within 3 layers of the topic threads on a topic: "9.11 terrorist attacks" (2001-09-
28 NHK News7 Topic #5), are shown in Figure 4 (a). In this example, the topic
class is consisted of 16 topics, and 16 identical video shots were extracted as key

images. As key images, we extracted Mr. Osama bin Ladin, Taliban, Afghanistan and so on.

Next, the 12 key images, which were extracted from a topic class made from topics within 3 layers of the topic threads on a topic: "People abducted by North Korea" (2002-10-16 NHK News7 Topic #1), are shown Figure 4 (b). In this example, the topic class is consisted of 36 topics, and 57 identical video shots were extracted as key images. As key images, we extracted the abductees, the abductee's family, the nuclear facility in North Korea and so on.

The extracted key images show that the images were derived correctly in relation to the contents of the topics. In these two examples, we were able to extract image sets that represented effectively the contents of the topics.

5 Conclusions

In this paper, we introduced a method to extract the key images for useful access to large news video archive by visualizing the semantic structure. The extraction of key images is realized by analyzing the semantic structure based on a "topic" and an "identical video shot". The topic segmentation and topic tracking/threading were realized by using relation between closed-caption texts described speech. On the other hand, the extraction of identical video shots was realized by using the similarity of images.

By a preliminary experiment, we observed the effectiveness of selecting key images and visualizing a topic by key images.

In the future, we will investigate intellectual structuring methods and visualizing methods based on the topic structure such as merger/branch of relations between topics. We will also try to use similar video shots for extracting a key image.

References

1. S. Kurohashi, and M. Nagao, "Japanese morphological analysis system JUMAN version 3.61," Kyoto University, 1999.
2. I. Ide, R. Hamada, S. Sakai, and H. Tanaka, "Semantic analysis of television news captions referring to suffixes," *Proc. of 4th Intl. Workshop on Information Retrieval with Asian Languages (IRAL'99)*, pp.37–42, 1999.
3. I. Ide, H. Mo, N. Katayama, and S. Satoh, "Threading news video topics," *Proc. of 5th ACM SIGMM Intl. Workshop on Multimedia Information Retrieval (MIR2003)*, pp.239–246, 2003.
4. F. Yamagishi, S. Satoh, T. Hamada, and M. Sakauchi, "Identical video segment detection for large-scale broadcast video archives," *Proc. of 3rd Intl. Workshop on Content-Based Multimedia Indexing (CBMI2003)*, pp.79–86, 2003.
5. H.D. Wactlar, M.G. Christel, Y. Gong, and A.G. Hauptmann, "Lessons learned from building a Terabyte digital video library," *IEEE Computer*, vol.32, no.2, pp.66–73, 1999.
6. M.G. Christel, A.G. Hauptmann, H.D. Wactler, and T.D. Ng., "Collages as dynamic summaries for news video," *Proc. of 10th ACM Intl. Conf. on Multimedia*, pp.561–569, 2002.

Author Index

Lecture Notes in Computer Science

For information about Vols. 1–3222

please contact your bookseller or Springer

Vol. 3273: T. Baar, A. Strohmeier, A. Moreira, S.J. Mellor (Eds.), <<UML>> 2004 - The Unified Modelling Language. XIII, 454 pages. 2004.

Vol. 3271: J. Vicente, D. Hutchison (Eds.), Management of Multimedia Networks and Services. XIII, 335 pages. 2004.

Vol. 3270: M. Jeckle, R. Kowalczyk, P. Braun (Eds.), Grid Services Engineering and Management. X, 165 pages. 2004.

Vol. 3269: J. Lopez, S. Qing, E. Okamoto (Eds.), Information and Communications Security. XI, 564 pages. 2004.

Vol. 3266: J. Solé-Pareta, M. Smirnov, P.V. Mieghem, J. Domingo-Pascual, E. Monteiro, P. Reichl, B. Stiller, R.J. Gibbens (Eds.), Quality of Service in the Emerging Networking Panorama. XVI, 390 pages. 2004.

Vol. 3265: R.E. Frederking, K.B. Taylor (Eds.), Machine Translation: From Real Users to Research. XI, 392 pages. 2004. (Subseries LNAI).

Vol. 3264: G. Paliouras, Y. Sakakibara (Eds.), Grammatical Inference: Algorithms and Applications. XI, 291 pages. 2004. (Subseries LNAI).

Vol. 3263: M. Weske, P. Liggesmeyer (Eds.), Object-Oriented and Internet-Based Technologies. XII, 239 pages. 2004.

Vol. 3262: M.M. Freire, P. Chemouil, P. Lorenz, A. Gravey (Eds.), Universal Multiservice Networks. XIII, 556 pages. 2004.

Vol. 3261: T. Yakhno (Ed.), Advances in Information Systems. XIV, 617 pages. 2004.

Vol. 3260: I.G.M.M. Niemegeers, S.H. de Groot (Eds.), Personal Wireless Communications. XIV, 478 pages. 2004.

Vol. 3258: M. Wallace (Ed.), Principles and Practice of Constraint Programming – CP 2004. XVII, 822 pages. 2004.

Vol. 3257: E. Motta, N.R. Shadbolt, A. Stutt, N. Gibbins (Eds.), Engineering Knowledge in the Age of the Semantic Web. XVII, 517 pages. 2004. (Subseries LNAI).

Vol. 3256: H. Ehrig, G. Engels, F. Parisi-Presicce, G. Rozenberg (Eds.), Graph Transformations. XII, 451 pages. 2004.

Vol. 3255: A. Benczúr, J. Demetrovics, G. Gottlob (Eds.), Advances in Databases and Information Systems. XI, 423 pages. 2004.

Vol. 3254: E. Macii, V. Paliouras, O. Koufopavlou (Eds.), Integrated Circuit and System Design. XVI, 910 pages. 2004.

Vol. 3253: Y. Lakhnech, S. Yovine (Eds.), Formal Techniques, Modelling and Analysis of Timed and Fault-Tolerant Systems. X, 397 pages. 2004.

Vol. 3252: H. Jin, Y. Pan, N. Xiao, J. Sun (Eds.), Grid and Cooperative Computing - GCC 2004 Workshops. XVIII, 785 pages. 2004.

Vol. 3251: H. Jin, Y. Pan, N. Xiao, J. Sun (Eds.), Grid and Cooperative Computing - GCC 2004. XXII, 1025 pages. 2004.

Vol. 3250: L.-J. (LJ) Zhang, M. Jeckle (Eds.), Web Services. X, 301 pages. 2004.

Vol. 3249: B. Buchberger, J.A. Campbell (Eds.), Artificial Intelligence and Symbolic Computation. X, 285 pages. 2004. (Subseries LNAI).

Vol. 3246: A. Apostolico, M. Melucci (Eds.), String Processing and Information Retrieval. XIV, 332 pages. 2004.

Vol. 3245: E. Suzuki, S. Arikawa (Eds.), Discovery Science. XIV, 430 pages. 2004. (Subseries LNAI).

Vol. 3244: S. Ben-David, J. Case, A. Maruoka (Eds.), Algorithmic Learning Theory. XIV, 505 pages. 2004. (Subseries LNAI).

Vol. 3243: S. Leonardi (Ed.), Algorithms and Models for the Web-Graph. VIII, 189 pages. 2004.

Vol. 3242: X. Yao, E. Burke, J.A. Lozano, J. Smith, J.J. Merelo-Guervós, J.A. Bullinaria, J. Rowe, P. Tiño, A. Kabán, H.-P. Schwefel (Eds.), Parallel Problem Solving from Nature - PPSN VIII. XX, 1185 pages. 2004.

Vol. 3241: D. Kranzlmüller, P. Kacsuk, J.J. Dongarra (Eds.), Recent Advances in Parallel Virtual Machine and Message Passing Interface. XIII, 452 pages. 2004.

Vol. 3240: I. Jonassen, J. Kim (Eds.), Algorithms in Bioinformatics. IX, 476 pages. 2004. (Subseries LNBI).

Vol. 3239: G. Nicosia, V. Cutello, P.J. Bentley, J. Timmis (Eds.), Artificial Immune Systems. XII, 444 pages. 2004.

Vol. 3238: S. Biundo, T. Frühwirth, G. Palm (Eds.), KI 2004: Advances in Artificial Intelligence. XI, 467 pages. 2004. (Subseries LNAI).

Vol. 3236: M. Núñez, Z. Maamar, F.L. Pelayo, K. Pousttchi, F. Rubio (Eds.), Applying Formal Methods: Testing, Performance, and M/E-Commerce. XI, 381 pages. 2004.

Vol. 3235: D. de Frutos-Escrig, M. Nunez (Eds.), Formal Techniques for Networked and Distributed Systems – FORTE 2004. X, 377 pages. 2004.

Vol. 3234: M.J. Egenhofer, C. Freksa, H.J. Miller (Eds.), Geographic Information Science. VIII, 345 pages. 2004.

Vol. 3233: K. Futatsugi, F. Mizoguchi, N. Yonezaki (Eds.), Software Security - Theories and Systems. X, 345 pages. 2004.

Vol. 3232: R. Heery, L. Lyon (Eds.), Research and Advanced Technology for Digital Libraries. XV, 528 pages. 2004.

Vol. 3231: H.-A. Jacobsen (Ed.), Middleware 2004. XV, 514 pages. 2004.

Vol. 3230: J.L. Vicedo, P. Martínez-Barco, R. Muñoz, M. Saiz Noeda (Eds.), Advances in Natural Language Processing. XII, 488 pages. 2004. (Subseries LNAI).

Vol. 3229: J.J. Alferes, J. Leite (Eds.), Logics in Artificial Intelligence. XIV, 744 pages. 2004. (Subseries LNAI).

Vol. 3226: M. Bouzeghoub, C. Goble, V. Kashyap, S. Spaccapietra (Eds.), Semantics of a Networked World. XIII, 326 pages. 2004.

Vol. 3225: K. Zhang, Y. Zheng (Eds.), Information Security. XII, 442 pages. 2004.

Vol. 3224: E. Jonsson, A. Valdes, M. Almgren (Eds.), Recent Advances in Intrusion Detection. XII, 315 pages. 2004.

Vol. 3223: K. Slind, A. Bunker, G. Gopalakrishnan (Eds.), Theorem Proving in Higher Order Logics. VIII, 337 pages. 2004.